Laos

Footprint Handbook

Joshua Eliot, Jane Bickersteth & Zee Gilmore

W9-DET-052

Vieng Thara
Town of Rvier
ng Vieng. LAOS. (856) 2052 870374
Email : viengthara@gmail.com

This was the earthly paradise that all the French had promised: the country that was one vast Tahiti, causing all the French who had been stationed there to affect ever after a vaguely disolute manner.

Norman Lewis in *A Dragon Apparent* on his arrival in Vientiane on a burning March day in 1950

3rd edition

Laos Highlights

See colour maps at back of book

❶ Luang Prabang
Perfectly formed little city with UNESCO World Heritage status

❷ Pak Ou Caves
4,000 images of the Buddha crammed into cliff-side caves with a river view

❸ Khouang-Sy Falls
Popular get-away from Luang Prabang with prospect of a cooling dip

❹ The Mekong
Mother river of Southeast Asia

❺ Muang Sing
Attractive base to visit minorities

❻ Caves at Vieng Xai
Communist Pathet Lao bolt-hole and command centre

❼ Plain of Jars
Perplexing giant stones littered over US-bombed grasslands

❽ Van Vieng
Way station en route to Luang Prabang with caves, rafting and trekking to elegant monasteries

CHINA

Phongsali

MYANMAR (BURMA)

Luang Namtha

Muang Xai

Xam Neua

Ban Houei Xai

Mekong River

Luang Prabang

Tranh Ninh Highlands

Sayaboury

Phonsavanh
Plain of Jars ❼

Nam Ngum Reservoir

Phonhong

Pakxan

VIENTIANE

THAILAND

Contents

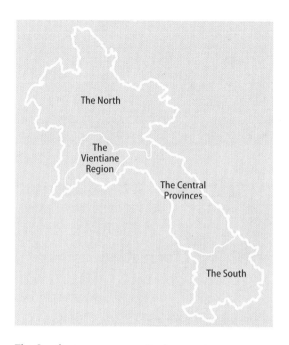

The North

The
Vientiane
Region

The Central
Provinces

The South

Inside front cover

Overview
Price guide

Inside back cover

Authors

A foot in the door

Plain of Jars *(right) Xieng Khouang's enigmatic giant stone jars*
World Heritage City *(below) Leafy Luang Prabang, the Mekong and Wat Long Khoun from Phousi*
Vang Vieng's *(previous page) Popular stopping-off place on the way to Luang Prabang and a good base from which to explore the countryside.*

Colonial legacy *(above) Villa Santi, a renovated French-era villa in Luang Prabang, now an elegant auberge*
Minority village *(right) Trekking opportunities, including visits to minority villages, are abundant in Laos, particularly in the north*

Introducing Laos

In Vientiane and Luang Prabang it is possible to pick up postcards depicting long-dead Laotian beauties with 'Forgotten Laos' emblazoned on the card. The makers mean one thing, but the message is rather different: Laos has hunkered down and escaped the developments that have marred other countries in the region. Laos has been forgotten. It has the innocence of an earlier age when time was not money, when life was savoured slowly, and when the joys of the moment triumphed over the desires of the future. Of course there's a good dose of romanticism here. Laos is poor, many people die younger than they would elsewhere, and the government struggles to find the means to take the country on a trajectory towards modernity.

The French didn't leave much behind when they gave Laos back to its inhabitants in 1954. But it is tempting to think the French contributed to the Lao sense of style. From the fine arts to the humdrum, there's something about the way the Lao do things you won't find on the other side of the Mekong. The French weren't here long enough to do much damage to Laos' natural resources, and the wars that followed put the country's wild lands out of bounds to business. The result is that Laos probably has the richest forests, the cleanest rivers and the freshest air of all the countries in Southeast Asia. Rafting, trekking, caving and climbing are nascent activities but have enormous potential.

The dominant cultural group in Laos are the Lao: lowland-living, wet-rice cultivating, Theravada Buddhists. But more than half the population comprise an array of hill peoples each with their own traditions, beliefs and practices. With the opening up of Laos' wild areas has come easier access to the country's minority groups. Trekking is blossoming, particularly in the north.

Luang Prabang in the north and Wat Phou in the south are special places, the first a living city and the second the monumental remains of a long-gone empire. But it is probably the country's vernacular architecture that is more memorable for the simple reason that in other countries it has been swept away in a maelstrom of redevelopment. Simple wooden village homes, colonial-era brick-and-stucco shophouses, and gently mouldering monasteries mark Laos out as different.

Highlights

A jewel in the crown

Luang Prabang is Laos' single greatest draw. A UNESCO World Heritage site and a former royal capital, sited in the mountainous north at the confluence of the Mekong and Nam Khan, its position alone makes it worth the journey. When you add what UNESCO describes as "the exceptional fusion of traditional architecture and urban structures built by 19th and 20th century European colonial rulers" and it becomes a place that really should not be missed. Luang Prabang shows the merit of missed opportunities: starved of funds for 40 years from the French withdrawal through to 1990, its eclectic mix of 16th-century monasteries and late 19th and early 20th century shophouses has survived with scarcely a pimple of redevelopment. UNESCO bestowing World Heritage status has, hopefully, meant that the core of the town, including the incomparable Wat Xieng Thong, will be protected. And there's more! Luang Prabang has great little guesthouses, excellent restaurants, and numerous opportunities for rewarding forays into the surrounding countryside, from the 4,000 Buddhas of the Pak Ou caves to the waterfalls at Khouang-Sy.

Bombed back to the Stone Age

Xieng Khouang was unfortunate to lie at the epicentre of one of the war in Indochina's nastier 'sideshows'. It was bombed to bits – something that is still all too evident from the crater-peppered landscape. The war may be over but day-by-day the number of maimed and killed rises as farmers plough up unexploded ordnance and young children play with the detritus of war. Another tragedy was the total destruction of Xieng Khouang town, bombed so thoroughly that not a single building survived, in the process obliterating all examples of one of the country's three religious architectural styles. However Xieng Khouang's mysterious giant stone jars did survive – some 300 of them littered over the eponymous Plaine de Jarres. Archaeologists argue over what they were for, but the Lao have always known the answer: the jars were left by King Khoon Chuong and his troops after they had used them to brew prodigious quantities of *lau-lao* to lubricate a stupendous victory celebration.

The Khmer in Laos

In the far south of Laos is a slice of history that belongs to another people: the Khmer. The Khmer empire of Angkor extended its power and influence over southern Laos, as well as large areas of central and northeast Thailand. Wat Phou is ample evidence of the economic might and artistic prowess of the Khmer, conveniently left in Laos for another people to exploit. It is a fabulous concoction of pavilions, causeways and sanctuaries dating from the 12th century.

A lower case capital

Finally, there is the capital, Vientiane. Like Xieng Khouang, this was also ravaged by war but during an era when military technologies were rather less destructive than those available to the US. In 1827, after King Chou Anou's failed and foolhardy attempt at defeating the Siamese, King Rama III ransacked the city, infuriated at the sheer effrontery of the Lao ruler. Wat Phra Kaeo and Wat Sisaket may still stand, but the former is without the famed Phra Kaeo, or Emerald Buddha, which now holds pride of place in Bangkok's Grand Palace. The result is that, with one or two exceptions, Vientiane is more of a French colonial outpost than a Lao city. It still, though, holds considerable charm. It is a low key place, restrained and understated, with simple shophouses and French villas, and a great position on the Mekong.

Khmer ruins (right) The main sanctuary of 12th-century Wat Phou, built by the Khmers of Angkor

Vientiane's most important site (below) That Luang, symbol of Lao nationhood and the country's most sacred Buddhist monument

Wat Xieng Thong (above) Luang Prabang and Laos' finest monastery, a glittering survivor of the Chinese raids of the 19th century

Don Deth (right) The Mekong islands of the south, land-locked Laos' own tropical riverside resort

Cymbals and gongs (next pages) Monks on the drum tower at a monastery in Ban Houei Xai

Lao weaving (top left) Of all Laos'
artistic traditions, perhaps none is more
varied and more vital than its weaving

Festival gathering (top right)
Drinking rice wine is a group activity
enjoyed on special occasions

Urban renewal (above) Pigs for
market, beer for sale: commerce comes
to Xieng Khouang, wiped off the map
by the bombings of 1969 and 1970

Travel Lao-style (right)   Arrive early,
secure a place, and be patient

Leafy capital (next page)
Sok Paluang, Vientiane's busy
southern bypass

Unofficial Laos

Air travel has come to be a pretty tedious affair in the modern world. Predictable and boring. In Laos, it is anything but. From the moment the stewardess on a Lao Aviation domestic flight offers you a boiled sweet – and looks askance when you decline – you have the sense that this could be different. Has the technology of pressurization not arrived in this small corner of Asia? Or is it just some quaint throwback to an era of aerodromes and airliners? The average air traveller might be rather more worried than amused when the Bangkok Airways ground staff in Luang Prabang inform you that visibility is so poor their aircraft can't land – whereupon the Lao Aviation girl then informs you with a gentle smile that their pilots (ex-military, you see) always deliver.

Boiled sweets & fog

It's much the same on land and river. Slip into one of the 'fast' river boats which feel like they are made of balsa wood and have engines the size of a small bovine, and slip on a lifejacket and crash helmet. Surreal! There are enough speedboat pilots for the country to mount its very own marine grand prix series. Long-distance bus journeys are another thing entirely. Schedules and journey times on many routes are, it seems, plucked from a random numbers table. Don't count on arriving at any particular hour – or day for that matter – and don't worry about it either. No one else will.

Faster by boat

Laos, we have said, is forgotten. It's poor. Global multinationals are not looking over their shoulders for another Microsoft to be born in the backstreets of Pakse. But as you trip, dust-caked, like some Victorian explorer, into a provincial town it's always slightly deflating to see schoolchildren emailing their pen pals across the world. Laos is disconnected in lots of ways, but incredibly connected in others. David Beckham is no stranger to the people of Laos.

Global Laos

Lao food is really pretty good. But if you are slightly squeamish about what you eat it's probably best not to ask, for two reasons. First because you will then discover that the delicious-looking rounds of white flesh sizzling over the glowing coals are not squid cunningly flown in from the coast several thousand kilometres distant, but pig's small intestine. And second, because having asked you will have little choice but to munch your way, smiling politely, through a slice. Or there's the conundrum over how bakers in the remotest of small towns can produce excellent baguettes. Then stuff them with what passes as pâté (another case of 'don't ask'). And then, if you wish, drizzle them with fish sauce. What Michelin-starred chef would think of that!

Don't ask!

Finally, there's the money to pay for all these delectables. Kip. Could Laos have a more appropriate name for its currency? Until 2002 the largest denomination note available was 10,000 kip – around US$1. Now the central bank has gone berserk and issued a 20,000 kip note. But even a 10,000 kip note will induce the average market stall holder to suck in his breath at your sheer pecuniary audacity. And then, brain dulled by too many Beer Laos, you find that the bill for your slap-up dinner comes to 387,500 kip – sufficient bank notes to stun an elephant – and you receive your change in three currencies, baht, US dollars and kip. Tcha!

Money talks

Essentials

Planning your trip

Where to go

Laos may not be on the travel itineraries of most international tourists, or in the brochures of many tour companies, but it is a priceless country with a great deal to offer the traveller. Notwithstanding the country's poverty and lack of development, it is civilized and refined with elegant towns, sophisticated cuisine, a leisurely pace of life, and a population among the most welcoming and relaxed in Asia. Laos has style.

On paper there might seem little to entice the visitor to Laos. Certainly the former royal capital of Luang Prabang – designated a World Heritage Site by UNESCO – is a fabulous little city. The capital Vientiane, along with the other Mekong towns of Pakse, Savannakhet and Thakhek, is also elegant with its French architectural heritage largely intact. Wat Phou, an outlier of the former Cambodian kingdom of Angkor, is highly satisfying while some visitors enjoy the enigmatic stone urns that litter the Plain of Jars. The Mekong islands in the far south are also a great place to read *War and Peace* at leisure. But above all, what visitors to this gem of a country tend to remember best of all are the warmth of the people, the leisurely pace of life, and the pleasure that comes from visiting a country which has so far successfully kept the more lurid and gauche aspects of the modern world at bay.

Timetabling a visit Because travelling in Laos can be a bit of a lottery, allowing some leeway in a schedule is strongly recommended. Assuming, for example, that it will be possible to catch a flight from Phonsavanh to Vientiane to connect with another from Vientiane to Bangkok, and from there to the US or Europe, is – to say the least – risky. The same goes for road transport, especially during the wet season. Those on organized tours have some distinct advantages in this regard. They will have the services of a local tour guide to apply pressure and perhaps supply gifts to free seats on overbooked planes. Local guides are also much more aware of when problems are likely to arise. A lone traveller, with no Lao, will find it hard to do the same deals and may be left floundering on the tarmac.

Nonetheless, a 2-3 week visit to Laos is sufficient to see much of the country – or at least that fraction of the country that it is possible to see. The main issue, perhaps, is how to couple a visit to the north with a trip to the south where Pakse, Champassak, Wat Phou and the Mekong Islands are to be found. Vientiane to Pakse is a journey of around 750 km and many people, because they have booked a flight into and out of Vientiane, have then to retrace those 750 km to catch their plane out. By air this is bearable; by road it may be testing one's patience. The alternative is to enter and exit at different ends of the country, which used to be impossible because visas stipulated the entry and exit points. But now it is possible to enter at Chiang Khong/Ban Houei Xai in the far north, travel south, and then exit at Pakse/Chongmek. There is also the option of entering or departing from Vietnam or from China (see box Overland connections with Laos on page 36).

Itineraries Laos doesn't have a great number of 'must see' places. In fact, for many people, just one: Luang Prabang. This doesn't mean that Laos isn't worth visiting; it's just that the charm of the country is not in the official and the institutional, but in the informal and unofficial. As a result, working out sets of itineraries doesn't make a great deal of sense because the informal and unofficial can't, by definition, be pinned down. The main issue, as noted above, is how to get about: by plane it is possible to hop from, say, Vientiane to Luang Prabang to Phonsavanh to Pakse and Champassak. Theoretically this would be possible in (a rushed) 10 days. By road, 3 weeks would be more likely.

When to go

The weather is best for travel during the relatively cool and dry winter months from November to March. Not only is the weather more pleasant at this time of year, but roads are also in better shape. Temperatures in upland areas like the Plain of Jars, the Bolovens Plateau and some towns in the north of the country can drop to below freezing in winter. From April onwards, temperatures can exceed 40°C in many lowland areas, although it remains dry through to May. From June or July, as the wet season wears on, so unsurfaced roads begin to deteriorate and overland transport in some areas becomes slower and more difficult. In the north, the months from March through to the first rains in May or June can be very hazy as smoke from shifting cultivators burning off the secondary forest hangs in the air. Not only does this mean that views are restricted but during the worst of days it can cause itchiness of the eyes as well as cancelled flights.

See Climate, page 304, for further details
See also www.weather.yahoo.com/ for daily weather reports

Essentials

Tours and tour operators

Andrew Brock Travel, 54 High St East, Uppingham, Rutland, LE15 9PZ, UK, T01572-821072. *Asian Journeys*, 32 Semolong Rd, Northampton NN2 6BT, T01604-234855, F234877. An organization offering tailor-made trips only. A company newsletter is available about expeditions. *Audley Travel Ltd*, 6 Willows Gate, Stratton Audley, Oxfordshire OX27 9AU, T01869-276200, F276214, www.audleytravel.com *Explore Worldwide*, 1 Frederick St, Aldershot, Hants GU11 1LQ, 01252-760000, www.exploreworldwide.com Arranges small group tours (average 16 people), with many different types of trip offered including cultural excursions, adventure holidays and natural history tours. *Gateway to Asia*, 545 High Rd, Wembley, Middlesex HA0 2DJ, T01283-821096, F820467, www.gateway-to-asia.co.uk/ *Guerba Expeditions*, Wessex House, 40 Station Rd, Westbury, Wiltshire, BA13 3JN, T01373-858956, F858351, www.guerba.co.uk *Magic of the Orient*, 2 Kingsland Court, Three Bridges Rd, Crawley, West Sussex RH10 1HL, T01293-537700, F537888, www.magic-of-the-orient.com *Maxwells Travel*, D'Olier Chambers, 1 Hawkins St, Dublin 2, Ireland, T01-6779479, F6793948. *Regent Holidays*, 15 John St, Bristol BS1 2HR, T0117-9211711, F9254866, www.regent-holidays.co.uk Tailor-made holidays. Recommended. *Silk Steps*, Tyndale House, 7 High St, Chipping Sodbury, Bristol BS37 6BA, T01454-888850, F888851, www.silksteps.co.uk Tailor-made tours and group travel arrangements. *Steppes East Limited*, 51 Castle St, Cirencester GL7 5ET, T01285-651010, F885888, www.steppeseast.co.uk *Symbiosis*, 113 Bolingbroke Grove, London SW11 1DA, www.symbiosis-travel.com/ An environmentally aware company that offers expeditions that respect traditional values and cultures.

UK & Ireland

Burma
Cambodia
Central Asia
China
Ethiopia
India
Indonesia
Malaysia
South Korea
Thailand
Vietnam

Laos

experience & explore

Tailor-made & Group Travel Arrangements

Silk Steps

Tel: 01454 888850 Fax: 01454 888851
Email: info@silksteps.co.uk
Web: www.silksteps.co.uk
Silk Steps Ltd, Tyndale House,
7 High St, Chipping Sodbury,
Bristol, BS37 6BA
England

Essentials

Specializes in tailor-made tours but also offers two Laos-centred itineraries: one based around the **Luang Prabang Boat Race Festival** in late August and also 'Laos Explored', which is an overview of the country's highlights. *Tennyson Travel*, 30-32 Fulham High St, London, SW6 3LQ, T020-7736 4347, F020-7736 5672, tennyson@visitvietnam.co.uk

USA   *Adventure Centre*, 1311 63rd St, Suite 200, Emeryville, CA 94608, T510-6541879, F6544200, www.adventurecenter.com A green company supporting 'Trees for Life' which aims to re-forest denuded areas such as Nepal. Offers seven different trips in Laos and Southeast Asia for 15-30 days. There are no Laos specific routes; all include excursions to neighbouring countries. *Global Spectrum*, 5683 Columbia Pike, Suite 101, Falls Church, Va 22041, T800 419 4446, info@asianpassages.com Specialists to Southeast Asia. *Journeys*, 107 Aprill Drive, Suite 3, Ann Arbor MI 46103, T734-6654407, F6652945, www.journeys-intl.com Two Laos trips offered: six-day 'Laos Odyssey' and 'Vientiane-Luang Prabang Highlights', which is a more focused six-day trip. *Himalayan Travel Inc*, 8 Berkshire Pl, Danbury, CT 06810, T203-7432349, F7978077, www.himalayantravelinc.com/ *Myths & Mountains*, 976 Tee Court, Incline Village, NV 89451, T800-670-Myth, T775-8325454, F8324454, travel@mythsandmountains.com *Nine Dragons Travel & Tours*, PO Box 24105, 2136 Fullerton Drive, Indianapolis, In 46214, T1-317-3290350, toll free within USA T800-9099050, www.nine-dragons.com

Australia   *Adventure World*, 3rd Floor, 73 Walker St, North Sydney, NSW 2060, T028913-0755, F029956-7707, info@adventureworld.com.au *Intrepid Travel Pty Ltd*, 11 Spring St, Fitzroy, Victoria, T1300-360667, F613-94-195878, www.intrepidtravel.com.au

Specialists in tailor-made journeys through Laos and across Indochina.

Steppes East

Travel Beyond the Ordinary

Steppes East Limited
51 Castle Street, Cirencester, Gloucestershire, GL7 1QD
Telephone: 01285 651010 Fax: 01285 885888
E-mail: sales@steppeseast.co.uk www.steppeseast.co.uk

Operated by Tennyson Travel Ltd fully bonded and licenced by the CAA

Visit Vietnam *for*
UNBEATABLE VALUE
We are the exclusive tour operator specialising in:
Vietnam, Cambodia, Laos and Myanmar
FLIGHTS, VISA, ACCOMMODATION, TOUR PACKAGES, TAILOR MADE PROGRAMMES AND GROUP TOURS

Tel: 020 7736 4347 tennyson@visitvietnam.co.uk
www.visitvietnam.co.uk
COLOUR BROCHURE 24hrs 020 7736 5672

Shiralee Travel, 32 Main Rd, PO Box 1420, Hermanus, 7200, South Africa, **South Africa**
T028-3130526, F3124507, liesel.maree@harveyworld.co.za

Apsara Tours, No 8 Wat Langkar St, Daun Penh, Phnom Penh, Cambodia, T85523-216 **Cambodia**
562/212019, F217334, www.apsaratours.com.kh

Bangkok Airways, 60 Queen Sirikit National Convention Center, New Ratchadapisek **Thailand**
Rd, Klongtoey, Bangkok 10110, T66 (0) 2229 3456, F66 (0) 2229 3450, reservation@bangkokair.co.th Operates tours in conjunction with several tour operators.

A good general site for those wishing to find a local tour company in Laos is **Special interest**
www.visitlaos.laopdr.com/Touroperatorlinks_files/content_files/main.htm **tour operators**

Essentials

Canoeing/rafting There are quite a few companies offering canoeing tours/trips in Laos – and this is likely to be a real growth area given the country's wealth of river resources. *Bolykhamsay Tour*, Ban Haisok, Hengboun Rd, PO Box 501, Vientiane, Lao PDR T(+856-21)-218373, F218373, T(+856-20)-511990 (mob), vanxayxay@hotmail.com, www.bolykhamsay.laopdr.com/ Local tour company running canoeing, trekking and cultural tours to Laos. *PaddleAsia*, 19/3 Thanon Rasdanusorn, Thambon Rasda, Amphur Muang 83000, Thailand, T/F66-76-240893, T01-8936558 (mob), www.paddleasia.com, organizes raft trips to Laos, with a maximum group size of 8 and prices starting at US$250.

Cycling *Cycling Southeast Asia*, www.cycling-sulawesi.com/laos.html. A handy site for anyone thinking of arranging their own cycling tour of Laos or going with a group.

Global Spectrum™
Travel Specialists to Southeast Asia

Asian Passages™
presents

Group and Individual Tours
Customized Adventures
Special Interest Itineraries
Volunteer Programs

5683 Columbia Pike
Falls Church, Virginia 22041
1 800 419 4446   703 671 9619

gspectrum@gspectrum.com

www.asianpassages.com

Viet Nam   Cambodia   Myanmar   Laos   Thailand

LAOS CAMBODIA VIETNAM
Group, Individual and Custom Tours
Representatives in Saigon, Ha Noi, Da Nang,
Vientiane, Phnom Penh & Siem Reap

We have satisfied clients from around the globe.
Wherever you are, you are in
good hands with Nine Dragons Travel & Tours

NINE DRAGONS TRAVEL & TOURS
Specialists in Asian Travel
tours@nine-dragons.com
www.nine-dragons.com

2136 Fullerton Drive, Indianapolis, IN 46214 USA
Local & International Calls 317-329-0350
Within the US Toll Free: 800-909-9050

Revelation Adventure Tours, Bicycle & Canoe Adventure Tours, PO Box 1763, Chelsea, Québec, J9B 1A1, Canada, www.revelationtours.com/ Canada-based firm offering bicycle tours in the north of Laos, as well as canoe tours. *Savanh Banhao Toursim*, 023 Luang Prabang Rd, Ban Akath Village, Sikhot District, Vientiane, Lao PDR, T/F (856-21)-251246, 218291, T(856-20)-516170 (mob), sldphthg@laotel.com, http://sht.laopdr.com/ Lao-based outfit specializing in cycling and river tours of Laos. *SpiceRoads.com*, www.spiceroads.com/tourleader.htm. Specialist tour company that only runs bicycling tours, including a range to Laos. Informative and valuable website.

Cultural tours *Absolute Asia*, 180 Varick St, 16th Floor, New York, NY 10014, USA, T(212)-6271950, F(212)-6274090, www.absoluteasia.com Offers various tours to Laos, some with an arts theme and others focusing on the natural environment. *Lao Travel Service*, 08/3 Lane Xang Av, Vientiane, T(+856-21) 216603/4, F216150, laotravl@laotel.com, www.laotravelservice.laopdr.com/. This long-established (for Laos) company has branches in Luang Prabang and Pakse and specializes in historical tours. Also has adventure and nature-oriented trips too.

Off-road tours *Luang Prabang Travel and Tour Co*, Vientiane Branch, 079 Sithan Neua, Luang Prabang Rd, P.O.Box 3686, T(856-21)-251370, F222614, thongxay@laotel.com, http://offroad.laopdr.com/ Specializes in off-road tours.

Finding out more

Information on Laos is not easy to come by. The National Tourism Authority of Laos does not have a global reach. The best bet is to browse Lao-related, or Lao-dedicated, websites. However even these are often out of date.

General tourism – related sites www.laopdr.com Portal for Lao websites with sections on accommodation and transport, also a travel and tourism section. Good place for background information. www.mekongcentre.com The official website of the Lao National Tourism Authority. Links to the Vientiane Times and a fair amount of background information. www.laolink.com French language website: good range of stories and information. www.visit-Laos.com/news/index.htm Stories, news, travel information (thin), links. www.laoembassy.com The Laotian embassy in Washington's site. Some useful information although the travel practicalities were out-of-date when we visited it last. www.netspace.net.au/~mrfelix/bsa/ For potential bicycle tourists – Mr Pumpy offers a blow by blow account of one route through the Mekong Delta and another through Laos to Vietnam. The routes are well explained and the pitfalls are highlighted. www.pata.org/ The Pacific Asia Travel Association, better known simply as PATA,

Let's explore **Laos** with **APSARA TOURS**

Contact us for the finest travel arrangement in Cambodia, Vietnam, Laos, Myanmar and Thailand

APSARA TOURS
No. 8 Wat Langkar St, Khan Daun Penh, Phnom Penh, Cambodia
Tel: 855 23 212 019 / 216 562
Fax: 855 23 217 334
E-mail: apsaratours@apsaratours.com.kh
apsaratours@bigpond.com.kh
Website: www.apsaratours.com.kh

with a useful news section arranged by country, links to airlines and cruise lines, and some information on educational, environmental and other initiatives.

www.lib.utexas.edu/dls/index.html Up-to-date maps of Asia showing relief, political boundaries and major towns.

Maps

www.nationalgeographic.com National Geographic's cartographic division, which takes maps from their current Atlas of the world.

www.expediamaps.com/ US biased but still pretty comprehensive. Key in a town and wait for it to magically appear.

www.weather.yahoo.com/ Provides weather information for Vientiane and eight other towns in Laos.

Weather & geographical information

www.rainorshine.com/ A simple but effective weather site with five-day forecasts for 800 cities worldwide.

www.vientianetimes.com The website for Laos' only (bi-weekly) English language newspaper. Past issues available and excellent links to other Laos-relevant sites.

Newspapers, news & the media

www.nationmultimedia.com/ Homepage for *The Nation,* one of Thailand's main English language daily newspapers with some coverage of Laos.

www.bangkokpost.net/ Homepage for the *Bangkok Post* including back issues and main stories of the day with some coverage of Laos.

www.oanda.com/converter/classic Select your two currencies by clicking on a list and the exchange rate is provided.

Currencies

www.global.lao.net/ LaoNet is a virtual community for Lao students and students of Laos worldwide. It is not linked to the government and is based outside the country. Good information; can be dense.

General sites

www.coombs.anu.edu.au/ Assorted material from the Research School of Pacific and Asian Studies at the Australian National University in Canberra.

www.nbr.org Papers on Asia covering strategic, economic and political issues.

www.leidenuniv.nl/ Library of slides of Laos and other Southeast Asian countries.

www.asiasociety.org Homepage of the Asia Society with papers, reports and speeches as well as nearly 1,000 links to what they consider to be the best educational, political and cultural sites on the Web.

History & culture

Language

Lao is the national language but there are many local dialects. French is spoken by government officials and hotel staff, and many educated people over 40. Most government officials and many shopkeepers have some command of English.

See Footnotes, page 312, for useful words and phrases. See also Background, page 296, and Books, page 307

Lao is closely related to Thai and, in a sense, is becoming more so as the years pass. Though there are important differences between the languages, they are mutually intelligible. To many Thais, Lao is a rather basic version of their own more sophisticated language – they often describe it as 'primitive'. Of course the Lao vehemently reject, and resent, such a view and it represents, in microcosm, the 'big-brother-little brother' relationship that exists between the two countries and peoples. (It is not accidental that the Lao of the poverty-stricken northeast of Thailand are often regarded as country bumpkins in Bangkok.) Today, though, many Lao watch Thai TV, their antennae aimed to receive transmissions from the west. As a result Thai expressions are becoming more common and familiarity with Thai is spreading. Even written Thai is more in evidence. As Thailand dominates mainland Southeast Asia in economic terms (they

Essentials

are the largest investor in Laos) this linguistic imperialism is seen by Thailand's critics as just another facet of a wide ranging Thai cultural colonization of Laos.

Disabled travellers

Laos is not an easy country for the disabled traveller; pavements are often uneven, there are potholes galore, pedestrian crossings are ignored, ramps are unheard of, lifts are few and far between, and escalators are seen only in magazines. On top of this, numerous other hazards abound, among the most dangerous of which must number the tuk-tuk drivers, whose philosophy on road safety remains either undeveloped or eccentric. However while there are scores of hurdles that disabled people will have to negotiate, the Lao themselves are likely to go out of their way to be helpful. After all, one of the legacies of the war in Indochina is a large population of amputees.

Some travel companies are beginning to specialize in exciting holidays, tailor-made for individuals depending on their level of disability. For those with access to the internet, a Global Access - Disabled Travel Network Site is **www.geocities.com/Paris/1502** It is dedicated to providing information for 'disabled adventurers' and includes a number of reviews and tips from members of the public. For inspiration, you might want to read *Nothing Ventured* edited by Alison Walsh (Harper Collins), which gives personal accounts of worldwide journeys by disabled travellers, plus advice and listings.

Gay and lesbian travellers

Laos, unlike Thailand, does not have a hot gay scene – but there is more gay activity than one might expect, and also some bars and clubs where gays congregate (largely in the capital, Vientiane). The Lao government is intent on avoiding the mushrooming of the gay and straight sex industry, as occurred in Thailand, so that today the country has become a byword for sex tourism. There is talk of harsh penalties being introduced by the government to prevent this occurring. Openly gay behaviour is contrary to local culture and custom and visitors should not flaunt their sexuality. The word 'day' is rarely used; instead the Thai word *katoey* (meaning 'lady boy') is used to describe men with effeminate characteristics. For a list of bars and clubs where gays congregate, and meeting places for gays see: **www.utopia-tours.com/vientian.htm**; **www. travelandtranscendence.com/g-laos.html**

Student travellers

In the past, the Lao government has not been overly eager to attract student travellers. It has not wanted to suffer from the problems that Thailand has encountered, where hoardes of tourists descend upon 'hotspots', spending little money and generally degrading the place (or that, at least, was the generally accepted view). However, in recent years, this generally anti-backpacker attitude has moderated and the government has come to realize that backpackers do spend money, that they bring income to places where other forms of development are lacking, and that today's backpackers are tomorrow's big spenders. The result is that many more students are visiting the country, and its reputation as a cracking place to enjoy a cheap, culturally-rich and wonderfully relaxing stint during a gap year or summer holiday is growing. That's all to the good. But there are few savings that come from being a student in Laos. In short, don't expect massive savings on travel, entry fees and such like.

ISIC Anyone in full-time education is entitled to an International Student Identity Card
See www.isic.org (ISIC). These are issued by student travel offices and travel agencies across the world

Children and babies

Younger travellers are more prone to illness abroad, but that should not put you off taking them. More preparation is necessary than for an adult and perhaps a little more care should be taken when travelling to remote areas because children can become more rapidly ill than adults (but often recover more quickly).

Diarrhoea and vomiting are the most common problems so take the usual precautions, but more intensively. Make sure all basic childhood **vaccinations** are up to date as well as the more exotic ones. Children should be properly protected against diphtheria, whooping cough, mumps and measles. If they have not had the disease, teenage girls should be given rubella (german measles) vaccination. Consult your doctor for advice on BCG inoculation against tuberculosis: the disease is still common in the region. Protection against mosquitos and drug prophylaxis against malaria is essential.

Many children take to "foreign" food quite happily. Milk may be unavailable. Powdered milk may be the answer; breast feeding for babies even better.

Upper respiratory infections such as colds, catarrh and middle ear infections are common – antibiotics could be carried against the possibility. **Outer ear infections** after swimming are also common – antibiotic ear drops will help.

The treatment of **diarrhoea** is the same as for adults except that it should start earlier and be continued with more persistence. Children get dehydrated very quickly in the tropics and can become drowsy and uncooperative unless cajoled to drink water or juice plus salts. Oral rehydration has been a lifesaving technique in children.

Protect children against the sun with a hat and high factor tanning lotion. Severe sunburn at this age may well lead to serious skin cancer in the future.

Essentials

and offer special rates on all forms of transport and other concessions and services. They sometimes permit free admission to museums and sights, at other times a substantial discount on the entrance charge. The ISIC head office is: ISIC Association, Box 9048, 1000 Copenhagen, Denmark, T45-33939303.

Travelling with children

Many people are daunted by the prospect of taking a child to Laos. Naturally, it is not something which is taken on lightly; travelling is slower and more expensive and there are additional health risks for the child or baby. But it can be a most rewarding experience, and with sufficient care and planning it can also be safe. Children are excellent passports into a local culture. You will also receive the best service, and help from officials and members of the public when in difficulty.

Sleeping At the hottest time of year, air conditioning may be essential for a baby or young child's comfort. This rules out many of the cheaper hotels, but air-conditioned accommodation is available in all larger towns. When the child is bathing, be aware that the water could carry parasites, so avoid letting him or her drink it.

Food & drink Be aware that expensive hotels may have squalid cooking conditions; the cheapest street stall is often more hygienic. Where possible, try to watch food being prepared. Stir-fried vegetables and rice or noodles are the best bet; meat and fish may be pre-cooked and then left out before being re-heated. Fruit can be bought cheaply: papaya and banana are excellent sources of nutrition, and can be self-peeled ensuring cleanliness. Powdered milk is available in provincial centres (most brands have added sugar). If taking a baby, breast feeding is strongly recommended. Powdered food can

Essentials

also be bought in some towns – the quality may not be the same as equivalent foods bought in the West, but it is perfectly adequate for short periods. Bottled water and fizzy drinks are also sold widely.

Transport   Public transport may be a problem; long bus journeys are restrictive and uncomfortable. There is a reasonable domestic air network. Chartering a car is the most convenient way to travel overland. But rear seatbelts are scarce and child seats even rarer.

Disposable   These can be bought in Vientiane, but are often expensive. If you are staying any
nappies   length of time in one place, it may be worth taking terry's (cloth) nappies. All you need is a bucket and some double-strength nappy cleanse (simply soak and rinse). Cotton nappies dry quickly in the heat and are generally more comfortable for the baby or child. They also reduce rubbish – Laos is not geared to the disposal of nappies. Of course, the best way for a child to be is nappy-free – like the local children.

Emergencies   Babies and small children deteriorate very rapidly when ill. A travel insurance policy
See page 60 for   which has an air ambulance provision is strongly recommended. When planning a
hospitals in Nong Khai   route, try to stay within 24 hours' travel of a hospital with good care and facilities. Many
and Udon Thani   middle class Lao people travel to Thailand for health care (usually to Nong Khai or Udon Thani), and are suspicious of the ability of hospitals even in the capital of dealing with more than the most basic problems. Expats also leave the country for health care, usually for Bangkok or Udon Thani.

Sunburn   **Never** allow your child to be exposed to the harsh tropical sun without protection. A child can burn in a matter of minutes. Loose cotton clothing, with long sleeves and legs, and a sunhat are best. High-factor sun-protection cream is essential.

Checklist   Baby wipes; child paracetamol; disinfectant; first-aid kit; flannel; immersion element for boiling water; decongestant for colds; instant food for under-one-year-olds; mug/bottle/bowl/spoons; nappy cleanse, double-strength; ORS (Oral Rehydration Salts) such as *Dioralyte*, is the most effective way to alleviate diarrhoea (it is not a cure); portable baby chair, to hook onto tables (not essential but can be very useful); sarong or backpack for carrying child (and/or light weight collapsible buggy); sterilizing tablets (and container for sterilizing bottles, teats, utensils); cream for nappy rash and other skin complaints such as *Sudocrem*; sunblock; factor 15 or higher; sunhat; terry's (cloth) nappies, liners, pins and plastic pants; thermometer; zip-lock bags for carrying snacks, etc.

Flying with   Check out the facilities when booking your flight as these vary with each aircraft. *British*
kids   *Airways* now has a special seat for under 2s; check which aircraft have been fitted with
Visit: www.babygoes2.   them when booking. Pushchairs can be taken on as hand luggage or stored in the
com   hold. Skycots are available on long-haul flights. Take snacks and toys for in-flight entertainment and remember that swallowing food or drinks during take-off and landing will help prevent ear problems.

Suggested   Pentes, Tina and Truelove, Adrienne (1984) *Travelling with Children to Indonesia and*
reading   *South-East Asia*, Hale & Iremonger: Sydney. Wheeler, Maureen *Travel with Children*, Lonely Planet: Hawthorne, Australia.

Women travellers

While women travelling alone can generally face more potential problems than men or couples, these are far less pronounced in Laos than in most countries. Women have considerable autonomy in Laos (although this does not apply to some of the hill peoples) and while their status is not equal to that of men, the level of bias is comparatively small. Women play a critical role in trade, household and reproductive decision-making, they are prominent in Lao history, and even the Lao language is notable for its lack of gendered pronouns. Some scholars have even argued that men and women are equal. This is difficult to sustain and on the other side of the coin it is notable that the practice of Buddhism accords men a higher status, and in national politics women play a very minor role. But the relative power, autonomy and status of women means that it is rare for women to be harassed. Nonetheless women should take care to dress modestly, especially in the smaller, more provincial towns. Here in particular, skimpy tops and micro-shorts still arouse in locals the sort of embarrassed shock their urban counterparts have had to get used to. Women should also take the usual precautions, like avoiding, if possible, travelling alone at night.

Working in the country

Work is not easily available in Laos. There is a vibrant expat community, mostly of aid workers (with NGOs or bilateral/multilateral agencies) as well as the usual diplomatic corps. But unlike Thailand there is little scope for people to, for example, stay here for a few months and teach English.

For those proposing to live in Laos, the Vientiane Guide published by the Women's International Group is highly recommended

Useful websites www.ncvo-vol.org.uk/ Umbrella group representing voluntary organizations – some 500 – in the UK. **www.vso.org.uk/** VSO, UK. **www.ozvol.org.au/** Australian Volunteers International.

Before you travel

Getting in

Travelling in Laos is far simpler than it used to be. Visas can be obtained in a matter of days from any Lao embassy or consulate. For those who enter via the Friendship Bridge or arrive at Vientiane's Wattay Airport or Luang Prabang Airport visas are available on arrival for a modest fee (see below for details).

Regulations for tourists and business people seem to have settled down over the last few years. However visitors must be ready for the possibility that new or altered regulations have come into force since this book was researched. Over the last few years the trend has been towards greater openness. In 1991, 6,920 tourists visited the country; in 1995, 360,605; and in 1999, 614,279. Numbers have continued to increase during 2000 and 2001. Independent travel on public transport is easy (though not always comfortable), visas are cheaper and easier to get, entry and exit regulations have eased, visa extensions are easily arranged, and many more private hotels, guesthouses and tour companies have opened up for business.

In the past getting a tourist visa for Laos was quite a palava. Now the system, thankfully, is much simpler, easier and cheaper. Most Lao embassies will issue 30-day tourist visas. However many visitors to Laos arrange a visa in a neighbouring country, usually Thailand but also Cambodia, China, Myanmar and Vietnam. Furthermore, at the main gateways into Laos (the Friendship Bridge, and Vientiane and Luang Prabang aiports) it is possible to arrange a visa on arrival.

Tourist visas

Visas on arrival Visas on arrival are issued at **Vientiane's Wattay Airport**, the **Friendship Bridge** crossing near Nong Khai/Vientiane, and also at **Luang Prabang Airport** which has recently been upgraded to international status. The price in mid-2002 was US$30. Note that US dollars and Thai baht only are accepted in payment and a passport photograph is also required. **NB** Very occasionally the visa on arrival system in suspended. In April 2001, during the Party Congress, the Ministry of the Interior, worried about security, suspended the system – but didn't tell the Ministry of Foreign Affairs. The result: 40-odd tourists stranded at Wattay Airport who then had to take a plane back to Bangkok. Once in Laos, it is a simple matter to extend visas by visiting the immigration office in Vientiane. See the section on Visa extension, below.

Thailand **Bangkok** Most people visiting Laos travel through Thailand and, as a result, Bangkok is the best place to arrange a visa – although this is only necessary if you are thinking of entering the country at a point other than the Friendship Bridge or Vientiane or Luang Prabang airports. The Laos embassy in Bangkok (see box, page 29; open 0900-1200, 1400-1630, weekdays) issues one month visas in three working days; there is also a one day express service. However, as the embassy is fairly inaccessible, and considering the cost and time of negotiating Bangkok's roads, many visitors find it easier to arrange their visa through one of the Thai capital's many travel agents, who usually add only a 200-300 baht charge on top of the basic cost. The greatest concentration of tour agents is along and around Khaosan Road in Banglamphu, but agents in other tourist areas will also arrange visas at similar rates.

Nong Khai Nong Khai is the nearest town of any size to the Friendship Bridge spanning the Mekong. A number of tour companies have, over the years, sprung up to provide travellers to Laos with visas.

Chiang Khong It has been possible for a few years now to obtain visas in Chiang Khong and cross the Mekong from here to Ban Houei Xai. In Chiang Khong town itself *Ann Tour*, 6/1 Sai Klang Road, T/F053-791218 is recommended, while close to the ferry pier 1 km north of town are *Chiang Khong Tour* and *Nam Khong Travel* which provide a similar service. A photocopy of your passport is needed and the process usually takes one working day. Visas on arrival are not available at the Chiang Khong/Ban Houei Xai crossing point.

Nakhon Phanom and **Mukdahan** These two towns are across the Mekong from Thakhek and Savannakhet respectively, where it is possible to enter Laos. While visas on arrival are not available at these crossing points, agencies in the two towns will arrange visas for around US$30 for 15 days or US$50-60 for a 30-day visa.

Chiang Mai, **Ubon Ratchathani**, **Udon Thani** and **Khon Kaen** Tour agencies in Chiang Mai in Northern Thailand, and Ubon Ratchathani and Udon Thani in Northeast Thailand, will arrange visas for a fee. There is a Lao consulate in Khon Kaen (see box, page 29), also in Northeast Thailand, where tourist visas can be arranged.

Other Visas are available from Lao embassies in Cambodia, Myanmar (Burma), Vietnam and
neighbouring China and consulates in Vietnam (Ho Chi Minh City and Danang) and China (Kunming).
countries See box on page 29 for contact details.

Transit visas Usually valid for 7-10 days and can be obtained by tourists with a confirmed onward airline ticket. These are available from Lao embassies in Bangkok, Hanoi, Phnom Penh, Beijing, and Yangon (Rangoon) and from Lao consulates in Kunming (China), Ho Chi Minh City (Saigon, Vietnam) and Danang (Vietnam). As with regular tourist visas you

Embassies and consulates

Australia 1 Dalman Crescent, O'Malley, Canberra, T612-62864595, F62901910

Belgium Avenue de la Brabanconne, 19-21 b 1000 Bruxelles T322 734166

Cambodia 15 Mao Tse Tung Boulevard, PO Box 19, Phnom Penh, T855 23-982632, F720907

China Sanlitun Dongsie Jie, Beijing (Peking), T861-65231224, F65326748; inside Camelia Hotel, Kunming, T0871-3176624.

France 74 Raymond Poincare, Paris T331-45530298, F47275789

Germany Am Lessing 6, 5330, Koenigwinter, Bonn T49 222321501, F22233065

Indonesia Jn Kintamani Raja, Kuningan Timur, Jakarta, T6221-5202673, F5229601

Japan -3-3-22, Nishi Azabu, Minato-ku, Tokyo, T8103 54112291, F3-54112293

Malaysia 1 Lorong Damai Tiga, Kuala Lumpur, T603 2483895, F3-2420344

Myanmar (Burma) A1 Diplomatic Headquarters, Taw Win Road, Yangon (Rangoon), T951 222482, F227446

Sweden Badstrandvagen 11, Stockholm, T468 6182010, F6182001

Thailand 520-502/1-3 Ramkhamhaeng Soi 39 (Pracha-Uthit Road), Bangkapi, Bangkok, T662-5383696 or T5396667-9, F5396678 and in Khon Kaen, 19/1-3 Phothisarn Road, T6643 223698

USA 317 East 51st Street, New York, T1212 8322734, F7500039. 2222 S Street, Washington, T1202 3326416

Vietnam 22 Tran Binh Trong, Hanoi, T844 8269746, F8228414; 93 Pasteur Street, Ho Chi Minh City (Saigon), T848 -8297667; 12 Tran Qui Cap Street, Danang, T051-821208.

Essentials

can pay extra for an 'express' service. **NB** Transit visas cannot be extended (see Overstaying, below).

Business and visitors' visas valid for 30 days may be obtained from Laos' embassies and consulates, although the Lao Embassy in Bangkok often operates as an intermediary. Visitors' visas can be extended for a further 30 days while business visas can be indefinitely extended for repeated 30-day periods. The visa must be approved in Vientiane and requires a formal request from a business, governmental organization or family or friend in Laos. Approval for issuing the visa is sent to the appropriate embassy from Vientiane. A business visa allows travel throughout Laos, with multiple entries and exits. Business visas are renewable in Vientiane.

Business & visitors' visas

Visa restrictions on points of entry and exit Visas used to state the entry and exit points where the visa was to be used. This requirement was lifted in 1996 and visas now permit visitors to enter and leave at any border post open to foreigners.

Visa extensions Visas can be extended in Laos for a further 30 days at the cost of US$3 per day. This can be paid in kip or US dollars. You will need one passport photo. The Immigration office in the Ministry of the Interior opposite the Morning Market in Vientiane can process visa extension applications in a day. The staff here are pleasant and issue extensions politely and with little fuss – if you are particularly friendly and spend some time chatting with the young men they may even issue you the extension in a few hours. But if they take objection to you they can insist on two or more days!

Visitors who overstay are fined when they leave the country, currently US$5 per day beyond the visa's expiry date

Visas for Thailand With recent changes to Thailand's visa regulations it is no longer necessary for nationals of most countries to obtain a visa in Vientiane before entering the kingdom. If crossing by land, visas are issued at the Friendship Bridge. However, two month visas are available from the Thai Embassy on Thanon That

Luang in Vientiane and at the Thai Consulate in Savannakhet. It takes one day to process an application. Agency rates: if you intend to apply through one of the many visa agencies in Vientiane, it will take 24 hours to process and the cost will be around 700 baht.

Visas for China The Chinese Embassy, Wat Nak, Vientiane T021-315103, is open 0900-1130 for visa applications. Sixty day visas take three days to process (although for an extra charge, applications can be turned round in on the same day or the following day). Agency rates: same day, US$40; 24 hours, US$75; 72 hours, US$45.

Visas for Vietnam Visas for Vietnam are available from the embassy in Vientiane and the consulate in Savannakhet. They take three days to process, although for an extra fee can be turned round in 48 hours. Agency rates: 48 hours, US$95; 72 hours, US$55.

Visas for Cambodia Visas for Cambodia are available from the embassy in Vientiane. A same day service is available for an extra fee; it usually takes 24 hours. Agency rates: same day, US$40; 24 hours US$30.

Passport photographs It is useful to take several passport photographs with you for visa extensions, applications for other visas, etc.

Registering arrival and departure In most towns in the north of the country it used to be necessary to register your arrival and departure. Although this process was discontinued in 1999, some travellers report that they have, on occasion, had to have their passports stamped by police, at various sites including Pak Beng. Local immigration authorities sometimes have their own rules. Usually there is no fee, although there have been some reports of local immigration/police officers extracting unofficial fees. The lesson seems to be: be flexible and be prepared.

Insurance Always take out travel insurance before you set off and read the small print carefully. Check that the policy covers the activities you intend or may end up doing. Also check exactly what your medical cover includes, i.e. ambulance, helicopter rescue or emergency flights back home. Also check the payment protocol. You may have to cough up first (literally) before the insurance company reimburses you. It is always best to dig out all the receipts for expensive personal effects like jewellery or cameras. Take photos of these items and note down all serial numbers.

You are advised to shop around. *STA Travel* and other reputable student travel organizations offer good value policies. Young travellers from North America can try the International Student Insurance Service (ISIS), which is available through *STA Travel*, T1-800-7770112, www.sta-travel.com Other recommended travel insurance companies in North America include: *Travel Guard*, T1-800-8261300, www.noelgroup.com *Access America*, T1-800- 2848300; *Travel Insurance Services*, T1-800-9371387; *Travel Assistance International*, T1-800-8212828; and *Council Travel*, T1-888-COUNCIL, www.counciltravel.com Older travellers should note that some companies will not cover people over 65 years old, or may charge higher premiums. The best policies for older travellers (UK) are offered by **Age Concern**, T01883-346964.

Customs **Duty free allowance** 500 cigarettes, two bottles of wine and a bottle of liquor can be brought into the country duty free. There is a small but well-stocked duty-free shop on the Lao side at Tha Duea – and at Wattay Airport.

Export restrictions Laos has a strictly enforced ban on the export of antiquities and all Buddha images.

No inoculations are required except a cholera vaccination if coming from an infected area. It is advisable to take full precautions before travelling to Laos. Hospitals are few and far between and medical facilities are poor. Expats living in Laos tend to fly to Bangkok or even further afield should they need hospitalization or sophisticated medical care. Tetanus, polio, hepatitis, rabies, typhoid and cholera injections are recommended.

Vaccinations
See Health, page 60, for further details

What to take

Travellers usually tend to take too much, especially to a place like Laos which is not noted as a shopping Mecca. In Vientiane it is possible to buy most toiletries as well as things like photographic supplies and peanut butter. Luang Prabang, Savannakhet and Pakse also stock most basic items. Outside these cities little is available beyond items like soap, washing powder, batteries, shampoo, and the like.

See Health, page 61, for a medical checklist

Suitcases are not appropriate if you are intending to travel overland by bus. A backpack, or even better a travelpack (where the straps can be zipped out of sight), is recommended. Travelpacks have the advantage of being hybrid backpacks-suitcases; they can be carried on the back for easy porterage, but they can also be taken into hotels without the owner being labelled a 'hippy'.

In terms of clothing, dress in Laos is relatively casual – even at formal functions. Suits are not necessary. However, though formal attire may be the exception, dressing tidily is the norm. There is a tendency, rather than to take inappropriate articles of clothing, to take too many of the same article. Laundry services are cheap and rapid.

Checklist Bumbag; earplugs; first-aid kit; insect repellent and/or electric mosquito mats, coils; international driving licence; passports (valid for at least six months); photocopies of essential documents; shortwave radio; spare passport photographs; sun protection; sunglasses; Swiss Army knife; torch; umbrella; wet wipes; zip-lock bags.

Those intending to stay in budget accommodation might also include: cotton sheet sleeping bag; money belt; padlock (for hotel room and pack); soap; student card; toilet paper; towel; travel wash.

Money

Travellers' cheques denominated in US dollars and pounds sterling can be changed in major centres. The Euro was causing a certain amount of confusion during 2001 and early 2002 but it will also doubtless soon become widely accepted. Banks are generally reluctant to give anything but kip in exchange for hard currency. US dollars and Thai baht can be used as cash in most shops, restaurants and hotels. A certain amount of cash (in US dollars or Thai baht) can also be useful in an emergency. Keep it separate from your travellers' cheques.

There are no ATMs in Laos

The unit of currency is the **kip**. The kip has plummeted in value over the last few years. In the mid-1990s there were 1,200 kip to the US dollar. Because the kip has been so volatile over recent months foreign currency rates for hotels and other services have fluctuated wildly. Be prepared for further significant change in the costs of goods and services.

Currency
Conversion rates
in October 2002:
US $1, 7,562 kip;
UK £1, 11,720 kip;
1 Euro, 7,378 kip;
1 Thai baht, 173 kip
For latest rates, see
www.xe.com/acc/

Denominations in notes used to start at the diminutive – and useless – one kip. Ten, 20 and 50 kip notes have also become useless objects of veneration. Fifty kip is worth next to nothing. The lowest commonly used note is the 500 kip note. More useful are the 1,000, 5,000, 10,000 and the recently issued 20,000 kip notes. But even the latter, the highest denomination note available, is worth just US$2. As a result, pockets tend to bulge with huge wads of kip. It is partly because of the sheer inconvenience of

Essentials

carrying pockets full of Lao notes that people sensibly opt for Thai currency, or US dollars, instead. There are no coins in circulation.

Exchange
Most shops and restaurants will give you kip for US dollars or Thai baht

It is getting much easier to change currency and travellers' cheques in Laos. There are now a host of foreign banks – mostly Thai – with branches in Vientiane (Siam Commercial Bank, Thai Farmers Bank, Standard Chartered and more). *Le Banque pour Commerce Exterieur Lao*, the *Lao Mai Bank*, and the *Phak Thai Bank* change most major international currencies (cash) and travellers' cheques denominated in US dollars and pounds sterling. There is a slight but barely significant difference in the rates of exchange offered by banks and money changers.

Foreign banks sometimes display **ATM** signs. But these are not do-it-yourself ATMs. Money is withdrawn by counter staff and charged at 3%. It makes sense, if you are arriving from Thailand, to draw a few thousand baht out of an ATM before arriving in Laos. Note that some banks charge a hefty commission of US$2 per travellers' cheque, so it is sensible to take travellers' cheques in larger denominations. While banks will change travellers' cheques and cash denominated in most major currencies into kip, some will only change US dollars into Thai baht, or US dollars cash. (In other words, some banks will not change pounds sterling into Thai baht or US dollars – just kip.) It is easier to carry US dollars cash in small denominations or Thai baht when travelling, changing them as you go.

The government scrapped its multi-tier exchange rate system a while ago and with its demise the formely flourishing currency black market also disappeared. However with the catastrophic fall of the Thai baht in mid-1997, so the kip was dragged down too and the government began rounding up private money changers in Vientiane to try and stop the decline. As a result, the black market was given a new lease of life. However the situation has since returned to 'normal'. The Lao kip tends to shadow the Thai baht but with a rather quaint one week delay.

More expensive items, for example, tours, car hire, hotels, etc, tend to be quoted in dollars (or baht) while smaller purchases are quoted in kip. Thai baht are readily accepted in most towns but it is advisable to carry kip in rural areas (buses, for example, will usually only accept kip). It is quite normal to be quoted a price in kip, US dollars and baht. Nor is it unheard of to pay for a meal in three different currencies and certainly to be handed a bill quoting, for good measure, the total in kip, baht and US dollars.

The kip is non-convertible, so once you leave Laos any remaining notes are useless unless you can pass them on to someone about to enter the country.

Credit cards

Now that Laos has reformed its banking laws and welcomed foreign investment, so payment by credit card is becoming easier – although beyond the larger hotels and restaurants in Vientiane and Luang Prabang do not expect to be able to get by on plastic. American Express, Visa, Mastercard/Access, Bangkok Bank and MBF cards are accepted in a limited number of more upmarket establishments. Note that a commission is charged by some places on credit card transactions. If they can route the payment through Thailand then a commission is not levied; but if this is not possible, then 3% is usually added. *Le Banque pour Commerce Exterieur Lao* will advance cash on credit cards but only after they have telexed Bangkok for clearance. They charge for the cost of this extra administration.

Currency regulations

There are no restrictions on the import or export of foreign currencies other than Thai baht: a maximum of 100,000 baht can be imported. The Lao kip is a non-convertible currency, but inside Laos it is now almost as much in demand as US dollars and baht.

Cost of living

The budget traveller will find that a little goes a long way in Laos. Numerous guesthouses offer accommodation at around US$2-3 a night (often considerably less if you're sharing) and more and more are beginning to throw in free water and bananas. Food-wise, the seriously strapped can easily manage to survive healthily on US$2-3 per day, so an overall daily budget (not allowing for excursions) of US$4-5 should be more than enough for the really cost-conscious. For the less frugally minded, a daily allowance of $8-10 should see you relatively well-housed and fed, while at the upper end of the scale, there are usually plenty of accommodation and restaurant opportunities for those looking for Lao-levels of luxury. A mid-range hotel (attached bathroom, hot water, and a/c) will normally cost around US$20 per night. A good meal at a restaurant, perhaps US$5-10.

The cost of travelling around Laos depends largely on your chosen method of transport. The variety of available domestic flights means that the bruised bottoms, dust-soaked clothes and stiff limbs that go hand-in-hand with some of the longer bus/boat rides can be avoided by those with thicker wallets and deeper pockets. Air travel costs are standardized, and the same prices are offered by all travel agents (or should be). Foreigners pay more than locals. Boats traditionally formed the cornerstone of domestic travel requirements. Now though, as more of the country becomes accessible by land (although beware the rainy season, when some previously adequate roads become at best treacherous and at worst impossible), the popularity of boat travel has diminished while the cost has rocketed. Although heavily influenced by the price of fuel, boat travel remains generally costly. As the roads improve and journey times diminish, buses have emerged above both planes and boats as the preferred (not to mention most reasonably priced) transportation option.

Cost of travelling
For air, bus and boat fares, see pages 44, 47 and 101 respectively

Essentials

Getting there

Most visitors to Laos enter either through **Vientiane's Wattay Airport** or via the **Friendship Bridge** at **Tha Deua**. Foreign visitors can also enter Laos at **Thakhek, Savannakhet, Chongmek** and **Ban Houei Xai** (all to/from Thailand); **Lao Bao** and **Cau Trea** (from Vietnam); and **Boten** (from China). As of early 2002, the borders with Myanmar (Burma) in the north and Cambodia in the south were still **closed** to foreigners.

Entry/exit points

Air

Bangkok is the main gateway to Vientiane. If you want to visit Bangkok as well as Laos, the best way is to include the Bangkok-Vientiane sector on your long haul ticket. This is a cheaper option than purchasing tickets separately in Bangkok. There are daily flights between **Vientiane** and **Bangkok** operated by *THAI* and *Lao Aviation*. Expats in Vientiane prefer to take the *THAI* flight, for reasons of both safety and comfort. However, foreign embassies are now a little more relaxed about their staff travelling on *Lao Aviation* and the airlines' French-built ATRs (which operate on the Vientiane-Bangkok route) are said to be airworthy. While the official fares are slightly different both can be purchased from travel agents for US$115 one-way, US$230 return. International flights purchased in Laos can be paid for using credit cards: Amex and Visa only. *Bangkok Airways* has recently started flying from **Bangkok** to **Luang Prabang**, via **Sukhothai** (the latter also in Thailand). *Lao Aviation* now also run a twice-weekly service (Thursdays and Sundays) between **Chiang Mai**, in Northern Thailand, and **Vientiane**, via **Luang Prabang** (US$71.40 one-way).

From Thailand & the rest of the world
There are no direct flights to Laos from North America or Europe

For cheap flights, try www.fly4less.com www.flynow.com www.dialaflight.com www.what'sonwhen. com

While most visitors to Laos fly into Vientiane, the preferred route in and out of Laos for many is via the Thai city of **Udon Thani** in Northeast Thailand, about 50 km south of the Friendship Bridge. This is because the single domestic airfare between Udon and Bangkok is a third that of the international fare between Vientiane and Bangkok, while the differential between the return fares is one half. In addition there

▶▶ Discount flight agents

Australia and New Zealand

Flight Centres, *82 Elizabeth St, Sydney, T13-1600; 205 Queen St, Auckland, T09-309 6171. Also branches in other towns and cities.*

STA Travel, *T1300-360960, www.statravelaus.com.au; 702 Harris St, Ultimo, Sydney, and 256 Flinders St, Melbourne. In NZ: 10 High St, Auckland, T09-366 6673. Also in major towns and university campuses.*

Travel.com.au, *80 Clarence St, Sydney, T02-929 01500, www.travel.com.au*

UK and Ireland

Council Travel, *28a Poland St, London, W1V 3DB, T020-74377767, www.destinations-group.com*

STA Travel, *86 Old Brompton Rd, London, SW7 3LH, T020-74376262, www. statravel.co.uk They have other branches in London, as well as in Brighton, Bristol, Cambridge, Leeds, Manchester, Newcastle-Upon-Tyne and Oxford and on many university campuses. Specialists in low-cost student/youth flights and tours, also good for student IDs and insurance.*

Trailfinders, *194 Kensington High Street, London, W8 7RG, T020-79383939.*

North America

Air Brokers International, *323 Geary St, Suite 411, San Francisco, CA94102, T01-800-883 3273, www.airbrokers.com Consolidator and specialist on RTW and Circle Pacific tickets.*

Council Travel, *205 E 42nd St, New York, NY 10017, T1-888-COUNCIL, www. counciltravel.com Student/budget agency with branches in many other US cities.*

Discount Airfares Worldwide On-Line, *www.etn.nl/discount.htm A hub of consolidator and discount agent links.*

International Travel Network/Airlines of the Web, *www.itn.net/airlines Online air travel information and reservations.*

STA Travel, *5900 Wilshire Blvd, Suite 2110, Los Angeles, CA 90036, T1-800-777 0112, www.sta-travel.com Also branches in New York, San Francisco, Boston, Miami, Chicago, Seattle and Washington DC.*

Travel CUTS, *187 College St, Toronto, ON, M5T 1P7, T1-800-667 2887, www.travelcuts.com Specialist in student discount fares, Ids and other travel services. Branches in other Canadian cities.*

Travelocity, *www.travelocity.com Online consolidator.*

---

are three flights a day between Bangkok and Udon – although the evening flight arrives too late to make it to the Friendship Bridge before it closes at 1800 (check the *Thai airways* domestic timetable at **www.thaiair.com**). It might seem a bit of a palava, but the service works very efficiently and is, in fact, pretty hassle-free. From Udon Thani there are a/c buses that run direct from the airport to the **Friendship Bridge** (40 minutes). At the bridge, buy a ticket for the shuttle bus for 10 baht and on reaching Lao immigration apply for a visa on arrival (see Visas on arrival, page 27, for details). From the Lao side, taxis and tuk-tuks wait to ferry people into Vientiane (150-200 baht, 20 minutes). All in all, the difference in time between flying direct to Vientiane or taking the Udon/Friendship Bridge option is probably just one hour because immigration at Wattay Airport tends to be slower. Should you arrive in Udon too late to reach the bridge before it closes at 1800, there is a wide range of hotels and guesthouses to choose from.

From Vietnam   There are flights between **Vientiane** and **Hanoi** and **Vientiane** and **Saigon** (Ho Chi Minh City) operated by *Lao Aviation* and *Vietnam Airlines*. *Lao Aviation* operate six flights a week (not Monday) between Hanoi and Vientiane and one flight a week to Saigon (Friday).

The Vientiane-Phnom Penh route has two direct return flights a week, on Monday and Friday.

The only connection with China is with *Lao Aviation* which offers one flight a week (on Sunday) between **Kunming** and **Vientiane** (US$105 one-way). The *Lao Aviation* route map displays a service between Luang Prabang and Kunming, but this seems to be wishful thinking.

From China

There used to be one *Lao Aviation* flight a week between **Yangon** (Rangoon) and **Vientiane**. It was suspended in 1999.

From Myanmar (Burma)

Silk Air used to offer a service between **Singapore** and **Vientiane** while *Malaysian Airlines* had operated flights between **Kuala Lumpur** and **Vientiane**. These have both been suspended but the intention is to restart the services when conditions allow.

From Singapore & Malaysia

Thai Airways is the agent for ***Lao Aviation*** in Bangkok: 491/17 Ground Floor, Silom Plaza, Silom Road, Bangkok, T02-2369822, F02-2369821. Tickets bought in Bangkok on *Lao Aviation* are **not** refundable in Laos. *Lao Aviation*'s office in Chiang Mai (Thailand) is at 2/115 Rajchapuak, Huaykaew Road, T053-404033, F053-223400. In Hanoi, Vietnam: Apt no. 8 B3b, Giang Vo, 269 Kimma Street, T04-8464873, F04-8464874. In Ho Chi Minh City (Saigon), Vietnam: 181 Habai Trung Street, Quan 3, T/F08-8226990. In Phnom Penh, Cambodia: 85 Sihanouk Avenue, Khana Tonle Basak, T/F023-216563. In Kunming, China: N.96 East Dong Feng Dong Road, Camelia Hotel, T871-312748.

Useful websites www.thaiair.com Thai Airways site. Useful for checking flight timetables to Udon Thani from Bangkok (domestic) and to Vientiane (international). www.bangkokair.com Home page of *Bangkok Airways* which now flies between Bangkok and Luang Prabang (see page 21 for contact details).

Road and river

The **Thai-Lao Mittaphab (Friendship) Bridge** opened in 1994 (see page 70). Crossing the border at Tha Deua is very easy. The bridge is open Monday-Sunday 0800-2200. Immigration and customs are on both sides of the bridge and a shuttle bus transports visitors across (10 baht). Tuk-tuks and taxis wait at both customs houses to take visitors either on to Vientiane, 20-40 minutes (150-200 baht) or to Nong Khai in Thailand. The cheapest way into Vientiane from the bridge is to board a No 14 bus. These run every half-hour or so until 1700 and terminate at Vientiane's Morning Market or *talaat sao*. Note that it is necessary to bargain particularly assiduously on the Thai side of the frontier. Buses and taxis from Vientiane leave from the Morning Market. **NB** Do not travel with anybody else's belongings. Should the bridge have closed, there are plenty of hotels and guesthouses in the nearby Thai town of Nong Khai.

From Thailand
A second bridge over the Mekong, linking Savannakhet to Mukdahan in Thailand, is due for completion in 2005

There is an official border post on the Mekong River at the Thai town of **Nong Khai** with a crossing to **Tha Deua** (25 km from Vientiane) but this is only open for locals; tourists must use the bridge.

There are regular ferries 0800-1700 Monday-Friday and 0800-1200 Saturday across the Mekong between **Thakhek** and **Nakhon Phanom** (Thailand).

Ferries run between Hua Wiang, 2 km north of **Chiang Khong** (Thailand) and **Ban Houei Xai**.

Regular ferries between **Savannakhet** and **Mukdahan** (Thailand) 0830-1700 Monday-Friday, 0830-1230 Saturday.

Essentials

▶▶ Overland connections with Laos

As the Lao authorities have eased restrictions on overland access for foreigners, so the number of access points has multiplied. This table is designed to help make sense of border crossings and provide cross references to the relevant sections of text. In 2002 the borders with Cambodia and with Myanmar (Burma) were closed to foreigners.

Border crossings with Thailand
*Ban Houei Xai – Chiang Khong
(see page 184)*
*Vientiane/Tha Deua – Nong Khai
(see page 101)*

*Thakhek – Nakhon Phanom
(see page 197)*
*Savannakhet – Mukdahan
(see page 203)*
*Pakse – Chongmek/Ubon Ratchathani
(see page 229)*

Border crossings with Vietnam
*Lac Xao (Route 8) – Cau Treo
(see page 193)*
*Savannakhet/Xepon – Lao Bao
(Route 9) (see page 203)*

Border crossings with China
Boten – Mengla (see page 175)

It is possible to cross the Mekong to **Chongmek** (Thailand) from **Pakse** (see page 229 for details). The completion of a new bridge over the Mekong at Pakse has made this journey considerably quicker.

From Vietnam The most popular crossing point between Vietnam and Laos is at **Lao Bao**, northwest of Hué in Vietnam and east of Savannakhet in Laos, situated in the Annamite chain of mountains which forms a spine separating Laos and Vietnam (see Xepon, page 205, for further details about this crossing point). From the border, entering Laos, the last bus to **Savannakhet** leaves at 1500, arriving 2400, with no food stops.

In recent years, a more northerly border with Vietnam has opened to foreign travellers, 80 km from the Vietnamese town of Vinh. The Vietnamese border town is **Cau Trea**, and on the Lao side, the nearest town is **Lak Xao (Muang Kham Keut)**. There is no accommodation on the Vietnamese side, but there is a choice of guesthouses in Lac Xao (one hour from the border by 'jumbo', see page 192).

From China From China the frontier is close to the Lao town of **Boten**. The nearest Chinese town is **Mengla**. (To get to Mengla, take a bus from Jinghong, six hours.) From Mengla there are frequent buses to the border (Mohan) from 0730. At the frontier it is possible to change remaining yuan into Lao kip. There are no money changing facilities on the Lao side of the border although *Vieng Champa Tour* will convert US dollars cash at a poor rate of exchange. Around midday buses arrive to take new arrivals on to towns like Luang Namtha and Udom Xai (Muang Xai). While the border with China near **Muang Sing** is not a legal crossing point we have had several reports of travellers who were successful in crossing here.

From Cambodia & Myanmar (Burma) Officially, foreigners are currently not permitted to either enter or leave Laos via Cambodia or Myanmar (Burma). From Cambodia, the entry point is at **Muang Saen**, across the Mekong River from **Phumi Khampong Sralan**. There is also a border crossing at **Xieng Kok**, on the Mekong, into Myanmar (Burma) but this, likewise, is closed to foreigners. However, there have been reports of travellers being granted a visa here and entering Myanmar (Burma).

Touching down ◀◀

Emergencies *Ambulance: T195.* **Fire brigade:** *T190.* **Police:** *T191.*
IDD code *T00856*
Directory Enquiries *T16 or T170 for international*
Official time *Seven hours ahead of GMT.*
Official language *Lao, Thai is understood, as is French and English in the main tourist areas.*
Hours of business *Government offices: 0800-1700 Monday-Friday but often closed for two hours at lunchtime (usually 1200-1400).* **Banks:** *0800-1200, 1400-1500 Monday-Friday; some banks also open on Saturday mornings.* **Shops:** *0900-1700 Monday-Saturday and some on Sunday.*
Voltage *220 volts, 50 cycles in the main towns. 110 volts in the country. Two-pin sockets are common so adaptors are required. For sensitive equipment it is best to use a voltage regulator. Blackouts are common outside Vientiane and many smaller towns are not connected to the national grid and only have power during the evening and early night.*
Weights and measures *Metric along with local systems of measurement.*
Type of plug socket *Same as Thailand – two-pin socket.*

Essentials

Touching down

Airport information

Wattay International Airport is about 6 km from Vientiane. Until a couple of years ago Wattay Airport was a throwback to an earlier age of aviation when pilots were aviators and airports were airfields. There wasn't an escalator or moving walkway in sight. Sadly for those with a nostalgic turn of mind, this is all in the past. A new, Japanese-financed (but Lao-designed) terminal was opened a couple of years back, fully air-conditioned and painted in soothing – and very 21st-century – grey. There's even an escalator as well as a small number of air bridges for the few airplanes that require such advanced technology. While in some sense this is a shame, most people will regard it as an advance. Visitors can now complete their visa application forms in air-conditioned comfort while listening to piped international music. (But all is not lost: the old terminal has now become the domestic terminal.) The runway was extended to 2,700 m even before the terminal buildings were finished and it is now equipped with international standard landing equipment. The airport also has a restaurant, hotel booking counter, foreign exchange desk, duty free shop, gift shop, and post office. In other words, most of the things that you could possibly want from an airport. Visas on arrival are available at Wattay Airport (see Visas, page 27). Depending on the numbers of tourists arriving and needing such a visa, the process usually takes about 30 minutes and is fairly efficient and pretty painless. If you intend coming back to Laos it is handy to take a few extra forms with you so you can fill one in before landing.

Flight information: T212066

International airport tax: US$10. Domestic airport tax: 5,000 kip.

Airport tax

By bus Local buses operate from Luang Prabang Road outside the airport every 45 minutes. **By taxi** Metered taxis available. Fares payable in US dollars, baht or kip. Expect to pay around 10,000 kip depending on destination. **By tuk-tuk** Around 5,000 kip to the town centre; it may be necessary to walk out onto the main road to catch one (they usually wait near the airport entrance).

Transport to town

Tourist information

See Finding out more, page 22, for a list of useful websites

Until independent privately owned tour operators were permitted to set up shop in 1991, there was a tourist information vacuum in Laos. The official government-run **National Tourism Authority of Lao** (Lane Xang Avenue, Vientiane, T021-212251, F212769, www.mekongcenter.com) is not renowned for its skills in information dissemination. The best source of up-to-date information is from recent travellers, whose comments and advice is documented in scrapbooks in Nong Khai guesthouses (across the river in Thailand). At the speed with which events are moving in Laos, these sources become outdated very quickly. Certain tour agencies in Bangkok also keep bulletin boards of up-to-date records and travellers' tips, although these informal sources are becoming less necessary as travelling becomes easier and information on travelling is more widely available. In Vientiane it is also possible to pick up two modestly handy and informative magazines geared to tourists: *Discover Laos* and *Muong Lao*, the latter published by LNTA.

There is a local telephone directory, called *How to Call Us and Our Friends*, which lists the numbers of expats living in Vientiane as well as aid agencies and embassies.

Maps

See also Getting around, page 48

The **Women's International Group** (WIG) produce the *Vientiane Guide*; very useful and full of up-to-date information and good maps (see Books, page 309, for further details). Another useful book is the *Guide to Wats in Vientiane*. State-produced maps of Vientiane, Luang Prabang, Pakse, Savannakhet and other major towns (major is used advisedly) are available but often in limited supply. Local maps and guides mentioned above are available at several shops and hotels in Vientiane.

Tours In the past, tours allowed little flexibility in terms of accommodation, itinerary or mode of transport. This has changed and most outfits allow you to customize their package (including choice of accommodation) depending on budget.

Local customs and laws

Clothing Informal, lightweight clothing is all that is needed, although a sweater is vital for the highlands in the winter months. An umbrella is useful during the rainy season. Sleeveless shirts and singlets, shorts and short skirts are generally frowned upon. When visiting monasteries (wats) women should keep their shoulders covered. In general, 'scruffy' travellers are frowned upon. One of the main reasons why tourism was tightly controlled in Laos is because of the perceived corrosive effects that badly dressed tourists was having on Lao culture. The assumption is that scruffy dress is a reflection of character. While there has been a relative opening up of the country over the last few years, this does not mean that many officials do not continue to subscribe to this belief.

Conduct **Wats** Lao monks are said to be not as disciplined as Thai monks – probably owing to the effects of 15 years of communism – but Buddhism has undergone a revival. If talking to a monk your head should be lower than his. Avoid visiting a wat around 1100 as this is when the monks have their morning meal. It is considerate to ask the abbot's permission to enter the *sim* and shoes should be removed before entry. When sitting down, feet should point away from the altar and main image. Arms and legs should be fully covered when visiting wats. A small donation is often appropriate (kneel when putting it into the box).

Forms of address Lao people are addressed by their first name, not their family name, even when a title is used.

Visiting minority villages: house rules

- *Etiquette and customs vary between the minorities. However, the following are general rules of good behaviour that should be adhered to whenever possible.*
- *Dress modestly and avoid undressing/changing in public.*
- *Ask permission before photographing anyone (old people, pregnant women and mothers with babies often object to having their photograph taken).*
- *Only enter a house if invited.*
- *Do not touch or photograph village shrines.*
- *Do not smoke opium.*
- *Avoid sitting or stepping on door sills.*

- *Avoid excessive displays of wealth and be sensitive when giving gifts (for children, pens are better than sweets).*
- *Avoid introducing Western medicines.*
- *Do no sit with the soles of your feet pointing at other people (ie sit cross-legged).*
- *Do not buy heirlooms.*
- *Cover yourself when bathing in public.*
- *Buy new handicrafts to support village industries.*
- *Don't openly embrace or kiss.*
- *Always offer to pay for food or accommodation.*
- *Don't speak loudly.*

Essentials

Greeting The *nop* or *wai* – with hands together and head bowed, as if in prayer – remains the traditional form of greeting. Shaking hands, though, is very widespread – more so than in neighbouring Thailand. This can be put down to the influence of the French during the colonial period whereas Thailand was never colonized.

In private homes Remove your shoes. When seated on the floor you should tuck your feet behind you. Try not to pat children on the head, as it is considered the most sacred part of the body.

General Pointing with the index finger is considered rude.

Visiting minority villages It is becoming increasingly popular for travellers to Laos to visit minority villages. This raises a whole series of questions about conduct which cannot be covered in a general discussion because of cultural differences between the Lao and the upland peoples, and between the many different upland peoples. There is certainly a case for advising that visitors, where possible, employ the services of a local guide. Just as was the case in northern Thailand when trekking became popularized there, the actions of a few are tarring the reputation of the many. In more than a few cases, visitors have no idea how to behave with minority people. Many seek to buy drugs, female travellers potter around scantily clad, they have little notion of local customs, where not to go, what not to bring (many bring sweets), and so on. Because the numbers of travellers visiting minority villages has exploded in recent years this has become quite a serious problem. See also box above

In Laos, who eats when is important. At a meal, a guest should not begin eating until the host has invited him or her to do so. Nor should the guest continue eating after everyone else has finished. At a family gathering, the eating order is dictated by age: mother and father take the first food, and then each child in order of their descending age. It is also customary for guests to leave a small amount of food on their plate; to do otherwise would imply that the guest was still hungry and that the host had not provided sufficient food for the meal. **Eating**

Sensitivity pays when taking photographs. Be very wary in areas that have (or could have) military importance – such as airports, where all photography is prohibited. Also **Photographs** be careful when photographing official functions and parades without permission. Always ask permission before taking photographs in a monastery.

Tipping It is not common practice, even in hotels. However it is normal practice to tip guides and some more expensive restaurants, mostly in Vientiane, appreciate a 10% tip if service charge is not included on the bill.

Prohibitions Beyond the usual and obvious prohibitions – drugs, firearms and such like – visitors should be sensitive to the political and religious situation in Laos. Open criticism of the government should be avoided and proselytizing is not appreciated. Deportation or detention – or both – will be the likely result.

Responsible tourism

Most international tourists come from a handful of wealthy countries. This is why many see tourism as the new 'imperialism', imposing alien cultures and ideals on sensitive and unmodernized peoples. The problem, however, is that discussions of the effects of tourism tend to degenerate into simplifications – culminating in the drawing up of a checklist of 'positive' and 'negative' effects. Although such tables may be useful in highlighting problem areas, they also do a disservice by reducing a complex issue to a simple set of rather one dimensional 'costs' and 'benefits'. Different destinations will be affected in different ways; these effects are likely to vary over time; and different groups living in a particular destination will feel the effects of tourism in different ways and to varying degrees. At no time or place can tourism (or any other influence) be categorized as uniformly 'good' or 'bad'. Tourism can take a young Australian backpacker on US$10 a day to a guesthouse in a small town in northern Laos, a family to a first class hotel in Luang Prabang where a room can cost more than US$100 a night, or a businessman or woman to Vientiane.

Some tourists are attracted to Laos because of its exotic 'tribal' hill peoples. When cultural erosion is identified, the tendency is to blame this on tourists and tourism who become the so-styled 'suntanned destroyers of culture'. The problem with views like this is that they assume that change is bad, and that indigenous cultures are unchanging. It makes local peoples victims of change, rather than masters of their own destinies.

Tourist art, both material (for instance, sculpture) and non-material (like dances) is another issue where views over the impacts of tourism sharply diverge. The mass of inferior 'airport' art on sale to tourists demonstrates, to some, the corrosive effects of tourism. It leads craftsmen and women to mass-produce second rate pieces for a market that appreciates neither their cultural or symbolic worth, nor their aesthetic value. Yet tourism can also give value to craft industries that would otherwise be undermined by cheap industrial goods. So, some people argue that the craft traditions of Laos may be given a new injection of vitality by the demands that tourism is increasingly creating. Indeed, this has already happened: witness the re-birth of top quality textile production.

The environmental deterioration that is linked to tourism is due to a destination area exceeding its 'carrying capacity' as a result of overcrowding. But carrying capacity, though an attractive concept, is notoriously difficult to pin down. A second dilemma facing those trying to encourage greater environmental consciousness is the so-called 'tragedy of the commons', better described in terms of Chinese restaurants. When a group of people go to a Chinese restaurant with the intention of sharing the bill, each customer will tend to order a more expensive dish than he or she would normally do – on the logic that everyone will be doing the same, and the bill will be split. In tourism terms, it means that hotel owners will always build those few

How big is your footprint?

- *Learn about the country you're visiting.*
- *Start enjoying your travels before you leave by tapping into as many sources of information as you can.*
- *Think about where your money goes – be fair and realistic about how cheaply you travel. Try and put money into local people's hands; drink local beer or fruit juice rather than imported brands and stay in locally-owned accommodation.*
- *Open your mind to new cultures and traditions. It can transform your holiday experience and you'll earn respect and be more readily welcomed by local people.*
- *Think about what happens to your rubbish - take biodegradable products and a water filter bottle. Be sensitive to limited resources like water, fuel and electricity.*
- *Help preserve local wildlife and habitats by respecting rules and regulations,*

such as sticking to footpaths, not standing on coral and not buying products made from endangered plants or animals.
- *Use your guidebook as a starting point, not the only source of information. Talk to local people, then discover your own adventure!*
- *Don't treat people as part of the landscape, they may not want their picture taken. Put yourself in their shoes, ask first and respect their wishes.*

***NB**: This is taken from the* Tourism Concern *website which also provides further elaboration of the points noted here. The code was developed from a Young Travellers' conference in April 2001 but is not aimed only at young travellers. As they say: "It applies to everybody who loves travelling, whether on a budget holiday or staying in a luxury community run centre".*

more bungalows or that extra wing, to maximize their profits, reassured in the knowledge that the environmental costs will be shared among all hotel owners. So, despite most operators appreciating that over-development may 'kill the goose that lays the golden eggs', they do so anyway. But many areas of Laos have few other development opportunities and those with beautiful landscapes and/or exotic cultures find it difficult not to resist the temptation to market them and attract the tourist dollar. And why shouldn't they?

One of the ironies is that the 'traveller' or 'backpacker' finds it difficult to consider him or herself as a tourist at all. This, of course, is hubris built upon the notion that the traveller is an 'independent' explorer somehow beyond the bounds of the industry.

Tourism Concern, a UK-based charity, works to resolve some of the issues sketched out above in a constructive manner. As they say on their website: "We look at the way tourism affects the people and environments in tourism destination areas. Tourism Concern raises awareness of tourism's impact with the general public, with government decision-makers and within the tourist industry itself – and we provide a unique information base for campaigners and students of tourism." It is possible to subscribe to their magazine, *In Focus* by writing to Tourism Concern, Stapleton House, 277-281 Holloway Road, London N7 8HN. Subscription rates vary between £12 and £25. Or visit their website: www.tourismconcern.org.uk

Pressure groups

Safety

Crime rates are very low but it is advisable to take the usual precautions. Most areas of Laos are safe – a very different state of affairs from only a few years ago when foreign embassies advised tourists not to travel along certain roads and in certain areas (in particular Route 13, between Vientiane and Luang Prabang, and Route 7 between

See page 27 for information on women travelling alone

Essentials

Phonsavanh and Route 13). Today these risks have effectively disappeared. There was a spate of bombings in Vientiane in 2000 that may have been linked to the Hmong resistance movement (although some people suspected a disaffected group within the ruling party). However these seem to have stopped just as mysteriously as they started. There has been a reported increase in motorcycle drive-by thefts in Vientiane, but these and other similar crimes are still at a low level compared with most countries.

Travel advisories
Check on conditions before travelling at **www.fco.gov.uk/travel/countryadvice**, the **UK Foreign & Commonwealth Office**'s travel warning section, or at **www.travel.state.gov/laos.html**, the **US State Department**'s continually updated travel advisory.

Road safety
As the number of motorized vehicles increases and their speeds rise, so road accidents are also escalating. The US State Department's travel advisory puts it like this: "Traffic in Laos is chaotic, and road conditions are very rough. Many drivers are unlicensed and uninsured. Theoretically, traffic moves on the right, but vehicles use all parts of the road. Cyclists pay little or no heed to cars on the road. Motorcycles carry as many as five people, greatly impeding the drivers' ability to react to traffic. The evening hours are particularly dangerous. Road construction sites are poorly marked, have no advance warning, and can be difficult to see at night. Roads are poorly lit, many vehicles have no operating lights, few bicycles have reflectors, and it is common for trucks to park on unlit roads with no reflectors." As the hiring of motorbikes by tourists is becoming more popular so tourist injuries are also increasing. The utmost care should be taken.

The Golden Triangle
The Golden Triangle, in certain areas, has risks because of the opium trade and the lawlessness that goes with this.

Mines
Xieng Khouang province, the **Bolovens Plateau**, **Xam Neua**, and areas along the **Ho Chi Minh Trail** are littered with *bombis* – small anti-personnel mines and bomblets from cluster bomb units. There are also many large unexploded bombs; in many villages they have been left lying around. They are very unstable so **DO NOT TOUCH**. Five to 10 people are still killed or injured every month in Laos by inadvertently stepping on ordnance, or hitting 'pineapple' bomblets with hoes.

Where to stay

Sleeping
See also box on page 43
Rooms in Laos are rarely luxurious and standards vary enormously – you can end up paying double what you would pay in Bangkok for the same level of facilities and service. However the hotel industry is expanding rapidly: many older buildings are under renovation, and new hotels are springing up – some in conjunction with overseas companies. Only the *Tai-Pan*, *Royal Dokmaideng*, *Settha Palace*, *Novotel*, *Lao Plaza* and *Lane Xang* in Vientiane and the *Villa Santi*, *Phou Vao*, *Villa Santi Resort* and *L'Hotel Souvannaphoum* in Luang Prabang come into the first class bracket. Of these only the *Novotel*, *Lao Plaza*, *Souvannaphoum*, *Villa Santi* and the *Phou Vao* (in Luang Prabang) could be said to approach international standards in terms of the range of facilities on offer. That said, there is a reasonable choice of hotels of different standards and prices in Vientiane, Luang Prabang and Pakse and an expanding number of budget places in many towns on the fast-developing tourist trail.

The majority of guesthouses and hotels have fans and attached bathrooms, although more and more are providing a/c where there is a stable electricity supply

Hotel classifications

L *US$100+*

First class plus: *business services, sports facilities (gym, swimming pool etc), Asian and Western restaurants, bars, and discotheques. Only a handful of hotels in Vientiane and a couple in Luang Prabang could be said to meet this level of facilities. The most expensive hotel in Vientiane is the Lao Plaza at US$120 (rack rate) and in Luang Prabang the* Souvannaphoum, Villa Santi *and* Phou Vao *which charge around US$100.*

AL *US$60-100*

First class: *business services, sports facilities (gym, swimming pool etc), Asian and Western restaurants, bars, and discotheques. Only hotels in Vientiane and Luang Prabang will conform to international standards of 'First Class'. Bear in mind that most hotels in Laos are small and cannot support a wealth of facilities and amenities; the 'gym' may be basic, the business suite quaintly rudimentary. Nonetheless they should be comfortable and may well make up in terms of personal service and friendliness what they lack in size and grandeur.*

A *US$30-60*

Tourist class: *all rooms will have air-conditioning and an attached bathroom, very occasionally a swimming pool, restaurant, 24-hour coffee shop/room service and cable films and/or satellite television.*

B *US$15-30*

Economy: *air-conditioning, attached bathrooms with hot water. Restaurant and room service.*

C *US$8-15*

Budget: *probably air-conditioned, attached bathroom. Bed linen and towels, and there may be a restaurant.*

D *US$4-8*

Guesthouse: *fan-cooled rooms, possibly attached bathroom facilities. Mixture of bathroom technologies from Asian to Western. Bed linen and towels. Rooms will probably be small, facilities few.*

E *US$2-4 and* **F** *US$<2*

Guesthouse: *fan-cooled rooms, shared bathroom facilities. Asian toilets. Variable standards of cleanliness.*

Essentials

(and others are installing their own generators) to cater for the needs of the growing tourist trade. Smaller provincial towns, having previously had only a handful of hotels and guesthouses – some of them quaint French colonial villas – are now home to a growing number of rival concerns as tourism takes off. In rural villages, people's homes are enthusiastically transformed into bed and breakfasts on demand. While the evidence is of deep and wide change in the tourist infrastructure, Laos still has a long way to go before it approaches international standards. To put the country in to perspective: there are more beds on offer, and a wider range of services and facilities, in single Thai beach resorts like Pattaya and Phuket than in the whole of Laos.

Until the mid 90s, Laos was a relatively expensive place for budget travellers. While mid-range hotels offered reasonable value for money compared with Thailand, guesthouses at the lower end of the market were overpriced. However, as independent tourism has expanded and the number of guesthouses has increased, so the ensuing price wars have kept costs competatively low. In addition the fall in the value of the kip has meant that, in international terms, Laos has become cheaper since the last edition of this book was published. While Vientiane may still have little to offer the budget traveller, many towns in the North – such as Vang Vieng, Muagn Ngoy, Muang Sing, Pak Beng, and Luang Nam Tha – have a large choice of very cheap, and in some cases very good accommodation, including dorm beds. A double in a guesthouse can be found for 20,000 kip, around US$2 at the early-2002 rate of exchange. In addition many towns, especially in the north, have rock-bottom dorm rooms that many Lao use for around 8,000 kip per bed (less than US$1). See Cost of living, page 32, for further details.

Getting around

Laos is a large country with a small population: some five million people inhabit an area of 237,000 sq km – roughly the size of the United Kingdom. It is also very poor and has been ravaged by a terrible war, experiencing, in the process, some of the heaviest bombing the world has ever witnessed. Couple this with the mountainous terrain and a tropical climate of seasonal torrential rains, and it is no wonder that road construction poses a considerable challenge in many areas. The government of the Lao People's Democratic Republic was also cut off from the West from 1975 – when the Lao People's Revolutionary Party finally ousted the Royal Lao Government – until the mid-1980s, when it hesitatingly embraced a programme of economic reform and international integration. All this means that roads in Laos are not exactly 'good', but they are slowly improving. The accessibility of the further flung towns and villages can depend to a certain extent on the time of year, and also sometimes the willingness of passengers to get out and help build the very road the bus is meant to be driving along.

Practicalities Quite a few bus, truck, tuk-tuk and taxi drivers understand the rudimentaries of English, French or Thai, although some of them (especially tuk-tuk drivers) aren't above forgetting the lowest price you thought you'd successfully negotiated before hopping aboard! It is best to take this sort of thing in good humour. Even so, in order to travel to a particular destination, it is a great advantage to have the name written out in Lao. Map reading is out of the question, and many people will not know road names, even if it's the road right outside their front door. However, they will know where all the sights of interest are – for example wats, markets, monuments, waterfalls, etc.

Air

Many of Laos's major towns are serviced by *Lao Aviation*. Tickets can be purchased from their office in Vientiane. All flights using *Lao Aviation*, whether domestic or international, have to be paid for in US dollars by foreigners. Kip are not acceptable. You can pay using Thai baht or, depending on the location of the aviation office, some other Western currencies, but you use their exchange rate which is usually unfavourable. All prices are quoted in US dollars. (*Lao Aviation* accept Visa and Amex on their international routes.) The 2002 prices listed below are for one-way fares, inclusive of 5% tax.

From Vientiane Pakse US$95, Ban Houei Xai US$88, Muang Xai (Oudomxai) US$71, Savannakhet US$61, Xam Neua US$70, Luang Namtha via Luang Prabang US$80, Xieng Khouang/Phonsavanh US$44, Luang Prabang US$55, Sayaboury US$42.

From Luang Prabang Luang Namtha US$37, Muang Xai US$28, Ban Houei Xai US$46, Xieng Khouang US$35, Phongsali US$46.

From Pakse Savannkhet US$44, Luang Namtha-Ban Houei Xai US$41.

Lao Aviation fly three types of aeroplane: French-built ATR 72s, and Chinese-built Y-7s and Y-12s. The latter two hardly inspire confidence and some foreign embassies in Vientiane request that their staff do not fly on the Y-7s and Y-12s, viewing them as simply too risky. This was also applied to the ATR-72s until quite recently, because they were inadequately maintained. In May 1998 a plane carrying a high-level military delegation from Vietnam crashed over Xieng Khouang. In 2000 the US Embassy was advising its personnel to limit domestic travel on *Lao Aviation* to essential travel only because of "serious concerns about the operation of Lao Aviation, particularly regarding its safety standards and maintenance regime". This has since changed and – at least on the ATRs – the view is that safety has improved. In *Muong Lao*, the company's in-flight magazine, there is a long section explaining in anorak detail the maintenance regime for each type of plane.

Notwithstanding all of these concerns, flying is still the quickest and most convenient form of travel. In addition the most reliable, comfortable and newest machines – the ATR-72s – operate on the most popular routes (Vientiane-Bangkok and Vientiane-Luang Prabang).

Lao Aviation, at least on its minor domestic routes, seems to operate on the rather charming principle of *c'est la vie*. Planes are overbooked, underbooked, leave 30 minutes early, two hours late, or not at all. The official Visit Laos website used to admit that 'timetables cannot be relied upon' and exhorts visitors to 'please be flexible'. Some passengers have even been ticketed (in Lao) to towns they had no wish or intention of visiting – presumably on the basis that they might like the places. As a tourist this can be amusing, even enchanting; as a businessman or woman it can be thoroughly frustrating. Letters from readers do, however, show a marked reduction in the number of complaints about the efficiency or otherwise of *Lao Aviation* and this is, presumably, because the company is becoming more professional as each year passes.

River

It is possible to take river boats up and down the Mekong and its main tributaries. The Mekong is navigable from Ban Houei Xai on the border with Thailand downriver to south of Pakse. *En route* boats stop at Luang Prabang, Vientiane, Thakhek and Savannakhet as well as other smaller towns and villages. But there is no scheduled service and departures may be limited during the dry season. Boats leave at the last minute, and speaking Lao is definitely an advantage here. Boats are basic but cheap. Take food and drink and expect somewhat crowded conditions aboard. Prices vary according to size of boat and length of journey. Downriver from Luang Prabang to Vientiane takes four days, travelling up to 10 hours a day. There are plenty of boats available from Luang Prabang, travelling up or downriver. The most common riverboats are the *hua houa leim*, with no decks, the hold being enclosed by side panels and a flat roof; note that metal boats get very hot.

While river transport remains important in a country with lots of rivers and few roads, it seems to be in terminal decline. As roads are upgraded and the cost of road transport goes down and speed goes up, so travellers are abandoning the river for the road. This means that scheduled passenger ferries on some routes are a thing of the past – although it is still possible to charter a vessel, but the price is relatively high.

Myths
and Mountains
LAOS
Inside the culture,
myths and charm of Laos

Journeys of a Lifetime
www.mythsandmountains.com
800-670-6984

▶▶ **Motorcycling Laos**

Riding a motorbike around Laos is not as daunting as you might think and the freedom is a big plus. The easiest option is to rent a bike in the country, which can be done in Vientiane. Expect to pay US$20-25 for a good quality 250 cc off-road bike. Alternatively, bikes can be brought in from neighbouring countries: one or two bike hire shops in Chiang Mai can arrange paperwork to accompany their bikes (with some notice) to cross into Laos. To bring your own bike into the country, a carnet can be obtained from your home country and used at immigration. Without a carnet, travel agents on the Laos side (at Ban Huay Xai, the Friendship Bridge, Vientiane and Pakse) can arrange for the customs and immigration paperwork to be completed (usually for US$40, for a 15-day bike "passer"). Finally it is possible to buy a bike in Laos: cheap Chinese bikes or pricier Thai-made Japanese machines.

The roads vary in condition from dirt tracks in the north, to potholed asphalt, to smooth 'highways' in reasonably good condition (eg much of Route 13 south of Vientienne). But wherever you travel, at the end of the day a long massage and a good cushion will be required. Fuel is cheap and readily available. Out of the cites the main traffic problems will be slow tractors, chickens with a death wish and, of course, a few slow moving tourist buses.

A good map is essential. The Golden Triangle Rider *map of Laos is the best and can be bought in most major cities in Laos and Thailand. It is sensible not to ride alone – mainly due to the possibility of mechanical failure and the lack of parts and competent mechanics, especially those able to fix larger bikes. (In Vientiane Feurds on Samsenthai Road is the best source of parts and expertise.) It is wise to carry some basic tools and spares, and a good first aid kit is also an essential item. For further information check out* **www.gt-rider.com**

Information supplied by Philip Bower.

Road

Bicycle & motorcycle hire

Bicycles are available in many towns and are a cheap way to see the sights. Chinese bikes tend to be better than Thai ones. Many guesthouses have bikes for rent. There are an increasing number of motorcycles available too.

Bicycle touring
www.netspace.net.au/~mrfelix/bsa/ is a good website to check out

Long-distance bicycle touring is not common in Laos. However there is great potential: the roads are not heavily used (as they are, for example, in neighbouring Thailand), and traffic speeds are modest. That said, traffic volumes are increasing and road knowledge is limited (see Road safety, page 41).

Bus/truck
During the rainy season (June -December) expect journey times to be longer than quoted; indeed some roads may be closed altogether

It is now possible to travel to most areas of the country by bus, truck or *songthaew* (converted pick-up truck) in the dry season, although road travel in the rainy season can be trickier if not downright impossible. That said, road conditions have improved in many areas over the years since we last updated this book. Many of the roads have been repaired or upgraded, making journeys along them infinitely more comfortable, as well as faster.

There is a variety of forms of public transport on Laos's roads, and also a rather intriguing north-south divide. In the north, Nissan and Mitsubishi trucks are used as pick-ups and these are often the fastest form of land-based public transport. For longer journeys, big Langjian (Chinese) trucks are sometimes used. On the long routes, such as Vientiane/Luang Prabang to Xam Neua/Nam Nouan/Vieng Thong, they use Chinese trucks colourfully converted into buses with a wooden structure on the back, divided wooden seats and glassless windows. In some more remote places (Xam Neua to

Bus fares (2002)

Public buses

Vientiane to	Distance	Duration	Fare	Departure time
Airport	6 km	-	400 kip	Every 30 mins
Tha Deua	29 km	-	700 kip	
Ban Thalat (bus #09)	87 km	-	2,500 kip	0630, 0800, 0930
Van Vieng (bus #01)	160 km	-	4,000 kip	0700, 1030, 1330
Kasi (bus #04)	230 km	-	7,000 kip	0800
Luang Prabang	420 km	-	26-40,000 kip	0700, 0800, 0930, 1100, 1300, 1700
Pakxan	159 km	-	5,000 kip	0700, 1100, 1400
Thakhek	360 km	-	12,000 kip	0400, 0500, 0600
Savannakhet (bus #36)	490 km	-	20,000 kip	0730, 1000
Pakse (bus #35)	770 km	-	26,000 kip	0800, 1100, 1230

All departures from the Morning Market

Private buses

Vientiane to	Distance	Duration	Fare	Departure time
Pakxan	159 km	2.30 hours	5,000 kip	0700
Thakhek	360 km	5.30 hours	15,000 kip	0700
Savannakhet	490 km	7.30 hours	20,000 kip	0700
Xam Neua	900 km	36 hours	50,000 kip	0700
Xieng Khouang	490 km	-	50,000 kip	0730
Udom Xai	550 km	18 hours	40,000 kip	0600
Luang Prabang	400 km	10 hours	30,000 kip	0700, 0800, 0930

All departures from the Nong Duang Market

International buses

Vientiane to	Fare
Danang (Vietnam)	US$28
Hanoi (Vietnam)	US$25
Hue (Vietnam)	US$25

Vieng Xai, for instance), ancient jeeps are common. In the south of the country, Japanese-donated buses are used although you may see the occasional shiny Volvo bus.

Journey times are always, and inevitably, delayed by toilet stops, loading, unloading and overloading so vehicles, seemingly, never pick up any speed. Expect bus times sometimes to vary considerably from those quoted in the travelling text – one journey may be twice or half as long as another on the same stretch of road, in the same season, and with the same type of vehicle. For example, on our way up to Xam Neua from Nam Nouan it took under three hours. But the return journey took six hours, because our bus picked up 36 bulging bags of rice and thereafter crawled.

Though it may be possible to travel by road to many areas of the country this is not to imply that road travel is a breeze. Many roads or parts of road are unsealed, buses are overloaded, and breakdowns, though not *enormously* frequent, aren't wholly uncommon, either. However, that the situation has improved drastically over recent years can be measured by the fact that 'rot taay' – 'dead' vehicle – is now no longer as familiar an expression among travellers as 'kop jai'. For some connections you may need to wait a day and journeys can vary enormously in the length of time they take, depending on the weather conditions. Travellers can often negotiate a price if travelling by truck and it seems to be quite easy to hitch. Note that close to half of government expenditure is on transport and communications – and much of that on road construction and improvement. Roads are being upgraded and new vehicles slowly introduced so, in theory, journey times should only get shorter. But bear in mind a piece from the *Vientiane Times* of 1 September 1999: "A Vietnamese truck travelling along Road No 8 between the Theun-Hinboun Hydropower Project site and Lak Sao . . . skidded on the unsealed road for about 10 km before overturning." Scary.

Car/car hire Car hire is anything from US$40-80 per day, depending on the vehicle, with the first 150 km free, then US$10 every 100 km after that. Price includes a driver. *Asia Vehicle Rental*, T021-217493 in Vientiane, very reliable. The cheapest option in many towns is simply to hire a tuk-tuk, either by the hour or the day. While these are not comfortable for long distance travel they are fine for reaching destinations out of town.

Taxi Metered taxis are common in Vientiane, where there is a good telephone taxi company. Taxis are not so common outside the capital, although there are cars for charter.

Tuk-tuk/ saamlor/ trishaw Saamlors (literally '3 wheels') or trishaws can be hired in most towns, although they are becoming increasingly rare in Vientiane. Negotiate the price before boarding – it may be helpful to get someone to write your destination down. Outside Vientiane a short trip around town should cost 3,000-4,000 kip depending on the town, the distance, and your bargaining skills. The majority of motorized 3-wheelers known as 'jumbos' or tuk-tuks (a name derived from the noise they make) are large motorbike taxis with two bench seats in the back; Thai-style tuk-tuks are also making their presence felt.

Hitchhiking This is well worth trying and unlike Thailand, for example, drivers are likely to stop. At some border crossings it is the only way to secure transport although in such instances it is usual to pay for the journey. Note, though, that there are very few vehicles in Laos and almost no private cars – expect to hitch on lorries. Reports from travellers indicate that hitching is productive. Because public transport can be limited in more out-of-the-way spots and at certain border crossings, hitching is sometimes the only option.

Maps of Laos & Southeast Asia A decent map is an indispensable aid to travelling. Although maps are usually available locally, it is sometimes useful to buy a map prior to departure to plan routes and itineraries. Below is a select list of maps. Scale is provided in brackets.

Regional maps Bartholomew: *Vietnam, Laos and Cambodia* (1:2,000,000);

AVR ASIA VEHICLE RENTAL Co.,Ltd.

Fully Licensed Rental & Leasing Service.

- Full Insurance through AGL.   - Provincial & cross border travel.
- Self drive or with driver.   - Business, Project, Private leasing...
- All types of vehicles.
- Specialists in 4x4 travel.

Tel: (856-21) 217493-223867, Fax : (856-21) 217493.
Mob : (856-20) 511070-511293- 514867.
Address : 354-356 Samsenthai Rd.
Vientiane Lao P.D.R.
www.avr.laopdr.com, Email : avr@loxinfo.co.th

; *Southeast Asia* (1:5,800,000). Globetrotter: *Vietnam, Laos and Cambodia* (1:1,900,000). ITM (International Travel Maps): *Laos*; *Southeast Asia* (1:6,000,000). Nelles: *Vietnam, Laos and Cambodia* (1:1,500,000); *Southeast Asia* (1:4,000,000).

Other maps *Tactical Pilotage Charts* (TPC, US Airforce) (1:500,000); *Operational Navigational Charts* (ONC, US Airforce) (1:500,000). Both of these are particularly good at showing relief features (useful for planning treks); less good on roads, towns and facilities.

Locally available maps It is sometimes possible to get hold of sheet maps at a scale of 1:100,000 last updated at the beginning of the 1980s and based on French-produced originals. Rather easier to find is a five-sheet country set at a scale of 1:1,000,000. Both are produced by the Service Geographique National. There is also a series of locally produced town maps which covers the major settlements of Vientiane, Luang Prabang, Thakhek, Savannakhet and Pakse. Perhaps the best map of Vientiane is the colourful *Map of Vientiane* produced by the Women's International Group.

Map outlets The best selection in the UK is available from *Stanfords*, 12-14 Long Acre, London WC2E 9LP, T020-7836 1321, www.stanfords.co.uk Also recommended is *McCarta*, 15 Highbury Place, London N15 1QP, T020-7354 1616.

Keeping in touch

Communications

Internet cafés have been popping up all over the shop in Laos for the last couple of years. Dicey connections are getting better, although speed is not a phenomenon closely related with the internet here. There is often fierce rivalry between neighbouring outlets, and the ensuing price wars only benefit the customer. Popular with travellers and locals alike, you may well find yourself surrounded by excitable saffron-robed monks – hotmail really is a universal language.

Internet
Internet cafés are listed under Communications in each town's directory

International service: the outbound service is inexpensive but long term foreign residents cast aspersions on its reliability; they prefer to have mail hand-delivered by people going to Bangkok. Postal rates in 2002 were:

Post

Postcards	Asia	2,500 kip	Europe	2,700 kip	USA	3,200 kip
Letters (10g)	Asia	3,300 kip	Europe	3,500 kip	USA	4,000 kip
Letters (20g)	Asia	3,600 kip	Europe	4,000 kip	USA	5,000 kip

Contents of outgoing parcels must be examined by an official before being sealed. Incoming mail should use the country's official title, *Lao PDR*. EMS or Express Mail Service is available from main post offices in larger towns.

A telephone and **fax service** is available at the *International Service Centre*, Settathirath, Vientiane, international telephone service open 24 hours a day, fax service open daily 0730-2130 and faxes are received 24 hours a day. Mark incoming faxes with receiver's telephone number and recipient will be informed immediately.

Poste restante: there is a poste restante at the central post office in Vientiane.

Freight forwarders: for advertisements of freight and packaging companies in Vientiane, see the *Vientiane Times*, published every other day and available in several outlets around the capital and in many hotels and guesthouses.

Telephone   **Local** All major towns are now linked by phone and many places have fax facilities, particularly guesthouses and hotels. Call 178 in Vientiane for town codes.

International Most towns in Lao have at least one telephone box with IDD facility, except for those towns which have no telephone connection. The one drawback is that you must buy a phonecard. Because these are denominated in such small units, even the highest value card will only get you a handful of minutes talk time with Europe. All post offices, telecommunications offices and many, many shops sell phone cards. If ringing Laos from Thailand, dial 007 before the country code for Laos.

Media

Newspapers/
magazines
*The Vientiane Times is
also on the web at
www.vientianetimes.
com*

Vientiane Times, established in 1994, is published every other day and costs 4,000 kip. It provides quirky pieces of information and shouldn't have any Pulitzer Prize hopefuls too worried about its razor-sharp investigative reporting. Looking at the development of this newspaper over the years it does seem to have honed its headlines somewhat. The April 1996 issue, for example, had, as its lead story – and with apparently no irony: 'First Lao Telephone Directory – A Milestone for Communications'. Looking at the April and May 1999 issues, the headlines range from 'Foreign Ministry Condemns NATO Bombing of Chinese Embassy in Belgrade', through to a real winner in 'Introducing Cardamom Cropping in Phongsaly'. Even foreign stories seem to be selected on a rather hit-and-miss basis. In July 2001, for example, one of the lead overseas pieces was 'Sardinians protest loss of sea link to mainland'. Local expats find the most intriguing section of the newspaper Streetwise where locals are interviewed about their views on some topic of the day. Here, when it's simply too hot to think, they just seem to recycle old stories.

Discover Laos is a monthly publication. *Newsweek* and *The Economist* are available, as is the French language *Le Renovateur* (4,000 kip). The *Bangkok Post* (costing more than its cover price of ฿20) is the most recent addition to newstands which previously stocked only government-controlled Lao language newspapers and *Pravda* in Russian and French. The Lao Government *Khao San Pathet Lao News Bulletin* is produced daily in English and French and yields journalistic treats such as 'Sayaboury province exceeds radish production forecast' and 'Message of solidarity to Havana'. They can be found blowing around hotel lobbies.

Television   This is becoming increasingly popular as more towns and villages get electricity. Even Vientiane's poorest communities sport forests of aluminium antennae orientated to receive signals from across the Mekong. (Thai broadcasts can be received in the Mekong basin – that is where most of the population centres are to be found – but not in mountainous areas, which includes Luang Prabang.) The national TV station broadcasts in Lao but there is a distinct preference for Thai soaps and game shows. Thailand's Channel 5 gives English subtitles to overseas news. Many homes have VCRs imported from Thailand, and some upmarket hotels also subscribe to Asia's Star TV (which transmits news as well as sports, music, film and general channels). In rural areas there is concern at the effects that a growing penchant for pornographic videos is having among Laos' youth.

Radio   The Lao National Radio broadcasts news in English. The **BBC World Service** can be picked up on shortwave on 11.955 MHz and 11.750 (25 m band); 9.740 MHz (30 m band); 7.145 MHz (41 m band); 6.195 MHz (48 m band) and 3.195 MHz (76 m band). **Voice of America** also broadcasts (see below). Every day in many of the cities and towns loudspeakers blare out broadcasts of the municipal radio station. These days, socialist slogans have been replaced with commercials for soft drinks, washing powder

Laos dialling codes

International code for Laos *00 856*
If phoning Laos from Thailand, you must
*dial **007** before the country code of **856***

Regional dialling codes
***031** Attapeu*
***084** Ban Houei Xai*
***086** Luang Namtha*
***071** Luang Prabang*
***081** Muang Xai (Udom Xai)*
***031** Pakse*
***054** Pakxan*
***088** Phongsali*
***061** Phonsavanh*
***034** Salavan*
***074** Sayaboury*
***041** Savannakhet*
***031** Sekong*
***051** Thakhek*

***023** Vang Vieng*
***021** Vientiane*
***064** Xam Neua*
***061** Xieng Khouang*
***20** Mobile numbers*
*You can also call **178** in Vientiane for town
codes*

Useful numbers
***16** Operator*
***170** International operator*
***190** Fire*
***191** Police*
***195** Ambulance*

Dialling tones
***Ringing** double ring, repeated regularly*
***Engaged** equal tones, separated by equal
pauses*

and toothpaste. The **BBC World Service's Dateline East Asia** provides probably the best news and views on Asia. Also with a strong Asia focus are the broadcasts of the **ABC** (Australian Broadcasting Corporation).

Short Wave Radio British Broadcasting Corporation (BBC, London) Southeast Asian service 3915, 6195, 9570, 9740, 11750, 11955, 15360; Singapore service 88.9MHz; East Asian service 5995, 6195, 7180, 9740, 11715, 11750, 11945, 11955, 15140, 15280, 15360, 17830, 21715. **Voice of America** (VoA, Washington) Southeast Asian service 1143, 1575, 7120, 9760, 9770, 15185, 15425; Indonesian service 6110, 11760, 15425. **Radio Beijing** Southeast Asian service (English) 11600, 11660. **Radio Japan** (Tokyo) Southeast Asian service (English) 11815, 17810, 21610.

Food and drink

Glance at the World Bank's World Development Report and Laos appears as one of the globe's poorest countries. On this basis, few would imagine that beneath the statistics of destitution is a country with a rich cuisine and a (reasonably) flourishing restaurant industry. Lao food is like Thai food - but different. There may not be quite the variety of dishes, but if you have had your gastronomic interest stirred by Thai cuisine, then Lao food will do the same. Moreover – and this is a big plus over neighbouring Thailand – Laos was also fortunate to have been colonized by France. While the French may not have left much in the way of railway lines and steel mills, they did leave a gastronomic legacy which is still evident from the simple baguette to some really stylish restaurants. There is also another plus: no Pizza Hut, no McDonald's and no KFC. So: come ready to eat and enjoy from the simple market stall to restaurants with crisp linen napkins and obsequious waiter.

NB Urban areas have access to safe water, but all water should be boiled or sterilized before drinking. Cheap bottled water is widely available – as are fizzy drinks.

Less than a third of rural areas have safe water. Do not swim in stagnant water for risk of bilharzia. Restaurant food is, on the whole, hygienically prepared, and as long as street stall snacks have been well cooked, they are usually fine and a good place to sample local specialities.

Cuisine
The best places to try Lao food is often from roadside stalls or in the markets

There are many similarities between Lao and Thai food, although it is slightly less influenced by Chinese cuisine. Lao dishes are distinguished by the use of aromatic herbs (including marijuana) and spices such as lemon grass, chillies, ginger and tamarind. Coconut fat is used sparingly. Food takes a long time to prepare and does not keep well, which goes some way to explaining why many restaurants do not offer local dishes, or if they do, they demand advance warning.

The staple Lao foods are **glutinous rice** (*kao niao*) and **fermented fish** or *pa dek*, often laced with liberal spoons of *nam pa*, or fish sauce. *Nam pa* – like *nam plaa* in Thailand, *nuoc mam* in Vietnam, and *ngan-pyaye* in Myanmar (Burma) – is an essential element of Laotian gastronomic life. No meal would be complete without a small dish of *nam pa*, and it is spooned onto almost any savoury dish. To make *nam pa*, freshwater fish are packed into containers and steeped in brine. (Elsewhere, fish sauce is made mostly from small saltwater fish species, but because Laos is landlocked, freshwater fish are used in their place.) The resulting brown liquid – essentially the by-products of slowly putrifying fish – is drained off and bottled. *Pa dek* is *nam pa* with knobs on – or rather *nam pa* with small chunks of fermented fish added, often with rice husks too. It tends to be used in cooking rather than as a condiment and is usually kept in an earthenware pot – often outside as the aroma is so strong!

Being a landlocked country, most of the fish is fresh from the Mekong. Mutton (goat) is practically unheard of and beef (water buffalo) expensive, so most of the dishes are variations on two themes: **fish and bird**. There is also a health/technological reason for this: without refrigerators, anyone slaughtering a cow, pig or water buffalo needs to be sure there are enough buyers to purchase all the meat in one day. Outside big towns there is neither the demand nor refrigerators to warrant such a slaughter – except when there is a festival and other significant events, like a wedding. But the Lao cookbook does not stop at chickens and turkeys (there are thousands of turkeys in Luang Prabang, thanks to an esoteric aid project which farms them). The rule of thumb is that if it has wings and feathers, it's edible. In some areas, such as Luang Prabang, the province's birds have long since been eaten. In the south, where the forests have not (yet) been denuded, wild foods are more plentiful and it is not unusual to see pangolin, deer and turtle on the menu.

The most common **vegetables** are aubergines, tomatoes, cucumbers and lettuce, often cooked together, pureed and eaten with sticky rice. Soups are eaten at the middle or end of a meal but never at the beginning. They are usually a mixture of fish and meat infused with aromatic herbs. One would have thought, in a place like Laos, that **fruit** would be on every menu. But, perhaps because familiarity breeds contempt, many restaurants will have no fruit of any kind – even at breakfast and particularly in places not geared to foreigners.

Laap, also meaning 'luck' in Lao, is a traditional ceremonial dish made from (traditionally) raw fish or meat crushed into a paste, marinated in lemon juice and mixed with chopped mint. It is said to be similar to Mexican *cerviche*. It is called *laap sin* if it has a meat base and *laap pa* if it's fish based. Beware of *laap* in cheap street restaurants – sometimes it is concocted from raw offal and served cold; this should be consumed with great caution. *Phanaeng kai* is stuffed chicken with pork, peanuts and coconut milk with a dash of cinnamon. *Kai ping* is grilled chicken eaten with sticky rice.

There are several different types of **soup** – including *keng no mai* (bamboo shoot soup), *keng khi lek* (vegetable and buffalo skin), *ken chut* (without pimentos) *keng kalami* (cabbage soup with fish or pork), *kenghet bot* (mushroom soup).

Distinctive fruits

◀◀

Custard apple (or sugar apple) Scaly green skin, squeeze the skin to open the fruit and scoop out the flesh with a spoon. Season: June-September.

Durian (Durio zibethinus) A large prickly fruit, with yellow flesh, about the size of a football. Infamous for its pungent smell. While it is today regarded by many visitors as simply revolting, early Europeans raved about it. Banned from hotel rooms throughout the region, and beloved by most Southeast Asians, it has an alluring taste – some maintain it is an addiction. Season: May-August.

Jackfruit Similar in appearance to durian but not so spiky. Yellow flesh, tasting slightly like custard. Season: January-June.

Mango (Mangifera indica) A rainforest fruit which is now cultivated. Widely available in the West; in Southeast Asia there are hundreds of different varieties with subtle variations in flavour. Delicious eaten with sticky rice and a sweet sauce. Season: March-June.

Mangosteen (Garcinia mangostana) An aubergine-coloured hard shell covers this small fruit which is about the size of a tennis ball. Cut or squeeze the purple shell to reach its sweet white flesh which is prized by many visitors above all others. Southeast Asians believe it should be eaten as a chaser to durian. Season: April-September.

Papaya (Carica papaya) A New World Fruit that was not introduced into Southeast Asia until the 16th century. Large, round or oval in shape, yellow or green-skinned, with bright orange flesh and a mass of round, black seeds in the middle. The flesh, in texture and taste, is somewhere between a mango and a melon. Some maintain that it tastes 'soapy'. Season: Year round.

Pomelo A large round fruit the size of anything from an ostrich egg to a football, with thick, green skin and pith, and flesh similar to grapefruit, but less acidic. Season: August-November.

Rambutan (Nephelium lappaceum) The bright red and hairy rambutan – rambut is the Malay word for 'hair' – with its slightly rubbery but sweet flesh is a close relative of the lychee of southern China. Season: May-September.

Salak (Salacca edulis) A small pear-shaped fruit about the size of a large plum with a rough, brown, scaly skin (somewhat like a miniature pangolin) and yellow-white, crisp flesh. It is related to the sago and rattan trees.

Tamarind (Tamarindus indicus) Brown seedpods with dry brittle skins and a brown tart-sweet fruit which grow on a tree introduced into Southeast Asia from India. The name is Arabic for 'Indian date'. The flesh has a high tartaric acid content and is used to flavour curries, jams, jellies and chutneys as well as for cleaning brass and copper. Season: December-February.

Essentials

There is a well-ingrained **Vietnamese** culinary tradition and **Chinese** food is never hard to find. Feu, Vietnamese noodle soup, is itself an import from China but often masquerades in Laos as a Lao dish. It is usually served with a plate of raw vegetables. Most restaurants outside the main towns do not have menus but will nearly always serve feu and laap or local specialities. Indeed their generic name is raan khai feu – restaurants that sell feu.

The Lao are partial to **sweets**: sticky rice with coconut milk and black beans (which can be bought in bamboo tubes in the markets) and grilled bananas are favourites.

The best Lao cookbook is Phia Sing's Traditional Recipes of Laos (Prospect Books: Totnes, Devon, UK, 1995).

The French in Laos left a legacy of sophisticated cuisine. French food is widely available, with street cafés, serving delectable fresh croissants, baguettes, pain au chocolat and a selection of sticky pastries, which can be washed down with a powerful cup of **French legacy**

▶▶ Restaurant classifications

Expensive *US$10+ for a meal. A 3-course meal in a restaurant with pleasant decor. Beers, wines and spirits available.*

Mid-range *US$5-10 for a meal. Two courses, reasonable surroundings.*

Cheap *US$2-5 for a meal, probably only*

a single course, surroundings spartan but adequate.

Seriously cheap *Under US$2. Single course, often makeshift surroundings such as a street kiosk with simple benches and tables. In many cases a simple meal will cost less than US$1.*

Essentials

Lao coffee. The Lao however have a habit of eating *baguette* sandwiches with fish sauce sprinkled on top – these are available in Vientiane, Savannakhet and Pakse. Menus in many of Vientiane's restaurants still have a distinctly French flavour to them – frogs' legs included. Vintage Bordeaux and Burgundies occasionally emerge from the cellars of restaurants too – although most of the fine vintages have now been consumed. Hotels in main towns often provide international menus and continental breakfasts. Even in small towns it is easy enough to create a continental breakfast: baguettes are widely available, wild honey can usually be tracked down, and fresh Bolovens' coffee is abundant (although tragically 'Nescaf' seems to be making insidious inroads). Some people recommend taking a jar of jam or peanut butter to spread on the baguettes. The Lao prefer theirs either with 'pat,' – more like spam – or with thick and sweetened condensed milk. It may be significant that while the French left to their former colonies in Southeast Asia the art of baking and great coffee, the British bestowed such practical things as railways and roads. Perhaps this says something about their respective national characters.

Eating out
Expect to pay US$2-10 per head for a meal in main towns and less outside. By eating Lao food in local restaurants it is possible to pay US$1 or less for a meal

Food in Laos is surprisingly good – for a country so poor. Perhaps this is something that the French have left behind in the heart of every Lao. Or perhaps it was always there. Really classy restaurants are only to be found in Vientiane and Luang Prabang, and especially the former. Good French and Italian cuisine are available in both cities. Salads, steaks, pizzas and more are all on offer. Expect to pay anywhere upwards of US$5 for a reasonable meal. A better bet in terms of value for money are the Lao restaurants. Again, however, restaurants at the top end of the scale are really only to be found in Vientiane and Luang Prabang. Expect to pay around US$5.

Far more prevalent are lower-end Lao and Chinese-Lao restaurants, to be found in every town. Food in these places is usually good and excellent value for money. You'll find a cold beer and a good range of vegetarian and meat-based dishes all for US$3-5. In towns on the tourist trail these local restaurants are complemented by places geared to the vicarious demands of tourists. Here you'll find fruit smoothies, burgers and more – for anywhere between US$2 and US$5. Finally, right at the bottom end – in terms of price if not necessarily in terms of quality – are stalls that sell, for example, baguettes with fillings, simple single dish meals, and more, for a dollar or two.

Drink
Imported beer, wines and spirits can be found in hotels, restaurants, bars and nightclubs but are not particularly cheap. *Beer Lao* is a light lager (although the alcohol content is 5%) best served ice-cold. In towns without power it is normal to add ice although most places now are on the grid. *Beer Lao* also has the advantage of being reasonably priced: from a little less than US$1 for a large bottle, depending on the restaurant or bar. Chinese beer is cheaper still and can be found in the northern provinces. French wines can be purchased (at a price) in some supermarkets and quite a few restaurants.

The local brew is rice wine and is drunk from a clay jug with long straws. The white variety is called *lau-lao* – 'Lao alcohol' – and is made from fermented sticky rice. Red lau-lao – or *fanthong* – is fermented with herbs. Bottled lau-lao is also widely available, *Sticky Rice* being the best brand; always ensure that the screw-top bottles are sealed.

Soft drinks & bottled water

Soft drinks are expensive – they are imported from Thailand. A can of coke in a stall costs about 3,000 kip, a bottle some 1,500 kip. *Nam saa*, weak Chinese tea, is always served with strong coffee and is free. There is now local fresh milk production, so milk and yoghurt are available. **Bottled water** is widely available and produced locally, so it is cheap (about 1,000 kip for a litre).

Shopping

Popular souvenirs from Laos include minority or hilltribe artefacts and textiles, which are sold pretty much everywhere, and are (unsurprisingly) cheapest in the villages not specifically geared towards tourism. As far as 'best buys' go, it really does boil down to a simple matter of taste, although many women stock up on **silks**, which are easily found in the majority of markets. The smaller, less touristy towns will sell them cheapest (at about 30,000 kip a length). Most markets offer a wide selection of patterns and embroidery to choose from, and perhaps one of the best places to go is Ban Phanom Handicraft Weaving Loom, just outside Luang Prabang. Vientiane and Luang Prabang offer the most sophisticated line in boutiques, where you can get all sorts of clothes from the utterly exquisite to the frankly bizarre. Those on a more frugal budget will find some tailors who can churn out a decent pair of trousers (your best bet would be the tailor's attached to *Travel Online Internet and Email* on Sisavangvong in Luang Prabang, or the little shop operated by the owner of *Amphone Guesthouse* in Vang Vieng), but be aware that Thailand remains streets ahead in tailoring proficiency.

Antique textiles from northern Laos sell from US$40 upwards. It is hard to find 'antique' textiles in good condition as old *pha sin* (sarongs) are worn over new ones for work or bathing and so wear out quickly. Carol Cassidy in Vientiane (see page 97) has revived high quality traditional weaving and her weavers are producing work of an exceptionally high quality. Prices, though, can run into thousands of US dollars for these museum-quality pieces.

A wide variety of modern materials are sometimes used to make the *pha sin*, the Lao **sarong**, and *pha baeng*, or **shawl**, worn by Lao women. The latter became high-fashion in Bangkok in the early 1990s, after the Thai princess Mahachakri Sirindhorn took to wearing them on her return from Laos. The bridal *sin* is a popular buy; it is usually plain with a single motif repeated over most of the material, but with an elaborate border. Gold and silver thread, *tdinjok*, is often woven into the border pattern. Lao weavers have been isolated from external influences and have maintained many of their original patterns and styles. Most of the materials are sold in weaving villages or are available from markets in the main towns. For more background on Lao textiles see page 294.

Making **silverware** is a traditional craft in Laos – most of it is in the form of jewellery and small silver pots (though they may not be made of silver). Luang Prabang is reputed to produce the best silverware (see page 142) but this may just reflect received wisdom rather than reality. The finest silversmiths, with a few exceptions, work out of Vientiane. Chunky antique **'tribal' jewellery**, bangles, pendants, belts and earrings, are often sold in markets in the main towns, or antique shops in Vientiane.

Craftsmen in Laos are still producing **wood carvings** for temples and coffins. Designs are usually traditional, with a religious theme. Craftsmen produce carved panels and statues for tourists, which are available in outlets in Vientiane.

Essentials

Bargaining While bargaining is common in Laos – in the market or in negotiating a trip on a saamlor or tuk-tuk for example – it is not heavy duty bargaining. The Lao are extremely laid back and it is rare to be fleeced. Having said that, beware the tuk-tuk drivers in Lak Xao, and some of the more transparent petitions for more money 'for medicine' you'll hear in some pockets of the country where opium is abundant. Approach bargaining with a sense of fun. The higher quality handicrafts can usually be found in Luang Prabang and Vientiane, although prices will be correspondingly high. Some of the best bargains are to be found when you're not looking for them, among the local villages.

Entertainment and nightlife

If you are looking for evenings out at cultural events, or are keen to dance the night away, Laos is not the place for you. Until five or so years ago, the country seemed to shut down from about 2100. Even today, anywhere outside the capital is unlikely to provide much in the way of night time revelry. Excepting perhaps the odd lock-in in Luang Prabang's Maylek pub, a quiet evening sipping Lao beer by the Mekong is as good as it gets.

The pace of life in Laos is slow; certainly nothing is super-developed – you can count even the number of cinemas on one hand, so the nearest you should expect to get to seeing the hottest new Hollywood blockbuster would generally be the nightly videos shown at some guesthouses. All this, of course, is part of the inherent appeal of the country and most visitors wouldn't have it any other way.

Bars & discos Most larger towns have bars and 'discos'. But a Lao disco is usually a place where live rather than recorded music is played. In 1996 the government tried to crack down on what was felt to be Thai cultural imperialism and stipulated that bands had to play at least 70% Lao music (as opposed to Thai or Western). They also banned karaoke bars for the same sort of reason: moral depravity. This latter edict seemed to be weakly enforced in smaller towns and may have been lifted by the time this book is on the shelves. There is a growing number of bars and clubs in Vientiane, and a handful in the other major centres (mostly geared to locals rather than the foreign/expat markets).

Holidays and festivals

The list below is not exhaustive, but does include the most important festivals. There are many Chinese, Vietnamese and ethnic minority festivals which are celebrated in Laos and there are many regional variations

Being of festive inclination, the Lao celebrate New Year four times a year: the international New Year in January, Chinese New Year in January/February, Lao New Year (Pimai) in April and Hmong New Year in December. The Lao Buddhist year follows the lunar calendar, so many of the festivals are movable. The first month begins around the full moon in December, although Lao New Year is celebrated in April. There are also many local festivals (see under individual regions).

The **baci** ceremony is a uniquely Lao *boun* (festival) and celebrates any auspicious occasion – marriage, birth, achievement or the end of an arduous journey for instance. The ceremony dates from pre-Buddhist times and is therefore animist in origin. It is centred around the *phakhouan*, a designer-tree made from banana leaves and flowers (or, today, some artificial concoction of plastic) and surrounded by symbolic foods. The most common symbolic foods are eggs and rice – symbolizing fertility and fecundity. The *mophone* hosts the ceremony and recites memorized prayers, usually in Pali, and ties cotton threads (*sai sin*) around the wrists of guests symbolizing good health, prosperity and happiness. For maximum effect, these strings must have three knots in them. It is unlucky to take them off before at least three days have elapsed and custom

Calendar

◀◀

The Gregorian calendar is the official calendar for administration, but many traditional villages still follow the lunar calendar. The Lao calendar is a mixture of Sino-Vietnamese and Thai-Khmer. It is based on the movement of the sun and moon and is different to the Buddhist calendar used in Thailand. New Year is in December, but is celebrated in April when the auspices are more favourable. As in China, each year is named after an animal. Weeks are structured on the waxing and waning of the moon and days are named accordingly.

dictates that they never be cut. Many people wear them until, frayed and worn, they fall through sheer decrepitude. All this is accompanied by a *ramvong* (traditional circle dance) which is accompanied by traditional instruments – flutes, clarinets, xylophones with bamboo crosspieces, drums, cymbals and the *kaen*, a hand-held pipe organ that is to Laos what the bagpipes are to Scotland.

New Year's Day (1st: public holiday) celebrated by private *baci* throughout the country. *Pathet Lao Day* (6th: public holiday) parades in main towns. *Army Day* (20th: public holiday). *Boun Pha Vet* (movable) to celebrate King Vessanthara's reincarnation as a Buddha. Sermons, processions, dance, theatre. Popular time for ordination. | **January**

Magha Puja (movable) celebrates the end of Buddha's time in the monastery and the prediction of his death. It is principally celebrated in Vientiane and at Wat Phou, near Champassak. *Chinese New Year* (movable, January/February) celebrated by Chinese and Vietnamese communities. Many Chinese and Vietnamese businesses shut down for three days. | **February**

Women's Day (8th: public holiday). *People's Party Day* (22nd: public holiday). *Boun Khoun Khao* (movable) harvest festival, local celebration centred around the wats. | **March**

Boun Pimai (13-15th: public holiday) to celebrate Lao New Year. The first month of the Lao New Year is actually December but festivities are delayed until April when days are longer than nights. By April it's also hotting up, so having hosepipes levelled at you and buckets of water dumped on you is more pleasurable. The festival also serves to invite the rains. Pimai is one of the most important annual festivals, particularly in Luang Prabang (see page 94). Statues of the Buddha (in the 'calling for rain' posture) are ceremonially doused in water, which is poured along an intricately decorated trench (*hang song nam pha*). The small stupas of sand, decorated with streamers, in wat compounds are symbolic requests for health and happiness over the next year. It is celebrated with traditional Lao folksinging (*mor lam*) and the circle dance (*ramwong*). There is usually a three-day holiday. Similar festivals are celebrated in Thailand, Cambodia and Burma. | **April**

Labour Day (1st: public holiday) parades in Vientiane. *Visakha Puja* (movable) to celebrate the birth, enlightenment and death of the Buddha, celebrated in local wats. *Boun Bang Fai* (movable) or the rocket festival, is a Buddhist rain-making festival (see box above). Large bamboo rockets are built and decorated by monks and carried in procession before being blasted skywards. The higher a rocket goes, the bigger its builder's ego gets. Designers of failed rockets are thrown in the mud. The festival lasts two days. | **May**

Children's Day (1st: public holiday). | **June**

Essentials

▶▶ Bun Bang Fai: the Lao Sky Rocket Festival

Perhaps Laos' best known festival is the bun bang fai or Sky Rocket festival. This is celebrated across Laos and in Thailand's northeastern region (which is also Lao) between May and June – the end of the dry season. The festival was originally linked to animist beliefs, but through time it also became closely associated with Buddhism. The climax of the festival involves the firing of massive rockets into the air to ensure bountiful rain by propitiating the rain god Vassakarn (or, as some people maintain, Phya Thaen), who also has a penchant for fire. The rockets can be 4 m or more long and contain as much as 500 kg of gunpowder. As well as these bang jut *rockets, there are also bang eh – rockets which are heavily and extravagantly decorated and which are not fired, and just for show. Traditionally the rockets were made of bamboo; now steel and plastic storm pipes are more commonly used in Thailand such is the size*

of bang jut. *Specialist rocket-makers commissioned months before hand have taken over from the amateurs of the past. The rockets are mounted on a bamboo scaffold and fired into the air with much cheering and shouting – and exchanging of money as gambling has become part and parcel of the event.*

Traditionally, bun bang fai *were local festivals when neighbouring villages would take it in turns to bear the cost. The rockets were made by Buddhist monks who were the only people with the time and knowledge to build the gunpowder-packed rockets. It was far more lewd and wild than today. Men wearing phallic symbols would parade through the village, drunken groups would dance wildly imitating sexual intercourse, and young men and women would take the opportunity to meet and court. At the same time, young boys would be ordained and monks blessed.*

June/July **June/July** *Khao Phansa* (movable) is the start of Buddhist Lent and is a time of retreat and fasting for monks. These are the most usual months for ordination and for men to enter the monkhood for short periods before they marry. The festival starts with the full moon in June/July and continues until the full moon in October. It all ends with the *Kathin* ceremony in October when monks receive gifts.

August *Lao Issara* (13th: public holiday), Free Lao Day. *Liberation Day* (23rd: public holiday). *Ho Khao Padap Dinh* (movable) is a celebration of the dead.

September *Boun Ok Phansa* (movable) is the end of Buddhist Lent and the faithful take offerings to the temple. It is in the '9th month' in Luang Prabang and the '11th month' in Vientiane, and marks the end of the rainy season. Boat races take place on the Mekong River with crews of 50 or more men and women. On the night before the race small decorated rafts are set afloat on the river.

October *Freedom from the French Day* (12th: public holiday) which is only really celebrated in Vientiane only.

November *Boun That Luang* (movable), is celebrated in all Laos' *thats*, although most enthusiastically and colourfully in Vientiane (see page 94). As well as religious rituals, most celebrations include local fairs, processions, beauty pageants and other festivities.

December *Hmong New Year* (movable). *Independence Day* (2nd: public holiday), military parades, dancing, music

Sport and special interest travel

Activity-wise, Laos is hardly the place for extreme sports enthusiasts, and despite the rafting opportunities available from Vang Vieng, there's actually not much 'white' in watersports here. However, the enormous popularity of floating lazily down the Nam Xong, stopping every so often to get out of your inner tube and explore a cave or two, is indisputable, and people come back for more time and again. Canoeing is also on offer, but gear yourself up for a pleasant if rather tame day out rather than a foam flecked white knuckle ride.

See Specialist tour operators, page 21, for further details

Essentials

There are some very good caving opportunities in the karst areas of the central provinces, but these are scarcely on the average tourist itinerary and need a good deal of initiative to explore – see page 195 for details of caves in the Thakhet area). We don't know of any tour operators who have done much more than dabbled in this field. For further information see the following websites: www.speleo.nl/laos; www.mmadventure.com; and www.rainierpubs.com

Caving

There are no specialist companies – as far as we are aware – offering rock-climbing tours to Laos. However the following websites offer some pointers and guidance: www.simonfoley.com/climbing/laos.htm, www.planetfear.com/climbing/forum/t.html?t=424, and www.geocities.com/wee_rocks/laos.html. The last site here – for *Wee's Rock Climbing School* – took an expedition to Luang Prabang in 2000 and says: "Climbing in Laos is in the very beginning stage, none of the locals climb, nobody really knows anything…"

Climbing

Laos currently has three courses: a quaint little one close to Vientiane; a rather better course about 2 km before the Friendship Bridge, at the 16 km mark; and a better one still at the hideous *Dansavanh Resort* outside the provincial capital of Tulakhom, around 60 km from Vientiane. There are also plans afoot to open another course attached to the *Champassak Palace Hotel* in Pakse, but it's unlikely that any moves in that direction will be made before 2003.

Golf

Treks are offered in abundance, and the most northerly parts of the country are especially geared up for this sort of activity, although there are plenty of opportunities in places further south such as Luang Namtha, Muang Sing, and even (in a rather elementary way) around the Bolovens Plateau, in places like Tad Lo. Plans to develop treks around Kasi have yet to be approved, although word on the street is that if the current ideas take off, the packages on offer should be jolly good.

Trekking

Health

The health care in Laos is varied: there are some decent private and government clinics and hospitals, but as with all medical care, first impressions count. If a facility is grubby and staff wear grey coats instead of white ones, then be wary of the general standard of medicine and hygiene. If you do get ill, the hospitals and clinics listed under the main centres in this book are the most highly regarded in the country. If they cannot treat you they will know where you·should be sent.

See Travelling with children, page 25, for further information on children's health

Medical services are restricted by a lack of trained personnel and facilities and standards are poor – particularly at district and rural level. There is only one doctor to every 4,545 people. Emergency treatment is available at the Mahosot Hospital and Clinique

Medical facilities

Settathirath in Vientiane (see page 103) but better facilities are available in Thailand. The Australian and Swedish embassies have clinics – both charge a small fee – for smaller problems (see page 103). Emergency evacuation to Udon Thani (Thailand) can be arranged at short notice. It is wise to carry a first aid pack in case of emergency. Pharmacies are usually poorly stocked. The likelihood of finding good medical care diminishes very rapidly as you move away from larger towns. Especially in the rural areas there are systems and traditions of medicine wholly different from the Western model and you will be confronted with less orthodox forms of treatment such as herbal medicines and acupuncture, not that these are unfamiliar to most Western travellers.

Hospitals in Thailand Nongkhai-Wattana General Hospital, 1159/4 Prajak Road, Nong Kha, T66-42 465201-8. Aek Udon International Hospital, 555/5 Posri Road, Udon Thani, T66-42 342555.

Before you go   Ideally, you should see your GP or travel clinic at least six weeks before your departure for general advice on travel risks, malaria and vaccinations. Make sure you have travel insurance, get a dental check (especially if you are going to be away for more than a month), know your own blood group and if you suffer a long-term condition such as diabetes or epilepsy make sure someone knows or that you have a Medic Alert bracelet/necklace with this information on it.

Vaccinations for your Laos trip	Vaccination	Recommended
	Polio	Yes if none in last 10 years
	Tetanus	Yes if none in last 10 years (but after five doses you have had enough for life)
	Typhoid	Yes if none in last three years
	Yellow Fever	The disease does not exist in Vietnam. However, the authorities may wish to see a certificate if you have recently arrived form an endemic area in Africa or South America.
	Rabies	Yes if travelling to jungle and/or remote areas
	Hepatitis A	Yes - the disease can be caught easily from food/water
	Japanese Encephalitis	May be advised for some areas, depending on the duration of the trip and proximity to rice growing and pig-farming areas.
	BCG	We are not sure how much protection this vaccination gives the traveller against lung tuberculosis but I would currently advise people to have it in the absence of any better alternative.

Malaria in Laos   The deadly *P.falciparum* malaria, in a form that is resistant to chloroquine, exists in all of the country except the capital, Vientiane. The choice of malaria prophylaxis will need to be something other than chloroquine for most people, since there is such a high level of resistance to it. Always check with your doctor or travel clinic for the most up-to-date advice.

Anti-malarials Important to take for the key areas. Specialist advice is required as to which type to take. General principles are that all except Malarone should be continued for four weeks after leaving the malarial area. Malarone needs to be continued for only seven days afterwards (if a tablet is missed or vomited seek specialist advice). The start times for the anti-malarials vary in that if you have never taken Lariam (Mefloquine) before it is advised to start it at least 2-3 weeks before the entry to a malarial zone (this is to help identify serious side-effects early). Chloroquine and Paludrine are often started a week before the trip to establish a pattern but Doxycycline and Malarone can be started only 1-2 days before entry to the malarial area. **NB** It is risky to buy medicinal tablets abroad because the doses may differ and there may be a trade in false drugs.

Mosquito repellents Remember that DEET (Di-ethyltoluamide) is the gold standard. Apply the repellent every 4-6 hours but more often if you are sweating heavily. If a non-DEET product is used, check who tested it. Validated products (tested at the London School of Hygiene and Tropical Medicine) include *Mosiguard*, Non-DEET *Jungle formula* and non-DEET *Autan*. If you want to use citronella remember that it must be applied very frequently (that is hourly) to be effective. If you are a popular target for insect bites or develop lumps quite soon after being bitten, carry an Aspivenin kit. This syringe suction device is available from many chemists and draws out some of the allergic materials and provides quick relief. For anti-malarial tablets, see above.

Items to take with you

Sun block The Australians have a great campaign, which has reduced skin cancer. It is called Slip, Slap, Slop. Slip on a shirt, Slap on a hat, Slop on sun screen.

Pain killers Paracetomol or a suitable painkiller can have multiple uses for symptoms but remember that more than eight paracetamol a day can lead to liver failure.

Ciproxin A useful antibiotic for some forms of travellers diarrhoea (see below).

Immodium A great standby for those diarrhoeas that occur at awkward times (that is before a long coach/train journey or on a trek). It helps stop the flow of diarrhoea and in my view is of more benefit than harm. (It was believed that letting the bacteria or viruses flow out had to be more beneficial. However, with Immodium they still come out, just in a more solid form.)

Pepto-Bismol Used a lot by Americans for diarrhoea. It certainly relieves symptoms but like Immodium it is not a cure for underlying disease. Be aware that it turns the stool black as well as making it more solid.

MedicAlert These simple bracelets, or an equivalent, should be carried or worn by anyone with a significant medical condition.

For longer trips involving jungle treks, taking a clean needle pack, clean dental pack and water filtration devices are common-sense measures.

Websites Foreign and Commonwealth Office (FCO) (UK) **www.fco.gov.uk** This is a key travel advice site, with useful information on the country, people, climate and lists the UK embassies/consulates. The site also promotes the concept of 'Know Before You Go'. It also encourages the purchase of travel insurance and appropriate travel health advice. It has links to the Department of Health travel advice site, see below.

Further Information
Further information on health risks abroad, vaccinations etc may be available from a local travel clinic

Department of Health Travel Advice (UK) **www.doh.gov.uk/traveladvice** This excellent site is also available as a free booklet, the T6, from Post offices. It lists the vaccine advice requirements for each country.

Medic Alert (UK) **www.medicalalert.co.uk** This is the website of the foundation that produces bracelets and necklaces for those with existing medical problems. Once you have ordered your bracelet/necklace you write your key medical details on paper inside it, so that if you collapse, a medical person can identify you as someone with epilepsy or allergy to peanuts etc.

Blood Care Foundation (UK) **www.bloodcare.org.uk** The Blood Care Foundation is a charity 'dedicated to the provision of screened blood and resuscitation fluids in countries where these are not readily available.' They will dispatch certified non-infected blood of the right type to your hospital. The blood is flown in from centres around the world.

Public Health Laboratory Service (UK) **www.phls.org.uk** This site has up-to-date malaria advice guidelines for travel around the world. It gives specific advice about the right drugs for each location. It also has useful information for those who are pregnant, suffering from epilepsy or planning to travel with children.

Centers for Disease Control and Prevention (USA) **www.cdc.gov** This site from the

Essentials

US Government gives excellent advice on travel health, has useful disease maps and details of disease outbreaks.

World Health Organisation www.who.int The WHO site has links to the WHO Blue Book (it was Yellow up to last year) on travel advice. This lists the diseases in different regions of the world. It describes vaccination schedules and makes clear which countries have Yellow Fever Vaccination certificate requirements and malarial risk.

Tropical Medicine Bureau (Ireland) **www.tmb.ie** This Irish-based site has a good collection of general travel health information and disease risks.

Fit for Travel (UK) **www.fitfortravel.scot.nhs.uk** This site from Scotland provides a quick A-Z of vaccine and travel health advice requirements for each country.

British Travel Health Association (UK) **www.btha.org** This is the official website of an organization of travel health professionals.

NetDoctor (UK) **www.Netdoctor.co.uk** This general health advice site has a useful section on travel and has an 'ask the expert', interactive chat forum.

Travel Screening Services (UK) **www.travelscreening.co.uk** This is the author's website. A private clinic dedicated to integrated travel health. The clinic gives vaccine, travel health advice, email and SMS text vaccine reminders and screens travellers who have returned, for tropical diseases.

Books & leaflets *The Travellers Good Health Guide* by **Dr Ted Lankester** (ISBN 0-85969-827-0). *Expedition Medicine* (The Royal Geographic Society) **Editors David Warrell and Sarah Anderson** (ISBN 1 86197 040-4). *International Travel and Health* **World Health Organisation**, Geneva (ISBN 92 4 158026 7). *The World's Most Dangerous Places* by **Robert Young Pelton, Coskun Aral and Wink Dulles** (ISBN 1-566952-140-9).

The Travellers Guide to Health (T6) can be obtained by calling the Health Literature Line on 0800 555 777. Advice for travellers on avoiding the risks of HIV and AIDS (*Travel Safe*) available from Department of Health, PO Box 777, London SE1 6XH. *The Blood Care Foundation* order form PO Box 7, Sevenoaks, Kent TN13 2SZ T44-(0)1732-742427.

On the road

The key viral disease is **Dengue fever** (see page 64), which is transmitted by mosquitos that bite during the day. The disease is like a very nasty form of the flu with 2-3 days of illness, followed by a short period of recovery, then a second attack of illness. The south of Laos suffered a serious epidemic of Dengue in 1998. Westerners very rarely get the worst haemorrhagic form of the disease. Bacterial diseases include **tuberculosis** (TB) and some causes of the more common traveller's **diarrhoea**.

Diarrhoea & intestinal upset
This is almost inevitable. One study showed that up to 70% of all travellers may suffer during their trip

Symptoms Diarrhoea can refer either to loose stools or an increased frequency; both of these can be a nuisance. It should be short lasting but persistence beyond two weeks, with blood or pain, require specialist medical attention

Cures Ciproxin (Ciprofloaxcin) is a useful antibiotic for bacterial traveller's diarrhoea. It can be obtained by private prescription in the UK which is expensive, or bought over the counter in Vietnam pharmacies. You need to take one 500 mg tablet when the diarrhoea starts and if you do not feel better in 24 hours, the diarrhoea is likely to have a non-bacterial cause and may be viral (in which case there is little you can do apart from keep yourself rehydrated and wait for it to settle on its own). The key treatment with all diarrhoeas is rehydration. Try to keep hydrated by taking the right mixture of salt, sugar and water. This is available as Oral Rehydration Salts (ORS) in ready-made sachets or can be made up by adding a teaspoon of sugar and a half teaspoon of salt to a litre of clean water. Drink at least one large cup of this drink for each loose stool. You can also use flat carbonated drinks as an alternative. Immodium and Pepto-Bismol provide symptomatic relief.

Prevention Be careful with water and ice for drinking. Ask yourself where the water came from. If you have any doubts then boil it or filter and treat it. There are many filter/treatment devices on the market. Food can also transmit disease. Be wary of salads (what were they washed in), re-heated foods or food that has been left out in the sun, having been cooked earlier in the day. There is a simple adage that says wash it, peel it, boil it or forget it. Also be wary of unpasteurized dairy products, these can transmit a range of diseases from brucellosis (fevers and constipation), to listeria (meningitis) and tuberculosis of the gut (obstruction, constipation, fevers and weight loss).

Symptoms Malaria can cause death within 24 hours and Laos can be considered a high-risk country. It can start as something just resembling an attack of flu. You may feel tired, lethargic, headachy; or worse, develop fits, followed by coma and then death. Have a low index of suspicion because it is very easy to write off vague symptoms, which may actually be malaria. All clinics in Laos can test for malaria quickly and reliably. If you come down with a fever, get tested as quickly as possible.

Malaria & insect bite prevention

Cures Treatment is with drugs and may be oral or into a vein depending on the seriousness of the infection. Remember ABCD: Awareness (of whether the disease is present in the area you are travelling in), Bite avoidance, Chemoprohylaxis, Diagnosis.

Prevention This is best summarized by the B and C of the ABCD, bite avoidance and chemoprophylaxis. Wear clothes that cover arms and legs and use effective insect repellents. Use a mosquito net dipped in permethrin as both a physical and chemical barrier at night in the same areas. Guard against the contraction of malaria with the correct anti-malarials (see above). The Royal Homeopathic Hospital in the UK does not advocate homeopathic options for malaria prevention or treatment.

Symptoms If you go diving make sure that you are fit to do so. *The British Scuba Association* (BSAC), Telford's Quay, South Pier Road, Ellesmere Port, Cheshire CH65 4FL, United Kingdom, T01513-506200, F506215, www.bsac.com, can put you in touch with doctors who do medical examinations. Protect your feet from cuts, beach dog parasites (larva migrans) and sea urchins. The latter are almost impossible to remove but can be dissolved with lime or vinegar. Keep an eye out for secondary infection.

Underwater health

Cures Antibiotics for secondary infections. Serious diving injuries may need time in a decompression chamber.

Prevention Check that the dive company know what they are doing, have appropriate certification from *BSAC* or *Professional Association of Diving Instructors* (PADI), (Unit 7, St Philips Central, Albert Rd, St Philips, Bristol BS2 0TD, T0117-3007234, www.padi.com), and that the equipment is well-maintained.

Symptoms White Britons are notorious for becoming red in hot countries because they like to stay out longer than everyone else and do not use adequate sun protection. This can lead to sunburn. Aloe vera gel is a good pain reliever. Long-term sun damage leads to a loss of elasticity of skin and the development of pre-cancerous lesions. Many years later cancers may develop. There is the milder basal cell carcinoma which, if detected early, can be treated by cutting it out or freezing it. The much nastier malignant melanoma may have already spread to bone and brain at the time that it is first noticed.

Sun protection
Follow the Australians' advice: Slip, Slap, Slop

Prevention Sun screen. SPF stands for Sun Protection Factor. It is measured by determining how long a given person takes to 'burn' with and without the sunscreen product on. So, if it takes 10 times longer to burn with the sunscreen product applied, then that product has an SPF of 10. If it only takes twice as long then the SPF is 2. The higher the SPF the greater the protection. However, do not just use higher factors just to stay out in the sun longer. 'Flash frying' (desperate bursts of excessive exposure), as it is called, is known to increase the risks of skin cancer.

Dengue fever **Symptoms** This disease can be contracted throughout Vietnam. In travellers this can cause a severe flu-like illness which includes symptoms of fever, lethargy, enlarged lymph glands and muscle pains. It starts suddenly, lasts for 2-3 days, seems to get better for 2-3 days and then kicks in again for another 2-3 days. It is usually all over in an unpleasant week. The local children are prone to the much nastier haemorrhagic form of the disease, which often leads to their death.

Cures The traveller's version of the disease is self-limiting and forces rest and recuperation on the sufferer.

Prevention The mosquitoes that carry the Dengue virus bite during the day, unlike the malaria mosquitoes. Which sadly means that repellent application and covered limbs are a 24-hour issue. Check your accommodation for flower pots and shallow pools of water, since these are where the dengue-carrying mosquitoes breed.

Hepatitis **Symptoms** Hepatitis means inflammation of the liver. Viral causes of the disease can be acquired anywhere in Laos. The most obvious symptom is a yellowing of your skin or the whites of your eyes. However, prior to this, all you may notice is itching and tiredness.

Cures Early on, depending on the type of hepatitis, a vaccine or immunoglobulin may reduce the duration of the illness.

Prevention Pre-travel hepatitis A vaccine is the best bet. Hepatitis B (for which there is a vaccine) is spread through blood and unprotected sex. Both can be avoided. Unfortunately there is no vaccine for hepatitis C, or the increasing list of other Hepatitis viruses.

Tuberculosis This old disease is still a significant problem in many areas. The bus driver coughing as he takes your fare could expose you to the mycobacterium.

Symptoms Cough, tiredness, fever and lethargy.

Cures At least six months treatment with a combination of drugs is required.

Prevention Have a BCG vaccination before you go and see a doctor early if you have a persistent cough, cough blood, fever or unexplained weight loss.

Sexual health The range of visible and invisible diseases is awesome. Unprotected sex can spread HIV, Hepatitis B and C, Gonorrhea (green discharge), chlamydia (nothing to see, but may cause painful urination and later female infertility), painful recurrent herpes, syphilis and warts, just to name a few. You can cut down the risk by using condoms. Commercial sex workers in Laos may have high levels of HIV.

If you do stray, consider getting a sexual health check on your return home

The health section was written by **Dr Charlie Easmon** MBBS MRCP MSc Public Health DTM&H DOccMed Director of Travel Screening Services.

The Vientiane Region

Introducing the Vientiane Region

In 1563, King Setthathirat made the riverine city of Vientiane the capital of Laos. Or, to be more historically accurate, Wiang Chan – the 'City of the Moon' – became the capital of Lane Xang. In those days it was a small fortified city on the banks of the Mekong with a palace and two wats, **That Luang** and **Wat Phra Kaeo** (built to house the Emerald Buddha). The city had grown prosperous from the surrounding fertile plains and taxes levied from trade going upriver. As Francis Garnier put it, this was the "former metropolis of the kingdom of Laos".

Today Vientiane is, perhaps, the most charming of all Southeast Asia's capital cities. Cut off from the outside world and foreign investment for much of the modern period, its colonial heritage remains largely intact. This is a capital that is more lower case than upper case. While the last few years may have brought greater bustle and activity, it is still a quiet city of tree-lined boulevards where the image of the past is reflected in the present. Walking or bicycling remain pleasant ways to navigate the town – 'city' is too grand a word for Vientiane – but it is still large enough to support

Things to do in the Vientiane Region

① Bicycle or catch a *tuk-tuk* up to **That Luang**, the holiest Buddhist shine in Laos.

② Visit **Wat Sisaket**, a beautiful, cloistered monastery insulated from the noises of the surrounding streets.

③ Return perplexed from **Xieng Khuan**, 25 km east of Vientiane, a confused concoction of deities, half-deities and pseudo-deities.

④ Raft, trek and explore the caves around the attractive town of **Van Vieng**, way station on the road to Luang Prabang.

⑤ Take pleasure in a cold beer after a long, hot day at one of the **bars on the Mekong**, and watch the sun set over the river.

a slate of excellent restaurants, a good number of attractive bars, a handful of clubs, and some serviceable hotels.

Around Vientiane are a number of places of interest, some of which make for worthwhile stopovers or weekend retreats, including **Lao Pako** and **Nam Ngum**. **Vang Vieng** and **Kasi** both lie on the road north to Luang Prabang and have become popular way stations. But with improvements to the road some travellers have been tempted to travel non-stop. If you can, make time for Van Vieng, an attractive town in itself and an excellent base from which to explore the surrounding countryside with its caves, waterfalls and minority villages, and attendant activities such as trekking and rafting.

Vientiane

Phone code: 021
Colour map 2, grid B2
Population: under
200,000 (city); 600,000
(municipality)

The Apollo astronauts couldn't see it from space. You'd probably miss it from a low-flying plane. Vientiane is a capital that wears its national status lightly. If Vientiane were human she would be unassuming and understated, she would wear sensible shoes, and blend in with her surroundings. This is what makes the city so charming: no well-known fast-food outlets; no progressive trance; no mass transit system; no 100,000-seat stadiums. Vientiane is created in proportions that the human mind can readily comprehend. It will take you half a day to get a grip of the city's layout, another half day to fill in many of the blanks. By the end of the third day you will be striding the pavements and cycling the streets as if you belong here.

Ins and outs

Getting there

Most visitors arrive in Vientiane by air, the great bulk on one of the daily connections with Bangkok. For details on arriving and transport from Vientiane's Wattay Airport see page 33. It is now very easy to arrive 'overland', taking the Friendship Bridge which lies just 20 km downstream from the capital. Visas are available on arrival via the bridge. For details on crossing at the bridge and visa formalities see pages 70 and 33. The closest Thai town of any size to the bridge is Nong Khai. Shuttle buses ferry people across the bridge and they operate every 20 mins, 0830-1730. These buses stop at the Thai and Lao immigration posts where a small fee may be payable. Tuk-tuks (small carts with engines) and taxis are available to take people on to Vientiane. There are always plenty of both. The cheapest way into town is to board a No 14 bus. These run every half-hour or so until 1700 and terminate at Vientiane's Morning Market or *talaat sao*. For destinations beyond Vientiane, most people either travel by bus (slow but cheap) or plane (quick and still cheap by Western standards). Boats do travel up the Mekong to Luang Prabang but there are no scheduled services and the journey takes several days.

Getting around

See Transport, page
99, for further details

Although Vientiane is the capital of Laos, it is no Bangkok. It is small and manageable, with a population of less than 200,000, and getting around is fairly easy. The core of the city is negotiable on foot and even outlying hotels and places of interest are accessible by bicycle. For many, bicycling will be the most appealing option. Although it can be debilitatingly hot at certain times of the year, there are no great hills to struggle up. If bicycling doesn't appeal, a combination of foot and tuk-tuk is the best way to explore the city. There is a limited city bus service but it really serves outlying destinations in the Vientiane Plain rather than the city proper. There are motorbikes for hire and taxis are also available, although these are mainly used for longer journeys and day trips.

Orientation

See page 95 for advice
on maps of Vientiane

The capital is divided into *ban* or villages, mainly centred around their local wats, and larger *muang* or districts: **Muang Sikhottabong** lies to the west, **Muang Chanthabouli** to the north, **Muang Xaisettha** to the east and **Muang Sisattanak** to

Arriving at night

It takes some skill to arrive in Vientiane late at night. The last domestic flight touches down at around suppertime, 1830; the final Lao Aviation international connection at 1915. So no one finds themselves stranded at the airport in the wee hours. Buses also arrive in the late afternoon or early evening and the Friendship Bridge closes at 2200. If by some fluke you do find yourself arriving later than you expected the city is safe to walk around, and there are usually tuk-tuk drivers snoozing in their machines who will willingly take your money. The bus station at the morning market is, in any case, just a 10-15 minute walk from the centre of town. Many of the more up-market hotels have 24-hour security and it's usually possible to raise someone from bed at the guesthouses too.

the south. Vientiane can be rather confusing for the first-time visitor as there are few street signs and most streets have two names – pre- and post-revolutionary. The names of major streets – or *thanon* – usually correspond to the nearest wat. Traffic lights and wats serve as directional landmarks. But because Vientiane is so small and compact it doesn't take long to get to grips with the town and the best way to do this is either on foot or by bicycle.

Tourist information

Lao National Tourism Company, 08/2 Lane Xang Av, T216671, F212013. In the past this office has lacked information, or, for that matter, courtesy. However, a few staff training sessions from some Dutch students of tourism have paid off, and the staff are now very friendly and want to help any way they can. Their inability to speak much English is still a bit of a barrier, but there are several English language leaflets to pick up.

History

Vientiane is an ancient city. There was probably a settlement here, on a bend on the left bank of the Mekong, in the 10th century. But given that Laos' history is so murky, much of our knowledge about the city before the 16th century is thin – and dubious. Scholars do know, from the chronicles, that King Setthathirat decided to relocate his capital here in the early 1560s. It seems that it took him four years to build the city, constructing a defensive wall (hence 'Wiang', meaning a walled or fortified city), along with Wat Phra Kaeo and a much enlarged That Luang.

Vieng Chan remained intact until 1827 when it was ransacked by the Siamese – explaining why many of its wats are of recent construction. Francis Garnier in 1860 wrote of 'a heap of ruins' and having surveyed the 'relics of antiquity' decided that the "absolute silence reigning within the precincts of a city formerly so rich and populous, was ... much more impressive than any of its monuments ...". A few years later, Louis de Carne wrote of the vegetation that it was like "a veil drawn by nature over the weakness of man and the vanity of his works ...". The city was abandoned for decades, erased from the maps of the region. The city was only conjured back into existence by the French who commenced reconstruction at the end of the 19th century. They built rambling colonial villas and wide tree-lined boulevards, befitting their new administrative capital, Vientiane. At the height of American influence it was renowned for its opium dens and sex shows.

▶▶   Bridging the Mekong

In April 1994, King Bhumibol of Thailand and the President of Laos, accompanied by prime ministers Chuan Leekpai of Thailand and Australia's Keating opened the first bridge to span the lower reaches of the Mekong River, linking Nong Khai in Northeast Thailand with Vientiane in Laos. The bridge took a long time to materialize. It was first mooted in the 1950s, but war in Indochina and hostility between Laos and Thailand scuppered plans until the late 1980s. Then, with the cold war ending and growing rapprochement between the countries of Indochina and Asean, the bridge, as they say, became an idea whose time had come.

The 1,200 m-long Friendship Bridge, or Mittaphab, was financed with US$30 mn of aid from Australia. It is a key link in a planned road network that will eventually stretch from Singapore to

Beijing. For land-locked Laos, it offers an easier route to Thailand and through Thailand to the sea. For Thailand, it offers an entrée into one of the least developed countries in the world, rich in natural resources and potential. While for Australia, it demonstrated the country's Asian credentials. The Thais would like to build two further bridges. One will probably link Savannakhet and Mukdahan; final agreement was reached at the end of 2001 and it should be completed by 2005. The Lao and Thai governments have also signed a memorandum of understanding to build a bridge between Thakhek and Nakhon Phanom although Vientiane is decidedly cool about the prospect. They worry that bridges not only bolster trade, but also bring consumerism, crime, prostitution and environmental degradation.

Modern Vientiane   Today Vientiane is a quiet capital. The population of the Vientiane Municipality in 2000 was a whisker under 600,000. However, this includes a number of districts and villages outside the city proper. Vientiane itself has a population of under 200,000. Before 1970 there was only one set of traffic lights in the whole city and even with the arrival of cars and motorbikes from Thailand in recent years, the streets are a far cry from the congestion of Bangkok. Unlike Phnom Penh and Saigon there are only scattered traces of French town planning; architecture is a mixture of east and west, with French colonial villas and traditional wooden Lao buildings intermingled with Chinese shop houses and more contemporary buildings. Some locals worry that foreign investment and redevelopment will ruin the city. Already some remarkably grotesque buildings are going up although officials do seem aware that there is little to be gained from creating a Bangkok in microcosm.

Sights

Most of the interesting buildings in Vientiane are of religious significance. All tour companies and many hotels and guesthouses will arrange city tours and excursions to surrounding sights.

That Luang   Situated on Thanon That Luang, this is considered Vientiane's most important site and the holiest Buddhist monument in the country. The golden spire looks impressive at the top of the hill, 3 km northeast of the city. According to legend, a stupa was first built here in the third century AD by emissaries of the Moghul Emperor Asoka and it is supposed to have contained a relic of the Buddha (his breast bone). But excavations on the site have only located the remains of an 11th/13th-century Khmer temple and this earlier provenance is doubtful in the

24 hours in the city

We say this more than once in this book: the charm of Laos lies in the fact that you can't find an espresso at three in the morning or a nightclub meeting your strange desire for techno. There's little point reaching for your Palm organizer and mapping out a day minutely planned to the last moment. But, for what it's worth…

Get up at dawn and wander out on to the streets to watch the city's monks collecting alms from crouching women and girls (rarely men). After the final victory of the Pathet Lao in 1975 monks were encouraged – none too gently – to work for their living. Depending on your budget either buy a baguette from one of the roadside carts or get a Lao coffee and croissant or baguette from one of the cafés around the Nam Phou Fountain. If it's the hot season and it is still not too late in the day, **hire a bicycle** from one of the shops near the Nam Phou Fountain or from your guesthouse. Ride north on Lane Xang Avenue and That Luang Road to **That Luang**, the symbol of Lao nationhood and one of the holiest sites in the country. The ride back into town is slightly downhill, all the better if the day is hotting up. Near the bottom of Lane Xang Avenue are Vientiane's two finest monasteries as well as the **Morning Market** or *Talat Sao*. Begin with the market. Among the cornucopia of stalls and shops with tack from Thailand and China, and textiles and silver from Laos, is a reasonable café. Re-charged, head to **Wat Sisaket** and **Wat Phra Kaeo**. If your engagement with Buddhist architecture cannot stretch to two monasteries head for the first of these: much more satisfying with its shaded cloisters and elegant, perfectly-proportioned *sim*. By now it is probably time for lunch. Save the big spend for the evening and tuck into some roadside barbecued chicken – and make sure that's a thin and scrawny Lao bird and not one of the plump, hormone-filled creatures from Thailand. The stalls around the Morning Market are usually a good bet.

Doing nothing much at all may seem the most enticing prospect during the hot season. But if it's reasonably cool, or you are incomprehensibly full of energy, one nice outing is to bicycle downstream along the **Mekong**. A track (no cars) follows the Mekong beginning at around Kilometre 5 – cut in off the main road along one of the many paths and ride for as long as you like. The path is shaded by trees, passes monasteries and attractive riverside houses. There are shops for cold drinks and snacks along the way.

Make sure you get your bike back (if you need to) before the sun has set and make your way to **Quai Fa Ngum** and the Mekong. Until recently enterprising Lao would set up small groups of tables right on the banks of the river and serve beers and snacks to locals and visitors. In mid-2002 the government had fenced off the river (some Grand Plan is in the offing), forcing the riverside stalls closer to the road, but it is still a pleasant place to begin the evening's revelries. After a few beers use those tens of thousands of kip you saved at lunch and have dinner at *Le Nadao*, *Le Silapa*, *Café Colombo*, or *Cote D'Azur* (see our entries for details). To round off the day, *Sticky Fingers* is good for cocktails and coffee, and the *Chess Club* for live music and alcohol.

The Ventiane Region

extreme. It was built in its present form, encompassing the previous buildings, in 1566 by King Setthathirat, whose statue stands outside. Plundered by the Thais and the Chinese Ho in the 18th century, it was restored by King (Chao) Anou at the beginning of the 19th century. He added the cloister and the Burmese-style pavilion containing the That Sithamma Hay Sok.

It was again carefully restored by l'Ecole Francaise d'Extrême-Orient, whose conservators also restored parts of Angkor Wat, at the beginning of the

20th century. The stupa was rebuilt yet again in 1930, as many Lao disapproved of the French restoration. The reliquary is surrounded by a square cloister, with an entrance on each side, the most famous on the east. There is a small collection of statues in the cloisters including one of the Khmer king Jayavarman VII. The cloisters are used as lodgings by monks who travel to Vientiane for religious reasons and especially for the annual That Luang festival (see page 94).

The base of the stupa is a mixture of styles, Khmer, Indian and Lao, and each side has a *hor vay* or small offering temple. The second tier is surrounded by a lotus wall and 30 smaller stupas, representing the 30 Buddhist perfections. Each of these originally contained smaller golden stupas but they were stolen by Chinese raiders in the 19th century. The 30 m-high spire

Vientiane

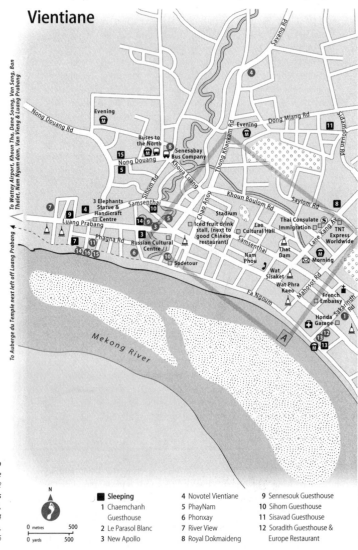

N

0 metres 500
0 yards 500

Sleeping
1 Chaemchanh
  Guesthouse
2 Le Parasol Blanc
3 New Apollo

4 Novotel Vientiane
5 PhayNam
6 Phonxay
7 River View
8 Royal Dokmaideng

9 Sennesouk Guesthouse
10 Sihom Guesthouse
11 Sisavad Guesthouse
12 Soradith Guesthouse &
  Europe Restaurant

dominates the skyline and resembles an elongated lotus bud, crowned by a stylized banana flower and parasol. It was designed so that pilgrims could climb up to the stupa with walkways around each level. There was originally a wat on each side of the stupa but only two remain: **Wat Luang Nua** to the north and **Wat Luang Tai** to the south. While That Luang may be the most important historical site in Vientiane, most visitors will feel that it is not the most interesting, impressive or beautiful, largely because it seems to have been constructed out of concrete. Both Wat Sisaket and Wat Phra Kaeo (see below) are more memorable. Nonetheless, it is important to appreciate the reverence with which the *that* is held by most Laotians – indeed, by most Lao including the many millions who live in neighbouring Thailand. The *that* is the proto-type for the distinctive Lao-style angular chedi which can be seen in northeast

The Ventiane Region

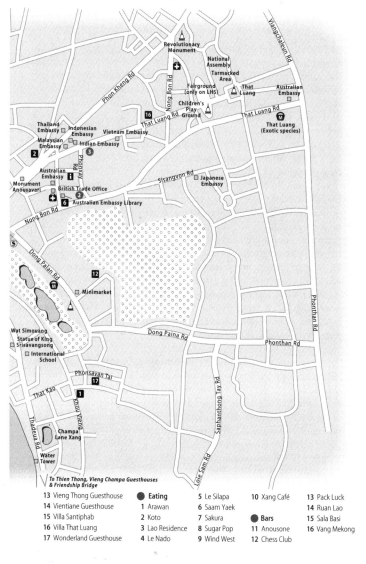

13 Vieng Thong Guesthouse	● **Eating**	5 Le Silapa	10 Xang Café	13 Pack Luck
14 Vientiane Guesthouse	1 Arawan	6 Saam Yaek		14 Ruan Lao
15 Villa Santiphab	2 Koto	7 Sakura	● **Bars**	15 Sala Basi
16 Villa That Luang	3 Lao Residence	8 Sugar Pop	11 Anousone	16 Vang Mekong
17 Wonderland Guesthouse	4 Le Nado	9 Wind West	12 Chess Club	

Thailand as well as across Laos. A booklet about the wat is on sale at the entrance.
■ *Tue-Sun 0800-1200, 1300-1600 (except 'special' holidays). 1000 kip.*

Revolutionary Monument Also known as the **Unknown Soldiers Memorial**, this monument is located just off Phon Kheng Road. Echoing a *that* in design, it is visible from the parade ground (which resembles a disused parking lot), in front of That Luang. This spectacularly dull monument, a landmark on top of the hill, was built in memory of those who died during the revolution in 1975.

The **Pathet Lao Museum**, to the northwest of Wat That Luang, is only open to VIPs and never to the public. But there are a few tanks, trucks, guns and aircraft used in the war lying in the grounds, which can be seen from the other side of the fence.

Monument Anousavari
The top affords a bird's eye view of the leafy capital

At the end of Thanon That Luang and the top of Lane Xang is the Oriental answer to Paris's Arc de Triomphe and Vientiane's best known landmark, the monstrous Monument Anousavari. It is called the Anou Savali, officially renamed the Pratuxai or Victory Gate, but is affectionately known as 'the vertical runway'. It was built by the former regime in memory of those who died in the wars before the Communist takeover, but the cement ran out before its completion. Refusing to be beaten, hundreds of tonnes of cement – part of a US aid package to help with the construction of runways at Vientiane's Wattay Airport – were diverted up Thanon Lane Xang to finish off the monument in 1969. The glittering golden dome in the distance is the expensive, Russian-built opera house, which is now only used during National Day celebrations.

The interior of the Monument Anousavari is reminiscent of a multi-storey car park (presumably as a counterpoint to the parade ground by the Revolutionary Monument), sporadically decorated with graffiti daubed on top of unfinished Buddhist bas-reliefs in reinforced concrete. The frescoes under the arches at the bottom represent mythological stories from the Lao version of the Ramayana, the Phra Lak Pralam. Until 1990 there was a bar on the bottom floor; today Vientiane's young hang out on the parapet, listening to the *Lambada* in Lao. ■ *Mon-Fri 0800-1100, 1400-1630, but these hours seem to be posted only for fun. 1000 kip.* Souvenir shops at ground level and up the monument charge exorbitant rates; bargain hard.

Wat Sisaket Further down Thanon Lane Xang is the **Morning Market** or **Talaat Sao** (see below under markets) and beyond, where Thanon Setthathirat meets Thanon Lane Xang, is one of Vientiane's two national museums, **Wat Sisaket**. Built in 1818 during the reign of King Anou, it is one of the most important buildings in the capital. A traditional Lao monastery, the buildings survived the Thai sacking of the town in 1827 (perhaps out of deference to its having been completed only 10 years before the invasion), making it the oldest wat complex in Vientiane. The main sanctuary, or sim, with its sweeping roof has many stylistic similarities with Wat Phra Kaeo (see below): window surrounds, lotus-shaped pillars and carvings of deities held up by giants on the rear door. The **sim** contains 2,052 Buddha statues (mainly terracotta, bronze and wood) in small niches in the top half of the wall. There is little left of the Thai-style jataka murals on the lower walls but the depth and colour of the originals can be seen from the few remaining pieces. The ceiling was copied from temples King Anou had seen on a visit to Bangkok. The standing image to the left of the altar is believed to have been cast in the same proportions as King Anou. Around the *sim*, set into the ground, are small *bai sema* or boundary stones.

The sim is surrounded by a large courtyard, which originally had four entrance gates (three are now blocked). The cloisters shelter 120 large Buddhas in the attitude of subduing Mara (see page 292), plus a number of other images in assorted mudras, and thousands of small figures in niches, although many of the most interesting Buddha figures are now in Wat Phra Kaeo. Most of the statues are 16th-19th century, but there are some earlier images. Quite a number were taken from local monasteries during the French period, and have ended up here. The cloister walls were originally decorated with murals. Behind the sim is a large trough, in the shape of a naga, used for washing the Buddha images during the water festival (see page 57). The whole ensemble – sim plus cloister – is washed in a rather attractive shade of caramel and with the terracotta floor tiles and weathered roof presents a most satisfying sight. An attractive Burmese-style library, or *hau tai*, stands on Thanon Lane Xang outside the courtyard. The large casket inside used to contain important Buddhist manuscripts but they have now been moved to protect them against vermin. Wat Sisaket is the home of the head of the Buddhist community in Laos, Phra Sangka Nagnok. Sadly Wat Sisaket is badly in need of restoration. ■ *Tue-Sun 0800-1200, 1400-1600. 1000 kip. No photography in the* sim.

Just behind Wat Sisaket is an entire complex of superbly preserved colonial houses in a well maintained garden, where the French ambassador resides. The cathedral was built in 1928.

Wat Phra Kaeo

The building was expertly reconstructed in the 1940s and 1950s and is now surrounded by a garden

Almost opposite Wat Sisaket on Thanon Setthathirat is the other national museum, **Wat Phra Kaeo**, also known as **Hor Phra Kaeo**. It was originally built by King Setthathirat in 1565 to house the Emerald Buddha (or *Phra Kaeo*), now in Bangkok. He brought the image from Chiang Mai where he had previously been king. Wat Phra Kaeo was never a monastery but was kept for royal worship. The Emerald Buddha was removed by the Thais in 1778 and Wat Phra Kaeo was destroyed by them in the sacking of Vientiane in 1827. Francis Garnier, the French explorer, who wandered the ruins of Vieng Chan in 1860 describes Wat Phra Kaeo "shin[ing] forth in the midst of the forest, gracefully framed with blooming lianas, and profusely garlanded with foliage". Louis de Carne in his journal, *Travels in Indochina and the Chinese Empire* (1872), was also enchanted, writing when he came upon the vegetation-choked ruin that it "made one feel something of that awe which filled men of old at the threshold of a sacred wood".

The **sim** stands on three tiers of galleries, the top one surrounded by majestic, lotus-shaped columns. The tiers are joined by several flights of steps and guarded by nagas. The main, central (southern) door is an exquisite example of Lao wood sculpture with carved angels surrounded by flowers and birds. This door, is the only notable remnants of the original wat. (The central door at the northern end, with the larger carved angels supported by ogres, is new.) The sim now houses a superb assortment of Lao and Khmer art and some pieces of Burmese and Khmer influence, mostly collected from other wats in Vientiane.

Notable pieces *3, 4, 17*: bronze Buddhas in typical Lao style; *294, 295*: Buddhas influenced by Sukhothai-style (Thailand), where the attitude of the walking Buddha was first created (see page 292); *354*: Buddha meditating – made of lacquered wood shows Burmese influence, 18th century; *372*:

wooden, Indian-style door with erotic sculpture, dating back to the 16th century, originally from the Savannakhet region; *388*: copy of the Phra Bang, the revered statue associated with the origins of Buddhism in Laos (see page 247); *416*: a Khmer deity with four arms; *412, 414, 450*: also Khmer pieces; *415*: is a hybrid of Vishnu and Buddha; *430, 431*: are 18th-century copies of the famous Khmer apsaras, the celestial nymphs of Angkor; *698*: this stone Buddha is the oldest piece of Buddhist art in Laos, sixth to ninth century; *collection of stelae*: inscribed in Lao and Thai script, including one with a treaty delineating a 16th-century agreement between Siam and Lane Xane. An unusual exhibit is the "Atom Struck Tile" found on the site of Sairenji Temple, Hiroshima.

A short description of each exhibit is given in French and Lao. The garden has a small jar from the Plain of Jars (see page 155), which was transported by helicopter down to Vientiane. ■ *Mon-Sun 0800-1200, 1300-1600. 1000 kip. No photographs in the* sim.

Adjacent to the museum is the **old royal palace**, today the presidential palace, closed to the public.

That Dam Travelling north on Chanta Koummane, the distinctive brick That Dam, or **Black Stupa**, can be seen. It is renowned for the legend of the seven-headed naga, which is supposed to have helped protect the city from Thai invaders (conveniently forgetting that the city was comprehensively sacked by the Thais in 1827). The naga now lies dormant, waiting for another chance to fail. The stupa was renovated in 1995 but still has its former uncared for feel.

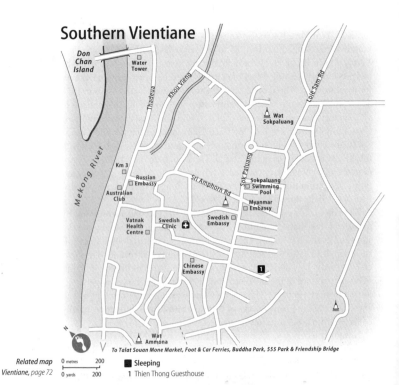

Southern Vientiane

Don Chan Island
Water Tower
Thadeua
Khou Vieng
Toie Sam rd
Wat Sokpaluang
Km 3
Russian Embassy
Sri Amphorn Rd
Sok Paluang
Sokpaluang Swimming Pool
Australian Club
Myanmar Embassy
Vatnak Health Centre
Swedish Clinic
Swedish Embassy
Chinese Embassy
1
Mekong River
Wat Ammona
To Talat Souan Mone Market, Foot & Car Ferries, Buddha Park, 555 Park & Friendship Bridge

Related map
Vientiane, page 72

0 metres   200
0 yards   200

■ Sleeping
1 Thien Thong Guesthouse

In the centre of town, on Samsenthai near the stadium, this place was formerly **National** called the Revolutionary Museum but in these post-revolutionary days it **Museum** has been redesignated a National Museum. To emphasize the change of emphasis it has also recently moved to a new building, but continues to display the country's history from earliest times, mostly in the form of photographs depicting the 'wicked colonial years and the struggle for freedom'. As in most countries trying to build a sense of national identity after a divisive and destructive civil war, history is carefully patrolled and, if necessary, sanitized. There are also some mini jars from the Plain of Jars in the museum's grounds. ■ *Mon-Sun 0800-1200, 1300-1600 (but these hours are interpreted flexibly). 3000 kip.*

Facing the National Museum on the other side of the road is the **Lao National Culture Hall**. If this is reflective of Lao attempts to protect and/or promote culture then they might as well give up. A hideous piece of masonry partly funded, it would seem, by multi-lateral organizations.

Parallel to Samsenthai is Setthathirat and Wat Ong Teu (with bright orange **Wat Ong Teu** monks' quarters). Constructed by King Setthathirat in the 16th century, it was *The name of* ransacked by the Siamese in 1827 and then rebuilt during the late 19th and *the monastery,* 20th centuries. The wat houses one of the biggest Buddhas in Vientiane, *Wat Ong Teu, means* weighing several tons, which sits at the back of the sim. The wat is also noted *Temple of the Heavy* for its magnificent *sofa* and ornately carved wooden doors and windows with *Buddha* motifs from the Phra Lak Pralam (the Ramayana). The monastery runs one of the larger Buddhist schools in Laos and the Deputy Patriarch, Hawng Sangkharat, of the Lao monastic order lives here. The wat comes alive every year for the That Luang festival – originally a ceremony where nobles swore allegiance to the king and constitution, which amazingly has survived the Communist era (see page 94).

A short walk away, on the banks of the Mekong (junction of Chao Anou and **Wat Chan** Fa Ngoum), is Wat Chan, or **Wat Chanthabuli**. Unfortunately, it was wrecked by the marauding Thais in 1827 – only the base of a single stupa remains in front of the sim. The stupa originally had Buddha images in the 'Calling for Rain' attitude on each side (see page 292); only one remains. Inside the reconstructed sim is a remarkable bronze Buddha from the original temple on this site. The wat is also renowned for its panels of sculpted wood on the doors and windows.

For those who have had their fill of Theravada Buddhist wats, there is a fine **Chua** Mahayana Buddhist *chua* (pagoda) just off Khoun Boulom, near Chao **Bang-Long** Anou. The Chua Bang-Long is tucked away down a narrow lane and was established by Vientiane's large and active Vietnamese population. Before the outbreak of the Second World War it was said that Vientiane had more Vietnamese residents than it did Lao. A statue of the Chinese goddess Quan Am (see box page 78) stands in front of a Lao-style *that* which, in turn, fronts a large pagoda – almost Cao Dai in style. The pagoda has been extensively renovated and embellished over the last few years. Not far away, at the intersection of Samsenthai and Khoun Boulom is another, much smaller and more intimate, pagoda.

Further east of town on Simoung is **Wat Simoung**. It contains the town foun- **Wat Simoung** dation pillar (*lak muang*), which was erected in 1563 when King Setthathirat established Vientiane as the capital of the kingdom of Lane Xang. It is believed

The Ventiane Region

▶▶ The story of Quan Am

Quan Am was turned onto the streets by her husband for some unspecified wrong doing and, dressed as a monk, took refuge in a monastery. There, a woman accused her of fathering, and then abandoning, her child. Accepting the blame (why, no one knows), she was again turned out onto the streets, only to return to the monastery much later when she was on the point of death – to confess her true identity. When the Emperor of China heard the tale, he made Quan Am the Guardian Spirit of Mother and Child, and couples without a son now pray to her. Quan Am's husband is sometimes depicted as a parakeet, with the Goddess usually holding her adopted son in one arm and standing on a lotus leaf, the symbol of purity.

to be an ancient Khmer boundary stone, which marked the edge of the old Lao capital. The sim was reconstructed in 1915 around the foundation pillar, which forms the centre of the altar. In front of the altar is a Buddha, which is thought to have magical powers and is often consulted by worshippers. Wat Simouang may not be charming, refined or architecturally significant but in some senses it is the most important monastery in the capital. Street hawkers selling offerings of fruit, flowers, candles and incense line the surrounding streets, supplying the scores of people who come here hoping for good fortune. In the grounds of the wat are the ruins of what appears to be a Khmer laterite chedi. ■ *1,000 kip.*

Statue of King Setthathirat Just beyond Wat Simoung, where Setthathirat and Samsenthai meet, is the statue of King Setthathirat, the founder of Vientiane. The original statue was carved by a Lao sculptor, which apparently made the king look like a dwarf. Consequently it was destroyed. It was replaced by the present statue (there's a copy of it in Luang Prabang) which was, peculiarly, donated by the Russians. Just as strangely, the statue survived the revolution.

Excursions

Buses, trucks and pick-ups to destinations around Vientiane all leave from the station next to the Morning Market; it is also possible to hire a car (around US$45 per day). Taxis can be hired for the day from the Morning Market or outside one of the main hotels and cost around 100,000 kip per day for excursions outside Vientiane. Also, see car hire, page 99.

East and South

Bicycling downstream
See Transport, page 99, for bicycle hire details
A neat outing is to bicycle downstream along the banks of the Mekong. Cycle south on Tha Deua Road until Km 5 and then turn right down one of the tracks (there are a number) towards the river bank. A path, suitable for bicycles, follows the river beginning at about Km 4½. There are monasteries and drinks sellers en route to maintain interest and energy.

Xieng Khuan Otherwise known as the **Garden of the Buddhas**, Xieng Khuan is a few kilometres beyond **Tha Deua** and 25 km east of Vientiane (on Route 2), close to the frontier with Thailand. It has been described as a Laotian Tiger Balm Gardens with reinforced concrete Buddhist and Hindu sculptures of Vishnu, Buddha, Siva and various other assorted deities and near-deities.

There's also a bulbous-style building with three levels containing smaller sculptures of the same gods. The garden was built in the late 1950s by a priest-monk-guru-sage-artist called Luang Pu Bunleua Sulihat, who studied under a Hindu rishi in Vietnam and then combined the Buddhist and Hindu philosophies in his own very peculiar view of the world. He left Laos because his anti-communist views were incompatible with the ideology of the Pathet Lao (or perhaps because he was just too weird) and settled across the Mekong near the Thai town of Nong Khai, where he proceeded to build an equally revolting and bizarre concrete theme park for religious schizophrenics – Wat Khaek. Luang Pu died in 1996 at the age of 72. Surprisingly, he remains very popular in Laos and northeastern Thailand. With Luang Pu's forced departure from Laos his religious garden came under state control and it is now a public park. Food vendors sell drinks and snacks. ■ *Mon-Sun 0800-1700. 2,000 kip, plus an extra charge for cameras. Getting there: 1 hr by bus no 14 (1,000 kip); the bus stops first at the Friendship Gate border and then at Xieng Khouane (a further 1½ km). For returning to Vientiane, there is a bus stop in front of the Garden. Alternatively it is possible to charter a tuk-tuk or, indeed, cycle because the road follows the river and is reasonably level the whole way.*

555 Park (Saam Haa Yai) These are extensive, but rather uninspiring, gardens, with Chinese pavilions, a lake and a small zoo, 14 km down Thanon Tha Deua (Route 2) from Vientiane. In the 1980s, a white elephant was captured in southern Laos. Revered in this part of the world for their religious significance, it had to be painted to ensure it was not stolen on the way to the capital. Formerly kept in the Saam Haa gardens, it has since been moved to a secret location somewhere in Vientiane and is paraded in front of the crowds to marvel at during the That Luang festival. White elephants are not really white, but pink.

Lao Pako This lies 50 km northeast of Vientiane, on the banks of the Nam Ngum (off Route 13). See page 104 for details.

Kaysone Phimvihane Museum If the National Museum is your idea of a fun way to spend a few hours then the Kaysone Phomvihane Museum will make you giddy with excitement. It commemorates the exploits and leadership of the Lao PDR's equivalent of Vietnam's Ho Chi Minh. Kaysone was certainly the critical character in Laos' recent history: revolutionary fighter, inspired leader, and statesman. Now this dedicated museum is mostly visited by Lao schoolchildren as part of their education. ■ *Getting there: a bus south on Route 13 from the Morning Market and get off about 500 m past the Km 5 mark. As they say: you can't miss it.*

Tad Leuk waterfall This is a two-hour drive east in the direction of Pakxan. There's a surfaced road to Thabok (the waterfall sign is easily seen on the left) and then a dirt track leads the 20 km to the waterfall (the last 5 km or so is rough), a drive of about one hour – 90 km in total from Vientiane. The falls (and Tad Leuk Don) are well indicated. It is a good picnic spot, with swimming possible in the lake behind the waterfall. There's also a restaurant here but as there's no electricity hot food is off the menu: just papaya salad, fresh bamboo soup and beer and soft drinks. As well as the river, rapids and pools there's a forest track with bird-watching possibilities. There is even speculation about wild elephants, though this would seem optimistic. In 2000, it is said that 2,000 local and overseas visitors came here, not a huge number, and most concentrated at the weekend and on public holidays.

The Ventiane Region

Prabat Phonsanh   About 80 km down the Pakxan road, is Prabat Phonsanh, built on a plug of volcanic rock in the middle of a coconut plantation. It is known for its footprint of the Buddha and has a statue of a reclining Buddha – a mudra rarely seen in Laos. Houei Nhang Forest Reserve, on Route 13 South, has a nature trail through lowland semi-evergreen forest. Mouse deer, porcupines and civet cats have been spotted here.

Friendship Bridge   The observation area by the Mekong River makes a good picnic spot. It would be possible to take lunch in Thailand for visitors with multi-entry visas. Forms need to be filled in and travel across the bridge is by minibus. Tuk-tuks wait at the other end. ■ *Take bus no 14 from Vientiane's main bus station, 1,000 kip.*

North

Dane Soung   About 30 km from Vientiane, on the Luang Prabang road is Dane Soung. Too steep for tuk-tuks, it tends to be only private cars and motorbikes that make it here. Turn left at the 22 km mark towards Ban Houa Khoua. Dane Soung is 6 km down the track and is only accessible in the dry season. Large fallen rocks form a cave with Buddhist sculptures inside. On the left of the entrance is a footprint of the Buddha. A popular spot with locals at the weekend.

Nam Suong rapids & waterfall   These are 40 km north on Route 13. Turn left at the Lao-Australian Livestock Project Centre and right before the bridge: there is an absurdly out-of-place, Surrey-style picnic spot by the lake. For the rapids and waterfall, turn left before the bridge along a precipitously narrow track – they are only impressive during the rainy season.

Kaukhanna waterfall   Another lesser-known hot-spot is the Kaukhanna waterfall, campsite and restaurant. About 18 km from Vientiane along the Phonhong road, turn off for a further 11 km. Tuk-tuks normally only head that way on public holidays, so a private car or taxi may be necessary to get here. ■ *6,000 kip car entry plus 1,000 kip per person.*

Vientiane Zoo   Close to the district capital of **Tulakhom**, around 55 km north of Vientiane on Route 10, is this zoo. Really it shouldn't be called Vientiane Zoo at all, but quite a few Vientiane residents come out here at weekends and it is all they've got. One might expect the worst; in fact it's not too bad. For some reason the deer and especially the kangaroos have the best deal: large enclosures with lots to keep their minds off their incarceration. The latter breed like billy-o just to show how very happy they are. The bears and large cats have the worst of it, and the crocodiles just lounge around looking crocodilian. The tiger is a sad creature which, even if he could breed without a mate, probably wouldn't be able to work up the necessary enthusiasm. The great prize is a white elephant (extremely holy in Buddhist terms) which is fed vast quantities of bananas by merit-seeking Lao and which must seriously annoy his grey partner. There's a café and picnic area. It is a long way to go for a mediocre zoo. ■ *Mon-Sun 0800-1700. 10,000 kip, 3,000 kip for children. Getting there: travel south on Route 13 and then take the left fork at Km 5 (Ban Xaysavang) onto Route 10; the zoo is just off the road at the 55 Km mark (it is well signposted), just before Tulakhom town. Take a public bus bound for Tulakhom and ask to be let off at the 'Suan Sat Wiang Chan'.*

Near the village of Houei Thone, 63 km up the road to Luang Prabang (Route 13) is this home to the remains of either a 16th-century Lao Buddhist shrine or, just possibly, an 11th-century Mon sanctuary. There is a grouping of high relief images of the Buddha carved into the cliffs here. There is also a second group of sculptures 20 km further on still. The name Vang Sang means Elephant Palace and this is reputed to be linked to the presence of an elephants' graveyard in the vicinity. ■ *Getting there: take a bus heading north along Route 13 towards Luang Prabang and alight at the Km 62 marker where there is a sign to the shrine. From here a dirt track leads the 2 km to the shrine itself.*

Vang Sang

See page 104 for Ban Thalat and Nam Ngum Dam, 90 km from Vientiane on Route 13 to Luang Prabang. See also page 106 for Vang Vieng, about 150 km north on the road to Luang Prabang, Route 13.

Further north along Route 13

The Ventiane Region

Essentials

Sleeping

Vientiane has just 3 hotels – the *Novotel Vientiane*, *Lao Plaza Hotel*, and newcomer *Settha Palace* – which could really be considered international grade (and that term is used loosely), but there are a large number of very well run, and elegant, converted former colonial villas as well as some good mid-range places. Just a handful of years ago it would also have been accurate to write that there are also few budget places to stay, but this has eased considerably. More expensive hotels (this includes mid-range places) usually insist on payment in US$ or Thai baht, although most guesthouses will take kip, or a combination of the 3 currencies. As a rule of thumb, hotels priced over US$30 (ie our **A** category and above) accept major credit cards.

■ *on maps, pages 72, 76, 82, and 84*
Price codes: see inside front cover

   The accommodation listed below is divided into 4 sub-sections. Most of the hotels and guesthouses are listed under City centre. Vientiane is not a large city and all these places are within a 10-15 min walk of the Nam Phou Fountain and the main concentration of restaurants, shops, internet cafés and bars. The remaining 3 groups of accommodation are ordered geographically. West of city centre includes those hotels upstream on the Mekong, mostly on the road towards the airport. Northeast of city centre includes a small group of hotels out towards That Luang. With a bicycle it takes just 10-15 mins to get into the centre of town, or less. Finally, Southeast of the city centre, downstream on the Mekong, is another small number of hotels and guesthouses. It is worth emphasizing that Vientiane is not Bangkok: even those places not in the City centre category will be a short tuk-tuk drive (10 mins) from the centre or a modest cycle ride.

L *Lao Plaza Hotel*, 63 Samsenthai, T218800/1, F218808, lph@laoplazahotel.com, www.laoplazahotel.com 3 restaurants, fitness centre (for which there are expansion plans), pool, nightclub, conference centre, satellite TV, IDD telephones, shopping arcade, most major credit cards accepted (but the hotel doesn't change TCs). This Thai-managed, 140-room monstrosity is no doubt useful for business visitors but seems rather incongruous in Vientiane. However, it undoubtedly offers the best range of facilities in the country and unlike the *Novotel* also has a central location. Non-guests may also use the hotel's facilities for a set fee.

City centre

AL *Settha Palace*, 6 Pang Kham, T217581-2, F217583, settha@laonet.net, www. setthapalace.com The only French hotel in town, Settha Palace was built in 1936 and opened as a hotel in 1999. Its French architecture, colonial décor, period furniture and landscaped gardens are really lovely, and sit more easily with the fundamental essence of Vientiane than the glitz and glamour of the other top level hotels, while providing the same level of convenience for both business and leisure guests. Its Belle Epoque Restaurant provides the most mouth-watering French cuisine. Recommended.

A *Tai-Pan*, 22/3 François Ngin Rd (off Fa Ngoum), T216906-9, F216223, www.travelao.com, taipan@loxinfo.co.th Restaurant, bar, basic gym and small pool. Most major credit cards accepted, a/c, restaurant, free airport pick-up. Built in the mid-1990s and perhaps the best of the centrally located places to stay with lots of bars and restaurants close by. While it has that international 'could be anywhere' feel, it is nonetheless stylish and relaxed. The service is hard to fault and facilities are good. The lobby is rather more impressive than the 36 rooms, but they are reasonably well equipped rooms with IDD telephones and satellite TV. There is also a conference room and an increasingly popular bar. Room rates include a good breakfast.

A-B *Hotel Day Inn*, Pang Kham, T214792, F222984. A/c, restaurant, bike hire, good position in quiet part of town just to the north of the main concentration of bars and

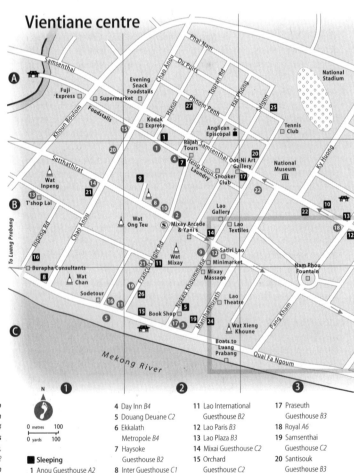

Vientiane centre

Detail map
*A Around Nam
Phou*, page 84
Related maps
*Vientiane,
  page 72
Southern
Vientiane,
  page 76*

■ **Sleeping**
1 Anou Guesthouse *A2*
2 Asian Pavilion *B4*
3 Chaleunxay *C5*
4 Day Inn *B4*
5 Douang Deuane *C2*
6 Ekkalath
  Metropole *B4*
7 Haysoke
  Guesthouse *B2*
8 Inter Guesthouse *C1*
9 Lani I *B2*
10 Lani II *A5*
11 Lao International
  Guesthouse *B2*
12 Lao Paris *B3*
13 Lao Plaza *B3*
14 Mixai Guesthouse *C2*
15 Orchard
  Guesthouse *C2*
16 Phornthip
  Guesthouse *B1*
17 Praseuth
  Guesthouse *B3*
18 Royal *A6*
19 Samsenthai
  Guesthouse *C2*
20 Santisouk
  Guesthouse *B3*
21 Saysana
  Guesthouse *B1*

restaurants. Run by a friendly Cambodian, it is a renovated villa, with attractive, airy, clean and large rooms, excellent bathrooms, good value, restaurant serving tasty food. Recommended. **A-B** *Lani I*, 281 Setthathirat (set back from the road next to Wat Hay Sok), T214919, F215639. A/c, restaurant (excellent Chinese, cooked by Lani's father on request), outside bar. This auberge was one of the first to open in Vientiane and remains popular with those who have been acquainted with the country since it began to open up in the late 1980s. It is clean and well run, set in a quiet garden, with telex and fax services. Because rooms are often taken by long-term visitors, booking in advance is recommended. The rooms on the ground floor can be dark. This is an elegant almost urbane place, with a good central position yet set back from the road in a quiet compound next to a wat. Bicycles for hire. But along with these plus points is an important negative: it is unjustifiably overpriced given the much better choice of accommodation now.

B *Anou*, 1-3 Heng Boun, T213630-1, F213632, anouhotel@microtec.com.la Fairly recently renovated with welcoming elevator, credit cards accepted. The *Anou* has the

The Ventiane Region

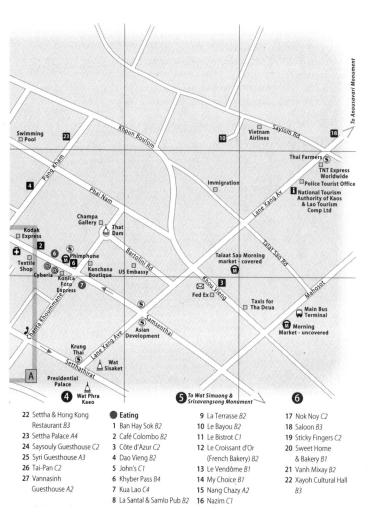

22 Settha & Hong Kong Restaurant *B3*	**● Eating**	9 La Terrasse *B2*	17 Nok Noy *C2*
23 Settha Palace *A4*	1 Ban Hay Sok *B2*	10 Le Bayou *B2*	18 Saloon *B3*
24 Saysouly Guesthouse *C2*	2 Café Colombo *B2*	11 Le Bistrot *C1*	19 Sticky Fingers *C2*
25 Syri Guesthouse *A3*	3 Côte d'Azur *C2*	12 Le Croissant d'Or	20 Sweet Home
26 Tai-Pan *C2*	4 Dao Vieng *B2*	(French Bakery) *B2*	& Bakery *B1*
27 Vannasinh	5 John's *C1*	13 Le Vendôme *B1*	21 Vanh Mixay *B2*
Guesthouse *A2*	6 Khyber Pass *B4*	14 My Choice *B1*	22 Xayoh Cultural Hall
	7 Kua Lao *C4*	15 Nang Chazy *A2*	*B3*
	8 La Santal & Samlo Pub *B2*	16 Nazim *C1*	

same owners as the *Phousi Hotel* in Luang Prabang. Rooms here are standard hotel style, clean and serviceable but impersonal. Facilities include satellite TV; attached restaurant serves Lao and European cuisine with live traditional music. **B** *Asian Pavilion*, 379 Samsenthai, T213430/1, F213432, asianlao@loxinfo.co.th Major credit cards accepted, a/c, restaurant. This hotel offers 50 very average rooms and, overall, is a very average hotel. But there could be a surprise in store for some guests: those elegant curtains don't hide fantastic views over the Mekong but a bare brick wall. It's only notable attributes are its history and the enthusiasm of the staff. It used to be the *Hotel Constellation* and the original owner, a colonel in the Royal Lao Army, was sent to a re-education camp after the victory of the Pathet Lao in 1975. He was one of the last prisoners to be released in 1988 whereupon he reclaimed his hostelry, renamed it the *Vieng Vilai*, and set up shop once more. **B** *Douang Deuane*, Nokeo Koummane Rd, T222301-3, F222300, douangdeuane@pan-laos.net.la Credit cards accepted, a/c, restaurant, opened in 1996. From the exterior this looks an unremarkable place, but the rooms are very good: parquet wood floors, excellent bathrooms, satellite TV and a decent size, central position. The room rates have remained competitive. Recommended. **B** *Ekkalath Metropole*, Samsenthai (not far from That Dam), T2134201, F215628. Some a/c. The more expensive rooms have breakfast included in the room rate. Cheaper rooms are housed in the guesthouse attached to the hotel – very basic with no hot water but fairly clean. The rooms in the main block are about the size of the Serengeti, with ugly metal doors, some with attached sitting area ('suite' would be too grand a word for these spartan affairs). Bleak, although the hairy looking electrics in some of the bathrooms might end up jazzing up your stay. Professional electricians should either stay away or ask for a job. **B** *Hotel Lao*, 53/9 Heng Boun, T2192801,

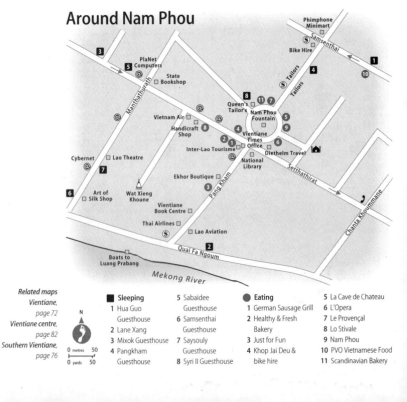

Around Nam Phou

■ Sleeping		● Eating	
1 Hua Guo Guesthouse	5 Sabaidee Guesthouse	1 German Sausage Grill	5 La Cave de Chateau
2 Lane Xang	6 Samsenthai Guesthouse	2 Healthy & Fresh Bakery	6 L'Opera
3 Mixok Guesthouse	7 Saysouly Guesthouse	3 Just for Fun	7 Le Provençal
4 Pangkham Guesthouse	8 Syri II Guesthouse	4 Khop Jai Deu & bike hire	8 Lo Stivale
			9 Nam Phou
			10 PVO Vietnamese Food
			11 Scandinavian Bakery

F219282. 30 enormous a/c rooms, opened in early 1999. The owners are planning to set up credit cards facilities. Satellite TV, telephone, mini-bar, even a hairdryer in the attached bathrooms. Friendly staff still enthused with the idea of working in the service sector. **B** *Lane Xang*, Fa Ngoum, T214100-7, F214108. Major credit cards accepted, a/c, international restaurant, pool, nightclub, bar, putting green, badminton and tennis courts, snooker hall, sauna, fitness centre. This place is the original 'luxury' hotel in Vientiane, built by the Soviets shortly after the victory of the communists in 1975. Its retro-hip Soviet fittings and furniture have now sadly been ripped out to make way for a more contemporary look. The up side is that the rooms are now extremely good value, with excellent bathrooms, making it the best value accommodation in town, with a great central position on the river.

B-C *Inter Guesthouse*, 24-25 Fa Ngoum/Chou Anou (next to Wat Chan), T213582. A/c, good restaurant (excellent steak). Thai-owned hotel with 20 rooms that will not win any local beauty contests. The rooms here have deteriorated over the last few years and while they are reasonably clean have a shabby appearance. On the plus side, good attached hot water showers. Noisy nightclub close by is probably a little more than just a nightclub, judging by the number of very friendly young ladies who congregate here. Needs love and investment. **B-C** *Lao Paris*, 100 Samsenthai, opposite *Lao Plaza Hotel*, T213440, F216382. A/c, private bathrooms with hot water, some with TV in room. Clean but uninspired, cheaper rooms on top floor are drab, central location. **B-C** *Vannasinh Guesthouse*, 51 Phnom Penh Rd (off Samsenthai), T/F218707. Some a/c. Huge warren-like house, clean, large rooms and well managed, with friendly staff (good English and French spoken), bicycles for hire. Well priced and very popular, but avoid the breakfast. Recommended.

C *Chaleunxay Hotel*, Khou Vieng Rd (opposite the Forestry Department), T223407, F223529. Newly converted into a hotel, Chaleunxay nevertheless has a laid back, ramshackle, slightly untidy air that persists despite the brace of cleaners whose jobs never seem to be quite done. Endearing. Temperamental hot water supply. Very friendly staff, and convenient location very close to the Morning Market and bus station. **C** *Haysoke Guesthouse*, 1-2 Heng Boun, T219711/22, F219755. Fairly new Chinese establishment, large, clean rooms with TV, mini bar and a/c. Attractively furnished with rattan, hot water bathroom attached, family suites available. **C** *Hua Guo Guesthouse*, 359 Samsenthai, T216612. Some a/c, some private bathrooms and hot water. Basic and rather unfriendly Chinese-run guesthouse. Bikes and motorbikes for rent, bargaining possible. **C** *Lao International Guesthouse (LIG)*, 015/2 François Ngin Rd, T/F216571. Sign reads Lao Sakonh Guest House. The handful of rooms here are mixed: some with a/c, some with attached bathrooms, some with hot water. Those on the ground floor are rather dark, better on the upper floors. Towels provided. Annoying electronic bird alarm on main door. Downstairs is a Vietnamese restaurant, French and English spoken, bicycles and motorbikes for hire. **C** *Orchard Guesthouse*, 33 Fa Ngoum Rd, T252825, F216588. A new establishment that has friendly staff, spotlessly clean and nice rooms with fan or a/c. It's slap bang on the noisy Fa Ngoum Rd, though, so great for deep sleepers. Tiled roof onto which you can bring table and chairs if the mood takes you. Lovely view of the river. Owners hope to open a restaurant in due course. **C** *Pangkham Guesthouse*, 72/6 Pang Kham, T/F217053. Another Chinese-run guesthouse. More expensive rooms have a/c, all rooms have hot showers, cheaper rooms have no windows. Basic, clean rooms in featureless block, service is drone-like. Building is currently being extended, bikes for hire. **C** *Phornthip Guesthouse*, 72 Inpeng Rd, T217239. Some a/c. A quiet, family-run and very friendly guesthouse, almost always full (pre-booking is recommended). Perhaps a trifle overpriced (a function, no doubt, of its popularity), there's a courtyard at the back, but no garden. Large rooms, attached bathrooms, bicycle hire for 15,000 kip per day. To get to it, turn down the alley just next to *Sodetour*. Recommended. **C** *Saysana Guesthouse*, Chao Anou, T218636. A/c, major credit card accepted, restaurant, beauty salon, car rental, ancient telephones with antique switchboard. The *Saysana* looks smarter than it is. The *Victory Disco* is very popular. The hotel blurb sells Vientiane as 'the land of virginal valuable outstanding artistic culture', which is quite a string of words. **C** *Saysouly Guesthouse*, 23 Manthathurath, T218383-4, F223757, saysouly@hotmail.com Some a/c. Some rooms with western bathrooms attached, including hot water. This is the only guesthouse in town to have cooking facilities. A well-maintained suite of 4 doubles open out onto a sitting and dining area, with attached kitchen equipped with 2 electric rings. Motorbike for hire at US$10 per day. Very clean. Recommended. **C** *Settha Guesthouse*, 80/4 Samsenthai, T213241, F215995. A/c, restaurant. Chinese-run guesthouse attached to the *Hong Kong Restaurant*. Central location opposite the swish *Lao Plaza Hotel*. Good sized rooms with clean bathrooms and hot water, efficiently managed, lacking in ambience. **C** *Syri Guesthouse*, Quartier Chao Anou (near the stadium), T212682, F219191. A/c, some en-suite bathrooms, very hot water, clean sheets daily. Rooms here are average and unexciting and the old building is looking rather run-down. However, family-run and friendly, leafy entrance, quiet street, 1st floor sitting area, guests can use the kitchen, bikes for hire for US$1 per day. **C** *Syri II Guesthouse*, T241345, T020-61697 (mob), syri2@hotmail.com, just off Nam Phou circle a few doors down from the *Scandinavian Bakery*. Riding on the success of *Syri I*, this handsome 4-storey house offers a range of rooms and steep twisting staircases. The more expensive rooms have a/c and en-suite bathrooms and are nicely furnished, but the cheaper rooms with small wall fans and shared bathrooms are barely larger than the double beds they hold and gloomy without windows. The house is cluttered with an interesting array of bizarre objects.

C-D *Praseuth Guesthouse*, 312 Samsenthai, T217932. This nondescript building contains 10 small a/c rooms, many without windows. Walls and floor are wooden which enhances the gloomy feel, but facilities are clean. Some rooms with attached bathrooms. Bikes for hire. Central location. **C-D** *Samsenthai Guesthouse*, 15 Manthathurath, T212116. Some a/c, restaurant attached, some private bathrooms, some hot water. This hotel is a bit of a mixed bag. The cheaper rooms were grubby and depressing on our last visit, while the top-end rooms were large but didn't stretch to great cleanliness, either. The overall impression is not good though: a hideous block with a fusty aroma. Central location. **C-D** *Santisouk Guesthouse*, 77/79 Nokeo Koummane (above *Santisouk Restaurant*), T215303. A/c. 9 rooms, some with shared facilities, others with attached showers. All are clean but the shared bathroom is pokey and a bit grungy. Those situated over the popular restaurant below can be noisy too, but good value at this rate.

D *Mixai House*, 39 Nokeo Koummane, T217023. Basic, gloomy rooms but clean with fans. Large, separate bathroom with hot water. Large reception/lounge area with TV. Feels like university halls. Bicycle hire 5,000 kip per day.

E *Mix-o-k Guesthouse*, Setthathirat. Happy yellow paint inside, this place is great – spotless rooms, soft mattresses, good double and twin rooms, and it's right next to an internet café for those virtual trips home. And the owner speaks good English. Excellent value. Recommended. **F** *Sabaidee Guesthouse*, Setthathirat, the cheap price reflects the facilities. Turquoise, swimming pool-esque rooms with fans. Proprietor speaks reasonable English if cajoled out of his habitual grump. Communal washrooms, and always a queue.

AL *Novotel Vientiane*, Samsenthai, near the junction with Luang Prabang, T213570, F213572, novotellao@loxinfo.co.th A/c, restaurant, pool, room rate includes breakfast, but tax is on top, most major credit cards accepted. Until the opening of the *Lao Plaza Hotel* this was Vientiane's best place to stay. It is a large international-style hotel, with a good range of facilities including gym, tennis court, sauna, Lao massage, disco, business centre, snooker hall and games room. For tourists it suffers from a poor location on the edge of town towards Wattay Airport (free airport transfer). The building itself is so characterless as to be virtually DOA, but it is popular with business people because it works.

West of city centre
Upstream, towards the airport

B *New Apollo*, 69A Luang Prabang, T213244, F213245. A/c, Visa and Amex credit cards accepted. Large but rather plain rooms with sitting area, elevator, restaurant with live music every night. This is a rather monstrous hotel in terms of its architecture which has gone through several incarnations (usually a bad sign). Popular with East Asian tourists and businessmen who seem to enjoy the nightclub here. It suffers from being on the main road out to the airport. **B** *River View*, corner of Fa Ngoum and Sithan Neua, T2162446, F216232. A/c, restaurant, this hotel sounds as though it might be attractive: don't be deluded. Painted lurid pink and green on the exterior, the lobby is filled with brightly painted umbrellas, glass knick-knacks, uncomfortable furniture and mouse droppings. The 32 rooms are pretty dismal too. In short, it's a lot to endure for a river view. **B-C** *Villa Santiphab*, Nong Douang. A/c, restaurant (order meals, no menu), friendly and small hotel in an old villa, 4 rooms with attached bathrooms.

C *Auberge du Temple*, 184/1 Ban Khounta (west of town, off road to Wattay Airport down towards the river, 100 m west of *Novotel*), T/F214844. Some a/c, some with own bathrooms. This is a really stylish auberge owned by a Frenchman. It's a converted villa in a large compound, with verandas, relaxed and sophisticated, a few km out of the town centre, but worth it. Try to get one of the quieter rooms at the back of the villa. There is also one dorm room containing 5 beds (**F**). Bicycle and motorbikes for rent. Recommended. **C** *Sennesouk Guesthouse*, 100 Luang Prabang, T213375, F217449. Some a/c, restaurant, just west of *Novotel Hotel* on airport side so a little out of town. Rooms are OK and some have attached western bathrooms. But there is a nightclub next door and it can be noisy when the restaurant is in full swing. **C-D** *Sihom Guesthouse*, T214562. 27 Sihom Rd. Mixture of rooms: some with TVs, some with a/c. All with rattan furniture and huge hot water bathrooms attached. Opened in early 1999 so rooms are in excellent condition, café out front serving snacks and drinks. Good value for fan rooms. Recommended.

D *Vientiane Guesthouse*, Luang Prabang, T212928. Some a/c, no hot water, restaurant (downstairs from hotel). Situated on the busy main rd out to the airport, not a place noted for its style or ambience. In crying need of a good overhaul. **E** *PhayNam*, 48 Nong Douang, T216768. Crumbling old house up a long driveway. 10 rooms with a/c, fridge, and attached bathrooms but no hot water. Clean but dismal atmosphere with moulding walls and old blankets. Another budget choice.

A-B *Royal Dokmaideng*, Lane Xang, T214455, F214454. A/c, major credit cards accepted, restaurant, pool, not far from the Anousavari Monument, opposite the Morning Market. A refurbished hotel of 80 rooms with a Chinese feel to it – heavy furniture, marble and high pressure Karaoke Bar. They also do a good line in blurb: 'brilliantly greets guests, sincerity broadcast thousand miles'. At this price there are several other places which offer more ambience and a better location – a placeless place.

Northeast of city centre
Towards That Luang

B *Villa That Luang*, 307 That Luang, T413370, F412953. A/c, restaurant. Another converted villa with large and attractively furnished rooms (sitting area). Laundry is included in the room rate, about 1500 m north of town centre almost at That Luang itself. Well run with friendly staff. **B-C** *Lani II*, 268 Saylom (set back from the road, entrance opposite the T-junction), T213022, F215639. A/c, private bathrooms, hot water, food available if ordered in advance. This is the sister guesthouse to *Lani I*. It is clean, quiet and friendly with an attractive garden and, on balance, just as good as *Lani I*. Quite a few long term visitors, so advance booking advisable. Bicycles for hire. Recommended. **B-C** *Le Parasol Blanc*, behind National Assembly, close to Anousavari Monument (not very well marked), T216091, F215444. A/c, restaurant (see comments in the restaurant listing, below), good sized pool. This is a very attractive leafy haven. Spacious rooms with wooden floors and sizeable bathrooms, some look onto the garden, with sitting area in front. The most expensive rooms are alongside the pool. Charming place, well run, mostly patronized by French visitors. Recommended. **C** *Sisavad Guesthouse*, 93/12 Sisavad Neua, north of town, near the Monument, T/F212719. Major credit cards accepted, restaurant, pool, en-suite shower rooms with hot water. Slightly out of town, its big selling point being its pool. If you don't require a pool then it can only really be billed as 'adequate'. Mostly caters to Asian tourists.

E-F *Phonxay*, Nong Bon Rd. Some a/c. Large, very ugly and very run down but at the same time refined in a derelict way. Looks like it can't exist for much longer, but it's still going strong and will probably outlast them all. Only for the hardened traveller.

Southeast of city centre
Downstream

B *Vieng Thong Guesthouse*, Ban Phiawat, opposite Wat Phiavat in a side street, T/F212095. Family-style house, large rooms with country-cottage feel – thick duvets, rattan furniture, china tea-sets. All rooms with hot water showers, nice garden with café and big aviary, pleasant but perhaps a little expensive. Car for hire.

C *Chaemchanh Guesthouse*, 78 Khou Vieng, T312700. A/c, airy, rather run-down villa with 8 large rooms with attached bathrooms (hot water), set in an extensive garden compound. This guesthouse is about 1,500 m from the town centre just off the raised, tree-lined Khou Vieng, but is accessible by bicycle. A peaceful and attractive place to stay. **C** *Soradith Guesthouse*, 150 Ban Dong Palan, 15 mins walk from Morning Market, T/F41365. A/c, hot water, TV, fridge, 10% discount for longer stays, welcoming owner. Ten clean but boring rooms in a modern building in a well kept garden. A quiet spot down a side street. The 'complex' incorporates MVT – *Music Vientiane Café* and the excellent *Europe* restaurant. Mountain bikes for hire here at US$2 per day. **C** *Thien Thong*, Sok Paluang, T313782, F312125. A/c, good food. 13 clean rooms with tiled hot water shower rooms attached and fridge. House is in an attractive and leafy compound about 1,500 m from the town centre, so bicycles needed. Recommended. **C** *Wonderland Guesthouse*, Phonsavan Tai (off Khou Vieng, southeast of town), T312894. A/c, restaurant, small guesthouse in private villa down a quiet lane some way from the centre of town. Attractive garden, birds, verandas, clean and 10 good-sized rooms with attached bathrooms. Consider staying here if you don't mind (or prefer) being out of the town centre – easily accessible by bicycle along attractive, tree-lined Khou Vieng, but no bikes for hire here.

E-F *Vieng Champa*, Tha Deua, south of town, just up from the Australian Club, T314412. Some of the cheapest rooms in Vientiane. Stone cells with old twin beds, all fan cooled, communal showers and toilets. Grubby and decaying.

Wats (monasteries)

It is possible to stay in monks' quarters at Wat Sisaket, Lane Xang, in exchange for informal English lessons.

There are 3 service apartment operations in Vientiane, all on Luang Prabang Rd out towards the airport. (Note that many hotels and guesthouses will also provide good deals for long-term guests.) Alternatively, rent a house or villa: names of rental agencies are usually listed in the *Vientiane Times*.

AL *Parkview Executive Suites*, Luang Prabang Rd, 1 km upstream from the *Novotel* towards the airport, T250888, F250777, parkview@laotel.com The swishest place to stay – this is where World Bank consultants spend their generous allowances. A/c, large pool, tennis courts, gym and sauna, satellite TV, and restaurant. At around US$1,500 per month or more for a cosy 1- or 2-bedroom apartment this costs more than a room in the best hotel. **A** *Khunta Residence*, around 2 km along Luang Prabang Rd towards the airport from the *Novotel*, T251199, F251198. A step down from the *Parkview* but better for families with a more relaxed atmosphere and larger apartments. There's also a pool, fitness centre and tennis court. **A-B** *Mekong Hotel*, Luang Prabang Rd, opposite the *Parkview Executive Suites*, T212938, F212822, www. avipclub.com/laos/mekong/ This is the least attractive option. The hotel itself is a pretty hideous affair, and we do not list it, but they do have have some well-priced apartments for rent.

Eating

Mid-range *Dao Vieng*, Heng Boun. Large menu, good reputation, popular at lunchtime. *Kua Lao*, 111 Samsenthai, T215777. Tastefully refurbished colonial house turned restaurant provides sophisticated atmosphere for quality Lao and Thai food. Avoid the set menu. Good Lao music accompaniment. Some locals believe that the restaurant has sold its Lao culinary credentials to the tourist dollar but most visitors to Laos will enjoy their meal here. Pricey for Laos. *Lane Xang Restaurant*, Quai Fa Ngoum, overlooks the river and produces Lao specials such as baked moose, grilled eel, baked turtle. Some international dishes also available. See also Traditional dance, page 94. *Lao Residence*, That Luang, just beyond Anousavari Monument, T413562. Classy Thai/Lao restaurant, though not as good as *Kua Lao*. Patrons can drink in the garden of this converted private house and then eat in the a/c restaurant. This is another restaurant which some locals refuse to patronize because it has become too touristy. The food is moderated to suit the palate of the foreigner and the downplaying of traditional Lao dishes in favour of Thai cuisine also reflects the origins of many of the clientele. *Mekong*, Tha Deua, not far from the Australian Club, in the direction of the bridge, T312480. Good food overlooking the Mekong, drinks on the balcony at sunset, Lao and international cuisine.

Lao
● *on map, pages 72, 82, and 84*
Price codes:
see inside front cover

Cheap *Just for Fun*, 57/2 Phang Kham, opposite *Lao Aviation*. Good Lao food with vegetarian dishes, selection of coffees and soft drinks and the largest selection of teas in Laos, if not Southeast Asia. The atmosphere is relaxed with a/c, newspapers and comfy chairs (also sells textiles and other handicrafts). No smoking. Recommended.

Seriously cheap *Souk Vi Mane* (meaning 'Life in paradise'), near That Dam, on southeast side, 50 m away on Chanta Khoummane. Run by an elderly lady who speaks good French this is an excellent little place with some of the best vegetable soup in Laos. Very good value.

There are a number of noodle shops in Chinatown along Khoun Boulom, Heng Boun and Chao Anou all of which have a palatable array of vermicelli, *muu daeng* (red pork), duck and chicken.

Mid-range *Ban Hay Sok*, Heng Boun. Excellent Lao and Chinese cuisine in a/c splendour including abalone, shark's fin and other speciality dishes. The chef is reputed to have formerly worked for the Laotian royal family. Recommended. *Hong Kong*, Samsenthai, T213240, F215995. Behind what must once have been a petrol station is an ostentatious and quite smart Chinese restaurant specializing in Cantonese and seafood cuisine.

Indian   **Mid-range** *Café Colombo*, 153 Setthathirat Rd, T222227. Newly opened and, on a recent visit, the best Indian/Sri Lankan restaurant in the country. An extensive menu, but the food is more than the usual curry-house fare. Relaxing and classier than *Nazim's*. Recommended. **Cheap** *Khyber Pass*, Samsenthai, next to the *Asian Pavilion*. This places covers most of the South Asian possibilities and serves Halal, Indian and Pakistan food. Open from 1000 until late. *Nazim*, Fa Ngoum, T223480. Authentic Indian (North and South Indian) and Halal food. Fast overtaking their competitors and becoming the most popular place to eat South Asian food in Vientiane. Their popularity has seen them open another restaurant in Vang Vieng as well as a branch in Luang Prabang. A real winner, both for taste and price.

Japanese   **Expensive to mid-range** *Koto*, Phonxay St, T412849. Another good Japanese restaurant but without the reputation of the *Sakura*; a touch cheaper. *Sakura*, Luang Prabang, Km 2/Soi 3, T212274 (see map). Regarded as the best Japanese food in town. Expensive for Vientiane but good value for Japanese food anywhere else. The restaurant is in a converted private house.

Vietnamese   **Seriously cheap** *Nang Chazy*, 54/2 Chao Anou/Heng Boun. Good Vietnamese stall
Served in many of the food. *PVO Vietnamese Food*, 344 Samsenthai, opposite *Hua Guo*. Baguettes stuffed
stalls in the with your choice of paté, salad, cheese, coleslaw, vegetables and ham. For those too
Chinatown area lazy to go to the Vietnamese Embassy, they offer a Vietnam visa service here. Bikes and motorbikes for rent too. For cheap Vietnamese food, there's a good selection of stalls near the ticket office for buses to Vietnam, on Sisangvon Rd, a couple of km north of the centre but worthwhile if that's your yen.

International   **Expensive** *L'Opera*, Nam Phou Circle, T215099. A/c Italian restaurant run by 2 Italians
Quite a few places who employ an English chef. Unfortunately, cold and overpriced but with delicious
listed here under ice-cream, wide range of pizza and pasta dishes, also barbecue steaks. Stick with the
International also specials. Same ownership as restaurants of same name in Bangkok and Manila.
serve good Lao/Thai
food and a handful
are also **Expensive to mid-range** *Le Nadao*, Ban Donmieng. This place is difficult to find but
experimenting with definitely worth every second spent searching the back streets of Vientiane in the dark.
fusion cuisine Sayavouth, who trained in Paris and New York, produces simply delectable French cuisine: soups, venison, lamb, puddings. Fantastic. But room for just 15 diners (although there are reports that he has recently expanded his operation), so you may be disappointed. Recommended. *Lo Stivale* (formerly *Deli Café*), Setthathirat, just west of Nam Phou. Extensive Italian menu with good pizzas, pastas, steaks and desserts. Attentive service in airy, stuccoed a/c restaurant.

Mid-range *Cote D'Azur*, 63/64 Fa Ngoum, T217252. Featuring Le Chef Jean Marc, formerly of *Le Provençal*. Comes highly recommended by resident expats, fine selection of dishes from the south of France and a variety of excellent pizzas baked in the restaurant's in-house pizza oven. Steaks are the best in town. *Europe*, Dong Palan, left just before Wat Dong Palan, T413651. Run by Swiss, serving Swiss, French, Italian and local food. Classiest restaurant in town for quality of food, but not particularly attractive surroundings. 1200-1400, 1800-2300, closed Mon. *KhopJai Deu*, Setthathirat, on the corner of Nam Phou. Garden seating, good atmosphere at night with soft lantern lighting, and an eclectic menu of Indian, Italian, Korean and international dishes. The best value are the local Lao dishes. Also serves draft or bottled beer at a pleasant a/c bar, where there are four computers and internet access. Recommended. *Le Parasol Blanc*, behind National Assembly building and attached to guesthouse of the same name. Extensive (and good) French menu and some Lao dishes, including Mekong fish. Reasonably priced. Attractive leafy environment, some a/c tables too. *Le Provençal*, Nam Phou Circle, T217251. Large French restaurant, with beamed ceiling, attempting (unsuccessfully) to recreate rural France. However, food is good, especially salad and steaks. Extensive wine list. Good value. Open 1130-1400, 1830-2230, closed Sun afternoons. *Le Silapa*, 17/1 Sihom Rd, T219689. Great little French restaurant, newly opened just on the western edge of the town centre (10--15 mins' walk from Nam Phou fountain. Haute cuisine and every bottle of wine purchased means a donation for a Lao child in distress. Closed most of Jul, otherwise open for lunch and dinner, Mon-Sat. *Le Vendôme*, Soi Inpeng, run by a Frenchman whose son trains the Lao bicycle squad, as good as any 1-star Michelin restaurant in France. A/c inside and an outside terrace, 1 of the best restaurants in town, good ambience, mouth-watering menu of fish, deer, rabbit, steaks, pizzas, soufflés, and salads. Choice of wines. As well as breeding good bicyclists, the propietor is also renowned for his shouting – his staff are said to live in perpetual fear. Recommended. *Nam Phou*, 20 Nam Phou Circle, T216248. French, upmarket and quietly sophisticated, with staggering French wine list. Recommended. *Saysana Steakhouse, Pub and Restaurant* (formerly *Win West*), opposite Russian Cultural Centre by traffic lights, Luang Prabang Rd. Quite good food, live music in Western-style surroundings, buffet lunch, happy hour. *Sticky Fingers*, François Ngin Rd (opposite the *Tai Pan Hotel*), small restaurant and bar with just a handful of tables serving Lao and International dishes including good salads, burgers and such like. Run by a friendly Australian lady and popular with expats. Recommended.

Mid-range to cheap *Le Bayou*, Setthathirat, T222227. Popular American diner style brasserie and bar, generous helpings of pizza, sandwiches, cracking steaks, excellent range of salads, burgers, French desserts and fruit drinks. Good for late evening coffee and drinking (the draft beer is well priced), also open for breakfast. Children's menu available, French speaking (same owner as *Le Vendôme*), pricey, but well worth every penny. Open 1100-0000. Recommended. *La Cave de Chateau*, Nam Phou. A new restaurant in this well-patronized location around the Nam Phou Fountain. Wine and cheese plus French specialities.

Cheap *Arawan*, 472-480 Samsenthai (not far from Wat Simoung/statue of king). The oldest French restaurant in Vientiane, run by a Corsican, good selection of cheeses ('flomages') and wines – but short on atmosphere and clientele, bar. *Le Bistrot*, 10/3 François Ngin, opposite *Tai-pan Hotel*. Bistro food and breakfast in friendly atmosphere, French-Lao run with good menu including French chicken and beef dishes and various attempts at fusion cuisine. *Inter*, Chao Anou (part of hotel). Locally renowned for its steaks; Lao food on advance order. *2 Mixay Arcade*, Setthathirat. Vietnamese, Lao and French food. Small place, with music as loud as the place is smelly. *La Santal*, 101 Setthathirat. Lao, Thai, French and Italian food including fish, steaks and pizzas in a/c restaurant. *Santisouk*, 77/79 Nokeo Koummane, entrance to stadium just off Samsenthai. This place doesn't look much, but the food is good for the price. Extensive French menu, reasonably priced sizzling steaks. Also serves good breakfast. Not particularly friendly staff and has gone down in our view since the last edition of this guide. *Sabaidee*, diagonally opposite *PlaNet Computers* on Setthathirat. Good, cheap Lao food which you might find yourself absent-mindedly sharing with one of the many resident cats or rabbits. *The Saloon Restaurant*, Pang Kham, opposite *Lao Plaza*,

T212990. Asian and western food, Belgium specialities, videos shown. *La Terrasse*, 55/4 Nokeo Koummane, T218550. Highly recommended French restaurant. Reasonable prices with excellent 'plat du jour' each day, good selection of French wine. Some rather out of character Mexican food also served. *Xang Café*, tucked away between *Sodetour* and Wat Inpeng. This place has obviously tried to cover every possible culinary possibility with an extensive menu with choices from Mexico, Europe, the Middle East and Asia. Over 22 different coffees available including 3 imbibed with alcohol, herbal teas and a wide vegetarian choice. Food is average to good, but the seating is uncomfortable as customers are perched on high stools. Hard to relax. *Xayoh Cultural Hall*, Nokeo Khoummane. The name of this place gives little hint of the cuisine. Attractive bar and restaurant next to the hideous Lao National Cultural Hall (hence the name). Salads, pizzas, burgers plus Lao/Thai food. The restaurant's speciality is their Sunday roast; beef and Yorkshire pud etc for homesick Englishmen and women.

Vegetarian   *Just for Fun* (see above under Lao restaurants). Although not a vegetarian restaurant, it produces excellent vegetarian food. Two other restaurants which do good lines in vegetarian dishes are the *Xang Café* (see above under International), providing a plethora of vegetarian options from around the world, and the *Nazim Indian Restaurant* (see above under Indian).

Cafés

Bakeries, breakfast & snack food   **Mid-range** *Scandinavian Bakery*, 74/1 Pang Kham, on Nam Phou Circle. Delicious pastries, bread, cakes and sandwiches. Tables outside and 2 floors inside (a/c). Friendly *farang* chef/baker, who made the cake for the President of Tanzania's daughter's wedding (photo to prove it). Great place for a leisurely breakfast of coffee and pastries, with English-language newspapers provided. Pricey for Laos but a necessary European fix for many expats. Daily 0700-1900. Recommended. **Mid-range to cheap** *Healthy & Fresh Bakery* (formerly *Much 'n' More*), Setthathirat, 0700-2100 (although also dependent on the mood of the owners, closed on Sun). Good selection of tasty pastries, bagels sandwiches, pizzas, yoghurts and more, but *Scandinavian Bakery* ultimately wins on variety and popularity. **Cheap** *Le Croissant d'Or*, top of Nokeo Koummane. French bakery, small selection and on the pricey side. *My Choice Restaurant*, Setthathirat Rd (on corner of Chou Anou), a/c ice-cream parlour and restaurant, not much ambience. **Seriously cheap** *SugarPop*, T213182, Sihom Rd. 50s American ice-cream parlour, very kitsch with neon lights and plastic seating, unsettling Thai pop music, but marvellous array of Walls ice-cream desserts and an eclectic collection of Eastern and Western foods including pizzas, hamburgers, noodles, rice and spaghetti. Very popular with little Lao children and their fathers.

Pavement cafés   Pavement cafés on Chao Anou include **Cheap to seriously cheap** *Liang Xiang Bakery*, *Sweet Home* and *Nai Xiang Chai* (good juices and shakes). **Seriously cheap** *Fresh fruit iced drinks* (safe ice), Chao Anou Rd. Also nearby on this road are coffee shops and bakeries. *Nok Noy*, on corner of Fa Ngoum and Nokeo Koummane. A good choice for a cheap baguette breakfast with coffee.

Food stalls   Food stalls in the evening along Quai Fa Ngoum (the river road); cheap food in an incomparable setting (although the government seems intent on redeveloping the river frontage and squeezing out the small cafés and bars). The *Dong Palane Night Market*, on Dong Palane near the cinema, is also a good place to go for Lao stall food. There are various other congregations of stalls and vendors around town, most of which set up shop around 1730 and close down by 2100.

Bars

The bars of the debauched pre-revolutionary days have faded into legend: *The Purple Porpoise*, the *White Rose* pick-up joint and the renowned *Les Rendezvous des Amis*, run by Madame Lulu, which reportedly offered patrons "warm beer and oral sex", are now only dim memories.

There are a number of bars-cum-stalls which set up in the evening along Quai Fa Ngoum (the river road); a good place for a cold beer as the sun sets and the evening breeze picks up. A new promenade has sprung up on the banks of the river, and quite a few restaurants have moved the short distance to exploit the better views offered by this river frontage. Another row of riverfront bars can be found along the dirt track running upstream from the *Saam Yacek Restaurant* (the continuation of Fa Ngoum). These include the *Anousone*, *Ruan Lao*, *Vang Mekong* and *Sala Lao*. Most also serve food, but their position is better

Belle-Ile Creperie and Pub, 21 Lane Xang, Thu-Sun 1700-2400 (or later, unofficially), has good music and is very popular after 2200. *John's Restaurant* has become a firm favourite with expats for a beer at sunset (or anytime!); it also serves a range of good Lao and international dishes. *KhopJai Deu* on Setthathirat (near the corner with Nam Phou) is probably the most popular bar at the moment. There's a 'garden' close to the road with piped music and draft beer. Note that it is a pick-up joint too. Also serves food (see Lao restaurants above). *Lane Xang Restaurant* (part of *Lane Xang Hotel*), almost opposite the hotel on Quai Fa Ngoum, garden bar. *Sala Basi*, river road downstream from *River View Hotel*, a simple bar built on a wooden platform above the Mekong, cane chairs and cold beer, a great place to drink, read and otherwise chill out. *Sala Beer Lao* (Beer Lao House), opposite the Evening Market at Thong Khankam, saloon bar featuring occasional performances by Lao band Sapphire and other live acts, the closest thing in Vientiane to a rock 'n' roll pub – as opposed to discos with live bands. *Samlo Pub*, Setthathirat, owned by a Belgian, good ambience, popular meeting place for expats (good place for coffee after dinner), snooker, darts, pizza-type food. *Saysana Steakhouse Pub and Restaurant*, opposite *Malic Cyber Café* on Luang Prabang, Vientiane's first pub, live band. *Sticky Fingers*, François Ngin Rd (opposite the *Tai Pan Hotel*), small and intimate bar and restaurant run by an Australian lady. Popular with ex-pats, recommended. *Sunset Bar* (aka *The End of the World*), end of Fa Ngoum, open wooden house overlooking the Mekong with good atmosphere, another favourite meeting place for expats to watch the sunset. *Tai-pan Hotel*, 2-12 François Nguin Rd, bar in the lobby which occasionally hosts groups of consultants discussing the latest poverty statistics and how best to gauge human development.

Entertainment

Bands & discos Many of the discos in town, both in hotels and independent set-ups, feature live bands usually playing a mixture of Lao and Thai music and cover versions of Western rock classics. Unless otherwise stated, the bands play 7 nights a week, most between 2000 and midnight. *Anou Cabaret*, Heng Boun, very popular, friendly but crowded and loud, 1 of the best live bands in town. *Dao Vieng*, 40 Heng Boun, disco above restaurant. *Saysana Club*, *Saysana Hotel* (ground floor), Chao Anou. *Viengratry May*, Lane Xang, live music, quite expensive. *Olympia*, *Lane Xang Hotel*, operates at the weekends. *Apollo Nightclub*, *New Apollo Hotel*, Luang Prabang, live music, popular. *Friendship Disco*, *Mekong Hotel*, Luang Prabang, opposite the Regent Centre, Chinese-run nightclub with live music. *Chess Club*, Sakarindh Rd. Live music and entrance charge plus a bar thrown in 'for free'. Bands play Lao and Thai pop songs and covers. Watch precision dancing by NGO workers and Lao colleagues. Great fun. *Pack Luck*, Sakarindh Rd, next door to the *Chess Club*. Loud music, women of ill repute plus the odd gay. Was the happening place, but the buzz has gone. *Sprite Club*, Samsenthai, between Khoun Boloum and the creek, large disco with live band. *Muang Lao*, Muang Lao Hotel, Tha Deua, good band. There are several clubs on Luang Prabang, towards the airport. The *Marina*, the *Rainbow* and the *Blue Star Disco* popular with the Lao, good live band playing Lao, Thai and western music. *Wind* [*sic*] *West Pub and Restaurant*, Luang Prabang Rd, just past the petrol station. This pseudo-Western bar serves steaks and some Lao dishes, and a live band plays rock 'n' roll some nights.

Cinema Sadly, the old **Theatres de Spectacles** which survived through to the early 1990s and were enthusiastically attended have gone the way of the communes. Before 1975, Bruce Lee was the star of the moment, then the Indian screen idol Shashi Kapoor filled the hearts of the average Lao teenager. In these old cinemas, Lao voice-overs were dubbed in live every night by a team of skilled local dubbers who handled up to 3 voices each and tried to put everything in the local context. There were considerable variations in the script from 1 show to the next. During the screening of a western, a cowboy might inquire of another "Wher've you ridden fram boy?" Reply: "Ah've come fram the Morning Market". Now the average middle-class Lao watches Thai videos.

The **American Embassy**, That Dam, shows a movie every Wed at 1930, US$3. The **Australia Club**, on Tha Deua, shows a laser video every Sun at 1900. Programmes for these shows are usually listed in the *Vientiane Times*.

Traditional dance *Lane Xang Restaurant* offers an excellent traditional dance show, accompanied by Lao musicians, while you eat, every night 1900-2145. *Natasin Lao School*, Phoun Hang, near the stadium, traditional dance. *Royal Dokmaideng Hotel* organizes traditional dance nights at the hotel. The *Asian Pavilion Restaurant* provides traditional dance shows every night. Many of the restaurants in the more upmarket hotels do likewise.

Videos Occasional Sunday videos are shown in *Xang Café* and some other bars.

Festivals

October *Freedom of the French Day* (12 Oct). A public holiday, see page 58. *Boun Souang Heua* (Water Festival and boat races), full moon, end of Buddhist Lent. A beautiful event. Candles are lit in all the homes and thousands of banana-leaf boats holding flowers, tapers and candles are floated out onto the river. This is preceded by candle-lit processions around the city's wats and through the streets. On the second day, boat races take place, with 50 or so men in each boat; they power up the river in perfect unison. An exuberant event, with plenty of merry-making.

November *Boun That Luang* (movable). Celebrated in all of Vientiane's *thats* – but most of all at That Luang (the national shrine). Pilgrims pay homage to the Buddha and there is a candlelit procession around the stupa. A week-long carnival surrounds the festival with fireworks, music and dancing. The entertainments range from dodgems to 'freak' shows, a fascinating cavalcade of people and events.

Shopping

The Chinese quarter is around Chao Anou, Heng Boun and Khoun Boulom and is a lively spot in the evenings.

Books
(see also Maps below) *Government Bookshop*, Setthathirat, mainly Lao books but some English research books, plus a few maps. Also small selection of maps and books on Laos in the *Lane*

Xang Hotel and at *Lani I*. **Vientiane Book Centre** (previously *Raintree Books*), 54/1 Pangkham Rd, T212031, F212031, offers the best selection in town and there are now 4 branches: Pang Kham, opposite *Lao Aviation*, Nokeo Khoummane, *Lao Plaza Hotel* and *Novotel*. Raintree was the first English-language bookshop in Laos. Selection of coffee-table books, book exchange welcomed, glossy magazines and maps also available here as well as publications for Lao PDR specialists, including the Lao census, UNDP publications, and photocopies of various 'grey' literature publications. Books can also be found in some of the handicraft shops listed below, and some guesthouses.

Clothing

Yani, Mixay Arcade, Setthathirat, French designed fashion using local fabrics, good quality and good value (by European standards), small selection of handicrafts. *Mandarina*, Samsenthai, T223857, beautiful contemporary fashions in Lao silk, great colours, designed by stylish half-French Isabelle Souvanlasy. *Ek Hor boutique*, Pangkhamk, T517247, F416677. A small shop boasting a high quality selection of clothes and handicrafts, with prices to match.

Galleries

Kuanming Art Gallery, 265 Samsenthai. *Lao Gallery*, 108/2 Samsenthai, exhibits local artists. *Champa Gallery*, by That Dam (next to US Embassy), T216299, an attractive French colonial house, mostly the work of Canadian artist Monique Mottahedeh and her family (who own the gallery) but some local work and a few handicrafts. *Oot-Ni Art Gallery*, 306 Samsenthai, with another door on Heng Boun, T215911. A real Aladdin's cave of handicrafts and artefacts on the 1st floor including cottons and silks. Quite pricey, but worth a look. Also have a branch in the Morning Market, *Yen Kham Handicraft Shop*. *T'Shop Lai Gallery*, Wat Inpeng Soi, funky studio exhibiting local sculptures and art; artists can be seen at work every day except Sun. Media include coconut shells, wood and metal, proceeds from sales are donated to Lao Youth projects.

Handicrafts & antiques

The main shops are along Setthathirat, Samsenthai and Pang Kham. The **Morning Market** is certainly worth a browse, with artefacts such as appliquéd panels, decorated hats and sashes, basketwork – both old and new, small and large – wooden tobacco boxes, sticky-rice lidded baskets, axe pillows, embroidered cushions and a wide range of silver work. There is a custom-built **handicraft village** in the triangle where Luang Prabang and Samsenthai roads meet – there are also some sterilized food stalls here. *Lao Handicrafts*, 43/2 Setthathirat, mostly cloths and cotton goods like bags and wallets. *Mai Phuong*, 43/3 Setthathirat, old handicrafts and also some antiques. *Mixay Boutique*, Setthathirat, Ban Mixay, range of wooden and textile products. *Ekhor Boutique*, Pang Kham Rd, textiles, clothes and handicrafts. *Moradok – Inside Asia*, Sibounheuang Rd 201/18, wooden products. *Vanxay Art Handicraft*, Samsenthai, antique and modern materials. *Somsri Handicrafts*, 20 Setthathirat, with a fair selection of crafts and antiques upstairs. *Lao Handicraft*, 72/5 Pang Kham, mainly wood carvings. *Union des Entreprises d'Artisanat Lao Export-Import*, Phon Kheng (about 500 m north of the Monument Anousavari), large selection of materials from the north and the south. *Namsin Handicrafts*, Setthathirat, wooden objects. *Nang Xuan*, 385 Samsenthai, selection of opium pipes, silver boxes, Lao jewellery and Vietnamese trinkets. *Lao Culture and Antiquity Gallery*, 397 Samsenthai. *Nguyen Ti Selto*, 350 Samsenthai, Lao and Vietnamese antiques. *Phonethip Handicrafts and Ceramics*, 55 Saylom. *Hand Made Studio*, 78 Nokeo Koummane Rd, pottery, painting, carvings and silverware. *Putri Champa*, Setthathirat, Lao-Indonesian arts and decorations. Lovely stuff. Mon-Sat 1000-1900. *Mandalay*, François Ngin Rd (opposite *Taipan Hotel*), sophisticated furniture and furnidhings shop. *T'shop Lai*, Soi Inpeng (next to *Le Vendôme* restaurant), classy shop selling Lao arts and handicrafts; a clear notch above the run-of-the-mill shops and stalls selling cloth bags and wooden spoons.

The Ventiane Region

Jewellery & silverware   Many of the stones sold in Vientiane are of dubious quality, but silver and gold are more reliable. Gold is always 24 carat, so darker in colour and softer, but is good value. Silver is cheap but not necessarily silver. Nevertheless, the selection is interesting, with amusing animals, decorated boxes, old coins, earrings, silver belts. Wide selection in the Morning Market. Silver, gold and gem shops on Samsenthai, concentrated in the stretch opposite the *Asian Pavilion Hotel*, and some gold shops further west towards the Chinese quarter. *Fa Watthana*, 121 Khoun Bouloum Rd, T215630, konfa@laotel.com Traditional and contemporary designs. *Yani*, in Mixay Arcade, has some choice pieces. *Moradok – Inside Asia*, Sibounheuang Rd 201/18, some silverware here. *Lane Xang* at Carol Cassidy for top of the range silver designer-ware. *Doris Jewelry*, 2 shops in *Lao Plaza Shopping Centre*, stocks silverware, gems and antiques.

Maps   Government produced tourist/town maps available from *Venus*, Samsenthai (oppo-
(see also site *Asian Pavilion Hotel)*. The best tourist map is the map of Vientiane produced by the
Books above) Women's International Group (WIG), unfortunately not widely available anymore – try the Morning Market or Phimiphone minimarket. The only map of Vientiane in wide circulation is an advertising vehicle. But it's a nicely produced 3-D map available gratis at the airport and around town. Rather large, and not particularly useful from a tourist viewpoint, but it makes a nice souvenir. (It is also sold in some places – with the 'free' cunningly snow-flaked out. Rather than get peeved, why not support small business enterprise in Laos?)

Markets   Vientiane has several excellent markets. The **Morning Market** (**Talat Sao**) off Lane Xang is the biggest and the best – it's busiest in the mornings (from around 1000), but operates all day. There are money exchanges here (quite a good rate), and a good café selling western food, soft drinks and ice-cream sundaes. It sells imported Thai goods, electrical appliances, watches, stationery, cosmetics, a selection of handicrafts (see above), an enormous choice of Lao fabrics, and upstairs there is a large clothing section, silverware, some gems and gold and a few handicraft stalls. There is also an interesting produce section – **Talat Khua-Din** – the other side of the bus stop. **Talat Thong Thum**, on the corner of Khoun Khum and Dong Miang, is the largest produce market. It is sometimes known as the evening market as it was built to replace the evening market in Nong Douang, but is busiest in the mornings. **Other markets** Talat Simuang, Fa Ngoum/Simuang; **Talat That Luang**, south of parade ground; **Talat Dong Palane**, Dong Palane (near the cinema); **Koudin**, near the bus station – cheaper than the Morning Market (although barter hard!), this spot comes alive from 0500-0600 and is good for handicrafts and clothes,

Photo processing   *Konica Plaza*, 110/5 Samsenthai. *Kodak Express*, *Venus Colorlab* next to *Konica Plaza*, Samsenthai and 2 on Heng Boun. Many more dotted around the town and in the Morning Market.

Tailors   There are many Vietnamese tailors along Samsenthai and Pang Kham (north of Nam Phou fountain), good at copying. *Queen's Beauty Tailor*, by the fountain, is quite good for women's clothes, but allow at least a week. *Adam Tailleurs*, 72 Pang Kham. *La Fantasie*, 55 Pang Kham. *Nova*, 64 Samsenthai. *TV Chuong*, 395 Samsenthai. There are also a few tailors in the Morning Market.

Textiles   *Lao Women's Union Projects*, Nam Phou Pl, handwoven cottons with traditional designs, some made up into cushion covers, bags, dressing gowns. *Kanchana*, 102 Samsenthai, That Dam Sq or Ban Nongtha Tai, handwoven silks and cottons. *The Textile Centre* (*Lao Handicraft and Garment Co*), Luang Prabang (next to the statue of the 3 elephants), pottery and textiles, Government run and tends to be the stop-off point for

Ikat production

◀◀

In the handicraft shops and at the morning market in Vientiane, it is possible to buy distinctively patterned cotton and silk ikat. Ikat is a technique of patterning cloth characteristic of Southeast Asia and is produced from the hills of Burma to the islands of Eastern Indonesia. The word comes from the Malay word mengikat which means to bind or tie. Very simply, bundles of warp or weft fibres, and in one Balinese case both, are tied with material or fibre (or more often plastic string these days), so that they resist the action of the dye. Hence the technique's name – resist dyeing. By dyeing, retying and dyeing again through a number of cycles it is possible to build up complex patterns. This initial pre-weaving process can take anything from two to 10 days, depending on the complexity of the design. Ikat is distinguishable by the bleeding of the dye which inevitably occurs no matter how carefully the threads are tied; this gives the finished cloth a blurred finish. The earliest ikats date from the 14th-15th centuries.

To prepare the cloth for dyeing, the warp or weft is strung tight on a frame. Individual threads, or groups of threads are then tied together with fibre and leaves. In some areas wax is then smeared on top to help in the resist process. The main colour is usually dyed first, secondary colours later. With complex patterns (which are done from memory, plans are only required for new designs) and using natural dyes, it may take up to six months to produce a piece of cloth. Today, the pressures of the market place mean that it is more likely that cloth is produced using chemical dyes (which need only one short soaking, not multiple long ones – six hours or so – as with some natural dyes), and design motifs have generally become larger and less complex. Traditionally, warp ikat used cotton (rarely silk) and weft ikat, silk. Silk in many areas has given way to cotton, and cotton sometimes to synthetic yarns.

The Ventiane Region

tour groups. **Lao Cotton**, on Luang Prabang (and a branch on Samsenthai), T215840, out towards Wattay airport, approximately 500 m on right from *Novotel Hotel*, good range of material, shirts, handbags and housecoats, ask to see the looms. **Lao Textiles** by Carol Cassidy, Nokeo Koummane, T212123, F216205, ccassidy@laotel.com Exquisite silk fabrics, including ikat (see box) and traditional Lao designs, run by an American, from a beautifully renovated colonial property, pricey, but many of the weavings are really museum pieces, dyeing, spinning, designing and weaving all done on premises (and can be viewed), custom-made pieces available on request, exclusive silver jewellery from *Lane Xang* also available. Recommended. **The Art of Silk**, Manthathurath, T214308, opposite *Samsenthai Hotel*, large selection of old and new weaving, small museum of old pieces of weaving, baskets and a loom, not cheap, but worth a visit. Every hue and design available in the **Morning Market**. **Hmong Handicrafts**, Samsenthai, opposite the *Asian Pavilion Hotel*, appliquéd quilts, bedspreads and cushion covers. **Ekho Boutique**, next to *Diethelm Travel*, also some silver and woodwork. **Satri Lao**, 79/4 Setthathirat, opposite *PlaNet Computers*, handicrafts, silk, wood, gallery, library and tea-shop. **Mandonna**, 342 Samsenthai, silk and cotton Lao textiles and accessories.

Charcuterie *Arawan*, Samsenthai, next to restaurant, just before Wat Simuang on right hand side. Good choice of French cheese, salamis and patés, olives, French wine, pasta, chocolate and coffee. **Vinotheque La Cave**, 354 Samsenthai, T217700, French wine shop with large range of wine, run by Claude Monnier, who serves aperitifs with cheese. **Supermarkets** *Phimphone Minimart*, Samsenthai, good choice of bread, cheese, wine and other European food, as well as Russian caviar, 1 branch opposite and another alongside the *Ekkalath Metropole Hotel*. **Simuang Minimarket**, Samsenthai,

Western goods

east end of Wat Simuang. Small *minimarket* next to bakeries on Chao Anou, sells western goods. *Friendship Intershop*, 92/3 Samsenthai, alcohol and soft drinks. *Foodland Minimarket*, 117 Chou Anou. *Lao Phanit Supermaket*, 104 Khoun Boulom. *Yoghurt Shop*, Heng Boun, makes fresh yoghurt daily. *Riverside Minimarket*, Fa Ngoum. The vast supermarket in the **Morning Market** building sells everything from pastries to Chinese bicycles.

Sport

Cross-country running

Vientiane Hash House Harriers, the local Hash, meets at the Nam Phou Fountain every Sat at 1600. Transport to Hash site available from there. Family Hash every Mon at 1700. Meeting point varies so check the noticeboard at the *Australia Club* or *Phimphone Minimart*.

Golf

Santisuk Lane Xang Golf Club, Km 14, Tha Deua, T812022. 9-hole course, open to the public 0700-1800, modest green fee, caddies available. Get there by taking bus no 14 from the Morning Market or 20,000 kip by tuk-tuk, although your best bet might be to catch one of the regular buses, as it's on the road to Tha Dua border crossing. *Vientiane Golf Club*, Km 6, Rd 13 South, T515820, Mon-Sun 0630-sunset, clubs for hire. To get there, turn right at Peugeot showroom 6 km south of town, left after bridge, right at fork, right at top of hill. *Dansavanh Resort*, Vientiane office at 168 Luang Prabang Rd (opposite the entrance to the airport), T217594. This new 18-hole course, around 60 km from town on Route 10 towards Tulakhom, is rather better than the Vientiane courses.

Gyms

Several hotels in town permit non-residents to use their fitness facilities for a small fee, including the *Tai Pan Hotel* (rather basic), the *Lao Plaza Hotel*, the *Lane Xang* and the *Novotel*.

Massage & saunas

Many **local wats** have herbal saunas, which can be used by prior arrangement. Lao massage is softer than Vietnamese; a cross between acupressure and chiropractice. Donation in region of 4,000 kip would be appreciated. Avoid washing for 4-5 hrs afterwards, to allow the herbs to soak in. *Wat Sok Paluang*, Sok Paluang. To get there, walk through the small stupas to the left of the Wat; the sauna is a rickety building on stilts on the right-hand side, recognizable by the blackened store underneath. Herbal sauna, followed by herb tea (2,000 kip), massage by 2 young male masseuses (4,000 kip), peaceful leafy setting in the compound of Wat Sok Paluang; a very relaxing experience. *Hutpraseuth Health and Beauty Centre*, off Khou Vieng Rd, near the German Embassy (see map). This is a great massage place, off the beaten track and therefore only really patronized by locals and a few expats. Traditional herbal saunas, a range of excellent massages, and various other health sessions. Recommended. *Wat Sri Amphorn*, Sri Amphorn. *Mixay Massage*, Nokeo Koummane, Lao massage (US$5 per hr), facials, manicure, pedicure, sauna, 1700-2100. *Vatnak Health Centre*, south of town, beyond the Australia Club, T312628. Good for a hard Thai massage. *Sauna and Massage Rooms*, Chao Anou, pleasant setting with cooing white doves. Sauna 4,000 kip, massage 15,000 kip per hr; there is herbal tea to sip or fruit juices can be bought.

Snooker

Kaonhot, Sakharin, 3 full-size snooker tables. Also tables on Heng Boun. *Visay Snooker*, next to the *Ekkalath Metropole Hotel*.

Swimming

Lane Xang Hotel, Fa Ngoum. *Australia Club*, Km 4 Tha Deua Rd, members only (monthly membership available, US$40), attractive, large pool in lovely position next to the river, western food available, recommended. *Sokpaluang Swimming Pool*,

Sokpaluang, south of centre (see South Vientiane map), Mon-Sun 0800-2000, 9,000 kip for the day, costumes for hire, good sized pool for serious swimmers, paddling pool for children, restaurant and bar. Other hotels which open their pools to non-residents for a small fee include: the *Royal Dokmaideng*, the *Lao Plaza Hotel* and the *Novotel*.

Vientiane Tennis Club, inside the stadium. Floodlit courts open until 2100. 3,000 kip per hr, equipment for hire, bar. **Tennis**

Tour operators

Diethelm Travel, Nam Phou Circle, Setthathirat, T213833, F215920, ditralao @laotel.com *Four Season*, 21 Khoun Boulom Rd, T217711, F217712, souriyo_a@hotmail.com *Inter-Lao Tourisme*, 07/073 Luang Prabang Rd, T214232, www.interlao.laopdr.com *Joy Travel*, 121/3 Sethathirath Rd, T215584, joytrvl @laoTel.com *Lao Asian Trails*, Unit 5, Baan Sokpaluang, Muang Sisatanak, PO Box 8430, T/F351789, www.asiantrails.com *Lao Tourism Company*, 8/2 Lane Xang Av, T216671, laotour@laotel.com *Lane Xang Travel* , 3/8 Hengboun Rd, T212469, F215804, laxtrvel@pan-laos.net.la, lxtrvel@laoTel.com *Raja Tour*, 3 Hong Boun, T213633, rajatour@laotel.com *Sodetour*, 114 Fa Ngoum, T216314, F216313, sodetour @laotel.com *Thang Nam Tours*, Tha Deua, T313660, 313863, F351052, www. thangnam.laopdr.com Offers a range of tours incorporating Vientiane, Luang Prabang and Phonsavanh. *That Luang Tour*, 28 Kham Khong, T215809, F215346. *Nakornluang Travel Centre*, 53/8 Heng Boun, T223862, 222749, F214130. *Viengchampa*, 005 Khou Vieng, Rd, T216225, vcptour@laoTel.com *Xaysomboune Travel & Villa Muong Khong Hotel*, 122 That Luang, T/F451849, www. xbtravel-vlmkhotel.laopdr.com – offers a variety of tours all over Laos.

Transport

Unlike most capital cities in Southeast Asia, Vientiane is easy to get around and most places of interest – from sights to hotels and restaurants – are accessible on foot. While traffic has increased substantially over the last 5 years or so, it is nothing like Bangkok or Saigon and bicycling remains the best and most flexible way to negotiate the city.

See also Ins and outs, page 68

Bicycle hire For those energetic enough in the hot season, bikes are the best way to get around town. Many hotels and guesthouses have bikes available for their guests (eg *Lani I*, *Syri*, *Hotel Day Inn*, *Lao-Paris*, *Pangkham*, *Mixai* and *Tai Pan*). There are also several bike hire shops around town, sometimes attached to restaurants, sometimes to shops specializing in other things. These include: *Minimart*, Samsenthai; the Yoghurt shop next to MIC, Heng Boun; the *Scandinavian Bakery*, Nam Phou Circle; and KhopJai Deu, Setthathirat, corner of Nam Phou Circle. Expect to pay about 15,000-20,000 kip per day depending on the state of the machine. Markets, post offices and government offices usually have 'bike parks' where it is advisable to leave your bike. A small minding fee is charged. **Local**

Bus Around central Vientiane and to outlying areas, most leave from the bus station by the Morning Market or Talaat Sao. Destinations, distances and fares are listed on a board in English and Lao. Bus No 14 goes to the Friendship Bridge (1,000 kip), Tha Deua and the Garden of the Buddhas. Note that there is really no city bus service as such – most link the city with local destinations outside Vientiane proper.

Car hire It is not essential to hire a driver but in the event of an accident it is always the foreigner's fault. Rates vary according to state and model of vehicle and also whether out-of-town trips are planned. Expect to pay about US$50-90 per day. *Asia Vehicle Rental*, 354-356 Samsenthai Rd, T217493, avr@loxinfo.co.th, www.avr.kopar.com Saloons and 4WDs for daily, weekly or longer-term hire, self-drive or with driver. *Burapha*, 14 Quai Fa Ngoum, T216600. *Jo Rumble Asia Vehicle Rental*, 08/3 Lane Xang Av, T/F217493. *Lane Xang Hotel*, Fa Ngoum, T214100. *Mr Seuth*, T412785. *Samsenthai Hotel*, T212116. *Phimphone Minimart*, 110/1 Samsenthai, T216963. *KPP Transport Services*, T20514825. Many hotels and guesthouses will also have cars for hire.

Motorbike hire About US$10 per day for a basic Honda 70, US$20-25 for a good 200 cc off-road bike. Several guesthouses and restaurants have motorbikes for hire including: *Auberge du Temple*, 184/1 Ban Khounta; *Lao International Guesthouse*, 015/2 François Ngin Rd; *Hua Guo*, 359 Samsenthai; *Saysouly*, 23 Manthathurath; *PVO Vietnamese Food*, 344 Samsenthai. A number of other places rent out motorbikes including: *Kham Tan*, Setthathirat, opposite Wat Xieng Khoune, T614201. *Vientiane Motors*, 35/1-3 Setthathirat. *Phimphone Minimart*, Samsenthai, T216963.

Saamlor These will soon be as rare as hen's teeth in Vientiane. There are a few around the Morning Market and also at outlying markets.

Taxi Taxis are mostly found at the Morning Market or around the main hotels. There are also usually a few parked near the Nam Phou Fountain. Newer vehicles have meters but there are still some ageing jalopies. Flag fall is 8,000 kip. A taxi to Tha Deua from the Morning Market costs 30,000 kip; to the airport US$5. There is a good telephone taxi service: T350000.

Tuk-tuk There are 2 main tuk-tuk stands, 1 close to the Morning Market and another on Chao Anou where it crosses Heng Boun. Tuk-tuks can be chartered for longer out-of-town trips (to a maximum distance of around 25 km) or for short journeys of just a km or so. Expect to pay less than 1,000 kip per person for a 2-3 km ride within the city. There are also share tuk-tuks available which run along regular routes taking in the city's main streets. Tuk-tuks are available around the Nam Phou Fountain area until 2330 but are quite difficult to hire after dark in other areas of town. To stop a vehicle, simply flag it down.

Long distance **Air** Wattay Airport lies 6 km west of the town centre, T212066. Vientiane is the hub of Laos's domestic airline system and to travel from the north, south or vice versa it is necessary to change planes here. See page 37 for more information on the airport.

Transport to and from the airport There are no buses, except from the main road outside the airport (500 kip, every 45 mins). Only taxis are allowed to pick up (US$5 to the centre of town, 20 mins) although tuk-tuks can drop off. But tuk-tuks can be taken from the main road and sometimes lurk at the far side of the airport parking area, near the exit (20,000 kip). Most Lao take the share tuk-tuks into town; these cost 2,000 kip per person – simply follow the crowds. The dual carriageway into town is 1 of only a handful of such stretches of road in the country.

Bus/truck Vientiane's main bus terminal is next to the **Morning Market** or Talaat Sao, on the eastern edge of the city centre. This serves destinations within Vientiane Province. Most departures are in the morning and can leave as early as 0400, so many travellers on a tight schedule have regretted not checking departure times the night before. There is a useful map at the station, and bus times and fares are listed clearly in Lao and English. **Paksan** (159 km) 2 hrs (6,000 kip), **Laksao** (350 km) 8 hrs, buses leave at 0400, 0500 and 0600 only (50,000 kip), **Thakhek** (360 km) 6 hrs (15,000 kip),

Boat fares (2002)

	Duration	Fare	Departure time
Speedboat			
Vientiane – Pak Lai	4 hours	80,000 kip	0800, 1500
Vientiane – Luang Prabang	-	160,000 kip	0900
Slow boat			
Vientiane – Pak Lai	24 hours	30,000 kip	-
Vientiane – Luang Prabang	4 nights	80,000 kip	-

Savannakhet (490 km) 8-9 hrs (25,000), **Salavan** (360 km) 16 hrs (45,000 kip), **Pakse** (750 km) up to 19 hrs (35,000 kip). **Friendship Bridge** 45 mins, buses leave every 20 mins from 0650-1710 (1,000 kip). For destinations north of Vientiane services include: **Kasi** (230 km) 6 hrs (8,500 kip) and **Van Vieng** (160 km) 4 hrs (6,000 kip). Buses to **Luang Prabang** depart at 0700, 0830, 1030, 1300 and 1700 and the journey takes 10-12 hrs. The 600 km stretch of road to Luang Prabang was upgraded at the end of 1996. In the past, rather than being plagued by pot holes the road was plagued by bandits, who posed a very real danger. But since the upgrading the military presence on the road has increased here significantly and UN cars and trucks regularly use this stretch, which is a sign that the international community in Vientiane consider it safe. The most comfortable buses are run by private companies, but these offer only a limited service. The *Senesabay Bus Company*, which has its office on Sihom Rd close to Talaat Laeng, runs between 1 and 3 services a day south to **Savannakhet**, with stops at Pakxan and Thakhek (25,000 kip). It also operates a 35,000 kip service to Pakse four times a day. For buses to Vietnam, see below.

Taxi For **Tha Deua** and the **Friendship Bridge**, taxis leave from outside the front of the covered Morning Market. Taxis for other destinations and for charter are also available here.

Boat Boats to the north (**Luang Prabang**) leave from Kao Liaw village about 8 km west of Vientiane. Departures are usually in the morning between 0800 and 0900 but it's best to visit the boat landing at Ban Kao Liaw before your intended day of departure to negotiate a price and check on times. Note that because so few people take the boat option (this even applies to Laotians) there are no standard fares, but for the slow boat to Luang Prabang expect to pay around 140,000 kip. There is no regular service south as the roads have been upgraded. Even the journey north is not regularly made anymore as Route 13 north is largely considered safe. Most travellers prefer the road option as they can stay in Vang Vieng on their way to Luang Prabang. The journey upriver to Luang Prabang takes 4-5 days, 3-4 days downriver. During the wet season, when the river is high, boats do sometimes make the entire journey north to Luang Prabang but at other times of year there is a change of boat at **Pak Lai** (it is possible to shorten the journey by taking a speedboat from Pak Lai – 5 hrs instead of 2 days and nights). The large boats for the first leg leave Luang Prabang most days, carrying passengers and cargo. Wooden boats are preferable to corrugated iron, as it gets very hot during the day. Take a blanket, warm clothes (cold at night) and *plenty* of food and drink. There are shops in Pak Lai to restock (and some very basic guesthouses – see page 186). Note that women travellers may not sit on top of the boat and the trip is not comfortable. The stretch from Pak Lai to Luang Prabang is quite rough and passengers are asked to walk along the bank for the particularly dangerous bits.

The **speedboat** option is a noisy one (and for the fearless – everyone wears motorcycle helmets and life jackets after not just one fatal accident a few years back).

Speedboats carry about 6 people and not much baggage and like the slow boats depart from the landing at Ban Kao Liaw. There are services to **Pak Lai** and **Luang Prabang** and the journey to Luang Prabang takes about a day.

International connections by road

Vietnam The second border to be opened to foreigners travelling to Vietnam from Laos can be reached by a single 350-km bus journey from Vientiane. 3 buses a day (at 0400, 0500 and 0600) leave for the Vietnamese border at **Lak Sao** (50,000 kip). The journey is not easy as the roads are for much of the way unsurfaced. The first 3½ hrs on Route 13 are comfortable, but then the bus heads inland on Route 8, and the journey can take anything up to 8 hrs to reach the border. Buses leave from Sisangvon Rd near the intersection with Nong Bon Rd where the ticket offices are also to be found. There are services to **Hanoi**, **Danang** and **Hue**. Appropriately, there is also a good selection of Vietnamese restaurants here too, around the ticket offices.

Thailand via the Friendship Bridge See Bus and Taxi above for details of transport to the bridge, and page 70 for crossing into Thailand.

Directory

Airline offices *Lao Aviation*, 2 Pang Kham (Fa Ngoum end), T212050, F212065, laoaviation@lao-aviation.com, for international flights, and T212057 for domestic connections. *Lao Aviation* also have an office at Wattay Airport, T512000, Mon-Fri 0800-1200, 1300-1600, Sat 0800-1200. *Lao Aviation* operate as agents for *Air France* and *China Southern Airlines*. Obtaining domestic flights can be difficult, with reconfirmation needed 24 hrs in advance in person. *Thai*, Pang Kham (in front of *Lao Aviation*), T216143, Mon-Fri 0800-1200, 1300-1700 Sat 0800-1200. *Vietnam Airlines*, booking offices, 225 Saylom Rd, T222370, F222370, and on Setthathirat, also office in *Lao Plaza Hotel*. *Malaysian Airlines*, *Lao Plaza Hotel*, T218816. *Silk Air*, *Royal Dokmaideng Hotel*, T217492. *Royal Air Cambodge* (the *Cambodian Airline*), T218816, F218815, 2nd floor *Lao Plaza Hotel*.

Banks
See Money, page 31, for further details on changing money in Laos

There are now quite a number of exchange booths scattered across the centre of town, usually attached to banks. They are open 7 days a week, usually 0830-1530. In addition there are more than half a dozen money changers at the Morning Market, some open 7 days a week. *Banque Pour le Commerce Exterieur*, 1 Pang Kham, traditionally offers the lowest commission (1½%) on changing US$ TCs into US$ cash; there is no commission on changing US$ into kip. *Joint Development Bank*, 33 Lane Xang (opposite market). *Lao May Bank*, 39 Pang Kham (opposite *Phimphone Minimart*). *Setthathirat Bank*, Setthathirat Rd. With the loosening of banking regulations a number of Thai banks have set up in Vientiane. Many are situated along Lane Xang Av. They all offer efficient and competitive exchange facilities: *Thai Military Bank*, 69 Khoun Boulom. *Siam Commercial Bank*, Lane Xang. *Bangkok Bank*, 28/13-15 Hat Sady. *Thai Farmers Bank*, Lane Xang. *Thipphachanh Vongxay Exchange*, near *Phimphone Minimart* offers an efficient service. *Bank of Ayudhya*, Lane Xang (past the Morning Market travelling towards the Anousavari Monument). *Krung Thai*, Lane Xang. Shop around, as some banks will charge commission on both cash and TCs (1-3%) and others not. *Mini Mart* on Samsenthai also changes cash, as do many shopkeepers in the capital.

Communications **Internet:** Internet cafés are now beginning to open up all over the place, many on Setthathirat Rd, and the trend looks set to continue. Generally open 0800-2200/2300. Shopping around for the best price is a good idea given the snail-paced connection speeds. It's lucky that most offer coffee and other drinks and have newspapers, because there's lots of hanging around. Consider sauntering in with *War & Peace* and a sleeping bag. A couple of the nicer places to try include: *PlaNet Computers*, 205 Setthathirat, planet@laonet.net, Mon-Fri 0830–2300, Sat-Sun 0900-2300, and *Star-net*, Mixay, T504550. The owner of *Star-net*, Somphane Sihavong, is very helpful and speaks good English. You shouldn't have to pay more than 150 kip per min. *Advance Information Internet Café*, 386 Samsenthai Rd, T217509, is one of the cheapest options. **Post Office**: Khou Viang/Lane Xang (opposite Morning Market), T216425. Poste restante, local and international telephone calls, and fax services (see page 49 for more detailed information). They also offer a good packing service and a philately counter where any stamp collecting desires can be quenched. *DHL*, 52 Nokeo Khoummane Rd, T216830, 214868. *TNT Express Worldwide*, 8/3 Lane Xang Av, T214361. *UPS*, 12/26 Nong Bon. *Transpack Lao*, That Luang Tai. *State Enterprise for Construction and Shipping*, 105 Khoun Boulom. *Federal Express*, Khou Vieng. *Lao Freight Forwarder*, Km 3, Tha Deua Rd, T313321, laoffimp@laotel.com **Telephone**: International telephone office, Setthathirat, near Nam Phou, telephone service open 24 hrs a day, fax service open 0730-2130.

Australia, Nehru, Quartier Phone Xay, T413600. **Myanmar (Burma)**, Sok Paluang, T314910. **Cambodia**, Tha Deua Km 2, T314952, F312584. **China**, Wat Nak, T315103. **Czechoslovakia**, Tha Deua, T315291. **France**, Setthathirat, T215258, F215250. **Germany**, 26 Sok Paluang, T312111. **India**, That Luang Rd, T413802. **Indonesia**, Phon Kheng, T413910. **Japan**, Sisavangvong, T414400, F414403. **Malaysia**, That Luang, T414205. **Sweden**, Sok Paluang, T315018, F315001. **Thailand**, Phon Kheng, T217158, F216998 (consular section on That Luang), Mon-Fri 0830-1200: 2-month Thai visa costs 300 baht (only baht acceptable), it takes 3 days to process. **UK**, no embassy but operates through the Australian Embassy. **USA**, That Dam (off Samsenthai), T212580, F212584. **Vietnam**, That Luang, T413400, 0800-1045, 1415-1615: US$50 for a 1-month visa – you must wait 3 days.

Embassies & consulates

101/3 Samsenthai, 1-day service, also dry cleaning.

Laundry

Clinics: *Australian Clinic*, Australian Embassy, T413603, Mon, Tue, Thu and Fri 0800-1200 and 1400-1700, Wed 0830-1200. *Swedish Clinic*, Sok Paluang (near Swedish Embassy), T315015, Mon, Tue, Wed and Fri 0800-1200, 1400-1600, Thu 0800-1200. *International Clinic*, Mahosot Hospital, Setthathirat, T214022, Mon-Sun, 24 hrs a day (said to be staffed by Cubans). **Hospitals**: *Clinique Setthathirat*, next to That Luang, T413720. **NB** The Australian and Swedish embassies have clinics for emergencies. For more serious medical problems it is advisable, if possible, to travel to Thailand. There are several very good hospitals in UdonThani, 2 hrs from Vientiane across the Friendship Bridge (see page 70 for details). **Pharmacies**: Khoun Boulom and Samsenthai.

Medical services

Churches: *Vientiane Evangelical Church*, Luang Prabang, on way to airport. Sun services in Lao, 1000.

Places of worship

Immigration: Phai Nam (Morning Market end), Mon-Fri 0730–1200, 1400–1700. A visa extension takes 1 day to process, you need 1 photograph, 500 kip for application form and US$1 per day extension. **Police Station**: Setthathirat, in emergency, T212707 or 190. **Police Tourist Office**: Lang Xang Av (next to the National Tourism Authority of Laos office), T251128. **National University of Laos (NUL)**: *Dong-Dok*, 10 km north on Route 10.

Useful addresses

The Ventiane Region

Around Vientiane

Lao Pako
Colour map 2, grid B2

Lao Pako lies 50 km northeast of Vientiane, on the banks of the Nam Ngum (off Route 13). There is a 'nature lodge' here established by an Austrian couple a few years back. The owners have 50 ha of land, through which they have cut paths and planted trees. A lovely place to retreat to, for swimming, trekking, rafting and walks to local Lao villages – and very reasonably priced.

Sleeping and eating Accommodation is in a Lao-style longhouse (**D-E**) or in single bungalows overlooking the river. The **cheap** restaurant here serves excellent Lao and European food. Can be crowded at weekends. For further information T222925 (radio phone) or F212981.

Transport Take bus no 19 from Vientiane's Morning Market (they leave at 0700, 1100 and 1400) towards Pakxan along Route 13 and get off at Som Sa Mai, 1 hr. From Som Sa Mai take a local boat to Lao Pako (another 25 mins).

Nam Ngum Dam and Ban Thalat

Colour map 2, grid B2

The Nam Ngum Dam, 90 km from Vientiane, is the pride of Laos and figures prominently in picture postcards. It provides electricity for much of the country and exports to Thailand are the country's second biggest foreign exchange earner. No photographs are allowed at the dam wall or the HEP plant.

Many people believe that the dam was built with Soviet aid and assistance following the victory of the Communists in 1975. In fact construction began in the 1960s under the auspices of the Mekong Development Committee and was funded by the World Bank and Western nations. Indeed a large slice of the country's aid budget went into the construction of the dam. The dam was officially opened in the early 1970s.

The lake is very picturesque and is dotted with hundreds of small islands. After the victory of the Communists two of the islands came in handy as open prisons for the most 'culturally polluted' of Vientiane's population. Two thousand drug addicts, prostitutes and other assorted hippies and low life were rounded up and shipped out here. One island was allocated for men and the other for women. In addition to the islands, huge semi-submerged tree-trunks pose an additional navigational hazard, as no one had the foresight to log the area before it was flooded. The untapped underwater cache of timber has been spotted by the Thais looking for alternative sources for their lucrative timber trade. Sub aqua chainsaws are used to take out the 'treasure'. For all their skills, it is necessary to bargain hard with boatmen before boarding to cross the lake. Boats from Nam Ngum Dam to Ban Pao Mo on the other side take around two hours. Boats can also be hired out, and again, barter hard to get a good hourly rate. Vang Vieng is two hours' ride from the dam.

Ban Thalat is a small market town (the word 'thalat' means market) on the southwest shores of the reservoir, a few kilometres from the dam. It is interesting mainly for the minority peoples who come here to market their produce and in reality it is a rather grotty and sad place with a handful of mediocre restaurants, a few ramshackle trinket stalls and a fisheries station. Boats are available for hire either to visit the reservoir's islands or to reach the *Dansavanh Resort* (see Sleeping below).

A *Dansavanh Nam Ngum Resort*, T217594, F252650, www.dansavanh.net Malaysian and Lao Government joint-venture. Phase 1 of this monstrous development is now ready, and incorporates a hotel with 209 rooms, Chinese and Thai restaurant, health centre, video games and casino as well as a recently opened golf course. Frankly, it's quite hideous. It was gruesome from the start, but now it's beginning to crumble even though it's not finished (a water theme park is planned). If you are tempted by the glossy brochure and the raft of amenities, there's just one piece of advice: resist! The biggest irony of all is that it tries to sell itself as an eco-tourist option. A second irony, almost as large, is that Dansavanh means 'Heavenly Land'.

Sleeping
■ *on map*
Price codes:
see inside front cover

C *Japanese Bungalows*, a/c, hot water bungalows. These are so-called because they were originally erected to house the Japanese engineers who worked on the dam. They are now available for tourists. They are situated away from the lakeside, not far from the dam itself.

D *Done Dok Khounkham Resort*, on an island in the lake, 6 rooms only, bathrooms en suite, basic but clean, electricity only after 1830, restaurant across a small bay (limited food, no alcohol – take your own), boat tours and fishing trips organized, isolated and quiet. **D** *Floating Hotel*, run by *Nam Ngum Tours*, a/c, hot water. The rooms here are fine, with attached bathrooms, and there is a decent floating restaurant close by (see below). **D** *Nam Ngum Dam Hotel* (on the right after the long bridge on the way to the dam), seafood restaurant in hotel.

E *Santipab*, on an island in the lake, rooms with attached bathrooms. A deteriorating guesthouse, cleanliness clearly not featuring as a priority and no electricity; tend to overcharge for the boat trip out there.

Nam Ngum & Ban Thalat

The Ventiane Region

Sleeping
1 Dansavanh NamNgum Resort
2 Done Dok Khounkham Resort
3 Floating Hotel, Japanese Bungalows & Nam Ngum Dam
4 Lao Pako Resort
5 Santipat

Eating **Mid-range** *Lao Food Raft*, next to *Floating Hotel*, tasty food, friendly staff.

Transport The most direct route to the dam from Vientiane is along Route 13, turning right at Phonhong at the strategically-placed concrete post in the middle of the road. Then head left to the village of Ban Thalat – where the market is worth a browse – then right across the narrow bridge to the dam, about 4 km up the road. There is an alternative route through much prettier countryside on Route 10 out of Vientiane, across the Nam Ngum by ferry. Turn right at the end of the road for the dam. *Dansavanh Nam Ngum Resort* also run a shuttle service from Vientiane and the Friendship Bridge to their resort (400 baht one way). **Bus** There is a direct bus to the Nam Ngum Dam which departs from the Morning Market in Vientiane daily at 0700, 3 hrs. Alternatively take 1 of the buses that leave every 2 hrs or so from the Morning Market to Ban Thalat, 2½ hrs (3,500 kip), and then a taxi or tuk-tuk on to Nam Ngum. **Taxi** By taxi (US$30).

Vang Vieng

Phone code: 021
Colour map 2, grid A2

Like its cousin in the north, Muang Sing, Vang Vieng has become one of the most popular destinations for travellers in recent years, flocking here in their hundreds. While Vang Vieng is undoubtedly an attractive town, an additional reason why it has become so popular is because it is a convenient stop-off point on the gruelling journey to Luang Prabang.

Situated 160 km north of Vientiane on the much improved Route 13, the drive to Vang Vieng follows the valley of the Nam Ngum north to Phonhong and then climbs steeply onto the plateau where Vang Vieng is located. The area around Vang Vieng is particularly picturesque, with its craggy karst limestone scenery, riddled with caves, crystal-clear pools and waterfalls. As many visitors have remarked, in the early morning the views are reminiscent of a Chinese Sung Dynasty painting. The caves are renowned in local mythology (see below). The area around Vang Vieng is inhabited by the Hmong and Yao hill peoples and the town itself is also attractive.

Sights There are a number of 16th- and 17th-century **monasteries** in town of which the most notable are **Wat That** at the northern edge of the settlement and **Wat Kang**, 100 m or so to the south. There is also a **market** that stocks a limited range of postcards, Lao language texts, fabrics, baskets and shoes. But Vang Vieng is best known for its limestone caves and of these **Tham Chang** is most renowned of all. Tham Chang penetrates right under the mountain and is fed by a natural spring – perfect for an early morning swim. From the spring it is possible to swim into the cave for quite a distance – bring a waterproof torch, if possible. The cave is said to have been used as a refuge during the 19th century from marauding Chinese Ho bandits and this explains the cave's name: 'loyal' or 'steadfast' (*chang*) cave (*tham*). Most visitors must pay a 1,000 kip entrance fee at the *Vang Vieng Resort* to gain access to the caves and to swim in the pools (although it is possible to cross the rickety bridge by the *Nam Song Hotel* which goes halfway across the river for 200 kip, wade across the rest – during the dry season – and arrive at the caverns from a different point). For your entrance fee you not only get into the caves but the recently installed lighting system will also be turned on.

There are many **more caves** in the vicinity of town, most to the west and north. It is possible to hire a bicycle in Vang Vieng (around 5,000 kip per day), take it across the river for 200 kip and cycle to the caves and villages the other side of the Nam Xong as all the sites are between 2 km and 15 km from Vang Vieng. Alternatively you can catch a 'Lao-style' tractor on the far side of the river (1,000-4,000 kip depending on distance – bargain hard). Each cave has an entrance fee of 2,000 kip and many have stalls where you can buy drinks and snacks. You can buy hand-drawn maps from the town, but all the caves are clearly signposted in English from the main road so these maps are not truly necessary.

Tour guides are available for hiking in the hills, rafting, visiting the caves and minority villages (see *NongBot Restaurant* and *Dokkhoun Guesthouse*), 15,000 kip for one day, or 50,000 kip overnight. Inner tubes can be rented for

Hiking, rafting & floating

The Ventiane Region

Vang Vieng

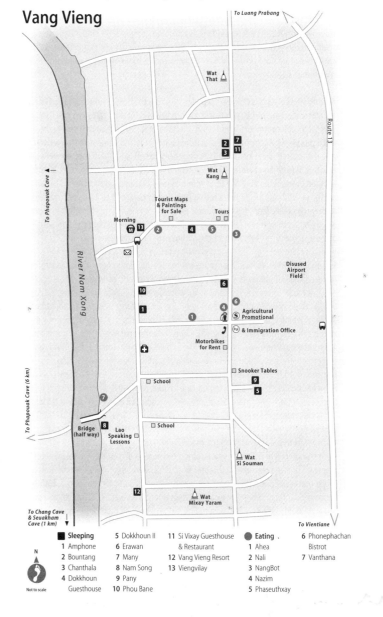

Sleeping
1 Amphone
2 Bountang
3 Chanthala
4 Dokkhoun Guesthouse
5 Dokkhoun II
6 Erawan
7 Many
8 Nam Song
9 Pany
10 Phou Bane
11 Si Vixay Guesthouse & Restaurant
12 Vang Vieng Resort
13 Viengvilay

Eating
1 Ahea
2 Nali
3 NangBot
4 Nazim
5 Phaseuthxay
6 Phonephachan Bistrot
7 Vanthana

N
Not to scale

5,000 kip per day – you can then take a tuk-tuk upriver to either Km 4½ or Km 7 and float lazily back to Vang Vieng (up to 3½ hours worth of floating).

Sleeping
■ *on map*
Price codes:
see inside front cover

To accommodate Vang Vieng's surge in popularity, numerous guesthouses and western-style restaurants have sprung up, so there is no shortage of good quality budget accommodation. On the last count there were over 25 guesthouses, 2 hotels and 1 resort. Unfortunately, there isn't much individuality in their design, although quite attractive multi-floored villas with sweeping exterior staircases are in vogue. The majority are clean with tiled floors (deadly when wet), en-suite showers and toilet, and contain little besides a double bed, a simple table and a fan. Several offer hot water, while the cheapest provide shared bathrooms. The owners are wise to the needs of travellers and many offer a laundry service, guides, rent bicycles and inner tubes (for the river) and sell maps of the area. They are good sources of information regarding the caves and other sights in the vicinity of town. Below is by no means an exhaustive list of guesthouses available.

B *Vang Vieng Resort*, a Chinese-owned resort close to Tham Chang, T219380. Bar and noodle restaurant, some chalets with bathrooms, no a/c and the rooms smell musty. The resort has control of Tham Chang, the cave, and has erected concrete steps and put lights inside. As a result it has lost its natural beauty and visitors are charged to get into the resort (1,000 kip), then to get into the cave (2,000 kip), and then again to take pictures. **B** *Nam Song Hotel*, T213506, with its own milestone at the gate. Beautiful location overlooking the Nam Xong within its own spacious grounds, but has a 'prison camp' feel with security lights, a roving Doberman guard dog and a French manageress, who is no less fear-inspiring. Rooms are small and clean with en-suite bathrooms, but overpriced as they offer nothing special when compared with the competition. The use of the a/c wrests an extra US$5 from patrons; expensive restaurant.

E *Amphone* T511180. Nicer than many alternatives, although nothing particularly out of the ordinary. Spotless rooms with hot water en-suites and a friendly proprietor, who also just happens to be a dab hand at knocking up beautifully tailored trousers, shorts and skirts in his shop opposite. Recommended. **E** *Bountang*, next to *Chanthala*, large 3-storey white villa with weaving loom and handicrafts in the garden. Choice of cold-water and hot-water showers. **E** *Chanthala*, next to Wat Kang. The cheapest rooms in Vang Vieng, shared toilet facilities, clean. **E** *Dokkhoun*, T511032, around the corner from the bus station, 2-storey villa with balcony area, clean rooms with en-suite bathrooms, tour guide service available from 1000-1800, car for rent, very popular. **E** *Dokkhoun II*, T219393, down a short lane in front of the disused airfield. Born out of *Dokkhoun I's* popularity this monster of a building boasts 3 floors and countless identical, large and clean rooms. Another favourite with travellers. **E** *Erawan*, T/F511093, erawan_van@hotmail.com Restaurant and guesthouse. Run by an Englishman and his Lao wife, this place is a hotbed of (mainly Israeli) tourists and is a font of useful information on things to do in the area. Rooms are similar to all the others in town, but this place also boasts a ping-pong table and TV, and is always buzzing with people. Restaurant menu is disappointingly international, but food is good, if quite pricey. **E** *Many*, opposite *Bountang*. This is one place that does not fit the Vang Vieng mould, an exotic choice. Rooms come with posters of semi-naked women and fancy crystal lampshades. The guesthouse is located at the back behind a beaded curtain, intimate lighting. Recommended if only for its individuality. **E** *Pany*, next door to *Dokkhoun II*. Offers one of the best deals for large doubles with hot water en-suite bathrooms (cheaper rooms have cold water only). The downside is that it can get noisy at night from the crowds next door. **E** *Phou Bane*, close to the market and the bus station. Restaurant (good), nice garden to lounge in. One of the original guesthouses in Vang

Vieng which may lend the place atmosphere, but the rooms are not as clean or well-equipped as others; shared shower and toilet downstairs. Nonetheless, a friendly place. **E** *Sivixay*, in newish block, clean rooms with bathrooms, cold water only, towels supplied. **E** *Viengvilay*, T511177. Bit of a mixed bag, this one: all rooms are reasonably clean and have attached bathrooms, and some on the second floor offer spectacular views of the mountains,

In 2002 there were more than 25 restaurants with English menus and food in Vang Vieng. We have only mentioned a few by name, below. However, there is a string of eating places along the road heading up east from the market and many others dotted around the town; fresh noodle soup and rice from the market.

Eating
● *on map*
*Price codes:
see inside front cover*

The Ventiane Region

Cheap *Nazim*, Indian (Halal food), T511214, open 1100-2300. Established in 2001 on the back of the popularity of its sister restaurants in Vientiane and Luang Prabang, this place has already proved a hit with its extensive menu and delicious food. *Phonephachan Bistrot*, this one is run by a French Canadian from Quebec, stylish interior with his own impressive photographic portraits of minority peoples, magazines, coffee-table books and French novels available to read, includes a bar. French and Lao food, excellent oven-baked pizzas and a large variety of pancakes and cheeses. Recommended. *Sivixay*, T219360. French-owned restaurant and bar, rather plain interior, has satellite TV, and old magazines to read. Offers an assortment of French and Lao dishes, good food. Tthe owner, Patrick Beaufort, has lived and worked in Thailand, Vietnam, and Vientiane. Interesting stories to tell, but service is mediocre.

Seriously cheap *Ahea*, T511141. This sweet little place is set away from the main strip and offers a good line in decent, cheap I ao food. The milkshakes are to die for, and stopping here can offer a welcome break for any traveller looking to escape the crowds. *Nali*, opposite the market, run by a Vietnamese family with the best coffee and banana shakes in town, friendly service. Recommended. *NangBot*, very hot Thai curries, but service is slack and unfriendly; guides available for trekking. *Phaseuthxay*, serves traditional Lao food in a charming but basic setting. Friendly service and good grub. *Vanthana*, next to *Nam Song Hotel*, covered wooden shelter overlooking the river, beautiful location to watch the sun set behind the limestone peaks and truck drivers washing their vehicles in the Nam Xong. Simple Lao dishes and a few Western favourites.

Bus/truck These leave from the Morning Market in Vientiane; the road is new and in good condition, 3½ hrs (6,000 kip). Also, **pick-ups** leave throughout the day for around 8,000 kip. There are now 5 buses a day that leave for **Vientiane** at roughly 0530, 0550, 0610, 1300 and 1430. The upgrading of the road from Vang Vieng to **Luang Prabang** from Vang Vieng was finally completed at the end of 1996. Journey time is around 7 hrs. Check on safety before travelling as in the past buses on this leg of the route north have been periodically ambushed by bandits. One bus a day leaves for Luang Prabang (40,000 kip) at 0900 or else catch a Vientiane-Luang Prabang bound bus when it passes through town. Route 13 continues north 60 km to Kasi. **Bicyle hire** Many bicycles for rent along the road east up from the market (5,000 kip per day). **Motorbike hire** The Vietnamese café, next to the telecom office, rents motorbikes for US$10 per day.

Transport
160 km to Vientiane

Kasi

This is one of those towns which seems to exist for no better reason that people need to rest and have a bite to eat. It is a trucking stop on Route 13 and as it is only 60 km north from Vang Vieng – a much more attractive town – it entices

Colour map 2, grid A2

few people to linger here longer than necessary. If you do find yourself there, there is plenty of interest to be had by walking around local ethnic villages. The children learn English at school and welcome the opportunity to talk to strangers.

According to some of the locals, the countryside around Kasi boasts what is reputedly the second-largest cave in the world – **Khoun Lang**. To date this has been a well-kept secret, although according to the owner of Vang Vieng's *Erawan Guesthouse*, three experts from UNESCO were due to survey it in 2002 to ascertain whether it would be safe for tourism. On the cards if the green light is given are plans for a walking tour through the jungle and by the river. Delightfully, the introduction of tourists to the area looks set to be done in a traditionally Lao style, with trips incorporating local food and living, including showers in the river and such like.

Sleeping & eating   Rooms are available in Kasi at several guesthouses, the most popular of which is the **E** *Somchith*, Route 13 Main Rd. A small place above a restaurant in the centre of town. **E** *Somchith II* has now been opened 50 m further down the road.

Transport   **Bus/truck** There are connections with **Vang Vieng** to the south (2 hrs) and north to **Luang Prabang** (4 hrs). As the town lies on the main highway it is easy enough to flag down a north or southbound bus.

The North

Introducing the North

Much of the northern region of Laos is rugged and mountainous, a remote borderland with a significant minority population of **hill peoples**. Until recently, in some areas at least, the only way to travel was by boat, along one of the **rivers** – many fast-flowing – which have cut their way through this impressive landscape. Today road travel is much improved, although still not easy. The key centre of the North is the old royal capital of **Luang Prabang**, one of the world's most beautiful cities. To the east is the **Plain of Jars**, a former stronghold of the Pathet Lao, while to the north are a string of small towns which are becoming increasingly popular places to visit. The North is rapidly becoming one of the highlights of a visit to Laos. **Eco-resorts** in peaceful forest settings, **treks** to upland minority villages, icy dips in mountain streams, and **rafting** down innumerable mountain streams are all becoming *de rigueur* as tourist numbers rise and local people cotton on to the peculiar desires of foreigners.

Things to do in the North

① Saunter through the old royal capital of **Luang Prabang** and imagine what cities used to be like. Take time, particularly, to absorb the character of the incomparable **Wat Xieng Thong.** Then climb **Phousi**, Luang Prabang's holy mountain, to claim a mental map of the city.

② Take a boat upstream to see the cliff-side **caves at Pak Ou**, stuffed with 4,000 images of the Buddha.

③ Take a dip in the **Khouang-Sy falls**, 30 km south of Luang Prabang.

④ Construct your own hypothesis for the creation of Xieng Khouang's **giant stone jars**.

⑤ Watch Xam Neua's women make some of Laos' most **beautiful textiles**.

⑥ Explore the **caves of Vieng Xai**, former stronghold of the Pathet Lao.

⑦ Walk and take on more ambitious treks from the upland town of **Phongsali**.

⑧ Use the attractive hill town of **Muang Sing** as a base for exploring the hill villages and minority peoples of the area.

The North

Luang Prabang

Phone code: 071
Colour map 2, grid A2
Population: 10,000
Altitude: 300 m

Luang Prabang is a sleepy town which lies on the upper Mekong, at its conflu-ence with the Nam Khan. It is known for its magnificent temples, particularly the former royal Wat Xieng Thong, and is dominated by Phousi – the 'marvel-lous mountain' – which sits in the middle of the town. This is the town that visi-tors often remember with the greatest affection. Its rich history, incomparable architecture, relaxed atmosphere, good food, friendly population and stunning position mark Luang Prabang out as exceptional. Even the local attitude to crime and punishment is laid-back, as evidenced by the Nam Pha 'free-range' jail, where prisoners are reportedly reluctant to be released. Cycling or walking around town in the early evening, this royal 'city' feels more like a small, provin-cial town – which, in effect, is what it is. Children play in the streets and women cook while old men lounge in wicker chairs and young boys play takro. The great fear, of course, is that all this will change.

Ins and outs

Getting there

See Transport, page 186, for further details

Until quite recently visitors to Luang Prabang were advised by Vientiane's foreign consular staff to fly rather than risk the road journey. This was because vehicles on the stretch of road between Vientiane and Luang Prabang, and particularly from Kasi north, were periodically attacked by bandits. These attacks have now stopped and the road is safe. In addition, Route 13 has been upgraded and the journey is a rela-tively painless 8-9 hrs. Easier still is to fly from Vientiane to Luang Prabang; there are several daily connections. There are also air connections with Phonsavanh, Ban Houei Xai, Muang Xai (Udom Xai) and Luang Namtha. International connections with Bangkok (via Sukhothai) and Chiang Mai in northern Thailand fly twice weekly. A service to Singapore has been under discussion for some time but is still to materi-alize. There are overland connections with other destinations in northern Laos including Sayaboury, Nong Khiaw, Xieng Khouang (Phonsavanh), Xam Neua, Luang Namtha, Muang Xai, Muang Ngoi and Pak Mong. A third option is to travel by river, although this is becoming less and less popular, as road conditions improve. None-theless a fair number of travellers choose to travel between Ban Houei Xai (close to the Thai border) and Luang Prabang via Pak Beng. There are also boats between Luang Prabang and Vientiane via Pak Lai and to Muang Ngoi and Nong Khiaw via Muang Khua.

Getting around

See also Transport, page 143

Luang Prabang is a small town and the best way to explore the 'city' proper is either on foot or by bicycle. The city authorities have, in the recent past, banned foreigners from hiring bicycles (as well as motorcycles). That this ban has now been lifted is no guarantee that it won't happen again, but there are tuk-tuks and saamlors available for hire, and anyway, strolling about drinking in this beautiful town is a real pleasure. Buses provide links with out-of-town destinations (although the service is limited and intermittent), and there are also boats and minibuses for charter and motorbikes for hire.

Best time to visit

The best time to visit Luang Prabang is from Dec to Feb. The most popular time to visit the town is during the comparatively cool months of Nov and Dec. By Feb the weather is hotting up and the views are often shrouded by a haze produced by shifting cultivators using fire to clear the forest for agriculture. This does not really clear until May or, sometimes, Jun. During Mar-Apr, when visibility is at its worst, it can cause soreness of the eyes as well as preventing airplanes from landing.

Tourist information

Luang Prabang Tourism, T212198, F212728, on the corner opposite the Post Office may appear to be a tourist office, but in fact it is just a state-owned tour company, providing little information, except a map for sale, open Mon-Sat. The official tourist office is next to the provincial office on Phothisarath Rd (not far from the *Souvannaphoum Hotel*) but there are only 2 people here who are useful to non-Lao speaking visitors (one speaks French, the other some English) and they are rarely available. There is also an **Information and Cultural Service** almost opposite Wat Mai at 72 Sisavangvong Rd, T212198. As many visitors arrive on tours there is considered to be little need for a tourist information service.

If you really do need some information, hotels and guesthouses (or other travellers) are often the best bet.

As a tourist, probably the best city map is one of a series of 5, compiled by the National Geographic Department of Laos. It can be bought in the shop next to the handicraft shop, along from the *Phousi Hotel* and almost opposite the Central Market. In 2000, a 3D city map was released, although it's not really practical for travellers as it's large and cumbersome, but it makes an attractive souvenir.

Maps

History

Louang Prabang was established as the royal capital by Fa Ngoum, the first monarch of Lane Xang, the Land of a Million Elephants, in the 14th century. The name of the city refers to the holy *Pra Bang*, Laos's most sacred image of the Buddha which was given to Fa Ngoum, Laos's greatest King, by his father-in-law the King of Cambodia. The city had already been the seat of local kingdoms for about 600 years. According to legend, the site of the town was chosen by two resident hermits and was originally known as Xieng Thong – 'Copper Tree City'. The ancient name for Luang Prabang was Chawa, which translates as Java.

In the 18th century there were more than 65 wats in the city; many have been destroyed over the years but over 30 remain intact. The continuing splendour and historical significance of the town led UNESCO to designate it a World Heritage Site at the end of 1995. In terms of size, Luang Prabang hardly deserves the title 'city' – the capital district has a population of a little more than 20,000, and there are probably barely 10,000 inhabitants in the town proper. (That said, there's also a sizeable itinerant population who are not counted as residents in the city.) But in terms of grandeur the appellation is more than deserved.

The English travel writer Norman Lewis described Luang Prabang in 1950 as a "tiny Manhattan, but a Manhattan with holy men in yellow robes in its avenues, with pariah dogs, and garlanded pedicabs carrying somnolent Frenchmen nowhere, and doves in its sky. Down at the lower tip, where Wall Street should have been, was a great congestion of monasteries."

The North

In some respects even more evocative than Lewis, James McCarthy, an otherwise rather plodding recorder of events and sights, wrote of Luang Prabang at the end of the 19th century:

"In a clear afternoon, Luang Prabang stood out distinctly. At evening the pagoda spires and the gilded mouldings of the wats, glancing in the light of the setting sun, added their effect to that of the natural features of the landscape – and caused in me a feeling of irresistible melancholy. Since my visit in February 1887, Luang Prabang had passed through much suffering. It had been ravaged by the Haw; its people had been pillaged and murdered or driven from their homes, and the old chief had only been rescued by his sons forcing him to a place of safety. The town seemed doomed to suffer, for within two months past it had again been burned, and, more recently still, about 500 of its inhabitants had died of an epidemic sickness."

Luang Prabang has been successively pillaged, razed and rebuilt over the years – the last invaders were the Chinese Ho (or Haw) in the mid-1880s. Virtually all traces of older structures have disappeared as they were built of wood and susceptible to fire and the vagaries of climate.

King Setthathirat moved the capital to Vieng Chan (Vientiane) in 1563 – now the political hub of modern Laos. Luang Prabang's importance diminished in the 18th century, following the death of King Souligna Vongsa and the break-up of Lane Xang, but it remained a royal centre until the Communist takeover in 1975. During the low point of Laos' fortunes in the mid-19th century when, following the defeat of King Anou at the hands of Rama III's forces, virtually all of Laos had become tributary to Bangkok, only Luang Prabang maintained a semblance of independence. The tiny kingdom, shorn of most of its hinterland, paid tribute to Bangkok (Siam), Hué (Vietnam) and Peking hoping to play one off against the next. This approach to foreign affairs neatly mirrors the country's strategy since 1975. What the king in Luang Prabang did not envisage, however, was the arrival of a power stronger than all three of these: the French.

The French and the British competed diligently for control of mainland Southeast Asia. France's piece of the cake became French Indochina and their attempt to wrest control of Laos from Siamese suzerainty was linked to the energy, perseverance and force of will of one man: Auguste Pavie. Contemporary accounts describe Pavie as 'thin and weak-looking' but this physical demeanor disguised a man of extraordinary abilities. He was appointed French vice-consul in Luang Prabang in May 1886 at which time he had already accumulated an impressive 17 years experience in Cambodia and Cochin China (south Vietnam). (Many colonial officials were dead before they had worked for 10 years, such were the demands of life in the East.) Pavie had, according to Martin Stuart-Fox in his *A history of Laos* (1997) not only acquired a comprehensive knowledge of the people, cultures and languages of the area, but also a deep dislike of the Siamese. His part in securing Laos for France was achieved when he rescued King Unkham from marauding Ho and Tai bandits in 1887. The protecting Siamese and their Lao soldiers had departed the city leaving Pavie with the opportunity to save the day. He plucked the aged king from a burning palace, escaped downstream and was rewarded when the king requested France's protection. With this began the dispossession of the Siamese by the French.

Luang Prabang was a religious as well as a trading centre. But it seems that to begin with Theravada Buddhism here creatively combined ritualistic elements from the Hinduist and animist past. Mendez Pinto in his account of 1578, describes Luang Prabang (or what historians take to be Luang

Mekong monsters, real and imagined ◀◀

It is said that the pla buk, the giant catfish of the Mekong, was only described by western science in 1930. That may be so, but the English explorer and surveyor, James McCarthy, goes into considerable detail about the fish in his book Surveying and exploring in Siam which was first published in 1900 and draws upon his travels in Siam and Laos between 1881 and 1893. He writes:

"The month of June in Luang Prabang is a very busy one for fishermen. Nearly all the boats are employed on fishing, each paying a large fish for the privilege. Two kinds of large fish, pla buk and pla rerm, are principally sought after. ... A pla buk that I helped to take weighed 130 pounds; it was seven feet long and four feet two inches round the body; the tail measured one foot nine inches. The fish had neither scales nor teeth, and was sold for 10 rupees. The roe of this fish is considered a great delicacy. The fish is taken in...June, July and August, when on its upward journey. Returning in November, it keeps low in the river, and a few stray ones only are caught."

McCarthy also recounts the story of a mythical river-serpent of the Mekong:

"It lives only at the rapids, and my informant said he had seen it. It is 53 ft long and 20 ins thick. When a man is drowned it snaps off the tuft of hair on the head [men wore their hair in this manner], extracts the teeth, and sucks the blood; and when a body is found thus disfigured, it is known that the man has fallen victim to the nguak, or river serpent, at Luang Prabang."

Prabang), having 24 religious sects and writes that there is "so great a variety and confusion of diabolical errors and precepts, principally in the blood sacrifices they employ, that it is frightful to hear them". The royal chronicles of the 16th century describe successive attempts to erase these sects from the kingdom.

Despite the demise of the monarchy (King Savang Vatthana and Crown Prince Vongsavang both died in re-education camps after the Pathet Lao came to power in 1975) and years of revolutionary rhetoric on the city tannoy, its dreamy streets have somehow retained the aura of old Lane Xang. In 1926 American Harry Franck found paradise in Luang Prabang when he wrote in his book *East of Siam* that "it is not a city at all, in the crowded, noisy, Western sense, but a leisurely congregation of dwellings of simple lines, each ... with sufficient ground so that its opinions or doings need not interfere with its neighbours. In short, Luang Prabang town is in many ways what idealists picture the cities of Utopia to be ...".

Today Luang Prabang is an easy-going provincial city. The great fear, of course, is that all this will change. In the early 1990s it was suggested that a highway be constructed from Vientiane, through Luang Prabang, to the Chinese border. This horrified many people who feared that Luang Prabang would become little more than a trucking stop between Thailand and China, inundated with singlet-wearing drivers and tourists. Fortunately, with UNESCO's designation of Luang Prabang as a World Heritage site the scope for redevelopment is, now, limited. The old town – essentially the promontory – is fully protected while elsewhere only limited redevelopment and expansion is permitted (no building, for example, can be higher than three storeys). Nonetheless, economists at the Asian Development Bank, with grand designs for the Greater Mekong Subregion as it is known, have their eyes on this quiet corner of the world.

Sights

The sights are conveniently close together in Luang Prabang. Most are walkable – the important ones can be covered leisurely within two days – but a bike is the best way to get around. When visiting the wats it is helpful to take a guide to obtain entry to all the buildings, which are often locked for security reasons. Without a guide, your best chance of finding them open is early in the morning.

Royal Palace
The palace itself is modest; its contents, spectacular

Also called the **National Museum**, the Royal Palace is right in the centre of the city on the main road, Phothisarath, which runs along the promontory. This allowed royal guests ready access from the Mekong. Unlike its former occupants, the palace survived the 1975 revolution and was converted into a museum the following year. It replaced a smaller wooden palace on the same site. The palace is not old: building started in 1904, during the reign of Sisavang Vong, and took 20 years. Although the bulk of the construction was completed by 1909, the two front wings were extended in the 1920s and

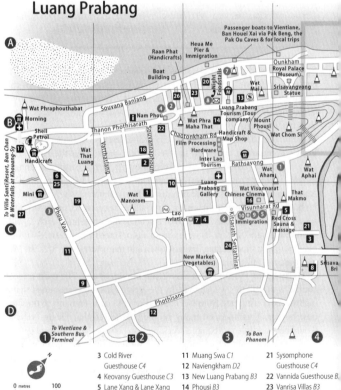

Luang Prabang

| Metres / Yards scale | 0 metres 100 / 0 yards 100 |

Detail map
A Luang Prabang detail, page 120

Sleeping		
1 Bane Lao C2	3 Cold River Guesthouse C4	11 Muang Swa C1
2 Boun Gning Guesthouse B2	4 Keovansy Guesthouse C3	12 Naviengkham D2
	5 Lane Xang & Lane Xang Travel C4	13 New Luang Prabang B3
	6 Le Parasol Blanc B1	14 Phousi B3
	7 Mano Guesthouse C3	15 Phou Vao D2
	8 Manilath Guesthouse C4	16 Rama C3
	9 Manoluck D1	17 Silivong Vanh B1
	10 Mouang Luang C2	18 Souvannaphoum B2
		19 Suankeo Guesthouse C1
		20 Suankeo II Guesthouse A3
		21 Sysomphone Guesthouse C4
		22 Vannida Guesthouse B.
		23 Vanrisa Villas B3
		24 Vieng Keo Guesthouse & Restaurant C3
		25 Villa Sin Xay Guesthouse & Restaurant C1

a new, more Lao, roof added at the same time. These later changes also saw the planting of the avenue of palms and the filling in of one of two fish ponds. As local residents saw the ponds as representing the 'eyes' of the capital, the blinding of one eye was taken as inviting bad fortune by leaving the city unprotected. The subsequent civil war was taken as a vindication of their fears. The palace is Khmer in style – cruciform in plan and mounted on a small platform of four tiers. It was built by the French for the Lao King, in an attempt to bind him and his family more tightly into the colonial system of government. The only indication of French involvement can be seen in the two French lilies represented in stucco on the entrance, beneath the symbols of Lao royalty. Indeed the palace, in many respects, is more foreign than Lao: it was designed by a French architect; built by masons from Vietnam; embellished by carpenters from Bangkok; and funded by the largesse of the colonial authorities.

The museum contains a collection of 15th/17th-century Buddha statues, including the famous Golden Buddha and artefacts from many of the wats in Luang Prabang such as the Khmer bronze drums from Wat Visoun.

On the right wing of the palace, as you face it, is the kings' private chapel, containing a copy of the **Pra Bang** – the Golden Buddha from which the city derived its name. The Buddha is in the attitude of Abhayamudra or 'dispelling fear' (see page 292). The original image is reportedly kept in a bank vault. It is 90% solid gold, stands 83 cm high and weighs around 50 kg. Reputed to have originally come from Ceylon (and said to date from any time between the first and ninth centuries), the statue was brought to Cambodia in the 11th century and was then taken to Lane Xang by King Fa Ngoum, who had spent some time in the courts of Angkor and married into Khmer royalty. An alternative story has the Pra Bang following Fa Ngoum to the city: it is said that he asked his father-in-law, the King of Angkor, to send a delegation of holy men to assist him in spreading the Theravada Buddhist faith in Lane Xang. The delegation arrived bringing with them the Pra Bang as a gift from the Cambodian King. The Pra Bang's arrival heralded the capital's change of name, from Xieng Thong to Nakhon Luang Prabang – 'The great city of the big Buddha'.

In 1563 King Setthathirat took the statue to Lane Xang's new capital at Vientiane. Two centuries later in 1779 the Thais captured it but it was

26 Viradesa & Wat That
   Guesthouses *B2*
27 Vongvichith
   Guesthouse *C1*

● Eating
1 Blue Room Café *B4*
2 Indochina Spirit *B2*
3 Malee Lao Food *C1*
4 Nam Phou *B2*
5 Nazim *C3*
6 Noodle Soup with
   Duck Shop *C3*
7 Pasaneyam Coffee
   Shop *A2*
8 Sakounna *B3*
9 Visoun *C3*
10 Yong Khoune *C3*

returned to Laos in 1839 and rediscovered in the palace chapel in 1975. The Pra Bang is revered in Laos as its arrival marked the beginnings of Buddhism in Lane Xang. The **Wat Ho Prabang** – whose untidy foundations are to the right of the entrance to the Royal Palace – was designed to house the statue but it was never completed (presently being restored). The intended building was designed by the Royal Secretary of the time, paid for by small donations sent in from across the country and begun in 1963. The chapel also contains four other Khmer Buddhas, ivories mounted in gold, bronze drums used in religious ceremonies and about 30 smaller Buddha images, surrounding the Pra Bang, which came from temples all over the city.

The main entrance hall of the palace was used for royal religious ceremonies, when the Supreme Patriarch of Lao Buddhism would oversee proceedings from his gold-painted lotus throne. The room to the immediate right of the entrance was the king's reception room, also called the Ambassadors' Room. It contains French-made busts of the last three monarchs, a model of the royal hearse (which is kept in Wat Xieng Thong) and a mural by French artist Alex de Fontereau, depicting a day in the life of Luang Prabang in the 1930s.

To the left of the entrance hall is the reception room of the king's secretary, and beyond it, the queen's reception room, which together house an eccentric miscellany of state gifts from just about every country except the UK. Of particular note are the moon rock presented to Laos by the US following the Apollo 11 and 17 lunar missions and a rifle inlaid with pearl – a present from Soviet premier Leonid Brezhnev in 1963. Also in this room are portraits of the last king, Sisavong Vattana, Queen Kham Phouy and Crown Prince Vongsavang, painted by a Soviet artist in 1967.

The coronation room, to the rear of the entrance hall, was decorated between 1960 and 1970 for Sisavong Vatthana's coronation, which was postponed because of the war. The walls are a brilliant red with Japanese glass mosaics embedded in a red lacquer base with gilded woodwork and depict scenes from Lao festivals. To one side of the carved howdah throne, with its gold three-headed elephant insignia, a huge candle, the same height as the

Luang Prabang detail

Sleeping
1 Lamach Guesthouse & Restaurant
2 L'Auberge Calao
3 Mme Chanthip Guesthouse
4 Pa Phai Guesthouse
5 Phounsab Guesthouse
6 Say Nam Khan Guesthouse
7 Sayo
8 Sikhanmuang
9 Villa Santi

Eating
1 Baan Khily Café & Paper Gallery
2 Bousavanh
3 Café des Artes
4 Chansamone
5 Duang Champa & Bar

king, stands guard; to the other, a tall pot to hold the crown. To the right of the throne, as you face it, are the ceremonial coronation swords and a glass case containing 15th- and 16th-century crystal and gold Buddhas, many from inside the 'melon stupa' of Wat Visoun. Because Luang Prabang was constantly raided, many of these religious artefacts were presented to the king for safekeeping long before the palace became a national museum.

In comparison, the royal family's private apartments behind are modestly decorated. They have been left virtually untouched since the day they left for exile in Xam Neua province. The king's library backs onto the coronation room: Savang Vatthana was a well-read monarch, having studied at the *Ecole de Science Politique* in Paris. Behind the library, built around a small inner courtyard are the queen's modest bedroom, the king's bedchamber and the royal yellow bathroom with its two regal porcelain thrones standing side by side. The remaining rooms include a small portrait gallery, the children's bedroom, dining room and a corridor containing the royal sedan chair which carried the king to religious ceremonies. Domestic rooms, offices and library are located on the ground floor beneath the state apartments.

Just to the left of the palace is the small and very modest Winter Palace. Visitors often wonder about the use and name of this building: it was built as a refuge to which women could retire in the days before and after childbirth. Finally, in the near, left hand corner (southern) of the compound, is the Luang Prabang Conference Hall. This was built for the coronation of Savang Vatthana, an event which never came to pass – the 1975 revolution interrupted preparations. Cultural events – dance, drama, puppet shows – are staged at the Royal Theatre, next to the museum (see Entertainment, page 140, for further details). ■ *Mon-Sun 0800-1100, 1330-1600. 10,000 kip. Shorts, short-sleeved shirts and strappy dresses are prohibited, as is photography.*

Further down Phothisarath, next to the Royal Palace, is Wat May (Wat Mai). **Wat May** This temple was officially called Wat Souvanna Phommaram and was the home of the Buddhist leader in Laos, Phra Sangkharath. The royal building, inaugurated in 1788, has a five-tiered roof and is one of the jewels of Luang Prabang. It took more than 70 years to complete. The façade is particularly interesting: a large golden bas-relief tells the story of Phravet (one of the last reincarnations of the Gautama or historic Buddha), with several village scenes including depictions of wild animals, women pounding rice and people at play. The interior is an exquisite amalgam of red and gold; the supporting pillars are similar to those in Wat Xieng Thong and Wat Visoun. The central beam at Wat May is carved with figures from Hindu mythology – the story of the birth of Ravanna and Hanuman. It was the home of the Pha Bang from 1894 until 1947. During *Pimay* (new year) the Pha Bang is taken from the Royal Palace and

Mekong

Boats to
Pak Ou

Wat
Xieng
Thong

Wat
Khi Li

Wat
Pak Khan

6 Khaem Khong
7 Khemkhane Food Garden
8 Le Potisan
9 Le Saladier
10 Luang Prabang Bakery
11 Olé Olé

12 Scandinavian Bakery & Planet Computers
13 View

● Bars
13 Mekong Star

The North

installed at Wat May for its annual ritual cleansing. It is returned to the Palace on the third day. ■ *2,000 kip.*

Mount Phousi

If you want to watch the sun go down, get to the top of Phousi early – but don't expect to be the only person there

Directly opposite the Royal Palace is the start of the steep climb up Phousi, a popular place to come to watch the sun set over the Mekong, illuminating the hills to the east. As you start the ascent, to the right is **Wat Pa Huak**, a disused wat suffering from years of neglect. It is usually locked but occasionally monks will open the building for a small donation. It is worth the trouble because the monastery has some fine 19th-century murals. From Wat Pa Huak, 328 steps wind up **Phousi**, a gigantic rock with sheer forested sides, surmounted by a 25 m-tall chedi. The summit affords a splendid panoramic view of Luang Prabang and the surrounding mountains. The Mekong lies to the north and west and the city to the southeast. Near the anti-aircraft gun, a sign used to warn visitors not to point their cameras towards the east; this was not for religious reasons, but because beyond the Nam Khan bridge lies Luang Prabang's secret weapon: the airport. Luang Prabang was probably sited at this point on the Mekong, in part at least, because of the presence of Phousi. Many capitals in the region are founded near sacred hills or mountains which could become local symbols of the Hindu Mount Mahameru or Mount Meru, the abode of the gods and also the abode of local tutelary spirits. ■ *Admission at western steps: 8,000 kip.*

Apart from being a magnificent spot from which to watch the sun go down, Phousi is culturally and symbolically very important. In the 18th century it was covered in monasteries and **Wat Chom Si**, built in 1804, still sits on the summit. Its shimmering gold-spired stupa rests on a rectangular base, ornamented by small metal Bodhi trees. Next to the stupa is a little sanctuary, from which a candle-lit procession descends at the Lao New Year festival, *Pimai*, accompanied by effigies of *Nang Sang Kham*, the guardian of the new year, and *Naga*, protector of the city. The drum, kept in the small *hor kong* on the east side of the hill, is used only on ceremonial occasions. The path going down from next to the ack-ack cannon leads to **Wat Tham Phousi**, which is more like a car port than a temple, but which is home to a rotund Buddha, *Kaccayana* (also called Phra Ka Tiay). At the top of the steps leading out of the wat stand a pair of tall cacti, planted defiantly in the empty shell casings of two large US bombs – the local monks' answer to decades of war.

Down a path to the north of Wat Tham Phousi is **Wat Siphouttabath**, just off the central road running along the promontory, which contains a 3 m-long footprint of the Buddha. Most of Luang Prabang's important wats are dotted along this main road, Phothisarath.

Wat Sene, further up the promontory, was built in 1718 and was the first sim in Luang Prabang to be constructed in Thai style, with a yellow and red roof, and lacks the subtlety of earlier Lao temples. Sen means 100,000 and the wat was built from a local donation of 100,000 kip. The donor is said to have discovered 'treasure' in the Khan River – quite what this was is unclear. The exterior may lack subtlety, but the interior is delicate and rather refined, painted red, with gold patterning on every conceivable surface. At the far end of the wat compound is a building containing a large, gold, albeit rather crudely modelled, image of the Buddha in the 'calling for rain' mudra (standing, arms held stiffly down). Note the torments of hell depicted on the façade of the building (top, left).

Further north on Xienthong Road is **Wat Xieng Thong Ratsavoraviharn**, usually known as just Wat Xieng Thong, set back from the road and at the top of a flight of steps leading down to the Mekong. The striking buildings in the tranquil compound are decorated in gold and post-box red, with imposing tiled roofs, intricate carvings, paintings and mosaics – making this the most important and finest royal wat in Luang Prabang. It was built by King Setthathirat in 1559, and is one of the few buildings to have survived the successive Chinese raids that marked the end of the 19th century. It retained its royal patronage until 1975 and has been embellished and well-cared for over the years – even the crown princess of Thailand, Mahachakri Sirindhorn, has donated funds for its upkeep. The sim is a perfect example of the Luang Prabang-style, with its low, sweeping roofs in complex overlapping sections. The eight central wooden pillars have stencilled motifs in gold and the façade is finely decorated. At the rear of the sim is a mosaic representation of the Thong copper tree in glass inlay. This traditional technique can also be seen on the 17th-century doors of Wat Ing Hang, near Savannakhet in south Laos. The interior of Wat Xieng Thong is decorated with rich frescoes and dharma wheels on the ceiling.

Wat Xieng Thong
This monastery was a key element in Luang Prabang's successful submission to UNESCO for recognition as a World Heritage site

Behind the sim are two red *hor song phra* (side chapels): the one on the left houses a rare Lao reclining Buddha in bronze, dating from the construction of the monastery, which was shown at the 1931 Paris Exhibition. The red exterior mosaics on the hor song phra, which relate local tales, were added in 1957 to honour the 2,500th aniversary of the Buddha's birth, death and enlightenment. The other *hor song phra* houses a standing image of the Buddha which is paraded through the streets of the city each pimai (new year) and doused in water. A small stone chapel with an ornate roof stands to the left of the sim.

The *hor latsalot* (chapel of the funeral chariot) is diagonally across from the sim. The grand 12 m-high gilded wooden hearse, with its seven-headed serpent was built for King Sisavang Vong, father of the last sovereign, and carried his urn to the stadium next to Wat That Luang (see below) where he was cremated in 1959. It was built on the chassis of a six-wheel truck by the sculptor, Thid Tun. The mosaics inside the chapel were never finished but the exterior is decorated with scenes from the Ramakien, sculpted in enormous panels of wood and covered with gold leaf. The *hor kong* at the back of the garden was constructed relatively recently in the 1960s and near it is the site of the copper tree after which Wat Xieng Thong took its name. ■ *5,000 kip.*

At the far northeast end of Phothisarath is **Wat Pak Khan**, which is not particularly noteworthy other than for its location overlooking the confluence of the two rivers. It is sometimes called the Dutch Pagoda as the sculptures on the south door are of figures dressed in 18th- and 19th-century Dutch costume.

This is better known as **Wat Vixoun** and is on the south side of Mount Phousi, next to the *Siensavan Cinema*, an eccentric-looking Chinese-built cinema, with painted nagas climbing around the pillars. Rumour has it that the Chinese owners have gloriously renovated the interior, but that they have not received permission to reopen as a cinema. Wat Visunnarat is a replica of the original wooden building constructed in 1513. Destroyed by marauding Chinese tribes, it was rebuilt in 1898, although it is still very medieval looking. The sim is virtually a museum of religious art, with the numerous Buddha statues it exhibits: most are more than 400 years old and have been donated over the years by locals. It also contains the largest Buddha in the city and old stelae engraved with Pali scriptures (called *hiu chaluk*). The big stupa, commonly known as **That Makmo** ('melon stupa'), was built by Queen

Wat Visunnarat

The North

Visounalat in 1504. It is of Sinhalese influence with a smaller stupa at each corner, representing the four elements. The arch on the northwest side of the sim is original, the only piece remaining of the 16th-century building. ■ *5,000 kip.*

Wat Aham, next door, was built by a relative of the king in 1823. The interior has rather beautiful pillars and roof and overbearing modern murals of the torments of hell, as well as a panoramic view of Luang Prabang. The two huge Bodhi trees outside are important spirit shrines.

Wat Phra Maha That Close to the *Hotel Phousi* on Phothisarath, is this typical Luang Prabang wat, built in the 1500s and restored at the beginning of the 20th century. The ornamentation of the doors and windows of the sim merit attention with their graceful, golden figures from the *Phra lak phra lam* (the *Ramayana*). The pillars, ornamented with nagas, are also in traditional Luang Prabang style. The front of the sim was renovated in 1991.

Wat Phra Bath Behind the market at the far northwest end of Phothisarath is Wat Phra Bath (or Phraphoutthabat Tha Phralak). The original wooden temple on this site dated back to the 17th century, but most of the present structure was built in 1959 by the local Chinese and Vietnamese community. It is worth a visit for its picturesque position above the Mekong. It is renowned for its huge Buddha footprint – '*bath*' is the Pali word for footprint.

Wat That Luang Close by, behind the stadium, is **Wat That Luang**. A royal wat, built in 1818 by King Manthaturat, it contains the ashes of the members of the royal family. Note the bars on the windows of the sim in wood and gold leaf, typical of Luang Prabang. The gold stupa at one end of the compound is the mausoleum of King Sisavang Vong, the last king. He is remembered fondly in Luang Prabang and many offerings are left at his stupa. The stone stupa contains relics of the Buddha and is the site of the Vien Thiene (candlelit) festival in May. There are also some traditional style *kuti*, or monks quarters, with carved windows and low roofs. When James McCarthy visited Wat Luang at the end of the 19th century, he was told of the ceremonies that were performed here on the accession of a new 'chief'. In his book *Surveying and exploring in Siam* (1900) he writes that the "... Kamus assembled and took the oath of allegiance, swearing to die before their chief; shot arrows over the throne to show how they would fight any of its enemies, and holding a lighted candle, prayed that their bodies might be run through with hot iron and that the sky might fall and crush them if they proved unfaithful to their oaths."

Wat Manorom South of Wat That Luang (between Phou Vao and Kisarath Settathirat) is Wat Manorom. It was built by the nobles of Luang Prabang to entomb the ashes of King Samsenthai (1373-1416) and is notable for its large armless bronze Buddha statue, one of the oldest Laotian images of the Buddha, which dates back to 1372 and weighs two tonnes. Locals maintain that the arm was removed during a skirmish between Siamese and French forces during the latter part of the 19th century. The monastery has an attractive weathered look and the usual carved doors and painted ceilings. While it is not artistically significant, the temple – or at least the site – is thought to be the oldest in the city, dating back, so it is said, to the reign of Fa Ngoum.

Wat Phra Phone Phao This wat, the Monastery of Phao Tree Forest Hill, is 3 km out of town to the east, near Ban Phanom. Looking as though it is made of pure gold from a distance, this wat is rather disappointing close up. The small huts to the right of the entrance are meditation cells or kutis. The wat's construction, funded by donations from Lao living abroad and overseas Buddhist federations, was started in 1959. But the building, modelled on the octagonal Shwedagon Pagoda in Yangon (Rangoon), was only completed in 1988. The names of donors are inscribed on pillars inside. The inner walls are festooned with gaily painted gory frescoes of macabre allegories by a local equivalent of Hieronymus Bosch. Lurid illustrations depict the fate awaiting murderers, adulterers, thieves, drunks and liars who break the five golden rules of the Buddhism. The less grotesque paintings document the life of the Buddha and these extend right up to the fifth floor. On the second level, it is possible to duck through a tiny opening to admire the Blue Indra statues and the view of Luang Prabang. ■ *Mon-Sun 0800-1000, 1300-1630.*

A guide to Luang Prabang's secular buildings

Traditional Lao The traditional Lao house is rectangular, supported on timber stilts, with a two-sided steep roof and built of bamboo, wood or daub. The stilts help to protect the occupants against wild animals at night and also help to keep the living area dry, especially during the rainy season. The underside also provides a shaded spot for working during the day, as well as area for storage. Living above ground is said to be a characteristic of the Lao and a 16th-century Lao text, the *Nithan Khun Borom*, records that the Lao and Vietnamese Kingdoms of Lane Xang and Dai Viet agreed to demarcate their respective zones of influence according to house style: people living in houses raised on stilts would owe allegiance to Lane Xang, those living on the ground, to Dai Viet.

The traditional Lao house is divided into three principal sections, recognizable from the exterior: the sleeping room, the veranda, and the kitchen. Under the main roof is the sleeping area and the very characteristic veranda is contiguous to it. The kitchen is linked to the main building by an open deck commonly used for bathing and washing. Roof, gables, rafters and balustrade are ornamented with lots of *savoir-faire*. The building process of traditional Lao houses was governed by strict rules: its orientation, the date when building could commence, the setting of the wooden piles, and so on, had to conform to spiritual guidelines.

French colonial The French introduced new technologies and materials into house construction, in particular the fired brick and the ceramic roof tile. Traditionally, these materials were reserved for wat construction – explaining why almost all buildings of pre-colonial vintage in Laos today are religious. The main characteristics of French colonial architecture are: extensive roof area to protect against sun and rain; large window openings, paned and shuttered; verandas; arcades; a monumental entrance; a fireplace and chimney breast; brick and wooden decorative details expressing different construction systems (for instance, columns, capitals, rafters and lintels) and ceramic roof tiles.

Lao-French colonial As French influence grew, so Lao builders began to incorporate some aspects of French design into their constructions. For example, some houses which in all other respects conform to the traditional Lao house style, have French openings and a grandiose doorway leading to a flight of impressive stairs.

French colonial-Lao In the same way as Lao builders adopted some French elements, so French architects and builders embraced Lao stylistic features. This is most evident in the use of temple-style ornamentation, on the roof for example.

International-modern Many houses are now built of concrete and the bungalow has become common. In many cases, traditional Lao architectural motifs and designs are merely made from concrete rather than the traditional wood. But concrete has also allowed some innovations in design: cantilevers, flat roofing, pre-fabricated elements and geometric ornamentation are all linked in part to the change in building medium from wood and bamboo, to concrete. 'International modern' includes both domestic buildings and compartments (shophouses).

Lao contemporary Lao contemporary houses tend to fall into two categories. Either they are respectful of traditional Lao style; or they embrace modern design and construction materials wholesale. Houses in the first category can be seen to be part of an evolution of the traditional Lao house: the main entrance has shifted to the gable side, the veranda is smaller, while the open area between the piles below the main house is enclosed with brick or concrete walls and has physically become part of the house. Wood is still used for exterior facing for the first floor, but the walls of the ground level floor are made from stone and bricks. This is the most common form of house built today.

The second category of Lao contemporary house is built entirely of brick and concrete and most Lao consider it to be more luxurious.

The North

Luang Prabang walking tour

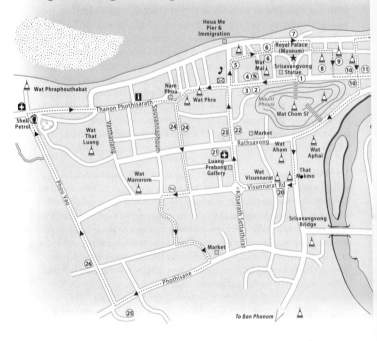

1 Start of tour	8 Wat Xieng Muang	15 Wat Xieng Thong
2 Traditional Lao house	9 Traditional Lao house	16 Bamboo house
3 Gendarmerie	10 Compartment buildings	17 Auberge Calao
4 Lao Bank	11 Princess Guesthouse	18 Lao houses with French
5 Lao-French colonial house	12 French colonial school	colonial influence
6 Lao-French colonial house	13 Villa Santi	19 School of Fine Arts
7 Royal Taxes office	14 Diethelm Travel Agent	20 Red Cross office

0 metres   60
0 yards   60

A walking tour of Luang Prabang's architectural heritage

This is a suggested walking tour of Luang Prabang's architectural highlights. To begin with it may be worth climbing Phousi or taking a stroll along the Mekong and Nam Khan river roads to get a better idea of the layout of the town. With a town as small as Luang Prabang it is easy enough just to set out and find your own route, following whatever appeals. The map marks some of the more significant buildings – other than the usual monasteries – and can be used to help explore the city. However, we have also provided a two-stage foot/bicycle tour. The first stage, which can be walked, concentrates on the peninsula and the streets that form the original core of the city. The second part of the tour is best undertaken by bicycle and covers the outer streets.

The **start of the tour** (1) is on Thanon Phothisarath in front of the Royal Palace. Historically, the area to the west of the palace was considered the noble quarter of town, the east was inhabited by the middle classes, while the working class lived around the foot of Phousi.

Walking tour: the peninsula
See related map on page 126

The North

Walking from the Royal Palace along Phothisarath southwest towards the Post Office, the first building that deserves special note is the **traditional Lao house** (2) in front of Wat Mai.

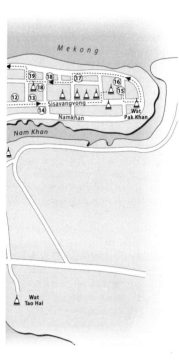

This is a construction on stilts with a closed veranda. Continuing along Phothisarath, on your left, is the **Gendarmarie** (3), a French colonial building constructed of bricks with gables on the façade. On the other side of the road is the **Lao Bank** (4), another example of a French colonial building.

Turn right onto Kitsarath Setthathirat Road and walk down towards the Mekong. Past the post office, on the right, is a Lao house showing French colonial influences – our **Lao-French colonial** (5) classification. Take the first road on your right to see more examples of traditional Lao houses. In some cases the formerly open ground level area has been enclosed to increase the habitable space, using a variety of different materials – bricks, wood and bamboo, for example. (This is also very common in Thailand. Traditionally the under-house area was used for weaving and lounging during the hottest hours of the day. At night, animals were corralled under the house. Fires were also lit here at night at the coldest times of year.) At the very end of this street, just beside the Royal Palace, are two opulent

21 French colonial hospital
22 Lao-international style market
23 International modern compartment buildings
24 Lao-French colonial buildings
25 Phou Vao Hotel
26 Lao contemporary buildings

Lao-French colonial style houses (**6**). Turn left to reach the Mekong River road and then right to walk along the river bank. The **Royal Taxes office** (**7**) lies behind the Royal Palace. To see some truly beautiful examples of traditional architecture, enter **Wat Xieng Muang** (**8**) and take the exit into the alley behind the temple. Opposite the wat is a **traditional Lao house** (**9**).

Continue back up to Phothisarath, turn left and take a look at the **compartment buildings** (**10**) on both sides of the street. These skillfully combine commercial and residential functions under the same roof, much like the Chinese 'shophouse' found throughout Southeast Asia. The ground floor is usually a business, often a shop or trading outlet, but sometimes a seamstress or even a mechanical workshop. Here the 'compartments' are built in a variety of styles, but mainly French colonial and Lao-French colonial. The Lao traditionally never lived and worked in the same building; they always ran their businesses from some other location, even if it was a street-side stall just a few yards away from their home. It is therefore safe to assume that these compartments were used by Chinese and Vietnamese immigrants.

Walking on towards the tip of the peninsula, there are several other notable buildings including the **Princess Guesthouse** (**11**), the **French colonial school** (**12**) on the left hand side of the road, the **Villa Santi** hotel (**13**) also on the left and the **Diethelm agency office** (**14**) on the right. At **Wat Xieng Thong** (**15**) take the exit from the monastery on the east side to look at the very modest **bamboo house** (**16**) down the alley.

At the tip of the peninsula, turn back along the Mekong river road. On the left is the **Auberge Calao** (**17**), an example of a renovated colonial building and the only Portuguese building on the peninsula. Immediately after the auberge, take the first road on your left and then turn right. Along this road, at the first intersection, are two very fine **Lao houses with French colonial influences** (**18**). Past the intersection further along the same street, the **School of Fine Arts** (**19**), a Lao traditional style building with two adjoining roofs is one of the few structures in Luang Prabang showing this architectural design. Turn right to return to the Mekong river road along which are a number of buildings showing various degrees of international influence.

Walk across the peninsula to the Nam Khan river road and then follow the road around Phousi. Along the road are a number of examples of Lao traditional and Lao-French colonial buildings. Turn right on to Visunnarat Road and facing Wat Visunnarat, the **Lao Red Cross Office** (**20**) is worthy of note.

Turn right on to Kitsarath Setthathirat and walk back towards the market and the centre of town. Along this street is the **French colonial hospital** (**21**), the **Lao international style market** (**22**), and the **international modern compartment buildings** (**23**) facing the market. At the post office intersection, turn left onto Phothisarath and follow the road until it reaches the *L'Hotel Souvannaphoum* on the left. The next street on the left has a number of **Lao-French colonial buildings** (**24**), showing French influences on Lao architecture.

Bicycle tour: the outer city
See Local transport, page 143, for further details on bicycling and bicycle hire

From here, the route is best completed by bicycle. These outer streets, away from the original core of the city, have a number of recently constructed hotels and large villas. The buildings, though perhaps not beautiful to the western eye, illustrate the way in which Lao architecture is using modern materials and incorporating modern design elements and architectural motifs.

Bicycle southwest out of town along Phothisane Road to the intersection with Phou Vao Road. Set on the top of the small hill here is one of Luang

Prabang's most modern buildings, the **Phou Vao Hotel (25)**. Turn right on to Phou Vao Road and bicycle towards the river. Along here are a number of **Lao contemporary buildings (26)** as well as the French colonial slaughterhouse. Return to town along Phothisarath Road.

Excursions

Many hotels and restaurants organize tours to the surrounding area. Visitors may find this much simpler with a tour operator, as roads remain unmarked and Lao people outside Luang Prabang are not used to tourists and few speak English or French.

The right bank of the Mekong

The **monasteries and villages on the right bank** (West) of the Mekong are accessible by boat from the landing areas downstream from the Royal Palace. For anyone who does not fancy spending three hours on a boat travelling to and from the Pak Ou caves, this makes for an enchanting half-day excursion. ■ *Ferry service to the other side of the river drops you near Wat Chom Phet. Do remember to fix a return time with the ferryman. 30,000 kip return.*

The first stop is usually Wat Long Khoun at the top of a flight of steps leading up from the river bank almost opposite Wat Xieng Thong. This wat was built in two stages and was renovated by the École Française de l'Extrême Orient in January 1994 at a cost of 400,000 FF. The oldest section is at the back and dates from the 18th century. The beautifully sculpted door was made in 1937. The *sim* on the river side of the compound is a delightful building. Small, well-proportioned and intimate, it has some vibrant murals. On the exterior, either side of the main doorway, are two bearded warriors, swords slung over their backs. They would seem to be representations of Chinese soldiers (Ho or Haw). The kings of Lane Xang are said to have come on three-day retreats to this spot, to prepare for their coronation. ■ *4,000 kip.* **Wat Long Khoun**

Wat Tham, literally 'cave monastery', is 100 m or so upstream from Wat Long Khoun, above a dilapidated *sala*. A well-trodden path leads there. The wat is a limestone cave temple with stairs and balustrades cut out of the stone. The interior is very dark but is worth exploring, as it is stacked with ancient, rotting Buddha images. A resident monk, with the aid of dim torches, will lead visitors down into the airless cavern pointing out rock formations and Buddha **Wat Tham**

The North

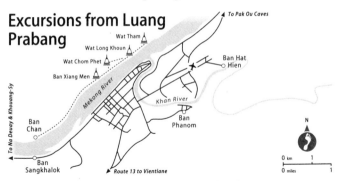

Excursions from Luang Prabang

To Pak Ou Caves
Wat Tham
Wat Long Khoun
Wat Chom Phet
Ban Xiang Men
Ban Hat Hien
Mekong River
Khan River
Ban Phanom
To Na Deuay & Khouang-Sy
Ban Chan
Ban Sangkhalok
Route 13 to Vientiane

N

0 km   1
0 miles   1

images. Fearful that the torches may not be powered by long life batteries, visitors may emerge into the light with a degree of relief. Not for the claustrophobic. ■ *4,000 kip.*

Wat Chom Phet & Wat Xiang Men Leading from Wat Long Khoun downstream is another well trodden track. A plaque incongruously announces that the route was repaired with a contribution from Condé Nast publications. Before reaching the small community of Ban Xiang Men a stairway leads up to Wat Chom Phet, a hilltop *sim* offering fine views over the Mekong and Luang Prabang. The site has been apparently abandoned as a religious site although the mouldering *sim* and kiltering chedis give the place a rather attractive 'lost wat in the forest' feel. This place, like elsewhere hereabouts, also has a profusion of apricot-coloured lilies. Walking on downstream, the track passes through **Ban Xiang Men**, a peaceful village where households cultivate the exposed river banks during the dry season, taking advantage of the annual deposition of silt. Wat Xiang Men dates from the last century and stands at the foot of a bamboo-clad slope near the centre of the village. ■ *4,000 kip.*

About 1 km downstream, in a clearing in the middle of the forest, is the **royal cemetery**. There are sculptures depicting members of the royal family who could not be cremated for religious reasons, such as children who died as infants and victims of contagious diseases. It is hard to find a local guide willing to take you there as most are terrified of ghosts.

Also on the right bank are two hills – **Phou Thao** and **Phou Nang**, named after Luang Prabang's very own Romeo and Juliet (everyone has one). Thao Phouthasene and Nang Kang Hi were two lovers who died in tragic but romantic circumstances only to find themselves transformed into rock and incorporated in the local landscape. The hills are said to look like a man and woman sleeping next to each other.

Ban Chan Ban Chan is a few kilometres downstream from Luang Prabang (about 15 minutes by boat) or 4 km on the road beyond the evening market to Ban Sangkhalok and a short crossing by boat (villagers will paddle you across). The village is known for its local pottery industry and mostly produces *thongs* (large water storage jars) and salt pots. ■ *Getting there: boats regularly cross the river – although the fare varies depending on the number of passengers. Alternatively charter a boat for a couple of hours (about 60,000 kip).* It is possible to cross over to Wat Long Khoun, walk downstream and catch another boat back to the Luang Prabang bank of the river either at Ban Xiang Men or Ban Chan. Or the circuit can be completed in the reverse direction. There are a couple of food stalls in Ban Xiang Men.

The Nam Khan and east of town

Ban Phanom Ban Phanom, or Tit Cliff Village, is 3 km east of Luang Prabang. This is a 300-year-old weaving village where shawls (*pha biang*) and sarongs (*pha sin*) are made from silk and cotton. The 100-odd families in Ban Phanom are members of the Lu minority who originated from Yunnan in Southern China. They were traditionally the king's weavers, soldiers and palace servants. Because they have integrated with modern Lao society, they do not take kindly to being referred to as tribals. Although best known for its weaving, the village's main economic activity is rice cultivation. A few years ago cloth was sold from a street market in the middle of the village but this now only operates at weekends. However some of the larger producers have turned their houses into small shops and it is possible to buy lengths of cloth at any times.

Henri Mouhot's tomb lies about 2 km beyond Ban Phanom, at the top of a bank looking down into the Nam Khan, a tributary of the Mekong. The French explorer Henri Mouhot stumbled across Angkor Wat in 1860 but succumbed to a malarial attack in Luang Prabang on 10 November the following year. Resident foreign aid workers spent months searching for the grave before rediscovering it in 1990. The tomb was not constructed until six years after his death, in 1867, and was designed by another French explorer, Doudart de Lagrée. In 1990 the town of Mouhot's birth, Montbéliard, donated a plaque inscribed, simply, 'Proud of Our Son'. The French government has granted an allowance for its upkeep. ■ *Getting there: by saamlor (20,000 kip) to Ban Phanom and a bit beyond or by bicycle or by boat (45,000 kip). Ask villagers in Ban Phanom for directions; small boys will sometimes show visitors the way.*

Ban Hat Hien

This village is on the airport road; fork right before the terminal and at the end of the road is Luang Prabang's knife-making village. Residents beat scrap metal over hot stoves to make blades and tools. The flames are fanned by bellows, originally made from teak tubes and operated with plungers – but several craftsmen use old 155-mm Howitzer propellants and say their "little presents from the US come in very handy". One shed is stacked with hundreds of old car batteries from which the lead is extracted and poured into moulds for ball bearings and gunshot. The results of their labours can be seen in the markets in town. From the nearby Nam Khan, villagers harvest 'seaweed' – which is dried, fried and eaten with sesame. *Khai pehn* from Luang Prabang is sold all over the country. ■ *Getting there: saamlor (15,000 kip).*

Upstream on the Mekong

Pak Ou Caves
Colour map 1, grid C3

The Pak Ou Caves are perhaps the most popular excursion from Luang Prabang and are 25 km upstream from the city. There are two series of caves set in the side of a limestone cliff opposite the mouth of the Mekong's Nam Ou tributary (Pak Ou means 'Mouth of the Ou'). The lower caves are named Tham Thing and the upper, Tham Phum. Both the caves and the many Buddhas within have been renovated with Australian funds. The lower cave is really a deep overhang, while the upper cave, a hundred or so steps up, is more of a cave, with a corpulent, rather unattractive image at the entrance. Torches are available, but candles make it possible to see reasonably well after your eyes have become accustomed to the dark. The two sacred caves, supposedly discovered by King Setthathirat in the 16th century, are studded with thousands – the official figure is 4,000: 2,500 in the lower cave and 1,500 in the upper – of wood and gold Buddha images; some are thought to be more than 300 years old. It is likely, though, that these caverns were associated with spirit (*phi*) worship before the arrival of Buddhism in Laos. Many of the images are in the distinctive attitude of the Buddha calling for rain (with arms held by the side, palms turned inwards). For years the caves, which locals still believe to be the home of guardian spirits, were inhabited by monks. The king visited them every New Year and stayed at Ban Pak Ou on the opposite bank of the Mekong, where there is a royal wat with beautiful old murals on the front gable. The famous French traveller Francois Garnier visited the caves on his travels in the 1860s. The caves are one of the main venues for Pimay in April, when hundreds make the pilgrimage upriver from Luang Prabang. During the dry season the river shrinks, exposing huge sandbanks, which are improbable gold fields. Families camp out on the banks of the Mekong and pan for gold, most of which is sold to Thailand. Boats will stop at Ban Pak Ou, across the water from the caves, where enterprising villages have set up thatched stalls serving sticky rice, barbecued mekong fish and somtam, plus cold drinks and snacks. **NB** Although resthouses, tables and a basic toilet have been built below the upper cave, there is no restaurant and no drinks stall at the caves themselves. ■ *8,000 kip, free for children. Getting there: charter a boat from Tha Heua Me or at one of the stairways down to the river along Manthatourath where boatmen wait for business. The going rate for the journey – about 2 hrs upstream and 1 hr down with stops* en route *– is US$10-20. Boats vary in size, but the larger ones can take up to 8 people. Note that many restaurants, hotels, guesthouses and tour companies will arrange this trip and it is probably better to do it this way. Tuk-tuks cost about US$20 too.*

Lao for 'cheers':
seung dium

Xang Hai is 20 km upstream from Luang Prabang, on the way to Pak Ou caves and a popular stop-off. The name of this village translates as 'making wine pots' and on the beach villagers *brew lau-lao*, a moonshine whisky. In the rainy season they grow glutinous or 'sticky' rice and in the dry season they ferment it in water and yeast. The distilled 'wine' is sold illegally in Luang Prabang. The village has now become rather touristy with scores of stalls selling textiles, ceramics, souvenirs from Thailand, opium pipes and weights, ethnic clothes – and some *lao-lao* too. But it remains a friendly place and villagers are delighted to give visitors a tasting session. ■ *Getting there: see Pak Ou Caves (above). Accommodation: if you want to stay longer, villagers will put visitors up for the night.*

Downstream on the Mekong

Waterfalls at
Khouang-Sy
Wildly romantic and
highly recommended

These waterfalls are 30 km south of Luang Prabang on a tributary of the Mekong. The falls, though not high, are enormously beautiful at all times of year. In the summer, the water cascades so gently over the various tiers of the falls that it's possible to scramble behind the curtains of water without getting wet. In the rainy season, the water roaring down the mountain catch at the imagination, and could form the backdrop for any Indiana Jones or James Bond adventure. Best of all, and despite appearances, it's still possible to take that left-hand path halfway up the falls and strike out through the pouring torrents to make for the heart of the waterfall. To do so involves climbing through hammering water and dripping caves before making for the main sheet of water itself, and climbing up as it pounds on your shoulders and back. The coating of deposits and the lush vegetation makes the falls appear almost organic from a distance. The UNDP has cleared a path to the falls which then winds on right up to the top, and there are a large number of vendors selling snacks and drinks and some souvenirs – the local village's economy seems to increasingly depend on tourist business. The pools above the falls are sheltered and comparatively private and make a wonderful spot for a swim (it is no longer permitted to swim in the lower pools). ■ *8,000 kip. Getting there: travel agents run tours here, US$50 (including lunch). Alternatively, charter a tuk-tuk, about 100,000 kip (US$10) there and back, though make sure you agree on a time with the tuk-tuk driver to return while you are still in Luang Prabang or he is likely to invent a 'meeting' he needs to hurry back for once you arrive at the waterfalls! Buses do run to Khouang Sy from the bus terminal by the stadium, but the journey takes up to 2 hrs. An alternative to taking a tuk-tuk is to travel by boat and tuk-tuk. Slow boats take 1 hr down and 2 hrs back up river, stopping at Ban Muang Khai (a pretty little village), where it is necessary to take a tuk-tuk the last*

6 km or so to the falls (about US$20). A third possibility is to take a speedboat there and back. The problem is that they are not permitted to leave from Luang Prabang itself, so pick one up downstream at Tha Leua Sing Kaeo (about 3 km downstream) – they can be arranged at Ban Don, a few kilometres upstream. This may all sound rather convoluted, but a journey by speedboat is an exhilarating experience (crash helmets compulsory)!

Further afield

These villages are within a shortish motorcycle ride (but see Local transport, page 143) of Luang Prabang. **Ban Longlan** is east of town. To get there, take the main road upstream. At Ban Pak Xuang, just before the bridge over the river Xuang (Pak Xuang means 'Mouth of the Xuang'), turn right to follow this tributary of the Mekong. Just before reaching Ban Kokvan turn right onto a track. This leads to Ban Natan. From here an even smaller track leads off to the left. It follows the Houai Hia, a small stream, between two mountains and works its way upwards to the mountain village of Ban Longlan. Allow two hours to get there. Few tourists visit this village so dress modestly and be especially sensitive.

Hmong villages

Another Hmong village downstream from Luang Prabang is **Ban Long Lao**. Take the road southwest from town and after about 8 km turn left (after Ban Lekpet and before Ban Naxao). At the radio transmitter carry straight ahead rather than turning right – which leads to a waterfall. The road climbs steeply, passing a small dam and ends at the village of Long Lao. Again this is a village visited rarely by tourists.

Essentials

Sleeping

The accommodation listed below is divided into three sections. The peninsula and town centre includes the old part of town – the peninsula, designated as a World Heritage Site by UNESCO – as well as the commercial heart of Luang Prabang around the post office as far downstream as *L'Hôtel Souvannaphoum*. South of the town centre includes all hotels and guesthouses outside this core area but still within the city boundaries. Note, though, that even hotels right at the edge of this area, such as the *Phou Vao*, are only a 15-20 min walk from the main concentration of bars and restaurants. Finally there is just one hotel in our Out of town category where transport is required.

■ *on maps, pages 118 and 120 Price codes: see inside front cover Road names are not widely used, and there seems to be some confusion over precisely what some of the roads are called*

The restored colonial villas on the peninsula and the *Phou Vao* tend to get booked up, particularly during national holidays – during Songkran hotels and guesthouses can almost charge what they like. In view of demand, if you are thinking of plumping for the upper range it is advisable to arrange accommodation in advance. There are plenty more hurriedly constructed budget guesthouses springing up than those listed below, particularly in the narrow streets between the post office and the river and now also inland from Phothisarath. Slightly more upmarket guesthouses are also multiplying. Many new establishments can be found on the tip of the peninsula heading towards Wat Xieng Thong and in the quiet streets around Phou Vao.

AL *L'Hôtel Souvannaphoum*, Phothisarath, T212200, F212577, sunaphum@ laotel.com VISA cards and TCs accepted, a/c, restaurant (see Eating below), hot water. The hotel consists of 2 restored villas, owned by *Inter-Lao Tourism*, full of interesting *objets d'art*, set in an attractive, large garden. *La Residence* (or *tuk mai* to the

Peninsula & town centre

staff), has 20 twin rooms in French colonial style with balconies, cool wooden floors, marble bathrooms and attractive (if sometimes glaringly white) décor. *La Villa* (more expensive) has 2 exceptionally stylish, very large rooms but the other rooms in this part of the hotel, though serviceable, are not so attractive. **AL** *Villa Santi Hotel*, Sisavangvong, T252158, F252157, www.villasantihotel.com A/c, restaurant (see below), free pick-up from airport if you call in advance. This is a restored early-20th-century private house of Princess Khampha and because it was built as a house, each room is a different size. There are 11 rooms in the old building and 14 rooms in a second stylishly-built 'annexe'. The newer rooms have baths and showers, the older rooms are more traditional. A charming place, full of character, efficiently run, attractive seating areas in the garden, lobby or on the balcony. The daughter of the official Royal Cook rustles up mouthwatering French cuisine in the Princess Restaurant. Guests will also be able to exploit the facilities of its sister establishment, the *Villa Santi Resort* (see Out of town, below).

A *L'Auberge Calao*, river road, T212100, F212100. A/c, restaurant (see below), 5 twin rooms in this beautifully restored 1902 building, with an incomparable position overlooking the Mekong. Four rooms are on the 1st floor with verandas above the river. Clean, relaxed and well run, although the original management have moved on. **A** *Phousi*, Kitsarath Setthathirat, T212717/8, F212719. A/c, restaurant, credit cards accepted. This hotel was upgraded and expanded in the mid-1990s. Twin rooms with wooden floors and decent shower rooms, satellite TV, extensive garden with seating area, traditional music on the garden terrace in the evenings, good central location. **A-B** *Say Nam Khan*, overlooking the river near Wat Sene, T/F212976. Attractive renovated building with a homely feel created by its friendly owners, white paint and wooden furnishings, 14 clean a/c rooms, although the inner ones are quite dark. Private bathrooms and hot water. Sitting on the terrace overlooking the Nam Kham drums home what a lovely setting it is.

B *New Luang Prabang Hotel*, Sisavangvong, T212264, F212804. Four floors and 15 rooms in a rather ugly building (even if you close your eyes to the rather grotty red carpet on the 1st floor), walls decorated with the odd piece of local tapestry. A/c rooms quite pricey for what they are, but the real selling point is the bar-terrace on the roof (although it seems to be a well kept secret which has yet to be 'found' by tourists). Free pick-up to and from the airport. **B** *Sayo Guesthouse*, Sotikoumman Rd, T252614. Seriously lovely: when Villa Santi is full they point all their disappointed guests in this direction, and it's not hard to see why. Beautifully and tastefully decorated with local fabrics and woodwork, polished wooden floors and furniture, and boasting a fantastic view over Wat Xieng Muang, you can watch the monks go about their work, carving and painting and woodwork. 10 rooms altogether, the newer annexe is well suited to families with children older than toddlers, as a flight of stairs in each room leads up to another half level for the children's beds. Highly recommended.

D *Phounsab Guesthouse*, 6/7 Sisavangvong Rd, T212975. 11 rather shabby rooms in this town guesthouse, all with a/c. The friendly owner has adequate English, breakfast provided, bikes for hire, tuk-tuk and boat tour service, and good place to meet other travellers. **D** *Madame Chanthip Guesthouse*, 97/5 Ban Wat Nong, T252079. Good vegetarian restaurant attached (serving some meat!) and great iced fruit drinks. **D-E** *Chaluensouk*, Chaotonkham Rd. Basic rooms, very clean, all with hot water ensuites. Free bottle of drinking water given daily, double rooms only, some with a/c. **D-E** *Kounsavan*, Chaotonkham Rd, T212297. Green is the colour at this beautifully situated guesthouse. Easy to miss because it's half way down a sleepy looking street, it's definitely worth stumbling upon this oasis of tranquillity. Green grass garden, flowers, balconies, hot water showers, some rooms with ensuites, this place is enormously friendly, and within easy striking distance of the town centre. Recommended.

E *Sikhanmuang*, Manthatourath Rd. A great option if you get one of the better rooms with a terrace. 1st floor rooms can smell, and on the second floor, you have to share bathrooms, but they're good, clean, simple rooms with wooden floors, presided over by friendly owners with broken English. **E** *Lamach*, Sisavangvong, T252079. A 2-storey building with double and twin rooms. Simple but clean with fan, shared toilet and hot shower. The café serves vegetarian food in the garden outside. A very friendly woman who speaks excellent English and French helps run the place. **E** *Suankeo II*, just behind the post office. This is one of the best of the budget choices. Recommended. **E** *Vanrisa Villas*, just around the corner from *Viradesa*, T/F212925. A little gem, with teak floors, large, characterful and immaculate rooms and friendly owners. The downstairs houses beautiful handicrafts and antiques. Recommended. **E** *Viradesa*, T252268. This venture has expanded into 2 hostels on the same street diagonally opposite each other off the river road and both called *Viradesa*. This one is run by an Irishman and his Lao wife, who are a good source of local knowledge for information-hungry travellers. Some rooms have their own good-sized hot water bathrooms (some over-the-top touches), others have shared facilities, all with portable fans. This previously sleepy street is becoming increasingly popular with tourists, and has even been (somewhat ambitiously!) referred to as the Khao San Rd of Laos. Good value. Dorm rates (10,000 kip) available in mammoth 12-bed dorms in the basement. A film is shown every evening at the bar, and is a popular crowd puller. **E** *Wat That Guesthouse*, 2/27 Ban Wat That, T212913. Next door neighbour and arch rival of *Viradesa Guesthouse*, this is also a nice place. No ensuite facilities, all the showers and toilets are located at the back. Very clean rooms, boasting some idiosyncratic home-made bedside lamps. The one 3-bed dorm gives the impression of sleeping in a tree house – very Robinson Crusoe! Owners speak good English and can offer advice on what to see and do.

E-F *Phonethavy*, Chaotonkham Rd. A pleasant option, whose friendly proprietess speaks extremely good English. Very clean with cool, tiled floors, the beds are comfortable and some rooms have ensuites while there are also communal facilities. **F** *Pa Phai*, opposite Wat Pa Phai. Guesthouse run by an elderly lady who speaks good English and French. Attractive little place with a shady garden and a veranda on the 1st floor. 10 clean rooms (separated only by rattan walls), very clean bathrooms, bikes for rent and same day laundry service. Recommended.

AL *Phou Vao*, Phou Vao, T212194, F212534, phouvao@hotmail.com A/c, restaurant, pool, credit cards accepted. Recently renovated and now under the management of the very upmarket *Pansea* group. This hotel, set on a hill slightly out of town, provides good views from the bedroom balconies. Although the building itself is nothing to write home about, the 58 rooms are now beautifully decorated, providing very comfortable accommodation. **AL-A** *Mouang Luang*, Boun Khong Rd, T/F212790, vicogrp@loxinfo.co.th Credit cards accepted, a/c, restaurant, pool. New, rather grandiose and lavish 2-storey reinterpretation of traditional Lao architecture in cement. There are 35 beautifully decorated rooms here with polished wooden floors, marble bathrooms and enthusiastic staff endeavouring to make their mark on the Luang Prabang hotel scene. Lao and European food in the restaurant, small kidney-shaped pool, which has, the local rumour mill reports, been built without any cleaning system. Small English language book stall.

South of town centre

The North

A *Le Parasol Blanc*, vicogrp@loxinfo.co.th 30 rooms set in secluded grounds. A modern construction with teak finish. **A** *Manoluck* (sometimes *Manoruck*), 121/3 Phou Vao Rd, T212250, 212509, F212508. Credit cards accepted, a/c, restaurant, new, quasi-classical hotel. Rooms are OK with polished wooden floors but a surfeit of ostentatious furnishings in the lobby, slightly overdone but comfortable. **A** *Naviengkham*, 4 Phothisane Rd, T212439, F212739. A bit out of the way, a/c, restaurant, characterless but functional rooms.

B *Muang Swa*, Phou Vao, T212263. A/c, restaurant. The rooms in the *Muang Swa* have bathrooms attached, but are bare and a trifle dingy for the price. There is also a rather dodgy nightclub here – beware of being fleeced by the girls.

B-C *Ban Lao*, Souvannaphum Rd, T252078, BanLao@laotel.com Some a/c. An impressive white mansion with large double rooms and polished wooden floors in the main building, some with bathrooms attached and some with shared facilities. New annexe with reasonable, clean rooms, attached facilities (hot water showers) and satellite TV. Pleasant gardens, restaurant set above a large, artificial pond serving French and Asian cuisine, good value for money. **B-C** *Lane Xang*, Visunnarat, next door to *Lane Xang Travel*, T212794. Some a/c. This attractive chalet-style hotel is run by *Lane Xang Travel Co*. Clean doubles (cheaper ones have no bathroom), good views of Wat Visunnarat, let down by a dingy restaurant.

C-D *Villa Sin Xay*, Phou Vao, T212587. Some a/c. Single, double and twin rooms, some with attached hot water bathrooms. Cheaper rooms have fans and outside toilets. Disinterested staff, nice gardens, and attached restaurant (8,000 kip, the food is good but the staff are semi-detached). **C-D** *Boun Gning Guesthouse*, 109/4 Ban That Luang, T212274. Attractive balcony, triples available, rooms quite bare and gloomy (some rather dirty), but friendly and helpful English-speaking management. The UNDP office is next door, so there are often UN workers staying here – interesting if you want to find out more about Laos. **D** *Vannida Guesthouse*, Ban That Luang, T212374. 10 rooms in a rambling old house with cooling balconies. Some rooms have attached bathrooms but most have fans and outside facilities. Garden with seating, sauna available in the evening; characterful. Recommended. **D** *Mano Guesthouse*, Phamahapasaman Rd, T253112. Brand new and spotless, with a tiled ground floor and wooden upstairs, this place is a relaxed and charming, family run option, offering some a/c. Ideal for chess enthusiasts, as into one of the stone tables outside is carved large chess set. Owners speak good English and some French.

E *Chanthy Banchit Guesthouse*, T252538. Ground floor rooms have ensuites while the upstairs share washing facilities. All rooms are charming and fairly similar. The big wooden table on the upstairs terrace is a good place to unwind with a drink if you're too tired to venture out. **E** *Manilath Guesthouse*, near the bridge to the airport, T212371. A pleasant guesthouse down a quiet lane in village close to the river. Friendly staff, decent clean rooms some with attached bathrooms. **E** *Som Chit*, Ban Thatluang 97/6 (near the hospital), T212522. Quiet place with fan rooms and friendly staff. **E** *Suankeo*, just behind Wat Manorom, T212965. This guesthouse is set in beautiful gardens with hammocks, plum and mango trees, a pond and a little bridge. Simple double rooms with bamboo walls, mosquito nets, fan, separate toilet and hot water showers. The owner is a friendly young Lao woman called Sonemany and speaks good English. Her father runs *Suankeo II*. **E** *Vongvichith*, just off Phou Vao, T212902. Opened in Feb 1999, a beautiful white villa with balcony and polished wooden floors. Large, clean doubles with separate toilet and hot shower, and a grand staircase for a budget guesthouse. Recommended – if a little out of the way.

E-F *Sysomphone*, Ban Visoun 22/4, T252543. Situated off Chao Xomphou at the end of one of the little roads that lead down to the Nam Khan, this buzzing little guesthouse is fast attaining legendary status. Already possibly the most popular joint in town for backpackers, this place is dripping with free bananas and bottled water, and offers clean rooms and bathrooms, oodles of hot water, and buckets of atmosphere. The proprietor, Somphone, is a man in a million whose English is great, and who bends over backwards to accommodate his guests. His specialities include rustling up bicycles or tuk-tuks at bargain prices, and entertaining his guests with card tricks well into the night. Go armed with a spare passport photograph, as he likes to keep whopping great photo albums of his guests, which make for entertaining viewing while proving how small the travelling world is. Highly recommended. Diagonally opposite is **E-F** *Cold River Guesthouse*, another goodie, offering the same free bananas and bottled water, and a merry mass of travellers. **E-F** *Vieng Keo*, Kitsarath Setthathirat (just round the corner from the *Rama*), T212271. Attractive old building but scruffy rather basic fan rooms with concrete floors. Some rooms have private facilities but others share the bathrooms downstairs in the courtyard (cold water only); comfortable beds. Balcony with plenty of comfy chairs, good place to recover and meet other travellers, but some grumpy staff. Also known as the 'Chinese Guesthouse', as it's a big old Chinese house. The *Viengkeo* restaurant next door offers standard fare. **F** *Keovansy*, Wisunalat (next to *Lao Aviation*), T252195. Basic doubles with fan and separate toilet and shower. Breakfast area with crazy red linoleum flooring. Very friendly staff; not much English spoken. **F** *Rama*, near Wat Visunnarat, Visunnarat Rd, T212728, lbtravel@laotel.com. Hot water (of sorts), basic but large, fan rooms, adequate but bare, friendly owner with good English. Noise is a problem here, with planes overhead during the day and a nearby nightclub at night.

AL *Villa Santi Resort*, Ban Na Dui, T252157, F212158, www.villasantihotel.com A new **Out of town** 55-room resort under the same management as *Villa Santi Hotel* had its 'soft' opening in early 2002 and should be fully open by the time this book hits the shelves. 6 km from town on the road to Kuang-Si falls, this resort, set in 10 ha of beautiful countryside, backing onto a local village and fields of rice paddys, could hardly be more dreamy. Part funded by a World Bank loan (which plays an important role in developmental projects in Laos to help local communities), the resort, 15 mins from the airport, is set to boast tennis, badminton, riding, sauna and swimming facilities, a fully-equipped gym, along with massage and aerobics services. A spa is planned. Shuttle buses into town are scheduled to leave every 30 mins throughout the day. Recommended

Eating

Luang Prabang produces a number of culinary specialities which make good souvenirs. They are, however, more likely to be found in the local market than in the restaurants. The most famous is *khai pehn*, dried 'seaweed', mainly from the Nam Khan, which is mixed with sesame and eaten nationwide. It is particularly good fried as a sandwich between garlic and sesame. *Chao bong*, a mildly hot pimento purée, is also popular throughout the country. Other delicacies include: *phak nam*, a watercress which grows around waterfalls and is commonly used in soups and salads; *mak kham kuan* (tamarind jam) and *mak nat kuan* (pineapple jam). Baguettes can be bought at many roadside stalls.

● *on maps, pages and Price codes: see inside front cover*

Perhaps the best – at least in terms of ambience – places to eat are the cafés and restaurants along the Mekong River, where the procession of boats and people make for fascinating viewing. The food can also be pretty good. Some enterprising souls have opened a row of French restaurants on Sisavangvong. Although there is little to distinguish between them, they are tastefully decorated with a combination of traditional Lao handicrafts and western styles. Lantern-lit at night they harness a good atmosphere and serve Lao fare along with mainly French and some Italian dishes. They are not budget options though.

Lao & French

Expensive *L'Hôtel Souvannaphoum*, Phothisarath. Lao dishes with French influences, good selection of wine, a smartish restaurant in a beautiful setting – covered veranda looking out over the garden. Fish, duck and quail are all usually on the menu.

Mid-range *Duang Champa*, Nam Khan, open 0900-2300, Lao and French food in a trendy restaurant. Produce is flown in (good range of cheeses), salads, sorbets, adapted Lao dishes, bar downstairs, overlooking the Khan River. *Le Potisan*, Sisavangvong Rd. A pleasant, airy setting with tiled floors and local tapestries decorating the walls. 13 different kinds of pizza and good steaks on the menu here. *Phousi* (*Phousi Hotel*), Kitsarath Setthathirat, set menu, also bar food. *Villa Santi, Princess Restaurant*, Sisavangvong. Attractive 1st floor restaurant in this airy villa, providing good choice of Lao and French food. The chef is the daughter of Phia Sing (chef to the Royal Family); his recipes have been translated and published (see Food, page 308 for publication details).

Cheap *Ban Lao*, behind Wat Manorom. Big purpose-built restaurant which largely caters for tour groups. Mostly Lao and some French cuisine served here. *Bouasavanh*, Manthatourath, Lao and Thai food, set on a terrace overlooking the river. *Café des Arts*, Sisavangvong, T252162, enormously pleasant and reasonably priced little French restaurant. Menu includes steaks, burgers, salads and tarts as well as a good line in creme caramel. Also provides some Lao food. Artwork for sale on the walls. *Chansamone*, Sisavangvong, next to *Diethelm Travel*. French and Lao cuisine, lovely service by 2 sisters, excellent soups, interesting anti-opium UNDP drawings on the walls. *Dao Fa Creperie*, Sisavangvong Rd. The name says it all: recently opened creperie run by the elegant Mathilde with excellent savoury and sweet crepes, a good selection of teas and coffees, fab ice creams and soothing jazz accompaniment. *Indochina Spirit*, Phothisarath Rd. Colonial building with an attractive courtyard. Lots of ambience and an extensive menu embracing Lao and Italian food from pizza to Luang Prabang dishes and including a vegetarian selection. On the tour group itinerary but don't be put off; it's a very nice place to eat with reasonable food, although it is pricey compared with other places. A Lao band plays here in the evening. *Khaem Khong*, Manthatourath, one of the better river restaurants. *Khemkhane Food Garden*, Nam Khan Rd, T212447. Does a good line in spicy foods – very pleasant terraced setting overlooking the Nam Khan. A local band sometimes tips up to blast guests with traditional Lao music. *Le Saladier*, Sisavangvong Rd (opposite side of street from *Phounsab Guesthouse*). Excellent salads, specials every evening, good desserts, although service can be slow, bordering on the desultory. *Malee Lao Food Restaurant*, Phou Vao. Lao dishes, including Luang Prabang specialities, the *laap* is particularly recommended. *Park Hovay Mixay Restaurant*, Dothikhoummane. Lao restaurant with a/c room plus a large open area. A small army of waiters bring reasonable Lao/Thai/Chinese food to your table. Popular with Luang Prabang's wealthier locals although the tour buses that occasionally congregate are offputting. *Riverside Sunset Restaurant*, Souvanabanlang Rd, T252026. Charming rustic setting serving fairly standard Lao fare. A good place for a drink as the sun sets. *Sakounna*, next to the old post office. Welcoming restaurant, good selection of Lao and some western dishes, tables on the street, with lanterns in the evening. The best fruit juices in town (especially lemon) are made here.

Seriously cheap *Nam Phou*, Thanon Phothisarath, opposite Wat That, rice with a choice of 3 to 7 dishes, great value. *New Luang Prabang Hotel*, Sisavangvong,

T212264, offers a decent selection of Lao and European food. *Sathaphon*, near *Villa Sinxay*, on the corner of the street. Basic dishes and an English menu, good value. *Som Chanh Restaurant*, down by the Mekong on Souvanabanlang Rd. This restaurant looks nice and interesting, split as it is between the 2 sides of the road. But poor food and poorer stomachs for the sampling were the order of the day on our last visit, which no amount of lovely river view could make up for.

Seriously cheap *Visoun*, Visunnarat Rd opposite *Rama Hotel*. Reasonable Chinese, Thai and European dishes, but portions are on the small side. *Yong Khoune*, Visunnarat Rd, diagonally across from *Rama Hotel*. Chinese and Thai food, excellent fish dishes and good breakfasts (they serve a delicious Luang Prabang muesli – their own concoction of fruit, nuts, yoghurt, and cornflakes), popular with helpful management. They also run a second-hand bookshop inside.

Chinese

Cheap *Nazim Indian Restaurant*, opposite Wat Visunnarat, T252263. Expanding from their base in Vientiane, and the harbinger of the third outlet in Vang Vieng, Luang Prabang's first Indian restaurant appears to be a roaring success: by 2000 it is crowded with *falang*. The menu offers a huge selection of authentic Indian food from both north and south of the country and Halal dishes. The management and the chefs are all Indian which ensures that the food is of excellent quality. The servings are huge, and the service is efficient; the interior remains a little bare. *Nesha's*, near Mt Phousi. On our last trip this fabulous little place had yet to hit the big time with tourists. But as who-ever goes in emerges singing its praises, and its varied dishes are utterly delicious as well as reasonably priced, it's bound to be catapulted high in the popularity stakes before long.

Indian

Mid-range *L'Auberge Calao*, river road. Light American lunches – hamburgers, open sandwiches, ice-cream etc – served here. Lao food only provided for groups in advance (set menu). Restaurant open 0630-2100. Good breakfasts. *Phou Vao* (hotel), Phou Vao Rd. This is the restaurant attached to the *Phou Vao Hotel* which is set on a hill outside town with great views over the city. Good Lao and Continental à la carte menu, buffet breakfasts.

International

The restaurant at the *Lamach Guesthouse* on Sisavangvong serves vegetarian food in the garden outside as does the *Madame Chanthip Guesthouse* at 97/5 Ban Wat Nong. The latter is better, although meat seems to creep in from time-to-time. **Seriously cheap** *Unnamed vegetarian*, Sisavangvong, behind *Villa Santi*. Excellent Lao food and amazingly good prices.

Vegetarian

Cafés

Café Ban Vat Sene, a seriously nice option, whose white walls and polished dark wooden floors, tables and chairs give the place a breezy, colonial air. The food (French) is a treat. Good place for herbal teas. *Healthy and Fresh*, Sisavangvong, relatively expensive but utterly delicious array of foods. Gets hot inside, so if you can bag one of the 4 tables outside, you're doing well. *Luang Prabang Bakery*, 11/7 Sisavangong, 3 doors to the right of the *Phounsab Guesthouse* (when facing entrance). Croissants, lemon bars, raisin slices, brownies, muffins, coffee, rolls, to eat on premises or to takeaway. Also sells muesli, making it a good place for breakfast. Reasonable prices and really lovely owner who talks good English. Also a popular joint in the evenings, thanks to an extensive Lao menu with a limited (but apparently delicious) side line in pizzas. *Pasaneyam Coffee Shop*, on the corner of Thanon Kitsalat, facing the river. An excel-lent little stall, best in the early morning. An elegant old man serves delicious sweet Lao

Cafés, bakeries & breakfast

The North

coffee/ovaltine combinations, and arranges an alternate pattern of swiss roll cakes and baguettes on his wooden bench. He puts on a fine show welcoming his guests, pouring the coffee and enticing you to drink more. *Scandinavian Bakery*, Sisavangong. Ice-cold a/c café with only 2 tables. Wide range of Danish pastries, croissants, quiches, pies, and cream cakes, filtered coffee and yoghurt. Foreign language newspapers available to read. Visitors can also log onto the internet upstairs at *PlaNet*.

Food stalls   A tempting choice of early evening stalls is to be found on Kitsarath Settathirat, towards the river. Roast chicken and sticky rice – a Lao favourite – are among the foods on offer.

Bars

There are several anonymous wooden platforms built over the bank of the Mekong on Manthatourath, which makes for an incomparable place to have a beer at sunset. *La Villa* (*L'Hotel Souvannaphoum*) has a very attractive bar area, with colonial rattan chairs and lovely décor, dress reasonably smart. *Visun Bar*, opposite *Rama*, good selection of beer, Chinese and local wines and spirits. *Villa Santi* and *L'Auberge Calao* both provide attractive settings for a drink, as do the restaurants along the river road – the *Duang Champa* provides an extensive choice of spirits.

Pubs   The idea of dedicated pubs appears to be a new one in Luang Prabang, but one that may well catch on quickly if the popularity of *Maylek*, LP's first pub, is anything to go by. Designed by a French Canadian architect with a definite eye for dim lighting and artfully arranged modern furniture, it's a surreal experience walking into a place such as this, which would be more at home in London's Covent Garden. Its steep prices, too, are more akin to London than Luang Prabang. As it enjoys the privilege of being the last watering hole to shut at night, lock in (from about 2330) normally sees a good few drinkers hunching over their cocktails until the early hours.

Entertainment

Cultural shows   Dance, theatre, puppet shows and *baci* ceremonies are staged at the Royal Theatre, next to the national museum. A variable insight into Lao culture (65,000 kip/person).

Discos   Occasional disco at *Muang Swa Hotel*. Live band with traditional Lao dancing, including line dancing. While the locals love it, not many tourists are seen here. 15,000 kip entry..

Festivals

April   *Pimay* (movable: public holiday) is celebrated in Laos during Apr. This festival has special significance in Luang Prabang, as it was the royal capital; certain traditions are celebrated in the city which are no longer observed in Vientiane. People from all over the province, and even further afield, descend on the city. The newly crowned Miss New Year (*Nang Sang Khan*) is paraded through town, riding on the back of the auspicious animal of the year. Pimay is the time when the tutelary spirits of the old year are replaced by those of the new. In the past the King and Queen would symbolically clean the principal Buddha images in the city's main wats – like Wat Xieng Thong and Wat May – while masked dancers would prance through the streets re-enacting the founding of the city by 2 mythical beasts. Day 1: bazaar market trade fair in streets around the post office; sprinkling of Buddha statues with water; release of small fish into Mekong from pier behind Royal Palace – a symbolic gesture, hoping for good luck in the New Year; construction of sand stupas on western bank of Mekong, at Mong Khoum, next to

The scholar, the king, the riddle and the severed head

Songkran in Luang Prabang is probably Laos' festive highlight. Processions, parties, competitions, music and dance, and drunken cavorting characterize this drawn out celebration of birth and renewal. In the grand procession that marks the festival's high point, the oddest element among the drummers and dancers, Lao beauties and ancient monks, is a papier maché head on a golden tray. The head is that of a four-faced god-king named Phanya Kabilaphom. This king, who emerges from deep in that part of Lao culture where history meets mythology, was prone to setting riddles. (There's one in every society.) Any challenger had seven days to solve the riddle. If they failed, they would lose their heads. If they won they could have, not the usual king's daughter, but the king's head. As is the way with these things, after many futile attempts by quickly headless competitors, one young scholar managed to answer the king's riddle.

What that riddle was Lao mythology does not tell, but we do know that the youth used his facility with vulture language. The king nobly accepted defeat. But the victor was deeply worried about what would happen when the blood from Phanya Kabila's head touched the ground. After all, was he not a god as well as a king? It would burn all the world's crops and boil the oceans of the world. So the king, usefully, suggested that the severed head be placed on a gold salver. He also suggested that the head be entrusted to the keeping of his seven daughters and brought out once a year and carried in procession. Each daughter was allotted a day of the week and a magical mount. In 1998 the procession fell on a Tuesday so the magical mount was Tuesday's daughter's beast – a wild boar. The beauties who follow the severed papier maché head of King Phanya Kabila are the daughters of this long-dead king.

Wat Xiang Men; fireworks in the evening. Day 2: first procession from Wat That to Wat Xieng Thong; dance of the masks of Pou Nheu Nha Nheu and Sing Kaeo Sing Kham; fireworks and festivities in the evening. Day 3: second procession from Wat Xieng Thong to Wat That; procession of monks; baci celebrations across town (see Festivals, page 56); fireworks in evening. Day 4: The Royal Palace Pha Bang is moved to Wat May. Day 5: all day traditional washing of Pha Bang at Wat May. Day 7: Pha Bang Buddha returned to Wat May. Days 9-11: Wat Xieng Thong Phraman image brought outside temple for ritual washing.

May *Vien Thiene* festival (movable) is the candlelit festival.

August *Boat races* (movable) celebrated in Luang Prabang in Aug unlike other parts of the country, where they take place in Sep. Boats are raced by the people living in the vicinity of each wat.

Shopping

Art galleries Quite a few little operations are popping up now, as the German owner of *Baan Khily Café and Paper Gallery*, Phothisarath, a few doors down from *Diethelm Travel Agent*, opened his place, trained all his staff, and then had to watch when most of them went off with their newly learnt skills to set up on their own. This is a *sa* paper crafts centre (*sa* is a rough, leaf-effect paper). The 1st floor sells scrolls, temple stencils, paper lanterns, cards and second-hand foreign language books. On the second floor there is a small art gallery and a comfortable balcony café that sells drinks and overlooks the string of wats on Sisavangong. *Nora Gallery*, 9/7 Sisavangvong. Exhibits work by local artists.

The North

Baskets   The best collection can be found in several shops along Sisavangvong, near *Villa Santi*.

Books   A small selection of second-hand books available at *Baan Khily Café & Paper Gallery*, Phothisarath, and you can also buy and exchange them at *Luang Prabang Bakery*. New English language paperbacks for US$10 each can be bought at **Mouang Luang Hotel**.

Handicrafts   There is a handicraft market, geared to tourists, close to the intersection of Phou Vao and the river roads, by the Shell petrol station. A row of shops lines Phothisarath Rd, upriver from the *Savannaphum Hotel*, selling tribal textiles, baskets, silverware, cross bows, earrings, betel boxes and more. *Raan Phat*, opposite Wat Phra Maha That. Eclectic assortment of dusty rice baskets, spoons, bird traps, weaving paraphernalia, textiles and some clothing. Next door, on a balcony, is an **Antique Shop**, with similar goods. **Luang Prabang Gallery**, Kitsarath Setthathirat. Quirky collection of handicrafts/antiques. **Luang Prabang Handicraft Shop**, Sisavangvong, offers a good range of silks and cottons, handicrafts and silver. The high quality is reflected in the high prices. Rather surprisingly, they can't make their fabrics into trousers, but can knock you out a skirt in a day. **Satri Lao Silk**, Sisavangvong, T219295, satrilao@hotmail.com   Truly beautiful silks and handicrafts for sale. Expensive, but definitely worth a look.

Markets   The **Central Market** (Dala Market) is housed in a concrete market building in the middle of town. It is mostly imported goods on sale here, but there are a few stalls selling silver boxes and belts and a handful with textiles. A couple of stalls sell loom parts and yarns for weaving. The busiest time of day is 0900-1100, but it is still open up to 1700 or 1800, depending on shopkeepers. The **New Market** on Phothisane sells mostly fruit and vegetables, and will soon be moving to grander quarters on the same road, a little further out. At the **Street Market**, near the Post Office on the stretch of Kitsarath Setthathirat that runs down to the Mekong, hill tribes sell fruit, wild honey, roots and tubers, fresh and dried fish, and knives and other ironmongery made by the smiths of Ban Hat Hien. In the evening, food stalls also set up shop here. This area bustles with activity; it seems to be an important trading and trans-shipment area. Boats dock at Heua Me pier to unload their goods. Again near the Post Office, opposite the *New Luang Prabang Hotel*, is the **Mong Market** selling mainly fabrics and tapestries. There is also a **Morning Market** (*talat sao*) at the downstream side of town, near the stadium.

Silver   One of Luang Prabang's traditional crafts is silversmithing. During the Communist era of 1975-89 many silversmiths turned to other occupations, such was the lack of demand. However, with the rise in tourism and the economic reforms demand has increased and many silversmiths have returned to their craft. Most tourists buy their silver – and other crafts – from the Central Market in Luang Prabang. However, almost none of the pieces on sale here is from the Luang Prabang area – despite what the marketeers might say. Most are made instead in Vientiane and trucked to the royal capital. Expert silversmiths like Thithpeng Maniphone maintain that these Vientiane-made pieces are inferior, and certainly the engraving and silverwork does appear cruder. **Thit Peng**, signposted almost opposite Wat That, workshop and small shop with jewellery and pots. The silversmith along the river, near the rear of the Royal Palace, produces good workmanship. His father made one of the King's crowns.

Weaving   Opposite Wat Phra Maha That, Central Market. Tribal peoples come into town to sell their wares from the roadside near the Central Market. The best collection of shops selling local textiles, both new and old, is along Sisavangvong. **Ban Phanom Handicraft Weaving Loom**, probably the best place to go for silks, to get there head out of town on the Phou Vao Rd, then turn right at the sign to the centre. The building itself is a large airy room filled with tables draped in hundreds of different silks and cottons, and you can see the women at work on their looms from the windows. Barter hard and you can come away with some spectacular materials.

Art Gallery, opposite Wat May, makes coffins as well as traditional woodcarvings. **Woodcarving**

Sport

Red Cross Sauna, opposite Wat Visunnarat, T212303. Massage 25,000 kip per hr (or **Sauna** 13,000 kip for ½ hr), traditional Lao herbal sauna, 10,000 kip. Daily 0900-2100 (1700-2100 for sauna). Bring your own towel/sarong. Also offers internet connection. The best and most professional massage outfit in town. *Anoudeth Setambath and Massage*, Souvanabanlang Rd, near the cluster of little streets peppered with guesthouses, T570471, 1000-2200, 22,000 kip for 1 hr of massage; sauna, 1700-2200, 6,000 kip per person. Some guesthouses including *Vannida* also offer steambaths.

Tour operators

Diethelm Travel, Phothisarath, T212277. *Inter-Lao Tourism*, Kitsarath Settathirath, T/F212024. *Lao Asian Trails*, Ban That Luang, Sisavangvong Rd, No 012 Unit ¼, Luang Prabang, T/F252257, www.asiantrails.com *Luang Prabang Tourism*, Phothisarath, T212198/9, F212728 (a government-run tour company). *Sodetour*, River road, T/F212092. *Lane Xang Tourism*, corner of Visunnarat, T/F212793. *Yong Khoune*, the restaurant on Visunnarat Rd. Organizes daily tours to the local sights, much cheaper than many of the travel agents or hotels.

Transport

Bicycle hire The best way to explore Luang Prabang and outlying places of interest is **Local** by bicycle. Many hotels, guesthouses and even restaurants offer bicycles for hire. *See also Ins and outs,* Expect to pay about 10,000-20,000 kip per day depending on the state of the machine. *page 114* (In 1999 the police banned the hiring of bicycles for an assortment of suspect reasons; there is the possibility that the ban could be reimposed.)

Motorbike hire When foreigners are not forbidden from hiring motorbikes, many guesthouses will hire out machines for around US$13 per day. Motorbikes can also be hired from the little shop opposite *Lao Aviation* and *Keovancy Guesthouse*.

Saamlor and tuk-tuk Lots around town, which can be hired to see the sights or to go to nearby villages. Barter hard!

Boats for local charter Boats for local charter, whether to the Pak Ou caves (see Excursions) or just to the other bank of the Mekong, are available from the 2 piers just downstream from the Royal Palace. Prices should be negotiated first. A boat to the Pak Ou caves (2 hrs upstream, 1 hr down) should cost about US$10-15.

Minibus with driver US$40 per day around Luang Prabang, US$60 per day if travelling further afield, available from several hotels and the tour companies.

Air Luang Prabang airport is about 2 km northeast of town; there is a standard 10,000 **Long distance** kip charge to take passengers into town although it is possible to walk. The new airport buildings and the lengthened and upgraded runway were paid for by Thailand. There is now an international service run by *Lao Aviation* between **Chiang Mai** and Luang

The North

Prabang once a week and **Bangkok Airways** has started a service between **Bangkok** and Luang Prabang, touching down at **Sukhothai** en route. *Silk Air* has been negotiating for rights to operate between Singapore and Luang Prabang for some time now, but as the Singapore-Vientiane service has been suspended this would seem to be some way off. Daily connections with **Vientiane**, twice a day, 50 mins, US$55. Early morning departures are often delayed during the rainy season, as dense cloud makes Luang Prabang airport inoperable until about 1100. In Mar and Apr, flights are sometimes cancelled due to the haze produced by the fires of shifting cultivators. Generally the *Lao Aviation* pilots manage to get their machines down, although *Bangkok Airways*, new to Luang Prabang, have been known to abandon their attempts. Flights to **Phonsavanh** daily at 0800, 30 mins (US$35), and connections with **Ban Houei Xai** (US$46), **Luang Nam Tha** (US$37). There is a standard 5,000 kip departure tax for all domestic flights, US$10 for international departures.

Transport to town: 10,000 kip per person in a shared tuk-tuk.

Speedboats depart from Ban Dom, 5 km from the Navigation Office (about 10,000 kip by tuk-tuk) Passengers are required to wear life jackets and crash helmets after an accident a few years back

Boat Luang Prabang was established at the confluence of the Mekong and Nam Khan because of the transport and communication opportunities that such a position affords in any otherwise mountainous and inaccessible area. However with the development of overland links and the upgrading, particularly, of the Vientiane-Luang Prabang road, river transport has languished. Nonetheless, while few passengers take the boat option south to Vientiane via Pak Lai, the route upstream to Ban Houei Xai via Pak Beng, on the border with Thailand, remains popular. Most boats leave from the 2 docking areas just downstream from the Royal Palace. The busier is the Heua Me Pier; the one slightly closer to the Royal Palace is only really used when the river level is low. A blackboard in the Navigation Office (0730-1130 and 1300-1600), situated on the banks of the Mekong a few hundred yards down from the Royal Palace, lists destinations and prices . **NB** prices are largely dependent on the price of gasoline. There are 3 departure areas which service the various destinations.

Boats to Vientiane via Pak Lai: departing from the Xieng Keo ferry port, 6 km from the Navigation Office (10,000 kip by tuk-tuk), the slow boat to Vientiane takes 3-4 days and costs 140,000 kip (69,000 kip to Pak Lai), while the speedboat takes a single day and costs 322,000 kip (150,000 kip to Pak Lai). (For details on the river journey from Vientiane to Luang Prabang see page 101.) Larger boats only go in the rainy season but try local boatmen as most boats making the journey take passengers even if they are commercial. It may be helpful to use a translator in order to negotiate the price. It can take several days of hanging around, while the freight is loaded. From Ban Pak Khone there are plenty of boats travelling south, but few people speak English and negotiating a fare is a tough business. The boat captains wait to get enough passengers on board and if they don't fill the vessel, they simply increase the fare. Many boats make an overnight stop at Pak Lai where there is basic guesthouse (see page 186). The stretch of river from Luang Prabang to Pak Lai is quite hazardous, with a fair number of rapids. The next significant settlement downstream is **Sanakham** (Xana Kham). It is possible to see working elephants on the journey between Pak Lai and Sanakham and Sanakham itself is quite an interesting place to stop. It supports 3 wats, one with a ruined stupa and another wat with an unusual Buddha image. There are a few restaurants here and one government guesthouse (**E**) but no one living there, so you need to ask around and are left to your own devices, once established. There is a river border crossing here to Chiang Khan in Thailand, but foreigners are not permitted to cross (although frequent boats ply the Mekong and it is said that no one asks for your passport). Boats from Sanakham are intermittent, and take about 8 hrs, arriving at the northern jetty. An alternative to the slow boat from Luang Prabang is to take one of the fast, noisy and rather more dangerous speedboats. These take just 8-10 hrs (but an exhausting and battering 8-10 hrs).

Boats to Ban Houei Xai via Pak Beng: it is becoming increasingly popular to enter Laos via Chiang Khong/Ban Houei Xai. However there is no road between Ban Houei Xai and Luang Prabang and the only way to get to Luang Prabang, or vice versa, is to take a flight or travel by river. Very slow boats, departing from the Navigation Office, with an overnight stop in Pak Beng, cost 100,000 kip all the way to Ban Houei Xai or 52,000 kip to Pak Beng. The much quicker alternative is to take one of the **speedboats** which depart from Ban Don Village, the journey to Pak Beng takeing 3 hrs (120,000 kip), with another 3 hrs to Ban Houei Xai (200,000 kip in total). It is also possible to charter a speedboat – normally hired out at a multiple of the regular number of passengers (6).

Boats to Muang Khua via Muang Ngoi/Nong Khiaw: there are also occasional boats that travel up the Nam Ou, which joins the Mekong north of Luang Prabang, to Muang Khua via Muang Ngoi/Nong Khiaw. However, like river transport elsewhere in Laos, improvements in roads and road transportation have meant that boats are now infrequent, especially when the river is low. A slow boat, departing from the Navigation Office, to Muang Khua should cost 94,000 kip, while the rate to Nong Khiaw is 61,000 kip. It may be necessary to charter a boat, and there are also occasional slow cargo boats. **Speedboats** also leave from Ban Don Village. Expect to pay 100,000 kip to Nong Khiaw. From Muang Ngoi/Nong Khiaw some vessels continue upriver to Muang Khua (198,000 kip all the way from LP to Muang Khua). Hazardous and uncomfortable but exhilarating travelling.

Road Bus transport has taken over from river travel as roads have improved and the vehicle stock has been modernized. There are two bus terminals. The **southern bus station** is on Phothisane Rd, past the turn-off for the *Pho Vao Hotel*, best reached by tuk-tuk (around 5,000 kip per person). To get to the **northern bus station**, cross the Srisavangvong Bridge and take the road towards the airport (tuk-tuk: around 10,000 kip per person).

Buses to Vientiane via Vang Vieng: 5 buses a day (0630, 0730, 1000, 1230 and 1700) leave for Vientiane from the southern bus station and take 8-10 hrs (60,000 kip, or 50,000 kip to Vang Vieng). In the past, vehicles on the road between Luang Prabang and Vientiane were subject to periodic attack by bandits, although the route has been considered safe for some time now (see page 100 for details).

Buses to Xieng Khouang (Phonsavanh) and Xam Neua via Nong Khiaw: the most direct route to Xieng Khouang and Phonsavanh is Route 7. However not only is this road in very poor condition but it is still regarded as a security risk and travellers should check on the situation before departing. At the time of writing, there were no bus services – only flights (US$35). An alternative, albeit rather longer, route to Xieng Khouang is via Nong Khiaw and Muang Ngoi (also reachable by boat, see above). Buses to Nong Khiaw/Muang Ngoi depart from the north bus station at 0900, 1130, 1330 and 1600, take 4 hrs and cost 25,000 kip. From here there are pick-ups to Pak Xeng and on to Phonsavanh via Vieng Thong on Route 1. There are basic places to stay in both Pak Xeng (near the bridge) and in Vieng Thong. The roundabout road from Luang Prabang to Phonsavanh is appalling – you may find yourself assuming the temporary mantle of road builder before being able to complete the journey; the journey may seem arduous (2-3 days) but the scenery is very rewarding, passing through many hilltribe villages. At the intersection of Route 1 and Route 6, which leads to Phonsavanh, is the small town of Nam Noen. Rather than turning south for Phonsavanh it is possible to catch a bus north to Xam Neua, if the state of the road permits.

Buses to Luang Namtha, Muang Xai and Muang Ngoi via Pak Mong: buses running north to Muang Xai (Udom Xai) – 4 hrs – via Pak Mong leave from the northern bus station 3 km out of town (take a tuk-tuk) towards the airport. They usually leave early morning. From Muang Xai there are buses onwards to Luang Namtha (Luang Pradang to Luang Namtha 8 hrs, 50,000 kip). The road to Muang Xai is good.

Directory

Airline offices   *Lao Aviation*, T212172. Visunnarat, down from *Rama*. It's a great source of tourist information. Takes VISA but not travellers' cheques. *Bangkok Airways*, at the airport.

Banks   *Lane Xang Bank*, near Wat May, changes US$ travellers' cheques into dollars or kip, Mon-Sun 0830-1200, 1330-1530 . Many of the jewellery stalls in the old market will change US$ and Thai baht – and also many of the restaurant and tourist shop owners. There are also numerous banks along Sisavangvong, all displaying their exchange rates on white boards outside. The various exchange offices belong to the same bank, but offer different exchange rates – so if money is an issue it's an idea to wonder around to find the best one.

Communications   **Internet**   Plenty of internet cafés are popping up all over the place, especially on Sisavangvong Rd. An internet rates 'war' is on the horizon and should help keep prices down. Still, it's worth knowing that different establishments charge different rates, as connection speeds leave a lot to be desired. *PlaNet Café*, 1 shop on Settathirat near the intersection with Rathsavong Rd, 1 on Sisavangvong, above the *Scandinavian Bakery*. Also on the main drag are *Malaylack Internet and Email* (just down from *Scandinavian Bakery)* who offer free Pepsi and a connection speed that is often faster than most; and *Travel Online Internet and Email*, a great favourite with the fashion-conscious, where the attached tailor's shop can rustle you up a fine pair of trousers in just hours. **Post Office and Telephone Office:** the old office on Phothisarath (opposite the *Phousi Hotel)* has closed and moved 100 m closer to the river. Mon-Fri 0830-1730. Express mail service, fax and international telephone facilities, philately section. There are many IDD call boxes around the post office and on Sisavangvong. Hotels and some guesthouses also allow international calls from their reception phones – about US$5 a min!

Medical services   Medical services in Luang Prabang are limited. The main **hospital** is on Kitsarath Settathirat. However, if you are caught seriously ill it is recommended that you make for Vientiane and, if necessary, for Thailand.

Useful addresses   **Immigration office**: opposite the *Rama Hotel* on Visunnarat Rd (T212435).

Around Luang Prabang

Nam Bak

Colour map 1, grid B3   The town of Nam Bak lies on the banks of the Nam Bak. It is a beautiful spot and is worth an overnight stop. The market is interesting in the very early morning, when hill people including Blue Hmong converge to sell exotic birds, insects, bats, and other forest species. There is a small wat on the left at the end of town as you come from Muang Ngoi, **Wat Tiom Tian**. From here there are good views of the surrounding countryside. There is a small children's graveyard behind the wat. On the other side of the bridge is a branch of Gerbera, a German NGO helping to recover and defuse Unexploded Ordnance (UXO); there are some fragments of landmines, rockets and other ordnance in the garden and front room on view. As this place is less regularly visited by tourists the NGO is rather more willing to discuss their work with tourists than the UK-based Mines Advisory Group (MAG) in Phonsavanh.

The road on to Muang Xai is beautiful, passing Blue Hmong villages.

F *Bounthiem*, canary yellow building opposite the wat at opposite end of town to the market. Five rooms of doubles and twins, clean, comfy mattresses in some rooms, mosquito nets, balcony area, fan (although electricity is only 1800-2200). Western toilet and scoop shower downstairs, friendly. Recommended. **F** *Vanmisay Guesthouse*, opposite the market. Doubles and triples, basic service, mosquito nets provided, toilet and bathrooms outside; friendly service. **F** *Khounvilay Guesthouse*, basic doubles, triples and twins. Quite scruffy with one enormously dirty squat toilet and a scoop shower out the back. Mosquito nets, cold drinks available. The wonderfully friendly family owners are likely to invite you to share their evening meal – an extravaganza of spices which is liable to blow your mouth away! Electricity 1800-2100.

Sleeping

There are 2 or 3 noodle shops, the best one opposite the market, *Han Nang Nit*. No English but very friendly service – good place to wait for the trucks onwards as they stop outside.

Eating

Bus/truck About 1 hr from **Muang Ngoi** by truck, good road. In theory, the trucks wait for the boats to arrive from Luang Prabang and Muang Khua. Trucks leave Nam Bak for Muang Ngoi (5,000 kip) at around 0700, and during the day when they're full. Be prepared to wait around for a few hrs. Regular connections with **Luang Prabang**; the bus leaves from Luang Prabang's northern bus station when full (0700-0800), 3 hrs (13,000 kip). The road runs parallel with the river for most of the journey. For **Muang Xai** (15,000 kip), you need to take a tuk-tuk to Pak Mong (3,000 kip), 10 km west of Nam Bak, and change there for a bus north to Muang Xai (12,000 kip, 3 hrs). Vehicles travelling east along Route 1 to **Nam Nouan** are not so frequent; best bet is the early morning, if at all.

Transport
94 km to Muang Xai

Banks An exchange by the market. **Useful information** Electricity: 1800-2200.

Directory

Muang Ngoi and Nong Khiaw

Muang Ngoi lies 20 km northeast of Nam Bak and is a delightful little village on the banks of the Nam Ou, surrounded by limestone peaks. There are, in fact, two settlements here: Muang Ngoi on the east bank of the Nam Ou and Nong Khiaw on the west. Sometimes the combined town is called one, sometimes the other – and sometimes, for no apparent reason, Nam Bak, which is a town some way to the northeast (see previous entry). One reason why Muang Ngoi/Nong Khiaw has become a popular stopping place for travellers is because of its pivotal position on the Nam Ou: many boats stop here. But most importantly, it is also a beautiful spot – the sort of place where time stands still, journals are written, books read, and stress is a deeply foreign concept. It is possible to swim in the river (women should wear sarongs) or walk around the town or up the cliffs. The bridge across the Nam Ou offers fine views and photo opportunities.

Colour map 1, grid B4

Tham Pha Thok (2 km away) and **Tham Pha Kwong** (3 km), two caves used by locals when the US bombed the area, and a small waterfall, **Than Mok**, are the most obvious attractions here. To get to the caves, either take a tuk-tuk (1,000 kip per person) or walk there: turn left out of the village heading towards Nam Bak and the Tham Pha Kwong caves are about half an hour's walk, up on the right. There is a shrine to the Buddha, various relics, and a pile of old ammunition and bombshells inside. Take a strong torch to explore the tunnel at the back.

Excursions

To get to **Than Mok**, in Sopkhong Village, you'll need to charter a boat. A boatload of five passengers should expect to pay around 15,000 kip each for

The North

the return trip (remember to set a return time). There's a 2,000 kip fee to see the waterfall, and some cheeky little child will likely charge you a further 5,000 kip to guide you there (40 minutes each way). Outrageous, perhaps, but without the child you might well not find it. It's best to go in the morning, so as not to have to rush the climb up to the falls or cut short your time there before darkness falls.

Sleeping
■ *on maps*
Price codes:
see inside front cover

E-F *Manipoon Guesthouse*, slightly grander rooms than the other guesthouses, separated by wooden walls rather than just bamboo. verandas offer an unspectacular view of nearby rooftops. Toilets out the back. Not worth the extra money. **F** *Mexay Guesthouse*, dirt cheap rooms, although food and people are less friendly than its more successful neighbour, *Sunset*. Organizes treks: 10,000 kip for a 1-day trek up the hill and over the valley, then down again. The view is spectacular, but beware the climb is steep. **F** *Phayboun Guesthouse*, first guesthouse on the left as you enter by road from the west. Solid building with reasonable doubles and twins, balcony, toilet and shower downstairs, restaurant attached with uninspiring food, quiet location, friendly owner, rats in abundance. **F** *Philasouk Guesthouse*, 2-floor simple wooden building by the river where the songthaews stop, with a restaurant downstairs. Very basic but clean twin rooms with mosquito nets. The whole house shakes when anyone moves. Basic toilet building behind the guesthouse. The girls have adopted the slightly perplexing practice of padlocking the only 2 toilets and then mislaying the key – so not for those with stomach problems. Electricity dusk-2300, noisy generator. **F** *Phosoi Guesthouse*, further down the road still and opposite the school. A small, rickety 2-floor structure with small doubles and twins, balcony, café downstairs, toilet and scoop shower in garden. **F** *Sainamou Guesthouse*, small, clean rooms separated by bamboo walls that do little to shut out the snoring of fellow guests. Friendly owners. Very cheap. Restaurant is well-positioned on the veranda overlooking the river but none except the trimmest of bottoms could sit comfortably on the tiny chairs provided, and there's precious little leg room, too. **F** *Sanhty Guesthouse*, a few doors down from the *Philasouk Guesthouse* and facing the river. Tiny twin rooms, squat toilet and shower out back, café downstairs. **F** *Somgnot Guesthouse*, on the same road a few doors down from the *Sanhty Guesthouse* and close to where the boats leave. Five 'spaces' – it's difficult to call them rooms – separated by bamboo screens, mattress on floor, oriental 'feel' with Indian paintings, run by a friendly old man with a little English – different! **F** *Sunset Guesthouse*, a charming, sprawling bamboo structure looking immediately out onto tables and sun umbrellas liberally arranged over the various levels of decking that serve as a popular restaurant in the evenings, and a good spot to read or write while soaking up the sun during the day. Slap bang on the bank of the river – you couldn't ask for a more picturesque setting or a better retreat from where to watch the sunset. Large, clean and pleasant toilet and scoop shower. Hard mattresses on the

Muang Ngoi (Nong Khiaw)

To Muang Khua
Truck Stop
Boats North & South
Nam Ou
To Vieng Thang & Nam Noen
School
Kaysone Monument
To Luang Prabang
To Pak Mong, Udom Xai & Luang Prabang

N
Not to scale

■ **Sleeping**
1 Manipoon
2 Mexay
3 Phayboun Guesthouse & Restaurant
4 Philasouk Guesthouse & Restaurant
5 Phosoi Guesthouse
6 Sainamou
7 Sanhty Guesthouse
8 Somgnot Guesthouse
9 Sunset

● **Eating**
1 Lao
2 Noodle Soupers
3 Vanmanyphong

floor, but definitely worth it. A great favourite with travellers. The food (European and curries) is good. Recommended.

Eating
● on map
Price codes:
see inside front cover

All the guesthouses have attached cafés. The food, though, is generally quite bland. A better option is to sample the noodle shops alongside *Philasouk* selling very tasty fried rice, sticky rice, and vegetables – ask to see their English menu. The quaintly named *Noodle Soupers Shop* is next door to the *Phosoi*.

Transport

It is far more pleasant to travel between **Luang Prabang** and Muang Ngoi by taxi boat (61,000 kip) than by bus. The river passes mountains, teak plantations, dry rice fields and a movable water-wheel mounted on a boat, which moves from village to village and is used for milling. But with the improvements that have been made to Route 13, road travel – both cheaper and quicker – has now become the preferred option for many.

Songthaew/truck Regular connections by songthaew with **Luang Prabang**, 3 hrs (14,000 kip). There are several departures a day for **Nam Bak**, 1 hr (5,000 kip), and on to **Muang Xai**. Alternatively, take one of the rather more regular songthaews to **Pak Mong**, 1 hr (8,000 kip) – there is a small noodle shop here – and then catch a vehicle on to Muang Xai, 2½ hrs (10,000 kip). Don't be surprised if there is a bit of a wait in Pak Mong. Travelling east on Route 1, there are buses to **Vieng Kham**, 2 hrs (12,000 kip), and **Nam Nouan** and from here south on Route 6 to **Phonsavanh** and the **Plain of Jars** (70,000 kip). It is usually necessary to stopover *en route*. There are guesthouses in Vieng Thong and Nam Nouan. In theory it is also possible to catch a bus northeast from Nam Nouan to **Xam Neua**, but this largely depends on the state of the roads and, therefore, the time of year. See Phonsavanh, page 155, and Xam Neua, page 163, for further details.

Boat There are occasional boats that travel up the Nam Ou, which joins the Mekong north of Luang Prabang, to **Muang Khua** via Muang Ngoi/Nong Khiaw (5 hrs, 45,000 kip). However, like river transport elsewhere in Laos, improvements in roads and road transportation have meant that boats are now infrequent, especially when the river is low. A speedboat to Muang Khua/Nong Khiaw from Luang Prabang should cost 100,000 kip (although it may be necessary to charter a boat) and there are also occasional slow cargo boats. From Muang Ngoi/Nong Khiaw some vessels continue upriver to Muang Khua (98,000 kip). Hazardous and uncomfortable but exhilarating travelling.

Useful information Electricity: 1830-2300.

Directory

Plain of Jars, Phonsavanh and Xam Neua

Apart from the historic Plain of Jars, Xieng Khouang province is best known for the pounding it took during the war. Many of the sights are battered monuments to the plateau's violent recent history. Given the cost of the return trip and the fact that the jars themselves aren't that spectacular, some consider the destination oversold. Indeed, any straw poll of visitors to the region will probably reveal a majority who feel disappointed by what they have seen – and doubtless slightly shell-shocked too at the sheer scale of the devastation. However, for those interested in modern military history, it's fascinating, and the countryside – particularly towards the Vietnam frontier – is beautiful. The jars, too, are interesting by dint of their very oddness: as if a band of giants' carousing had been suddenly interrupted, casting the jars across the plain in their hurry to leave.

20-Alternate

'20-Alternate' was the clandestine CIA headquarters near the Plain of Jars in northern Laos. It was so named to discourage journalists from going there, since it was but an 'alternate' air base, one of little importance. Also it was not shown on any maps. 20-Alternate was the staging base for General Vang Pao, the leader of the Hmong who fought the North Vietnamese for the Americans. At one time, during the height of the fighting, the 20-Alternate airfield was the busiest airport in the world with a landing or take-off every minute.

The North

Background

Xieng Khouang province has a murky history. This remote area was incorporated into the kingdom of Lane Xang by King Fa Ngoum in the 14th century but was often ruled by the Vietnamese (who called it Tran Ninh) because of its proximity to the border.

Travel agents and airlines tend to refer to Phonsavanh as Xieng Khouang, while Xieng Khouang is usually referred to locally as Muang Khoune, which leads to a good deal of confusion

As the Lao Aviation Y-12 turbo-prop begins its descent towards the plateau, the meaning of the term 'carpet bombing' becomes clear. On the final approach to the main town of **Phonsavanh**, the plane banks low over the cratered paddy fields, affording a T-28 fighter-bomber pilot's view of his target, which in places has been pummelled into little more than a moonscape. Some of the craters are 15 m across and 7 m deep. During the secret war against the North Vietnamese Army and the Pathet Lao, Xieng Khouang province received some of the heaviest bombing. The Plain of Jars was also hit by B-52s returning from abortive bombing runs to Hanoi as bombloads were jettisoned before heading back to the US air base at Udon Thani in northeast Thailand.

The MAG do not welcome tourists and their work should not be viewed as an 'attraction'

Tens of thousands of cluster bomb units (CBUs) were dumped on Xieng Khouang province in the 1960s and 1970s – as testified by the (former) scrap metal trade in CBU casings. Each unit was armed with 150 anti-personnel plastic 'pineapple' bomblets, which still regularly kill children and cripple adults. Hundreds of thousands of these bomblets – and their equally lethal cousins, impact mines, which the Lao call *bombis* – remain buried in Xieng Khouang's grassy meadows. One aid worker relates how in the mid-1980s, a specially designed, armour-plated tractor was terminally disabled by *bombis* while attempting to clear them from the fields. The UK-based Mines Advisory Group (MAG) is currently engaged in clearing the land of Unexploded Ordnance (UXO). They are beginning with schools and hospitals and then moving on to clear areas where fatalities are greatest. Villagers can also put requests in to have their back gardens cleared of ordnance. The fact that the MAG found a 500lb bomb close to their own HQ in Phonsavanh not very long ago illustrates the scale of the problem. Because the war was 'secret' there are few records of what was dropped and where – until someone is maimed. Often even the workings of the mines when they are uncovered is uncharted territory – the Americans used Laos as a testing ground for new ordnance and blueprints are unavailable.

Uncle Sam has, however, bequeathed to local people an almost unlimited supply of twisted metal. Bombshells and flare casings can frequently be seen in Xieng Khouang's villages where they are used for everything from cattle troughs and fences, to stilts for houses and water-carriers. In Phonsavanh steel runway sheets make handy walls while plants are potted out in shell casings. Research has shown that many villagers no longer see UXO as a problem. They have lived with it for over 20 years and more people die from malaria and in childbirth than they do from UXO.

At 1,000 m, the plateau area can be cold from December to March. The chief activity here is cattle rearing, although this has been much reduced by the aftereffects of the war. Xieng Khouang also supported tea plantations before the war and many French colonial settlers took to the temperate climate. Like the Bolovens Plateau to the south, the French colonial administration had visions of populating the Plain of Jars with thousands of hard-working French families. Only in this way, it was reasoned, could Laos be made to pay for itself. And only in the Plain of Jars and the Bolovens Plateau could French men and women be enticed to settle.

In the surrounding hills, the Hmong grew opium, which they traded to pedlars in Xieng Khouang town. Phonsavanh is the main town of the province today – old Xieng Khouang having been flattened – and its small airstrip is a crucial transport link in this mountainous region. The old town of Xieng Khouang – now rebuilt and renamed Muang Khoune – has a population of just a few thousand and Phonsavanh, 53,000. The whole province has a population of only around 250,000, a mix of different ethnic groups, predominantly Hmong, Lao and a handful of Khmu.

The province of Xieng Khouang is one of the poorest in an already wretchedly poor country. Government attempts to curtail shifting cultivation and encourage the Hmong to settle have been unsuccessful partly because there are no alternative livelihoods available that might induce the Hmong to change their swiddening ways. Travelling through the province there is a sense not just that the American air war caused enormous suffering and destruction, but that the following decades have not provided much in the way of economic opportunities.

Phonsavanh

The town offers little of interest other than the daily market, which is busy but rather undistinguished with the usual assortment of cheap Chinese bric-a-brac. The food market, behind the Post Office, is more lively and worth a wander. In fact the town is notable mainly for its sheer ugliness. It was only established in the mid-1970s and sprawls out from a heartless centre with no sense of plan, direction or pattern. Nonetheless, there are a fair few hotels and guesthouses in Phonsavanh for this is the only base available from which to explore the Plain of Jars.

Phone code: 061
Colour map 1, grid C4
It is cold here from Nov-Mar, several jumpers and a thick jacket are required

While Phonsavanh will win no beauty contests, it does have a rather attractive Wild West atmosphere. As journalist Malcolm Macalister Hall wrote in 1998: "I liked this ugly, rough-hewn town: for its unlikely invitations, its mad breakfasts, and the beautiful landscapes that surrounded it."

South of Phonsavanh, on two small hills, a pair of white and gold monuments can be seen. It is worth the short hike up, if only for the views they afford of the surrounding countryside. The monument on the left was built to commemorate the death of over one million Vietnamese troops in the war against the anti-communists. The newer monument to the right, more rounded in the Lao-style, was built later in memory of the Lao soldiers who died.

Tours If you arrive by air, the chances are you'll be inundated with official and unofficial would-be guides as soon as you step off the plane. Word on the street is to steer clear of 'Leon', his brother, and their chubby friend. At the other end of the spectrum, Vong from *LaneXang Travel* has had rave reviews from his groups, and chatters away about local legends and history. Alternatively, hotels, guesthouses and tour companies in town run tours to the Plain of Jars,

Muang Khoune (Xieng Khouang) and to Hmong villages to the northeast of Phonsavanh. A full day tour for four people, travelling about 30 km into the countryside, should cost up to US$60, although you may have to barter for it.

Excursions About 10 km southeast of Phonsavanh is the **Plain of Jars** (see page 155). Further southeast is the old city of **Muang Khoune** (**Xieng Khouang**) (see page 158). To the northeast, Route 7 runs to **Muang Kham** and the Vietnamese border (see page 159). Along this route are numerous Hmong villages; tour companies in town run trips out here. ■ *Getting there: public transport is limited and sporadic (see the entries for Muang Khoune, Plain of Jars and Muang Kham for more details). It's currently illegal to hire a tuk-tuk to get to the jars, and anyway, 4WDs are your best bet of making it successfully over the somewhat hairy roads out to the plains. As a rough guide, expect to pay in the region of US$30 for an English speaking guide to take 4 people, or US$60 with 7 people and a guide in a mini van. The cost of getting into each plain is 4,000 kip.*

The North

Sleeping
■ *on map*
Price codes:
see inside front cover
None of the streets in Phonsavanh are named – or at least the names aren't used. See the map on page 153 to check on the exact locations of the hotels and guesthouses

A *Auberge de la Plaine des Jarres*, T/F(Vientiane) 212613. In a spectacular position 1 km from the centre of Phonsavanh, on a hill overlooking town. More expensive in Oct-May. Restaurant, 16 attractive stone- and wood-built chalets with living room and fireplace, shower-room with hot water (sometimes), clean and comfortable, good food, lovely views, roses, geraniums and petunias planted around the chalets, the friendly owner speaks French.

B-C *Maly Hotel*, opposite *Inter-Lao Tourisme*, T312031, F312003. Startling green and aquamarine building. All rooms fully furnished with hot water bathrooms and a small (defused!) cluster bomb on the table. More expensive rooms are on the upper floors and come with satellite TV, sitting area and other luxuries. The lobby has a fireplace. Restaurant. Transport services available. The owner, Mr Sousath Phetrasy, also runs tours in the area and in the north from Xam Neua to the Burmese border at Xieng Kok. He spent his teenage years in a cave at Xam Neua during the war and has helped foreign researchers with projects in the region. He makes an excellent and knowledgeable guide. He speaks fluent English and German. Not a budget choice but recommended for the chance to meet the owner. **C** *Daophouan Hotel*, T312171. Opposite the food market. Large, clean doubles, with attached hot-water bathroom, breakfast included, but still overpriced, sterile and lacks atmosphere.

D-E *New Xieng Khouang Mai*, behind the dry market, T312049. Huge triples with attached (not very clean) bathroom; more expensive rooms have hot water. Staff friendly but seem to be on another planet; attached restaurant on main street. **D-E** *Phoudoi* (formerly the *Mittaphap*), T/F312048. Crumbling grey edifice flanked by a pair of shell casings opposite the *Lane Xang Bank*. Facilities include a restaurant (with considerable array of loudspeakers for karaoke), hot water showers (some shared) and their own generator which provides power 1800-2300. The most expensive room here is a suite with lurid blue satin bedcovers. Clean enough, excellent value for money, functional block.

E *Mouang Phouan*, T312046. 12 rooms in motel style with well-kept garden in front. A bungalow-style annexe with partitioned rooms and sitting area is situated down a quiet side street, also looking onto a little garden. Shared squat loos and wash area for annexe rooms, own toilets and washbasin in main hotel rooms. Hot water in thermos flasks provided; price includes breakfast and blankets offered in cold season. **E** *Panthavong*, T312099. Built in 2000 and a bit off the beaten track. Nothing special. **E** *Saengthavanh*, T211131. Clean, big and reputedly comfortable rooms with massive nets, cold showers. Friendly owners speak English and are taking further lessons at college. **E** *Van Aloun*, T312070. An ugly Chinese concrete house. Some rooms have their own bathrooms. Clean enough and friendly, although rooms a bit shabby now.

E-F *Kongkeo*, nice new house with large, clean rooms, some with ensuites, some with shared bathrooms. Rather excitingly, the shower on the roof is missing a bit of ceiling, so you can almost have a shower under the sun. But not quite, unless some doctoring has been done since our last visit. At the time of writing, several wooden huts were under construction out at the back, and looked very promising. See www.bostonreview.mit.edu/BR25.1/matteson.html "Remnants of War". The attached restaurant serves extremely cheap and equally spicy food. **F** *Dokkhoune*, T312189. 10 clean rooms with bare concrete floors and some with attached clean bathrooms. Sitting area, small balcony, substantial house with Russian shell casings in lobby, some used as plant pots. One of the better places to stay. **F** *Hay Hin*, T312252. Basic, but toilet paper and soap is provided. Warren-like, with rooms partitioned with hardboard. Upstairs, where there is a balcony and a communal sitting area, the rooms are slightly better. Tea provided, the manager does not speak English but is extremely enthusiastic. **F** *Phonsavanh Hotel*, T312206. Huge, clean rooms with attached bathroom, though the water supply is erratic. Sometimes quite noisy with parties downstairs. Doors with glass panels provide endless fun for nosy children; seems to be operating as a part-time brothel. **F** *Vinhthong*, T312047. Clean and serviceable rooms, some with enormous attached bathrooms. Friendly Vietnamese owner, display of shell casings, weapons and ammunition in lobby. Tours of the Plain of Jars organized. Excellent value. Recommended.

Phonsavanh

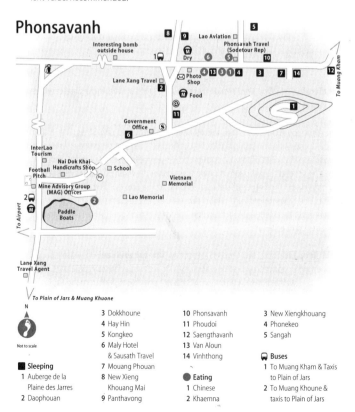

N
Not to scale

■ **Sleeping**
1 Auberge de la Plaine des Jarres
2 Daophouan
3 Dokkhoune
4 Hay Hin
5 Kongkeo
6 Maly Hotel & Sausath Travel
7 Mouang Phouan
8 New Xieng Khouang Mai
9 Panthavong
10 Phonsavanh
11 Phoudoi
12 Saengthavanh
13 Van Aloun
14 Vinhthong

● **Eating**
1 Chinese
2 Khaemna
3 New Xiengkhouang
4 Phonekeo
5 Sangah

🚌 **Buses**
1 To Muang Kham & Taxis to Plain of Jars
2 To Muang Khoune & taxis to Plain of Jars

The North

Eating
● *on map*
Price codes:
see inside front cover

Mid-range *Auberge de Plaine de Jarres*, reasonable menu of Lao dishes and some French food, somewhat overpriced given the competition.

Cheap *Chinese Restaurant*, a few doors down from *New Xieng Khouang*, hot Sichuan dishes are on the menu, a bit pricey, and be prepared to wait a long time.

Cheap to seriously cheap *Khaemna Garden Restaurant*, a fabulous setting by a lake overlooking a long stretch of rice paddies (don't forget your mosquito repellant). This place is just great. Super food (from the usual menu) and friendly service. Recommended. *Meuangphone*, on the same road as the *Chinese Restaurant* and a few doors down. A large restaurant that appears impersonal but the service is friendly and quick. Lao and western dishes. *New Xiengkhouang*, next door to *Van Aloun*. Flashy fairy lights out front, but the service is impossibly slow. Usual Falang fare and Lao dishes, bicycles can be hired here at an expensive US$2 per day. *Phonekeo*, limited menu with some dishes to raise the eyebrows, including Placenta Salad. "Chewy rubber" was the opinion of the only and regret-riddled patron we found, and he was talking about the chicken. *Sangah*, opposite the *Van Aloun Hotel*. Phonsavanh is not known for its gastronomic delights, but this is where many locals would choose to come if they had the choice. Thai, Lao and Vietnamese (good noodle soup) dishes all available as well as some Western fare including steak and chips. Enormous portions.

Seriously cheap *Phonsavanh Service*, next to the airport. Serves whisky, beer, nibbles and good noodle soup if you can avoid swallowing the flies.

Festivals

Dec *National Day* (second), horse-drawn drag-cart racing festival in Phonsavanh.

Dec/Jan *Hmong New Year* (movable) is celebrated in a big way in this area. Festivities centre around the killing of a pig and offering the head to the spirits. Cloth balls, *makoi*, are given by boys to girls they've taken a fancy to.

Shopping

Handicrafts *Noi Dok Khai Handicrafts Shop*, T312213, weavings, silks, carvings and baskets.

Tour operators

Lane Xang, on road south from the market. Helpful but no English spoken (other people in neighbouring shops may help interpret – eg the pharmacy). *Inter-Lao Tourisme*, slightly out of town, opposite the government office (see map). *Sodetour* have a representative who runs his own tours under the *Plain of Jars Travel Agency*. The office is on the corner of the road leading to the *Lao Aviation* office. Excellent English. The Government-run *Phoudoi Hotel* offers the cheapest tours in the area. But for the most knowledgeable tour guide, the owner of the *Maly Hotel* (see above) beats the competition.

Transport

Local **Jeep hire**: from *Hay Hin*, US$35 per day. **Tuk-tuk and taxi**: if it wasn't illegal, this method of transport would cost about 50,000 kip return fare to Plain of Jars. Taxis and tuk-tuks wait at both bus terminals. **NB** It is not possible to walk from the airport to the Plain, as there is a military base in between.

Long distance **Air**: the airport is about 5 km from town. 5,000 kip airport departure tax. A tuk-tuk to town is 6,000 kip per person. Twice daily connections with **Vientiane**, 40 mins (US$44), and 4 flights a week with **Luang Prabang**, on Mon, Wed, Fri and Sun, 25 mins (US$35). There is an exchange branch of the *Aroun May Bank* at the airport but don't count on it being open.

Bus: the most direct route to/from **Luang Prabang** is to take Route 7 west to Phou Khoun and then to travel north along Route 13, the recently upgraded 'highway' between Vientiane and Luang Prabang. However, at the time of updating, Route 7 was only intermittently open to buses. Its history is also dicey, as it used to be period-ically attacked by anti-government bandits. Things have quietened down, but it can take up to 2 days to negotiate as the condition of the road (unsealed) is terrible. It is often impassable in the wet season. The safer and longer alternative is to take Route 6 north to Nam Nouan (4-5 hrs, 23,000 kip), then travel west on Route 1 through Muang Ngoi to Pak Mong, and then to head south to Luang Prabang. It is usually nec-essary to stopover *en route*. There are guesthouses in Muang Ngoi, Vieng Thong and Nam Nouan.

Rather than turning south of Luang Prabang, it is also possible to continue west on Route 1 to **Muang Xai** (Udom Xai). To do this, take a bus north from Phonsavanh to Nam Nouen (4-5 hrs, 23,000 kip) and then west on Route 1 to Muang Ngoi and onwards to Muang Xai with a change at Pak Mong. It is usually necessary to stopover *en route*. There are guesthouses in Vieng Thong, Muang Ngoi (see page 147) and Nam Nouan. The trip to Luang Prabang from Phonsavanh, via Nam Nouen, costs 75,000 kip.

In theory, it should be possible to take a bus along Route 7 to Route 13 and then run south to **Vientiane** via Vang Vieng. However Route 7, as noted above, is still in very poor condition. Nonetheless, in the dry season there is 1 bus a day (180,000 kip) to Vientiane departing at 0830, but get there earlier to ensure your place on it (15-30 hrs, sometimes even longer!). Another way of reaching Vientiane – but again, in theory rather than practise – is to take Route 22 south to Pakxan, on the Mekong and then take one of the many buses which run along Route 13 to the capital. While there are plans to upgrade Route 22 south to Pakxan, which would greatly improve access with Vientiane, in 2002 it was still in a terrible state of repair with no bus services. Locals are not optimistic about it being upgraded in the near future.

There are regular taxis and buses and trucks to **Muang Kham** (3 hrs, taxi 12,000 kip or bus 10,000 kip), and trucks to **Nam Nouan** (4-5 hrs, 23,000 kip). From Nam Nouan there are buses north to **Xam Neua**. The upgrading of this road was completed in early 1999 and the journey can take as little as 2½-3 hrs and, as a result, it was possible to make the journey between Phonsavanh and Xam Neua in a day without an overnight stop *en route* – that is, if you started out early enough. Already, though, just a few rainy seasons have made the road not quite what it once was, and undertaking the journey could even be a lost battle. Check before setting off.

Banks *Lane Xang Bank*, opposite *Phoudoi Hotel*, changes cash and travellers' cheques, 0800-1200, 1330-1600. **Communications** Internet: at the time of writing, there was only 1 internet café in town, and it really wasn't worth waiting the eternity it took for the connection to fail. The going rate is astronomical because there's no elec-tricity half the time! Post office: opposite dry market. IDD call boxes outside. **Useful information** Electricity: 1830-2300. **Directory**

Plain of Jars

The 1,000 m-high, 1,000 sq km undulating plateau of the Plain of Jars (also known as Plaine de Jarres, or Thong Hai Hin), is about 50 km east to west. More than 300 jars survive, mainly (286, apparently) scattered on one slope – so-called 'Site One' or **Thong Hai Hin**. This site is closest to Phonsavanh (about 10 km) and has the largest jar – along with a small restaurant. For true jar lovers, Site Two (68 jars) known as **Hai Hin Phu Salatao** and Site Three (88 jars) called **Hai Hin Laat Khai** are about 30-40 km beyond Muang Khoune. A car is required to get to these outer sites. Note that while there are

Colour map 1, grid C5

The North

other assemblages of jars on the plain, most have not been cleared of UXO and visiting without a guide is not advised. ■ *Entrance fee to Plain of Jars: 4,000 kip. Restaurant.*

Origins of the jars

Most of the jars are 1-2½ m high, around 1 m in diameter and weigh about the same as three small cars. The jars have long presented an archaeological conundrum – leaving generations of theorists nonplussed by how they got there and what they were used for. Local legend relates that King Khoon Chuong and his troops from Southern China threw a stupendous party after their victory over the wicked Chao Angka and had the jars made to brew outrageous quantities of *lau-lao*.

However attractive the alcohol thesis, it is more likely that they are in fact 2,000-year-old stone funeral urns. The larger jars are believed to have been for the local aristocracy and the smaller jars for their minions. Some archaeologists speculate that the cave below the main site was hewn from the rock at about the same time as the jars themselves and that the hole in the roof possibly means the cave was used for cremation or that the jars were made and fired in the cave. But it's all speculation and their origins and function remain a mystery: the stone from which they are hewn doesn't even seem to come from the region. Closer to sites Two and Three are some half-hewn jars and archaeologists have postulated that they were carved here and then transported to Site One. The rock, apparently, is the same. Tools, bronze ornaments, ceramics and other objects have been found in the jars indicating that a civilized society was responsible for them – but no one has a clue which one, as the artefacts bear no relation to those left behind by other ancient Indochinese civilizations. Some of the jars were once covered with round lids and there is one jar with a rough carving of a dancing figure in the group facing the entrance to the cave.

Strategic battleground

Over the years a few jars have been stolen and a number have been transported by helicopter down to Vientiane's Wat Phra Kaeo and the back yard of the Revolutionary Museum. Local guides claim that despite four or five B-52 bombing raids every day for five years, the jars remained mysteriously unscathed; however, at the main site, several bomb craters and damaged jars show this to be a fanciful myth. During the heavy fighting on the Plain in the early 1970s, the Pathet Lao set up a command centre in the 'cave' next to the jars and then posed among the jars for photographs (which can be seen in the Revolutionary Museum in Vientiane). Around the entrance to the cave are numerous bomb craters as the US targeted the sanctuary in a futile attempt to dislodge the communists.

The Plain occupies an important niche in modern Lao history as it became one of the most strategic battlegrounds of the war. For General Vang Pao's Hmong, it was the hearthstone of their mountain kingdom; for the royalist government and the Americans it was a critical piece in the Indochinese jigsaw; for Hanoi it was their back garden, which had to be secured to protect their rear flank.

From the mid-1960s, neutralist forces were encamped on the Plain (dubbed 'the PDJ' during the war). They were supported by Hmong, based at the secret city of Long Tieng, to the southwest. US-backed and North Vietnamese-backed forces fought a bitter war of attrition on the PDJ; each time royalist and Hmong forces were defeated on the ground, US air power was called in to pummel from above. In mid-February 1970, American Strategic Air Command, on presidential orders, directed that B-52 Stratofortress bombers should be used over the PDJ for the first time. Capable of silently dumping more than a hundred 500-lb bombs from 40,000 ft, they had a devastating effect on the towns and villages. Half-a-million tonnes of bombs had been dropped on the PDJ by the end of the war – not including the thousands of tonnes jettisoned by bombers returning to bases in Thailand from Hanoi. But they had minimal effect on Communist morale. Even if the B-52s had managed to wipe out North Vietnamese and Pathet Lao forces, the US-backed troops were unable to reach, let alone hold, the territory. Hanoi had garrisons of reinforcements waiting in the wings.

On the Plain, the B-52 proved as inappropriate and ineffective a weapon as it later would on the Ho Chi Minh Trail. As the US bomber command increasingly turned its attention to the Trail, the Pathet Lao quickly seized the upper hand and retook the PDJ. The Communists were beaten back onto the surrounding hills and ridges a few more times by Vang Pao's forces and American bombers, but they kept swarming back. By March 1972, the North Vietnamese Army had seven divisions in Laos supporting the Pathet Lao. **Phu Kheng** ('Mountain of Courage' – the hill behind the new airport to the northwest), was the scene of some particularly hard fighting. It was here that the royalists, encamped on Phu Kheng, were trapped on two fronts by the Communists. When the Pathet Lao retook Xieng Khouang for the last time in 1973, they consolidated their position and bided their time.

The Plain today A vast aviation fuel depot was built next to the jars, early in the 1990s, to supply the huge new airbase just to the west. The base, designed by Soviet technicians, is the new headquarters for the Lao Air Force – which amounts to a grand total of nine Migs.

Plain of Jars

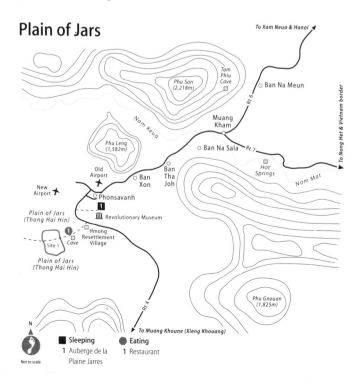

Along with the bomb craters that scar the landscape there are also patches of bare earth that have nothing to do with the Indochina conflict. These are avine free-fire zones. Local people clear the land of grass over an area of about 10 sq m and build a small hide. They then put sticky rice down and wait for the poor creatures to alight for a leisurely lunch before being blasted. The main season is after the first rains.

On the grasslands around the Jars are stumpy little flowers, known as '*Baa*' by the Hmong and '*dok waan*' by the Lao; they are eaten by local people – the stems are boiled to make a soup while the red buds are fried. Once the flower has bloomed (turning yellow), they are no longer tasty. *En route* to the Plain, the road passes through a **Hmong resettlement village**, distinctive for its style of housing – their homes are not built on stilts and there is no separate kitchen area on the side.

Transport Only accessible by vehicles from Phonsavanh (see Transport, page 154). It should be possible to drive to the Plain of Jars, see the Jars and return to town in 2 hrs. At the time of writing, tuk-tuks were barred indefinitely from ferrying customers around the plains, but should the ban be lifted a chartered tuk-tuk should cost about 50,000 kip. A more comfortable jeep is anything from US$35 for the day.

Muang Khoune (Xieng Khouang)

Colour map 1, grid C4 The original, old town of Xieng Khouang was destroyed during the war along with the civilization that went with it. The town was founded by Chao Noi Muang and was a stronghold for the Xieng Khouang royal family. In 1832 the Hmong mountain state of Xieng Khouang was annexed by Vietnam and renamed Tran Ninh. The king was marched off to Vietnam and publicly executed in Hué, while the population of Xieng Khouang was forced to wear Vietnamese dress.

Many important temples were built here in the distinctive Xieng Khouang style but these were completely obliterated by the American bombing. The religious architectural style of the province was one of the three main styles of Laos (Luang Prabang and Vientiane styles being the other two). The town was also the main centre for the French in this area during the colonial period and remnants of French colonial architecture are still in evidence.

Xieng Khouang was most heavily bombed during 1969 and 1970 when US air power was called in to reverse the success of the Communists' dry-season offensive on the Plain of Jars. In his book *The Ravens*, Christopher Robins interviews several former US pilots who describe the annihilation of the town in which 1,500 buildings were razed, together with another 2,000 across the plain. Three towns, he says, "were wiped from the map. By the end of the year (1970) there would not be a building left standing." During this time most villagers left their homes and lived in caves or in the forest. They subsisted on rice from China and Vietnam. So incessant was the bombing and strafing that peasants took to planting their rice fields at night.

The town, which is in fact little more than a village, was rebuilt after 1975 and renamed Muang Khoune, but today it holds nothing in the way of aesthetic charm and a sense of impermanence prevails; it consists of a row of wooden Lao houses and a market area. This, at least in the dry season, is Xieng Khouang province's equivalent of Dry Gulch. While Muang Khouane itself is spectacularly unimpressive, its position, surrounded by mountains, is noteworthy.

The North

Those excited about the prospect of visiting a unique collection of 500-year-old wats must, for the most part, be content with piles of 16th-century bricks. There is virtually nothing left of the 16th-century **Wat Phia Wat** (at the far end of town on the right hand side by the road), except the basement and several shrapnel-pocked Buddha statues. A half-hearted attempt at renovation remains barely noticeable. Walking up the hill, the French colonial remains of the Governor's house can be seen, with some old tile floors still in place and a hospital, patched together Lao-style. Next door to the Governor's house is a weaving school set up with UNDP money, teaching up to 60 students.

Two stupas perch on a pair of hills above the town. **That Chompet** – also known as That Dam – dates from the 16th century and is quite sizeable. The *that* is said to contain relics of the Indian emperor Asoka but this should be taken with a large drop of *nam pa*. But it does explain, perhaps, why the heart of the stupa has been hollowed out as thieves have searched – apparently in vain – for buried treasure. It is possible to scramble through the middle of the stupa. **That Phuane**, on the further hill, is smaller, with a square base. The centre of the stupa has also been dug out by treasure hunters.

Wat Si Phoum (opposite the market below the main road) was also destroyed by the war. A new inelegant wat has been built next to the ruined *that*. There is a small monastery attached to the wat. The market here holds little interest for the tourist, with nothing on sale but the bare essentials.

There is one small, very basic, hotel in town. Some of the Lao restaurants also accommodate travellers overnight; ask around. Good *feu* opposite the market.

Bus Daily bus connections with **Phonsavanh** from the morning market, 1-2 hrs (6,500 kip). Buses from Phonsavanh to Muang Khoune leave from the station just next to the Phonsavanh morning market, 1-2 km out of town towards Highway 4; take a tuk-tuk (4,000 kip per person). There are also trucks running between the 2 towns. **Tuk-tuk or taxi** Possible in the dry season.

Route 7 and Muang Kham

Route 7 heads east from Phonsavanh towards Muang Kham and the border with Vietnam. Attractive rolling hills and grassy meadows in the wet season, but very barren in the dry season, especially where the bomb craters have pock-marked the landscape. About 12 km east of Phonsavanh is the village of **Ban Xon** which lays claim to two famous daughters, Baoua Kham and Baoua Xi. These two heroines of the revolution are fêted for having shot down a US B-52 with small arms fire. War historians are very sceptical about this claim, but a Lao popular song was nonetheless written about them. The ballad is said to extol the beauty and courage of the women of Xieng Khouang.

The drive is an abject lesson in the potentially destructive nature of some forms of shifting cultivation. The figures are of dubious accuracy, but some authorities estimate that 100,000 ha of forest is destroyed each year in Laos by shifting cultivation. The government has had some success in reducing this from an estimated 300,000 ha in the 1970s, but it has been difficult to control. The difficulty in apportioning blame is that the Lao authorities would like to blame the minority shifting cultivators – especially the Hmong. Often swidden, or shifting cultivation, agriculturalists will cultivate land already logged-over by commercial timber firms for the simple reason that it is easier to cultivate. They then find themselves blamed for the destruction.

Route 7 winds its way down off the plateau along the **Nam Keua**, a fertile area where Hmong villagers grow rice and maize.

About 30 km east of Phonsavanh is the roadside Hmong village of **Ban Tha Joh**. For those wishing to visit a more traditional Hmong village, **Ban Na Sala** is 3 km up the road. Leave your vehicle at Ban Na Sala Mai on the road and walk south, up a very pleasant valley to the village. It is one of the best places to see the creative architectural and household application of war debris.

Muang Kham, 53 km east of Phonsavanh, is a small trading town in the centre of a large open valley on the route to Vietnam and China. Devastated during the war, it now has a thriving economy dealing in Vietnamese and Chinese goods. The valley is an important fruit and rice growing area. There's a market early every morning in the centre of town and there are also a couple of groups of stone jars close by. A simple restaurant serves noodle dishes.

More evidence of the dirty war can be seen. The intensity of the US bombing campaign under the command of the late General Curtis Le May was such that entire villages were forced to take refuge in caves. (Curtis Le May is infamously associated with bragging that he wanted to bomb the Communists 'back into the Stone Age'.) If discovered, fighter bombers were called in to destroy them. In the **Tam Phiu (Phiu Cave)**, overlooking the fertile valley near Muang Kham, 365 villagers from nearby Ban Na Meun built a two-storey bomb shelter and concealed its entrance with a high stone wall. They lived there for a year, working in their rice fields at night and taking cover during the day from the relentless bombing raids which killed thousands in the area. On the morning of 8 March 1968 two T-28 fighter-bombers took off from Udon Thani air base in neighbouring Thailand and located the cave mouth which had been exposed on previous sorties. It is likely that the US forces suspected that the cave contained a Pathet Lao hospital complex. Indeed, experts are at odds whether this was a legitimate target or an example of collateral damage.

The first rocket destroyed the wall, the second, fired as the planes swept across the valley, carried the full length of the chamber before exploding. There were no survivors and 11 families were completely wiped out. Local rescuers claim they were unable to enter the cave for three days, but eventually the dead were buried in a bomb crater on the hillside next to the cave mouth. Remains of their skulls, bones and teeth still litter the orange earth covering their makeshift grave. The interior of the cave was completely dug up by the rescue parties and relatives looking for their belongings and today there is nothing but rubble inside. It makes for a poignant lesson in military history and locally it is considered a war memorial. ■ *Getting there: the cave is to the west of the Muang Kham-Xam Neua road, just after the 183 km post. A rough track leads down to an irrigation dam, built in 1981.* An unexploded bomb lies embedded in the stream by the dam and the cave mouth is directly above.

Not far from Muang Kham, off the Vietnam road are two **hot springs** (*bor nam lawn*), on the Nam Mat. These are imaginatively named Bor Yai (Big Spring) and Bor Noi (Little Spring). They are said to have enormous potential for geothermal power but this is hard to believe as they do not appear to be particularly active. The murky water is distinctly uninviting but it is piped to showers and wooden tubs, where a therapeutic soak can be quite pleasant. They are locally known for their curative properties. ■ *Getting there: no buses go to the Hot Springs from Muang Kham, taxis may take you there for about 50,000 kip. See also Sleeping below.*

Nong Het is approximately 60 km from Muang Kham on the Vietnamese **Excursions**
border. It is deep in Hmong country and is an important trading post with
Vietnam, which is just a few kilometres down the road.

E *Hot Spring Guesthouse*, at the big hot spring, 2 bungalows, each with 4 rooms and 1 **Sleeping**
bathroom. **F** *My Xay Guesthouse*, opposite bus station in Muang Kham; serviceable
triples with bathrooms.

This area is accessible by truck, bus and sometimes songthaew. The only way to visit **Transport**
the minority villages *en route* to Muang Kham is by hiring a taxi. **Bus** From
Phonsavanh, buses to Muang Kham leave from the bus station near the market in the
centre of town (10,000 kip). **Taxi** It costs about US$35 to hire a jeep or taxi for the day
to visit the minority villages and other sights around Muang Kham.

Hua Phan and Phongsali Provinces

The North

*Hua Phan and Phongsali provinces were the base areas for the left-wing insur-
gency from the end of the 1940s until the final victory of the Pathet Lao over the
Royalist forces in 1975. Even before 1954, when the Geneva Agreement effectively ended French rule in Indochina, these provinces were under the control of the communists.* This was for two reasons. First, the proximity of
Phongsali and Hua Phan to Vietnam – the Lao Issara, the forerunners of the
Pathet Lao fled to Vietnam to take refuge with Ho Chi Minh's forces after
they had been initially defeated by the French in 1946. The second reason is
the sheer military difficulty of controlling an area that is so mountainous
and geographically fragmented – perfect territory for fighting a guerrilla war
against a technically and numerically superior enemy. Even in the early
1990s Phonsali felt like a country apart and to get to the provincial capital –
let alone outlying villages – involved a journey of more than three days by
boat. When the river was too low for boat travel the only means of access was
by helicopter, or on foot. Even today it is easy to appreciate why the communists chose to fight their war from this corner of Laos.

Xam Neua (Sam Neua)

Xam Neua is the capital of Hua Phan Province, known in Laos as a 'revolutionary province'. One of the poorest and most isolated areas of the country, it
has been sheltered from the free market ethos that has spilled into towns along
the Thai and Chinese borders.

Memories of the period when it was the base for the revolutionary struggle in
the 1950-70s are still close to the surface. The Lao Communist Party was
formed in Xam Neua in 1955 and the Pathet Lao had their headquarters in the
area as they confronted the right-wing government in Vientiane and the US.
American planes tried to dislodge the Communists from their mountain
redoubt, but protected in their caves they survived the onslaught. After the
war, senior members of the Royal Lao Government were sent to re-education
camps in the province. Loudspeakers in the market area blast music and propaganda from 0600 in the morning and there is a strong military presence. A
camp in the middle of town is off-limits to foreigners.

Phone code: 064
Colour map 1, grid B5
Population: 250,000
Altitude: 1,200 m
*Summer is pleasant in
Xam Neua but
temperatures at night
reach freezing in
winter. Bring a
pullover. The
mosquitoes are
monstrous,
precautions against
malaria advised*

Sights

The area is at its most pictureseque in October, when the rice is almost ripe

As the town was obliterated during the war and has been rebuilt since 1973, it is not terribly surprising that it offers little in the way of sights. Indeed Xam Neua's chief attraction is as a staging point for the caves at Vieng Xai. However the town's setting, at 1,200 m amid forested hills and rice fields, is pleasant enough. Walking a kilometre or two up Highway 6 which leads to Nam Bak and Phonsavanh affords excellent views of the town and an adjoining valley.

There is much evidence of swidden agriculture on the hillsides; indeed families practicing slash-and-burn can be found within a few minutes' walk of the central market. The **market** itself is good for hilltribe spotting – Hmong, Yao, Thai Dam (Black Thai), Thai Khao (White Thai), Thai Neua (Northern Thai) and other hill peoples can all be found buying and selling various commodities. There is also a strong Chinese and Vietnamese presence in the town. In the adjoining dry market, examples of the distinctive weaving of Xam Neua and Xam Tai can be found at reasonable prices along with goods trucked in from China and Vietnam.

Weaving

The province is known for its **weaving** and many houses have looms on their verandas. There are several workshops with four or five looms each; some of these use traditional vegetable dyes rather than the aniline (chemical) dyes which are the norm in most other areas. As far as is known from the somewhat sketchy evidence, Hua Phan was one of the 'cradle' areas for Lao weaving. This, combined with its remoteness, means that the diversity of designs produced in the province is second to none, as techniques that have become rare elsewhere are still practised here. The premier centre for weaving is at Xam Tai (local pronunciation, Xam Teua), 100 km to the southeast (see Excursions below).

Excursions

Exercise caution when travelling independently in Hua Phan: some of the authorities harbour a residual suspicion of westerners

Nam Tok Dat Salari is an excellent waterfall which zig-zags 100 m down a rock face, 36 km along Highway 6 to Nam Neun, visible on the left 3 km after the village of Ban Doan. The falls are difficult to miss as there are numerous empty houses and stalls by the road, used once a year by much of the population of Xam Neua when it decamps en masse to celebrate Pimai (Lao New Year) at the site. A track leads through the jungle on the right of the falls right to the top – a very good swimming and picnic spot.

Xam Tai lies 100 km to the southeast of Xam Neua, close to the Vietnamese border. It is the most famous weaving centre in the area, and is also said to be scenically beautiful. The road is bad and there is no guesthouse at Xam Tai. ■ *Getting there: you can try to charter a pick-up at the market, or hire a car at the Lao Houn Hotel.*

Sop Hao, 60 km east on the Vietnam border, features a trade fair each Saturday.

Sleeping

■ *on map*
Price codes: see inside front cover

E-F *Lao Houn*, next to the bridge over the Nam Xam facing the market, T312018. The formerly government-run hotel known as the *Sam Neua* or *No 1 Guesthouse* is now privatized and gradually improving. There are 28 rooms, some with attached bathrooms, varying from grubby downstairs to semi-clean upstairs. En-suite bathrooms were renovated a few years back and feature western toilet and hot shower. The communal bathrooms are dirty with no hot water, squat toilets and baths using bucket-and-scoop technology. There is a pleasant view of the town and hills from upstairs, the staff are friendly and one of the girls speaks good English. Restaurant, watch out for rats.

F *Dok Mai Dieng Guesthouse*, on the main road facing the market area, T312190. Two and 3-bed dormitory accommodation, priced per bed, shared bath and squat

The North

loo, basic. **F** *Phanxay*, big grey creepy-looking house on the main road just after it turns half-left away from the market area. Rooms with 3-4 beds and attached bathrooms. Moderately clean, light, more spacious than the other dormitory options; comfy chairs, restaurant. **F** *Phanhsam Guesthouse*, T312255. Vietnamese establishment, up the road from the *Dok Mai Dieng*. Doubles and 1 single, bedding a bit grungy, shared bath and squat toilet, with the best Italian manufactured hot water shower in Xam Neua, although accommodation is cramped. **F** *Thath Mouang* , T312141. Powder blue house just behind the *Phanxay*. Very friendly family with strings of singing and dancing children. Standard doubles and twins with towels provided, clean and airy, huge balcony area, shared western toilet and hot water shower. Recommended. **F** *Kheam Xam Guesthouse*, T312111. Opposite the *Lao Houn Hotel* on the corner, 3 floors, excellent views from top balcony, basic twins, large rooms, shared hot water shower and toilet, tiled floors, good restaurant downstairs.

Xam Neua is not going to win any gastronomic awards. One suspects this is a historical legacy: for decades the population have been more concerned with survival than conjuring up new dishes. The best service, though the food is average, is at the *Mit Sam Phan Restaurant*, the only place that seems to do chips. Their opening hours are erratic and they may be closed for days at a time. The *Sam Neua May Restaurant* very rarely has any food, but when they do they can serve up delicious fried noodles. **Cheap** *Phanxay Hotel Restaurant*, fair Lao and Chinese food, but none too clean. **Seriously cheap** Many noodle shops in the market area along the street adjacent to the river, of which *Joy's Place* (sign in English) is the best.

Eating
● *on map*
Price codes:
see inside
front cover

The North

Air The airport at Xam Neua has been recently upgraded and there are now daily or twice-daily connections with **Vientiane**, 1 hr 15 mins (US$70). The airport is 3 km from the centre of town on the road that leads to Vieng Xai and Vietnam, 3,000 kip in a tuk-tuk. All flights are subject to delay or cancellation due to the area's susceptibility to fog, especially during winter. *Lao Aviation*, T312023.

Transport

Xam Neua

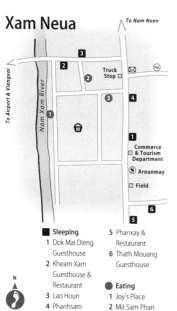

trucks: leave daily for **Nam Nouan**, where there are daily connections to **Phonsavanh** and, less regularly, to **Muang Ngoi**. The journey from Xam Neua to Nam Nouan takes 3-4 hrs, buses departing from opposite the post office at 0600 (excellent road); 6 hrs Nam Nouan-Phonsavanh (beware: the drivers tend to charge foreigners double on this route). Now the road from Xam Neua to Nam Nouan has been upgraded it might no longer be necessary to stay in Nam Nouan if you are coming from Phonsavanh. In the dry season, and if you leave early enough, you may be sufficiently lucky to make the journey in 1 day. If you are coming from Muang Ngoi it might be possible to catch an early bus, but more likely you will have to stay overnight in Vieng Thong, 3 hrs away. There are daily connections from Vieng Thong to Xam Neua and

■ **Sleeping**
1 Dok Mai Dieng Guesthouse
2 Kheam Xam Guesthouse & Restaurant
3 Lao Houn
4 Phanhsam Guesthouse
5 Phanxay & Restaurant
6 Thath Mouang Guesthouse

● **Eating**
1 Joy's Place
2 Mit Sam Phan
3 Sam Neua May

N
Not to scale

Phonsavanh. **Bus**: these leave from the market area regularly during the morning and into the early afternoon for **Vieng Xai**. It is said to be possible to hire **motorbikes** from the market in Xam Neua (US$ 15 per day).

Directory **Banks** *Arounmay Bank*, halfway along the main street, changes US$ and Thai baht. **Communications** There is a **post office** on the main street. The IDD call box is opposite.

Vieng Xai (Viengsay)

Colour map 1, grid B6

Most visitors to Vieng Xai and the caves stay in Xam Neua and make a day-trip out here

Most visitors to Vieng Xai and the caves stay in Xam Neua and make a day-trip out here

Vieng Xai and the surrounding countryside were strongholds for the left-wing insurgency. From 1964 onwards operations were directed from the cave systems at Vieng Xai, which proved an effective refuge from furious bombing attacks. At the height of the war, thousands of soldiers, government officials and their families occupied the valley at Vieng Xai and more operated from the surrounding region. The spectacular limestone karsts of the area are riddled with natural caves. Many were enlarged to create living quarters, offices, garages, supply depots, hospitals, schools and ammunition dumps. In the run-up to the fall of Vientiane there was even talk among the Pathet Lao leadership of making Vieng Xai an alternative capital, but this idea was dropped after 1975.

Ins & outs **Getting there** The village of Vieng Xai is 31 km east of Xam Neua on a road that branches off Route 6 to Sop Hao on the Vietnam border. The turn-off to the right is at Km 20. Pick-ups and passenger trucks shuttle between Xam Neua and Vieng Xai in the morning and a few in the early afternoon, but virtually none after 1500.

See Transport, page 167, for further details

Visiting the caves All the caves are within walking distance of the village. Visitors have to buy tickets for the caves (4,000 kip per person for each cave) from the Viengxay Cave Memorial Office, on the left-hand side of the government building. They may insist you take an attendant. On public holidays you can buy tickets at the entrance to the caves. The caves have been fitted with electric bulbs but you may find a torch useful. There is also a small museum in the village, behind the gold statue, which contains some interesting old photographs, many of them unlabelled. Ask the attendant to show it to you if he doesn't offer of his own accord.

Background Members of the Lao Issara who had fled to Vietnam after French forces smashed the movement in 1946 infiltrated areas of northeast Laos in 1947-49 under the sponsorship of the Viet Minh. The movement coalesced when Prince Souphanouvong, who had fled to Thailand, arrived in Hanoi and organized a conference in August 1950 at which the Free Lao Front and the Lao Resistance Government were formed. Thereafter, the Pathet Lao adopted strategies developed by the Viet Minh in Vietnam, who in turn drew on the strategies of Mao Zedong and the Chinese Communists: the establishment of bases in remote mountain areas, use of guerrilla tactics, exploitation of the dissatisfactions of tribal minorities and mobilization of the entire populations of liberated areas in support of the revolutionary struggle.

By the time of the Geneva Agreement of 1954 following the French defeat at Dien Bien Phu, Communist forces effectively controlled Hua Phan and Phongsali, a fact acknowledged in the terms of the settlement, which called for their regroupment inside these provinces pending a political settlement. The Pathet Lao used the breathing space afforded by this and the succession of coalition governments in the late 1950s and early 1960s to reorganize their operations. The Lao People's Revolutionary Party was formed at Xam Neua in 1955 and the Neo Lao Hak Sat, or National Front, was established in 1956. While Party President Prince Souphanouvong spent a good deal of time in Vientiane participating in successive coalition governments between 1958 and 1964, Secretary-General Kaysone Phomvihane remained in Hua Phan overseeing the political and military organization of the liberated zone.

The beginning of the American bombing campaign in 1964 forced the Pathet Lao leadership to find a safe haven from which to direct the war. Vieng Xai was chosen because its numerous limestone karsts contained many natural caves which could be used for quarters, while their proximity to each other inhibited attack from the air. Nevertheless, phosphorous rockets and napalm caused many casualties in the less fortified caves.

Previously, the valley had been home only to two small villages, Ban Bac and Nakay. The Pathet Lao leadership renamed the area Vieng Xai, meaning 'City of Victory' and it became the administrative and military hub of the revolutionary struggle. The first bombing raid on the area took place in 1965 and the caves were enlarged and reinforced with concrete from 1965 to 1967.

The village

Built in 1973, when the bombing finally stopped and the short-lived Provisional Government of National Union was negotiated, the former capital of the liberated zone is an unlikely sight. Surrounded by rice fields at the dead end of a potholed road, it features street lighting, power lines, sealed and kerbed streets and substantial public buildings – all in varying stages of decay. In the display window of an abandoned department store, a single mannequin still models a dusty sin and blouse. Just before the market and truckstop, a wonderful socialist-realist statue in gold-painted concrete pays tribute to those three pillars of the revolution: the farmer, the soldier and the worker. The worker has one boot firmly planted on a bomb inscribed 'USA'.

The main street divides as it reaches the top of the village to form a town 'square' which is in fact a triangle. At the apex is a war monument topped by a red star and along the base a yellow two-storey building houses government offices. The road that forms the southern side of the triangle leads past this building to the caves of **Kaysone** and **Nouhak**, while the road along the northern edge leads to the caves of **Souphanouvong** and **Phoumi**. Go right on the road along the base of the triangle to reach **Khamtai's cave** and what was once a recreation area, behind a sports ground with a derelict grandstand.

The caves

Five caves, those formerly occupied by senior Pathet Lao leaders Prince Souphanouvong, Kaysone Phomvihan, Nouhak Phounsavanh, Khamtai Siphandon and Phoumi Vongvichit, are officially open to tourists and the valley contains many other poignant reminders of the struggle. There is less war debris around than in Xieng Khouang, with the ubiquitous cluster bomb casings the most obvious example. The setting is a delight, with crags jutting vertically from fields of snooker-table green, and it is worth spending more time there than the one day required to see the caves. At present the site is run-down, having had virtually no maintenance since 1976, but moves have been underway to restore it since Kaysone's death in 1992 and desultory work is underway. Disneyland – watch out!

Each cave burrows deep into the mountainside and all of them feature 60 cm-thick concrete walls, living quarters, meeting rooms, offices, dining and storage areas. All but Khamtai's include an outside kitchen and at least two exits. Each cave also contains a centrally located 'emergency room', installed in case of a gas attack or similar eventuality. This consists of a fully sealed concrete bunker with room for 10 to 20 people, in the corner of which can be found the remains of a hand-cranked oxygen pump of Soviet manufacture. Below and outside the entrance to each cave, buildings house additional accommodation and meeting rooms. The occupants of the caves slept in these buildings, as raids rarely took place at night.

Until recently the original furniture and other items including books, maps and papers remained in the caves. The site is now slated for restoration under the auspices of the Kaysone Memorial Fund and almost all the furniture has been removed, leaving the caves bare. Restoration work was begun in 1997 and is ongoing.

To the right of the path leading to **Souphanouvong's cave**, or **Tham Than Souphanouvong**, stands a pink stupa, the tomb of the prince's son, who was captured and beaten to death by infiltrators a few kilometres away in 1967 at the age of 28. Inside the room used by the attendant below the cave, an ancient black and white photograph of Souphanouvong with Khruschev is stuck to the wall, while the next building contains a makeshift memorial to the prince decorated with a few dusty souvenirs of the USSR. Souphanouvong and Phoumi's caves both feature a 'garage cave' at the base of the karst, a cavity in the limestone large enough to accommodate a car.

Kaysone's cave or **Tham Than Kaysone** is reached by steps cut into the cliff face and extends over 100 m. Like the others there is a suite of rooms including a bedroom, meeting room and library. An interesting feature of Kaysone's cave is a long, narrow passage which connects the living quarters to a large meeting area which includes emergency accommodation for dozens of guests.

Khamtai's cave, or **Tham Than Khamtai**, is slightly different from the others. The first thing the visitor notices is a set of three bomb craters within metres of the entrance to the cave. The craters, now overgrown, are so close together they almost touch. Possibly inspired by their arrival, the entrance is shielded by an enormous, tapering slab of concrete, 4½ m high and nearly 2 m wide at the base. Inside, the cave is darker and more claustrophobic than the others, with no outside areas. The attendant may or may not lead you through a thick steel door at the bottom of some stairs well inside the cave. It gives access to a staircase which descends steeply before ending in a sheer drop of several metres to the floor of an underground theatrette.

A small distance from Khamtai's cave, and included in its entry price, is the large and obvious entrance to what is known as **Tam Xang Lot**, or 'cave that an elephant can walk through'. This natural cavern was used as a theatre, complete with stage, arch, orchestra pit and a concrete floor with space for an audience of several hundred. At the opposite end from the stage, a long passage featuring a number of stalactites and lit by daylight connects to the theatrette below Khamtai's cave.

Other caves   There are many abandoned caves around Vieng Xai which were obviously used during the war and at least one, on the left past Phoumi's cave, is quite extensive. The wisdom of fossicking about in them, given the attitude of local authorities, is debatable; unexploded bombs must also be assumed to be a risk whenever walking off the beaten track.

A conservation survey of the area in 1982 identified 95 caves of historical significance. Included in these was a former hospital complex approximately 15 km from Vieng Xai and a cave housing a school for children of government officials at Ban Bac. A separate cave complex at Hang Long, 25 km from Xam

Neua, housed the provincial government during the war years, but is now completely abandoned.

There is a fairly spectacular **waterfall** 8 km before Vieng Xai. About 3 km after **Excursions** the turn-off from Route 6, a swift stream passes under a steel and concrete bridge. A path just before the bridge leads off to the left, following the river downstream. It takes just a few minutes to reach the top of the waterfall, but the path leads all the way to the bottom, about 20 minutes' walk. Swimming is not advised.

F *Swampside Guesthouse*, perched on the lake behind the gold statue, 8 dorms, with 3 **Sleeping** beds in each, very basic and not very clean, toilet outside, shower in the lake, mediocre restaurant attached and filled with smoking Vietnamese men. **F** *Viengsay Guesthouse*. This place has a superb setting amid eucalyptus and Norfolk Island pines with views of surrounding karsts. To get there, follow the road that leads to Khamtai's cave but turn left at the football field; the hotel is the 1st building on the left. The hotel is the mouldering remnant of what were once comfortable quarters for visiting dignitaries and has been slated for renovation in anticipation of more tourist arrivals. Until then, it is extremely run-down. However, the hotel offers a few threadbare comforts, silk bedspreads and tea-sets in some rooms evoking past splendour. Doubles and triples available, ask for an upstairs room, common bath, food, beer and cigarettes available. Electricity 24 hrs.

A few noodle shops on the main street opposite the post office and in the market. **Eating** There is a restaurant attached to *Swampside*, but it is dirty and the food plain – although there are pleasant views of the lake.

Pick-ups and **passenger trucks** between Xam Neua and **Vieng Xai** leave from in **Transport** front of the market, around 8,000 kip one way (60-90 mins). It will cost around 100,000 *31 km to Xam Neua* kip to charter a pick-up if you have missed the last truck back to Xam Neua.

Communications Post office: in town, by the market. **Useful addresses** Police **Directory** **station**: behind the disued department store on the town square.

Muang Khua

This town is situated in the southern part of the province of Phongsali. Being *Colour map 1, grid B3* at the junction of the Nam Ou and Nam Phak, the town has long been a cross-roads between Vietnam and Laos. A French garrison was based in Muang Khua until 1954, when it was ousted by Vietnamese troops in the aftermath of the battle at Dien Bien Phu. For a brief period from 1958, Polish and Canadian officials of the Comité International de Contrôle were quartered in the town to monitor the ceasefire between the Pathet Lao and the Royal Lao government. Nowadays, Muang Khua is home to a burgeoning market in Vietnamese goods, trucked in from Dien Bien Phu: it not only lies on the Nam Ou but also on Route 4 – an important route into Vietnam.

It's a small town with three 'hotels' and very few restaurants. What it lacks in restaurants, it makes up for in pool tables; very small children show a frightening aptitude. Be prepared to have an instant audience if you try your hand. There is usually a box in which you are expected to make a donation.

There is a 30 m-long wood and iron pedestrian suspension bridge across the Nam Phak to a small village on the other side. Excellent views up and down the river but as the bridge tends to wobble, it is not for those who suffer from vertigo.

Muang Khouan is an attractive town to walk about, but be prepared for a group of children to join you on your saunter. The morning market sells fresh vegetables and meat; Akha women also sometimes come to the market. The goldsmith just off the main square is usually surrounded by a small group watching his very delicate work. There is a small new wat.

Excursions The Akha are the main hilltribe in the area. The nearest villages are 20 km out of town; you will need a guide if you want to visit them. The *Singsavanh Guesthouse* can arrange tours for around 80,000 kip per person for two days and one night, or about half that per day for trekking. The guides speak good English.

Sleeping
■ *on map*
Price codes:
see inside front cover

E-F *Singsavanh Guesthouse*, the best place on offer in Muang Khua. Clean and new concrete structure on the top of the hill next to the market. Basic twins and triples with mosquito net, some have toilet and shower attached. Very friendly with Cambodian staff. A dorm bed in the basement along with an eclectic collection of buffalo and deer heads is an experience. The basement turns into an English classroom in the evening. **F** *Chinese Hotel*, up the hill from the boat station, on the left, restaurant. There are 3-4 beds per room (no reduction for less people), mosquito nets, very dirty, no food, shared bathroom with squat toilets and showers, the building looks like it's been under construction for 20 years. **F** *Phoxay Guesthouse*, turn left at the top of the hill from the boat station and follow the sign. Good views of the town are the best thing going for this place. Basic and rather dirty rooms with squalid squat toilet out back. Dorm beds are the cheapest option. Security very poor.

Eating
● *on map*
Price codes:
see inside front cover

The *Nam Ou Restaurant* is up the mud slope from the beach – head for the yellow BeerLao flags; incomparable location for a morning coffee overlooking the river, English menu and friendly staff. The restaurant opposite the *Singsavanh* has tasty fried noodles and rice dishes, English menu. Noodles and baguettes available in the market.

Transport **Road** A little used and rough road – but beautiful as it goes through the mountains – runs northwest from Muang Khua to **Phongsali** (at least 3 hrs). Pick-ups for **Muang Xai** leave between 0700 and 0800 from outside the *Singsavanh* and later in the day if you're prepared to wait around, about 4 hrs (15,000 kip) – again, a beautiful ride.

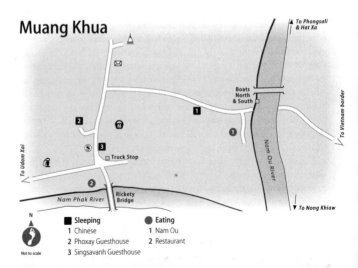

Muang Khua

Not to scale

Sleeping ■
1 Chinese
2 Phoxay Guesthouse
3 Singsavanh Guesthouse

Eating ●
1 Nam Ou
2 Restaurant

River Ferry boats travel north on the Nam Ou to **Phongsali** and south to **Muang Ngoi/Nong Khiaw**, leaving Muang Khua around 0700-0800. To Phongsali the journey takes approximately 6 hrs (45,000 kip for a slow boat), a beautiful trip, especially for birdwatching, with kingfishers everywhere. It is quite shallow in places and there is also a fair amount of white water. Take a blanket. Boats stop at **Hat Xa**, 20 km or so to the northeast of Phongsali. A jeep or truck transports travellers to Phongsali itself, just 20 km but 1½-2 hrs along a very bad road, especially in the rainy season (6,000 kip). Alternatively, it is possible to charter a jeep to take you to Phongsali for 50,000 kip. For boats south to Muang Ngoi, travel time is 4-5 hrs (98,000 kip).

You may find yourselves stuck in Hat Xa as there are no buses to Phongsali after mid-afternoon. Hat Xa now has a **F** guesthouse for a space in a bamboo shelter with a pillow and mattress. The Nam Ou River is the toilet and shower! The chief of Hat Xa runs the guesthouse along with a very pricey and basic restaurant, and the only shop with a fridge. Note there is no electricity in Hat Xa. There is a small noodle shop on the hill towards Phongsali which serves much better and cheaper fare.

Communications Post office: opposite the wat; turn right at the top of the hill. There is an IDD callbox at the top of the hill near the market. **Directory**

Phongsali

High up in the mountains, this northern provincial capital provides beautiful views and an invigorating climate. It is especially beautiful from January to March, when wildflowers and opium poppies bloom in the surrounding hills. The town can be cold at any time of the year – take some warm clothes. Mornings tend to be foggy and it can also be very wet.

Phone code: 088
Colour map 1, grid A3
Altitude: 1,628 m

Phongsali was one of the first areas to be liberated by the Pathet Lao in the late 1940s. The old post office (just in front of the new one), is the sole physical reminder of French rule. The architecture is a strange mix of Chinese post-revolutionary concrete style, Lao houses of wood and brick with tin roofs and bamboo or mud huts with straw roofs. The Chinese influence is very prominent here, mainly dating from the year when the new road network linked the town with the border. The town has a very different feel to the southern towns. New Chinese shophouses are under construction and the roofs are mainly galvanized iron. It is possible to buy apples, pears and even potatoes in Phongsali – the few restaurants along the only tarmacked road sell chips; a welcome relief after days of *feu*. The rice is steamed rather than sticky. **Sights**

The area is a potpourri of ethnicities, with between 22 and 26 minorities inhabiting the area, depending on how you define them. The principal groups are the Phou Noi, Akha, Lu, Yunnanese and Lao Seng. The so-called **Museum of Tribe** in front of the *Phongsaly Hotel* displays hilltribe costumes and photographs. Opening hours are erratic, but if you go there during the week and ask around, someone will probably open it for you. The town itself is home to about 20,000 people, mostly Lao, Phou Noi and Chinese. Anyone wishing to visit hilltribe villages is well advised to enlist a guide in Luang Prabang, as there are no travel agencies in Phongsali and transport options are very limited – the town boasts only one taxi.

Many paths lead out of town over the hills; the walking is easy and the views are spectacular. It is not possible to hire bikes, tuk-tuks or even ponies; there is little to do other than walk. There are a few pool tables in town and a basketball pitch **Activities** in the centre of town (play commences around 1700) so arrive with a long book and a willingness to mooch.

Some people trek north from Phongsali to Uthai, staying in Akha villages *en route*. During the rainy season, it may be possible to take a boat downriver from Uthai to Luang Prabang. Uthai is probably as remote and unspoilt as it gets.

Sleeping
■ *on map*
Price codes:
see inside front cover

C *Phou Fa*, turn right up the hill just past the *Phongsaly Hotel*. The hotel overlooks the town and has good views. Recently overhauled and now gone very up-market. Clean double rooms with attached bathrooms and 'supposed' hot water. Stone floor, large and gloomy restaurant, nightclub, and its best facility – a beer garden overlooking the town, an excellent spot for an afternoon beer. Friendly staff with excellent English. **F** *Phongsaly Hotel*, Chinese 4-storey monstrosity – the tallest building in town. Price is negotiable for longer stays. There are 2 floors of large and airy triple rooms, all with shared bathrooms. Excellent views from the roof and a good attached restaurant. The Chinese owner is rumoured to have come by his money by poaching elephants. **F** *Lucksoun*, opposite the *Phongsaly Hotel*, a 2-storey wooden house. Small, dingy and dirty twins and doubles (the price is per bed), mosquito nets provided, some rooms with no windows. The walls are planks of wood with good-sized gaps, shared bathrooms. A plus is the good restaurant downstairs. **F** per bed *Phongsali Guesthouse*, opposite the market, all rooms with 3-4 single beds, hard mattress, shared toilet and shower, rooms a bit dingy but clean. Sweeping views of the valley from rooms at the back, restaurant downstairs.

Eating
● *on map*
Price codes:
see inside front cover

Cheap   The restaurant at the *Phongsaly Hotel* has good food with the best chips in town. The *Lucksoun* also has a restaurant, cheap and good. A few doors down from the *Lucksoun* is a small Chinese restaurant with no menu. The *Phou Fa* has a big dining hall with an extensive menu. There are also *feu* stalls opposite the market.

Transport

Air   There is no reliable airline passenger service to Phongsali, as many flights are cancelled due to the relatively small number of prospective passengers – most visitors tend to get there by road.

Bus   All buses leave early (0730-1000) from the bus station next to the *Phongsaly Guesthouse*. Buses to **Hat Xa** leave 0700-0730; if you miss the morning departures you may have to wait another day. The road to **Muang Xai** (237 km, 38,000 kip) has been upgraded relatively recently, and is now in good condition. The journey to Muang Xai is about 9 hrs, but it is possible to break the journey at **Ban Na Noi** which lies at the intersection of the 2 roads going to Muang Khua and Muang Xai. There is a **F** guesthouse at Ban Na Noi offering simple rooms. An elephant farm near Km 14; elephants can sometimes be seen from the road.

Boat   Take a truck to Hat Xa (4,000 kip); boats leave in the morning for **Muang Khua**, 4-5 hrs. It can be cold and wet – wear waterproofs if you have them.

International connections with China   The most direct route between Phongsali and Luang Namtha is through

Phongsali

To Udom Xai & Chinese Border

Lane Xang

Kaysone Monument

Museum of Tribe

Buses to Hat Xa

To Hat Xa & Nam Ou River

N   Not to scale

■ **Sleeping**
1 Lucksoun
2 Phongsali Guesthouse
3 Phongsaly
4 Phou Fa

● **Eating**
1 Chinese

China and the road is in reasonable condition. However the Chinese border is only open for Lao and Chinese nationals.

Banks There is a branch of the Lane Xang Bank 20 m down from *Lucksoun*. It will only change US$ cash – the women in the market will give you a better rate. **Communications** Post Office: just down the road from the *Phongsaly Hotel* next to the Lane Xang Bank. There is an IDD call box on the opposite side of the road. **Useful information** Electricity: 1800-2200. **Directory**

The Western Route

The dusty provincial capital of Muang Xai is noteworthy for little more than the fact that it lies at overland crossroads. From here it is possible to travel southwest down Route 2 to Pak Beng. From Pak Beng there are boat connections using the Mekong to Luang Prabang and, upstream, to Ban Houei Xai and the border with Thailand. Travelling northwest from Muang Xai is the provincial capital of Luang Namtha. From here it is a shortish journey to Boten and the Chinese border or to the attractive upland settlement of Muang Sing – an excellent trekking base. Travelling southwest from Luang Namtha down Route 3 the road reaches the Mekong and the frontier with Thailand at Ban Houei Xai. Two rarely visited towns which lie off the main transport arteries are Sayaboury and Pak Lai. Sayaboury can be reached by road from Luang Prabang. From here, however, it is either necessary to turn around or continue south by boat. There are river connections along the Mekong, via Pak Lai, with Vientiane. When more people travelled between Vientiane and Luang Prabang this way, Pak Lai achieved some importance as a stopping-off point on the long journey; now it is largely bypassed.

Muang Xai (Udom Xai, Oudom Xai)

Muang Xai, the capital of Udom Xai province, is a hot and dusty town, but it makes a good stop-off point north or south. This provincial capital was razed during the war and the inhabitants fled to live in the surrounding hills; what is here now has been built since 1975 – which explains why it is such an ugly settlement. Since the early 1990s the town has been experiencing an economic boom as a result of its position at the intersection of roads linking China, Vietnam, Luang Prabang and Pak Beng, and commerce and construction are thriving. It also means that Muang Xai has a large population of Chinese and Vietnamese – something which appears to rile the locals. *Phone code: 081*
Colour map 1, grid B3

The village of **Ban Ting**, behind Muang Xai, is interesting to wander through and the wat just the other side of the stream has a ruined monastery. The wat at Ban Ting now includes quite a bizarre attraction – a life-size tree made of concrete featuring tin leaves, concrete animals in the foliage and two concrete reclining Buddhas on the topmost branches. The wat also includes a Buddhist high school for monks and offers a good view of the town and surrounding mountains. **Sights**

Ban Mok Kho is a Hmong village 16 km along Route 1 to Nam Bak where the inhabitants wear traditional dress and live in longhouses. ■ *Getting there: catch a ride on a pick-up going to Nam Bak, or negotiate a price with a taxi or tuk-tuk.* **Excursions**

The North

Sleeping

■ *on map*
Price codes:
see inside front cover

C *Hotel Fu Shan*, T312198. Two doors down from the *Sing Tong* and a step up in the friendliness stakes. Another Chinese establishment, bare doubles with attached shower and western toilet, hot water, TV and fan. Restaurant downstairs. **C** *Sai Xi*, opposite the post office. Some rooms with bathroom attached, hot water, TV and fan. A basic Chinese establishment where the staff continue to be blunt to the point of rudery; also noisy at night with partying clientele. **F** per bed in a 5-bed dorm on the 4th floor with communal (very dirty) toilet and shower 1 floor down. Good views of the town and hills beyond from the roof. **C** *Sing Tong*, opposite the market on the main street T312061, T071-212813, T/F021-412686. Attached bath and western toilet with hot water, towels and soap provided. Sometimes live pop music in the courtyard.

E *Linda Guesthouse*, T312147, downhill from the market and across the bridge. New 3-storey white building with gold frescos, clean, furnished rooms, some with bathroom attached, western toilet and hot water if you shower quickly (shampoo provided)! Rooms have fan and balcony, impressive lobby with comfortable sofa. The best Muang Xai has to offer at this price. Recommended. **E** *YangLu Guesthouse*, T312067. A few doors up from the *Sai Xi*. Large, bare rooms with attached hot water shower and toilet; a bit gloomy but friendly staff.

F *Dokbouadeng*, T312142. Attached hot water shower and toilet, small restaurant downstairs. **F** *Dongsanguane*, T312271. Dirty, bare rooms with shared toilet and shower, moulding walls. **F** *Lao-named Guesthouse*, T312253. Next to the *Phuxay*. Shabby but clean rooms, separate toilet and scoop shower, friendly owner, large selection of cheese crackers and cold drinks. **F** *Nong Leng*, between the *Singthong* and *Fu Shan*, disinterested staff but the rooms are clean with attached cold shower and Asian toilet. **F** *Phuxay*, T312140, downhill on the main street from the market and across the bridge, turn right after the petrol station (there is a sign at the petrol station), opposite the police counter-narcotics unit. Dirty, gloomy rooms with attached shower and toilet, nice garden with sitting area. **F** *Seuannalat*, next to *Linda Guesthouse*, T312384. Gloomy doubles with attached hot water and western toilet; also 5-bed dorms with shared toilet and shower.

Muang Xai (Udom Xai)

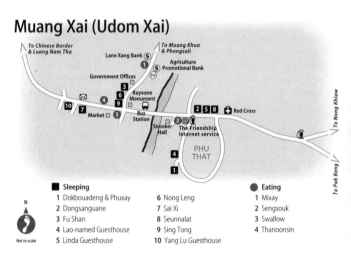

■ Sleeping		● Eating
1 Dokbouadeng & Phuxay	6 Nong Leng	1 Mixay
2 Dongsanguane	7 Sai Xi	2 Sengsouk
3 Fu Shan	8 Seunnalat	3 Swallow
4 Lao-named Guesthouse	9 Sing Tong	4 Thanoonsin
5 Linda Guesthouse	10 Yang Lu Guesthouse	

N
Not to scale

The North

Cheap *Thanoonsin*, next to the post office. Friendly service, menu in English, good basic Lao food and excellent cakes. **Seriously cheap** *Dokbouadeng* and *Seuannalat* guesthouses both have small cafés on the ground floor. *Mixay*, on the left about 100 m towards the *Lane Xang Bank*. Peaceful, has an English menu, very friendly staff and serves delicious hot pot. *Sengsouk*, opposite *Linda Guesthouse*. Has an English menu, delicious iced coffee with ovaltine, basic Chinese and Lao food. *Swallow Restaurant*, next to the market. English menu, clean, usual selection of Lao fare and egg dishes.

Eating
● on map
Price codes:
see inside front cover
Stalls in front of the
market sell beer and
snacks from nightfall

Air At the time of writing, all flights to Muang Xai had been suspended, although in the past, there have been daily connections with **Luang Prabang**, and 2 flights a week to Vientiane. Flights could well be resumed in the future, although the domestic time-table through to late 2002 gives no indication.

Transport

Road Bus/truck/songthaew: buses for the south to **Muang Houn** (4 hrs, 13,500 kip) and **Pak Beng** (5 hrs, 21,000 kip) leave from the bus station, which is situated opposite the market, 5 times a day, last truck around 0800. Attractive journey through a valley with paddy fields and many villages, on a bad road. From here, there are boat connections on to Ban Houei Xai west or Luang Prabang east (8 hrs). Pick-ups to Nateui (4 hrs, 12,000 kip), Boten (3 hrs, 15,000 kip) and Luang Namtha (4 hrs, 18,000 kip). The road passes Lao Soung and Hmong villages. Buses depart fairly frequently for **Muang Ngoi** (3 hrs) and **Nam Bak**. Direct buses leave for **Luang Prabang** (5 hrs, 20,000 kip). Route 4 goes north to **Muang Khua** (3-4 hrs, 15,000 kip) and there are also trucks to **Phongsali** – a gruelling ride (9 hrs, 38,000 kip).

   International connections with China: buses leave for the border at Boten (15,000 kip). For information on crossing into China, see page 36.

Banks *Lane Xang Bank*, downhill from the market on the main street on the left after 5-min walk. Changes US$, Chinese Yuan, French Francs and Thai Baht cash, and TCs. Smaller branch of the bank at back of market. Stalls in the market will give much better rates for cash exchange. **Communications** Post Office: opposite the *Sai Xi Hotel*, uphill from the market. International calls available. **Massage and sauna** Behind the *Phuxay Hotel*. Traditional Lao herbal sauna and massage offered by *Red Cross Centre*, weekdays 1600-2000, weekends 0800-1000, 1600-2000. **Useful information** Electricity: 24 hrs.

Directory

Pak Beng

This long thin strip of village is perched halfway up a hill, with fine views over the Mekong. Its importance lies in its location at the confluence of the Mekong and the Nam Beng. There is not much to do here but it makes for a good stop-over on the journey between Ban Houei Xai and Luang Prabang, or vice versa. The village is worth a visit for its traditional atmosphere and the friendliness of the locals, including various minorities. There's a good place to swim in the dry season, just downstream from the port – but be careful as the current is strong. There are also a couple of monasteries in town.

Colour map 1, grid C2

The locals are now organizing guides for **treks** to nearby villages. There is a three day/two night trek to Hmong villages for 1,400 baht with a car and an English-speaking guide. Ask at *Xaikhong Guesthouse* or *Bounmy Restaurant*.

Activities

The North

The North

Sleeping
■ on map
Price codes:
see inside front cover

D *Sarika*, completely rebuilt after a fire a few years back, this is an elegant structure on the steep cliff overlooking the river. Big, clean rooms with toilet and shower attached, tiled floors, restaurant downstairs. **F** *Xaikhong Pattana*, on the road above the customs buildings, take a sharp turn left as you come up from the pier. 2 floors of twins and doubles with an excellent view of the Mekong and a restaurant overlooking the river. Small but clean rooms, bamboo walls, tiled western toilets and a 'real' shower in the garden. But the staff are a bit dozy. **F** As you go up the hill on the main street there are 5 more newly-built, shaky wooden structures acting as guesthouses: the *Phanthavong* (left), *Dockhoune Angkhong* (right), *Monsavan* (left), *Monhmnay* (right) and *Mime* (right). All offer basic doubles or triples with mosquito nets, paper-thin walls and toilets and scoop showers out back. Look out for *Monsavan* on the left which has its toilets on the other side of the road perched precariously over the cliff. The guesthouses on the right have good views of the river.

Eating
● on map
Price codes:
see inside front cover

Sarika has an atmospheric restaurant downstairs with wonderful river views, fresh flowers on the table, amazing variety on the menu including cheese omelette, but interminably slow service. There are 5 or so restaurants lining the main road towards the river – *Pheth, Khoumniaw, Bounmy, Dockhoune* and *Chanhsamone*; all seem to have the same English menu offering basic Lao dishes, eggs and baguettes. The food is not especially memorable in any of them.

Entertainment

Three pool tables, one small 'cinema' – more a television really, showing Lao and Thai movies.

Transport

Bus/songthaews leave from the jetty for the route northwards to **Muang Houn**, 2 hrs (10,000 kip), and **Muang Xai**, 6-7 hrs (leaving in the morning) (21,000 kip). As direct songthaews to **Muang Xai** are few, an alternative is to take one to Muang Houn and then catch a rather more frequent departure from there to Muang Xai (for 13,500 kip). The road to Muang Xai is through spectacular scenery. There is no road between Pak Beng and Ban Houei Xai. The slow **boat** to **Ban Houei Xai** leaves at 0800 sharp from the port and takes all day (48,000 kip). The slow boat to **Luang Prabang** leaves around 0800 (52,000 kip). Speedboats to Luang Prabang (2-3 hrs) and Ban Houei Xai leave when full through the day until early afternoon. The fare for both journeys is 120,000 kip or 400 baht.

Directory

Banks There is no bank in town, but virtually all the guesthouses and restaurants will exchange cash Thai baht and US$. **Communications** Post Office: located up over the hill on the main road. **Useful information** Electricity: 1800-2200.

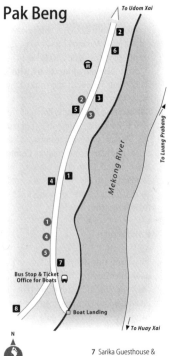

Pak Beng

To Udom Xai

To Luang Prabang

Mekong River

Bus Stop & Ticket Office for Boats

Boat Landing

To Huay Xai

N
Not to scale

■ **Sleeping**
1 Dockhoune Angkhong Guesthouse
2 Mime Guesthouse
3 Monhmany Guesthouse
4 Monsavan Guesthouse
5 Phanhthavong Guesthouse
6 Phuvien
7 Sarika Guesthouse & Restaurant
8 Xaikhong Pattana Guesthouse & Restaurant

● **Eating**
1 Bounmy
2 Chanhsamone
3 Dockhoune
4 Khoumniaw
5 Pheth

This is a new town (although it looks as old as any other), built in 1986 by the government to entice hill people down from the hills, in an attempt to stop them growing opium. There are quite a number of Blue Hmong in town.

Muang Houn
Colour map 1, grid B2

Sleeping F *Miss Manyvane*, a 2-storey concrete house, with a little balcony upstairs. Basic facilities, 4 rather mouldy twin rooms with tattered mosquito nets, shared toilet and scoop shower. The family lives downstairs. F *Lao named Guesthouse*, 2 doors up from *Miss Manyvane*. A wooden structure, basic twins with mosquito nets, shared toilet and scoop, shower, small café downstairs.

Eating There are just 2 places in town facing each other next to the market. Both serve noodles, eggs and sticky rice, no menu. Fresh baguettes available from the market in the morning.

Transport Regular **bus** connections with **Pak Beng** (2 hrs, 7,500 kip) and north to **Muang Xai** (4-5 hrs, 13,500 kip).

Directory **Useful information**: Electricity: 1830-0900.

The North

Nateui is a small roadside settlement at the junction of Route 3 and Route 1. Route 3 continues west to Luang Namtha and Ban Houei Xai while Route 1 runs north 18 km to the border settlement of Boten and then into China and Mengla. Nateui has become a stopover town for truck drivers making the drive from Luang Prabang, through Boten, to Mengla.

Nateui
Colour map 1, grid B2

Sleeping F Guesthouse on the main road; no traffic in the evening, so it is quiet. Reasonably good food served.

Transport There are infrequent **songthaew** connections with **Luang Namtha** (30,000 kip) and **Muang Xai** (12,000 kip) and rather more frequent departures for the border at **Boten**.

80 km to Muang Xai
18 km to Boten

Boten is 18 km north of Nateui, on the border with China, and is a similar sort of place to Nateui: it is a trucking stop for drivers making their way between Mengla in China and Luang Prabang. There are a couple of guesthouses here and a handful of noodle shops. At the weekend, the border handles no commercial traffic, so truck drivers sleep in their vehicles, or in one of the guesthouses. While Boten is not going to keep people hanging around for terribly long, the people here are very interesting!

Boten
Colour map 1, grid B2

Sleeping and eating F Guesthouse, small, unmarked, right on the border. Basic doubles and geared to Chinese, Vietnamese and Laotian truckers. Boten has a couple of *feu* stalls but little else.

Transport Infrequent **pick-ups** to **Luang Namtha** (10,000 kip) and **Muang Xai** (15,000 kip).

18 km to Nateui

International connections The border with China at Boten is open for international traffic, but no Chinese visas can be obtained here. Coming from China, you must get your Lao visa in Kunming. If you are coming from Luang Nam Tha or Muang Xai and heading for China, the earliest you can arrive is 1100. This means that when you cross into China you have to stay in **Mengla** (2 hrs away). Mengla is a nasty introduction to China, reverberating with the tiresome sounds of karaoke and prostitutes until the early hours. It is possible to reach the much nicer town of **Jinghong** (5-6 hrs from Mengla) if you stay in Boten and then make an early start.

Luang Namtha

Phone code: 086
Colour map 1, grid B2

This is yet another town that was obliterated during the war, and the concrete structures erected since 1975 have little charm. Like other towns in the north, the improvement in transport links with China and Thailand has led to burgeoning trade. The main attraction is the food market, where members of the many minorities who inhabit the area (including Thai Lu, Thai Dam, Lang Ten, Hmong and Khamucan) be found trading exotic species.

Excursions **Ban Nam Chang** is a Lang Ten village 3 km walk along a footpath outside town. Ask your way. The Lang Ten women are easily recognized – they wear their hair back and pluck their eyebrows when they turn 15, keeping them plucked from then on. Their clothes are black with coloured borders, and they wear a lot of delicate silver jewellery.

Ban Lak Khamay is quite a large Akha village 27 km from Luang Namtha on the road to Muang Sing. It was resettled from a nearby location higher in the hills in 1994 as part of government policy to protect upland forests. The community now grows teak and rubber trees commercially. The village chief speaks Lao. The settlement features a traditional Akha entrance; if you pass through this entrance you must visit a house in the village, or you are considered an enemy. Otherwise you can simply pass to one side of the gate. Other features of interest in Akha villages are the swing, at the highest point in the village and used in the annual swing festival, and the meeting house, where unmarried couples go to court and where newly married couples live until they have their own house. There is another, smaller Akha village a few kilometres on towards Muang Sing.

Trekking The NTA Lao/UNESCO Nam Ha Ecotourism Project is currently engaged in experimental treks to the **Nam Ha National Biodiversity Conservation Area** (8 km from town, past the airport). The aim of the project is to train local guides and to work with local villages in the area to develop remote 2- and 3-day trekking opportunities for visitors. They are happy to take with them small groups (4-8 people) of culturally sensitive travellers, and offer the chance to visit traditional villages, trek through various forest lands, take river trips and support local resource conservation efforts. ■ *Treks leave 3-4 times a week. Check with the Guide's Office, T211131, by Saikhong Longsack Guesthouse, for departure days; an information session about the trek is given the night before at 1600 at the Guide's Office. The price will cover the cost of food, water, transportation, guides, lodging and the trekking permit.*

Sleeping
■ *on map*
Price codes:
see inside front cover

There has been a sudden rush of guesthouses popping up here over the last few years, yet despite this, Luang Namtha remains a fair way down on the traveller's index of hot spots. **C-D** *Boat Landing Guesthouse and Restaurant*, T312398. Further out from town towards the airport than most other guesthouses, this place is happily located right on the river, very clean, and owners speak good English. Serves western and Lao food. **D-F** *Darasavath Guesthouse and Restaurant*, T211299. Twin and double roomed wooden bungalows with bamboo walls and ensuite bathrooms. Beautiful, very rustic, with locals working in the nearby fields. Friendly staff with decent English, free service to the bus station/airport (depending on whether you've stayed a couple of days). Discounts on group bookings, too. Good restaurant (see below). Recommended.

E *Cha Rueh Sin*, T312393. Bare, basic, but not uncharming rooms with bathrooms attached in a monster of a building. Breezy verandas overlooking parts of the town. **E** *Hong Tha Xay Som Boun Hotel*, T312079, F312078. Chinese-owned hotel with nice garden area, shop selling minority clothing, restaurant, bar and disco (noisy after 2000). However, the rooms are nothing special. Surely , with stone floors, ceiling fan, toilet and cold shower attached. Adequately clean. Their generator provides power until midnight. Overpriced. **E** *Khamanivong Guesthouse and Restaurant*, opened in Jul 2001, has lovely rooms with wooden floors and bamboo walls. Hard but comfortable beds, no fans. Communal toilets are, like the rooms, clean and well-maintained. Beautiful veranda, some spectacular views, depending on which side of the building you're on. Excellent restaurant (see below). **E** *Nongbouavieng Guesthouse and Restaurant*, T312359. Sad little rooms on the ground and 1st floors are a far cry from the lovely clean rooms with tiled floors and fans of the top floor, which have balconies and a spectacular view. Chinese fan decorations on the walls. The ensuites are bearable, while the communal bathrooms are hideously grotty. The brand new attached restaurant, however, is definitely worth a try (see below). **E** *Palanh*, T312439. Lovely clean rooms, big ones are airy and spacious with ensuite, smaller (and cheaper) ones have no attached bathrooms, but rather delightfully, you walk along the veranda to get to theirs. Very clean and rustic. Can buy drinks and snacks downstairs. Recommended. **E** *Unnamed Guesthouse*, not yet open, but looks extremely promising: chalet-like, with wide verandas and a pleasant view, friendly owners.

E-F *Bus Station Guesthouse*, T211090. Sweet little rooms, clean and airy. Hard beds, though. The place is extending and will soon boast 17 rooms. Ideally situated for an early morning start. **E-F** *Luang Namtha Guesthouse*, T312087, 312407. Opened in Feb 1999, this hotel is run by two Hmong brothers, one of whom speaks English. The house is an impressive building for

Luang Namtha

N

Not to scale

■ **Sleeping**
1 Bus Station Guesthouse
2 Cha Rueh Sin Guesthouse
3 Darasavath Guesthouse & Restaurant
4 Guesthouse
5 Hong Tha Xay Som Boun
6 Khammanivong Guesthouse & Restaurant
7 Luang Namtha Guesthouse & Restaurant
8 Many Chan Guesthouse & Restaurant
9 Palanh Guesthouse
10 Sai Khang Khang Langsack & Restaurant
11 Sinsavanh Guesthouse
12 Tian Fu Guesthouse & Restaurant
13 Unnamed Guesthouse

● **Eating**
1 Mani Van
2 Panda
3 Phonsay

The North

Luang Namtha, with a grand staircase. All rooms are beautifully clean and furnished with attached bathrooms, and balconies. They offer a free pick-up from the bus station if you telephone. Recommended. **E-F** *Sinsavanh Guesthouse*, T312328. An attractive wooden chalet with pleasant garden, the rooms inside are quite cramped, but attractive with wooden shutters and flowers, toilets and showers separate. Coffee, bread and snacks can be bought downstairs.

F *Guesthouse*, T211349. Not at all bad, and dirt cheap. Hard beds, though, and can smell of smoke. **F** *Many Chan Guesthouse*, T312209, opposite the smaller bus station. Small and gloomy rooms but reasonably clean with shared bathroom and toilet. Its good restaurant is getting expensive. Bikes hired for 8,000 kip per day. **F** *Saikhang Longsack Guesthouse*, T312257, next to the Kaysone monument. Large, clean rooms with attached toilet and shower, friendly staff. House is charming, with tiled floors and a breezy balcony overlooking the main street. **F** *Tian Fu Guesthouse and Restaurant*, T312360. Another Chinese (this time Sichuan) concern, the rooms are basic and gloomy. Try to get one on the 1st floor rather than upstairs, since the shared toilets and showers are located outside in the garden.

Eating
Price codes:
see inside front cover

Cheap *Darasavath Restaurant*, attached to the guesthouse (see above), serves the usual good selection of Lao foods (many restaurants here have exactly the same menus). Utterly dreamy, Robinson Crusoe-esque outside setting in a breezy 'bar' with thatched roof, wooden pillars with vines twined around them. The owner is happy to teach guests how to cook Lao-style if she's around. *Hongtha Xaysonboun Hotel* has a restaurant with English menu, good Lao and Chinese food.

Cheap *Khamanivong Restaurant*, attached to the guesthouse (see above), has a large selection of Lao and Thai food, all of which appears to be seriously good. The restaurant itself is tastefully decorated with tiled floors, brick walls, pebble stone pillars and rotating fans. Recommended.

Seriously cheap *Mani Van Restaurant*, is a friendly little café with an English menu serving snacks, coffee and fried noodles, wonderful chips, and conveniently located opposite the main bus station. Useful for those ever-delayed songthaews! *Nongbouavieng Restaurant*, attached to the guesthouse (see above), serves up a worthwhile selection of Lao and Chinese dishes in a lovely setting: a rickety old barn with wooden floors overlooking a 'lake' and rice paddies. Worth a go but don't forget your mozzie repellant! *Panda Restaurant*, T211304. A goodie – brand new, very clean, and small, with a hideous line in posters decorating the walls. Very cheap and tasty food. Friendly owner with good English. *Phonsay Restaurant*, has an English menu, with a wide selection of dishes, including Thai curries and spaghetti, but has moody staff with the weight of the world on their shoulders. *Sai Khang Khang Longsack Guesthouse*, T312257, attached clean restaurant with friendly staff and the usual selection of dishes. It seems to attract many Lao customers which is a good sign, and is popular with tourists, too. *Tailue Chinese Restaurant*, a favourite gambling haunt for the local men, serves good food, if a little greasy. Friendly and cheap.

Foodstalls The only noodle shop in town is next to *Kikham Feu* stalls by the main market and the morning market by the bus stop.

Sauna Herbal sauna not far from *Sengchanh film processing*. Sauna 10,000 kip; 50-min massage 15,000 kip. The towels they provide are utterly minging, so it's well worth bringing your own. 1630-1730.

Textiles *Paseutsin Shop*, sells the work of Luang Namtha's women – silk skirts, curtains, cushions etc. Mon-Fri 0830-1200, 1330-1600.

Bicycle hire Bicycles for hire from the *ManyChan Guesthouse* for 8,000 kip a day or 1,500 kip per hr.

Air The airport is 7 km from town (5,000 kip by tuk-tuk). Small planes fly to **Vientiane** daily except Mon and Fri at 1215 for US$80. Flights to **Luang Prabang** leave on Wed and Sun at 1700, US$37. There are 2 scheduled flights a week to **Ban Houei Xai**, Mon and Fri, at 1600, US$41.

Road The bus station and its ticket office (T312164, 0700-1600) are near the Morning Market. Pick-ups leave frequently for **Boten** (2 hrs, 10,000 kip) on the Chinese border via Nateui. Chinese visa required to cross into China (Meng La). This stretch of road is one of the more enjoyable bits of travelling in Laos. To **Muang Sing**, departures at 0800, 0900, 1000 and 1100 (2 hrs, 10,000 kip); pick-ups may depart throughout the rest of the day, depending on demand. To **Muang Xai**, 100 km, 2 services leave in the morning at 0800 and 1100 (4-6 hrs, 18,000 kip); 1 or 2 will leave if there is demand in the early afternoon. The road to **Ban Houei Xai** is unpaved and potholed. Daily departure at 0830, 8-10 hrs by pick-up in the dry season and almost impossible during rainy season (72,000 kip). The **Luang Prabang** service leaves at 0630 (4,000 kip). Buses to **Pakmong** are 30,000 kip, where connections (3,000 kip) may be caught to Nam Bak.

If you want to get somewhere pronto and there's no bus, it's worth speaking to some of the women in the nearby restaurants, as they might be able to arrange transport, although it will come at a price

River It is said to be possible to catch a fast boat from a point on the Namtha 7 km from Luang Namtha, to the Mekong at **Patha** (800,000 kip for the whole boat). There you have to change boats in order to travel north to **Ban Houei Xai** (Pak Ta). When chartering boats, beware of Captain Daolith, who overcharges for a boat which isn't even his.

Airline offices Lao Aviation, T312180, next to the *Lane Xang Bank* in town and another inside the departure hall at the airport, 7 km from town. Book flights 1 day in advance. **Banks** *Lane Xang Bank*, in the centre of town, takes TCs but at a sizeable commission and will change US$ cash, Chinese yuan and Thai baht. *The Agricultural Promotional Bank*, opposite the petrol station, will exchange cash but not TCs. There's a *BCEL* exchange opposite the Post Office that changes US$, yuan and baht at far more attractive rates. And there's also a ramshackle exchange in the bus station whose aim is heralded as 'to service our tourists' despite being almost always closed. **Communications** Internet: *PlaNet Computers* have a fully set up internet café but at the time of writing were still awaiting government permission to operate as LN's 1st cyber café. **Travel agents** *Champa Lao Travel*, T211396, F211397. A one-man band open Mon-Fri and closing for lunch. Good English, and helpful. **Useful information** Electricity: 1830-2200.

Muang Sing

Many visitors consider this peaceful valley to be one of the highlights of the north. Lying at the terminus of the highway in the far northwest corner of Laos, it is a natural point to stop and spend a few days recovering from the rigours of the road before either heading south or moving on to China (see International connections, page 182). The main activity for visitors is to hire bicycles and visit the hilltribe villages that surround the town in all directions – several guesthouses have maps of the surrounding area and trekking is becoming increasingly popular.

Colour map 1, grid B2

Muang Sing itself is little more than a village, situated on a picturesque upland plateau. This area is a borderland which has been contested by the Chinese, Lao and the Thai. At various points in the last few centuries it has come under the influence of the principality of Nan, now in Thailand, the Yunnanese of southern China and the Lao. While it is now firmly Lao territory there is the gnawing sense that the Chinese have invaded by stealth. The Chinese economic presence is all too evident.

Sights The town features some interesting old wooden and brick buildings and unlike nearby Luang Namtha and several other towns in the north it wasn't bombed close to oblivion during the struggle for Laos. An **old French fort** built in the 1920s is now off-limits to visitors, as it is occupied by the Lao army. The **market** is certainly worth a look early in the morning. It starts about 0545 and then begins to wind down after 0730. Along with the usual array of plastic objects, clothes and pieces of hardware, local silk and cotton textiles can be purchased. (In past years this was a centre for the opium trade.) Numerous hill peoples come to trade, including Akha, Mien and Hmong tribespeople along with Yunnanese, Thai Dam and Thai Lu – a highly colourful melange of peoples. The town is predominantly Thai Lu but the population of the district is 50% Akha, with a further 10% Thai Nua. Most Buddhist **monasteries** in the vicinity are Thai Lu in style. The most accessible is **Wat Sing Chai**, on the main road.

There are several NGOs as well as bilateral and multilateral development operations in the area. GTZ for example, the German aid agency, has an office in town where it displays the project's aims in a small exhibition.

Excursions to hilltribe villages
It is better not to visit hilltribe villages in late afternoon; this seems to be a private time and should be respected

The area around Muang Sing is home to many minorities who have been resettled, either from refugee camps in Thailand or from highland areas of Laos. The population of the district is said to have trebled between 1992 and 1996, although since then population growth has stabilized. As a result, it is one of the few places in northern Laos where **hilltribe villages** are readily accessible, either by bicycle or on foot. One possibility: at Km 103, turn right onto a dirt-road. After about 1½ km, you'll come to a Yao village and on the other hill, after another 10-minute walk, there is an Akha village.

About 4 km from Muang Sing on the road to the Chinese border is the (**E**) eco-tourist site/guesthouse, *Adima*, with several groups of four bungalows constructed in traditional Yao and Ikho style. It is under Dutch management, but has a charming group of nonplussed Lao staff! A calm and peaceful retreat surrounded by rice fields. Minority villages are literally on the doorstep. Guides are available for visiting villages and for trekking. ■ *Getting there: take a tuk-tuk (no more than 3,000 kip) to Oudomsin village, or hire a bike (some guesthouses or restaurants have basic maps). Adima is just beyond the village. Alternatively, the owner runs in and out of town about 3 times a day (depending on bus arrival times) and will pick you up from the bus station for 2,000 kip.*

Sleeping
■ *on map*
Price codes:
see inside front cover

E *Adima Guesthouse*, a little hard to get to, but seriously popular with travellers and definitely worth the effort. Walk 4 km towards China (!) and take a right (signposted to the *Adima*) – the guesthouse is another 500 m along here. Beautiful, peaceful bungalows; lovely open-air restaurant; fantastic position, and only a short walk from some hilltribe villages selling handicrafts. At the guesthouse, you can also pick up (for 6,000 kip) a walking guide booklet showing 5 routes to nearby villages, although if you get lost the villagers will point you in the right direction. There are only 10 rooms, which fill up quickly, so best to get there early. **E** *Inthanone Guesthouse*, about 1 km up from the bus station. Run by Lu tribe, traditionally styled thatched huts with attached clean toilet and shower, very friendly owners, a peaceful setting, away from the crowds of tourists in the village. Cows low at the window in the morning. **E** *Sengdeuane Guesthouse*, at the far end of town from the bus stop, a quiet spot. Shared bathroom outside, some rooms have iron doors which make the place resemble a dungeon, but an attractive view from the roof. There are also some newer, more luxorious, rooms out the back. **E** *Sing Xai Guesthouse*, just behind the market. Doubles and triples, attached bath with squat toilet and shower, mosquito nets, slow service but the rooms are fairly clean. In a beautiful spot by paddy fields. **E-F** *Daenneua Guesthouse*, and, next to it, **E-F** *Talu Guesthouse*, both new and clean, with *Daenneua* just edging ahead on the popularity front thanks to its friendly staff, slightly better rooms and laundry service.

F There is a row of 5 guesthouses in the centre of town with nothing to really distinguish between them, all offering basic, cramped double rooms with shared squat toilet and shower and paper-thin walls. These are the *Muang Sing Guesthouse*, *Viengphone Guesthouse* (2 rooms with own bathroom, good value), *Viengxai Guesthouse*, *Sengthong Guesthouse* and *Sengkhatiyavang Guesthouse*. **F** *SaengSavong Guesthouse*, behind the market. Aimed at Japanese travellers, the cheapest but smallest and dingiest rooms in Muang Sing with shared less-than-clean toilet and shower.

The North

Eating
● *on map*
Price codes:
see inside front cover

Cheap *Thamashath Restaurant*, new in 2001 and appropriately named (Thamashath means *the* view), this lovely place looks out over a panoramic stretch of the surrounding forests and mountains. Tasty food, too. **Seriously cheap** *Viengxai Guesthouse*, very good food, with some of the best chips in Laos, English menu, friendly service, reasonable prices. *Viengphone Guesthouse*, English menu, friendly service, good prices. *Sengthong Restaurant*, opposite *Viengxai Guesthouse*, has an English menu offering the usual fare, very slow service. The previous 3 restaurants are all popular at night and can get crowded. They are also prime places for the minorities to come and sell their wares. A quieter option is the restaurant at the *Sengdeuane Guesthouse* which has an English menu, nice garden setting with a pair of green parakeets and is popular with the locals.

Muang Sing

To Adima Guesthouse & Chinese Border
School
Bikes for hire
Stream
Wat Sing Jai
Tour Guide
Library
To Museum
Kaysone Monument
Lane Xang Bank Exchange Service
To Xieng Kok, Luang Nam Tha & Burmese Border
N
Not to scale

■ **Sleeping**
1 Daennuea Guesthouse
2 Inthanon Guesthouse (Lü Tribe)
3 Muang Sing Guesthouse
4 Saengsavong Guesthouse
5 Sengdeuane Guesthouse & Restaurant
6 Sengkhatiyavang Guesthouse
7 Sengthong Guesthouse
8 Sing Xai Guesthouse
9 Talu Guesthouse
10 Viengphone Guesthouse & Restaurant
11 Viengxai Guesthouse & Restaurant

● **Eating**
1 Sengthong

Tours & trekking   The *Viengxai Guesthouse* (and several other guesthouses) will arrange treks with a guide for US$15 per day per person, or US$20 per day with a car. Next to the small temple, Sam Lith offers his services as a guide with a car for US$50 per day in total.

Transport   **Local   Bicycles**: for rent from some of the guesthouses. There are also some bicycle hire shops on the main street. The going rate is 5,000 kip for 1 day. **Road**   The road from Muang Sing to **Luang Namtha** is asphalt but is sometimes broken – the terrain on this route is mountainous with dense forest. The only way to get to Muang Sing is by **truck** or **pick-up** from Luang Namtha, near the market. Vehicles leave throughout the day (2 hrs, 10,000 kip). Trucks also head southwest to **Xieng Kok** (15,000 kip) on the Mekong and the Burmese border several times a week. This 75-km stretch has recently been upgraded so the journey is no longer a gruelling 10-hr journey, but an easy 2½ hrs. Foreigners are not officially permitted to cross into Myanmar (Burma) here, but there have been reports of travellers being granted a visa and entering. **River**   It is sometimes possible to charter **boats** to head downstream on the Mekong to **Ban Houei Xai**, 3-4 hrs. This is expensive – around US$100-200. There is one guesthouse in Xieng Kok.

International connections with China   Muang Sing is the first or last stop in Laos, depending which way you are travelling, before/after the frontier with China. The border is 3 km on from the village of Oudomsin, around 10 km in all from Muang Sing. Pangthong Checkpoint at Km 106 was closed to foreigners for many years – only Lao and Chinese nationals could cross here – but is now open to all comers. There is a small morning market at the border selling fruit, baguettes and freshly made cookies. Pick-ups regularly make the journey to the border.

Directory   **Banks**   There is a small branch of the *Lane Xang Bank* to the right of the bus station to change cash and TCs. Almost all the guesthouses will exchange Thai baht, Chinese Yuan and US$. **Useful information**   Electricity: stops at 2200, so it's a good idea if you can time your arrival before then, as the guesthouses begin to shut up shop for the night. Otherwise you may have to go around banging on doors before you find a bed.

Ban Houei Xai (Houei Xai)

Phone code: 084
Colour map 1, grid B1

This town is in the heart of the Golden Triangle (see page 267) and used to derive its wealth from the narcotics trade as it is on the heroin route to Chiang Mai in Thailand. Today trade still brings the town considerable affluence, although it is rather less illicit. Timber is ferried across the Mekong from Laos to the Thai town of Chiang Khong and in exchange consumer goods are shipped back. Sapphires are mined in the area and, doubtless, there is also still a fair amount of heroin smuggling. Because this is a popular entry and exit point for tourists a considerable amount of money flows in from the numerous guesthouses and restaurants that have been built. However it seems that few people spend more than one night here – those who are entering Laos seem to want to get on and away from Thailand. The town has a large mix of different minorities.

Though the town is growing rapidly as links with Thailand intensify it is still small and easy enough to get around on foot. Most passengers dock close to the centre of town at the passenger ferry pier. The vehicle ferry pier is around 750 m further north (upstream) while the post office is about 500 m south, at the edge of town.

Sights   **Wat Chom Kha Out Manirath**, in the centre of town, is worth a visit if mainly for its views. The monastery was originally built at the end of the 19th century but because it is comparatively well endowed there has been a fair amount of rebuilding and renovation since then. There is also a large former French fort here, **Fort Carnot**, now used by the Lao army (and consequently out of bounds). Finally, the **Morning Market** can be entertaining. While there is little notable about the products on display, for many visitors who have entered from Thailand it will be their first experience of a Lao market. Local tribespeople come from the villages to sell their products in the market. To get there, take a tuk-tuk (3,000 kip). Ban Houei Xai is quite a good place to shop for Lao weaving and gems (see Excursions), as it is cheaper than Vientiane.

Excursions

There is a **sapphire mine** south of the town, near the fast-boat terminal. The miners pan in the morning and clean the stones in the afternoon, so the afternoon is the best time to visit.

Nam Chan is a pleasant village to visit, about 17 km from Ban Houei Xai. The Lanthen tribespeople who live here are well known for their textiles. Along the way, the road passes Hmong villages. ■ *Getting there: take a taxi from the Morning Market, 1 hr (80,000 kip for the whole vehicle).*

Ban Nam Keun, a small traditional village on the high plateau not far from the main town, is worth a visit for its natural beauty.

Sleeping
■ *on map*
Price codes:
see inside front cover

B-C *Mekong Lao Hotel*, Say Khong Rd, T211274, F211277, new and comfortable hotel with rather overfurnished rooms, views over the Mekong, a/c, TV, hot water showers. **C** *Thaveesinh*, on the main street, T312039/211502, second best in town now that the *Mekong Lao* has opened. A/c and fan rooms, TV and fridge, central location. **D** *Arimid Guesthouse*, at the northwest end of the town, T9804693. Extremely friendly service, the owners M and Mme Chitaly speak excellent French and a little English. Comfortable individual bungalows, bathroom attached, no hot water, nice garden area. Mme Chitaly will cook tasty Luang Prabang food and serve it to you at your bungalow. By far the most popular place in town.

D *Hotel Houei Sai*, Say Khong Rd, in the centre of town, T211064, with attached bathroom including hot shower. Lounge area on the 1st floor with pleasant view over the Mekong, basic but clean hotel, and friendly staff. **D** *Thanomsab Guesthouse*, Say Khong Rd (200 m from immigration checkpoint), T211095. Guesthouse in a private villa, some a/c rooms, hot water showers, clean. **D-E** *Manirath*, Say Khong Rd, in the middle of town, T211503, a/c rooms with attached bathroom including hot shower. Restaurant serving only breakfast. **E** *Sabaidee*, Khem Khong Rd, T211503, same management as *Manirath*. All rooms big and pretty similar, with ensuite hot showers and western toilets. Opened in 2001. Beds have been described as "heavenly"! Recommended. **F** *Muang Da*, a few doors along from *Houei Sai*, Chinese guesthouse with good food.

Ban Houei Xai

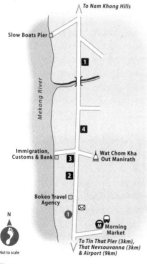

To Nam Khong Hills

Slow Boats Pier

Mekong River

1

4

Immigration,
Customs & Bank

3 Wat Chom Kha
Out Manirath

2

Bokeo Travel
Agency

✉

1

🚌 Morning
Market

*To Tin That Pier (3km),
That Nevsouvanna (3km)
& Airport (9km)*

N

Not to scale

■ **Sleeping**
1 Arimid Guesthouse
2 Houei Sai
3 Manirath
4 Thaveesinh Guesthouse

The North

Eating **Cheap** *Lao Zhang Sheng Co Ltd*, good Chinese, Lao and Thai food in a restaurant run by a Taiwanese man and his Thai wife. Noodle stalls everywhere.

Tour operators *Bokeo Travel*, next to *Bokeo Hotel*. English/French speaking, very helpful company with information on tours to villages and sapphire mines. *Lane Xang Travel* has international telephone service. *Phatthana Phoudoi Travel and Tours*, arranges tours to the mines and hilltribe villages and offers an international phone service – helpful people.

Transport **Air** *Lao Aviation*, T211026/211494. Connections with **Luang Prabang**, US$46, daily except Mon and Fri, and **Vientiane**, US$88, daily or twice daily. **Transport to town**: most hotels provide free transportation to and from the airport.

The **bus** station is located at the Morning Market, 2 km out of town; a **tuk-tuk** to town costs 3,000 kip. Route 3 to **Luang Namtha** (170 km) is still rather rough. Trucks depart in the morning at 0700, 0800, 0900 and 1000 (8-10 hrs, 72,000 kip). It is possible to break the journey halfway, in Vieng Phoukha.

River Daily boats to **Pak Beng** (halfway to Luang Prabang) and connections on to **Luang Prabang**. The slow boat to Pak Beng is raved about by many travellers, and leaves between 0800 and 1100 (6-7 hrs, 48,000 kip) from a jetty 1½ km north of town (a charming journey through lovely scenery – worth sitting on the roof for). Speedboats are a noisy, unrelaxing alternative; they leave from the jetty south of town, 3 hrs and 80,000 kip to Pak Beng. (There have been reports of unscrupulous boatmen claiming there are no slow boats in the dry season to encourage travellers to take their fast boats. This is usually untrue.) There are also boats that make the journey all the way from Ban Houei Xai to Luang Prabang – 2 days and 1 night, with the night spent in a simple guesthouse where the vessel moors, usually Pak Beng (52,000 kip). It is also possible to take a speedboat north along the Mekong to Xieng Kok on the Burmese border. This is not a legal border crossing point for foreigners, but from here you can take a truck to the northern Lao town of **Muang Sing**. To charter a boat could cost anything from US$100-200. In Jan 1999 the 30-seat, 19 m-long *Pak Oui* was launched at the Thai town of Chiang Saen, on the Mekong. It has been built to ferry tourists between Ban Houei Xai and Luang Prabang in more luxury than is usual (bucket seats, sun deck). However for the time being at least it is only taking passengers from Ban Houei Xai to Luang Prabang, not on the return journey, because it is not powerful enough to fight the current with a full complement of passengers. Expect to pay around US$200 with an overnight stay at the *Luangsay Lodge* in Pak Beng and all meals included. From time to time the odd passenger boat will make its way to **Xieng Kok** (200,000 kip), leaving 20 km out of Ban Houei Xai (20,000 kip for a whole tuk-tuk). The trip, though, is an upstream battle, so slow boats tend not to go on the whole. Chartering a boat is possible, but quite an investment at 800,000 kip. At Xieng Kok there's a row of new bungalows to the left of the boat drop, 40,000 kip per night for good rooms with verandas, bathrooms, mozzie nets and electricity 1800-2200. From Xieng Kok, it's possible to get to **Muang Sing** by bus (15,000 kip).

International connections **Boat**: small boats ferry passengers to and from **Chiang Khong** every 10-20 mins throughout the day (20 baht). **Thailand Immigration**: open 0800-1800. See Visas, page 28, for details on obtaining a visa in Chiang Khong.

Directory **Banks** *Lane Xang Bank*, in the middle of town. Changes TCs, US$ cash and baht, and offers a slightly better rate than the *Lane Xang Bank* beside the terminal where boats depart for Chiang Khong. **Communications** Post office: with telephone facilities about 500 m south (downstream) from the centre of town. **Useful addresses** Area code: 84. Immigration: at the boat terminal and the airport, Mon-Fri 0800-1800.

Sayaboury (Xayaboury)

Sayaboury is not on many visitors' agendas. This is partly because it is a difficult place to get to and partly because there doesn't seem any obvious reason
to make the effort. There is no road between Vientiane and Sayaboury and the
only way to get here from the capital is to take a boat upriver to Pak Lai and
then to catch a bus – if the road isn't washed away – from Pak Lai north to
Sayaboury (see Transport below). Rather easier is to catch a bus from Luang
Prabang through Muang Nan to the Mekong, cross the Mekong by ferry, and
then continue to Sayaboury – a comparatively painless 4-6 hour journey.
Having reached Sayaboury and sampled its limited enticements, it is then
necessary to retrace your steps or set out for Pak Lai and hope for a downstream boat to Vientiane.

Phone code: 074
Colour map 1, grid C2
Population: 300,000

These transport difficulties have given Sayaboury a rather charming forgotten feel. It may be the capital of a province covering over 16,000 sq km –
equivalent to the area of Hawaii or Northern Ireland – but it doesn't feel like it.
Perhaps reflecting this not really here/not really there atmosphere, Sayaboury
seems to have more alternative spellings than most – and this in a country
which is replete with imaginative transliterations. The following are just some
of the many ways in which the town and province are transliterated:
Sainyabuli, Xaignabouri, Sayaburi, Xayabury, Xaignabouli, Sayabouri and, as
used here (for no very good reason), Sayaboury. Even the government
appears to adopt a rather slap-dash approach to how the province's name is
rendered into English. The province is mountainous with Phu Khao Mieng,
Laos' ninth highest peak, just exceeding 2,000 m.

The town has a number of **monasteries** of which those of note, according
to local historians, are Wat Thin, Wat Pha Phoun, Wat Natonoy and Wat
Sisavang Vong, named after the king who reigned during the *de facto* Japanese
occupation of French Indochina. The location of the town on the Nam Houn
– a tributary of the Mekong – is also attractive.

In 1994 the National Tourism Authority recorded that the entire province had no
hotels or guesthouses. Fortunately things have changed, but only marginally. At last
count Sayaboury town had 2 hotels/guesthouses open to tourists. **F** *Pha Xang Hotel*,
restaurant and nightclub. Reasonable hotel in the centre of town close to the market
and post office. Rooms are clean with attached bathrooms (cold water only).
F *Hongvilai Guesthouse*, restaurant. South of the town centre on the banks of the
Houng River. This place has a better outlook than the *Pha Xang* but the rooms are not
quite as good – shared cold water bathrooms and not quite as clean. Even so, it
makes a nice spot to stay.

Sleeping

There are a number of restaurants, along with the usual noodle shops and stalls, near
the market and on the streets leading off the market. None is particularly noteworthy.
Simple Chinese and Lao dishes.

Eating

Air *Lao Aviation*, T412059. Connections with **Vientiane** daily, 1¼ hrs, US$42. On each
occasion the plane makes a round trip (ie Vientiane-Sayaboury-Vientiane).

Transport

Road/river There are no road links with Vientiane. The road south from Sayabouri
only goes as far as Muang Ken Thao, close to the border with Thailand. This road passes
through Pak Lai, on the Mekong, where it is possible to catch a boat downstream to
Vientiane. The route north is more useful. From Luang Prabang, catch a bus through
Muang Nan to the Mekong (3-4 hrs). From here, catch a ferry across the river to Tha

The North

Deua and from this little riverside hamlet a bus onward to Sayaboury (1 hr). Buses leave daily each morning from Luang Prabang.

Directory **Banks** One bank in town, the *Lane Xang Bank*. It does not accept TCs but will change US$ cash. The rate of exchange is said to be poor. **Communications** Post and telephone office in the centre of town, on the other side of the road from the market.

Pak Lai

Colour map 2, grid B1 Pak Lai is not much more than a convenient place to stop on the long river journey between Vientiane and Luang Prabang and it grew up as a riverine equivalent to the trucking stop. There are a couple of guesthouses here, a few restaurants and shops, and a desultory branch of the *Lane Xang Bank*.

Pak Lai does enjoy a footnote in Laos' colonial history which is worth recounting. In 1887 Luang Prabang was attacked by a band of Chinese Ho and northern Tai bandits. Auguste Pavie, the newly appointed French vice consul, rescued King Unkham from his burning palace and escaped downstream to Pak Lai. Here they remained while the King recovered from the journey (he was old and frail) and Pavie researched the early history of Lane Xang. This piece of quick-thinking indebted the king to Pavie and therefore also to the French. Within five years of this heroic rescue Laos was French and the Siamese had lost control of what was formerly theirs.

Sleeping One government guesthouse, **F** *Savang*, 20 mins' walk from ticket office at the end of the village, next to a timber factory, friendly and helpful staff, but basic with shared facilities.

Transport **Road** The road north from here is in poor condition, although upgrading work is continuing. During the dry season (roughly Nov-May) buses run north to **Sayabouri** (5 hrs). During the wet season don't count on their being any overland public transport.

River Connections by river boat north (upriver) to **Luang Prabang** and south (downriver) to **Vientiane**. But note that due to the upgrading of Route 13 between Vientiane and Luang Prabang the river option has languished and there are no longer any scheduled boats and therefore no standard fare. In the wet season when the river is high boats make the entire journey between Vientiane and Luang Prabang, with just a stop in **Pak Lai** (a total journey time of 4-5 days upriver and 3-4 down). But in the dry season it is sometimes necessary to change boats in Pak Lai onto a smaller vessel. There are also speedboats – much quicker and much less relaxing. For further details on taking the boat between Vientiane and Luang Prabang via Pak Lai see page 101.

The Central Provinces

Introducing the Central Provinces

Laos' central provinces, sandwiched between the **Mekong** (and Thailand) to the west and the **Annamite mountains** (and Vietnam) to the east, are the least visited in the country. Travellers entering Laos from Vietnam, or leaving for Vietnam, cross the **border** via Lac Xao or Xepon but few choose to linger for long. This is a shame because the **scenery** here is stunning, with dramatic limestone karsts, enormous caves, beautiful rivers and forests. In time the central provinces may exploit their natural attributes, but for the moment this is a largely unexplored area for tourists. The two major towns in the central portions of the country are **Thakhek** and **Savannakhet**. Both benefit from **riverside locations** and are attractive places where a day or two can be spent happily sauntering through the towns' **monasteries**, exploring their markets and back streets, and undertaking forays into the surrounding countryside.

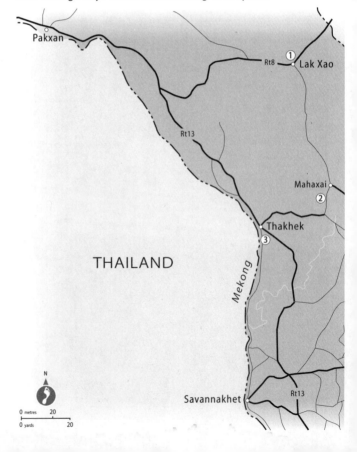

Things to do in the Central Provinces

① Rather than fly, take one of the more adventurous **overland routes to Vietnam**. Either catch a bus running over the the Annamite mountains through Lac Xao on Route 8 or via Xepon and Lao Bao on Route 9.

② Explore the **caves** around Thakhek, in the Mahaxai area.

③ Take a tuk-tuk out to **That Sikhot,** 7 km south of Thakhek, where Chao Sikhot is said to have come to a particularly grisly end.

④ Root – carefully – around the **Ho Chi Minh Trail**, if you have a yen for the detritus of war.

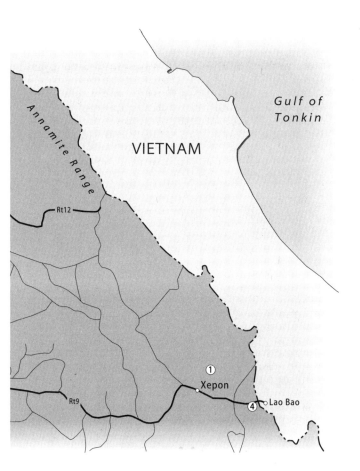

Pakxan (Paksan)

Colour map 2, grid B4   In the mid-1990s people used to stop in Pakxan to break the journey south (or north). But now that road upgrading has shortened the journey time between Vientiane and Thakhek to a bearable five to six hours, its one purpose in life, for most tourists, has been rendered obsolete. However, you might just find yourself stranded here when making your way to Vientiane from the Vietnamese border at Lac Xao. All Vientiane-bound buses leave in the early morning from the border, but it is possible to catch pick-ups and make your way to Pakxan by early evening.

Indulging in some futurology, there is also the possibility that Pakxan will find itself on the map in more than just the cartographic sense when – and if – proposed Route 22 is upgraded making it possible to reach Xieng Khouang, Phonsavanh and the Plain of Jars from Pakxan. This has been on the planner's desk for over a decade now and seems no closer to realization. There are other potential visitor draws, too, in the shape of **Wat Prah Bat**, an important pilgrimage site for Lowland Lao. Built in 1933, the stupa boasts a footprint of the Buddha as well as one of the largest drums in Laos. Every year, usually in July, Wat Prah Bat hosts a full moon festival. And for those travellers who already feel all 'templed out', there are several opportunities to explore the province's natural heritage by boat/canoe/kayak 50 km east of Paksan, where the **Nam Kading River** meets the Mekong.

Sleeping   **B** *Manolom Guesthouse*, located 2 km from the centre, as you enter from Vientiane.
Accommodation seems insufficient, given the number of backpackers passing through the town   Overpriced and unfriendly but they don't care, as they get the trade regardless of conditions! Basic with shared bathroom. **D-E** *B&K Guesthouse*, aross the river, along the 1st road on the right. The friendly owners of this new establishment speak very good English, and with clean rooms and ensuites, it's worth a try. **E** *Mandoney Guesthouse*, 500 m north of the bus station on Route 13. Big, white 3-storey building, a much better option than the *Phou Doi*, big clean doubles. **F** *Pakxan Phattana Hotel*, better known as the *Phou Doi*, 1 km south of the bus station, Route 13, T102. A/c, rather overpriced, simple rooms with shared bathrooms (clean though some of the rooms have leaky roofs, and lots of peep-holes).

Eating   There are many small restaurants along the main drag but few with English menus and mostly of poor quality and not particularly cheap. One alternative is *Vong Heuang Restaurant*, near the bus station.

Transport   **Road**   The bus stop is on Route 13 next to the bank. Connections with **Vientiane** (1-2
155 km to Vientiane   hrs, 6,000 kip), **Thakhek** (4-5 hrs, 15,000 kip) and **Savannakhet** (25,000 kip).
190 km to Thakhek

International connections   The border at **Lac Xao** (Km 20 in Lao) on the Lao side and **Cau Treo** on the Vietnamese side has been a legal border crossing point since Sep 1997. 3 morning buses a day leave for the border from **Vientiane** (at 0400, 0500 and 0600), which you can pick up in **Pakxan**. There are also occasional pick-ups from Pakxan to Lak Xao (30,000 kip); they first head south along the excellent Route 13, and then turn inland along the bumpy Route 8. From Lac Xao you can take a tuk-tuk to the border (1 hr, 30,000 kip for the whole tuk-tuk).

Directory   **Banks**   *Lane Xang Bank*, T212022, Route 13 (by the bus stop and market – incongruously new building in this setting).

Tham Hinboun

Heading east on Route 8 towards Lac Xao, the more adventurous visitor can encounter some of the most stunning landscapes in the entire country. However, independent travel here is not straightforward and will require some determination. After leaving the north-south Route 13, take Route 8 into the hills – with tremendous views over a karst landscape of pinnacles, cones and a patchwork of forest – to the small market town of **Nankinnot**. Turn right in the town and follow the dirt road (with difficulty, as it frequently divides and deteriorates) to the small riverside village of **Longphat**. No public vehicles seem to take this route. From Longphat, hire a boat for the 2-3 hour journey upstream to **Phonheng**. The boat trip to Phonheng is fascinating, with excellent views of impressive limestone cliffs along the way. The *Sala Hinboun Guesthouse* here is clean, has four double rooms and excellent food. It is not permanently staffed, so contact the owner, who lives in Nankinnot, before setting off for Phonheng.

This little known region contains some of the finest limestone karsts and caves in the world

Tham Hinboun is a further hour upstream and can only be described as sensational. The cave is so large that no one should suffer from claustrophobia. Returning south by boat, it is possible to continue downstream past Longphat and into the awesome Hinboun gorge. This is roughly 14 km long and for much of the distance vertical cliffs over 300 m high rise directly from the water on both sides. The gorge also has some historical significance, both during the Vietnamese War and, much earlier, with the discovery of some valuable religious documents. There is no white water but the river frequently flows quite fast. More impressive scenery then follows until the village of **Paktuk**, close to Route 13 where any journey can be continued.

Tham Nathan is another enormous cave set in this remote countryside, requiring a four-wheel drive vehicle and a good guide to find it. In the beautiful **Pathene Valley**, a visit to the rickety **Phontiou tin mine** is fascinating, but not encouraged by the Korean manager. A few kilometres past the mine, open panning is done by the local people, mainly of Vietnamese origin. They are allowed to sell their tin to the Phontiou mine. At the head of the valley a great limestone amphitheatre houses more caves.

Lac Xao (Lac Sao)

Sometimes called Muang Kham Keut (which is confusing because there is another Kham Keut – a village – 30 km west of Lac Xao), Lac Xao is a new town. It was established by the Lao army's Bolisat Phathana Khet Phoudoi (BPKP or Mountainous Area Development Company) back in 1968 in a remote and sparsely populated area close to the border with Vietnam. The original Kham Keut is located 30 km west of Lac Xao and is worth a visit *en route* as it is over 500 years old. The surrounding countryside is beautiful but if countryside isn't your thing, then Lac Xao itself has little else to recommend it beyond acting as a break in the journey overland to Vietnam.

Colour map 2, grid B5

Lac Xao retains a frontier, wild west atmosphere. In the distance looms a line of cliffs of which the last is locally known as Pa Pi Hai – or the 'Ghost that Cries'. There is a market and a post office in town, and a *BCEL Exchange* bank.

This part of Laos is one of the richest in terms of wildlife. Unfortunately for those who are trying to protect the country's forests and fauna – like the LXWC (below) – it also has great hydropower potential. The Nam Hinboun plant and the controversial Nam Theun II are situated close to Lac Xao and many fear that their construction will open up the region to yet more loggers and settlers. But it may be that the battle is already lost. The establishment of the town has enticed settlers into the area in any case and this has significantly increased the pressure on resources.

Lac Xao Wildlife Centre Close to the guesthouses is the Lac Xao Wildlife Centre (LXWC), a project run by the **Carnivore Preservation Trust** (F051-214366) to breed endangered cats (such as clouded leopards), civets, primates and bears indigenous to Laos. They have been operating since 1995 and currently have around 100 animals in their care. In return for a donation to their trust, they are happy to show visitors around.

The poverty of most local people means that US$5,000 for a sun bear (so that its gall bladder can be used) is almost too attractive a proposition to resist. The LXWC tries to buy these captured animals before they are sold to traders. They are then kept in captivity and bred so that at some future date when the natural environment is better protected they (and their young) can be released back into the wild. The LXWC has also been allotted 3,000 ha of forest by the BPKP as a future wildlife sanctuary although they don't have the resources to manage even this small area.

Another rare inhabitant of the area is the **Phi Tong Luang**, or the Spirits of the Yellow Leaves, better known as the **Mlabri**. This is a little known tribal group also present in very small numbers in Thailand (see box on page 193).

The local army of tuk-tuk drivers is also worth mentioning as a breed apart. The town's wild west atmosphere seems to have gone to their heads, so it's a question of holding on to your hats when in their care, and your wallets, too, as the handful we came across did their level best to fleece us.

Sleeping
■ on map
Price codes:
see inside front cover

There are now several relatively pleasant places to stay in Lac Xao. Previously, the only options were about 4 km south along Route 8B from the main town and market, where the **E** *Phoudoi Hotel* has a range of rooms in 3 buildings, and **E** Opposite is a fairly new guesthouse, with clean doubles. Now, though, there are a couple of guesthouses a stone's throw from the bus station, so no need to deliver yourself into the unscrupulous hands of the tuk-tuk drivers. **D** *Phoutthavong Guesthouse*, T341074. Spotless rooms with a/c or fans, tiled floor and wonderfully white, white paintwork and polished wooden furniture that sits at odds with the dusty atmosphere of the town. **D** *Souriya Hotel*, T341111, is another pleasant alternative with 20 spotlessly clean, simple rooms (some a/c) with TV and some baths (hot water). Friendly owner speaks quite good English. A motley selection of food, drink and toiletries is on sale in the foyer. **D** *Vongsouda Guesthouse*, T341035. Newish guesthouse with a/c, ensuites, western loos and hot water. Not most comfortable mattresses in the world, but rooms are clean and serviceable. Clean and airy lobby but real selling point is the large veranda outside the main entrance where you can sit and relax with a drink.

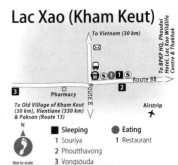

Lac Xao (Kham Keut)

To Vietnam (30 km)

To BPKP HQ, Phoudoi Hotel, Lac Xao Wildlife Centre & Thakhek

Route 8B

Pharmacy

To Old Village of Kham Keut (30 km), Vientiane (330 km) & Paksan (Route 13)

Airstrip

N

Not to scale

■ **Sleeping**
1 Souriya
2 Phoutthavong
3 Vongsouda

● **Eating**
1 Restaurant

Eating
● on map
Price codes:
see inside front cover

Only 1 restaurant, 200 m from *Phoutthavong Guesthouse*, on the same side of the road. Plenty of tables, in a pleasant if unextraordinary setting. Menu inclues a good line in

The Mlabri: the spirits of the yellow leaves

The elusive Mlabri 'tribe' represent one of the few remaining groups of hunter gatherers in Southeast Asia. They are also known as the Phi Tong Luang or 'Spirits of the Yellow Leaves' – when their shelters of rattan and banana leaves turn yellow they take this as a sign from the spirits that it is time to move on. The destruction of the forest means that the Mlabri have been forced to lead more sedentary lives, turning to settled agriculture in place of hunting and gathering.

Traditionally the Mlabri hunted using spears, but when stalking larger game, rather than throwing the weapon, they would brace it against the ground and allow the charging animal to impale itself on the point. In this way, the Mlabri were

able to kill the great saladang wild buffalo (Bos gaurus), as well as bears and tigers. Smaller game was more common however, and this was supplemented with tubers, nuts, honey and other forest products to provide a balanced diet. Many of the Mlabri's traditions are already on the verge of extinction. Hunting and gathering is no longer a tenable livelihood and disease and inter-marriage with other tribes is reducing their number. Perhaps this is no bad thing: as recently as the 1980s, a Mlabri was displayed in a cage in a Bangkok department store. Today, the problem is that the few Mlabri still alive, finding their forests impoverished, have been forced to become cheap labourers for groups such as the Hmong.

octopus and eel dishes and the drinks menu boasts both Red and Black label whisky. Outside veranda has a few tables with tree stumps for chairs.

Road Early morning connections to **Vientiane** at 0500, 0600 and 0800 (50,000 kip). **Transport** Throughout the day pick-ups depart for Route 13, and onwards north to **Pakxan**, 0700 (40,000 kip), and south to **Thakhek**, 0730 (30,000 kip). The road up into the mountains is excellent, partly because there is a hydropower dam here – the Nam Hinboum – and also because of the need to establish and maintain good infrastructural links with neighbouring countries. A road also snakes its way northwest through the mountains to **Xieng Khouang** and the **Plain of Jars**, but it is in a terrible state and is currently closed to all but the most intrepid. One traveller we met in Oct 2001 found himself physically making the road before the truck he was on could proceed. It is also (theoretically) possible to head south on Route 8B from Lac Xao and then onto Route 12 to go to **Thakhek** although there seems to be very little traffic on this abysmal road.

International connections It has been possible for foreigners to cross into **Vietnam** here since Sep 1997. Lac Xao (Km 20 in Lao) is the nearest settlement to the border on the Lao side and Cau Treo on the Vietnamese side. Pick-ups throughout the day to the border, 1 hr. You shouldn't have to pay more than 10,000 kip each if you can fill a whole tuk-tuk, but be prepared to barter hard. It's sometimes cheaper in the mornings, as there's a better chance the drivers will be able to pick up passengers for the return trip.

The Central Provinces

Thakhek (Muang Khammouan)

Phone code: 052
Colour map 2, grid B5

Thakhek is also known by its old name, Muang Khammouan; Khammouan is the province of which the town is the capital. Thakhek is sometimes translated as Indian (Khek or Khaek) Port (Tha), although it probably means Guest (Khaek) Port after the large number of people who settled here from the north. During the royalist period (through to the mid-1970s) it was a popular weekend destination for Thais who came here in droves to gamble. After the communist victory, when Laos effectively shut up shop, everything went very quiet. But the recent recovery of commercial traffic has brought some life back to this small settlement, although Thakhek remains a quiet town, set in beautiful countryside.

The origins of Thakhek can be traced back to the Cambodian-based kingdoms of Chenla and Funan which reached their heyday in the seventh century AD. But modern Thakhek was founded in 1911-12.

As in Savannakhet and Pakse, the locals are hoping that their town will be blessed by a bridge over the Mekong linking it with the Thai city of Nakhon Phanom. In June 1996 Vientiane and Bangkok signed a memorandum of understanding but the Lao are far less enthusiastic than the Thai. Transport and Construction Minister, Phao Bounaphon, frantically hedged his bets when he stated: "The bridge comes under the national plan of Laos, but the question of when it will be built depends on further study and financial factors." If it comes to fruition, Thakhek will be quiet no longer. To the northeast the impressive karst landscape of the Mahaxai area is visible (see Excursions).

Ins and outs

Getting there Flights between Vientiane and Thakhek have been discontinued – the improving quality of the road north to the capital makes flying unnecessary. Thakhek is across the Mekong from the Thai town of Nakhon Phanom and this is one of the points where it is possible for foreigners to cross between Thailand and Laos. The bus terminal is 2-3 km east of town on Route 13 at Talat (market) Souk Somboun, also known as Talat Lak Saam. Daily buses to Savannakhet (2½ hrs) and Pakse via Savannakhet. A new bus station is in the planning stage. Daily connections northbound service Vientiane (6-7 hrs) and Pakxan (4-5 hrs). Boats no longer run between Thakhek and Vientiane.

Thakhek

Getting around Tuk-tuks ferry people in from bus terminals and are available to hire for out-of-town trips. Thakhek itself is small enough to negotiate on foot or by bicycle.

Tourist information Inter-Lao Tourism is based at the *Khammouane Saykhong Hotel*. Open Mon-Sat 0800-1100 and 1300-1600.

Sleeping
1 Khammuan International
2 Khammouan Saykhong
3 Sooksomboon Guesthouse

Eating
1 Lao-named
2 Noodle Stall
3 Paransuk Prasod
4 Vanthiu

The Central Provinces

Sights

Two trains of thought generally divide visitor attitudes to Thakhek. There are few officially designated sights in town but some visitors consider it to be a gem of a settlement. Quiet and elegant with some remaining Franco-Chiinese architecture, including a simple fountain square, it has a fine collection of **colonial-era shophouses**, a breezy riverside position and a relaxed ambience. What locals must regard as the central business district at the river end of Kouvoravong Road is wonderful for its peeling buildings. Other visitors, on the other hand, look more critically at the dusty streets, seeing instead pockets of squalor with dilapidated buildings, and an uncharacteristic atmosphere of disinterest amongst the locals. There are three **markets** in Thakhek. The largest, Talat Souk Somboun (Talat Lak Saam) is out at the bus terminal, 2-3 km east of town. Tuk-tuks constantly ferry market-goers to and fro (3,500 kip). Talat Lak Song is at the eastern end of Kouvoravong Road, about 1½-2 km from the town centre. It is a mixed, largely dry goods market. Finally, north on Chaoanou Road, is the Talat Nabo.

Excursions

Visible from town is the karst landscape of the **Mahaxai area** to the north and east. Mahaxai itself is a beautiful small town 50 km east of Thakhek on Route 12. But even more beautiful is the scenery here: exquisite valleys and imposing limestone bluffs. A visit to Mahaxai should be combined with a visit to one or more of the spectacular caves mentioned below and some river excursions to witness the Se Bangfai gorges, or to enjoy the rapids further downstream. The *Government Guesthouse* has 10 large clean airy rooms, with attached shower, upstairs rooms are brighter. There is an attractive balcony overlooking the river, ideal for sitting and watching the world go by. Food is generally of high quality in the local noodle shops and foodstalls to be found in Mahaxai. To get there, take a songthaew from the Thakhek bus terminal (8,000 kip). Alternatively, charter a tuk-tuk which makes it easier to reach the caves. **NB** The last bus back to Thakhek leaves Mahaxai at 1500.

Mahaxai

Three caves can be visited on the way to Mahaxai, or as a day trip from Thakhek. **Tham Pha Ban Tham**, a cave containing Buddha images, lies 8 km from Thakhek. A local festival is held here during the fifth month of the Buddhist calendar. The cave itself is said to be inaccessible during the wet season. **Tham Xiang Lieb (Chiang Rieb)** is another cave at the foot of a limestone cliff, 12 km from Thakhek. The **Houai Xiang Lieb** flows from the cave and there are some prehistoric paintings on the cliff face. Again the cave is reportedly only accessible during the dry season. There is a third cave 15 km from Thakhek, **Tham Nong Ang**. This last cave is worth a visit if only to catch the cool breeze which rushes from within the rock and emanates at the cave entrance. Outside the cave is a shady, wooded picnicking area and a rather motley collection of animals. ■ *Getting there: a tuk-tuk should be around 100,000 kip for a 3-hr round trip to all 3 caves.*

Caves

    Tham En can be found to the south of Route 12, about 14 km towards Mahaxai. It is signposted only in Lao and can also be reached by tuk-tuk from Thahkek.

That Sikhot or **Sikhotaboun** is one of Laos' holiest sites and lies about 7 km south of Thakhek. The *that* is thought to have been built by Chao Anou at

That Sikhot

the beginning of the 15th century. It overlooks the Mekong and was restored in 1956. The *that* houses the relics of Chao Sikhot, a local hero, founder of the old town of Thakhek, and Chou Anou's son-in-law. According to local legend, Sikhot was an ordinary man who cooked some rice which he stirred with dirty – but as it turned out magic – sticks. When the local people understandably refused to eat the dirt-ridden rice he did so instead – and as a result was bestowed with Herculean strength. He conquered most of the surrounding area and took Vientiane whereupon he married the King of Vientiane's daughter. (The legend does not mention Chao Anou's name, but who wants to spoil a good story?) The king asked his daughter to discover whether Sikhot had any weakness. This she did, her husband foolishly revealing that he could only be killed through the anus. The King of Vientiane placed an archer at the bottom of Sikhot's pit latrine (a messy business that does not bear contemplating) and when the unfortunate Oriental Hercules came to relieve himself, was killed by an arrow up his anus. That Sikhot consists of a large gold *that* raised on a plinth (note the reliefs of the Buddha in various mudras along the base), with a viharn upstream built in 1970 by the last King of Laos. The whole is part surrounded by a high wall. Stalls selling drinks and some food are to be found under the trees to the left. The gate here is always open. Admission by donation (there is a wooden monk with alms bowl in front of the *that*). A further reason to come here is simply for the journey downstream along a quiet country road: bucolic Laos at its best. A major annual festival is held here in July. ■ *Getting there: by hired tuk-tuk (15,000 kip there and back) or by regular public tuk-tuk (stand at the intersection of Ounkham and Kouvoravong roads).*

Essentials

Sleeping
■ *on map*
Price codes:
see inside front cover

C *Khammouane Saykhong*, Setthathirat Rd (or Mekong Rd), T212216, F212370. A/c, restaurant. Large 1950s hotel with 50-odd rooms overlooking the Mekong. Had they designed the place with windows facing the river, rather than the doors, it would be possible to write 'river view' – but they didn't. Large, plain rooms, TV and fridge with rather run-down, though clean, bathrooms, hot water sometimes works, sometimes not. Not much English spoken, and the young male staff are very giggly. **C-D** *Sooksomboon Guesthouse* (formerly the *Sikhot Hotel*), Setthathirat Rd, T212225. A/c, restaurant. Attractive villa facing the Mekong and the place with the most character in Thakhek. The interior has been decorated with charm, the a/c rooms in the main house are best, with attached bathrooms, fluffy chairs, sometimes even asylum-esque padded walls, fridge and TV. Cheaper rooms in the motel-esque annexe, which is, well, motel-esque. **NB** Be prepared for a knock on the door around 0100; nightclubs close around that time and hookers and pimps go hunting.

D *Khammuan International* (formerly the *Chaleunxay Hotel*), Kouvoravong Rd, T212171. Some a/c, restaurant. Oldish villa with potential, but for some inconceivable reason the management decided that what guests really desire are small rooms without windows – so some of the a/c rooms are like caves. Attached bathrooms are good with hot water showers, rooms haven't seen a lick of paint in years, and the hotel has a large courtyard with a/c restaurant attached. Single rooms with super-powerful ceiling fans are available for the cheaper price. Best deal in town. **D** *Phou Doi*, Route 13, T212048, F212510. A/c, restaurant, inconvenient location 2 km east of town, not far from bus station, OK rooms but little character as this was only built a few years back.

Thakhek is not a place to come to for its cuisine. There is the usual array of noodle stalls – try the one in the town 'square' with its good fruit shakes. Warmed baguettes are sold at the 'square' in the morning.

Eating
● *on map*
Price codes:
see inside front cover

Mid-range Most restaurants are attached to hotels, of which the best, despite appearances, is that at the *Khammuan International*, but an exception is the small place downstream from the *Khammouane Saykhong Hotel* on the River Rd (only open in the evening), simple dishes and good fish. *Parsansuk Prasod*, River Rd. A 'floating' restaurant of sorts (although it looks as though it's about to sink), hard to miss the flashing fairy lights and loud Thai pop music, delicious fish by all accounts, but pricey.

Cheap *Lao-named restaurant*, on the corner of Ounkham Rd and the east-west street leading to Wat Nabo. English menu with Lao and some western dishes including hamburgers, but mainly centred around seafood. Popular with expats in the area, décor includes fully decorated Christmas tree year-round! *Vanthiu Restaurant*, Vietnamese, walk through the wine shop to get to the restaurant out back – see map for location. Friendly establishment, no English menu but some English dishes.

Seriously cheap *Huaphae Ponekham Restaurant*, T 213847. Another floating establishment that favours ear-splitting Thai music. Popular with the locals. Not for those with bland palettes.

Nothing geared to the weird predilections of visiting *farang* but functional basketry and such oddities as hand crafted buffalo bells available in Talat Lak Song. There are a few duty-free shops at the pier which stock Chinese 'champagne', French wines, spirits, perfume and cigarettes.

Shopping

Bus/truck The main bus terminal is about 2 km out of town, following the Kouvoravong road, close to Route 13. Tuk-tuks charge about 3,000 kip per person to ferry passengers townwards. A new bus station is planned to service Thakhek in the future, but no date has yet been set for the change of venue. Connections with **Vientiane** (6-7 hrs, 15,000 kip) and **Pakxan** (4-5 hrs, 15,000 kip). Several departures daily to **Savannakhet** (2½ hrs, 13,000 kip). For **Pakse**, take a bus or pick-up to Savannakhet and from there a bus leaves at 1330 for Pakse (20,000 kip). Route 13 has been recently upgraded and vehicles can travel at around 50-60 kph on this stretch.

Transport
190 km to Pakxan
139 km to Savannakhet
346 km to Vientiane

There is no longer a regular **boat** service to Vientiane.

International connections Thakhek is across the river from **Nakhon Phanom** in **Thailand**. Customs/Immigration Office by the pier open 0800-1200, 1300-1600 Mon-Sun. Boats regularly cross between the 2 towns (10,000 kip or 50 baht). Visas available from agents in Nakhon Phanom; US$30 for 15 days or US$50-60 for a 30 day visa. On arrival here from Thailand, you need to come already armed with a visa, as well as a 90 baht or 17,600 kip entry fee.

Banks *Banque Pour le Commerce Extérieur*, Kouvorvong Rd, just across from the post office, will change cash and TCs. *Lao Mai Bank*, Kouvoravong Rd (eastern end, opposite Talat Lak Song and about 1½-2 km from town centre), will change cash and TCs. There are also exchange counters at the bus terminal and the pier – cash only. **Communications** Post Office: Kouvoravong Rd (at crossroads with Nongbuakham Rd). **Telephone**: international calls can be made from the *Khammuan International* and *Khammouane Saykhong* hotels, and also from the post office.

Directory

Savannakhet

Phone code: 041
Colour map 2, grid C5
Population: 50,000

On the banks of the Mekong, Savannakhet – or Savan as it is usually known – is an important river port and the gateway to the south. At the starting point of the road to Danang in Vietnam (Route 9) and an important trading centre with Thailand, it is very commercial with a large Chinese and Vietnamese population.

Indeed, it is one of the only towns in Laos where there is still a sizeable Chinese population – most decided Communism did not sit well with their entrepreneurial instincts, and left. The population of the town proper is about 50,000, although the district as a whole supports well over 100,000 people. Across the Mekong, high-rise Mukdahan in Thailand may be cocking a snook at its poorer neighbour to the east, but Savannakhet has got a lot to offer that Mukdahan has bulldozed away in the name of modernization. It feels as though the country never left Savan: cows, buffalos, goats and chickens graze and wander around the urban area and a large portion of the town's French colonial roots still stand, moulding gently in the tropical climate. Whether this will last long is questionable. Construction of a bridge across the Mekong to Mukdahan under Japanese and Thai sponsorship has been due to commence for several years now, and the latest news is that it should be ready for use in 2005. There are also plans to upgrade the road east to Vietnam. However, it is not likely to be completed before 2003.

In 1989 US servicemen arrived in Savannakhet in their search for the remains of men missing in action (MIAs) and the whole town turned out to watch their arrival at the airport. Not realizing that the Lao bear absolutely no animosity towards Americans, the men kept their heads down and refused to disembark until the crowds dispersed. During the war against the Pathet Lao the Royal Lao Air Force operated out of Savannakhet and, towards the end of the conflict, even headquartered here.

Ins and outs

Getting there
See Transport, page 203, for further details

There are overland international connections from Savannakhet to both Thailand and Vietnam. But although it is possible to cross the Mekong from Mukdahan in Thailand and enter Laos through Savannakhet, few foreign travellers choose to do so. Rather more popular is to enter or leave Laos from Vietnam via Lao Bao. There are bus connections from Savan with Vietnamese towns including Danang, Dong Ha and Hué. Domestic links – for Laos – are good. There are daily air connections with Vientiane and Pakse, further south still. The government bus terminal is on the northern edge of town and from there buses leave daily for Vientiane via Thakhek (8 hrs all the way to the capital) and south to Pakse (6-8 hrs). A new private bus station currently offers connections with Pakse and Vientiane, and east with Lao Bao, Vietnam. The boats that used to be so useful when the roads were in a terrible state found most of their business evaporating as people responded to the improving roads by abandoning the river. There are now no scheduled ferry departures.

Getting around

Savan, while one of Laos' larger urban centres, is easy enough to negotiate on foot. Tuk-tuks, are the main form of local transport. Cars (with driver) and bicycles are also available for hire.

Wat Sounantha on Nalao Road has a three-dimensional raised relief on the outside of the front of the *sim* showing the Buddha, in the mudra of bestowing peace, separating two warring armies. **Wat Sayaphum** on the Mekong is rather more attractive and has several early 20th-century monastery buildings. It is both the largest and oldest monastery in town – although it was only built at the end of the 19th century. The monks of **Wat Sayamungkhun**, two of whom speak some English are also pleased to talk about their 50-year-old monastery. There is a large temple school here, and arriving during lessons can mean some impromptu English teaching.

Sights

Savan has quite a number of wats, none particularly notable unless 'watting' is a new experience

Savannakhet

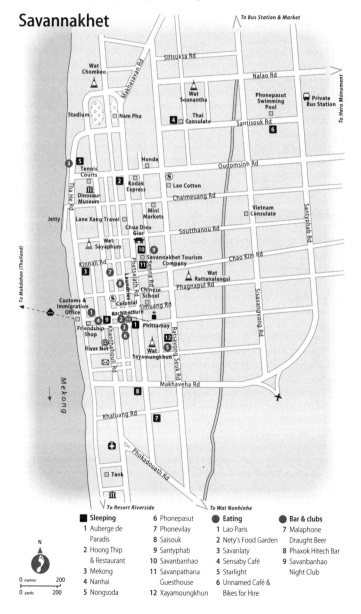

The Central Provinces

Sleeping
1 Auberge de Paradis
2 Hoong Thip & Restaurant
3 Mekong
4 Nanhai
5 Nongsoda
6 Phonepasut
7 Phonevilay
8 Saisouk
9 Santyphab
10 Savanbanhao
11 Savanpathana Guesthouse
12 Xayamoungkhun

Eating
1 Lao Paris
2 Nety's Food Garden
3 Savanlaty
4 Sensaby Café
5 Starlight
6 Unnamed Café & Bikes for Hire

Bar & clubs
7 Malaphone Draught Beer
8 Phaxok Hitech Bar
9 Savanbanhao Night Club

Savan's **colonial heritage** can be seen throughout the central part of town. Perhaps the most attractive area is the square east of the Immigration office between Khanthabouli and Phetsalath roads. Simuang Road, near the Catholic church, is also rewarding in this regard. Evidence of Savan's diverse population is reflected in the **Chua Dieu Giac**, a Mahayana Buddhist pagoda at the intersection of Soutthanu and Phetsalath roads which serves the town's Vietnamese population, and the Chinese school close to the Catholic church. In deference to Theravada tradition, the *chua* also has a *that* in the courtyard. The **central market** has moved from its former town location to a new site behind the government bus station north of the town. Talat Savan Sai's bustle is housed inside a brand spanking new building, built and managed by a Singaporean company, costing US$6 mn, complete with parking spaces, one of the few sets of escalators in Laos (although they don't work!), and even a western café. There is the usual selection of meat, vegetables, fruit, dry goods and fabrics, and an abundance of gold and silversmiths. For those unable to get to the Ho Chi Minh Trail, there is some rusting war scrap in the grounds of what used to be the **Provincial Museum** on the Khanthabouli Road and a tank just to the north (see map). The museum offers little terribly enlightening or interesting.

A recent addition to Savannakhet's list of attractions is the **Dinosaur Museum**, on Khantabouli Road, south of the stadium, which houses a collection of four different dinosaur and early mammalian remains, and even some fragments of a meteorite that fell to earth over 100 million years ago. The first fossils were unearthed in 1991 by a team of French and Lao scientists in the region. All exhibits are accompanied by explanations in Lao and French. The staff speak good English and French and are happy to explain their work.
■ *Mon-Fri 0800-1200, 1400-1600.1,000 kip.*

Excursions

That Inheng This holy 16th-century *that* or stupa is 12 km northeast of Savannakhet. It was built during the reign of King Sikhottabong at the same time as That Luang in Vientiane although local guides may try to convince you it was founded by the Indian emperor Asoka over 2,000 years ago. Needless to say, there is no historical evidence to substantiate this claim. The wat is the site of an annual festival (February or March) akin to the one celebrated at Wat Phou, Champassak (see page 230). ■ *Getting there: any of the regular tuk-tuks (30,000 kip) which ferry people between Savannakhet and Xeno go past the turn-off for That Inheng. It is a 3-km walk from the road. Alternatively hire a bicycle in town and cycle out here.*

Salt works Northeast of the city, a visit to the salt works makes for a good excursion. About 90% of Lao salt is produced here, either in large open saltpans or in an interesting Heath Robinson-like contraption where the saline solution is pumped into small metal trays over wood fires in open sheds!

Kengkok The main reason to come to this village, situated 60 km from Savan, is to see the beautiful surrounding countryside. ■ *Getting there: Kengkok is 35 km south along Route 13 and then 25 km off the road (turn left – 'inland'). The daily bus connection from Savan has been discontinued which means the only alternatives are hiring a car or a tuk-tuk (130,000-odd kip return), but make sure you remember to agree a pick-up time.*

A lesser-known Khmer site 75 km south of Savan along the Mekong, Ban **Ban Houan** Houan Hine, or *Stone House*, was built between the sixth and the end of the **Hine** seventh centuries. It does not begin to compare, however, with the better known Wat Phou outside Champassak. However a visit here can be combined with a visit to **That Phone**, a hilly Buddhist *that en route*. It was previously possible to travel by boat down the Mekong, but again improvements in road conditions, coupled with the more usual tourist disposition for pressing on elsewhere, has meant this is no longer an option. However, whereas the difficulty used to be in getting here without having to charter a car and driver, there is now a bus. ■ *Getting there: Ban Houan Hine lies 15 km off Route 13 (take Route 13 south, 60 km from Savan, and then turn right onto a track for a further 15 km – it is signposted from the main road 'Stone House Pillars'). The easiest method by far is by bus (13,000 kip). Departure times were unpindownable on our last visit, so best to ask around town.*

This is an enticing prospect for some visitors but getting here is not easy from **Ho Chi Minh** Savan and certainly is only possible as a day trip with a hired car. *Savanbanhao* **Trail** *Tourism* offer a day tour for US$140 with car and guide, or US$170 overnight. See Ho Chi Minh Trail, page 205, for further details.

Essentials

B *Auberge de Paradis (Sala Savan)*, by old market, T212445. 5 large, elegantly furnished, a/c rooms in this converted colonial villa. Wooden floors and rattan furniture, huge hot shower bathrooms attached. Recommended. **B** *Hoong Thip*, Phetsalath Rd, T212262, F 213230. A/c, satellite TV, dark rooms, big *mandi*-type bathrooms attached, breakfast included. Other services offered include sauna, car and driver hire ($25), and fairly pricey attached restaurant. **B** *Nanhai*, Santisouk Rd (their postal address, though, is 313RM Lasavong Rd), T212371, F212380. 6 floors, 42 rooms, karaoke bars, and dining hall. A prime example of a mainland Chinese hotel except the staff are quite polite here. Mainly used by Chinese businessmen, there is little atmosphere for the tourist. Rooms have a/c, TV, fridge, IDD telephones and en-suite bathroom but smell musty and unused, and the single rooms are minuscule. The pool has no water, which is a slight drawback. The hotel boasts the only lift in town. The Thai consulate is located here. **B** *Phonepasut*, Santisouk Rd, T212158/212190, F212916. A/c, hot water, restaurant, pool (US$1 for visitors), motel-like place with 2 courtyards. Rooms are clean with OK bathrooms, satellite TV, friendly and well run with support services like fax and international telephone. Situated 1 km from town centre in quiet street.

C-D *Mekong*, Tha He Rd, T212249. Some a/c. This place is housed in an attractive colonial villa on the Mekong, the rooms are large, generally clean, with good attached bathrooms. Mattresses vary hugely in comfortability, so a spot of testing is a good idea. The downside is that the Vietnamese management are diffident to the point of rudeness: ignore them and it's great. **C-E** *Savanbanhao*, Senna Rd, T212202, F212944. Some a/c. Centrally located hotel composed of 4 white houses set around a courtyard, with a range of rooms, most expensive with attached showers and hot water. Beware the water boiler of Soviet production, it is lethal. Large balcony, quiet compound and *Savanbanhao Tourism Company*, a tour firm, attached.

D *Nongsoda*, Tha He Rd, T212522. Oodles of white lace draped all over the house. Clean rooms with a/c and wonderfully hot water ensuites. **D** *Saisouk*, Makhavenha Rd, T212207. A real gem. This breezy new guesthouse has good sized twin and double rooms, immaculately furnished and spotlessly clean, some a/c, communal hot water

Sleeping
■ *on map, page 199*
Price codes:
see inside front cover

Savannakhet has a good selection of places to stay for US$5 and upwards but budget accommodation is scarce

bathrooms. Beautifully decorated with interesting objects d'art (including 3 telephones!), there are plenty of chairs and tables on the large verandas. Very friendly staff, no English. Laundry service. Recommended. **D-E** *Phonevilay*, 137 Phetsarath Rd. south of town centre, T212284. Some a/c. More expensive rooms with attached hot water showers, cheaper rooms have musty bathrooms, hard mattresses and are like cells, rude, disinterested staff. **D-E** *Savanpathana Guesthouse*, Senna Rd, next door to *Savanbanhao*, T213955. Ugly, grey building, bare and gloomy but clean rooms. No hot water, attached bathrooms with squat toilet and rusty shower, more expensive rooms upstairs are good value with a/c, although the 'VIP' rooms in their separate block are nothing to write home about with their tatty furniture and grubby albeit huge bathrooms. Predominantly male staff are helpful if they are not too busy watching Thai boxing on TV.

E *Resort Riverside*, about 2 km downriver past the post office, the sign reads *Savan Saikhong*, T212775. Beautiful location overlooking the river, pink and blue building overgrown with vines, provides simple doubles and twins. Cheaper rooms have cold water bathrooms and fan, while the most expensive have a/c, TV, fridge and hot water shower. Large garden with shady trees, pond, flowers and seating area, a bit far out of town but bikes for rent. Recommended. **E** *Santyphab*, Chaleunmouang Rd off Tha He Rd, 100 m from passenger pier to Thailand, T212177. Enormous rooms painted (albeit a very long time ago) a garish turquoise. Some a/c. Basic and very dirty but cheap rooms with attached cold water showers. You have to be a gymnast to get to some of the toilets! **E-F** *Xayamoungkhun* (in English the sign just reads 'Guest House'), 85 Ratsavong Seuk Rd, T212426. Some a/c. An excellent little hotel with 16 rooms in an airy colonial-era villa. Range of very clean rooms available, more expensive have hot water, a/c and fridge. Very friendly owners, a collection of secondhand books and magazines, centrally positioned, largish compound. Recommended. **F** Guesthouse at the bus station, basic dorm rooms but useful for catching the daily Vietnam bus which leaves at 0600.

Eating

● *on map, page 199*
Price codes:
see inside front cover

Several restaurants on the riverside serve good food and beer. The market also has stalls offering good, fresh food including excellent Mekong River fish dishes

Mid-range *SayChay*, 2nd floor of the Customs and Immigration building. One place to avoid, as despite the beautiful location overlooking the river the food is expensive and very uninspired.

Cheap *Happy Café*, at market 2 km north of town. Pleasant spot with western drinks and dishes, reasonable prices. *Savanlaty Restaurant*, breezy setting overlooking 'landscaped' courtyard. Lots of pictures of snakes and elephants too high up on the walls to see. *Unnamed Café*, opposite *Nety's Food Garden*. The freshest baguettes for breakfast, noodles and rice dishes, and a variety of fruit. English menu, bikes for hire.

Seriously cheap *Lao-Paris*, formerly the *Four Seasons Restaurant*, between the *Santyphab Hotel* and the Immigration Office. A crumbling building with 4 tables on the grey veranda and a dingy inside. Seriously tasty Farang fare and Lao/Vietnamese dishes, opens at 0800, serving a good cheap breakfast. Very friendly staff, offer information on local sites. *Nety's Food Garden*, east of Immigration Office, a mini 'hawker centre', awnings shield diners from the sun and a handful of stalls serve good and cheap single dish Lao, Vietnamese and Thai food. Recommended. *Sensaby Café*, next door to *Santyphab Hotel*. Cozy little café run by a young Chinese Lao woman. Good atmosphere at night. Good choice of western food including salads and ice-cream at very cheap prices, best milk shakes in town. Opening hours are erratic, best bet is in the evening, although they do offer breakfast. *Starlight*, opposite Wat Sayamung Khum, on the corner. Cheap and cheerful, and favoured by many westerners, don't expect any culinary masterpieces here, but the owners are a delight, and speak good English.

There are half a dozen large a/c discos in town, all of which have live bands and are **Bars & discos**
open 7 days a week. The largest, *Happy Night*, holds around 500 people and can sometimes be too popular to get into. *Savanbanhao Night Club*, across the street from the
Savanbanhao Hotel, 2100-2400. Hoong Thip also has discos. A nice friendly place with
a family atmosphere for an evening beer is *Malaphone Draught Beer*. Just up the road
from here is *Phakox Hitech*, an icy cool, dimly-lit bar, featuring live bands.

February *Than Ing Hang* (movable), similar to the festival at Wat Phou, Champassak **Festivals**
(see page 234).

Handicrafts Baskets available from the central market. There is a branch of *Lao Cot-* **Shopping**
ton on Ratsavong Seuk Rd.

Savanbanhao Tourism Co, Senna Rd, T/F212944, Mon-Sat 0800-1200 and 1330-1630, **Tour operators**
but rarely open and can't speak a word of English! Run tours and can arrange trips to
most sights in the area including overnight trips to a local village. *Lane Xang Travel*,
Kouravang Rd, T/F213775. *National Tourism Authority*, T/F212755.

Local Bicycle hire: from the *Resort Riverside* guesthouse, *Sensaby Café*, a stone's **Transport**
throw from the Immigration Office, or the *Unnamed* restaurant further up that road. *487 km to Vientiane*
The going rate is about 10,000 kip per day. **Car hire**: if you've time to shop around, it *139 km to Thakhek*
could be worth it: car and driver available from the *Hoongthip Hotel* (US$50 per day),
the *Nanhai Hotel* and from *Savannakhet Tourism company* (around $30). **Tuk-tuk**:
tuk-tuks of various shapes and sizes criss-cross town. They are locally known as
Sakaylab (as in Skylab) because they are said to resemble that piece of space hardware.
They may be more resilient and practical but certainly don't go as fast. 3,500 kip per
person for a local journey.

Long distance Air: Mon, Tue, Thu and Sat connections to **Vientiane** (US$61) and
Mon, Wed, Fri and Sun flights to **Pakse** (US$44). Flights to and from Vientiane will
sometimes operate via Pakse. The airport has undergone a revamp in anticipation of
servicing some international destinations as of 2002.

Road: the government bus terminal is on the northern edge of town. A tuk-tuk to the *There are no longer*
centre should cost about 4,000 kip. There is an information desk (some English) in the *any scheduled river*
station office, T212143. Daily connections with **Vientiane**, departing at 0630, 0800, *ferries to Vientiane*
0915, 1030 and 1230, good road, recently upgraded (8 hrs, 25,000 kip). Two departures
a day for **Pakse** departing 0630 and 1430 (6-7 hrs, 20,000 kip) – this road too has been
recently upgraded. Daily connections with **Thakhek** depart regularly 0730-1700 (2½
hrs, 13,000 kip), and **Xepone** at 0800.
    Since 1999, Savan has also been serviced by a **private bus station**, offering better
buses for the same price. As yet, only 2 routes are served by the 4 buses – northwards
towards Vientiane and eastwards to Lao Bao (see below). Private buses leave for
Vientiane at 0600 and 0700, and **Pakse** at 1430 and 2200.

International connections to Thailand and Vietnam Bus: there are daily connections with **Lao Bao** in Vietnam: government buses leave at 0600, and sometimes 1000
(25,000 kip), and private buses leave at 0700 and 1100. Buses to different destinations
in Vietnam leave on different days. Times, destinations and fares are all on a board outside the station office, tickets for sale in office, T212143. The journey to the border 236
km away is a 7-10 hr trip on a fairly rough track, and getting through customs and dealing with potential obstacles on the Thailand side means that it's impossible to state
how much longer it will take to get to Lao Bao itself. See Xepon below for further

The Central Provinces

details on crossing the border. Buses to **Danang**, a total distance of 508 km, operate 4 times a week on Tue, Wed, Fri and Sat (105,000 kip). These buses may also go to **Hué**, 409 km away. In addition to the Danang departures there are additional services to Hué on Mon, Thu and Sun (83,000 kip). Some buses to Hué and Danang travel via Dong Ha (329 km, 65,000 kip) and a dedicated Dong Ha bus is scheduled to leave at midnight, although has been known to leave as early as 2200. There is also a 1900 departure to Hanoi on Sat ($25).

Boat: to Thailand (**Mukdahan**), 5 or 6 departures throughout the day, Mon-Fri, 50 baht or 10,000 kip. On Sat and Sun there are just 3 boats at 1030, 1415 and 1600. The Customs and Immigration Office is near town centre on Tha He Rd, daily 0800-1200, 1300-1600. Visas for Laos available from agents in Mukdahan, US$30 for 15-day visa or US$50-60 for 30-day visa.

Directory **Airline offices** *Lao Aviation*, at the airport. **Banks** *Lao Mai Bank*, T212226, Khanthabouli Rd, Mon-Fri 0800-1200, 1300-1530. Also branches of the bank in the Post Office and another at the new market. A 3rd 5-storey branch is currently being constructed on the corner of Oudomsinh Rd, opposite the *BCEL*. *Banque pour le Commerce Exterieur Lao (BCEL)*, Oudomsinh Rd. Exchange counters around the market, any currency accepted, and at the pier (bad rate). The goldsmiths in the market regularly change money; all currencies bought and sold. You can exchange your excess kip here (good rates) and buy Thai baht. **Communications** Internet: *River Net and Computers*, next but one to the Post Office on Khanthabouli Rd, is owned by an Australian and his Lao wife and is the most useful internet café for travellers, offering reams of tourist-related information, from bus and ferry times to things to do. *Phitsamay OA Shop*, Chaluanmeung. **Post Office**: Khanthabouli Rd. Offers telephone and fax service (domestic and international), Mon-Sun 0800-2200. **Telephone**: in addition to Post Office, there are plenty of call boxes scattered around town (including 1 next to the Immigration office at the river). *Hoong Thip, Mekong, Nanhai* and *Phonepasut* hotels have IDD call service. **Embassies and consulates** **Vietnam Consulate**, Sisavangvong Rd. Open 0730-1100, 1400-1630, Mon-Sat, provides Vietnamese visas in 5 days, 2 photos and US$50 needed. **Thai Consulate**, *Nanhai Hotel*, 2-month visas take 3 days, 300 baht, 0830-1200 for applications, 1400-1530 for visa collection. **Places of worship** Catholic: mass daily at 0600 and 1900. **Useful addresses** Immigration office: for exit to Thailand at passenger pier. Mon-Fri 0830-1200, 1300-1600; on Sat, Sun and public holidays the office is open the same hrs but you must pay 50 baht per person for overtime for the officers!

Xepon (Sepon)

Colour map 3, grid A3 It is possible to cross into Vietnam by taking Route 9 east over the Annamite chain of mountains to **Lao Bao** (just over the border) and from there to the Vietnamese town of Dong Ha and the cities of Hué and Danang. The largest place on the Lao side of the frontier is Xepon. At first glance it might seem that there's not much to see and do here but as there is a government guesthouse travellers very occasionally use it as a stopping place *en route* to Vietnam, and those that do may be pleasantly surprised by what they find.

Excursions **That Salen** waterfall is 25 km north of Xepon. Tall and dignified, it's a pretty impressive spectacle. The owner of *Vieng Xai Guesthouse* will be able to get you there. The supremely fit have been known to hire bicycles.

Another waterfall, **Sakoy**, is about 4 km away by river, or 15 km by main road towards Vietnam. Wide without being high, it's nevertheless a great place for a picnic, and some travellers have even pitched camp here, situated as it is by the small village of Ban Sakoy, surrounded by coconut trees.

The town office, which acts as a sort of unofficial tourist office, can orchestrate a boat trip to a traditional Lao village, 2½ hrs away.

E *Vieng Xai Guesthouse*. A big house, wooden upstairs and concrete down, very clean, shared bathroom. Friendly owners who speak a little English. **F** per bed *Xepon Guesthouse*, very basic government-run 'hotel. These are the only 2 places to stay in the area within Laos, although accommodation is available just over the border in Lao Bao. | **Sleeping**

Road Buses: converted trucks leave for Xepon from **Savannakhet** daily at 0800 (6-7 hrs, 25,000 kip) and return to Savan the same day. It's also possible to jump on the various buses from Savan to **Vietnam** which also pass through Xepon, the cheapest option being the service to Lao Bao. | **Transport**

Crossing into Vietnam   The distance between the 2 immigration posts is about 1 km and motorbike taxis are available. From the Vietnamese immigration post to **Lao Bao** is another 3 km or so. Again, motorcycle taxis are available to carry weary travellers. We have received reports of long delays at this border crossing as paperwork is scrutinized and bags checked and double checked. The problem seems to be largely at the Vietnamese end of things. Don't be surprised if formalities take 3 hrs – and keep smiling!. | *The closest Vietnamese consulate is in Savannakhet. See page 204 for visa application details and opening hours*

The Central Provinces

Ho Chi Minh Trail

Throughout the Vietnam War, Hanoi denied the existence of the Ho Chi Minh Trail and for most of it, Washington denied dropping 1.1 million tonnes of bombs on it – the biggest tonnage dropped per sq km in history. The North Vietnamese Army (NVA) used the Trail, really a network of paths (trodden and cycled down by tens of thousands of men) and roads – some two-lane carriageways, capable of carrying tanks and truck convoys – to ferry food, fuel and ammunition to South Vietnam. Bunkers beneath the trail housed cavernous mechanical workshops and barracks. Washington tried everything in the book to stem the flow of supplies down the trail. | **History** *See Background, page 257, for a map showing the Ho Chi Minh Trail*

By 1966, 90,000 troops were pouring down the 7,000 km of Trail each year, and four years later, 150,000 infiltrators were surging southwards using the jungle network. Between 1966 and 1971, the Trail was used by 630,000 communist troops; over the same period, it was also the conduit for 100,000 tonnes of provisions, 400,000 weapons and 50,000 tonnes of ordnance. It was guarded by 25,000 troops and studded with artillery positions, anti-aircraft emplacements and SAM missiles.

The Trail wound its way through the Annamite mountains, entering Laos at the northeast end of the 'Panhandle', and heading southeast, with several access points into Cambodia and South Vietnam. The Viet Minh had used it as far back as the 1950s in their war against the French. The US airforce started bombing the Trail as early as 1964 in Operation Steel Tiger and B-52s first hit the Mu Gia pass on the Ho Chi Minh Trail in December 1965.

Carpet-bombing by B-52s was not admitted to by Lao Prime Minister Prince Souvanna Phouma until 1969, by which time the US was dispatching 900 sorties a day to hit the Trail. It is estimated that it took 300 bombs for each NVA soldier killed on the trail. The B-52 air strikes proved ineffective; they never succeeded in disrupting NVA supply lines for long.

In an effort to monitor NVA troop movements, the US wired the trail with tiny electronic listening devices, infra-red scopes, heat and smell-sensitive sensors, and locational beacons to guide fighter-bombers and B-52s to their target. The NVA carefully removed these devices to unused lengths of trail, urinated on them and retreated, while preparing to shoot down the bombers, which predictably arrived, on cue, from Clarke Field Air Base in the Philippines.

Creative US military technicians hatched countless schemes to disrupt life on the trail: they bombed it with everything from Agent Orange (toxic defoliant) to Budweiser beer (intoxicating inebriant) and dish-washing detergent (to make it into a frothing skid-track). In 1982 Washington finally admitted to dumping 200,000 gallons of chemical herbicides over the Trail between 1965 and 1966. The US also dropped chemical concoctions designed to turn soil into grease and plane-loads of Dragonseed – miniature bomblets which blew the feet off soldiers and the tyres off trucks. Nothing worked.

The US invasion of Cambodia in May 1970 forced Hanoi to further upgrade the Trail. This prompted the Pentagon to finally rubberstamp a ground assault on it, codenamed Lamson 719, in which South Vietnamese and US forces planned to capture the Trail-town of Tchepone, directly east of Savannakhet, and inside Laos. The plans for the invasion were drawn up using maps without topographical features.

In February 1971, while traversing the Annamite range in heavy rain, the South Vietnamese forces were routed, despite massive air support. They retreated leaving the Trail intact, 5,000 dead and millions of dollars-worth of equipment behind.

The Trail today Abandoned vehicles, bomb casings and, sometimes, gutted choppers and bombers, can still be seen along the Trail. There is more war debris on it than on the Plain of Jars as trucks cannot easily enter the area and pick up the scrap metal. Despite the herbicides, the mountainous region around the trail is still blanketed in dense tropical forest – much of it remarkably undisturbed. Because of its inaccessibility the forest has not been raided by the timber merchants. Many of the rare birds and animals found in the markets at Saravan are caught in this area. The Vietnam border area was more heavily populated before the war. Many of the tribal groups (mainly Lao Theung) were forced to move onto the Bolovens Plateau because of the heavy bombing of the Ho Chi Minh Trail.

Visiting the Trail
Nobody should go near the Trail without a guide as unexploded bombs abound

It is necessary to hire a Soviet jeep in order to cross the rivers because many of the bridges are broken and rivers are often impassable using other vehicles, especially during the rainy season. The trip can only be made in the dry season, November to March being the ideal time. The easiest access point to the Ho Chi Minh Trail is from Ban Tapung. For accommodation, see Xepon above. The local police discourage people visiting the trail without a guide because of the risk posed by unexploded ordnance. A guide will charge US$20-30 per day including meals and accommodation if required. (For example, from Savan it is possible to travel with a guide on public buses, staying overnight in Xepon.)

Transport Xepon is the nearest town (well, really a large village) to the trail. **Buses** for **Xepon** leave from **Savannakhet** at 0600 and 0800 (6 hrs, 25,000 kip). It would be possible to continue east from here and cross the border into Vietnam (see above).

The South

Introducing the South

Laos' southern provinces offer a varied array of enticements. Inland from the region's unofficial capital of **Pakse** is the **Bolovens Plateau**, an area that was earmarked by the French for settlement, was developed as a coffee producing area, and is becoming increasingly popular with tourists. Travelling south down the Mekong from Pakse, near the former capital of **Champassak**, are some of the finest Khmer ruins outside Cambodia – **Wat Phou**. Travelling downstream further still and the Mekong divides into a myriad of **channels** and **islands**. The largest of these, **Don Khong**, offers a wonderful escape from the world.

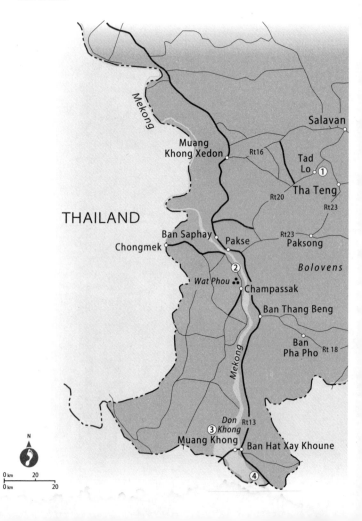

Things to do in the South

① Base yourself at **Tad Lo** and explore the peoples and natural attractions of the **Bolovens Plateau**.

② Take a day to discover Laos' own mini-Angkor – **Wat Phou** – and other smaller sanctuaries.

③ Chill out and forget about your troubles on the Mekong island of **Don Khong**.

④ Visit the stupendous **waterfalls** of **Li Phi** and **Khong Phapheng** – and hope to catch a glimpse of the Mekong's **freshwater dolphins**.

The Bolovens Plateau

The French identified the Bolovens Plateau as a prime location for settlement by hardy French farming stock. The soils are rich and the upland position affords some relief from the summer heat of the lowlands. Fortunately, their grand plans came to nought and although some French families came to live here they were few in number and all left between the 1950s and 1970s as conditions deteriorated. Even so, the area was developed as a coffee, rubber and cardamom growing area. Today it is inhabited by a colourful mix of ethnic groups, many displaced during the war and rather fewer due to recent dam building efforts. Tad Lo, particularly, is a popular tourist destination.

Exploring the Bolovens Plateau As tourism expands in Laos, so areas like the Bolovens are sure to become more accessible. For the moment though the tourist infrastructure is limited. Tour companies, especially in Pakse (see page 226), can organize trips. Alternatively, the best base is Tad Lo (see page 212). Other places near or on the Bolovens are Salavan, Attapeu and Sekong (see the respective entries), and guesthouses in these towns can also offer assistance and information. Note that it is not always possible to drive across the Bolovens Plateau from Salavan to Attapeu, even in the dry season. And in the wet season, parts of the new road recently constructed from Paksong come off the plateau.

The fertile farmland of the Bolovens Plateau has given Salavan province a strong agricultural base, supporting coffee and cardamom plantations. The road from Paksong to Pakse is known as the Coffee Road. Coffee was introduced to the area by French settlers in the 1920s and 1930s who made a quick exit as the bombing escalated in the 1960s. It is mainly exported via Pakse to Thailand, Singapore and, formerly, the USSR. Tea grown in this area is for local use. The Bolovens also has the perfect climate for durians, and villages (particularly on the road from Paksong to Pakse) are liberally dotted with durian trees. The fruit is exceptionally rich and creamy and in the peak season, between May and July, can be bought from roadside stalls for just 1,000 kip or so. Given its fertility, the plateau is now rapidly repopulating and new farms are springing up everywhere. To claim land, settlers need only erect a territorial fence.

During the bombing of the Ho Chi Minh Trail (see page 205), to the east, many hilltribes and other ethnic minority groups migrated to the Bolovens, which consequently has become an ethnographic goldmine with more than 12 obscure minority groups, including the Katou, Alak, Ta-Oy, Ya Houne, Ngai and Suk, living in the area. Most of the tribes are of Indonesian (or Proto-Malay) stock and have very different facial characteristics to the Lao; they are mainly animist (see page 284).

About 40 km south from Salavan on the Bolovens Plateau is **Tha Teng**, a village that was levelled during the war. Before that, it was the home of Jean Dauplay, the Frenchman who introduced coffee to Laos from Vietnam in 1920. Today the UNDP, in a joint venture with a private sector businessman, has set up a small wild honey processing factory. Villagers are paid for the combs they collect from jungled hills around Tha Teng. The carefully labelled 'Wild honey from Laos' is exported to European health food shops. There are several ethnic minority villages in the area.

The Ta-Oy village of **Ban Paleng**, not far from Tha Teng, is also fascinating – more so in February/March, when the animist Ta-Oy have their annual

The fall of Tha Teng: a personal view

In 1968, I read about the fall of Tha Teng to the Pathet Lao. The small article was buried in a back page of the newspaper. Not many Americans really cared about this loss or even knew where Laos was let alone Tha Teng.

In 1969 I was flying over Tha Teng in my Bird Dog – a Cessna 170 – which was used in my work as a Forward Air Controller (Code name, Raven 58) for the United States Air Force. All that was left of this town was about 20 homes lining a road on the northern edge of the Bolovens Plateau. The homes were gradually being overrun by heavy vegetation.

What was so important about this town that its loss would be reported in the United States? Tha Teng is strategically located on the northern edge of the Bolovens Plateau. Used as a military outpost, intelligence about enemy activity could be obtained. So, by occupying Tha Teng, the 'friendlies' – the Royal Lao Government – could, to a certain extent, control the gateway to the Bolovens. With its loss, the Pathet Lao and North Vietnamese could move more easily in their efforts to control the plateau.

The significance of the location of Tha Teng was well-known to the Pathet Lao. It was rumoured that there was a cave northeast of Tha Teng which could hold a battalion of troops and whose entrance was large enough to walk an elephant through. Elephants were used to haul heavy equipment, ammunition and supplies into the cave. But, from the air, the terrain looked flat. Even the military topological maps did not indicate the possibility of a cave.

However, on Thanksgiving Day 1969, I confirmed in fact the existence of that cave by 'clearing' away the 200-ft trees which protected its entrance. Further, it exposed a large permanent bivouac area in front of the cave entrance which provided facilities for at least a battalion-size unit. This staging area proved successful as the Pathet Lao captured the Bolovens during their campaign of 1970.

The war-that-wasn't in Laos was odd in more than just the sense that it wasn't a war. In Vientiane it was a common sight to see Pathet Lao soldiers coming down out of the mountains in full combat gear, including weapons, to obtain their daily rations. They could shop without concern of being captured and would then return to the mountains to join their combat units. These were the same soldiers that the Royal Lao army, who were also at the market, might be fighting later that same day.

Three days each year, the war would stop in southern Laos. Officials from Salavan would get in a truck and head south toward the plateau. At the edge of the Bolovens they would stop to let armed Pathet Lao (PL) get on their truck so they could continue to each village on the plateau. These PL guards would make certain that the officials would only go to the villages. As the officials visited each village, they would record the births, deaths and weddings which had taken place during the previous year. War, or no war, official government records had to be maintained. Following the three-day yearly truce, the war would resume.

Source: Ken Thompson, Raven 58, who flew as a FAC over Laos and Vietnam for over two years between 1968 and 1970.

The South

three-day sacrificial festival. A water buffalo is donated by each family in the village – built in a circle around the *kuan* (the house of sacrifice). The buffalo have their throats cut and the blood is collected and drunk. The raw meat is divided among the families and surrounding villages are invited to come and feast on it. The head of each family throws a slab of meat into the *lak khai* – a basket hanging from a pole in front of the kuan – so that the spirits can partake too. The sacrifice is performed by the village shaman, then dancers throw spears at the buffalo until it dies. The villagers moved from the Vietnam border area to escape the war, yet Ban Paleng was bombed repeatedly: the village is still littered with shells and unexploded bombs. **Ban Khan Nam Xiep** on the Coffee Road is also a Ta-Oy village.

The Katou villages such as **Ban Houei Houne** (on the Salavan-Pakse road) are famous for their weaving of a bright cloth used locally as pha sin – or sarongs. This village also has an original contraption to pound rice: on the river below the village are several water-wheels which power the rice pounders. The idea originally came from Xam Neua and was brought to this village by a man who had fought with the Pathet Lao.

Paksong (Pakxong)

Colour map 3, grid B3   The main town on the Bolovens Plateau is Paksong, a small market town 50 km east of Pakse. It was originally a French agricultural centre, popular during the colonial era for its cooler temperature. Paksong was yet another catastrophe of the war and was virtually destroyed. The area is famous for its fruit and vegetables; even strawberries and raspberries can be cultivated here.

Excursions   Not far from Paksong, 1 km off the road to Pakse, is **Tad Phan**, a dramatic 130 m-high waterfall. Take a track to the left off the main road at Ban Pak Kud, Km 38, and at the end of the track a path leads down to a good viewpoint halfway down the horseshoe-shaped gorge. This, like many waterfalls in southern Laos, is really spectacular. Salavan province also has a large hydroelectric power generating capacity – the Xe Xet barrage, next to the largest of the river's three magnificent waterfalls, supplies power to Pakse and some is exported to Thailand. There is a lovely guesthouse here, run by a Thai.

Sleeping   Best of the meagre choice on offer is **F** *Paksong Guesthouse*, originally built to house workers on a German development project. There are just 6 basic, rather damp but passable rooms. Shared *mandi* and toilet. Restaurant attached, serving cheap and simple food in a room not unlike a village hall.

Eating   The ubiquitous noodle shop.

Transport   **Bus/truck/pick-up** Regular connections with **Pakse** from 0600-1200 (1½-2 hrs,
50 km to Pakse   8,000 kip). Some Salavan-bound buses also travel via Paksong, although most buses take the faster Route 20 (this may change as the road improvements on Route 23 are completed). Buses to **Attapeu** leave at around 0830 and 1200 (3½-4½ hrs). One bus a day from Pakse passes through Paksong *en route* to **Tha Theng** and **Sekong**. Hitching is a possibility, although traffic on the recently surfaced – though quaintly somehow still potholed in places – Route 23 is light.

Tad Lo

Phone code: 031   Tad Lo is a popular 'resort' on the edge of the Bolovens Plateau, 30 km from
Colour map 3, grid B3   Salavan. There are three places to stay in this idyllic retreat, good hiking, an exhilarating river to frolic in (especially in the wet season) and elephant trekking. In the vicinity of Tad Lo there are also hilltribe villages and all three resorts can arrange visits. The Xe Xet (or Houai Set) flows past Tad Lo and there are two sets of cascades nearby. **Tad Hang**, the lower series, are overlooked by the *Tad Lo Resort* and *Saise Guesthouse* while **Tad Lo**, the upper, are a short hike away. The Xe Xet is yet another river being dammed in the area to produce hydropower for export to Thailand.

Alak villages There are two Alak villages, **Ban Khian** and **Tad Soung**, close to
Tad Lo. The Alak are an Austro-Indonesian ethno-linguistic group and their
grass-thatched huts with rounded roofs are not at all Lao in style and are distinct
from those in neighbouring Lao Theung villages. But most fascinating is the
Alaks' seeming obsession with death. The head of each household carves coffins
out of hollowed logs for himself and his whole family (even babies), then stacks
them, ready for use, under their rice storage huts. This tradition serves as a
reminder that life expectancy in these remote rural areas is around 40 (the
national average is a little over 50) and infant mortality upwards of 120 per 1,000
live births; the number one killer is malaria. ■ *All 3 guesthouses can arrange
guided treks to Ban Khian and Tad Soung. Anyone wishing to trek without a guide
might want to pop in to Tim's Restaurant for a quick chat to Soulideth (Tim's English-speaking husband). A great source of free and friendly information, he'll give
you a map which you can copy.*

Cave 1 km from Ban Khoua Set. Turn right into Sane Vang Noy, walk 4-5 km
off the road to a small mountain. There you will find a very old coffin still containing the remains of the old head of
the village, Sane Kham (named after
the mountain), who died over 100
years ago.

Ban Houay Houn Tours to this
coffee plantation and **weaving village**. ■ *Tours run by Saise Guesthouse – at 150,000 kip per tour, it's
best to set off in a group. Tim's Restaurant can also make arrangements
for you to get there, negotiating
directly with the tuk-tuk driver to keep
the price down.*

Buffalo ceremony This traditional
ceremony takes place in a nearby village on the first full moon in March
and is dedicated to the warrior spirit,
whom the local tribesmen ask for
protection. Villagers are happy for
tourists to come and watch (5,000
kip per person). The spectacle kicks
off at about 2000, with dancing, and
the next morning at 0500 the buffalo
is sacrificed. Throughout the day,
the entire village will share the meat
of the sacrificed animal as well as
leaving some choice pieces for the
spirits of the dead warriors in the
Ceremony House. ■ *Again, Tim's
Restaurant is the best place to go for
the low-down on this event.*

Elephant trekking This is an excellent way to see the area as there are few

Tad Lo

To Salavan (31 km)
To Pakse (85 km)
Route 20
Ban Houa Set
Track (1.5 km)
Path (3 km)
Ban Saen Wang
Tad Hang
Xe Xet
Tad Lo

N
Not to scale

3 Saise Guesthouse
4 Tad Lo Resort
   Bungalows
   & Restaurant

■ **Sleeping**
1 Bungalows
2 Green House
   (Guesthouse Saise)

● **Eating**
1 Restaurant
2 Tim's

roads on the plateau and elephants can go where jeeps cannot. It is also a thrill being on the back of an elephant. ■ *Can be organized by the guesthouses (50,000 kip).*

Sleeping
■ *on map*
Price codes:
see inside front cover

A-B *Tad Lo Resort*, T212105, ext 3325, or T021-213478, F021-216313; also bookable through *Sodetour* in Pakse,T212122. Reception is at the restaurant (not at the bunga-lows). Chalet-style accommodation (13 rooms) built right on top of the waterfalls. It is an attractive location (during the wet season) and the accommodation is comfortable – cane rocking chairs on the balconies overlook the cascades on the left bank. Elephant rides available. Good restaurant producing plenty of Lao food (as long as they think it's worth their while to open). Recommended.

E *Saise Guesthouse* (also *Sasay Guesthouse*), comprising 2 sections. The original 'white building' is looking somewhat run-down, but is otherwise adequate, with 3 simple rooms with fan and shared shower/toilet and 1 with attached bathroom. The more attractive, more expensive and peaceful option is the so-called *Green House* (the roof's a giveaway). Wooden chalet with 6 huge rooms, 4 with attached shower and toilet, and 2 of those with balconies overlooking the river. Originally owned by the government, the guesthouse has been taken over by a private company which is currently looking into opening more guesthouses and resorts in Tad Lo and the sur-rounding area. **E** *Bungalows*, probably the first of many such bungalows, these newly built rooms on stilts are clean and well maintained, with basic ensuite show-ers, and are a stone's throw from the popular restaurant overlooking the lower part of the Xe Xet.

Eating
● *on map*
Price codes:
see inside front cover

There are 3 small restaurants, as marked on the map, serving decent food at reasonable prices. **Seriously cheap** *Tim's restaurant*, named after the owner's wife, is the new-est of the lot, and a great source of both tasty food and good information. Speaking both English and French, and very aware of the problems too much money can bring the local people, the owner Soulideth is an authority on what to do in the area and how much it should cost.

Transport
31 km to Salavan
85 km to Pakse

Road Bus: the turning for Tad Lo is on Route 20, the recently upgraded road linking Pakse with Salavan. To get there, board a morning bus in Pakse bound for Salavan or vice versa (10,000 kip). Ensure that the bus is taking Route 20 and not the alternative Route 23 via Paksong. Most drivers know Tad Lo and will stop at **Ban Houa Set**. There is a blue sign here indicating the way to Tad Lo – a 1½-km walk along a dirt track and through the village of **Ban Saen Wang**. The bus takes about 2½ hrs. Buses depart from Ban Houa Set every 1-1½ hrs from about 0700-1330 to **Pakse** (10,000 kip) and also from about 0700-1500 to **Salavan** (40 mins, 6,000 kip). There's a daily service at 0830 to **Vientiane** (45,000 kip), and a single daily service to **Sekong** leaving between 0830-0900 (around 9,000 kip). There's also a Sun morning service to the Thai border, **Chongmek**, at about 0800-0900 (18,000 kip).

Salavan (Saravan)

Phone code: 034
Colour map 3, grid B3

The old French town of Salavan (also Saravan and Saravane) lies at the northern edge of the Bolovens Plateau and acts as a transport hub and trading centre for the agricultural commodities produced on the plateau. The Xe Don, which enters the Mekong at Pakse, flows along the northeastern edge of town.

Salavan is a charming town with no pretensions. Pigs and buffalo wander along the roads, children play in the streets and shops sell such practical goods as anvils, bicycle tyres, lengths of wire, transmission parts and brightly coloured functional plastic objects. There are few handicrafts or postcards in sight. Wandering through the town in the cool of the evening when people are at rest, talking, cooking and playing, it seems – despite the legacy of the war – to epitomize a more innocent past. If you happen to be walking past the market at 1700 or thereabouts, you may even find yourself invited to join the locals in a game of petang.

History Salavan was all but obliterated during the American war in Indochina. During the war, it changed hands several times as the Pathet Lao and forces of the Royal Lao Government fought for control of this critical town located on a strategic flank of the Ho Chi Minh Trail. The two sides, with the RLG supported by American air power, bombed and shelled the town in turn as they tried to dislodge one another. (There is a crude painting of the battle in the Champassak Museum in Pakse.) A few years ago there were piles of war scrap, including unexploded bombs, shells and mortars. Now cleared away, reminders of the war are largely confined to the memories of older residents (most are under 30) and the pages of books. But looking carefully can yield evidence: the awnings and umbrellas in the market are often made from parachute silk. The consequences of the shelling and bombing today, though, is that Salavan is a provincial capital with scarcely an ounce of physical beauty and almost no evidence of its French-era origins.

When US airforce pilots mounted bombing runs in Vietnam, their rules of engagement prohibited airstrikes within 500 m of a temple; in Cambodia, the margins were increased to 1 km. It has been said that in Laos such rules did not apply, but one retired US officer who was based there has written to us saying that "a complex web of rules [was] administered by levels of supervision stretching from the embassy in Vientiane, to Saigon, to Honolulu to the Pentagon, and included consultation with, and on the appropriate occasions approval by, the Lao government." Like Xieng Khouang, another critical town to the north, Salavan had one of the most beautiful temples in the country, **Wat Chom Keoh**, which was destroyed in an air raid in 1968. (The wat was commemorated on a postage stamp in the 1950s.)

The South

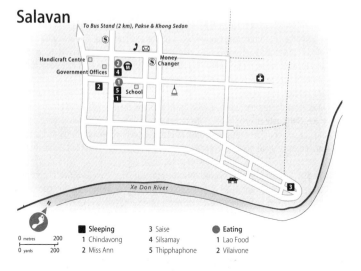

Salavan

To Bus Stand (2 km), Pakse & Khong Sedon

Handicraft Centre
Government Offices

Money Changer

School

Xe Don River

0 metres 200
0 yards 200

N

■ **Sleeping**
1 Chindavong
2 Miss Ann
3 Saise
4 Silsamay
5 Thipphaphone

● **Eating**
1 Lao Food
2 Vilaivone

Sights Today all that remains of Wat Chom Keoh are two forlorn and shell-pocked corner-posts, one ruined chedi and a dilapidated wat building decaying still further in the grounds of the Salavan general hospital. The **daily market** in the centre of town is worth a visit, mainly, admittedly, because there is little else to see apart from the new and usually closed handicraft centre. In past years the market was an environmentalist's nightmare: all manner of wild creatures, some listed as endangered, would end up here, either for the cooking pot or for the trade in live wild animals (see Background, page 305). Today the frisson of such sights is, fortunately, not on offer. There's the usual array of frogs and fish, and perhaps a wild bird or two, but not much else.

Excursions **Ban Nong Boua**, a beautiful lake near the source of the Xe Don, lies 18 km east of Salavan town. It is famed for its crocodiles which move into the river in the dry season (but remain out of sight). The road to Ban Nong Boua is too rough to be negotiated by tuk-tuk, which means it is necessary to charter a jeep or other sturdier vehicle.

Toum Lan is a katong village 46 km north of Salavan, notable for its longhouse and traditional weaving techniques (ask Mr Bousasone at *Saise Guesthouse* for details). A bus leaves for Toum Lan at 1400 and returns at 0700. Accommodation may be possible in the village (10,000 kip).

Sleeping
■ *on map*
Price codes:
see inside
front cover

D-E *Chindavong*, T211065. Established in 2000, on offer here are 2 different types of room. The 25,000 kip option is basic, with fans but no ensuites, whereas 70,000 kip will stretch to an a/c, ensuited, beautifully decorated, homely, bamboo-clad twin or double, complete with writing tables and 'chill out' area. The friendly owners' plans for 2002 include adding cheaper dorm rooms. Restaurant attached (no menu!). Recommended. **D-E** *Miss Ann Guesthouse*, no two rooms are the same, but all are basic, and if the surly service doesn't put you off, the ant infestation in the toilets might. **E** *Thipphaphone*, T211063. Clean (but musty) basic rooms with wooden walls. Decent mattresses, some a/c, some fans, spotless bathrooms, some ensuite, some communal. **E-F** *Saise Guesthouse*, 2½ km from the bus station at the other side of town (get there by tuk-tuk), T213775. Attractive guesthouse in arge garden compound. A/c rooms are of a good standard, fan rooms clean enough with large attached bathrooms (tank of water and dipper). Restaurant with limited menu, friendly management speak English and French – a useful source of information. **E-F** *Silsamay Guesthouse*, modern though not unattractive hotel in a central market location, 6 spacious and comfortable rooms with shared shower and toilet, 3 a/c rooms, 1 fan room has attached bathroom but no window. Tiled and beautifully clean throughout, balconies at front and back, friendly owner speaks some English. No water 2100-0600. Recommended.

Eating
● *on map*
Price codes:
see inside front cover

Most restaurants are situated around the market and there is little to choose between them. **Seriously cheap** Perhaps the tastiest is *Vilaivone*, a bamboo-clad place on the airstrip side of the market. *Lao Food*, by the market, offers Korean grilled meat among other things. Quite good. All restaurants serve much the same range of dishes.

Shopping The shop selling electrical goods has some tribal artefacts (probably overpriced, and being passed off as antiques). In and around the market basketry items and traditional cloth pieces can be found. A craft shop on the market square offers similar objects.

Bus/truck   The bus terminal is 2 km west of the town centre (tuk-tuk either way costs 3,000 kip). Not by any means a tourist hub, the reliability of buses is dicey at best in Salavan, but the scheduled connection times are as follows: **Pakse** at 0630, 0800, 1015, 1215 and 1300 (2½ hrs, 10,000 kip). **Sekong** at 0700 and 1300 (4 hrs, 9,000 kip). **Khong Xedon** at 0700, 1000, 1200, 1400 (3½ hrs, 9,500 kip). **Savannakhet** at 0630 (30,000 kip). **Tha Teng** at 1100 (6,000 kip). **Vientiane** at 0800 (40,000 kip). There are no buses further north than Toun Lan. Most buses from Pakse turn off Route 23 at Ban Houay He and travel to Salavan via Route 20 which goes past **Tad Lo** (see page 212). Before passing Tad Lo most buses stop for a while at the small market town of **Ban Lao Ngam** on the Houai Tapoung (46 km from Salavan, 79 km from Pakse). Route 20 is a new and comparatively fast road. Some buses, though, take the longer and rougher route via **Paksong** (Route 23). Trickier destinations to get to from Salavan include **Attapeu** (you have to go by bus to Sekong, then get the boat) and **Lao Bao** (the best way is via Savannakhet and then along Route 9).

Transport
116 km to Pakse
31 km to Tad Lo
76 km to Muang Khong Xedon
98 km to Sekong

Banks *Phak Tai Bank*, near the market, will exchange cash (US$ and Thai baht) and TCs. Open Mon-Fri. The shop selling cassettes and other electrical goods will also change money (marked on map as Money Changer). **Communications   Post Office**: in modern yellow building opposite the market. Local calls only from telephone exchange in same building. **Telecoms centre**: Mon-Sat, for international calls.

Directory

Continuing northwards from Tad Lo on Route 20, the road reaches **Ban Beng** after around 15 km. Turn right on to Route 23 – the 'Coffee Road'. From here the road climbs up to the lower slopes of the Bolovens Plateau. From Ban Beng, the road is poor as far as **Tha Theng**, although there are indications that upgrading is in the pipeline. From Tha Theng to **Sekong**, however, the road is 90% paved, although journey time has not come down much as the new bridges are not yet in place. The area is still largely forested with a sparse population concentrated along the road and mainly cultivating coffee. Buses and trucks usually stop at the local market centre of **Ban Tha Teng** (see Bolovens introduction, page 210, for information on some of the minority groups in the area around Tha Teng). Towards Sekong the land is more intensively cultivated; there is even some irrigated rice. This is also an area of resettlement with a number of new villages carving out a small area of civilized space in the forest. But the large logging yard and saw mill at **Ban Phon**, about 12 km north of Sekong, demonstrates what the local economy depends upon other than coffee: timber.

The Coffee Road

Sekong (Xekong, Muang Lamam)

Sekong – or Xekong – is a new town and capital of the province of the same name at the eastern edge of the Bolovens Plateau about 100 km south of Salavan and a similar distance north of Attapeu. It is situated on the Kong River – hence its name Xe (River) Kong – and was created comparatively recently when Attapeu province was divided. For the present anyone travelling between Salavan and Attapeu (but probably not vice versa) must stay overnight here as the first bus from Salavan does not arrive until the last for Attapeu has already departed (in fact a Pakse-bound bus, see Transport below). As roads improve and journey times drop it may become possible to make this trip without overnighting in Sekong.

Phone code: 031
Colour map 3, grid B4

The boat trip from Sekong to Attapeu is highly recommended

Those hoping to chance upon an unknown gem of a town should be prepared to be disappointed. In theory it would be a good base to explore the peoples and scenery of the Bolovens Plateau but there is simply no tourist infrastructure to make that possible. The market, centered on the bus terminal, has some rather pathetic wild animals, such as giant flying squirrels, for sale – more so than Salavan which has a more infamous reputation in this regard. There is a wat behind the market. The only reason to come here, other than out of sheer perversity, is to take a boat down the Xe Kong to the much more attractive town of Attapeu (see Transport, below).

Excursions About 25 km south of Salavan on the road to Attapeu near the Alak village of **Ban Mun Hua Mung** and lying on the Xe Nam Noi is a series of **waterfalls**. East of the bridge by 100 m is **Tad Houakone** and 4 km downstream is **Tad Phek**. A track leads from one to the other; during the dry season you can walk down river between the two. In between are a number of smaller falls.

Health warning Malaria is quite a serious problem in this area and precautions should be taken to avoid being bitten. If heading off the beaten track and away from immediate medical help for a few days, then it is recommended that an antidote is carried in the event of contracting malaria.

Sleeping
■ *on map*
Price codes:
see inside front cover

D *Sekong Souksamlane Hotel*, T214262. Popular with the local *falangs*, partly due to the attached restaurant – whatever you want, they'll try and accommodate it as long as the food is available at the local market. 16 rooms, 4 a/c, with attached shower, very functional and rather worn and dusty – OK for an overnight stop. The best rooms are upstairs; they have a balcony and get the mountain breeze. Electricity from 1800 to approximately 2100. One of the upstairs rooms is reputedly haunted. Some Malaysian UN officials drowned taking a boat downriver to Attapeu: they left their bags in their room and presumably come back every so often to try to retrieve them. One dorm room (4 beds), **E-F**. Rooms overpriced, but travellers need not get stung by these ambitious prices as there's now alternative accommodation in the shape of the new and very pleasant **E-F** *Sekong Guesthouse*, T211086.

Eating
● *on map*
Price codes:
see inside front cover

Cheap to seriously cheap *Phathip Restaurant*, opposite the *Sekong Hotel*. Owned by Nang Tu, a Vietnamese woman with considerable culinary expertise. The huge platters are a treat, especially the Vietnamese options. The front of the menu boasts all sorts of information about the area, which includes dire warnings about both the contamination of Sekong Province with the residue from the Vietnam War, and 'the odd grumpy *falangs* that for one reason or the other seem to be more or less resident in this forgotten corner of South-east Asia'. *Khamting Restaurant*, next to *Phathip* and another popular joint with the locals. **Seriously cheap** *Souksamlane Restaurant*, attached to *Sekong Hotel*, serves traditional Lao dishes and some European food. Tribal artefacts adorn the walls and are for sale. Noodle shops in and around the market.

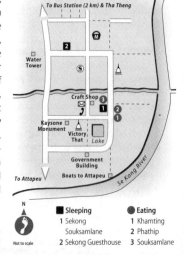

Sekong

To Bus Station (2 km) & Tha Theng

Water Tower

Craft Shop

Kaysone Monument

Victory That | Lake

Government Building

To Attapeu   Boats to Attapeu

Se Kong River

N

Not to scale

■ **Sleeping**
1 Sekong Souksamlane
2 Sekong Guesthouse

● **Eating**
1 Khamting
2 Phathip
3 Souksamlane

Shopping **Basketry** The *Sekong Hotel* sells woven basket 'backpacks'. A few baskets and textiles are for sale in the market and there is also a small craft shop selling weaving and textiles and a few other items.

Bus/truck The morning buses which are reputed to leave from outside the *Sekong Hotel* were not in evidence on our last trip, but are still worth asking about. Otherwise, the bus station lies 2½ km out of town (tuk-tuk 2,000 kip). Morning connections with **Salavan** leave at 0600 and 1330 (3 hrs, 10,000 kip), and **Pakse**, leaving at 0500 and 0630, via Paksong so it takes a little longer (5-7 hrs, 15,000 kip). No regular direct connections with Attapeu – it is necessary to take a Pakse-bound bus to the junction of the new road and then pick up a bus from Pakse bound for Attapeu, 4 hrs plus (but see Boat below). **NB** the buses to Attapeu don't leave from the bus station, so it's as well to ask where to wait on your arrival.

Transport
98 km to Salavan

Boat To **Attapeu** down the Xe Kong. Boats, which take about 4 people, need to be chartered privately. A beautiful and worthwhile trip, 7-8 hrs, upwards of 400,000 kip, depending on the price of gasoline.

Banks *Phak Tai Bank* changes cash (US$ and Thai baht only) into cash. **Communications** Post Office: yellow building not far from victory *that*. **Telephone**: Telecommunications centre next door to the Post Office, international calls possible. **Useful information** Electricity: 24 hrs – when it works.

Directory

In early 1999 the road between Sekong and Attapeu was being upgraded, at least as far as Km 52 where it meets the new road from Pakse/Paksong. From there on it varies between adequate and poor. About 16 km from this junction towards Paksong can be seen the spectacular 120-m high **Sekatamtok waterfall** which tumbles from the Xa Nam Noi. Road surfacing work appears to be slow which may in part be due to the fact that bridge construction which was meant to go hand-in-hand with road upgrading stopped in 1998 – due to the bridge contractor going to jail. For hitching, traffic is limited to construction traffic. Along the road from Ban Km 52 to Attapeu are clearings where new villages are being created for the 'upland' Lao. In a bid to resettle these people, the government is providing land, aid and resources for building and a space by the banks of the Xe Kong to grow vegetables and other crops to sell.

Attapeu

Attapeu has an altogether different character from the Bolovens Plateau as the region is predominantly Lao Loum rather than tribal. Attapeu is an attractive, leafy town positioned on a bend of the Xe Khong, at the confluence of the Xe Kaman. It is a pleasant place to walk around, with traditional wooden Lao houses with verandas and some French buildings. It was fought over by the Pathet Lao and RLG so in many respects it is a surprise the town is as attractive as it is. The people are friendly and traffic is limited. Vegetables are grown on the banks of the Xe Khong. A ferry takes passengers across the river.

Phone code: 031
Colour map 3, grid C4

According to ML Manich in his *History of Laos*, Attapeu should really be Itkapü. If so, then a translation of the town's name is Buffalo Shit. The non-Lao local people used to raise buffalo here and when asked what the place was called by the Lao, thought they were gesturing at a pile of buffalo excrement. The French, in their turn, transliterated Itkapü as Attapeu in a sort of Lao version of Chinese whispers. For a pile of dung the town, though, is remarkably picturesque.

The South

Outside Attapeu to the northwest is a clearing on the hilltop which marks the spot of a new hydropower scheme – the Houai Ho. Built by a Korean firm – Daewoo – labour from South Africa was employed to undertake a stupendous mining task: to dig a 740-m vertical shaft 4 m in diameter. Water is diverted down this shaft from a reservoir on the Bolovens Plateau to produce electricity for sale to Thailand. The timber from the area due to be flooded was removed by Vietnamese workers employed by a Thai logging firm. Truly an international enterprise.

Attapeu is not over-endowed with obvious sights of interest. As they say, it's the getting here which is important. The town has a 1930s vintage monastery, **Wat Luang**, but it's nothing to come here alone to see.

Health warning Malaria is quite a serious problem in this area and precautions should be taken to avoid being bitten. If heading off the beaten track and away from immediate medical help for a few days, then it is recommended that an antidote is carried in the event of contracting malaria.

Excursions For information on the surrounding area, visit the **Tourist Office** in the provincial hall, northwest of the town centre. They have large-scale relief maps of the area, good for hiking on or around the Bolovens Plateau. The office is run by Mr Phousavanh who is helpful and informative and will also offer his services as a guide. If intending to explore the countryside hereabouts, and use a guide, it is best to ask around. Other useful sources of information are Mr Bounkong who runs the *Pakong Restaurant* and Mr Boun Som at the *Sompasong Restaurant*.

The sleepy town of **Xaisetha** (Saisettha), which stretches along the north bank of the Xe Kaman, lies 12 km east of Attapeu along Route 18. There is regular transport from the east bank of the Xe Kong across from Attapeu.

Attapeu

N

0 metres 200
0 yards 200

■ **Sleeping**
1 Amphone Guesthouse (1)
2 Amphone Guesthouse (2)
3 Sooksomphone Guesthouse
4 Tavivan Guesthouse & Restaurant
5 Yingchokchay

● **Eating**
1 Noknoi
2 Pakong
3 Saisekaman
4 Sompasong
5 Unnamed Restaurants

Setthathirat's mysterious disappearance

The last great king of Lane Xang, Setthathirat (1548-71), see page 249, was reputedly murdered in a dastardly plot hatched in the town of Ongkaan – thought to be old Attapeu. He was enticed to the town by the prospect of two beautiful princesses, Nang Tapkaya and Nang Utumporn who wished to 'live with him'. (Whether this was a euphemism for more than a loose bed and breakfast arrangement is not clear.) There he was ambushed in the forest and, so it is said, murdered – although his body was never recovered. Locals believed that the King never died: his magical powers permitted him to survive and live at the bottom of the river from where he would, from time to time, emerge to perform great deeds.

A further 18 km along Route 18, 30 km in all from Attapeu, is the Alak village of **Pa-am** which sits directly on the Ho Chi Minh trail. War memorabilia freaks might be interested in the Soviet surface-to-air missile launcher (still apparently live), abandoned there by the Vietnamese. ■ *Getting there: charter a tuk-tuk (60,000-90,000 kip return) or take a morning truck.*

The Lao Loum village of **Ban Mai** lies 50 km southwest of Attapeu. From Ban Mai it's 6 km to **Ban Hinlat**. Find transport or walk. A further 6 km on is the **Xe Pha Waterfall** which lies on the Xe Pian. And another 9 km on from here, on the same river, are the **Xe Pang Lai Falls**. You may need a guide between the two falls – ask locally. It should be possible to arrange accommodation in either village. An alternative way of reaching Ban Mai may be to charter a boat from Attapeu to Xe Nam Sai and pick up a connection from there. ■ *Getting there: buses leave at 0800, 1200 and 1400 for Ban Mai, 1 hr, returning at 1600.*

Sleeping
■ *on map*
Price codes:
see inside front cover

A hotel with 100 rooms has been constructed but remains forlornly empty

B-C *Hotel Yingchokchay*, T212462. Opened in 2000, and a favourite with government officials and businessmen, this enormous building offers rooms from US$4 (with fan) to US$10 (a/c) for less financially strapped travellers. Lovely rooms – plain and simple, with dreamy mattresses and great ensuites. Breakfast included. **E** *Amphone Guesthouse 2*, halfway between the bus station and the town centre. Variety of 7 good rooms, most with attached bathrooms in a peaceful location not far from the river; cheaper 4-bed room with shared facilities outside (literally). Quiet, and gardens have potential. **E** *Sooksomphone Guesthouse*, no telephone. 16 decent airy rooms, some with ensuites, others with enormous beds and clean shared bathrooms (*mandi* and squat toilet). Owners speak some English and French. Food may be available, tours can be arranged to the surrounding area (but shop around first). Bicycles for hire (20,000 kip). Curfew at 2200. **E** *Tavivan*, T211090. 2 rickety but reasonably clean and surprisingly welcoming buildings with choice of fan or a/c, some rooms with verandas overlooking the new Tavivan restaurant. Great for large groups of travellers, the laid-back atmosphere of this place is not unreminiscent of university halls of residence. **F** *Amphone Guesthouse 1*, charming family-run simple set-up in a traditional wooden house. 6 spacious rooms with clean shared bathroom (*mandi*), basic meals provided and eaten with the family, peaceful garden. One of their sons was killed in a car accident not long before our last visit and they weren't sure whether or not to continue running a guesthouse. They so enjoy the company of travellers and we hope they will stay in operation. Recommended.

Eating
● *on map*

Cheap *Tavivan*, a dreary restaurant attached to the equally dreary guesthouse of the same name, serves such items as deer steak and sweet and sour fish.

The South

Seriously cheap *Pakong*, superb location down by the river. For anything other than the standard fare, it's best to order in advance. This place gets quite full. Mr Bounkong has plans to build some rooms on the same site and hopes to start tours to the surrounding area – a man to watch. Just up from *Souksomphone Guesthouse* towards the wat and almost opposite each other are a couple of places selling ready-made Lao food in pots. Cheap and good. There are a number of noodle shops including the friendly **Chambo Restaurant** and the **Sompasong**, where clothes can be re-stitched while you eat. Mr Boun Som at the *Sompasong* plans a more fully fledged restaurant and is a useful source of information.

Entertainment *Noknoi Restaurant* and *Saisekaman* pass for Attapeu's only 2 nightclubs. There may be live music and some food available, but the emphasis is on drinking.

Transport **Local Bicycle hire**: from the *Sooksomphone Guesthouse* (20,000 kip).

Truck/bus Efficiency around the bus station is simply not on the agenda, and although there are daily connections with the main tourist hubs, departure times are the stuff of great argument and debate. Prices are more definite, and a rough departure schedule is as follows, although checking on your arrival would be your best bet: daily connections with **Pakse** from the market at 0600 and 0900 (5-6 hrs, 20,000 kip). Previously, the 0600 minibus was said to be the quickest option as it goes pretty much non-stop If it goes at all. For **Sekong** (13,000 kip) and **Salavan** get off the bus at the junction with the new road and wait for a Pakse-Sekong bus. Most arrive too late to catch a connection on to Salavan the same day. The road is pretty poor, but it's an experience. From Sekong, there may be occasional trucks – it's a good journey, with excellent views of the Bolovens Plateau to the west. During the dry season (roughly Feb-Apr) there may be bus links to Attapeu along Route 18 – which links up with Route 13 between Pakse and Muang Khong. There's a 0800 service to **Vientiane** (55,000 kip), and 30 km away is the increasingly popular Pa-am (5,000 kip).

Boat From **Sekong** downriver (wet season only).

Directory **Banks** *Phak Tai Bank*, Mon-Fri 0830-1630, reputed to change US$ and Thai baht only, despite what it says. Money changers can be found around the market area – try the gold/jewellery shops. **Communications Post Office**: in town centre, Mon-Fri 0800-1200, 1300-1600. **Telephone**: Telecommunications centre next door to Post Office, Mon-Sat 0700-1700, international calls.

Pakse (Pakxe)

Phone code: 031
Colour map 3, grid B2
Population: over 50,000

Pakse is the largest town in the south and strategically located at the junction of the Mekong and Xe Don rivers. It is a busy commercial town, built by the French early in the 20th century as an administrative centre for the south. The town has seen better days but the tatty colonial buildings lend an air of old-world charm. Pakse is known locally for its large market. It is also the jumping-off point for visiting the old royal capital of Champassak, famed for its pre-Angkor, seventh-century Khmer ruins of Wat Phou (see page 233).

Ins and outs

Getting there
See Transport, page
229, for further details

Although Pakse is not on the border with Thailand, it is the largest Lao town close to the border crossing point at Chongmek. Boats ferry people across the Mekong and then buses take passengers on to the border. From the Thai side, buses continue on to Ubon Ratchathani in Thailand. Pakse is a local transport hub with daily air connections with Vientiane and 4 flights a week to Savannakhet. There are 2 bus terminals. Buses travelling north to Savannakhet (6-7 hrs), Thakhek and Vientiane (12-15 hrs) leave from Km 7 on Route 13 heading north. The southern terminal is south of town at Km 8 on Route 13. There are also bus services to a number of other towns in the south of Laos including Champassak (for Wat Phou), Don Khong, Salavan (Tad Lo), Attapeu and Sekong. Public passenger boats leave early in the morning for Champassak and Wat Phou, and also for Don Khong. They can also be privately chartered.

Getting around

Tuk-tuks wait to transport passengers from both bus terminals to the town centre (3,000 kip). Tuk-tuks and saamlors are the main means of local transport and can be chartered by the hr. Boats are available for charter from the jetty at the end of No 11 Rd. Cars are available for hire from some hotels and tour companies, and bicycles too (15,000-20,000 kip per day).

Tourist information

Office of Tourism Champassak, No 11 Rd, T212021, erratic hrs but try Mon-Sat from 0800.

The South

Background

According to ML Manich in his *History of Laos* (which, it must be said, is a liberal mixture of fact, fiction, fable and fantasy), the French decided to make Pakse the local administrative capital rather than Champassak because they wanted to rule the country without interference from the royal house of Champassak.

Two bridges span the Xe Don here. The single lane bridge downstream was built by the French in 1925 while the upstream structure was erected by the Soviet Union and was not completed until about 1990.

Presumably overcome with poetic inspiration, someone decided to name the town's roads as if they were highways: No 1 Road through to No 46 Road. The result, of course, is that no one knows where they live and tuk-tuk drivers are oblivious to road names. Even some hotel managers have no idea of the road outside their establishment.

Pakse, by anyone's standards, is not a seething metropolis – which, of course, gives it much of its charm. But it may be that this will change. There has been on-again, off-again talk of constructing a bridge across the Mekong here. It was rumoured at one point in the 1990s that the Japanese had allocated the funds and work was just weeks away from beginning – but still nothing has come of it. Locals can even point to the spot close to the stadium on Route 13 southeast of the town centre where the feeder road was to be constructed. If the bridge is ever built, Pakse will be firmly linked into the Thai economy and this, without question, will bring untold change. Locals, probably, will welcome and love it; romantic *farang* tourists will move on to some quieter corner of Laos. Even without the bridge, many people find they need to stay a night or two here.

Sights

Frankly, there's not that much to see in Pakse – at least so far as official sites are concerned. Locals tend to mention the **morning market**, slap bang in the centre of town. Even for Southeast Asia this is a major agglomeration of stalls and traders and it seems that Pakse exists for little else. It is best to get here between 0730 and 0800 when the place is in full swing. Although it continues to function throughout the day, it does so in a rather semi-detached fashion.

Champassak Museum This comparatively new 'sight' to grace Pakse is on No 13 Road (the main highway) running east out of town, close to the stadium. It opened in 1995 and displays pieces recovered from Wat Phou, handicrafts from the *Lao Heung* of the Bolovens Plateau, weaponry, musical instruments and a seemingly endless array of photographs of plenums, congresses and assemblies and of prominent Lao dignitaries opening hydropower stations and widget factories. Visitors are shown around by charming Lao guides who speak only limited English. Nor are the labels very informative. But it's still a treat for museum aficionados. ■ *0800-1130, 1300-1600, daily except public holidays. 3,000 kip*. Opposite the museum is yet another *that*-like **Heroes Monument**.

Wat Luang There are two score wats in town but none figures particularly high in the wat hall of fame. Wat Luang, in the centre of town, is the oldest. It was built in 1830, but the sim sports a kitsch pink and yellow exterior complete with gaudy relief work, since it was reconstructed and redecorated in 1990 at a cost of 27

Pakse

To Wat Donsamsib & North Bus Terminal

Don River

Mekong River

Sleeping
1 Champassak Palace & Restaurant
2 Champa Residence
3 Lankham
4 Pakse
5 Phonsavanh
6 Salachampa
7 Souksamran
8 Thaluang Guesthouse
9 Vannapha Guesthouse

Eating
1 Dok Faengdaeng
2 Dok Meui

0 metres 200
0 yards 200

million kip. (For most Western visitors this might seem like 27 million kip wasted, or worse. But contributing to the construction or renovation of a monastery brings merit to the contributor, accelerating their progression through the Buddhist cycle of birth and re-birth.) The hefty doors were carved locally. The compound was originally much larger, but in the 1940s, the chief of Champassak province requisitioned the land to accommodate a new road. To the right of the main entrance stands a stupa containing the remains of Khatai Loun Sasothith, a former Prime Minister who died in 1959. To the right of the sim is the monks' dormitory, which dates from the 1930s; the wooden building behind the sim is the monastic school – the biggest in southern Laos – and on the left of the entrance is the library, built in 1943. These earlier structures are, needless to say, the finest – at least for Western sensitivities. The compound backs on to the Xe Don. There are many more Lao monasteries in town. For those who desire a change there is also a Vietnamese/Chinese Mahayana Buddhist pagoda on No 46 Road, the **Linh Bao Tu Pagoda** and a **Church** on No 1 Road.

Situated on the road north towards Paksong, the Boun Oum Palace is now a hotel: the *Champassak Palace Hotel*. Before Thai hotel interests bought the place it was the half-finished palace of the late Prince Boun Oum of Champassak, the colourful overlord of Southern Laos and a great collector of objets d'art. He began constructing the house of his dreams in 1968 with the intention of creating a monument with more than 1,000 rooms. However, the Prince was exiled to France, before his dream was realized. Looking at the hotel it is hard not to conclude that his exile was wholly for the best, at least architecturally. Even so, the hotel is by far the largest structure in town, whether it has 1,000 rooms or not.

Boun Oum Palace

The South

Excursions

There are regular bus connections with Champassak; stay on the bus if you are travelling to Wat Phou. There are also public boats to Champassak, 1½ hours, and if your bartering skills are finely honed, you can get there for a song. Note that if chartering a boat, which makes sense in a larger group, a trip to Wat Phou can be combined with a visit to Um Muang (see below) in which case the boat will probably stop at Ban Wat Muang Kao, 4 km downstream from Champassak. Expect to pay about US$50-60 for boat hire for 15-20 people.

Wat Phou & Champassak
See main entry, page 230

3 Dorn Sok Dee
4 Elna
5 Ket Many
6 May Kham
7 Mengky Noodle Shop
8 Noodle Shop
9 Tae Feu Noodle Shop
10 Xuan Mai

Also known as **Muang Tomo** and **Oup Moung**, Um Muang is a lesser-known temple complex built at about the same time as Wat

Um Muang
See main entry, page 233

Phou on the opposite (left) bank of the Mekong . It lies 40 km from Pakse and is accessible by boat from town – access by bus is more difficult. Unlike Wat Phou, there are no public boats to Um Muang so it is necessary to charter one from the jetty at the end of No 11 Road. This makes sense in a big group of 10-15 so the cost of about US$50 can be split. Note that a trip to Um Muang can easily be combined with visits to Wat Phou and Champassak.

Muang Khao   Muang Khao lies on the opposite bank of the Mekong to Pakse and, as the name suggests – it means 'Old Town' – it was established before its larger brother but failed to take off when the French concentrated their attentions on Pakse. Muang Kao has a quaintness largely absent from Pakse. Most people come here *en route* to the Lao-Thai border at Chongmek but it does have some attractive buildings. You can also witness the deforestation of Laos as Thailand-bound timber trucks rumble past. ■ *Getting there: hire a boat from the pier, take the regular ferry, or one of the public passenger boats.*

Ban Saphay   This specialist silk-weaving village is 20 km north of town on the banks of the Mekong River. Here about 200 women weave (weaving is still women's work) traditional Lao textiles on hand looms. The designs, like the classic Lao *mut mee*, show clear similarities with those of northeastern Thailand, where the population are also Lao. However, there are also some unique designs. Prices obviously vary according to quality and intricacy but a sarong length (1½ m) costs about 35,000-50,000 kip. There is also an unusual statue of Indra, Ganesh and Parvati at the local wat. ■ *Getting there: the village is 5 km off Route 13, 20 km in total from Pakse. Public tuk-tuks (25,000 kip) travel from the 'terminal' on No 11 Rd near the port, especially in the morning.*

Ban Pha Pho   About 27 km from Ban Thang Beng on the road to Attapeu is Pha Pho, a Suay village known for its working elephants. The Suay are a tribal group renowned across Thailand and Laos for their elephant training abilities. There are more than 90 animals in the area which are used to move hardwoods and to transport rice. ■ *Getting there: by jeep from Pakse.*

Tours   There are a number of tour agencies in town. All will arrange tours to local sites like Um Muang, Wat Phou, Khong Island and Champassak. *Sodetour* arrange more adventurous tours to the Bolovens Plateau, for example. Costs vary considerably according to numbers. Tour companies and some hotels in town (for example *Souksam Lane*, *Salachampa* and *Champassak Palace*) will arrange day tours to Wat Phou, Tad Lo and the Khong Phapheng Falls.

Essentials

Sleeping   **AL-B** *Champassak Palace*, No 13 Rd, T212263, F212781. A/c, international restaurant.
■ *on map, page 224*   This is a massive chocolate box of a hotel with 55 rooms (looks like it should have 155).
Price codes: It was conceived as a palace for a minor prince (see Boun Oum Palace, page225, for fur-
see inside front cover   ther details) and is now operated by a Thai firm. Large rooms, ranging from economy to Presidential Suite; 40 more modern, less elaborate rooms were added in 2000. Friendly staff, a good terrace and the best facilities in town, including a fitness centre and karaoke bar and a great position above the Xe Don. Family rooms are a good deal but the place just can't seem to shake off the notion that it's a palace masquerading as a hotel. Plans are afoot to open a beer garden for the dry season, and 2003 may even see the opening of Laos' first golf course.

B *Champa Residence (Residence du Champa)*, No 13 Rd (on the main road east of town near the stadium and museum), T212120, F212765, champare@laotel.com A/c, pool planned for 1997, but it still hasn't materialized. 35 rooms in a new colonial style house, hot water and satellite TV, very clean and with some character. Attractive terrace and lush garden, visa cards accepted and tours arranged – it is run by *Sodetour* and the manager, Mr Kamphat Boua, is one of Pakse's 'Mr fixits'. New houses for longer term visitors are being constructed on the banks of the Mekong. Recommended.

C *Salachampa*, No 10 Rd, T212273, F212646. A/c, small hotel with just 15 rooms, the most characterful being in the 1920s main building: wooden floors, large, attached bathrooms with warm water showers – the upstairs rooms with balconies are best. There are also some additional, quaintly rustic, rooms in a 'new' extension. The hotel is run by Mr Nhouyvanisuong who bought the place in 1946; he speaks excellent French and reasonable English. Recommended for those looking for a touch of colonial elegance and friendly service. Tours organized from here. **C** *Souksamran*, No 10 Rd, T212002. A/c, good restaurant, clean small rooms, own bathrooms with hot water. Friendly staff although the words 'ambience' and 'character' do not spring to mind; more like 'functional'. However, it is good value. Car rental and boat tours available.

C-D *Lao Chaleun Hotel*, T251333, F251138. Opened in July 2001 on the corner of Rds 6 and 4, this place boasts 43 spotlessly clean and simply decorated a/c and fan rooms with TV and mini-bars. Some mattresses are distinctly better than others, so try a few before signing on the dotted line. A bit of an architectural eyebrow raiser, different areas of the hotel are separated by interesting part-walls under which you can duck to get to other corridors. The outer rooms have a communal veranda, and the plan is to add a bar to the open roof from where you can see a good chunk of the town. A restaurant is also on its way. **C-D** *Thaluang*, T251399, F212206, turn off Rd 13 at *Sodetour* onto Rd 24 and walk about 100 m. Opened in 2001, this guesthouse has a/c, TV, minibar, comfortable mattresses, clean serviceable rooms with large bathrooms and hot water. While there's nothing particularly distinguishing about the facilities here, it's pleasant enough and has friendly staff. Car available for rent.

D *Houy Nyang Kham Guesthouse*, near Km 5 off Route 13 (heading towards the southern bus terminal), T/F212755. Situated by a stream with hills in the background, makes for a nice spot. 5 dirty-looking cottages which actually house surprisingly clean rooms, with attached cold water showers and toilet, TV, restaurant, landscaped gardens, etc. The nightclub on the premises gets almost as noisy as the a/c, and is popular with the local ladies of the night. **D** *Lankham Hotel*, T251888. Off Rd 13 diagonally opposite *Lao May Bank*. The slightly haphazard, casual atmosphere of downstairs is not carried forward into the state of the rooms themselves, which are very clean and boast some of the most comfortable beds in town.

E *Vannapha Guesthouse*, near the hospital, T212502. 14 rooms, 7 a/c, with clean attached bathrooms. Fan rooms in the annexe are less clean, but still OK, the a/c rooms are nicely furnished in wicker and wood (1 even has a bath tub) and are good value. Friendly owner with some English also organizes car tours to nearby villages. Shady outdoor restaurant serves noodle and rice dishes. **E-F** *Pakse*, No 5 Rd (facing the market), T212131. A range of rooms in this ugly block, some a/c, some with attached bathrooms, none with hot water. Rooms are grubby and noisy and while it used to be relatively friendly it is now, reportedly, not even this. **E-F** *Phonsavanh Hotel*, No 13 Rd, T212842. This is 1 of the few places in town with backpacker prices but it has nothing else going for it bar its central location. Rooms are grubby and basic with partitions which don't go to the ceiling. Shared facilities, dismal feel and overpriced at that.

The South

Eating

• *on map, page 224*
Price codes:
see inside front cover

Lao/Vietnamese/Thai/Chinese Cheap *Dok Faengdaeng Restaurant*, No 11 Rd. Overlooks the Xe Don but the food here (Thai/Lao/Chinese) is only mediocre – it is mostly used for government functions and big parties, which just about says it all. *Dok Meui Restaurant*, T212062. Seriously good Chinese food accompanied by local music, flashing lights and lots of fake flowers. Friendly service. Mon-Sun 0800-2300. *Ket Many Restaurant*, 227 No 13 Rd, T212615. Chinese and Lao food from a limited menu in a/c restaurant, the deep fried frog and Mekong River fish have both been recommended, also serves European food (spaghetti etc), or why not sample the spicy sour virgin pork uterus? *May Kham*, No 13 Rd, close to the bridge across the Don River, about 100 m from Wat Luang. Many locals maintain this serves the best Vietnamese and Lao food in town, a/c restaurant but no pretensions, superb steamed duck and sweet and sour fish and morning glory stir fry. **Seriously cheap** *Don Keo Restaurant*, No 7 Rd, opposite the bank. Popular Thai food, a good spot to enjoy a beer. *Elna Restaurant – Café Crepe*, No 13 Rd, T213604. Good, cheap Lao food and crepes to die for. *Sai Khong*, end of No 9 Rd. This is really a bar but it also serves good food at lunch time and during the evening – the balcony overlooking the river is a good place to eat. *Xuan Mai*, open-air restaurant serving Vietnamese and Lao dishes, excellent value and very good.

Korean Mid-range *Korean Barbecue*, No 46 Rd (near corner with No 24 Rd), T212388. Classic Korean cook-it-yourself restaurant. **Seriously cheap** *Dorn Sok Dee Restaurant*, No 6 Rd. Justifiably popular for its Korean grilled meat dishes.

Noodles Seriously cheap *Mengky Noodle Shop*, No 13 Rd (close to *Phak Tai Bank*). Serves bowls of tasty duck and beef noodle soup. *Tae Feu Noodle Shop*, corner of 46 and 34 Rds, good Vietnamese noodle shop, clean and tasty.

Bakeries Crusty baguettes are available across town; great for breakfast with wild honey and fresh Bolovens' coffee.

Bars

The liveliest places in town are 2 bars with karaoke and music situated above the Mekong. The *Saeng Tawan* is near the jetty at the end of No 11 Rd while the *Sai Khong* is at the end of No 9 Rd. There is little to choose between them and Pakse's hippest dudes circulate between them. Some nights they are really jumping, other times they are empty. Girls sit with clients but it all seems in the best possible revolutionary taste.

Shopping

Morning Market (Daohuang Market), good for loads of unnecessary plastic and metal objects. Most people come here just to look but there are also some fun things to buy: tin watering cans, clay pots, textiles and sarongs, for instance.

Film A few shops on and around Rd No 7 and Rd No 10 where film can be developed.

Textiles Traditional handwoven silk cloth is available in the Morning Market. Many people, though, prefer to visit Ban Saphay where it is produced and buy lengths there – see Excursions, page 226, for further details. The *mut mee* ikat designs are similar to those produced across the border in the northeastern or Isan region of Thailand. However, here in Laos it is more likely that the cloth will be produced from home-produced silk (in Thailand, silk yarn is often interwoven with imported thread) and coloured using natural rather than aniline dyes.

Tour operators

The best sources of information remain the tour companies in town, although it is obviously in their interest to convince visitors that taking a tour is the best, possibly even the only, option. *Sodetour*, No 13 Rd, next door to the Vietnamese Consulate,

T212122, F212710. The local manager, Mr Booliep, is a mine of information. *Lane Xang Travel & Tours*, next to *Phonsavanh Hotel*, T/F212281. Bit of a rip-off joint, with 5 people desperately failing to do even 1 man's job. *Inter-Lao Tourisme*, *Champassak Palace Hotel*, T/F212778. *Phoudoi Travel Agency*, at *Champassak Palace Hotel*.

Local The main forms of transport are the **tuk-tuk** and **saamlor** (about 2,500 kip). Share tuk-tuks to local villages leave from the Morning Market and from the stop on No 11 Rd near the jetty. Tuk-tuks can also be chartered by the hr. For longer out-of-town journeys, hotels (eg *Souksam Lane* and *Champassak Palace*) and tour companies (eg *Sodetour*) have cars and minibuses (with driver) for charter. **Mountain bikes** can be hired on No 6 Rd. **Boats** can be chartered from the jetty at the end of No 11 Rd.

Long distance Air: daily connections with **Vientiane** (US$95); check with *Lao Aviation* for latest information (there is an office at the airport, T212252). 3-4 flights a week to **Savannakhet**, US$ 44. The airport is 2 km west of town: cross the bridge over the Don River by Wat Luang and continue straight up No 13 Rd.

Road: There are 2 **bus** terminals. Buses/trucks travelling north (to Savannakhet, Thakhek and Vientiane) leave from Km 7 on Route 13 heading north across the Xe Don. The southern terminal is at Km 8 also on Route 13, but heading south out of town. Tuk-tuks wait to transport passengers from both terminals to the town centre (you shouldn't have to pay more than 3,000 kip). Regular morning departures up until 1300 to most places; journey times are decreasing as the roads improve, and lists of departures can be found in many of the hotels and guesthouses. To **Vientiane**, they leave every couple of hrs from 0730 (12-15 hrs, 35,000 kip). To **Paksan** and **Thakhek**, there are 5 buses leaving between 0730-1230 (30,000 kip). To **Savannakhet**, there are also 5 buses (6-7 hrs, 20,000 kip). To **Champassak**, departures are at 0900 and 1200 (2 hrs, 10,000 kip); stay on the bus for **Wat Phou**, it stops in a village 2 km from the ruins. Other bus services include: **Don Khong** (4-5 hrs, 12,000 kip) and **Ban Nakasong** (for Don Deth, 11,000 kip), on a poor road; **Salavan** (Tad Lo) (1½ hrs, 10,000 kip); **Attapeu**, 0730 and 0900 (5 hrs, 20,000 kip); **Sekong**, 0630 and 0700 (15,000 kip), via Paksong or Salavan, changing at Ban Beng.

River: public **passenger boats** leave daily, early in the morning for **Champassak** and **Wat Phou**, 0730 (1½-2 hrs, 5,000 kip). For **Don Khong**, boats leave around 0700-0800, or 1400 (6-8 hrs, 15,000 kip). Alternatively, **charter boats** are available (for 15-20 people), US$50-60 for **Champassak**, US$140 for **Don Khong**.

International connections with Thailand It is possible to cross the border to **Ubon Ratchathani** in Thailand via **Chongmek**, from Pakse. Take a long-tailed passenger boats (1,000 kip) from the 'port' at the end of Rd No 11 across the Mekong to the village of Muang Kao. From Muang Kao, songthaews and ancient share taxis like Chevrolet Belairs wait to ferry passengers to the border at Chongmek (1½ hrs, 6,000 kip). This route is an important exit point for Lao timber and timber trucks rumble their way towards the border. There is a sizeable timber yard at Chongmek, in Thailand. At the border there is a post office and duty free shop. Customs formalities are very relaxed. Converted trucks wait to transport passengers to **Phibun Mangsahan** in Thailand (1½ hrs) and from there to **Warin Chamrap** (1 hr), just south of Ubon Ratchathani and about 90 km from the border.

Future roads to Vietnam and Cambodia Two new highways linking Pakse with **Danang** in Vietnam via the Bolovens Plateau and another crossing into Cambodia and Phnom Penh are under construction.

Transport

130 km to Muang Khong
50 km to Paksong
85 km to Tad Lo
40 km to Chongmek (Thailand)
38 km to Champassak
116 km to Salavan
250 km to Savannakhet

Pakse is the local transport hub and while it is easy enough to get to local centres like Salavan and Attapeu, to travel between local centres is more difficult and may require a journey back to Pakse

The South

Directory **Banks** *Phak Tai Bank*, No 13 Rd, changes US$, pound sterling and most currencies (cash), will give kip on a Visa Card. Mon-Fri 0800-1600. There is a branch of the *Phak Tai Bank* close to the bus station on Route 13, but they will only change cash. *Phak Tai branch bank*, near the market place, opposite *Pakse Hotel*, Mon-Fri 0830-1530, Sat 0930-1000. There are money changers in the market area. It is possible to change TCs on Sun at *Champassak Palace Hotel*, but the commission is hefty. **Communications** Internet: expect to pay around 500 kip per min. There are several internet shops, and no doubt more will soon be opening. *@D@M's*, Internet and email service, Rd 13; *Lankham Hotel* has about 5 computers; the Cannon photocopy shop is another potential, and there's another outlet worth trying near Wat Luang. **Post** Office: No 8 Rd, overseas telephone calls can also be made from here. Express mail service available. Note the ashtrays made from defused (one hopes) unexploded shells. **Telephone**: Telecommunications office for fax and overseas calls on No 1 Rd, towards No 13 Rd end. **Embassies & consulates** Vietnamese consulate, No 24 Rd, Mon-Fri 0800-1300, 1400-1630. Visas for Vietnam cost US$55 and take 4-5 days to process.

Champassak and Wat Phou

Phone code: 031
Colour map 3,
grid C2
Population:
under 50,000

The agricultural town of Champassak has a relaxed village ambience, stretching along the right bank of the Mekong for 4 km. It is the nearest town to the fantastic archaeological sight of Wat Phou, and now that it has enough comfortable accommodation it is a good base from which to explore Wat Phou and the surrounding area.

In 1970 Chao Boun Oum began work on yet another rambling palace on the outskirts of Champassak, but it was never finished as he was exiled to France in 1975. It is now the official residence of Champassak's squatter community. The Prince's brothers owned the two French-style houses along the main road running south.

Wat Phou

The archaeological site of Wat Phou is at the foot of the Phou Passak, 8 km southwest of Champassak. With its teetering, weathered masonry, it conforms exactly to the Western ideal of the lost city. The mountain behind Wat Phou is also called **Linga Parvata** as the Hindu Khmers thought it resembled a lingam – albeit a strangely proportioned one. The original Hindu temple complex is thought to have been built on this site 800 years ago because of the sacred phallic mountain symbol of Siva, the Hindu deity.

Ins & outs
See also Pakse
excursions, page 225

Getting there Wat Phou is just 8 km from Champassak. Local buses run from town to the ruins, either catch one from the central terminal or flag one down and ask the driver to drop you off at the entrance. Bags can be left with the helpful (English-speaking) staff while you explore the ruins. Alternatively, charter a tuk-tuk in Champassak (around 30,000 kip return – ask him to wait). If travelling by public boat from Pakse alight at Champassak and then take a bus or tuk-tuk; if on a chartered boat then it will probably dock at Ban Wat Muang Kao, some 4 km downstream from Champassak.

Information Admission to temple complex: 5,000 kip (goes towards restoration). Officially open daily 0800-1630, but they're happy to let you in if you get there for sunrise even as early as 0530. Foodstall on the gate. The UNDP and UNESCO have agreed to finance and assist the renovation of Wat Phou and to establish a museum to hold some of its more vulnerable artefacts. A team of archaeologists is based at the site.

Today, Linga Parvata provides an imposing backdrop to the crumbling temple ruins, most of which date from the fifth and sixth centuries, making them at least 200 years older than Angkor Wat. At that time the Champassak area was the centre of power on the lower Mekong. The Hindu temple only became a Buddhist shrine in later centuries. The French explorer, Francis Garnier, discovered Wat Phou in 1866 and local villagers told him the temple had been built by 'another race'. Unfortunately, not much is known about Wat Phou's history. Ruins of a palace have been found next to the Mekong at Cesthapoura (halfway between Wat Phou and Champassak – now an army camp) and it is thought the sixth-century Chenla capital was based there. The old city wall crosses the main road just before the ravine on the return to Champassak. Archaeologists and historians believe most of the building was the work of the Khmer king, Suryavarman II (1131-1150), who was also responsible for starting work on Angkor Wat, Cambodia. The temple remained important for Khmer kings even after they had moved their capital to Angkor. They continued to appoint priests to serve at Wat Phou and sent money to maintain the temple until the last days of the Angkor Empire.

Background

Wat Phou

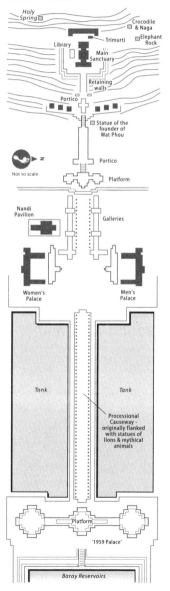

The king and dignitaries would originally have sat on the platform above the 'tanks' or baray and presided over official ceremonies or watched aquatic games. In 1959 a palace was built on the platform so the king had somewhere to stay during the annual Wat Phou festival (see below). The smaller house was for the king's entourage. A long avenue leads from the platform to the pavilions. The **processional causeway** was probably built by Khmer King Jayavarman VI (1080-1107), and may have been the inspiration for a similar causeway at Angkor Wat. The grand approach would originally have been flanked by statues of lions and mythical animals, but few traces remain.

1959 Palace & processional causeway

The South

Pavilions The sandstone pavilions, on either side of the processional causeway, were added after the main temple and thought to date from the 12th century (most likely in the reign of Suryavarman II). Although crumbling, with great slabs of laterite and collapsed lintels lying artistically around, both pavilions are remarkably intact, and as such are the most-photographed part of the temple complex. The pavilions were probably used for segregated worship for pilgrims, one for women (left) and the other for men (right). The porticoes of the two huge buildings face each other. The roofs were thought originally to have been poorly constructed with thin stone slabs on a wooden beam-frame and later replaced by Khmer tiles.

Only the outer walls now remain but there is enough still standing to fire the imagination – the detailed carving around the window frames and porticoes is well-preserved. The laterite used to build the complex was brought from Oup Moung, another smaller Khmer temple complex a few kilometres down river (see below), but the carving is in sandstone. The interiors were without partitions but it is thought they used rush matting. The furniture was limited, reliefs only depict low stools and couches. At the rear of the women's pavilion are the remains of a brick construction, believed to have been the queen's quarters. Brick buildings were very costly at that time. The original partitions were probably made of rush matting.

Nandi Above the pavilions is a small temple, the **Nandi Pavilion**, with entrances on
Pavilion & two sides. It is dedicated to Nandi, the bull (Siva's vehicle), and is a common
temple feature in Hindu temple complexes. There are three chambers and each
remains would originally have contained statues – but they have been stolen. As the hill begins to rise above the Nandi temple, the remains of six **brick temples** follow the contours, with three on each side of the pathway. All six are completely ruined and their function is unclear. Archaeologists and Khmer historians speculate that they may have been Trimurti temples. At the bottom of the steps is a **portico** and statue of the founder of Wat Phou, Pranga Khommatha. Many of the laterite paving stones and blocks used to build the steps have holes notched down each side – these would have been used to help transport the slabs to the site and drag them into position.

Main sanctuary The main sanctuary, 90 m up the hillside and orientated east-west, was originally dedicated to Siva. The rear section (behind the Buddha statue) is part of the original sixth-century brick building. Sacred spring water was channelled through the hole in the back wall of this section and used to wash the sacred linga. The water was then thrown out, down a shute in the right wall, where it was collected in a receptacle. Pilgrims would then wash in the holy water. The front of the temple is later – probably 8th-9th century – and has some fantastic carving: asparas, dancing Vishnu, Indra on a three-headed elephant (the former emblem of the kingdom of Lane Xang).

Around Wat Phou

Above the portico of the left entrance there is a carving of Siva, the destroyer, tearing a woman in two. The Hindu temple was converted into a Buddhist shrine (either in the 13th century during the reign of the Khmer king Jayavarman VII or when the Lao conquered the area in the 14th century) and a large Buddha statue now presides over its interior. Local legend has it that the Emerald Buddha – now in Bangkok – is a fake and the authentic one is hidden in Wat Phou; archaeologists are highly sceptical. There is also a modern Buddhist monastery complex on the site.

To the left of the sanctuary is what is thought to be the remains of a **small library**. To the right and to the rear of the main sanctuary is the **Trimurti**, the Hindu statues of Vishnu (right), Siva (central) and Brahma (left). Behind the Trimurti is the **holy spring**, believed by the Khmers to have possessed purificatory powers. Some of the rocks beyond the monks' quarters (to the right of the temple) have been carved with the figures of an elephant, a crocodile and a naga. They are likely to have been associated with human sacrifices carried out at the Wat Phou festival. It is said the sacrifice took place on the crocodile and the blood was given to the naga. Visitors in February (during the Wat Phou festival) should note that this practice has now stopped.

Around the sanctuary

Other excursions from Champassak

About 1 km from Ban Noi on the Mekong is Oup Moung. It is accessible from the main road south from Pakse at Ban Thang Beng, Km 30, from where a track (vehicle access possible) leads to Ban Noi and then onto the ruins. In colonial days, Oup Moung was a stopping point for ships travelling up river from Cambodia. But its main treasure is a sixth-century temple complex built at roughly the same time as Wat Phou. The site is an assortment of ruins, surrounded by jungle. A seven-headed sandstone naga greets you on arrival from the Mekong.

Oup Moung (Um Muang)
See also Pakse excursions, page 225

Like Wat Phou, the main temple is built of laterite and its carvings are in similar style to those of the bigger complex upriver. There are also remains of a second building, more dilapidated and moss-covered, making it difficult to speculate about its function. Hidden among the jungle are also the remains of two baray. Oup Moung is not on the same scale and nowhere near as impressive as Wat Phou, but stumbling across an unknown sixth-century Khmer temple in the middle of the jungle is nonetheless a worthwhile diversion. With great slabs of laterite protruding from the undergrowth and ancient sandstone carvings lying around the bushes, there is no doubt that a great deal lies undiscovered. Oup Moung is believed to be where the laterite blocks, used in the construction of Wat Phou, were taken from. ■ *Mon-Sun 0600-1630, 2,000 kip. Getting there: by boat from Champassak (60,000-80,000 kip); or by tuk-tuk, 30 mins, hire car or boat from Pakse (see Pakse entry).*

About 15 km southwest of Champassak is Don Talaat, which is worth a visit for its weekly market (Saturday and Sunday). It's renowned for the number of snakes on show. From here, the road continues to Chongmek and the border with Thailand.

Don Talat

One hour downriver from Pakse is this island, where Chao Boun Oum had his weekend house, which has lain abandoned since his exile to France.

Hao Pa Kho island

Essentials

Sleeping
■ *on map*
Price codes:
see inside front cover

B *Auberge Sala Wat Phou*, T213280. A/c, hot water, 10 large, clean rooms, all with attached shower and wc. The top front rooms have balconies. Stylish and the best place to stay in Champassak. Friendly but could nonetheless benefit from some improvements. Restaurant serves good but pricey food.

E *Bungalows*, about 2 km south of 'fountain circle' in Champassak is Wat That, which boasts 23 nagas guarding its entrance. There is a bungalow complex here, set on the banks of the river. 20 rooms, some with attached bathrooms. Restaurant. **E** *Dokchampa*, bamboo rooms with shared bathrooms and cold water. Good value restaurant. **E-F** *Khamphouy Guesthouse*, delightful family-run place. Fine bright rooms in the main house with shared facilities and 1 cottage (in the garden) of 2 rooms with attached shower. Clean, comfortable, friendly, relaxed. Bikes for hire – a bargain at 5,000 kip. Recommended. **E-F** *Saythong Guesthouse and Restaurant* riverside location. 5 basic rooms upstairs with shared *mandi* and toilet, with 6 more (3 a/c) out the back. These 6 have attached showers. Good food, ample portions.

Eating
● *on map*

Cheap See *Auberge Sala Wat Phou* above. **Seriously cheap** See *Dokchampa* and *Saythong* guesthouses above, plus a couple of noodle shops in the middle of town.

Festivals **February:** *Wat Phou festival* (movable, full moon of the third lunar month, usually Feb), lasts for 3 days with pilgrims coming from far and wide to leave offerings at the temple. In the evening there are competitions – football, boat racing, bullfighting and cockfighting, Thai boxing, singing contests and the like. There is also some pretty extravagant imbibing of alcohol.

Transport **Local** **Bicycle hire:** from guesthouses for 5,000 kip per day.

Road Champassak and Wat Phou lie on the west or right bank of the Mekong River, while the main road is on the east bank. The turning for the ferry is 34 km from Pakse, and the **bus** travels on the vehicle ferry, right into town. There's currently one official morning connection at 0730 from the southern bus terminal in **Pakse** (2 hrs, 10,000 kip), but as the Khong Islands increase in popularity, more services will be laid on. Otherwise take a bus bound for places further south, jump off at **Ban Thang Beng** on Route 13 and take a boat from Ban Muang across the Mekong to **Ban Phaphin** (1,000 kip). It is just as quick and far more entertaining to go by boat (see below). Heading

Champassak

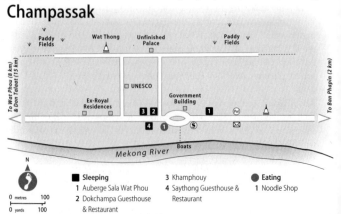

Sleeping
1 Auberge Sala Wat Phou
2 Dokchampa Guesthouse & Restaurant
3 Khamphouy
4 Saythong Guesthouse & Restaurant

Eating
1 Noodle Shop

The South

south from Champassak down towards the **Khong Islands**, most travellers hop on the boat, but if that's full or you're in a hurry, it's also possible to go by bus if you first get the ferry across to the east bank and grab a tuk-tuk to Ban Thang Beng. Once here, it's a bit of a lottery, as you will be taking the chance that there'll be space on the 0700 or 0900 Pakse-Don Khong services (which should come rumbling past at about 0725 and 0925 respectively).

Boat Regular **public boats** from the jetty at the end of No 11 Rd in **Pakse**. Most boats leave around 0700-0800 (2 hrs, 5,000 kip). Boats stop at Ban Phaphin, 2 km north of downtown Champassak; tuk-tuks from here into town cost 2,500 kip. Boats coming upstream from **Don Khong** arrive about 1400 and continue on to Pakse. A **chartered boat** from Pakse, for up to 6 people, could include a visit to Um Oup (Muang Moung) – see Excursions above, US$50-60. There's also a morning connection to **Don Khong** (8,000 kip). Setting off from Pakse around 0700-0800, it stops at **Champassak** 1½-2 hrs later. Be warned, though, that the turnaround time is speedy, and by the time this boat pushes off again, it's usually full to bursting and not apt to wait for any stragglers.

The Islands of the South

This area is locally known as See Pan Done, 'The 4,000 Islands'. Don Khong and Don Khone are two of these many islands littered across the Mekong right at the southern tip of Laos near the border with Cambodia. Half of the islands are sub-merged when the Mekong is in flood. Just before the river enters Cambodia it divides into countless channels. The distance between the most westerly and easterly streams is 14 km – the greatest width of the river in its whole 4,200-km course. The river's volume is swelled by the Kong, San Srepok and Krieng tributaries, which join just upstream from here. Pakha, *or fresh water dolphins, can sometimes be spotted in this area between December and May when they come upsteam to give birth to their young, but they are increasingly endangered.*

Don Khong and Muang Khong

Don Khong is the largest of the Mekong islands at 16 km long and 8 km wide. It's a tremendous place to relax or explore by bicycle. Don Khong's 'capital' is **Muang Khong**, a small former French settlement. While Muang Khong may be the district's main settlement it feels more like a village than a town, with only a few thousand inhabitants. Pigs and chickens scrabble for food under the houses and just 50 m inland the houses give way to paddy fields.

Phone code: 031
Colour map 3, grid C2
Population: 50,000

Getting there The bus journey from Pakse to Don Khong (2 hrs, 13,000 kip) on Route 13 is 120 km and, until recently, progress was excruciatingly slow. But by early 1999 practically the whole road was surfaced with only the bridges remaining to be completed; this, rather amazingly has now been done. The trip is worthwhile for the contrast it offers to conditions in northeastern Thailand, just 20 km or so west. Much of the area is still forested (large quantities of Lao timber are trucked to Thailand via Chongmek, west of Pakse) and villages are intermittent even on this road – the national artery for north-south communications. Paddy fields sometimes appear to be fighting a losing battle against the encroaching forest and most houses are roofed in thatch rather than zinc. At Ban Hat Xay Khoune a car ferry and boats wait to transport passengers across the Mekong to Don Khong and Muang Khong (price is included in the 13,000 fare.

Ins & outs
See Transport, page 239, for further details

The Cambodian border remains officially closed to foreigners

Sights There are two wats here. **Wat Kan Khong**, also known as Wat Phuang Kaew, is visible from the jetty: a large gold Buddha in the mudra of subduing Mara garishly overlooks the Mekong. Much more attractive is **Wat Chom Thong** at the upstream extremity of the village which may date from the early 19th century but which was then much extended during the colonial period. The unusual Khmer-influenced sim may be gently decaying but it is doing so with style and the wat compound, with its carefully tended plants and elegant buildings, is very peaceful. The naga heads on the roof of the main sim are craftily designed to channel water: it issues from their mouths. The old sim to the left of the main entrance is also notable – although it is usually kept locked because of its poor condition.

For early risers the **morning market** in Muang Khong is also worthwhile – if only to see the fish that are served in the restaurants here before they are consigned to the cooking pot. Note that the market only really operates between 0530 and 0730. If you are getting up for the market, it is worth setting the

The South

Mekong islands

To Pakse & Champassak ▲ To Pakse

Mekong River

Don San

Ban Houa Khong Lem

Boats from Pakse & Don Sai

Ban Houa Khong

Ban Dong

Don Hinyai

Don Khong

Rt 13

Wat Phu Khao Kaew

Tham Phu Khiaw

Muang Khong

Passenger /Car Ferry

Ban Naa

Airstrip

Ban Hat Xay Khoune

To Vietnam

Don Khamat

Ban Muang Saen Nua

Don Phuman

Ban Huay

Don Long

Don Som

Ban Khinak

Don Loppadi

CAMBODIA

Ban Nakasong

Ban Thakho

To Cambodia

Don Xang

Don Deth

Boat Landing

Don Tao

Khone Phapheng Falls

Railway Bridge

Ban Khone Nua

Don Khone

Li Phi Falls

Ban Khone Thai

Don Sadam

Don Sanla

Ban Hang Khon

Dolphins

N

0 km 3
0 miles 3

⊢ ┼ ⊣ + – disused railway

alarm clock even earlier to get onto the banks of the Mekong before 0600 when the sun rises over the hills to the east, picking out the silhouettes of fishermen in their canoes.

Most people come to Muang Khong as a base for visiting the **Li Phi** and **Khong Phapheng Falls** (see page 240). However the island itself is worth exploring by bicycle and deserves more time than it gets from most visitors. It is flat – except in the interior – the roads are quiet, so there is less risk of being mown down by a timber truck, and the villages and countryside offer a glimpse of traditional Laos. Most people take the southern 'loop' – a distance of about 25 km or 2-3 hours. The villages along the section of road from **Ban Muang Saen Nua** southwards are wonderfully picturesque. Few people bicycle the northern loop, which takes a full day (0800-1600) and is not so attractive as the south.

Excursions

Tham Phu Khiaw is tucked away among the forest of the **Green Mountain** in the centre of the island. It's a small cave, containing earthenware pots. Buddha images and other relics and offerings litter the site. Every Lao New Year (April) townsfolk climb up to the cave to bathe the images. Getting there is not particularly straightforward except during Lao New Year when it is possible to follow the crowds. Head 1½ km north from Muang Khong on the road until you come to a banana plantation, with a couple of wooden houses. Take the clearway just before the houses through the banana plantation and at the top, just to the left, is a small gateway through the fence. Here there is a fairly well defined path. Head up and along this and after 300 m or so, there is a rocky clearing. The path continues from the top right corner of this clearing. A further 200 m on there is a rocky mound that rolls up and to the left. Walk across it at about 1000 for about 20 m, when it levels out, and then head along this back to the forest. Keeping the rock immediately on the right, continue round and after 40 m there are two upturned tree trunks placed to mark the entrance to the cave. All this is about 15 minutes from the road!

About 6 km north of Ban Muang Saen Nua is a hilltop wat which is arguably Don Khong's main claim to national fame. **Wat Phu Khao Kaew** (Glass Hill Monastery) is built on the spot where there is an entrance leading down to the underground lair of the nagas – **Muang Nak**. This underground town lies beneath the waters of the Mekong and there are several tunnels that lead to the surface – another is at That Luang in Vientiane. Lao legend has it that the nagas will come to the surface to protect the Lao whenever the country is in danger. This means, to most Lao, whenever the Thais decide to attack. Some people believe that the Thais tricked the Lao to build *thats* over the holes to prevent the nagas coming to their rescue – the hole at Wat Phu Khao Kaew is likewise covered.

Pon's Restaurant (reliable and recommended), *Phoxai Don Khong Guesthouse* and *Soukson Guesthouse* can arrange boats to **Don Deth** or **Don Khone** (see next entry). Most leave around 0800 and cost up to 75,000 kip for up to 10 people, whether or not you return the same day. Day trips can be tailored to suit (for example – both falls, or dolphins and one fall). It is also possible to alight at Ban Nakasong, from where a chartered tuk-tuk (50,000 kip round trip) can be taken to the **Khone Phapheng falls** (see below). Boats return to Don Khong around 1600-1700, although check with your boatman, and be aware that they do have a habit of setting off with no thought to conducting a head count. The alternative is to cross to Hat Xay Khoune and walk to Route

13 and try for transport south (it can be limited) to Ban Nakasong and take a boat to Don Deth or Don Khone from there (3,000 kip per person).

Sleeping
■ *on map*
Price codes:
see inside front cover

A *Auberge Sala Done Khong*, T/F212077. A/c, this is the best place to stay on Don Khong. 12 large rooms in traditional wooden house (it was the holiday home of the previous regime's foreign minister), the best are in the main building on the 1st floor where there is an attractive balcony overlooking the Mekong. Attached bathrooms with hot water showers, clean and professionally run, tours arranged, bicycles for hire (15,000 kip), good food – very relaxing.

B *Villa Muang Khong*, T213011. T/F212503. 22 tidy a/c rooms in a bungalow complex, attached western bathrooms, hot water, garden, restaurant serving Lao and European food. 15,000 kip bicycle hire.

D *Souk Sun Guesthouse and Bungalow*, northern end of town near Wat Chom Thong, T212071. A range of rooms from well-designed a/c rooms with attached bathrooms to simple rooms with fans and shared facilities all around an attractive garden. The manageress, Mrs Khamsone, is clearly trying to cover all her options, and along with the wide array of accommodation will arrange boats to visit the falls to see the freshwater dolphins etc. She also runs one of the most popular guesthouses on Don Deth, which includes some of the cheapest accommodation on the island – a 4- bed dorm for 8,000 kip per bed).

E *Done Khong Guesthouse 1*, opposite the jetty, T214010. 3 rooms in raised wooden house, attractive sitting area which catches the morning and evening breeze, fans, shared toilets and showers (in fact like *mandis* – a barrel of water and dipper). Restaurant attached, French spoken by the owner. All starting to look a little tatty, friendly, bicycles for hire. **E** *Done Khong II*, quiet location 300 m out of town on the road to Muang Sen, with rice paddies and hills behind. 6 rooms with attached facilities and 4 rooms with shared facilities. Immaculate throughout. **E** *Mekong Guesthouse*, 14 beautifully simple and spotless fan rooms, some overlooking the Mekong, and all with comfortable mattresses. 3 rooms with a/c (80,000 kip). The detached showers and toilets are equally clean. Recommended. **E** *Pon's Guesthouse and Restaurant*, T214037. 5 fan rooms quaintly decorated, the best of which has a lovely Mekong-facing window. Bike hire for 10,000 kip. **E** *Villa Kang Khong*, T213529. Elegant family house converted in 1997 by the former manager of the *Auberge*

Muang Khong

To Ban Dong (10 km)
To Pon's Bungalows (250m)
Wat Chom Thong
To Ban Muang Saen Nua (8 km)
School
Mekong River
To Ban Hat Xay Khoune
Shops
Shops
Shops
Wat School
Wat Kan Khong

0 metres   50
0 yards   50

■ **Sleeping**
1 Auberge Sala Done Khong
2 Done Khong II
3 Done Khong Guesthouse & Restaurant
4 Mekong Guesthouse
5 Phoxai Guesthouse
6 Pon's Guesthouse & Restaurant
7 Souk Sun Guesthouse & Bungalow
8 Villa Muang Khong

● **Eating**
1 Noodle Shop
2 Restaurant
3 Souk Sun

Sala Done Khong. 9 rooms furnished with character and style, attached shower and toilet, beautiful wooden sitting area, breakfast served, lush garden, bicycles for hire, excellent value.

E-F *Phoxai Done Khong Guesthouse*, 7 basic but clean rooms painted a determined turquoise. Shared toilets correspondingly clean. Owner is friendly and can speak some English and organize tours. A good choice for the budget traveller. **E-F** *Pon's Bunga-lows*, beautiful location by the river, 200 m north of Wat Chom Thong. 6 a/c clean and comfortable rooms, some with attached bathrooms.

There is a growing number of simple noodle houses and a few more sophisticated places. Because there is no electricity most places only serve fish and chicken: killing a pig or cow requires a lot of hungry diners. For some reason, although many other towns and areas also make such a claim, Don Khong is renowned for the quality of its *lau-lao* (rice liquor).

Eating
● *on map*
Price codes:
see inside front cover

Mid-range to cheap *Souk Sun Chinese Restaurant*, attractive place built over the Mekong, only serves Chinese food including good local fish and tasty honeyed pork.

Cheap *Pon's Restaurant*, T214037. Good atmosphere, excellent food, try the fish soup. Recommended. *Villa Muang Khong Hotel Restaurant*, Lao and European food – a limited but good selection of dishes.

Seriously cheap *Done Khong Guesthouse*, the restaurant attached to this guest-house produces good food – nothing flash, just simple single-dish meals. It does a good line in pancakes, too, and despite advertising 'banana craps', the finished prod-uct is really very tasty! *Mekong Restaurant*, attached to the *Mekong Guesthouse*, this restaurant is pleasantly positioned near the bank of the Mekong, and provides legend-ary fare at wonderfully low prices.

December: *Boat Racing* (early in the month). This 5-day festival with boat races on the river opposite Muang Khong coincides with National Day on 2 Dec. A great deal of cel-ebration, eating and drinking.

Festivals

Local **Bicycle hire** from *Villa Khang Khong* and *Done Khong Guesthouse*, 10,000 kip per day. There are a few tuk-tuks in town but they are hardly required around tiny Muang Khong. It is, though, possible to **charter a tuk-tuk** for the trip to the far side of the island, load on a bicycle or two and then cycle back. An unreliable **bus** travels around the island, sometimes meeting the boat from Pakse.

Transport

Long distance **Truck/bus**: regular morning bus connections from **Pakse**, leaving at 0800 (4-5 hrs, 13,000 kip). Alternatively, catch a bus bound for Ban Khuak or Ban Nakasong and jump off at **Ban Hat Xay Khoune** and catch a boat from there (see below). When leaving Don Khong, a bus departs around 0800, but it's worth asking the guesthouse owners for the most recent transport information; for earlier departures, cross to Ban Hat Xay Khoune and pick up a bus from Nakasong (from 0600 onwards). See also Ins and outs, page 235.

Don Khong is approximately 120 km south of Pakse on Route 13

Boat: From **Ban Hat Xay Khoune** it is possible to take a **motorboat** (6,000 kip for the whole vessel divided by the number of passengers), or, for a cheaper crossing, take the **car ferry**. The ferries, which spend most of their time transporting ancient Russian Zil trucks loaded with Cambodian rosewood across the Mekong, are made from 2 old US pontoon boats on either side of an ageing diesel river boat with a pallet lying

The South

crossways over all 3 (1,000 kip). They leave from Ban Hat (1 km south of Hat Xay Khoune) and dock at Ban Naa (1 km south of Muang Khong). Public **passenger boats** (10,000 kip) leave **Pakse** at 0700-0730, depending on how quickly they fill up; leave **Champassak** where they stop en route 1½-2 hrs later; and finally arrive at Don Khong after a journey of 7-8 noisy hrs. Boats going upriver from Don Khong leave around 0700 and take a little longer. When arriving at Don Khong, it's best to alight at **Ban Houa Khong** and arrange transport from there to Muang Khong (buses and tuk-tuks wait here). Boats often continue to **Ban Muang Sen Nua**, although they may arrive considerably later as they tend to visit neighbouring islands first. Chartering a boat to/from Pakse costs around US$140 (maximum 20 people).

International connections Cambodia, on paper, is easily accessible. But the border is closed to foreigners and in any case this area of Cambodia is dangerous and travel is not advisable.

Directory **Banks** There is a basic bank in town, on the same side of the road as Wat Kan Khong and further south. Hrs are erratic and it accepts only US$ or Thai baht; guesthouses will also change cash at rates slightly poorer than market rate. **Communications** Post **Office**: opposite the jetty in centre of town. International dialling from here.

Don Khone and Don Deth

A number of companies run tours to the area, especially from Pakse (see Pakse Tours, page 226)

The islands of Don Khone and Don Deth are the pot of gold at the end of the rainbow for most travellers who head to the southern tip of Laos, and it's not hard to see why. And after the relative fever and bustle of Pakse, the transport headaches around the Bolovens Plateau, and the architectural wonder of Wat Phou, the bamboo huts that stretch along the banks of these two staggeringly beautiful islands are filled with contented travellers in no rush to move on.

Background For those who have travelled on the upper reaches of the Mekong, where, for much of the year it is a slow, lazy river, huge roaring waterfalls might seem rather out of character. But here, near the Cambodian border, the underlying geology changes and the river is punctuated by rapids and the Khone Falls. The name Khone is used loosely and there are in fact two impressive cascades in the area: the **Li Phi** (or **Samphamit Falls**) and **Khong Phapheng Falls** – the latter are the biggest in Southeast Asia and reputedly the widest in the world. Lt Francis Garnier was suitably impressed when he ascended the Khon cataract in 1860, his boatmen hauling their vessels "through a labyrinth of rocks, submerged trees, and prostrate trunks still clinging to earth by their many roots".

In the early 1990s environmentalists were horrified to read that there were plans afoot to build a five-star hotel, casino and golf course at Khong Phapheng. This has thankfully still not materialized, although the feeling is that it is only a matter of time before the big money arrives. Just to illustrate what crazy ideas some people have for Laos, the intention was to build a two-lane highway to link the resort with Pakse, and Pakse with Ubon Ratchathani. A heliport and landing strip were also planned. Fortunately the original investors pulled out of the monstrous scheme, although a memorandum of understanding is still in force. How such a scheme was ever considered may be linked to the fact that President Khamtai Siphandone was born in the area and his elder brother has links with Thai developers. Most locals like the idea: it will bring money and jobs. Most outsiders are aghast at the thought. At the party congress of 1996, Khamtai was unceremoniously ejected from his position as Prime Minister largely, it is said, because he had become too close to Thai big business. But in February 1998 he was appointed President.

The closest place to take a boat to **Li Phi Falls** is from Ban Nakasong, **Li Phi Falls** downriver from Ban Hat Xay Khoune, the crossing point to Don Khong. The boat trip down the fast-flowing channels between the many islands to **Don Khone** is very picturesque; the islands are covered in coconut palms, flame trees, stands of bamboo, kapok trees and hardwoods. The river is riddled with eddies and rapids and it demands a skilled helmsman to negotiate them. In the distance, a few kilometres to the south, are the Khong Hai Mountains which dominate the skyline and delineate the frontier between Laos and Cambodia.

Before putting into **Ban Khone Nua**, the main settlement on Don Khone, **Don Deth** 'port' is on the right, with what remains of its steel rail jetty. In the late 19th and early 20th centuries Don Khone served as an important bypass around the rapids for French cargo boats sailing upriver from Phnom Penh. Ports were built at the southern end (Don Khone) and northern end (Don Deth) of this string of rapids and cascades, and were linked by a 5-km stretch of narrow gauge **railway track**. This railway has the unique distinction of being the only line the French ever built in Laos, although whether a 5-km stretch of steel counts as a 'line' is a moot point. A colonial-style customs house still stands in the shadow of the impressive railway bridge at Ban Khone. On the southern side of the bridge lie the rusted corpses of the old locomotive and boiler car.

From the bridge, follow the path through Ban Khone Thai and then wind through the paddy fields for 1½ km (20 minutes' walk) to **Li Phi** (also called **Somphamit** and **Khone Yai**) falls, which are more a succession of raging rapids, crashing through a narrow rocky gorge. In the wet season, when the rice is green, the area is beautiful – in the dry season, it is scorching. From the main vantage point on a jagged, rocky outcrop, the falls aren't that impressive, as a large stretch of the falls are obscured. ■ *9,000 kip entry fee* .

One of the few places in the world where it is possible to see **freshwater dolphins** is also nearby, not far from the village of Ban Hang Khon. The walk **spotting** across Don Khone is some 4 km; bicycles can be hired by asking around. Boats are available at Ban Hang Khon to take you nearer the dolphins (40,000 kip per boat). Canadian Ian Baird runs the Lao Community Fisheries and Dolphin Protection Project here as he has been doing since 1993 on a budget of US$60,000 per year. He has enticed 44 villages in the area to help him protect the rare freshwater Irrawaddy dolphins (*Orcaella brevirostris*). In 1996 there were thought to be 30 dolphins, after which the numbers seemed to decline and, according to data collected in 1998 using sonar equipment, there were fears that there were as few as nine left. And this was thought to be the largest group in the Mekong. Posters that he had printed showing a mother and calf that 'drowned' after being caught in fishing nets are stuck up in many restaurants and guesthouses on Don Khong. The problem for Baird is that the Lao-Cambodian border transects the dolphin pool. Not only does this mean Baird has to organize a joint approach in a famously lawless area (at least on the Cambodian side), but Cambodian fishermen seem hooked on dynamite and hand grenade fishing technology – the piscine equivalent of the scorched earth approach. However, his efforts appear to be paying off, as it now appears that numbers are on the up again. ■ *The dolphins come here only during the winter months of Dec-May and the best chance of seeing them is morning (0800-1000) or afternoon (1400-1800).*

Khong Phapheng Falls

About 36 km south of Ban Hat Xay Khoune, the road down to **Khong Phapheng Falls** from Route 13 forks below Ban Thakho: one branch leads to a vantage point for a fantastic front-on view of the falls, while the other leads down to the bank of the Mekong, 200 m away, just above the lip of the falls. At this deceptively tranquil spot, the river is gathering momentum before it plunges over the edge. The 'front view' vantage point has a large wooden structure, built up on stilts, overlooking the cascades. When you see the huge volume of white water boiling and surging over the jagged rocks below, it is hard to imagine that there is another 10 km width of river running through other channels. A perilous path leads down from the viewpoint to the edge of the water. Unsurprisingly, the river is impassable at this juncture, as an 1860s French expedition led by adventurers Doudart de Lagrée and Francis Garnier discovered. Garnier wrote:

"There, in the midst of rocks and grassy islets, an enormous sheet of water leaps headlong from a height of 70 ft, to fall back in floods of foam, again to descend from crag to crag, and finally glide away beneath the dense vegetation of the forest. As the river at this point is about 1,000 yd in width, the effect is singularly striking."

It was said that a tongue of rock once extended from the lip of the falls, and the noise of Khong Phapheng – literally 'the voice of the Mekong' – crashing over this outcrop could be heard many miles away. The rock apparently broke off during a flood surge, but the cascades still make enough noise to justify their name. ■ *9,000 kip entry fee for foreigners, there are a number of food and drinks stalls here.*

The principal settlement near Khone Falls, and the last Laotian town of any size before the Cambodian border, is **Ban Khinak**.

Transport Most people get to the falls or see the dolphins by asking 1 of the guesthouses to arrange a trip. There is usually only time to see the dolphins and the railway, or the Li Phi Falls and the railway, or the Khong Phapheng falls. However, there is limited accommodation available for those who might wish to stay overnight (see Sleeping, below). For the Li Phi Falls, the dolphins and the other sights of Don Khone, most visitors take a boat from Muang Khong (Don Khong Island) to Ban Khone Nua and walk or bicycle from there. For the Khong Phapheng Falls most take a boat to Ban Nakasong and then charter a tuk-tuk or motorcycle from there (70,000 kip return). A cheaper option is to take the ferry to Ban Hat Xay Khoune, walk about 1 km to Route 13 and then hitch or catch a bus to Ban Thakho or Ban Nakasong. Note, though, that buses are very irregular.

Don Deth

■ Sleeping
1 Mr Boua Phanh Guesthouse & Restaurant
2 Mr Buon Yong's Paradise Bungalows
3 Mr Deng's Bungalows
4 Mr Lamphone's Huts & Restaurant
5 Mr Phong's Guesthouse & Restaurant
6 Santiphab Guesthouse & Restaurant
7 Mr Sidae's Bungalows
8 Souksan Guesthouse & Restaurant
9 Mr Tho's Bungalows
10 Mr Vong's Guesthouse & Restaurant

● Eating
1 Debudom Souk
2 Rasta Café
3 Rounlieng

From Don Khone, it is possible to hire a boat for the day, and visit the islands and go fishing.

Excursions

Ban Khinak **F** *Khone Phapheng Guesthouse*, near the market, basic rooms, some with bathroom attached. The *Khinak Hotel* which is also here seems to be closed until further notice.

Sleeping

Don Deth This island has really woken up to tourism in the last couple of years, and the riverbank is peppered with bamboo huts and restaurants geared to accommodate the growing wave of travellers that flood south to stop and recoup in this idyllic setting before heading back into the mêlée of living out of a rucksack for weeks on end. It's a great location for soaking up the sunrises and sunsets, not to mention the beaches and swimming that attract the hordes in the dry season. Campfires and Full Moon parties here are another major pull. Many people tend to make their choice of accommodation on the strength of a chance conversation had elsewhere on their travels, and this is as good a way to choose as any, as the accommodation is all cheap and usually much of a muchness. But if you're stuck, the following all have something of note about them.

■ *on map*
Price codes:
see inside front cover

B *Mr Phong's Guesthouse and Restaurant*, directly ahead of you, as you arrive at the boat landing. 6 attractive rooms built from natural materials. Shared facilities, restaurant similar to that in Don Khong which is under the same management.

E-F *Souksan Guesthouse and Restaurant*, at the northern end of the island at Houa Deth. Mrs Khamsone has cleared an area which now houses 20 or so twin and double rooms built from wood/bamboo with shared shower and toilets, and a legendary Chinese restaurant. This place justifiably claims to offer the best view of the sunset, and is a cracking place to chill out as you sip one of the many cocktails they serve. Water volleyball is a popular option here in the dry season.

F *Mr Buon Yong's Paradise Bungalows*, a really lovely option, somehow nicer than most of the other standard bungalows that litter the riverbank. **F** *Mr Lamphone's Huts and Restaurant*, 8 rooms on a quiet stretch of the river, complete with verandas and, importantly, hammocks. **F** *Santiphab Guesthouse and Restaurant*, idyllic setting just by the bridge that connects Don Deth with Don Khone, flanked by the Mekong on 1 side and rice paddies on the other – a friendly, timeless place that serves tasty fare along with buckets of atmosphere. **F** *Mr Sidae's Bungalows*, a really friendly, family feel to these 5 rooms, decorated with fresh flowers. The attached restaurant is also recommended. **F** *Mr Tho's Bungalows*, 10 rooms in standard Don Deth bungalow style. Mr Tho speaks good English, and isn't above using it to try and rip you off. **F** *Mr Vong's Guesthouse and Restaurant*, 4 very clean 2-bedroom bungalows with twin and double beds. Restaurant serves a somewhat limited range of dishes, mainly salads and fried meats. Can arrange boat tours – 80,000 kip to see the big waterfall (Khone Pa Pheng), 1½ hrs in a boat and a stop at the falls.

Don Khone Although Don Deth does attract the vast majority of tourists, Don Khone keeps its end up by offering some very pleasant accommodation alternatives. **D** *Auberge Sala Don Khone*, Ban Khone Nua. A former French hospital built in 1927, this place is now perhaps the nicest place to stay on the island. 2 traditional Luang Prabang style houses have been built in the grounds, with 6 rooms, all with attached shower and toilet, some with a/c. **F** *Next door to Auberge Sala Don Khone*, Mr Boun has built a thatched bungalow with 3 tidy rooms with shared facilities. **F** *Mr Khamphouy, Mrs Liem Phet and Mr Chan*, all run 'guesthouses' – really rooms in family homes. Ask around; other families will probably follow suit with rising demand.

The South

Eating   **Ban Nakasong** (the jumping-off point for Don Khone) There are 2 small thatched beach-side restaurants which serve good chicken noodle soup (*feu*). In the rainy season they move further up the bank. Small food and drinks stall just on the right, as you get off the boat.

Don Khone The best place to eat is the restaurant (**Seriously cheap**) opposite the *Auberge Sala Don Khone*, overlooking the river. Traditional Lao food, and some European – simple, but good and not too pricey.

Transport   **Bicycle hire** From near where the boat drops you. **Boat** From Ban Nakasong, 25 mins.

Boat/Bus/truck When leaving, it's necessary to hop on a boat to Ban Nagasong (30 mins, 5,000 kip per person) before the buses depart for Pakse, at 0600 and 0900 (11,000 kip). The earlier departure makes the best time (2 hrs) and usually has more room.

Directory   **Communications** No Post Office and no telephones. **Useful information** Electricity: none (although more and more properties are introducing battery charged lighting and there is the odd generator).

The South

Background

History

Scholars of Lao history, before they even begin, need to decide whether they are writing a history of Laos; a history of the Lao ethnic group; or histories of the various kingdoms and principalities that have, through time, been encompassed by the present boundaries of the Lao People's Democratic Republic. Historians have tended to confront this problem in different ways without, often, acknowledging on what basis their 'history' is built. It is common to see 1365, the date of the foundation of the kingdom of Lane Xang, as marking the beginning of Lao history. But, as Martin Stuart-Fox points out, prior to Lane Xang the principality of Muang Swa, occupying the same geographical space, was headed by a Lao. The following account provides a brief overview of the histories of those peoples who have occupied what is now the territory of the Lao PDR.

Archaeological and historical evidence indicates that most Lao originally migrated south from China. This was followed by an influx of ideas and culture from the Indian subcontinent via Myanmar (Burma), Thailand and Cambodia – something which is reflected in the state religion, Theravada Buddhism.

Being surrounded by large, powerful neighbours, Laos has been repeatedly invaded over the centuries by the Thais (or Siamese) and the Vietnamese – who both thought of Laos as their buffer zone and backyard. They too have both left their mark on Lao culture. In recent history, Laos has been influenced by the French during the colonial era, the Japanese during the Second World War, the Americans during the Indochinese wars and, between 1975 and the early 1990s, by Marxism-Leninism.

It is also worth noting, in introduction, that historians and regimes have axes to grind. The French were anxious to justify their annexation of Laos and so used dubious Vietnamese documents to provide a thin legal gloss to their actions. Western historians, lumbered with the baggage of western historiography, ignored indigenous histories. And the Lao People's Revolutionary Party uses history for its own ends too. The official three volume *History of Laos* is currently being written by Party-approved history hacks. The third volume (chronologically speaking) was published in 1989 and, working back in time, the first and second thereafter. As Martin Stuart-Fox remarks in his *A History of Laos*, "the communist regime is as anxious as was the previous Royal Lao government [pre-1975] to establish that Laos has a long and glorious past and that a continuity exists between the past and the present Lao state" (1997: 6). In other words, Laos has not one history, but many. Take your pick.

First kingdom of Laos

Myth, archaeology and history all point to a number of early feudal Lao kingdoms in what is now South China and North Vietnam. External pressures from the Mongols under Kublai Khan and the Han Chinese forced the Tai tribes to migrate south into what had been part of the Khmer Empire. The mountains to the north and east served as a cultural barrier to Vietnam and China, leaving the Lao exposed to influences from India and the West. There are no documentary records of early Lao history (the first date in the Lao chronicles to which historians attach any real veracity is 1271), although it seems probable that parts of present-day Laos were annexed by Lannathai (Chiang Mai) in the 11th century and by the Khmer Empire during the 12th century. But neither of these states held sway over the entire area of Laos. Xieng Khouang, for example, was probably never under Khmer domination. This was followed by strong Siamese influence over the cities of Luang Prabang and Vientiane under the Siamese Sukhothai Dynasty. Laos (the country), in effect did not exist; although the Laos (the people) certainly did.

The downfall of the kingdom of Sukhothai in 1345 and its submission to the new Siamese Dynasty at Ayutthaya (founded in 1349) was the catalyst for the foundation of what is commonly regarded as the first truly independent Lao Kingdom – although there were smaller semi-independent Lao *muang* (city states, sometimes transliterated as *meuang*) existing prior to that date.

Fa Ngoum and Lane Xang

The kingdom of Lane Xang (Lan Chang) emerged in 1353 under Fa Ngoum, a Lao prince who had grown up in the Khmer court of Angkor. Fa Ngoum is clearly an important man – that is, if the amount of space devoted to his exploits in the Lao chronicles is anything to go by. There is more written about him than there is about the following two centuries of Lao history. It is also safe to say that his life is more fiction than fact. Fa Ngoum was reputedly born with 33 teeth and was banished to Angkor after his father, Prince Yakfah, was convicted of having an incestuous affair with a wife of King Suvarna Kamphong. In 1353 Fa Ngoum led an army to Luang Prabang and confronted his grandfather, King Suvarna Kamphong. Unable to defeat his grandson on the battlefield, the aged king is said to have hanged himself and Fa Ngoum was invited to take the throne. Three years later, in 1356, Fa Ngoum marched on Vientiane which he took with ease and then on Vienkam which proved more of a challenge (see box, page 248). He is credited with piecing together Lang Xang – the Land of a Million Elephants (or, if not accented, the Valley of Elephants) – the golden age to which all histories of Laos refer to justify the existence (and greatness) of Laos.

In some accounts Lang Xang is portrayed as stretching from China to Cambodia and from the Khorat Plateau in present-day Northeast Thailand to the Annamite mountains in the east. But it would be entirely wrong to envisage the kingdom controlling all these regions. Lane Xang probably only had total control over a comparatively small area of present-day Laos and parts of Northeast Thailand; the bulk of this grand empire would have been contested with other surrounding kingdoms. In addition, the smaller *muang* and principalities would themselves have played competing powers off, one against another, in an attempt to maximize their own autonomy. It is this 'messiness' which led scholars of Southeast Asian history to suggest that territories as such did not exist, but rather zones of variable control, termed *mandalas* by OW Wolters (see the box on page 251).

Legend relates that Fa Ngoum was a descendant of Khoum Borom, "a king who came out of the sky from South China". He is said to have succeeded to the throne of Nanchao in 729, aged 31, and died 20 years later, although this historical record is, as they say, exceedingly thin. Khoum Borom is credited with giving birth to the Lao people by slicing open a gourd in Muong Taeng (Dien Bien Phu, Vietnam) and his seven sons established the great Tai kingdoms. He returned to his country with a detachment of Khmer soldiers and united several scattered Lao fiefdoms. In those days, conquered lands were usually razed and the people taken as slaves to build up the population of the conquering group. (This largely explains why, today, there are far more Lao in northeastern Thailand than in Laos – they were forcibly settled there after King Anou was defeated by King Rama III of Siam in 1827 – see page 250.) The kings of Lane Xang were less philistine, demanding only subordination and allegiance as one part of a larger *mandala*.

Luang Prabang became the capital of the kingdom of Lane Xang. The unruly highland tribes of the northeast did not come under the kingdom's control at that time. Fa Ngoum made Theravada Buddhism the official religion. He married the Cambodian king's daughter, Princess Keo Kaengkanya, and was given the Phra Bang (a golden statue, the most revered religious symbol of Laos), by the Khmer court.

▶▶ Cunning Fa Ngoum takes Vienkam

ML Manich in his History of Laos *relates a slightly fanciful but nonetheless entertaining story of how Fa Ngoum took Vienkam in 1356. The town was surrounded by an impenetrable thicket of bamboo and defended by a skilled commander, Phya Pao. Unable to take the town, he ordered his three generals to shoot arrows of gold and silver into the thicket for three days. Then he withdrew. The townspeople, scarcely believing their luck, cut down the bamboo to recover* the precious arrow heads and in so doing opened their city up to attack by Fa Ngoum. But rather than taking the city he invited Phya Pao to fight him in a single-handed elephant duel. They fought for so long without either one gaining an advantage that Fa Ngoum reinstated Phya Pao as governor of Vienkam. In the ensuing celebrations in Vientiane 10 elephants, 1,000 cows and 2,000 buffalo were slaughtered for the feast.

It is common to read of Lane Xang as the first kingdom of Laos; as encompassing the territory of present-day Laos; and as marking the introduction of Theravada Buddhism to the country. On all counts this portrait is, if not false, then deeply flawed. As noted above, there were Lao states that predated Lane Xang; Lane Xang never controlled Laos as it currently exists; and Buddhism had made an impact on the Lao people before 1365. Fa Ngoum did not create a kingdom; rather he brought together various pre-existing *muang* (city states) into a powerful *mandala*. As Martin Stuart-Fox writes, "From this derives his [Fa Ngoum's] historical claim to hero status as the founder of the Lao Kingdom." But, as Stuart-Fox goes on to explain, there was no central authority and rulers of individual *muang* were permitted considerable autonomy. As a result the "potential for disintegration was always present ..."

After Fa Ngoum's wife died in 1368, he became so debauched, it is said, that he was deposed in favour of his son, Samsenthai (1373-1416), who was barely 18 when he acceded the throne. He was named after the 1376 census, which concluded that he ruled over 300,000 Tais living in Laos: *samsen* means, literally, 300,000. He set up a new administrative system based on the existing *muang*, nominating governors to each, that lasted until it was abolished by the Communist government in 1975. Samsenthai's death was followed by a period of unrest. Under King Chaiyachakkapat-Phaenphaeo (1441-78), the kingdom came under increasing threat from the Vietnamese. How the Vietnamese came to be peeved with the Lao is another story which smacks of fable more than fact. King Chaiyachakkapat's eldest son, the Prince of Chienglaw, secured a holy white elephant. The emperor of Vietnam, learning of this momentous discovery, asked to be sent some of the beast's hairs. Disliking the Vietnamese, the Prince dispatched a box of its excrement instead, whereupon the Emperor formed an army of an improbably large 550,000 men. The Prince's army numbered 200,000 and 2,000 elephants. (Considering that the population of Lane Xang under Samsenthai was said to be 300,000 this beggars statistical belief. Still, it is a good story.) The massive Vietnamese army finally prevailed – two Lao generals were so tired they fell off their elephants and were hacked to pieces – and entered and sacked Luang Prabang. But shortly thereafter they were driven out by Chaiyachakkapat-Phaenphaeo's son, King Suvarna Banlang (1478-85). Peace was only fully restored under King Visunarat (1500-1520), who built Wat Visoun in Luang Prabang (see page 123).

Increasing prominence & Burmese incursions Under King Pothisarath (1520-48) Vientiane became prominent as a trading and religious centre. He married a Lanna (Chiang Mai) princess, Queen Yotkamtip, and when the Siamese King Ketklao was put to death in 1545, Pothisarath's son claimed the throne at Lanna. He returned to Lane Xang when his father died in 1548. Once again

Background

Kings of Lane Xang

Fa Ngoum	1353-1373	Pothisarath	1520-1548
Samsenthai	1373-1416	Setthathirat	1548-1571
Lan Kamdaeng	1417-1428	Saensurin	1572-1574
Phommathat	1428-1429	Mahaupahat (under	
Mun Sai	1429-1430	Burmese control)	1574-1580
Fa Khai	1430-1433	Saensurin	1580-1582
Khong Kham	1433-1434	Nakhon Noi (under	
Yukhon	1434-1435	Burmese control)	1582-1583
Kham Keut	1435-1441	Interregnum	1583-1591
Chaiyachakkapat-		Nokeo Koumone	1591-1596
Phaenphaeo		Thammikarath	1596-1622
(aka Sao Tiakaphat)	1441-1478	Upanyuvarat	1622-1623
Suvarna Banlang		Pothisarat	1623-1627
(aka Theng Kham)	1478-1485	Mon Keo	1627
Lahsaenthai Puvanart	1485-1495	Unstable period	1627-1637
Sompou	1497-1500	Sulinya Vongsa	1637-1694
Visunarat	1500-1520		

an elephant figured as a prime mover in the event: Pothisarath was demonstrating his prowess in the manly art of elephant lassoing when he was flung from his mount and fatally crushed. Asserting his right as successor to the throne, he was crowned Setthathirat in 1548 and ruled until 1571 – the last of the great kings of Lane Xang.

At the same time, the Burmese were expanding East and in 1556 Lanna fell into their hands. Setthathirat gave up his claim to that throne, to a Siamese prince, who ruled under Burmese authority. (He also took the Phra Kaeo – Thailand's famous 'Emerald' Buddha and its most sacred and revered image – with him to Luang Prabang and then to Vientiane. The residents of Chiang Mai are reputed to have pleaded that he leave it in the city, but these cries fell on deaf ears. The Phra Kaeo stayed in Vientiane until 1778 when the Thai general Phya Chakri 'repatriated' it to Thailand.) In 1563 Setthathirat pronounced Vieng Chan (Vientiane) the principal capital of Lane Xang. Seven years later, the Burmese King Bayinnaung launched an unsuccessful attack on Vieng Chan itself.

Setthathirat is revered as one of the great Lao kings, having protected the country from foreign domination. He built Wat Phra Kaeo (see page 75) in Vientiane, in which he placed the famous Emerald Buddha brought from Lanna. Setthathirat mysteriously disappeared during a campaign in the southern province of Attapeu in 1574, which threw the kingdom into crisis (see page 219). Vientiane fell to invading Burmese the following year and remained under Burmese control for seven years. Finally the anarchic kingdoms of Luang Prabang and Vientiane were reunified under Nokeo Koumane (1591-96) and Thammikarath (1596-1622).

Disputed territory

From the time of the formation of the kingdom of Lane Xang to the arrival of the French, the history of Laos was dominated by the struggle to retain the lands it had conquered. Following King Setthathirat's death, a series of kings came to the throne in quick succession. King Souligna Vongsa, crowned in 1633, brought long awaited peace to Laos. The 61 years he was on the throne are regarded as Lane Xang's golden age. Under him, the kingdom's influence spread to Yunnan in South China, the Burmese Shan States, Isan in Northeast Thailand and areas of Vietnam and Cambodia.

Background

Souligna Vongsa was even on friendly terms with the Vietnamese: he married Emperor Le Thanh Ton's daughter and he and the Emperor agreed the borders between the two countries. The frontier was settled in a deterministic – but nonetheless amicable – fashion: those living in houses built on stilts with verandas were considered Lao subjects and those living in houses without piles and verandas owed allegiance to Vietnam.

During his reign, foreigners first visited the country – the Dutch merchant Gerrit van Wuysthoff arrived in 1641 to assess trading prospects – and Jesuit missionaries too. But other than a handful of adventurers, Laos remained on the outer periphery of European concerns and influence in the region.

The three kingdoms After Souligna Vongsa died in 1694, leaving no heir, dynastic quarrels and feudal rivalries once again erupted, undermining the kingdom's cohesion. In 1700 Lane Xang split into three: Luang Prabang under Souligna's grandson, Vientiane under Souligna's nephew and the new kingdom of Champassak was founded in the south 'panhandle'. This weakened the country and allowed the Siamese and Vietnamese to encroach on Lao lands. *Muang*, which previously owed clear allegience to Lane Xang, began to look towards Vietnam or Siam. Isan *muang* in present-day Northeast Thailand, for example, paid tribute to Bangkok; while Xieng Khouang did the same to Hanoi and, later, to Hué. The three main kingdoms that emerged with the disintegration of Lane Xang leant in different directions: Luang Prabang had close links with China, Vientiane with Vietnam's Hanoi/Hué and Champassak with Siam.

By the mid-1760s Burmese influence once again held sway in Vientiane and Luang Prabang and before the turn of the decade, they sacked Ayutthaya, the capital of Siam. Somehow the Siamese managed to pull themselves together and only two years later in 1778 successfully rampaged through Vientiane. The two sacred Buddhas, the Phra Bang and the Phra Kaeo (Emerald Buddha) were taken as booty back to Bangkok. The Emerald Buddha was never returned and now sits in Bangkok's Wat Phra Kaeo (see page 75).

King Anou (an abbreviation of Anurutha), was placed on the Vientiane throne by the Siamese. With the death of King Rama II of Siam, King Anou saw his chance of rebellion, asked Vietnam for assistance, formed an army and marched on Bangkok in 1827. In mounting this brave – some would say foolhardy – assault, Anou was apparently trying to emulate the great Fa Ngum. Unfortunately, he got no further than the Northeast Thai town of Korat where his forces suffered a defeat and were driven back. Nonetheless, Anou's rebellion is considered one of the most daring and ruthless rebellions in Siamese history and he was lauded as a war hero back home.

King Anou's brief stab at regional power was to result in catastrophe for Laos – and tragedy for King Anou. The first US arms shipment to Siam allowed the Siamese to sack Vientiane, a task to which they had grown accustomed over the years. (This marks America's first intervention in Southeast Asia.) Lao artisans were frog-marched to Bangkok and many of the inhabitants were resettled in Northeast Siam. Rama III had Chao Anou locked in a cage where he was taunted and abused by the population of Bangkok. He died soon afterwards, at the age of 62. The cause of his death has been variously linked to poison and shame. One of his supporters is said to have taken pity on the king and brought him poison. Other explanations simply say that he wished himself dead. Still others that he choked to death. Whatever the cause, the disconsolate Anou, before he died, put a curse on Siam's monarchy, promising that the next time a Thai king set foot on Lao soil, he would die. To this day no Thai king has crossed the Mekong River. When the agreement for the supply of hydro-electric power was signed with Thailand in the 1970s, the Thai king was invited officially to open the Nam Ngum Dam, a feat he managed from a sandbank in the middle of the Mekong.

Background

Making space

Western historians like to think of kingdoms 'controlling' territory. In Southeast Asia such cut-and-dried spatial categorization made little sense until the early 20th century. This led the historian OW Wolters to suggest the word mandala *to describe the manner in which Southeast Asian kingdoms controlled territory:*

A mandala *"...represented a particular and often unstable political situation in a*

vaguely defined geographical area without fixed boundaries and where smaller centres tended to look in all directions for security. Mandalas *would expand and contract in concertina-like fashion. Each one contained several tributary rulers, some of whom would repudiate their vassal status when the opportunity arose and try to build up their own network of vassals."*

Over the next 50 years, Anou's Kingdom was destroyed. By the time the French arrived in the late 19th century, the virtually unoccupied city was subsumed into the Siamese sphere of influence. Luang Prabang also became a Siamese vassal state, while Xieng Khouang province was invaded by Chinese rebels – to the chagrin of the Vietnamese, who had always considered the Hmong mountain kingdom (they called it Tran Ninh), to be their exclusive source of slaves. The Chinese had designs on Luang Prabang too and in order to quash their expansionist instincts, Bangkok dispatched an army there in 1885 to pacify the region and ensure the north remained firmly within the Siamese sphere of influence. This period was clearly one of confusion and rapidly shifting allegiances. In James McCarthy's book of his travels in Siam and Laos, *Surveying and Exploring in Siam* (1900), he states that an old chief of Luang Prabang remarked to him that the city had never been a tributary state of Annam (North Vietnam) but had formerly paid tribute to China. He writes:

"The tribute had consisted of four elephants, 41 mules, 533 lbs of nok (metal composed of gold and copper), 25 lbs of rhinoceros' horns, 100 lbs of ivory, 250 pieces of home-spun cloth, one horn, 150 bundles of areca-palm nuts [for betel 'nut' chewing], 150 cocoanuts [sic] and 33 bags of roe of the fish pla buk [the giant Mekong cat fish, see page 306]."

Disintegration of the kingdom

The history of Laos during this period becomes, essentially, the history of only a small part of the current territory of the country: namely, the history of Luang Prabang. And because Luang Prabang was a suzerain state of Bangkok, the history of that kingdom is, in turn, sometimes relegated to a mere footnote in the history of Siam.

The French and independence

Following King Anou's death, Laos became the centre of Southeast Asian rivalry between Britain, expanding East from Burma and France, pushing west through Vietnam. In 1868, following the French annexation of South Vietnam and the establishment of a protectorate in Cambodia, an expedition set out to explore the Mekong trade route to China. Once central and North Vietnam had come under the influence of the Quai d'Orsay in Paris, the French became increasingly curious about Vietnamese claims to chunks of Laos. Unlike the Siamese, the French – like the British – were concerned with demarcating borders and establishing explicit areas of sovereignty. This seemed extraordinary to most Southeast Asians at the time who could not see the point of spending so much time and effort mapping space when land was so abundant. However, it did not take long for the Siamese king to realize the importance of maintaining his claim to Siamese territories if the French in the east and the British in the south (Malaya) and west (Burma) were not to squeeze Siam to nothing.

However, King Chulalongkorn was not in a position to confront the French militarily and instead he had to play a clever diplomatic game if his Kingdom was to survive. The French, for their part, were anxious to continue to press westwards from Vietnam into the Lao lands over which Siam held suzerainty. Martin Stuart-Fox argues that there were four main reasons underlying France's desire to expand West: the lingering hope that the Mekong might still offer a 'backdoor' into China; the consolidation of Vietnam against attack; the 'rounding out' of their Indochina possessions; and a means of further pressuring Bangkok. In 1886, the French received reluctant Siamese permission to post a vice consul to Luang Prabang and a year later he persuaded the Thais to leave. However, even greater humiliation was to come in 1893 when the French, through crude gunboat diplomacy – the so-called Paknam incident – forced King Chulalongkorn to give up all claim to Laos on the flimsiest of historical pretexts. Despite attempts by Prince Devawongse to manufacture a compromise, the French forced Siam to cede Laos to France and, what's more, to pay compensation. It is said that after this humiliation, King Chulalongkorn retired from public life, broken in spirit and health. So the French colonial era in Laos began.

What is notable about this spat between France and Siam is that Laos – the country over which they were fighting – scarcely figures. As was to happen again in Laos' history, the country was caught between two competing powers who used Laos as a stage on which to fight a wider and to them, more important, conflict.

Union of Indochina   In 1893 France occupied the left bank of the Mekong and forced Thailand to recognize the river as the boundary. The French Union of Indochina denied Laos the area which is now Isan, northeast Thailand, and this was the start of 50 years of colonial rule. Laos became a protectorate with a *résident-superieur* in Vientiane and a vice-consul in Luang Prabang. However, as Martin Stuart-Fox points out, Laos could hardly be construed as a 'country' during the colonial period. "Laos existed again", he writes, "but not yet as a political entity in its own right, for no independent centre of Lao political power existed. Laos was but a territorial entity within French Indochina." The French were not interested in establishing an identifiable Lao state; they saw Laos as a part and a subservient part at that, of Vietnam, serving as a resource-rich appendage to Vietnam. Though they had grand plans for the development of Laos, these were only expressed airily and none of them came to anything. "The French were never sure what to do with Laos", Stuart-Fox writes, "either the parts or the whole." Unlike Cambodia to the south, the French did not perceive Laos to have any historical unity or coherence and therefore it could be hacked about and developed or otherwise, according to their whim, as if it were a piece of brie.

In 1904 the Franco-British convention delimited respective zones of influence. Only a few hundred French civil servants were ever in Vientiane at any one time and their attitude to colonial administration – described as 'benign neglect' – was as relaxed as the people they governed. To the displeasure of the Lao, France brought in Vietnamese to run the civil service (in the way the British used Indian bureaucrats in Burma). But for the most part, the French colonial period was a 50-year siesta for Laos. The king was allowed to stay in Luang Prabang, but had little say in administration. Trade and commerce was left to the omnipresent Chinese and the Vietnamese. A small, French-educated Lao élite did grow up and by the 1940s they had become the core of a typically laid-back Lao nationalist movement.

Japanese coup   Towards the end of the Second World War, Japan ousted the French administration in Laos in a coup in March 1945. The eventual surrender of the Japanese in August that year gave impetus to the Lao independence movement. Prince Phetsarath, hereditary viceroy and premier of the Luang Prabang Kingdom, took over the leadership of the Lao Issara, the Free Laos Movement (originally a resistance movement against the Japanese). They prevented the French from seizing power again and declared Lao independence on 1 September 1945. Two weeks later, the north and south provinces were reunified and in October, Phetsarath formed a Lao Issara government headed by Prince Phaya Khammao, the governor of Vientiane.

France refused to recognize the new state and crushed the Lao resistance. King Sisavang Vong, unimpressed by Prince Phetsarath's move, sided with the French, who had their colony handed back by British forces. He was crowned the constitutional monarch of the new protectorate in 1946.

The rebel government took refuge in Bangkok. Historians believe the Issara movement was aided in their resistance to the French by the Viet Minh – Hanoi's Communists.

In response to nationalist pressures, France was obliged to grant Laos ever greater self government and, eventually, formal independence within the framework of the newly reconstructed French Union in July 1949. Meanwhile, in Bangkok, the Issara movement had formed a government-in-exile, headed by Phetsarath and his half-brothers: Prince Souvanna Phouma and Prince Souphanouvong. Both were refined, French-educated men, with a taste for good wine and cigars. The Issara's military wing was led by Souphanouvong who, even at that stage, was known for his Communist sympathies. Within just a few months the so-called Red Prince had been ousted by his half-brothers and joined the Viet Minh where he is said to have been the moving force behind the declaration of the Democratic Republic of Laos by the newly-formed Lao National Assembly. The Lao People's Democratic Republic emerged – albeit in name only – somewhere inside Vietnam, in August 1949. Soon afterwards, the Pathet Lao – literally, 'the Lao nation' was born. The Issara movement quickly folded and Souvanna Phouma went back to Vientiane and joined the newly-formed Royal Lao Government.

By 1953, Prince Souphanouvong had managed to move his Pathet Lao headquarters inside Laos and with the French losing their grip on the north provinces, the weary colonizers granted the country full independence. Retreating honourably, France signed a treaty of friendship and association with the new royalist government and made the country a French protectorate.

Independence

The rise of communism

While all this was going on, the king sat tight in Luang Prabang instead of moving to Vientiane. But within a few months of independence, the ancient royal capital was under threat from the Communist Viet Minh and Pathet Lao. Honouring the terms of the new treaty, French commander General Henri Navarre determined in late 1953 to take the pressure off Luang Prabang by confronting the Viet Minh who controlled the strategic approach to the city at Dien Bien Phu. The French suffered a stunning defeat which presaged their withdrawal from Indochina. The subsequent occupation of two North Lao provinces by the Vietnam-backed Pathet Lao forces, meant the kingdom's days as a western buffer state were numbered.

With the Geneva Accord in July 1954, following the fall of Dien Bien Phu in May, Ho Chi Minh's government gained control of all territory north of the 17th parallel in neighbouring Vietnam. The Accord guaranteed Laos' freedom and neutrality, but with the Communists on the threshold, the US was not prepared to be a passive spectator: the demise of the French sparked an increasing US involvement. In an operation that was to mirror the much more famous war with Vietnam to the East, Washington soon found itself supplying and paying the salaries of 50,000 royalist troops and their corrupt officers. Clandestine military assistance grew, undercover special forces were mobilized and the CIA began meddling in Lao politics. In 1960 a consignment of weapons was dispatched by the CIA to a major in the Royal Lao

French defeat

Background

Army called Vang Pao – or VP, as he became known – who was destined to become the leader of the Hmong.

US involvement & the domino effect

Laos had become the dreaded 'first domino', which, using the scheme of US President Dwight D Eisenhower's famous analogy, would trigger the rapid spread of Communism if ever it fell. The time-trapped little kingdom rapidly became the focus of superpower brinkmanship. At a press conference in March 1961, President Kennedy is said to have been too abashed to announce to the American people that US forces might soon become embroiled in conflict in a far-away flashpoint that went by the inglorious name of 'Louse'. For three decades Americans have unwittingly mis-pronounced the country's name as Kennedy decided, euphemistically, to label it 'Lay-os' throughout his national television broadcast.

Coalitions, coups & counter-coups

The US-backed Royal Lao Government of independent Laos – even though it was headed by the neutralist, Prince Souvanna Phouma – ruled over a divided country from 1951 to 1954. The Communist Pathet Lao, headed by Prince Souphanouvong, emerged as the only strong opposition. The growth of the Pathet Lao had been overseen and sponsored by North Vietnam's Lao Dong party since 1949. By the mid-1950s, Kaysone Phomvihane, later Prime Minister of the Lao PDR, began to make a name for himself in the Indochinese Communist Party. Indeed the close association between Laos and Vietnam went deeper than just ideology. Kaysone's father was Vietnamese, while Prince Souphanouvong and Nouhak Phounsavanh both married Vietnamese women. Entrenched in the northern provinces, Pathet Lao troops – supported by the Communist Viet Minh forces – made several incursions into central Laos and civil war erupted.

Government of National Union

Unable to secure cooperation with the Communists, elections were held in Vientiane in July 1955 but were boycotted by the Pathet Lao. Souvanna Phouma became Prime Minister in March 1956. He aimed to try to negotiate the integration of his half-brother's Pathet Lao provinces into a unified administration and coax the Communists into a coalition government. In 1957 the disputed provinces were returned to royal government control and in May 1958 elections were held. This time the Communists' Lao Patriotic Front clinched nine of the 21 seats in the Government of National Union. The Red Prince, Souphanouvong and one of his aides were included in a coalition cabinet and former Pathet Lao members were elected deputies of the National Assembly.

Almost immediately problems which had been beneath the surface emerged to plague the government. The American-backed rightists were rather shaken by the result and the much-vaunted coalition lasted just two months. The National Union fell apart in July 1958. Pathet Lao leaders were jailed and the right-wing Phoui Sananikone came to power. With anti-Communists in control, Pathet Lao forces withdrew to the Plain of Jars in Xieng Khouang province. A three-way civil war ensued, between the rightists, the Communists and the neutralists.

Civil war

CIA-backed strongman General Phoumi Nosavan thought Phoui's politics rather tame and with a nod from Washington he stepped into the breech in January 1959, eventually overthrowing Phoui in a coup in December and placing Prince Boun Oum in power. Confusion over Phoumas, Phouis and Phoumis led one American official to comment that it all "could have been a significant event or a typographical error".

Within a year, the rightist regime was overthrown by a neutralist *coup d'état* led by General Kong Lae and Prince Souvanna Phouma was recalled from exile in Cambodia to become Prime Minister of the first National Union. Souvanna Phouma incurred American wrath by inviting a Soviet ambassador to Vientiane in October.

Prince Souvanna Phouma: architect of independence and helmsman of catastrophe

Prince Souvanna Phouma was Laos' greatest statesman. He was Prime Minister on no less than eight occasions between 1951 and 1975 for a total of 20 years. He dominated mainstream politics during the turbulent years from independence until the victory of the Pathet Lao in 1975. But in the last analysis he was never able to preserve the integrity of Laos in the face of much stronger external forces. "Souvanna stands as a tragic figure in modern Lao history," Martin Stuart-Fox writes, a "stubborn symbol of an alternative, neutral, 'middle way'."

He was born in 1901 into a branch of the Luang Prabang royal family. Like many of the Lao élite he was educated abroad, in Hanoi, Paris and Grenoble, and when he returned to Laos he married a woman of mixed French-Lao blood. He was urbane, educated and, by all accounts, arrogant. He enjoyed fine wines and cigars, spoke French better than he spoke Lao, and was a Francophile – as well as a nationalist – to the end. In 1950 Souvanna became a co-founder of the Progressive Party and in the elections of 1951 he headed his first government which negotiated and secured full independence from France.

Souvanna made two key errors of judgement during these early years. First, he ignored the need for 'nation building' in Laos. And second, he underestimated the threat that the Communists posed to the country. With regard to the first of these misjudgements, he seemed to believe – and it is perhaps no accident that he trained as an engineer and architect – that Laos just needed to be administered efficiently to become a modern state. The belief that the government first had to try and inculcate a sense of Lao nationhood he either appeared to reject, or to ignore. The second misjudgement was his long held belief – until it was too late – that the

Pathet Lao was a nationalist and not a communist organization. He let the Pathet Lao grow in strength and this, in turn, brought the US into Lao affairs.

By the time the US began to intervene in Lao affairs, during the late 1950s, the country already – with hindsight – seemed to be heading for catastrophe. But in his struggle to maintain some semblance of neutrality and independence for his tiny country, he ignored the degree to which Laos was being sucked into the quagmire of Indochina. As Martin Stuart-Fox writes:

"He [Souvanna] knew he was being used, and that he had no power to protect his country from the war that increasingly engulfed it. But he was too proud meekly to submit to US demands – even as Laos was subjected to the heaviest bombing in the history of warfare. At least a form of independence had to be maintained...".

When the Pathet Lao entered Vientiane in victory in 1975, Souvanna did not flee into exile. He remained to help in the transfer of power. The Pathet Lao, of course, gave him a title and then largely ignored him as they pursued their Communist manifesto. Again, Martin Stuart-Fox writes:

"Souvanna ended his days beside the Mekong. He was to the end a Lao patriot, refusing to go into exile in France. The leaders of the new regime did consult him on occasions. Friends came to play bridge. Journalists continued to seek him out, although he said little and interviews were taped in the presence of Pathet Lao minions. When he died in January 1984, he was accorded a state funeral."

The above is a summary of the discussion of Souvanna Phouma in 'Suvanna Phuma and the Quest for Lao Neutrality', in Martin Stuart-Fox's Buddhist Kingdom, Marxist State: the Making of Modern Laos *(Bangkok: White Lotus, 1996).*

With US support, Nosavan staged yet another armed rebellion in December and sparked a new civil war. Kong Lae backed down, Souvanna Phouma shuffled back to Phnom Penh and a new right-wing government was set up under Boun Oum.

Zurich talks and the Geneva Accord　The new Prime Minister, the old one and his Marxist half-brother finally sat down to talks in Zurich in June 1961, but any hope of an agreement was overshadowed by escalating tensions between the superpowers. A year later an international agreement on Laos was hammered out in Geneva by 14 participating nations and accords were signed, once again guaranteeing Lao neutrality.

By implication, the accords denied the Viet Minh access to the Ho Chi Minh Trail. But aware of the reality of constant North Vietnamese infiltration through Laos into South Vietnam, the head of the American mission concluded that the agreement was "a good bad deal".

Another coalition government of National Union was formed under the determined neutralist Prince Souvanna Phouma (as Prime Minister), with Prince Souphanouvong for the Pathet Lao and Prince Boun Oum representing the right. It was no surprise when it collapsed within a few months and fighting resumed. This time the international community just shrugged and watched Laos sink back into the vortex of civil war. Unbeknown to the outside world, the conflict was rapidly degenerating into a war between the CIA and North Vietnamese jungle guerrillas.

The war that wasn't　With the Viet Minh denying the existence of the Ho Chi Minh Trail, while at the same time enlarging it, Kennedy dispatched an undercover force of CIA-men, Green Berets and US-trained Thai mercenaries to command 9,000 Lao soldiers. To the north, the US also supplied Vang Pao's force of 30,000 Hmong guerrillas, dubbed 'Mobile Strike Forces'. With the co-operation of Prince Souvanna Phouma, the CIA's commercial airline, Air America, ferried men and equipment into Laos from Thailand (and opium out). Owing to the clandestine nature of the military intervention in Laos, the rest of the world – believing that the Geneva settlement had solved the foreign interventionist problem – was oblivious as to what was happening on the ground. Right up until 1970, Washington never admitted to any activity in Laos beyond 'armed reconnaissance' flights over northern provinces. Richard Nixon, for example, claimed that "there are no American ground combat troops in Laos", which was stretching the truth to breaking point. Souvanna Phouma appropriately referred to it as 'the forgotten war' and it is often termed now the 'non-attributable war'. The willingness on the part of the Americans to dump millions of tonnes of ordnance on a country which was ostensibly neutral may have been made easier by the fact that some people in the administration did not believe Laos to be a country at all. Bernard Fall wrote that Laos at the time was "neither a geographical nor an ethnic or social entity, but merely a political convenience", while a Rand Corporation report written in 1970 described Laos as "hardly a country except in the legal sense". More colourfully, Secretary of State Dean Rusk described it as a "wart on the hog of Vietnam". Perhaps those in Washington could feel a touch better about bombing the hell out of a country which, in their view, occupied a sort of political never-never land – or which they could liken to an unfortunate skin complaint.

Not everyone agrees with this view that Laos never existed until the French wished it into existence. Scholar of Laos Arthur Dommen, for example, traces a true and coherent Lao identity back to Fa Ngoum and his creation of the kingdom of Lane Xang in 1353, writing that it was "a state in the true sense of the term, delineated by borders clearly defined and consecrated by treaty" for 3½ centuries. He goes on:

"Lao historians see a positive proof of the existence of a distinct Lao race (*sua sat Lao*), a Lao nation (*sat Lao*), a Lao country (*muong Lao*) and a Lao state (*pathet Lao*). In view of these facts, we may safely reject the notion, fashionable among apologists for a colonial enterprise of a later day, that Laos was a creation of French colonial policy and administration" (Dommen 1985:19).

Wars of the roses?

Post Second World War politics in Laos have been compared with the English Wars of the Roses: rival elements within one royal family, representing different political opinions, were backed by different foreign powers. By the early 1960s King Savang Vatthana was convinced that his centuries-old kingdom, now a pawn of conflicting superpower interests, was doomed to extinction. A speech made to the nation in 1961 reflects his despondency:

"Our country is the most peaceful in the world... At no time has there ever arisen in the minds of the Lao people the idea of coveting another's wealth, of quarrelling with their neighbours, much less of fighting them. And yet, during the past 20 years, our country has known neither peace nor security... Enemies of all sorts have tried to cross our frontiers, to destroy our people and to destroy our religion and our nation's aura of peace and concord... Foreign countries do not care either about our interests or peace; they are concerned only with their own interests."

American bombing of the North Vietnamese Army's supply lines through Laos to South Vietnam along the Ho Chi Minh Trail in East Laos (see page 205) started in 1964 and fuelled the conflict between the Royalist Vientiane government and the Pathet Lao. The neutralists had been forced into alliance with the Royalists to avoid defeat in Xieng Kouang province. US bombers crossed Laos on bombing runs to Hanoi from air bases in Thailand and gradually the war in Laos escalated. In his book *The Ravens* (1987), Christopher Robbins sets the scene:

"Apparently, there was another war even nastier than the one in Vietnam and so secret that the location of the country in which it was being fought was classified. The cognoscenti simply referred to it as 'the Other Theater'. The men who chose to fight in it were hand-picked volunteers and anyone accepted for a tour seemed to disappear as if from the face of the earth."

The secret war was conducted from a one-room shack at the US base in Udon Thani, 'across the fence' in Thailand. This was the CIA's Air America operations room and in the same compound was stationed the 4802 Joint Liaison Detachment – or the CIA logistics office. In Vientiane, US pilots supporting Hmong General Vang Pao's rag-tag army, were given a new identity as rangers for the US Agency for International Development; they reported directly to the air attaché at the US embassy. Robbins writes that they "were military men, but flew into battle in civilian clothes – denim cutoffs, T-shirts, cowboy hats and dark glasses ... Their job was to fly as the winged artillery of some fearsome warlord, who led an army of stone-age mercenaries in the pay of the CIA and they operated out of a secret city hidden in the mountains of a jungle kingdom ..." He adds that CIA station chiefs and field agents "behaved like warlords in their own private fiefdoms."

The most notorious of the CIA's unsavoury operatives was Anthony Posepny – known as Tony Poe, on whom the character of Kurtz, the crazy colonel played by Marlon Brando in the film *Apocalypse Now*, was based. Originally, Poe had worked as Vang Pao's case officer; he then moved to North Laos and operated for years, on his own, in Burmese and Chinese border territories, offering his tribal recruits one US dollar for each set of Communist ears they brought back. Many of the spies and pilots of this secret war have re-emerged in recent years in covert and illegal arms-smuggling rackets to Libya, Iran and the Nicaraguan Contras.

By contrast, the Royalist forces were reluctant warriors: despite the fact that civil war was a deeply ingrained tradition in Laos, the Lao themselves would go to great lengths to avoid fighting each other. One foreign journalist, reporting from Luang

Prabang in the latter stages of the war, related how Royalist and Pathet Lao troops, encamped on opposite banks of the Nam Ou, agreed an informal ceasefire over Pimay (Lao New Year), to jointly celebrate the king's annual visit to the sacred Pak Ou Caves, upstream from the royal capital (see page 131). Correspondents who covered the war noted that without the constant goading of their respective US and North Vietnamese masters, many Lao soldiers would have happily gone home. During the war, a US commander was quoted in a newspaper as saying that the Royalist troops were "without doubt the worst army I have ever seen", adding that they made the [poorly regarded] "South Vietnamese Army look like Storm Troopers".

Air Force planes were often used to carry passengers for money – or to smuggle opium out of the Golden Triangle. In the field, soldiers of the Royal Lao Army regularly fled when faced with a frontal assault by the Vietnam People's Army (NVA). The officer corps was uncommitted, lazy and corrupt; many ran opium-smuggling rackets and saw the war as a ticket to get rich quick. In the south, the Americans considered Royal Lao Air Force pilots unreliable because they were loath to bomb their own people and cultural heritage.

The air war The clandestine bombing of the Ho Chi Minh Trail (see page 205) caused many civilian casualties – so-called collateral damage – and displaced much of the population in Laos' eastern provinces. By 1973, when the bombing stopped, the US had dropped 2,093,100 tonnes of bombs on Laos – equivalent to 300 kg of explosives for every man, woman and child in the country. To pulverize the country to this degree 580,994 bombing sorties were flown. The bombing intensified during the Nixon administration: up to 1969 less than 500,000 tonnes of bombs had been dropped on Laos; from then on nearly that amount was dropped each year. In the 1960s and early 1970s, more bombs rained on Laos than were dropped during the Second World War – the equivalent of a plane load of bombs every eight minutes around the clock for nine years. This cost American taxpayers more than US$2 mn a day – but the cost to Laos was incalculable. The war was not restricted to bombing missions – once potential Pathet Lao strongholds had been identified, fighters, using rockets, were sent to attempt to destroy them. Such was the intensity of the bombing campaign that villagers in Pathet Lao controlled areas are said to have turned to planting and harvesting their rice at night. Few of those living in Xieng Khouang province, the Bolovens Plateau or along the Ho Chi Minh Trail had any idea of who was bombing them or why. The consequences were often tragic, as in the case of Tam Phiu Cave (see page 160).

In *The Ravens*, Robbins tells of how a fighter pilot's inauspicious dream would lead the commander to cancel a mission; bomber pilots hated dropping bombs and when they did, aluminium canisters were carefully brought back and sold as scrap. After the war, the collection and sale of war debris turned into a valuable scrap-metal industry for tribespeople in Xieng Khouang province and along the Ho Chi Minh Trail. Bomb casings, aircraft fuel tanks and other bits and pieces that were not sold to Thailand have been put to every conceivable use in rural Laos. They are used as cattle troughs, fence posts, flower pots, stilts for houses, water carriers, temple bells, knives and ploughs.

But the bombing campaign has also left a more deadly legacy – of unexploded bombs and anti-personnel mines. Today, over a quarter of a century after the air war ended, people are still dying and being maimed in the fields and forests of provinces like Xieng Khouang. The greatest irony of all, perhaps, is that most of Xieng Khouang was not even a military target – pilots would simply dump their ordnance so that they would not have to risk landing with their bomb bays packed with high explosive. Making farming in this part a Laos a highly dangerous occupation was simply one of those 'accidents' of war.

Within Laos the war largely focused on the strategic Plain of Jars, in Xieng Khouang province, and was co-ordinated from the town of Long Tieng (the secret city), tucked into the limestone hills to the southwest of the plain. Known as the most secret spot on earth, it was not marked on maps and was populated by the CIA, the Ravens (the air controllers who flew spotter planes and called in air strikes) and the Hmong.

Vietnam War

▶▶ **Raven FACs: a personal view**

Raven was the call sign used by Forward Air Controllers (FACs) in Laos. It came to designate, however, a special breed of FAC – someone who was highly motivated, aggressive, decisive, daring and exceptionally skilled and professional in his work. The mystique was heightened by the secrecy of the assignment. Pilots would leave Vietnam and seemingly disappear. This became clear when I read a personal advertisement in the Vietnam Veterans Newspaper requesting information about a Raven FAC I had known. When I called the person who placed the ad, he said that the last time he had seen the Major was at Bien Hoa. He said that he had not seen nor heard of him since. I told him that he had been 'undercover' in Laos.

The importance of the mission of the Raven is put in perspective by understanding first the mission of a FAC. Essentially, a FAC had three responsibilities: (1) to conduct air reconnaissance to obtain first-hand information concerning enemy locations, activity and threats; (2) to control and direct Air Force or Navy aircraft bombers or Army artillery on enemy targets; and (3) to control, direct and coordinate air strikes with ground troops for close air support.

The importance of the first responsibility was clearly demonstrated when I precluded an attack on Tuy Hoa by a North Vietnamese battalion. As a result of my daily flights over the mountains west of Tuy Hoa, I came upon a North Vietnamese battalion digging trench lines and bunkers, preparing for an assault on Tuy Hoa. In addition, I also observed trays of rice drying in the open down the side of the mountain and was thus able to pinpoint the enemy locations in the caves and bunkers nearby. As a result of these sightings, I declared a tactical emergency. That declaration resulted in an unlimited amount of air power being diverted for my use.

The FAC is in a position to have immediate information about troop movements and direct air power or artillery very effectively on the target. He is an on-scene commander with all the responsibilities and authority of that position. The FAC has the responsibility and right to over-rule even the orders of a general officer. I exercised that authority in Vietnam after I was assigned to Tuy Hoa.

The Pathet Lao were headquartered in caves in Sam Neua province, to the north of the plain. Their base was equipped with a hotel cave (for visiting dignitaries), a hospital cave and even a theatre cave.

The Plain of Jars (colloquially known as the PDJ, after the French Plaine de Jarres), was the scene of some of the heaviest fighting and changed hands countless times, the Royalist and Hmong forces occupying it during the wet season, the Pathet Lao in the dry. During this period in the conflict the town of Long Tien, known as one of the country's 'alternate' bases to keep nosy journalists away (the word 'alternate' was meant to indicate that it was unimportant), grew to such an extent that it became Laos' second city. James Parker in his book Codename Mule claims that the air base was so busy that at its peak it was handling more daily flights than Chicago's O'Hare airport. There was also fighting around Luang Prabang and the Bolovens Plateau to the south.

The end of the war Although the origins of the war in Laos were distinct from those which fuelled the conflict in Vietnam, the two wars had effectively merged by the early 1970s and it became inevitable that the fate of the Americans to the east would determine the outcome of the secret war on the other side of the Annamite Range. By 1970 it was no longer possible for the US administration to shroud the war in secrecy: a flood of Hmong refugees had arrived in Vientiane in an effort to escape the conflict.

Personnel had been spotted in the field by a commanding officer on a mountain top overlooking the valley. He was ready to open fire when I flew over and countermanded the order. In this case after the fact I realized that the artillery fire should have been carried out, as the people were in fact enemy. However, regardless of my lack of experience at the time, my order not to fire stopped the action of a field officer who was more experienced and of much higher rank.

But in time I gained the experience to differentiate clearly between 'friendlies' and the enemy. This ability was demonstrated when I directed air strikes on a 'friendly' outpost near Pakxong on the Bolovens Plateau. This time, when I spotted the troops, I knew they were enemy. However, after returning to Paksé, the CIA commander called me in and wanted to know why I had bombed one of his outposts. In fact, the outpost had been overrun, and after flying over the post at about 200 feet to confirm the identity of the troops, I did not hesitate to direct air strikes against it.

Whereas my error of judgement in Vietnam cost the life of one civilian who was killed following the infiltration of the town that evening by the troops I had saved from artillery fire, in Laos I saved the lives of many friendly troops.

Close air support was the most challenging of a FAC's responsibilities, since he had to maintain a continuing awareness of where the enemy was and where the friendlies were. In some situations, the FAC had to also consider the ordnance being delivered by the aircraft, and the reliability of the information being provided by the ground troops. In Vietnam I had to send an F-4 out to sea to drop its ordnance since the location of the friendly troops could not be clearly determined. In this case the ordnance was a 10,000 pound bomb. It was not quite appropriate for 'close air support' – especially when the location of the friendly troops was in doubt.

(This box was written by Ken Thompson, or Raven 58, who flew as a FAC in Vietnam and Laos over 26 months between 1968 and 1970. He was awarded two Distinguished Flying Crosses and a Bronze Star for valour.)

During the dying days of the US-backed regime in Vientiane, CIA agents and Ravens lived in quarters south of the capital, known as KM-6 – because it was 6 km from town. Another compound in downtown Vientiane was known as 'Silver City' and reputedly also sometimes housed CIA agents. On the departure of the Americans and the arrival of the new regime in 1975, the Communists' secret police made Silver City their new home. Today, Laotians still call military intelligence officers 'Silvers' – and from time to time during the early 1990s as Laos was opening up to international tourism, Silvers were even assigned as tour guides.

A ceasefire was agreed in February 1973, a month after Washington and Hanoi struck a similar deal in Paris. Power was transferred in April 1974 to yet another coalition government set up in Vientiane under the premiership of the ever-ready Souvanna Phouma. The neutralist prince once again had a Communist deputy and foreign affairs minister. The Red Prince, Souphanouvong, headed the Joint National Political Council. Foreign troops were given two months to leave the country. The North Vietnamese were allowed to remain along the Ho Chi Minh Trail, for although US forces had withdrawn from South Vietnam, the war there was not over.

The communists' final victories over Saigon (and Phnom Penh) in April 1975 were a catalyst for the Pathet Lao who advanced on the capital. As the end drew near and the Pathet Lao began to advance out of the mountains and towards the more populated areas of the Mekong valley – the heartland of the Royalist government – province after province fell with scarcely a shot being fired. The mere

▶▶ 'Over the fence' – with Raven

As a Raven Forward Air Controller (Raven FAC), I had the privilege of belonging to an élite group of pilots who flew covert operations in Laos in support of the Royal Lao Government. We would fly in support of the Royal Laotian Army or the CIA Special Guerrilla Units (SGUs).

SGUs were trained by CIA Country Team members. They were an élite fighting force designed to interdict movement of the North Vietnamese along the Ho Chi Minh Trail in the south or in areas around the Plain of Jars in the north. When they operated along the trail or in other forward locations, their supplies would be flown in by a Porter aircraft, piloted by Continental Air Service or Air America pilots. The advantage of this aircraft was that it could land and take off on a very short 'runway' – about 100 feet in length.

Normally, I would support the SGUs from the air, providing reconnaissance or fighter aircraft support. However, on one day they returned the favour. My airplane crashed in a rice paddy south of Attapeu. Nine North Vietnamese were across the paddy as I made a judicious move toward the opposite side. I knew that the SGUs were in the area near Attapeu, as I headed in that direction. As I came upon them, I recognized that they were friendly and shortly thereafter I was picked up by an Air America helicopter and flown to a nearby Lima Site (PS-38) for the night.

During the time of the Ravens, 1966 to 1975, there were only a total of 191 pilots. Very few Americans actually ever went into Laos – except along the Ho Chi Minh Trail. My time in Laos was quite enjoyable. Officially, I was a 'forest ranger' working for the Lao Government. In fact, I worked for the American Ambassador and was assigned to provide visual reconnaissance and direct air support for the Royal Laotian Army and the CIA SGUs.

And, there was much to discourage volunteers. The casualty rate was said to be 50%. The conditions were more harsh. And, then there were the drug dealers and gold dealers. (At that time it was illegal to trade in gold in the United States. One could only buy 'jewellery'. For that reason, contracted CIA pilots from Air America and Continental Air Service would be seen wearing heavy gold bracelets which were not much more than gold bars formed into a bracelet.)

But, I had volunteered to join the Air Force for the specific purpose of going to Vietnam and Laos. I had been a student at Ohio State University and was exempt from the draft. I was 26 years old when I joined the Air Force – just under the 26.5 age limit required of Air Force pilots. Having never flown before in my life I became a '90-day Wonder' as I received my commission as a second Lieutenant at Lackland Air Force Base in San Antonio, Texas. From Lackland I went to Laredo, Texas for Undergraduate Pilot Training. I completed my training in 1968, followed

arrival of a small contingent of Pathet Lao soldiers was sufficient to secure victory – though these soldier arrived at Wattay Airport on Chinese transport planes to be greeted by representatives of the Royal Lao government. It is even possible that they were not even armed. Nonetheless, rightist ministers, ranking civil servants, doctors, much of the intelligentsia and around 30,000 Hmong crossed the Mekong and escaped into Thailand, fearing that they would face persecution from the Pathet Lao. Many lived for years in squalid refugee camps, although the better connected and those with skills to sell secured US, Australian and French passports. For Laos, a large proportion of its human capital drained westwards, creating a vacuum of skilled personnel that would hamper – and still does – efforts at reconstruction and development. But while many people fled across the Mekong, a significant number who had aligned themselves with the Royalists decided to stay and help build a new Laos. They saw themselves as Lao patriots and their patriotic duty was to stay.

by 0-1 (Bird Dog) Special Operations Training, POW training and then on to the Philippines for Jungle Survival Training.

In Vietnam I was stationed at the Tuy Hoa MACV (Military Assistance Command Vietnam) compound where I flew in support of the Vietnamese Army. I volunteered for the Steve Canyon Program soon after arriving at Tuy Hoa. The Steve Canyon Program was named after 'Steve Canyon' – the flamboyant adventurist comic strip character. As I departed Bien Hoa Air Force Base near Saigon for Laos, I learned why it was called 'Steve Canyon'. The colonel who drove me to the airplane which would take me to my first stop in Thailand said: "Well, now all you have to look forward to is ... glory, money and medals!"

Ravens were a breed apart. They would wear what they wanted when flying – shorts and T-shirts, home-made flying suits or cowboy outfits. They would disregard the Air Force standards for flying time and clock as much as 150 to 200 hours a month.

The monetary rewards were appealing. While not the income a true 'mercenary' might receive – for example, US$50,000 or US$100,000 for flying certain cargo in Southeast Asia or the Middle East – the extra per diem income, free in addition to being paid for board and room, maids and cooks, and combat pay, was welcome. It could amount to an extra US$1,000 per month.

Arriving at Udon Air Force Base in Northeast Thailand, I was directed to a remote area of the base called 'Det-1'. The commander did not know much about what I would be doing, but he was responsible for maintaining my Air Force records, since when I went into Laos, I would be a 'civilian'. Flying into Laos was quite different from flying into other countries. To protect my destination, when I crossed the border I would radio: "Raven 58, crossing the fence." 'Laos' would never be mentioned.

Along with the AOC (Air Operations Center) commander, a radio operator, two airplane mechanics and a medic, I lived in the town of Pakse, in a large colonial villa. The living conditions were excellent. After flying out into the war zone each day and returning, I would go down town to a movie or to the Mekong Bar for dancing and music, or to an inviting sidewalk café for dinner.

I believed that the Lao knew who I was. But, I found out that many did not. While trying to make a call to Vietnam to speak with my future Vietnamese wife, Kim Chi, a new Air Force Lieutenant received the call and became inquisitive as to why I referred to myself as "Mister Thompson" rather than "Captain". Even military personnel in Vietnam, including Air Force Forward Air Controllers, did not know about the clandestine operations of the Ravens.

Source: Ken Thompson. See end of previous box for details.

Administration of Vientiane by the People's Revolutionary Committee was secured on 18 August. The atmosphere was very different from that which accompanied the Communist's occupation of Saigon in Vietnam the same year. In Vientiane peaceful crowds of several hundred thousand turned out to hear speeches by Pathet Lao cadres. The King remained unharmed in his palace and while a coffin representing 'dead American imperialism' was ceremonially burned this was done in a 'carnival' atmosphere. Vientiane was declared 'officially liberated' on 23 August 1975. The coalition government was dismissed and Souvanna Phouma resigned for the last time. All communications with the outside world were cut.

While August 1975 represents a watershed in the history of Laos, scholars are left with something of a problem: explaining why the Pathet Lao prevailed. According to Martin Stuart-Fox, the Lao revolutionary movement "had not mobilized an exploited peasantry with promises of land reform, for most of the country was under-populated and peasant families generally owned sufficient land for their subsistence needs. The appeal of the Pathet Lao to their lowland Lao compatriots was in terms of nationalism and independence and the preservation of Lao culture from the corrosive American influence; but no urban uprising occurred until the very last minute when effective government had virtually ceased to exist... The small Lao intelligentsia, though critical of the Royal Lao government, did not desert it entirely and their recruitment to the Pathet Lao was minimal. Neither the monarchy, still less Buddhism, lost legitimacy." (Stuart-Fox 1997: 164).

Stuart-Fox concludes that it was external factors, and in particular the intervention of outside powers, which led to the victory of the Pathet Lao. Without the Vietnamese and Americans the Pathet Lao, he hazards, would not have won. For the great mass of Laos' population before 1975, Communism meant nothing. This was not a mass uprising but a victory secured by a small ideologically committed élite and forged in the furnace of the war in Indochina.

Laos under communism

The People's Democratic Republic of Laos was proclaimed in December 1975 with Prince Souphanouvong as President and Kaysone Phomvihane as Secretary-General of the Lao People's Revolutionary Party (a post he had held since its formation in 1955). The king's abdication was accepted and the ancient Lao monarchy was abolished, together with King Samsenthai's 600-year-old system of village autonomy. But instead of executing their vanquished foes, the LPRP installed Souvanna and the ex-king, Savang Vatthana, as 'special advisers' to the politburo. On Souvanna's death in 1984, he was accorded a full state funeral. The king did not fare so well: he later died ignominiously while in detention after his alleged involvement in a counter-revolutionary plot (see below).

Surprisingly, the first actions of the new revolutionary government was not to build a new revolutionary economy and society, but to stamp out unsavoury behaviour. Dress and hairstyles, dancing and singing, even the food that was served at family celebrations, was all subject to rigorous scrutiny by so-called 'Investigation Cadres'. If the person(s) concerned were found not to match up to the Party's scrupulous standards of good taste they were bundled off to re-education camps.

Relations with Thailand, which in the immediate wake of the revolution remained cordial, deteriorated in late 1976. A military coup in Bangkok led to rumours that the Thai military, backed by the CIA, was supporting Hmong and other right-wing Lao rebels. The regime feared that Thailand would be used as a spring-board for a royalist coup attempt by exiled reactionaries. This prompted the arrest of King Savang Vatthana, together with his family and Crown Prince Vongsavang, who were all dispatched to a Seminar re-education camp in Sam Neua province. They were never heard of again. In December 1989 Kaysone Phomvihane admitted in Paris, for the first time, that the king had died of malaria in 1984 and that the queen had also died "of natural causes" – no mention was made of Vongsavang. The Lao people have still to be officially informed of his demise. (Some commentators – like Christopher Kremmer in his book *Stalking the Elephant Kings* published in 1997 – have used the incarceration of the King to mount a stinging critique of the current regime in Vientiane. However he does not adequately acknowledge the issue of the king's implication in a right-wing, counter-revolutionary plot.)

Re-education camps   Between 30,000 and 40,000 reactionaries who had been unable to flee the country were interned in remote, disease-ridden camps for 're-education'. The reluctant scholars were forced into slave labour in squalid jungle conditions and subjected to incessant political propaganda. Old men, released back into society after more than

15 years of 're-education' were cowed and subdued, although some were prepared to talk in paranoid whispers about their grim experiences in Xam Neua.

In 1986 Amnesty International released a report on the forgotten inhabitants of the re-education camps, claiming that 6,000-7,000 were still held. By that time incarceration behind barbed wire had ended and instead those held were 'arbitrarily restricted' rather than imprisoned. They were assigned to road construction teams and other public works projects. Nonetheless, conditions for these victims of the war in Indochina suffered from malnutrition, disease and many died prematurely in captivity. It is unclear how many died, but at least 15,000 have been freed. Officials of the old regime, ex-government ministers and former Royalist air force and army officers, together with thousands of others unlucky enough to have been on the wrong side, were released from the camps, largely during the mid to late 1980s. Most of the surviving political prisoners have now been reintegrated into society.Some work in the tourism industry and one, a former colonel in the Royal Lao Army, jointly owns the *Asian Pavilion Hotel* (formerly the *Vieng Vilai*) on Samsenthai Road in downtown Vientiane. After years of being force-fed Communist propaganda he now enjoys full government support as an ardent capitalist entrepreneur. The Lao, as scores of books like this one keep reminding their readers, are a gentle people and it is hard not to leave the country without that view being reinforced. Even the Lao People's Revolutionary Party seems quaintly inept and it is hard to equate it with its more brutal and sinister sister parties in Vietnam, China or the former Soviet Union. Yet five students who meekly called for greater political freedom in 1999 were whisked off by the police and have not been heard of since. So much for soggy ineptness.

Laos' recent political and economic history is covered in more detail under Modern Laos (see page 265). But, it is worth ending this short account of the country's history by noting the brevity of Laos' experiment with full-blown Communism. Just 10 years after the Pathet Lao took control of Vientiane, the leadership were on the brink of far-reaching economic reforms. By the mid-1980s it was widely acknowledged that Marxism-Leninism had failed the country and its people. The population were still dreadfully poor; the ideology of Communism had failed to entice more than a handful into serious and enthusiastic support for the party and its ways; and graft and nepotism were on the rise.

Reflecting on 10 years of 'reconstruction' — Background

A total of 300,000 Lao – 10% of the population and mostly middle class – fled the country's increasingly totalitarian regime between 1973 and 1975. From 1988, these refugees began to head back across the Mekong from camps in Thailand and to asylum in the US and France. More than 2,000 refugees were also repatriated from Yunnan Province in China. For those prepared to return from exile overseas, the government offered to give them back confiscated property so long as they stay at least six months and become Lao citizens once again. Thailand's Lao refugee camps are now part of history. One of the best accounts of this period is Lynellyn D. Long's *Ban Vinai: the Refugee Camp*. As a Jesuit priest who worked at the camp explained to the author: "Before they [came to the camps the refugees] had a life revolving around the seasons ... Here they cannot really work ... Here people make only dreams."

The refugee camps

Modern Laos

Politics

Laos underwent the political equivalent of an earth tremor in March 1991 at the Fifth Congress of the Lao People's Revolutionary Party (LPRP). Pro-market reforms were embraced and the politburo and central committee got a much-needed transfusion of new blood. At the same time, the hammer and sickle motif was quietly removed from the state emblem and enlightened sub-editors set to work on the national credo, which is emblazoned on all official documents.

This shift in economic policy and ideology can be traced back to the Party Congress of 1986, making Laos one of the very first countries to embrace 'perestroika'. As late General Secretary Kaysone Phomvihane stated at the Fourth Party Congress in 1986:

"In all economic activities, we must know how to apply objective laws and take into account socio-economic efficiency. At the present time, our country is still at the first stage of the transition period. Hence the system of economic laws now being applied to our country is very complicated. It includes not only the specific laws of socialism but also the laws of commodity production. Reality indicates that if we only apply the specific economic laws of socialism alone and defy the general laws pertaining to commodity production, or vice versa, we will make serious mistakes in our economic undertaking during this transition period" (General Secretary Kaysone Phomvihane, Fouth Party Congress 1986; quoted in Lao PDR 1989:9).

Under the horrified gaze of Marx and Lenin – their portraits still dominate the plenary hall – it was announced that the state motto had changed from "Peace, Independence, Unity and Socialism" to "Peace, Independence, Democracy, Unity and Prosperity". The last part is largely wishful thinking for the poorest country in Southeast Asia, but it reflected the realization that unless Laos turned off the socialist road fast, it would have had great difficulty digging itself out of the economic quagmire that 15 years' adherence to Marxism had created. In August 1991, at the opening of the People's Supreme Assembly, Kaysone Phomvihane, the late President, said: "Socialism is still our objective, but it is a distant one. Very distant." With that statement, Kaysone embraced – somewhat reluctantly, it must be said – the country's market-orientated policy known as *Chin Thanakan Mai* or 'New Thinking'.

President Kaysone Phomvihane died in November 1992, aged 71. (His right hand man, Prince Souphanouvong – the so-called Red Prince – died just over two years later on 9 January 1995.) As one obituary put it, Kaysone was older than he seemed, both historically and ideologically. He had been chairman of the LPRP since the mid-1950s and had been a prodigé and comrade of Ho Chi Minh, who led the Vietnamese struggle for independence from the French. After leading the Lao Resistance Government – or Pathet Lao – from caves in Sam Neua province in the north, Kaysone assumed the premiership on the abolition of the monarchy in 1975. But under his leadership – and following the example of his mentors in Hanoi – Kaysone became the driving force behind the market-orientated reforms. The year before he died, he gave up the post of Prime Minister for that of President.

His death didn't change things much, as other members of the old guard stepped into the breach. Nouhak Phounsavanh – a sprightly 78-year-old former truck driver and hardline Communist – succeeded him as President. Nouhak didn't last terribly long in the position and in February 1998 he was replaced by 75 year-old General Khamtai Siphandon – the outgoing Prime Minister and head of the LPRP. Khamtai represents the last of the revolutionary Pathet Lao leaders who fought the Royalists and the Americans.

With the introduction of the New Economic Mechanism in 1986 so there were hopes, in some quarters at least, that economic liberalization would be matched by political *glasnost*. So far, however, the monolithic Party shows few signs of equating capitalism with democracy. While the Lao brand of Communism has always been seen as relatively tame, it remains a far cry from political pluralism. Laos' first constitution since the Communists came to power in 1975, was approved in 1991. The country's political system is referred to as a 'popular democracy', yet it has rejected any significant moves towards multi-party reforms.

The Golden Triangle – the Lao connection

Since 1990, attempts have been made to combat the production and trafficking of illicit drugs – sizeable industries in Laos and one in which its mountain tribespeople excel. They contribute to the Golden Triangle's hard drugs output, providing at least 60% of the world's heroin supply. Laos is the third largest producer of opium after Burma and Afghanistan. The opium trade was legal in Laos until US pressure forced the government to outlaw it in 1971. The French quietly bought and sold the Hmong opium crop to finance their war efforts against Vietnam's Communists and the Americans turned a blind eye to the trade and allegedly fostered it too. During the 1960s, the drugs trade was run by a handful of high-ranking Royalist officers who became very rich.

Today, in Laos' northern provinces, the opium addiction rate of 50% in some villages is more than twice the literacy rate, and until recenly small parakeets (sachets) of opium have become an unofficial currency.

In October 1990, following accusations from the US State Department that the Lao government and military authorities were actively involved in the narcotics trade network, Laos agreed to co-operate with the US in narcotics control and US aid is providing US$20m to substitute cash crops – such as sesame, coffee and mulberry trees (for silk) – for Papaver somnifera (opium poppies) in the mountainous northeastern Houa Phanh province. By signing up for the war against drugs, Laos opened its empty coffers to a welcome flow of funds. Seizures of raw opium and heroin increased and opium confiscated from traffickers was ceremonially burned. Traffickers also began being convicted in the Lao courts.

Take the elections to the 108-seat National Assembly on 24 February 2002. All of the candidates standing for election had been approved by the LPRP's mass organization, the Lao Front for National Construction. While it is not necessary for a candidate to be a member of the LPRP to stand, they are closely vetted and have to demonstrate that they have a 'sufficient level of knowledge of party policy'. As with the previous elections to the National Assembly at the end of 1997, only one of the 108 deputies elected was not a member of the Lao People's Revolutionary Party. Who was this sole, brave symbol of political pluralism? The minister of justice. When President Khamtay Siphandone turned up to cast his ballot (voting is compulsory), one journalist asked him what the election would change. His answer: "There won't be any change."

On the dreamy streets of Vientiane, the chances of a Tiananmen-style uprising are remote. But the events of the late 1980s and early 1990s in Eastern Europe and Moscow did alarm hardliners – just as they did in Beijing and Hanoi. They can be reasonably confident, however, that in their impoverished nation, most people are more worried about where their next meal is going to come from than they are about the allure of multi-party democracy. Nonetheless when students or others are tempted to suggest that there might be another way they are swiftly rounded-up and disappear.

The greatest concern for the Lao leadership (and in this sense the country mirrors developments in many other countries of Asia) is what effect 'westernization' is having upon the population. The economic reforms, or so the authorities would seem to believe, have brought not only foreign investment and new consumer goods, but also greed, corruption, consumerism and various social ills from drugs to prostitution. This was starkly illustrated at the March 1996 party congress. Observers were expecting to find the congress reaffirm the policy of economic reform and rubber stamp it 'business as usual'. Instead one of the architects of the reform programme,

Background

Deputy Prime Minister Khamphoui Keoboualapha, was unceremoniously dumped. The reason? It was thought that he had become too close to Thailand and in particular to influential Thai investors. He was blamed more than most for the emergence of the various social ills that the leadership have been so desperate to stem. Khamphoui was rehabilitated in a leadership reshuffle in February 1998 but this was probably because the leadership reasoned that they needed people with some knowledge of economic policy to see the country through the Asian crisis. It would be surprising if the process of economic reform was reversed – although it will probably slow down from time to time reflecting domestic developments and concerns – largely because there is simply no alternative.

Foreign relations From the 1980s the government took steps to improve its foreign relations – and Thailand has been the main beneficiary. Historically, Thailand has always been the main route for international access to landlocked Laos. Survival instincts told the Vientiane regime that reopening its front door was of paramount importance. The 1990s began with an unprecedented visit by a member of the Thai royal family, Crown Princess Sirindhorn, and in 1994 the Friendship Bridge officially opened (see page 70) linking Laos and Thailand. The border disputes with Thailand have now been settled and the bloody clashes of 1987/88, when thousands on both sides lost their lives, are history. Thailand is Laos' largest investor and the success of the market reforms depend more on Thailand than any other country (but see

Provinces & provincial capitals

○ **Provinces**

1 Phongsali	10 Préfecture de Vientiane
2 Luang Namtha	11 Xieng Khouang
3 Bokeo	12 Bolikhamxai
4 Oudomxai	13 Khammouane
5 Luang Prabang	14 Savannakhet
6 Houa Phan	15 Salavan
7 Sayaboury	16 Sekong
8 Vientiane	17 Champassak
9 Xaysomboon	18 Attapeu

Development and underdevelopment ◀◀

	Laos	UK	USA
GDP (billions	1.7	1,415	9,837
GDP/capita (PPP$, 2000)	1,575	23,509	34,142
Life expectancy at birth (years)	53.5	77.7	77.0
Adult literacy rate (%)	48.7	99	99
Underweight children under 5 (%)	40	-	-
Total fertility rate (1995-2000)	5.3	1.7	2.0
Annual population growth	2.2	0.2	1.0
Doctors/100,000 population	1.2	164	279
Infant mortality/1,000 live births	90	6	7
Probability at birth of males living to 65 (%)	44.9	81.5	77.4
Probability at birth of females living to 65 (%)	50.0	88.3	85.7
Telephone mainlines per 1,000 population	8	589	700
CO2 emissions per capita (tonnes)	0.1	9.2	19.9

Source: Human Development Report 2002 (UNDP).

below on the economic crisis). Economic pragmatism, then, has forced the leadership in Vientiane to cosy up to Bangkok. This does not mean that relations are warm. Indeed, Vientiane is irredeemably suspicious of Thai intentions, a suspicion born of a history of conflict. This is nicely reflected in a tiff between the two countries in 2001 over a Thai film depicting Lao king Chao Anou in a less than favourable light (see box on page 279).

Laos is rapidly becoming a 'keystone' in mainland Southeast Asia (see Economy below) and sees its future in linking in with its more powerful and richer neighbours. To this end Laos joined the Association of Southeast Asian Nations (ASEAN) on 23 July 1997, becoming the group's second Communist member (Vietnam joined in July 1995). By joining, Vientiane is hoping to be in a better position to trade off the interests of the various powers in the region, thereby giving it greater room for manoeuvre. It was also hoped that tiny Laos would be able to develop on the economic coat tails of Southeast Asia's fast-growing economic 'tigers' – a hope rudely dashed by the region's economic crisis which began with the collapse of the Thai baht on 3 July 1997.

Relations have also thawed with China. Laos and China set up a bilateral trade agreement some years ago and this was followed by a defence co-operation agreement signed in 1993. The Chinese are now important suppliers of military hardware to the Lao. This has caused some worries in Vietnam, which shares a 1,300 km-long border with Laos and historically has had poor relations with China. As the old men of the Lao Communist Party, who owed so much to the Vietnamese, die off so their replacements are looking elsewhere for investment and political support. They do not have such deep fraternal links with their brothers in Hanoi and are keen to diversify their international relations.

Laos is also the only country in Indochina to have maintained relations with the US since 1975 – despite the fact that they never offered reparations or aid to the country. Washington even expected the Lao government to allocate funds to help locate the bodies of US pilots shot down in the war. When Vientiane pledged to co-operate with the US over the narcotics trade during Foreign Affairs Minister General Phoune Sipaseuth's meeting with US Secretary of State James Baker in October 1990, it agreed to step up the search for the 530 American MIAs still listed as missing in the Lao jungle. In mid-1993, tri-lateral talks between Laos, Vietnam and the US allowed for greater cooperation in the search for MIAs. Many of the unaccounted-for servicemen are thought to have been airmen, shot down over the Ho Chi Minh Trail which ran through Lao territory along the border with Vietnam. The MIA charity, based in Vientiane, has assumed quite a high profile and, in the absence of other US aid organizations, has become a major conduit for humanitarian assistance to the Lao government. In October 1992, America's diplomatic presence in Laos was upgraded to ambassadorial status from chargé d'affaires and at the end of 1997 a high-level US mission to Laos promised greater support in the country's bomb-defusing work. The US continues to provide technical and other assistance to Laos as the government tries to sort out this long-term legacy of the war. There was even talk of granting Laos Most Favoured Nation trading status. But, unwilling to put all its eggs in one basket, Vientiane has also courted smaller western countries, particularly Sweden (a long time friend), France, Germany and Australia.

Japan is now Laos' biggest aid donor, although Australia and Sweden are also very significant contributors. These days Washington and Tokyo offer more in the way of hope for the embattled regime than Moscow: in 1991, 100 Soviet economic and technical advisers were pulled out of the dilapidated flats they occupied on the outskirts of Vientiane and with their withdrawal from the country came the end of the era of Soviet aid. While Russia gave Vientiane some leeway before it had to pay back its rouble debt, the country's former lifeline with Moscow has become of scant importance to Laos' economic future.

As Laos turned to the West, Japan and Thailand for economic help, the government became more critical of its closest Communist ally, Vietnam. Following Vietnam's invasion of Cambodia in December 1978, thousands of Vietnamese moved into northern Laos as permanent colonizers and by 1978 there were an estimated 40,000 Vietnamese regulars in Laos. In 1987, 50,000 Vietnamese troops withdrew. With the death of President Kaysone Phomvihane in November 1992, another historical link with Vietnam was cut. He was half-Vietnamese and most of his cabinet owed their education and their posts to Hanoi's succour during the war years. In 1990 a Vientiane census found 15,000 Vietnamese living illegally in the capital, most of whom were promptly deported.

Laos is the only landlocked country in Southeast Asia and Vientiane is keen to pursue a cooperative 'equilibrium policy' with its neighbours. There is a widely held view that Laos – a small, poor, weak and land-locked country – is best served by having multiple friends in international circles. The leadership in Vientiane are in the tricky situation of having to play off China's military might, Thailand's commercial aggressiveness and Vietnam's population pressures, while keeping everyone happy. The answer, in many people's minds, is to promote a policy of inter-dependence in mainland Southeast Asia. In 1993 a western diplomat quoted by the French newspaper *Le Monde* said: "This country's only hope is to become, within the next 10 or 20 years, a bridge between its powerful neighbours, while at the same time managing to avoid being engulfed by either of them". That is proving to be no easy matter.

Economy

Until just a few years ago, if the world's financial markets crashed and international trade and commerce collapsed overnight, Laos would have been blissfully immune from the catastrophe. It would be 'farming as usual' the next morning. Since the mid-1980s, though, the government has gradually begun cautiously to tread the free-market path, veering off the old command system. Farms have been privatized and the state has to compete for produce with market traders at market prices. Many of the unprofitable state-owned businesses and factories have been leased or sold-off.

The logic for economic reform (about which, more below) and the integration of Laos into the regional – and world – economies was pretty compelling. During the decade of command planning from 1975 through to 1985 the economy grew at just 2.9% per year, barely sufficient to meet the needs of a growing population and not enough to fuel the desire for a better standard of living. The government's fear was that, like other communist countries, the failure to bring the Lao people a better standard of living might challenge the supremacy of the Lao People's Revolutionary Party. The decision to opt for reform seemed to be borne out as the economy picked up steam. During the early years of reform, between 1986 and 1990, the economy grew at 4.8% per year and from 1991-1995 increased again to 6.5% per year. However recent events have emphasized that economic liberalization also has its risks. The collapse of the Thai baht at the beginning of July 1997 also dragged down the Lao kip while Thailand's fall from economic grace caused Thai investment in Laos to evaporate (Thailand is Laos' largest foreign investor). 1998 saw zero growth and inflation escalated to nearly 100% as the government rather ineptly tried to control events. Economic nationalists who had remained quiet during the reformist years of the early and mid-1990s found their voice and began to highlight the dangers of over-zealous reform. Since then the economy has stabilized and in 2000 the government reported economic growth of 6-6½%. However many independent observers find this hard to believe and instead estimate that growth was probably in the range 2-3%. For a country where the population is expanding at about 2-3% too this speed of economic expansion is not going to lift many people out of poverty.

The country's greatest economic potential lies in its natural resources – timber, gold, precious stones, coal and iron – and hydro-power. It has been estimated that only 1% of the country's hydo-power potential of some 18,000 MW has so far been exploited and myriad schemes are being discussed (see below). Malaysian, Taiwanese, Chinese and Thai firms have been awarded timber concessions in the country, many of them working in collaboration with the Lao army which has become an important economic player. (Strict reafforestation commitments were written into the contracts although there are grave doubts about how far the agreements are honoured.)

But though Laos has embarked on a path of economic reform (notwithstanding current debates) and has, since the mid-1980s, attracted large sums (for it) of foreign investment, there is no getting away from the fact that Laos is still – in economic terms – an extraordinarily poor place. In 1995 the government published its first ever survey of consumption and expenditure, undertaken with the help of the UNDP. It showed what most people already knew: that people don't have much surplus income. On average, the survey showed, 62% of household income is spent on food. The survey also showed that Laos does not have the deep disparities that are so painfully visible in neighbouring countries like Thailand (but see Emerging inequalities below). Although two-thirds of households may be 'poor', two-thirds also have an income that lies within 50% of the median. Laos, then, is a fine example of 'shared poverty' – we are poor, but at least we are all poor.

A second expenditure and consumption survey (the so-called LECS II) was undertaken in 1997-98 and, in 2001, a participatory poverty assessment was published. These studies showed a number of worrying trends. First, a widening in spatial inequalities as some regions surge ahead and others get left in the economic doldrums. And second, a widening of inter-personal inequality as some individuals and households do very well out of the economic reforms, and others lag behind. The government is concerned that as the country 'embraces the market' it should not create a population of haves and have nots. The last lines of a World Bank analysis of the LECS II data concludes that a "key challenge facing policymakers developing a poverty reduction strategy for Laos will be to design policies that promote economic growth while keeping inequality in check." (World Bank 2001: 26).

▶▶ Landmarks of economic reform

1975   *December: full and final victory of the communist Pathet Lao.*

1982   *Reforms first touted.*

1985   *Pilot studies of financial autonomy in selected state-run industries.*

1986   *Decentralization of decision-making to the provinces including provincial tax administration. Freeing-up the market in rice and other staples.*
          November: *NEM endorsed by the Party Congress.*

1987   *Restrictions on the cross-provincial movement of agricultural produce abolished; barriers to external trade reduced.*
          June: *prices of most essentials market-determined.*

1988   *Forced procurement of strategic goods at below market price abolished; reduction in public sector employment; tax reforms introduced; private sector involvement in sectors previously reversed as state monopolies permitted; introduction of new investment law.*
          March: *prices of fuel, cement, machinery and vehicles freed; tax reforms enacted; state and commercial banking sectors separated; state enterprises made self-reliant and autonomous; explicit recognition of the rights of households and the private sector to use land and private property.*
          June: *nationwide elections held for 2,410 positions at the district level.*
          July: *multiple exchange rates abolished; liberal foreign investment code introduced;*
          payment of wages in kind abolished.

1989   ***June:*** *second tax reform enacted.*
          October: *first joint venture bank with a foreign bank begins operation, the JointDevelopment Bank.*

1990   ***March:*** *privatization ('disengagement') law introduced.*
          June: *key economic laws covering contracts, property, banking and inheritance discussed by National Assembly.*
          July: *State Bank (Central Bank) of the Lao PDR established and fiscal management of the economy formally handed over to the new bank.*

1992   *Thai Military Bank begins operating a full branch in Vientiane.*
          January: *Commercial Bank and Financial Institutions Act introduced.*

1993   *Accelerated privatization programme announced.*
          December: *removal of last quantitative restrictions and licensing requirements for imports.*

1994   ***March:*** *new investment and labour laws passed in March by the National Assembly, to be enforced within 60 days. As an incentive to foreign investors, the investment law lowers some import taxes and the tax on net profit, streamlines the approval process, and ends the foreign investment period limit of 15 years.*

1997   *Government tries to control currency transactions in the wake of Thailand's economic collapse*
          April: *new land law introduced authorising transfer of land titles to relatives and use as collateral in obtaining bank loans.*
          July: *Laos joins the Association of Southeast Asian Nations*

2000   *Direct foreign investment approvals decline from a peak of US$2.6 bn in 1995 to just US$20 mn in 2000.*

Sources: Rigg, Jonathan (1997) Southeast Asia: the human landscape of modernization and development, *London: Routledge, and other sources.*

Laos made the jump from a sleepy agrarian economy hidden behind a façade of socialism to a reforming economy like China and Vietnam's in the 1980s. In English this change is rather blandly named the New Economic Mechanism (NEM). Locally, the more evocative terms *chin thanakaan mai* ('new thinking') and *kanpatihup setthakit* (the 'reform economy') are used. The origins of the NEM can be traced back to 1982 when the possibility of fundamental reform of the economy was first entertained by a small group within the leadership. For the next three or four years the debate continued within this small circle and it was not until 1985 that the NEM was actually pilot-tested in the Vientiane area. The success of the reforms there led to the NEM being presented at – and adopted by – the critical Fourth Party Congress of 1986. The NEM encompasses a range of reformist policies, much like those adopted in other countries from Russia to Vietnam: a move to a market determination of prices and resource allocation; a shift away from central planning to 'guidance' planning; a decentralization of control to industries and lower levels of government and the encouragement of the private sector; the encouragement of foreign investment and the promulgation of a new investment law allowing 100% foreign ownership; a lifting of barriers to internal and external trade.

Former President Kaysone Phomvihane shouldered much of the blame for the miserable state of the economy, admitting that the Party had made mistakes. At the Congress in 1991 he set the new national agenda: Laos had to step up its exports, encourage more foreign investment, promote tourism and rural development, entice its shifting cultivators into proper jobs and revamp the financial system. In doing so he prioritized the problems but offered no solutions bar the loosening of state control and the promotion of private enterprise.

The first task for the government was to stabilize the value of the local currency, the kip and introduce market 'discipline' so as to eliminate a booming currency black market. So from 1986, when economic reforms were first introduced, Laos eliminated six of its seven official exchange rates to create a unified market-related rate. By the early 1990s the kip had stabilized at around 700 to the US$. The once-booming black market all but disappeared. Although still a non-convertible currency, the kip was as much in demand in Laos as the US dollar and Thai baht. This helped put Laos on a more commercially competitive footing. Unfortunately for supporters of economic reform, the collapse of the Thai baht and the consequent fall in the value of the kip encouraged the Lao government to reintroduce currency controls (see Reform in a period of economic crisis, page 277).

What Laos was able to achieve by introducing the NEM was a very rapid reorientation of its economy. But the question to be asked is: 'what exactly was being reformed?' The assumption is that Laos, as a so-called transitional economy, was making – is making – the transition from communism to capitalism, from state to market. This, though, misses the point that in 1986 there was remarkably little in Laos to reform. The great majority of the population were poor farmers (and they still are, around 85%) and the country's industrial base was almost non-existent. There were almost no communes to break up; and there was no large state industrial sector to dismember. It all meant that the task of the Lao leadership has been comparatively easy when compared with, say, Vietnam. In a sense, Laos was never socialist except in name and so the shift to a market economy involved not a move from socialism to capitalism, but from subsistence to capitalism.

This doesn't mean that reform has been a doddle, because although Laos may not have had to undo years of socialist reconstruction and development, there was also little that the leadership could build on to promote modernization. There are few skilled workers, there is a great dearth of engineers and graduates, the stock of roads is woefully thin, large slices of the country are almost impossible to reach, there is little domestic demand to fuel industrialization, there are few entrepreneurs and there are even fewer people with the money to invest in new ventures. In other words, Laos is short of most of the elements that constitute a modern economy and most of the people that make it tick.

Agriculture Rice is the staple food crop, cultivated by 75% of the population, and nearly three-quarters of Laos' farmers grow enough to sell or barter some of their crop. Output has more than doubled since 1980 and the country now produces 2.2 million tonnes of rice a year from 690,000 ha of paddy land. Moreover, the Fifth Five-Year Development Plan (2001-2005) states that rice production remains 'the most fundamental issue' for the country.

While Laos may be land rich, this does not mean that everyone necessarily has enough to eat, and the achievement of food security is one of the government's priority objectives. Nationally the Lao PDR has achieved food self-sufficiency but at the regional, and more important village and intra-village levels, national self-sufficiency does not equate with local food security. For the country as a whole around 40% of the population are undernourished. At a crude regional level, the north is in rice deficit, the centre is self-sufficient, and the south is in rice surplus. But this masks considerable intra-regional variation. For example, Sekong, in the south, is traditionally a rice deficit province, as is Xieng Khouang in the centre. As we move down the scale levels from national to regional, provincial, district and village there are likely to be important variations in terms of food security. Even households that are in production surplus may face a consumption deficit due to their having to sell a portion of production to meet demands for cash or to pay off debts.

The main agricultural areas are on the Mekong's floodplains, especially around Vientiane and Savannakhet. The government has been successful in expanding the area capable of producing two rice crops a year by upgrading and developing the country's irrigation infrastructure. Cotton, coffee, maize and tobacco are the other main crops and the production of these and other 'industrial' crops such as soya and mung beans has increased in recent years. On the Bolovens Plateau in the south, rice, coffee and cardamom – 500 tonnes of the latter is produced a year – are grown. Fisheries and livestock resources are being developed – the cattle population has risen from 446,900 head in 1990 to 986,600 a decade later.

While shifting cultivators continue to pose a 'problem' to the government, their numbers have dropped substantially since 1985 as the land allocation programme has been enthusiastically implemented. This is reflected by the fact that they are now said to cut down 100,000 ha of forest a year now, compared with 300,000 in the early 1980s. The situation has improved dramatically since the mid-1970s when Hmong General Vang Pao complained to a *National Geographic* reporter that "In one year a single family will chop down and burn trees worth US$6,000 and grow a rice crop worth US$240." He demanded the Hmong get their share of fertile, irrigated land – a share they are still waiting for.

Centuries of war and 15 years of Communism had little impact on the self-reliant villages of rural Laos. The government's attempts at cooperativization proved unpopular and unworkable. Just before the cooperativization programme was abruptly suspended in mid-1979 there were 2,800 cooperatives accounting for perhaps 25% of farming families. But even these figures overestimate the role of cooperatives at that time, for many were scarcely functioning. The little work that has been undertaken on agriculture during this period has shown that even when cooperatives were functioning, their members were reluctant participants and there was a good amount of foot-dragging and petty obstructionism. The reasons why cooperatives were such a failure are numerous. To begin with and unlike China and Vietnam, there were almost no large landlords, there was little tenancy and there was abundant land. The inequalities that were so obvious in neighbouring countries simply did not exist in Laos. Second, most farmers were subsistence cultivators; capitalism had barely made inroads into the Lao countryside and the forces of commercialization were largely absent. Further and third, the LPRP provided little support either of a technical or financial kind. As a result, farmers – largely uneducated and bound to their traditional methods of production – saw little incentive to change. In some areas it was not so much a lack of interest in cooperatives, but a positive dislike of them. There were reports of farmers slaughtering their cattle, burning their

Number of tourist arrivals ◀◀

1990	14,400
1991	37,613
1992	87,571
1993	102,946
1994	146,155
1995	208,271
1996	422,324
1997	465,197
1998	502,198
1999	614,279
2000	723,705

fields and eating their poultry, rather than handing their livestock or crops over to the Party. By mid-1979, when the policy was suspended, the leadership in Vientiane had concluded that their attempts at cooperativization had been a disaster.

Since the suspension of the policy, the government has effectively returned to a free enterprise system in the countryside. Farmers now, effectively, own their land and, since a new land law was approved by the National Assembly in April 1997, they can pass it on to their children and use it as collateral to get a bank loan. They can produce whatever crops they like and can sell these on what has become virtually a 'free market'. Lao farmers, though they may be poor and though technology may be antiquated, are in essence no different in terms of the ways they work than their kinsfolk over the Mekong in Thailand.

Laos, as books constantly reiterate, is poor. While it is tempting to mouth those favourite words 'poor but happy', there can be little doubt that the major challenge facing the country is how to promote development. There are few people – whether government ministers or shifting cultivators, businessmen or hawkers – who do not fervently hope that their children will be better off than they. And 'better off' means richer. Laos is playing a game of catch-up. As Houmpheng Souralay of the Foreign Investment Management Committe said to Singapore's *Sunday Times*, "We want to catch up with our neighbours like Thailand, Cambodia and Vietnam." But, he significantly added, only if those "investments are wholesome and do not erode our cultural identity".

Major development constraints are the shortage of skilled workers and capital, an undeveloped communication system (just 3,900 km of tarred roads), poor educational and health resources, rugged terrain and low population density. Even with some 40% of public expenditure going into infrastructure the challenge of linking people to the market and the state remains supremely important. Without roads and transport farmers cannot obtain inputs for agriculture, cannot market any surplus production and cannot increase their incomes. In the history of Southeast Asia there is no development which has not done more to sponsor, support and sustain the region's economic revolution than better communications.

Traditionally, one of Laos' most important sources of foreign exchange was receipts from over-flight rights, as the Bolovens Plateau lies on the flight path from Bangkok to Hong Kong and Tokyo. Nearly 100 international flights traverse Lao airspace every day and in the mid-1990s the government was receiving US$300 for each one: a total of almost US$11 mn a year. But, today, rather more important and one of the country's biggest foreign exchange earners is hydro-power. Much of this comes from the Nam Ngum Dam, north of Vientiane, and from the Xeset Dam in southern Laos. These

Building up the economy

Background

▶▶ **Facing up to reality**

In March 1995, the Bangkok Post *reported the story of a new Lao face cream and the television commercial used to promote it. In the commercial, a woman using the cream is regarded by her friend with the exclamation "Wongdevan, you look so beautiful!" and then asked confidentially about the secret of her physical transformation. Laos subsequently began to greet friends looking rather the worse for wear with the stock phrase "My, Wongdevan, you look so beautiful!"*

Unfortunately, the actress in the commercial happened to be the girlfriend of an influential Lao, and in a fit of pique, no doubt believing the joke cast aspersions on his own taste in women, he had a new law introduced banning satirical jokes based on Lao TV commercials – with offenders liable to a fine of 2,500 kip. Latest reports are that the joke is more popular than ever, and sales of the face cream are sluggish.

generate not only electricity, but more than US$20 mn a year in exports to Thailand.

Plans are underway to further exploit the potential of the Mekong and its tributaries and over 60 projects have been slated for development over the next decade. The biggest proposed project is the Pa Mong Dam, 20 km upstream from the capital. If built, the resultant flooding would require the relocation of more than 6,000 people and the price tag is an estimated US$2.8 bn, a vast sum for a country with a GDP of just US$1.7 bn (2000). The decision to build the dam rests with the Mekong River Commission, whose members include Laos, Thailand, Cambodia, Myanmar and Vietnam. Laos has been dubbed the 'battery' or 'Kuwait' of Southeast Asia and the government has signed various deals with Thailand and Vietnam to sell electricity.

A few years ago these grand hydo-power plans all seemed eminently sensible: energy-hungry Thailand's economy was rapidly growing and Laos was well placed to meet its needs. But there were two issues that the Lao government and its international advisers failed to take sufficiently into account. The international environmental lobby and an economic slow-down. The US$1.5 bn Nam Theun 2 Dam, for example, has been delayed by discoveries of rare bats and birds and for years financial backing from multi-lateral agencies like the World Bank and the Asian Development Bank was held up. The dam, which is now expected to be operational in 2006, will flood an area of 450 sq km on the Nakai Plateau in central Laos. The World Bank, now all too conscious that its environmental credentials have been tarnished by dam developments in India and elsewhere, has gone out of its way to ensure that all the required environmental and other studies are undertaken. And the collapse of the Thai economy in mid-1997 also brought into question the economic rationale for the project.

But the Nam Theun 2 Dam is not quite the open-and-shut case it might appear, with the international environmental lobby on the side of local people and cuddly animals and the dastardly World Bank supporting shadowy businessmen and the interests of international capital. When local people were asked their views of the dam, many apparently welcomed it. An official explained that they did not want to stay "sitting on the porch in torn clothes, playing the *kaen* [a type of bamboo pan pipe] and having our picture taken by tourists" (*The Economist*, 30.8.97). Even some environmentalists argued that having the dam might be preferable to having the forests logged. For without the money that can be earned from selling electricity to Thailand one of the few alternatives is selling wood.

Most of Laos' new enterprise has been in the service sector – there is little evidence that the reforms have prompted a significant increase in manufacturing activity. Most industry in Laos is small scale – rubber shoes, matches, tobacco processing, brewing and soft drinks and ice manufacturing. Saw-milling and timber processing account for the majority of factories. To give an idea of how limited Laos' industrial base is, the government's compendium of 'basic' statistics notes that in 2000 the country produced 250,000 boxes of chalk and 400,000 blocks of soap. Altogether, industry employs only a few thousand people and accounts for a tiny fraction of the gross domestic product. However, this is gradually changing, albeit from an extremely low base: textile manufacturers have set up shop in the country and garments are now one of Laos' most valuable export (see below).

With the odds stacked against it, the government cannot afford to be choosy when it comes to investment. Several hundred foreign investment contracts have been approved since the government adopted a more liberal investment code in 1988, many of them textile factories and enterprises in the tourism sector. Unlike most of its Southeast Asian neighbours, Laos' embryonic garment industry is not subject to quotas from markets in the US and the European Community. The supposed 'flood' of foreign investment in this sector has been nothing more than blue jeans and T-shirt manufacturers from Thailand, Hong Kong, Macao and France, relocating to avoid export restrictions.

In an effort to make the business climate more attractive, the state bank now supplies credit to all sectors of the economy. Provincial banks have been told to operate as autonomous commercial banks. State enterprises have been warned that if their bottom line does not show a profit, they are out of business. Provinces are free to conclude their own trading agreements with private companies and neighbouring countries – which generally means Thailand.

Tens of thousands of people work for the government in a top-heavy and sometimes corrupt bureaucracy. Civil servants are paid the equivalent of US$20-40 per month while domestic servants working for expatriate families receive double this figure, or more. No wonder official corruption and profiteering are on the increase – there is little else to explain the new houses and cars in the capital.

Background

Reform in a period of economic crisis

While Laos might be poor it was not insulated from the effects of Asia's economic crisis. Indeed, it is the reforms of the years since 1986 which has made the country vulnerable to developments beyond its borders. The Lao kip was dragged down by the depreciation of the Thai baht and lost value from US$1 = 978 kip in December 1996 to US$1 = 1,780 kip in November 1997. By March 1999 it had sunk still further to US$1 = 4,200 kip and in November 1999 the unofficial rate of exchange was US$1 = 7,600 kip. At the end of 2002 there were around 10,000 kip to the US$. In fact there is no currency in Southeast Asia, with the exception of the Burmese kyat, which has lost more value.

As the currency lost value the government lost its nerve and slapped on currency controls and rounded up the private money changers who have been operating for years in Vientiane. The governor of the Lao central bank blamed "speculative attempts by opportunists" for the kip's collapse. The trade deficit widened and eight state-owned banks became effectively insolvent. Inflation during 1997 rose from 11% in January to 27% in September and in 1998 continued to escalate to reach 100% by the end of the year. There was also a sharp downturn in investment (remember, Thailand is Laos' largest foreign investor). From a peak of US$2.6 bn in approved projects in 1995, investment dropped to just US$150 mn in 1997 and shrunk still further to US$20 mn in 2000.

The leadership held very different views on how to deal with the crisis. The so-styled 'conservatives' in the politburo wanted the government take a step back from the market and emphasize domestic resources. Reformists wanted further liberalization – à la the IMF – and to extricate the country from the economic mess by integrating still more rapidly into the regional and world economies. The outcome of this debate, in typically Lao style, was a bit of both. The leadership took their foot off the pedal of economic reform but did not substantially reverse what was already in place. It also seems that they may have realized the futility of trying to rein back trade with neighbouring Thailand and China given their lack of control in many areas of the economy.

What is perhaps most surprising about Laos' economic malaise is the absence of any public disturbances. With the economy contracting, inflation running at more than 100%, banks broke, foreign investment evaporating and the government apparently clueless and helpless as to what to do, one might have expected just a little more public debate and criticism. After all, Thailand and South Korea both saw a change of government, Malaysia the trial and imprisonment of its deputy prime minister Anwar Ibrahim and Indonesia the violent dumping of Suharto, president of more than three decades. Laos may be renowned for the relaxed and forgiving ways of its people, but it is hard not to wonder, 'for how much longer?'

Fears of dependency on Thailand Thailand is Vientiane's lifeline to the outside world. Just two years after their last bloody border dispute in 1987-88, the old enemies patched up their differences. The Thai Crown Princess Sirindhorn visited Laos in early 1990 – the first visit by a member of the Thai royal family for 15 years – and Thailand lifted a ban on the export of 200 'strategic goods' to Laos, which had been in place since 1975 and which covered everything from military equipment to food and bicycles. The two old foes agreed to build the Mittaphab – or Friendship – bridge across the Mekong linking Vientiane with Nong Khai in Northeast Thailand. The bridge was built with Australian assistance and opened in 1994 (see page 70). However, fears of Laos becoming a Thai commercial colony has led the government to extend an extremely cautious welcome to Thai proposals to build another bridge at Savannakhet in the southern 'panhandle', which would provide a link west with the northeastern Thai town of Mukdahan and from there with southern Vietnam. Following prodding from the ADB and the Thai government this bridge appeared to get the final go-ahead in November 2001 and it is expected to be completed by 2006. There is also talk of a bridge linking Chiang Khong in Thailand's north with Ban Houai Xai, allowing Thailand easier access to the rich market of Yunnan in southern China.

Thais have emerged as the biggest foreign investors in Laos. A number of Thai commercial banks have set up in Laos, along with businessmen, consultants and loggers. Young Lao who previously attended universities in the Soviet bloc are now being dispatched to Thai universities. The warming of relations between Bangkok and Vientiane has raised some eyebrows: sceptics say Laos' wealth of unexploited natural resources is a tempting reward for patching things up. Laos has about two million ha of forest – 400,000 ha of which is teak and other high quality timber – and it is disappearing fast. But to its credit, Thailand has prioritized aid to Laos and has signed joint ventures in almost every sector – from science and technology to trade, banking and agriculture. Thai businessmen have partially taken over the state beer and brewery and the Thai conglomerate Shinawatra (owned by the current Thai prime minister) has been given telecommunications concessions. Nonetheless, Thai diplomats are only too aware of the poor reputation that their businessmen have in Vientiane. They are regarded as over-bearing and superior in their attitude to the Lao and rapacious, predatory and mercenary in their business dealings. The Thai government has even run courses to try and improve business behaviour. But Thai perceptions of their neighbours are deeply entrenched. As one Thai critic once remarked: "Thai cultural diplomacy starts with the assumption that Thai culture is superior."

To understand Laos' fears of Thailand it is necessary to look back in history. Until the French absorbed Laos into Indochina, Laos came under Thai suzerainty and indeed the Siamese saw Laos as a junior, rather primitive, colony of theirs. When

History matters

In July 2001 the Lao ambassador to Thailand threatened unspecified retaliation if a planned film depicting a Thai heroine's glorious struggle against the invading army of Lao King Chao Anou offended the Lao people. He didn't specify what might happen but there was talk in Vientiane of a boycott of Thai goods. The Lao ambassador said he would have to see if the king, revered in Laos as someone who stood up to the Thais, 'is depticted in a disgraceful way'. The film will be a historical drama retelling the story of how Khunying Mo, the wife of the deputy governor of Korat in Northeast Thailand, organized the population of the city to thwart the invading army of Chao Anou in 1827. Chao Anou was later defeated by the Siamese army who raced north from Bangkok. He escaped to Hué in Vietnam but was later sent back to Bangkok a prisoner, where he died in 1829.

Historians continue to argue whether there is any veracity in this account of Khunying Mo's exploits, but that would seem to be beyond the point. It is part-and-parcel of school history lessons, rather like the story of the ride of Paul Revere to the Americans.

While it might seem odd for a Communist government to get hot under the collar about a king who lived and died more than 1½ centuries ago, when it comes to Lao-Thai relations the merest hint of a slight can cause great offence. Moreover, the Thais can also be very sensitive when it comes to film producers playing around with their history. It is still not possible to see Yul Brunner as King Mongkut cavorting with Anna Leonowens in The King and I. When 20th Century Fox released a remake of the film, Anna and the King with Jodi Foster as Anna, it too was banned.

the foolhardy King Anou of Vientiane tried to recreate the great 14th-century Lao kingdom of Fa Ngoum and invaded Siam he was soundly thrashed in a battle at Korat, in northeast Thailand, and then saw his capital Vientiane plundered, sacked and razed by Siamese forces – a fact which explains why today this ancient city is so devoid of architecture pre-dating the French period. Anou was captured and later died in captivity. Needless to say, Thai and Lao history is at odds on this period of history: Thai accounts paint Anou as a rebel; those written by Lao historians characterize him as a national hero. (This partly explains the emotional response of the Lao to a Thai producer's decision to make a film of these historical events – see the box History matters, above.)

It is only with this background in mind that Lao fears of Thai commercial hegemony can be fully appreciated. When, in 1988, former Thai Prime Minister Chatichai Choonhaven expressed a desire to turn Indochina "from a battlefield into a market place", this was viewed by many Lao – and some more thoughtful Thais – as tantamount to a threat of commercial invasion. (The theme was returned to in 1995 when a senior Thai diplomat, Suridhya Simaskul, remarked to the journalist Michael Vatikiotis, "We have passed the stage of turning battlefields into markets; now the market itself has become the battlefield.") Thailand, its own natural resources denuded through years of thoughtless exploitation, was hoping to pillage Laos' resource-rich larder. In July 1989, state run Radio Vientiane broadcast a commentary, presumably officially sanctioned, stating: "Having failed to destroy our country through their military might [referring to the Ban Rom Klao border conflict of 1987-88], the enemy has now employed a new strategy in attacking us through the so-called attempt to turn the Indochinese battlefield into a marketplace..." It is this fear of Thailand and of over-dependence on Thailand, which has prompted the Lao government to do its utmost to try and diversify its commercial links. In a rather novel departure from the usual state of affairs, the Lao are also more scared of Thai cultural pollution, than western cultural pollution. The similarities between the two countries and the fact that many Lao households watch Thai television, make Thailand seem more of a risk. In 1993, former president and Pathet Lao veteran Phoumi Vongvichit warned against the dangers of prostitution, 'depraved' dancing and gambling. The source of these threats to pristine Lao culture was Thailand. Newspaper reports even dubbed the Mittaphaap Bridge the AIDS Bridge, because it was expected that the bridge would bring prostitution and AIDS to the country.

Dependency on aid & development aims

Laos depends heavily on imports – everything from agricultural machinery and cars to petrol products, textiles and pharmaceuticals – 75% of which are financed by foreign aid. Western bilateral donors are enthusiastically filling the aid gap left by the Socialist bloc. Countries and private donors are falling over each other to fund projects; NGOs are homing in and multi-lateral development banks are offering soft loans and structural adjustment programmes. As Laos' foreign debt is mostly on highly concessional terms, it is not crippled by repayment schedules. But with development banks accelerating their project-funding, fears are mounting that Laos is teetering on the edge of a debt trap.

The share of foreign assistance to GDP has nearly tripled since the mid-1980s. In 1985-86 it stood at 6%, by 1988 had reached 10% and in 2000 was over 16%. This translates into a figure equivalent to around two-thirds of the country's export earnings, or US$50 per person per year. By 1990, Vientiane's capacity to absorb this aid was being swamped, its ministries overwhelmed by one of the highest per capita aid inflows in the developing world. While western economic advisers have been touting investment strategies, project co-ordination and quality have suffered in the rush.

The country and its foreign strategists are looking to four distinct areas for future income. The first concentrates on mining and energy. Laos already has three HEP dams that generate power for export to Thailand and others are planned. The latest, built by South Korea's Daewoo group in southern Laos, began exporting electricity to Thailand in April 1998 (see page 219). Mining rights to some of Laos' huge lignite reserves have been sold to Thai investors. Other untapped mineral resources include reserves of gold, gemstones and iron ore, while foreign companies have undertaken preliminary searches for oil. The second area of interest is agriculture and forestry. Investors are looking at growing feed grains like soya beans and maize for export to Thailand. Raw timber exports are being replaced by processed wood industries. More enlightened analysts also see Laos as a potential large exporter of organic agricultural products – after all, agriculture in the country has never had to rely on biochemical inputs or genetically engineered seeds. The third potential area for development is tourism but the government is wary of Laos going the same way as Thailand. The fourth and final strategy – and the most ambitious – is for Laos to become the 'service centre' between China, Vietnam, Cambodia and Thailand (see Laos as the 'keystone' of mainland Southeast Asia, below).

Emerging inequalities & human development

As in neighbouring Vietnam, the economic reforms are beginning to widen inequalities in society. Most of those who are doing well live in towns or at least close to one of the country's main roads. This means that off-road communities, and especially those in highland areas, are finding that – at least in relative terms – they are becoming poorer. In addition, because it is mostly minority Lao Soung and Lao Theung who live in these marginal areas, the economic reforms are widening inequalities between ethnic groups. One foreign aid worker was quoted in the *Far Eastern Economic Review* at the beginning of 1996 saying: "When they come down to Vientiane, where the lowland Lao [the Lao Loum] live, it's like Hong Kong to them. Here's money, here's development. In their own villages, there's nothing." As in Vietnam, the need to ensure that the economic reforms bring benefits to all and not just a few, is a key political question. The leadership are acutely aware that widening inequalities could fuel political discontent and this is perhaps one reason why the government seems so intent on increasing the number of members of the National Assembly from ethnic minorities.

The data that are available indicate that inequalities are widening. The first living standards survey was released in 1995 and showed what most people already knew: that Laos was a poor but relatively egalitarian place. The latest living standards survey, undertaken in 1997/98, shows that this equality is being eroded as the economic reforms progress. In Vientiane 'only' 14% of the population are officially designated 'poor'. But in the northern provinces of Hua Phanh and Oudomxai it is 70% and 65% respectively.

The government claims its "programme for the basic elimination of illiteracy among the masses", launched in 1984, was "an outstanding success". Literacy rates are still low – 47% in 1999. Adult education has been expanded, schools upgraded, 62 classrooms built "for 1,600 tribal youths" and a new university has been set up in Vientiane. But while the government has been busy building schools, the quality of education has slipped further: they cannot afford to pay teachers or buy textbooks.

Health care has suffered for the same reasons. Infant and under-five mortality rates are some of the highest in the world, the former estimated at 96 per 1,000 live births. Half of those who do survive suffer malnutrition, nearly all contract malaria, diarrhoea, respiratory and intestinal diseases and life expectancy at birth is still just 54 years (1998).

In what sceptics might view as an ultimately futile effort, the leadership in Vientiane have chanced upon an economic future for their country: as the 'keystone' or 'crossroads' of Southeast Asia. Nor is it just Lao leaders who are drumming up enthusiasm for this notion. The Asian Development Bank (the Asian arm of the World Bank) is at the forefront of developing – and funding – what has become known as the Greater Mekong Sub-region or GMS. This will link southwest China, Thailand, Myanmar, Cambodia, Vietnam and Laos. And within this scenario, Laos is the crucial pivotal country through which most road and rail links will have to go. There is talk of a 'Golden Quadrangle' (as opposed to the infamous Golden Triangle) – even of a Golden Land. This reference draws on ancient Indian texts which talked of *Suvarnaphum* – a Golden Land – which encompassed modern-day Thailand, Laos, Myanmar and probably Peninsular Malasia and parts of Indonesia too. Like most grand ideas, it looks great on paper but putting it into practice is something else. Indeed, Laos' current economic problems are in no small part due to its cosying-up to Thailand and integration into the regional economy of mainland Southeast Asia.

Laos as the 'keystone' of mainland Southeast Asia Background

Culture

People

More than three-quarters of the population are subsistence farmers and only a tenth of its villages are anywhere near a road. Nearly one child in five dies before its fifth birthday, 87% of villages are afflicted with malaria, 80% by diarrhoea and cars seem to have a longer life expectancy than people. More than one third of the population aged over 15 cannot read or write, the diet is inadequate, sanitation poor and only a quarter of the population have access to safe drinking water. Debilitating and fatal diseases, from malaria to bilharzia, are endemic in rural Laos while the health and education systems are limited. In northern provinces the opium addiction rate is double the literacy rate.

Ethnic groups

A summary of the origins, economy and culture of the major groups is provided on pages 284-289

Laos is less a nation state than a collection of different tribes and languages. The country's enormous ethnic diversity has long been an impediment to national integration. In total there are more than 60 minority tribes which are often described as living in isolated, self-sufficient communities. Although communication and intercourse may have been difficult – and remains so – there has always been communication, trade and inter-marriage between the different Lao 'worlds' and today, with even greater interaction, the walls between them are becoming more permeable still.

Laos' ethnically diverse population is usually – and rather simplistically – divided by ecological zone into three groups: the wet rice cultivating, Buddhist Lao Loum of the lowlands, who are politically and numerically dominant, constituting over half of the total population; the Lao Theung who occupy the mountain slopes and make up about a quarter of the population; and the Lao Soung, or upland Lao, who live in the high mountains and practise shifting cultivation and who represent less than a fifth of Laos' total population. The terms were brought into general usage by the Pathet Lao who wished to emphasize that all of Laos' inhabitants were 'Lao' and to avoid the more derogatory terms that had been used in the past – such as the Thai word *kha*, meaning 'slave', to describe the Mon-Khmer Lao Theung like the Khmu and Lamet. Stereotypical representations of each category are depicted on the 1,000 kip note, see illustration opposite.

The French viewed the Lao (not to put too fine a point on it) as if they were at times an exasperating child. But, as Virginia Thompson put it in the late 1930s, "For the rare Frenchman who sees in the Laotians a silly, lazy and naïve people, there are hundreds who are charmed by their gentle affability ...". It was this affability which Henri Mouhout noted in the 1860s and which led some Frenchmen to express their concern as to what might happen to the Lao if the uncontrolled immigration and settlement of Siamese, Vietnamese and Chinese was permitted. (Norman Lewis in *A Dragon Apparent* said much the same about Frenchmen who had gone native: "Laos-ized Frenchmen are like the results of successful lobotomy operations – untroubled and mildly libidinous.") By the Second World War towns like Vientiane and Thakhek already had larger populations of Vietnamese than they did of Lao and had the Japanese occupation and independence not nipped French plans in the bud, Laos might well have become a country where the Lao were in a minority.

Although the words have a geographical connotation, they should be viewed more as contrasting pairs of terms: *loum* and *theung* mean 'below' and 'above' (rather than hillsides and lowland), while *soung* is paired with *tam*, meaning 'high' and 'low'. These two pairs of oppositions were then brought together by the Pathet Lao into one three-fold division. Thus, the Lao Theung in one area may, in practice, occupy a higher location than Lao Soung in another area. In addition, economic change, greater interaction between the groups and the settlement of lowland peoples in hill areas, means that it is possible to find Lao Loum villages in upland areas, where the inhabitants practise swidden, not wet rice, agriculture. So, although it is broadly possible to characterize the mountain slopes as inhabited by shifting cultivating Lao Theung of Mon-Khmer descent, in practice the neat delimitation of people into discrete spatial units breaks down and as the years go by is becoming increasingly untenable.

Lao Loum It has been noted that the Lao who have reaped the rewards of reform are the Lao Loum of T'ai stock – not the Lao Theung who are of Mon-Khmer descent or the Lao Soung who are 'tribal' peoples, especially Hmong but also Akha and Lahu. Ing-Britt Trankell, in her book *On the Road in Laos: an Anthropological Study of Road*

Population density

Province	Population ('000s)	Area km²	Population Density/km²)
Attapeu	97	10,320	9
Bokeo	126	6,196	20
Bolikhamxai	182	14,863	12
Champassak	558	15,415	36
Houa Phan	272	16,500	17
Khammouan	303	16,315	19
Luang NamTha	128	9,325	14
Luang Phrabang	406	16,875	24
Udom Xai	234	15,370	15
Phongsali	170	16,270	10
Salavan	285	10,691	27
Savannakhet	748	21,774	34
Sayaboury	325	16,389	24
Sekong	71	7,665	9
Vientiane (municipality)	583	3,920	149
Vientiane (province)	319	15,927	20
Xieng Khouang	223	15,880	14
Xayasomboun special region	60	7,105	8
Whole country	5,091	236,800	21

Source: National Statistical Centre, State Planning Committe (2000)

Construction and Rural Communities (1993), writes that the Lao Loum's "sense of [cultural and moral] superiority is often manifested in both a patronizing and contemptuous attitude toward the Lao Theung and Lao Sung, who are thought of as backward and less susceptible to socio-economic development because they are still governed by their archaic cultural traditions".

During the sixth and seventh centuries the Lao Loum arrived from the southern provinces of China. They occupied the valleys along the Mekong and its tributaries and drove the Lao Theung to more mountainous areas. The Lao Loum, who are ethnically almost indistinguishable from the Thais of the Isan region (the Northeast of Thailand), came under the influence of the Khmer and Indonesian cultures and sometime before the emergence of Lane Xang in the 14th century embraced Theravada Buddhism. The majority of Lao are Buddhist but retain many of their animist beliefs. Remote Lao Loum communities still usually have a *mor du* (a doctor who 'sees') or medium. The medium's job description is demanding: he must concoct love potions, heal the sick, devise and design protective charms and read the future.

Today, the Lao Loum are the principal ethnic group, accounting for just over half the population, and Lao is their mother tongue. As the lowland Lao, they occupy the ricelands of the Mekong and its main tributary valleys. Their houses are made of wood and are built on stilts with thatched roofs – although tin is far more popular these days. The extended family is usually spread throughout several houses in one compound.

There are also several tribal sub-groups of this main Thai-Lao group; they are conveniently colour-coded and readily identifiable by their sartorial traits. There are, for example, the Red Tai, the White Tai and the Black Tai – who live in the upland valley areas in Xieng Khouang and Hua Phan provinces. That they live in the hills suggests they are Lao Theung, but ethnically and culturally they are closer to the Lao Loum.

Population by ethnic group

Group	Official category	% of total population
T'ai	Lao Loum	55
Mon-Khmer	Lao Theung	35
Tibeto-Burman	Lao Soung	10

Lao Theung The Lao Theung, consisting of 45 different sub-groups, are the descendants of the oldest inhabitants of the country and are of Mon-Khmer descent. They are sometimes called *Kha*, meaning 'slave', as they were used as labourers by the Thai and Lao kings and are generally still poorer than the Lao Loum. Traditionally, the Lao Theung were semi-nomadic and they still live mainly on the mountain slopes of the interior – along the whole length of the Annamite Chain from South China. There are concentrations of Akha, Alak and Ta-Oy on the Bolovens Plateau in the south (see page 210) and Khamu in the north.

Most Lao Theung still practise slash-and-burn, or shifting, agriculture and grow dry rice, coffee and tobacco. They would burn a small area of forest, cultivate it for a few years and then, when the soil was exhausted, abandon the land until the vegetation had regenerated to replenish the soil. Some groups merely shifted fields in a 10-15 year rotation; others not only shifted fields but also their villages, relocating in a fresh area of forest when the land had become depleted of nutrients. To obtain salt, metal implements and other goods which could not be made or found in the hills, the tribal peoples would trade forest products such as resins and animal skins with the settled lowland Lao. Some groups, mainly those living closer to towns, have converted to Buddhism but many are still animist.

The social and religious beliefs of the Lao Theung and their general outlook on health and happiness, are governed by their belief in spirits. The shaman is a key personality in any village. The Alak, from the Bolovens Plateau (see page 213) test the prospects of a marriage by killing a chicken: the manner in which it bleeds will determine whether the marriage will be propitious. Buffalo sacrifices are also common in Lao Theung villages and it is not unusual for a community to slaughter all its livestock to appease the spirits.

Viet Minh guerrillas and American B-52s made life difficult for many of the Lao Theung tribes living in East Laos, who were forced to move away from the Ho Chi Minh Trail. By leaving their birth places the Lao Theung left their protecting spirits, forcing them to find new and unfamiliar ones.

Lao Soung The Lao Soung began migrating to Laos from South China, Tibet and Burma, in the early 18th century, settling high in the mountains (some up to 2,500 m). The Hmong (formerly known as the Meo) and Yao (also called the Mien) are the principal Lao Soung groups.

The Yao (or Mien) The Yao mainly live around Nam Tha – deep inside the Golden Triangle, near the borders with Thailand, Burma and China. They are best-known as craftsmen – the men make knives, crossbows, rifles and high-quality, elaborately designed silver jewellery, which is worn by the women. Silver is a symbol of wealth among the Yao and Hmong.

The Mien or Yao are unique among the hilltribes in that they have a tradition of writing based on Chinese characters. Mien legend has it that they came from 'across the sea' during the 14th century, although it is generally thought that their roots are in South China where they originated about 2,000 years ago.

Background

Lao, Laos and Laotians

Most Lao are not Laotians. And not all Laotians are Lao. 'Lao' tends to be used to describe people of Lao stock. There are, in fact, several times more Lao in neighbouring Northeastern Thailand – roughly 20 million – than there are in Laos with a total population of some 5 million of whom perhaps a little over a half are ethnic Lao. At the same time not all Laotians – people who are nationals of Laos – are ethnic Lao. There are also significant minority populations including Chinese, Vietnamese, the Mon-Khmer Lao Theung and the many tribal groups that comprise the Lao Soung. After a few too many lau-lao it is easy to get confused.

The Mien village is not enclosed and is usually found on sloping ground. The houses are large, wooden affairs, as they need to accommodate an extended family of sometimes 20 or more members. They are built on the ground, not on stilts and have one large living area and four or more bedrooms. As with other tribes, the construction of the house must be undertaken carefully. The house needs to be orientated appropriately, so that the spirits are not disturbed and the ancestral altar installed on an auspicious day.

The Mien combine two religious beliefs: on the one hand they recognize and pay their dues to spirits and ancestors (informing them of family developments); and on the other, they follow Taoism as it was practised in China in the 13th and 14th centuries. The Taoist rituals are expensive and the Mien appear to spend a great deal of their lives struggling to save enough money to afford the various life cycle ceremonies, such as weddings and death ceremonies. The Mien economy is based upon the shifting cultivation of dry rice, maize and small quantities of opium poppy.

Material culture The Mien women dress distinctively, with black turbans and red-ruffed tunics, making them easy to distinguish from the other hilltribes. All their clothes are made of black or indigo-dyed homespun cotton, which is then embroidered using distinctive cross-stitching. Their trousers are the most elaborate garments. Unusually, they sew from the back of the cloth and cannot see the pattern they are making. The children wear embroidered caps with red pompoms on the top and by the ears. The men's dress is a simple indigo-dyed jacket and trousers, with little embroidery. They have been dubbed "the most elegantly dressed but worst-housed people in the world".

The Akha have their origins in Yunnan, southern China, and from there spread into Burma (where there are nearly 200,000) and Laos and rather later into Thailand.

The Akha (or Kaw)

The Akha are shifting cultivators, growing primarily dry rice on mountainsides but also a wide variety of vegetables. The cultivation of rice is bound up with myths and rituals: the rice plant is regarded as a sentient being and the selection of the swidden, its clearance, the planting of the rice seed, the care of the growing plants and finally the harvest of the rice, must all be done according to the Akha Way. Any offence to the rice soul must be rectified by ceremonies.

Akha villages are identified by their gates, a village swing and high-roofed houses on posts. They have no word for religion but believe in the 'Akha Way'. They are able to recite the names of all their male ancestors (60 names or more) and they keep an ancestral altar in their homes, at which food is offered up at important times in the year such as New Year, during the village swing ceremony and after the rice harvest.

At the upper and lower ends of the village are gates which are renewed every year. Visitors should walk through them in order to rid themselves of the spirit of the jungle. The gates are sacred and must not be defiled. Visitors must not touch the

Background

▶▶ Papaver Somniferum: the opium of the people

The very name the Golden Triangle, is synonymous in many people's minds with the cultivation of the opium poppy (Papaver somniferum). It is a favourite cash crop of the Lahu, Lisu, Yao and Hmong (the Akha only rarely grow it). The attractions of cultivating the poppy are clear: it is profitable, can be grown at high altitudes (above 1,500 m), has low bulk (important when there is poor transport) and does not rot. Today, most opium is grown in Myanmar (Burma) and Laos, and then often traded through Thailand to the world's drug markets.

The opium poppy is usually grown as part of a rotation, alternating with maize. It is sown in September/October (the end of the wet season) and 'harvesting' stretches from the beginning of January through to the end of March. Harvesting

occurs after the petals have dropped off the seed heads. The 'pod' is then carefully scoured with a sharp knife, from top to bottom, allowing the sap to ooze through and oxidize on the surface of the pod. The next day, the brown gum is scraped off, rolled into balls, and wrapped in banana leaves. It is now ready for sale to the buyers who travel the hills.

Though a profitable crop, opium production has not benefited the hilltribes. It makes those who grow it criminals, and opium addiction is widespread – among the Hmong it is thought to be about 30 percent of the population. Efforts to change the ways of the hilltribes have focused upon crop substitution programmes (encouraging farmers to cultivate crops such as cabbages) and simple intimidation.

Zones of poppy cultivation in Laos, Myanmar & Thailand

gates and should avoid going through them if they do not intend to enter a house in the village. A pair of wooden male and female carved figures are placed inside the entrance to signify that this is the realm of human beings. The two most important Akha festivals are the four-day Swinging Ceremony celebrated during August and New Year when festivities also extend over four days.

Material culture Akha clothing is made of homespun blue-black cloth, which is appliquéd for decoration. Particularly characteristic of the Akha is their head-dress, which is adorned with jewellery. The basic clothing of an Akha woman is a head-dress, a jacket, a short skirt worn on the hips, with a sash and leggings worn from the ankle to below the knee. They wear their jewellery as an integral part of their clothing, mostly sewn to their head-dresses. Girls wear similar clothing to the women, except that they sport caps rather than the elaborate head-dress of the mature women. The change from girl's clothes to women's clothes occurs through four stages during adolescence. Unmarried girls can be identified by the small gourds tied to their waist and head-dress.

Men's clothing is much less elaborate. They wear loose-fitting Chinese-style black pants and a black jacket which may be embroidered. Both men and women use cloth shoulder bags.

Today the Akha are finding it increasingly difficult to follow the 'Akha Way'. Their complex rituals set them apart from both the lowland Lao and from the other hilltribes. The conflicts and pressures which the Akha currently face and their inability to reconcile the old with the new, is claimed by some to explain why the incidence of opium addiction among the Akha is so high.

The Hmong (or Meo)

Origins The Hmong are probably the best-known tribe in Laos. In the 19th century, Chinese opium farmers drove many thousands of Hmong off their poppy fields and forced them south into the mountains of Laos. The Hmong did not have a written language before contact with Europeans and Americans and their heritage is mainly preserved through oral tradition. Hmong mythology relates how they flew in from South China on magic carpets. Village story-tellers also like to propagate the notion that the Hmong are in fact werewolves, who happily devour the livers of their victims. This warrior tribe now mainly inhabits the mountain areas of Luang Prabang, Xieng Khouang and Xam Neua provinces where they practise shifting cultivation.

Economy and society Until a few years ago, other Lao and the rest of the world knew the Hmong as the Meo. Unbeknown to anyone except the Hmong, 'Meo' was a Chinese insult meaning 'barbarian' – conferred on them several millennia ago by Chinese who developed an intense disliking for the tribe. Returning from university in France in the mid-1970s, the Hmong's first highly qualified academic decided it was time to educate the world. Due to his prompting, the tribe was rechristened Hmong, their word for 'mankind'. This change in nomenclature has not stopped the Hmong from continuing to refer to the Chinese as 'sons of dogs'.

Nor has it stopped the Lao Loum from regarding the Hmong as their cultural inferiors. But, again, the feelings are reciprocated: the Hmong have an inherent mistrust of the lowland Lao – exacerbated by years of war – and Lao Loum guides reluctantly enter Hmong villages.

The Hmong value their independence and tend to live at high altitudes, away from other tribes. This independence in addition to their association with poppy cultivation and their siding with the US during the war has meant that of all the hilltribes it is the Hmong who have been most severely persecuted. They are perceived to be a threat to the security of the state; a tribe that needs to be controlled and carefully watched.

Hmong villages tend not to be fenced, while their houses are built of wood or bamboo at ground level. Each house has a main living area and two or three sleeping rooms. The extended family is headed by the oldest male; he settles family disputes and has supreme authority over family affairs. Like the Karen, the Hmong too are spirit worshippers and believe in household spirits. Every house has an altar, where protection for the household is sought.

As animists, the Hmong believe everything from mountains and opium poppies to cluster bombs, has a spirit – or *phi* – some bad, some good. Shamans – or witch-doctors – play a central role in village life and decision making. The *phi* need to be placated incessantly to ward off sickness and catastrophe. It is the shaman's job to exorcise the bad *phi* from his patients. Until modern medicine arrived in Laos along with the Americans, opium was the Hmong's only palliative drug. Due to their lack of resistance to pharmaceuticals, the Hmong responded miraculously to the smallest doses of penicillin. Even Bandaids were revered as they were thought to contain magical powers which drew out bad *phi*.

The Hmong are the only tribe in Laos who make batik; indigo-dyed batik makes up the main panel of their skirts, with appliqué and embroidery added to it. The women also wear black leggings from their knees to their ankles, black jackets (with embroidery) and a black panel or 'apron', held in place with a cummerbund. Even the youngest children wear clothes of intricate design with exquisite needlework. Traditionally the cloth would have been woven by hand on a foot-treddle/back-strap loom; today it is increasingly purchased from markets.

The White Hmong tend to wear less elaborate clothing from day to day, saving it for special occasions only. Hmong men wear loose-fitting black trousers, black jackets (sometimes embroidered) and coloured or embroidered sashes.

The Hmong particularly value silver jewellery; it signifies wealth and a good life. Men, women and children wear silver – tiers of neck rings, heavy silver chains with lock-shaped pendants, ear-rings and pointed rings on every finger. All the family jewellery is brought out at New Year and is an impressive sight, symbolizing the wealth of the family.

In the dying days of the French colonial administration, thousands of Hmong were recruited to help fight the Vietnamese Communists. Vang Pao – known as VP – who would later command 30,000 Hmong mercenaries in the US-backed war against the Pathet Lao, was first picked out by a French colonel in charge of these '*maquisards*' or 'native movements'. Later, the Hmong were recruited and paid by the CIA to fight the Pathet Lao. Under General VP, remote mountain villagers with no education were trained to fly T-28 fighter-bombers. It is said that when these US aircraft first started landing in remote villages, locals would carefully examine the undercarriage to see what sex they were.

An estimated 100,000 Hmong died during the war – even after the Pathet Lao's 'liberation' of Vientiane in 1975, Hmong refugees, encamped in hills to the south of the Plain of Jars, were attacked and flushed out by Vietnamese troops. Stories of chemical weapons being used against them (most notably 'yellow rain') were found to be US propaganda as the suspected biological agents, trichothecane mycotoxins, supposedly dumped on Hmong villages by the government, were identified as bee faeces. Swarms of over-flying bees have a habit of defecating simultaneously when they get too hot, showering the countryside with a sticky, yellow substance.

When the war ended in 1975 there was a mass exodus of Hmong and today more than 100,000 live in the US – mostly on the west coast and in Minnesota. A small group of Hmong, led by Vang Pao, optimistically fought the Lao government until quite recently, and there are probably still a small number of disaffected Hmong who cling to the cause. But they have lost what credibility they may have had and while Hmong in the US regularly lobby politicians they are increasingly out of touch with the situation in Laos. The rebels' biggest public relations disaster came in 1989 when they shot dead several Buddhist monks while attacking a government convoy on the road to Luang Prabang. While there was a spate of bombings in Vientiane in 2000 that was probably linked to the Hmong resistance they are increasingly only a minor irritant to the government in Vientiane. Where the US-based Hmong are important, though, is in the money they remit to their relatives in Laos.

Following liberation, Hmong refugees continued to pour into Thailand, the exodus reaching a peak in 1979 when 3,000 a month were fleeing across the Mekong. Thousands also ended up in the US and France, fresh from the mountains of Laos: unsurprisingly they did not adapt easily. Various stress disorders were thought to have triggered heart attacks in many healthy young Hmong – a condition referred to as Sudden Unexplained Nocturnal Death Syndrome. In *The Ravens*, Robbins comments that "in a simpler age, it would have been said that the Hmong are dying of a broken heart".

Other communities

The largest non-Lao groups in Laos are the Chinese and Vietnamese communities in the main cities. Many of the Vietnamese were brought in by the French to run the country and stayed. In more recent years, Vietnam also tried to colonize parts of Laos. The Vietnamese are not well-liked: one of the few rude words in the Lao language refers to them. The Chinese have been migrating to Laos for centuries and are usually traders, restaurateurs and shop-owners. With the relaxation in Communist policies in recent years, there has been a large influx of Thais; most are involved in business. In Vientiane there is also a small community of Indians running restaurants, jewellery and tailors' shops. The majority of the Europeans in Laos are embassy staff or involved with aid projects and oil prospecting companies and live on the south and east side of Vientiane.

Architecture

The architecture of Laos reflects its turbulent history and has strong Siamese/Thai, Burmese and Khmer influences. Philip Rawson, in his book *The Art of Southeast Asia* (Thames & Hudson), goes so far as to state that "The art of Laos is a provincial version of the art of Siam." This is unjustified in so far as art and architecture in Laos, though it may show many links with that of Siam/Thailand (unsurprisingly as over the centuries the two countries have, at various times, held sway over parts of each other's territory), also has elements and styles which are unique to it. Unfortunately, little has survived because many of the older structures were built of wood and were repeatedly ransacked by the Siamese/Thais, Chinese and Vietnamese and then bombed by the Americans. Religious buildings best exhibit the originality of Lao art and architecture.

Like Thailand and Myanmar (Burma), the stupa is the most dominant architectural form in Laos. In its classic Indian form, it is a voluptuous half round – a hemisphere – very like the upturned begging bowl that it is supposed to symbolize. This is surmounted by a shaft representing the Buddha's staff and a stepped pediment symbolizing his folded cloak. In Thailand the stupa has become elongated while in Laos it is also more angular, with four distinct sides. They are referred to as *that* (rather than *chedi*, as in Thailand).

In addition to the *that*, a Lao monastery or *wat* (*vat*) will also have a number of other buildings of which the most important is the *sim* or ordination hall (in Thai, *bot* or *ubosoth*). See the box on page 290 for a short rundown on the main structures found in an orthodox Lao *wat*.

Architectural styles

Lao wats are generally less ornate and grand than those in Thailand, although the temples of Luang Prabang are stunning, with their layered roofs that sweep elegantly towards the ground. There are three main styles of temple architecture in Laos: Luang Prabang, Vientiane and Xieng Khouang. The last of these was almost lost forever because of the destruction wrought on the city of Xieng Khouang during the war (see page 158). Fortunately one or two examples exist in Luang Prabang.

The Vientiane style is influenced by the central Thai-style, with its high, pointed and layered roofs. Most of the main sanctuaries are rectangular and some, such as Wat Phra Kaeo in Vientiane, have a veranda around the entire building – a stylistic

Background

▶▶ The Lao wat

There is no English equivalent of the Lao word wat or vat. It is usually translated as either monastery or temple, although neither is correct. It is easiest to get around this problem by calling them wats. They were, and remain to some extent, the focus of the village or town; they serve as places of worship, education, meeting and healing. Without a wat, a village cannot be viewed as a 'complete' community. The wat is a relatively new innovation. Originally, there were no wats, as monks were wandering ascetics. It seems that although the word 'wat' was in use in the 14th century, these were probably just shrines, and were not monasteries. By the late 18th century, the wat had certainly metamorphosed into a monastery, so sometime in the intervening four centuries, shrine and monastery had united into a whole. Although wats vary a great deal in size and complexity, there is a traditional layout to which most conform.

Wats are usually separated from the secular world by **two walls**. Between these outer and inner walls are found the **monks' quarters** or dormitories (kutis), perhaps a drum or **bell tower** (hor kong) that is used to toll the hours and to warn of danger and, in larger complexes, schools and other administrative buildings. Traditionally the kutis were placed on the south side of the wat. It was believed that if the monks slept directly in front of the principal Buddha image they would die young; if they slept to the left they would become ill; and if they slept behind it there would be discord in the community of monks.

The inner wall, which in bigger wats often takes the form of a **gallery** or

Generalized plan of a wat

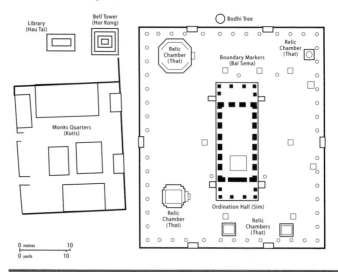

feature imported from Bangkok. Most of the larger sim have a veranda at the back as well as at the front. Vientiane's wats have higher roofs than those in Luang Prabang, the buildings are taller and the entrances more prominent. The steps leading up to the main entrance are often guarded by nagas or nyaks, while the doorways themselves are usually flanked by pillars and topped with intricately carved porticoes. That Luang, in Vientiane, historically provided a template for most Lao stupas and its unique shape is found only in Laos and some areas of North and Northeast Thailand.

cloister (phra rabieng) lined with Buddha images, represents the division between the worldly and the holy, the sacred and the profane. It is used as a quiet place for meditation. Within the inner courtyard, the holiest building is the **ordination hall** or **sim**, reserved for monks only. This is built on consecrated ground, and has a ring of eight stone tablets or boundary markers (bai sema), sometimes contained in mini-pavilions, arranged around it at the cardinal and subcardinal points and shaped like stylized leaves of the bodhi tree, often carved with representations of Vishnu, Siva, Brahma or Indra, or of nagas. Buried in the ground beneath the bai sema are stone spheres – and sometimes gold and jewellery. The bai sema mark the limit of earthly power. The ordination hall is characteristically a large, rectangular building with high walls and multiple sloping roofs (always odd in number) covered in glazed clay tiles (or wood tiles, in the north). At each end of the apex of the roof are dok sofa, or 'bunches of flowers', which represent garuda grasping two nagas (serpents) in its talons. Chao faa, flame-like protrusions are attached to the extreme edge of the downward slope of the roofs. Inside, often through elaborately carved and inlaid doors, is the main Buddha image. There may also be numerous subsidiary images. The inside walls of the sim may be decorated with murals depicting the Jataka tales or scenes from Buddhist and Hindu cosmology. Like the Buddha, these murals are meant to serve as meditation aids. It is customary for pilgrims to remove their shoes on entering any Buddhist building (or private house for that matter). Many complexes have secondary chapels, or **hor song phra** attached to the main sim.

Also found in the inner courtyard may be a number of other structures. Among the more common are that (chedis), tower-like **relic chambers** which in Laos and parts of Northeastern Thailand (which is also Lao in terms of culture) take the distinctive lotus bud form. These can be built on a massive scale (such as That Luang in Vientiane, see page 70), and contain holy relics of the Buddha himself. More often, thats are smaller affairs containing the ashes of royalty, monks or pious lay people.

Another rarer feature is the **library** or scripture repository (hau tai), usually a small, tall-sided building where the Buddhist scriptures can be stored safely, high off the ground. Salas are open-sided **rest pavilions** which can be found anywhere in the wat compound; the sala long tham or **study hall** is the largest and most impressive of these and is almost like a sim or viharn without walls. Here the monks say their prayers at noon.

Sometimes wats have a boat house to shelter the local boat used in the annual boat race.

In rural villages wats often consist only of a sala, or meeting hall.

It seems that wats are often short-lived. Even great wats, if they lose their patronage, are deserted by their monks and fall into ruin. Unlike Christian churches, they depend on constant support from the laity; the wat owns no land or wealth, and must depend on gifts of food to feed the monks and money to repair and expand the fabric of its buildings.

As in other Buddhist countries, many of the stupas contain sacred relics – bones or hairs of the Buddha, or the ashes of kings.

The Luang Prabang architectural style has been influenced by North Thai temples. The roofs of the main sanctuaries are very low, almost touching the ground – best exemplified by the magnificent Wat Xieng Thong in Luang Prabang. The pillars tend to narrow towards the top, as tree trunks were originally used for columns and this form was copied when they started to be constructed of stuccoed brick. The wats

▶▶ **Mudras and the Buddha image**

An artist producing an image of the Buddha does not try to create an original piece of art; he is trying to be faithful to a tradition which can be traced back over centuries. It is important to appreciate that the Buddha image is not merely a work of art but an object of and for, worship. Sanskrit poetry even sets down the characteristics of the Buddha – albeit in rather unlikely terms: legs like a deer, arms like an elephant's trunk, a chin like a mango stone and hair like the stings of scorpions. The Pali texts of Theravada Buddhism add the 108 auspicious signs, long toes and fingers of equal length, body like a banyan tree and eyelashes like a cow's. The Buddha can be represented either sitting, lying (indicating paranirvana), or standing, and (in Thailand) occasionally walking. He is often represented standing on an open lotus flower: the Buddha was born into an impure world, and likewise the lotus germinates in mud but rises above the filth to flower. Each image will be represented in a particular mudra or 'attitude', of which there are 40. The most common are:

Abhayamudra – dispelling fear or giving protection; right hand (sometimes both hands) raised, palm outwards, usually with the Buddha in a standing position.

Varamudra – giving blessing or charity; the right hand pointing downwards, the palm facing outwards, with the Buddha either seated or standing.

Vitarkamudra – preaching mudra; the ends of the thumb and index finger of the right hand touch to form a circle, symbolizing the Wheel of Law. The Buddha can either be seated or standing.

Dharmacakramudra – 'spinning the Wheel of Law'; a preaching mudra symbolizing the teaching of the first sermon. The hands are held in front of the chest, thumbs and index fingers of both joined, one facing inwards and one outwards.

Bhumisparcamudra – 'calling the earth goddess to witness' or 'touching the earth'; the right hand rests on the right knee with the tips of the fingers 'touching ground', thus calling the earth goddess Dharani/Thoranee to witness his enlightenment and victory over Mara, the king of demons. The Buddha is always seated.

Dhyanamudra – meditation; both hands resting open, palms upwards, in the lap, right over left.

Other points of note:

Vajrasana – yogic posture of meditation; cross-legged, both soles of the feet visible.

Virasana – yogic posture of meditation; cross-legged, but with the right leg on top of the left, covering the left foot (also known as paryankasana).

Buddha under Naga – a common image in Khmer art; the Buddha is shown seated in an attitude of meditation with a cobra rearing up over his head. This refers to an episode in the Buddha's life when he was meditating; a rain storm broke and Nagaraja, the king of the nagas (snakes), curled up under the Buddha (seven coils) and then used his seven-headed hood to protect the Holy One from the falling rain.

Buddha calling for rain – a common image in Laos; the Buddha is depicted standing, both arms held stiffly at the side of the body, fingers pointing downwards.

often have a veranda at the back and the front. The most famous wats in Luang Prabang and Vientiane were built with royal patronage. But most wats in Laos were and are, constructed piece-meal with donations from the local community. Royal wats can be identified by the number of *dok sofa*: more than 10 'flowers' signifies that the wat was built by a king.

The Xieng Khouang style appears to be an amalgam of Vientiane and Luang Prabang influences. The *sim* is raised on a multi-level pediment, as with Vientiane-style *sim*, while the low, sweeping roofs are similar to *sim* in Luang Prabang.

Bhumisparcamudra – calling the earth
goddess to witness. Sukhothai period,
13th-14th century.

Dhyanamudra – meditation.
Sukhothai period, 13th-14th century.

Abhayamudra – dispelling fear or
giving protection. Lopburi Buddha,
Khmer style 12th century.

Vitarkamudra – preaching, "spinning
the Wheel of Law". Dvaravati Buddha,
7th-8th century, seated in the
"European" manner.

Abhayamudra – dispelling fear or
giving protection; subduing Mara
position. Lopburi Buddha, Khmer style
13th century.

The Buddha 'Calling for rain'

Arts and crafts

Lao art is well known for its wealth of ornamentation. As in other neighbouring Buddhist countries, the focus has been primarily religious in nature. Temple murals and bas-reliefs usually tell the story of the Buddha's life – the jataka tales. There has never been the range of art in Laos that there is in Thailand, as the country has been

Weaving fundamentals

Colours/dyes:	*red, orange, indigo and yellow*
Motifs, animal:	*naga/nyak (river serpent),* hong *(mythological goose-like bird),* naak *(dragon),* to mom *(deer),* siharath *(elephant lion),* singh *(lion)*
Motifs, geometric:	*zig-zag, triangles, spirals*
Motifs, natural:	*trees, flowers*
Motifs, other:	*palace buildings,* that *(stupas)*
Primary pieces:	*sin/phaa sin (wrap around sarong worn by women usually finished with a separate hand woven border),* pha baeng *(shoulder cloth or shawl),* pha tai luuk *(shawl worn by mothers to carry their infants),* pha mon *(head scarf) wedding corsage, funeral outfits.*

NB The above is very generalized; different weaving traditions of the country use different motifs, colours, techniques and designs.

n constantly dominated and influenced by foreign powers. Much of it has been destroyed over the centuries, as plundering neighbours ransacked towns and cities. The *Ramayana*, the Indian epic, has become part of the Lao cultural heritage and is known as the *Phra Lak Phra Lam* (see page 297). Many of the doors and windows of temples are engraved with scenes from this story, depicting the struggle between good and evil. Prime examples are the huge teak shutters at Wat Xieng Thong in Luang Prabang.

Sculpture Sculpture in Laos is more distinctive in style; the best pieces originate from the 16th to 18th centuries. Characteristic of Lao Buddha images is a nose like an eagle's beak, flat, extended earlobes and tightly curled hair. The best examples are in Wat Phra Kaeo and Wat Sisaket in Vientiane.

The 'Calling for Rain' mudra (the Buddha standing with hands pointing towards the ground, arms slightly away from the torso) is distinctively Lao (see page 77). The 'Contemplating the Tree of Enlightenment' mudra is also uniquely Lao – it depicts a standing Buddha with hands crossed in front of the body. There are many examples in the Pak Ou Caves, on the Mekong, 25 km upstream from Luang Prabang (see page 131).

Textiles Of all Laos' artistic traditions, perhaps none is more varied and more vital than its handwoven textiles. These inevitably show some stylistic links with Thailand, but in many respects Laos' tradition is richer and certainly the cloth being produced in Laos today is far finer, more complex and more technically accomplished than any currently being woven in Thailand (although there are those in Thailand who would dispute this, assuming – wrongly – that Thailand is more advanced than Laos in every regard).

Weaving is a craft almost entirely performed by women and it has always been a mark of womanhood. Traditionally, a girl was not considered fit for marriage until she had mastered the art of weaving and the Lao Loum women were expected to weave a corsage for their wedding day. Today these traditions are inevitably less strictly adhered to and there are also a handful of fine male weavers. (Indeed, it has been suggested that these few male weavers produce better – or at least more adventurous – work than their female counterparts because they are less constrained by tradition and more willing to experiment with new designs.) Even so, a skilled weaver is held in high regard and enjoys a position of respect. Cloth is woven

Background

The 'lost wax' process

A core of clay is moulded into the desired form and then covered in beeswax and shellac. Details are engraved into the beeswax. The waxed core is then coated with a watery mixture of clay and cow's dung, and built up into a thick layer of clay. This is then fired in a kiln, the wax running out through vents cut into the clay. Molten bronze is poured into the mould where it fills the void left by the wax and after cooling the mould is broken to reveal the image.

from silk, cotton, hemp and a variety of synthetic materials (mostly polyester) – or in some combination of these.

The finest weaving comes from the north. Around Xam Neua (and especially near Xam Tai), the Lao Neua produce some outstanding pieces. These were handed down through a family as heirlooms, stored in lidded stone jars to protect them from insects, moisture and sunlight and only worn on special occasions. But the recent history of this area forced people to sell their treasured textiles and few remain *in situ*. Indeed it was feared that the art of traditional weaving had been lost entirely in the area. Only the work of some NGOs and committed supporters has resuscitated high quality weaving in the area (and in Vientiane where some of the finest weavers now live and work). Lao Neua textiles are usually woven with a cotton warp and a silk weft and pieces include *pha sin* (sarong), *pha baeng* (shawl) and blankets. Various methods are employed including *ikat* (see the box on page 219) – where cotton is used as the Lao Neua consider that indigo dye does not take well on silk – and supplementary weft techniques. Pieces show bold bands of design and colour and the *pha sin* is usually finished with a separate handwoven border. Among the designs are swastika motifs, *hong* (geese), diamond shapes, *nyak* (snake) heads, lions and elephants.

The Lao Loum of the Luang Prabang area also have a fine weaving tradition, different from that of the far north and northeast. *Pha sin* produced here tend to have narrow vertical stripes, often alternating between dark and light. Silk tends to be used throughout on the finer pieces, although the yarn may be imported rather than locally produced and it is coloured using chemical dyes. Motifs include zig-zags, flowers and some designs that are French in inspiration.

Around Pakse in the south and also in central Laos around Savannakhet and Thakhek, designs are influenced by the Khmer and closest to those produced in the Isan region of northeast Thailand. *Matmii* ikat-woven cotton cloth is most characteristic. Designs are invariably geometric and today it is unusual to find a piece which has not been dyed using chemicals. Designs are handed down by mothers to their daughters and encompass a broad range from simple *sai fon* ('falling rain') designs where random sections of weft are tied, to the more complex *mee gung* and *poom som*. The less common *pha kit* is a supplementary weft ikat, although designs are similar to those in *matmii*. *Pha fai* is a simple cotton cloth, in blue or white and sometimes simply decorated, for everyday use and also used as part of the burial ceremony, when a white length of *pha fai* is draped over the coffin.

Literature

Lao literature is similar to Thai and is likewise also influenced by the Indian epic the *Ramayana*, which in Laos is known as the *Phra Lak Phra Lam* (see box, page 297). Scenes from the Phra Lak Phram Lam can often be seen depicted in temple murals. The first 10 jataka tales, recounting the last 10 lives of the Gautama Buddha (the historic Buddha), have also been a major inspiration for Lao literature. The versions that are in use in Laos are thought to have been introduced from Lanna Thai (northern Thailand, Chiang Mai) in the 16th century, or perhaps from the Mon area of present day Myanmar and Thailand. In these 10 tales, known as the *Vesantara Jataka*, the Buddha renounces all his earthly possessions, even his wife and children. Although the jataka tales in Laos are clearly linked, in religious terms, with Buddhism and therefore with India, the stories have little in common with the Indian originals. They draw heavily on local legends and folklore and have merely been incorporated within a religious literary milieu. They are essentially animist tales provided with a Buddhist gloss.

Traditionally, as in other parts of Southeast Asia, texts were recorded on palm leaves. The letters were inscribed with a stylus and the grooves darkened with oil. A palm leaf manuscript kept under good conditions in a well-maintained *hau tai* or library can last 100 years or more.

With the incorporation of Laos into French Indochina at the end of the 19th century, the Lao élite effectively renounced traditional Lao literature in favour of the French language and French artistic traditions. Many of the Lao élite were educated in France and those that were not still enjoyed a French-style education. The upshot was that Lao literature came to be looked down upon as primitive and simplistic and most scholars wrote instead in French.

As with traditional songs, much Lao poetry has been passed down the generations and remains popular. *Sin Xay* is one of the great Lao poems and has been written down (although many have not) and is found in many temples.

In 1778 the Thais plundered Laos and along with the two most sacred Buddha images – the Phra Bang and the Phra Kaeo (Emerald Buddha) – they pillaged a great deal of Lao religious literature and historical documents. Most Lao manuscripts – or *kampi* – are engraved on palm leaves and are 40-50 cm long, pierced with two holes and threaded together with cord. A bundle of 20 leaves forms a *phuk* and these are grouped together into *mat*, which are wrapped in a piece of cloth.

Language

See also box Transcribing Lao, page 298; Language, page 23; and Useful words & phrases, page 312

The official language is Lao, the language of the ethnic majority. Lao is basically a monosyllabic, tonal language. It contains many polysyllabic words borrowed from Pali and Sanskrit (ancient Indian dialects) as well as words borrowed from Khmer. It has six tones, 33 consonants and 28 vowels. Lao is also spoken in Northeast Thailand and North Cambodia, which was originally part of the kingdom of Lane Xang. Lao and Thai, particularly the Northeast dialect, are mutually intelligible. Differences have mainly developed since French colonial days when Laos was insulated from developments of the Thai language. French is still spoken in towns – particularly by the older generation – and is often used in government but English is being increasingly used. Significant numbers of Lao have been to universities and colleges in the former Soviet Union and Eastern Europe, so Eastern European languages and Russian are also spoken, but not widely.

Many of the tribal groups have no system of writing and the Lao script is similar to Thai, to which it is closely related. One of the kings of the Sukhothai Dynasty, Ramkhamhaeng, devised the Thai alphabet in 1283 and introduced the Thai system of writing. Lao script is modelled on the early Thai script and is written from left to right with no spacing between the words.

Like many other newly independent countries, the leadership in the Lao PDR have attempted to make Lao the national language, in fact as well as in rhetoric. An oft-quoted phrase is 'Language reveals one's nationhood, manners reveals one's lineage'. Because Lao is so similar to Thai, there has also been a conscious attempt to maintain a sense of difference between the two countries' languages. Otherwise,

The Lao Ramayana: the Phra Lak Phra Lam

The Phra Lak Phra Lam *is an adaptation of the Indian Hindu classic, the Ramayana, which was written by the poet Valmiki about 2,000 years ago. This 48,000 line epic odyssey – often likened to the works of Homer – was introduced into mainland Southeast Asia in the early centuries of the first millennium. The heroes were simply transposed into a mythical, ancient, Southeast Asian landscape.*

In Laos, as in Thailand, the Phra Lak Phra Lam *quickly became highly influential. In Thailand this is reflected in the name of the former capital of Siam, Ayutthaya, taken from the legendary hero's city of Ayodhia. Unfortunately, these early Thai translations of the Ramayana, which also filtered into Laos, were destroyed following the sacking of Ayutthaya by the Burmese in 1767. The earliest extant version was written by Thai King Taksin in about 1775.*

The Lao, and Thai, versions of the Ramayana, closely follow that of the original Indian story. They tell of the life of Ram (Rama), the King of Ayodhia. In the first part of the story, Ram renounces his throne following a long and convoluted court intrigue and flees into exile. With his wife Seeda (Sita) and trusted companion Hanuman (the monkey god), they undertake a long and arduous journey. In the second part, his wife Seeda is abducted

by the evil king Ravana, forcing Ram to wage battle against the demons of Langka Island (Sri Lanka). He defeats the demons with the help of Hanuman and his monkey army and recovers his wife. In the third and final part of the story – and here it diverges sharply from the Indian original – Seeda and Ram are reunited and reconciled with the help of the gods (in the Indian version there is no such reconciliation). Another difference from the Indian version is the significant role played by Hanuman – here an amorous adventurer who dominates much of the third part of the epic.

There are also numerous sub-plots which are original to the Phra Lak Phra Lam, *many building upon local myth and folklore. In tone and issues of morality, the Lao and Thai versions are less puritanical than the Indian original. There are also, of course, differences in dress, ecology, location and custom.*

Hanuman
Adapted from Hallet, Holt (1890) A Thousand Miles on an Elephant in the Shan

Background

some people believe, there exists the danger that Laos might simply become culturally absorbed within Greater Thailand. As scholars have pointed out, the cultural flows have essentially been one way: most people in Laos can understand Standard Thai, but few Thais (except in the Northeastern region) can understand Lao. Linguistically, Lao and Thai are both dialects of the same root language, but neither is the dialect of the other. (Many Thais view Lao as a linguistic off-shoot of Thai, and hence subordinate to Thai. Understandably, people in Laos take offence at this intimation.)

Because of this delicate intersection of nationality, identity and language, there has been a studied attempt to establish language principles for Lao that clearly separates it from Thai. To begin with it was necessary to establish an accepted, national version of spoken Lao (there are significant differences between areas). In other words, to produce Standard Lao which could be taught in schools, promoted in the media, and used in government. This effort at language engineering can be dated from the 1930s, and saw further refinements in the 1940s, 1950s, 1970s and 1990s. (Note that these attempts to develop Standard Lao bridge the colonial, royalist and communist periods.) While this has been successful to the extent that Lao remains

▶▶ Transcribing Lao: playing with words

How to transcribe the Lao language is a vexed issue which even the French never really worked out in some 50 years of trying. It is common to find three or four transcriptions of a town's name – Salavan, Saravane and Saravan; or Muang Khammouane, Mouang Khammouan and Muang Khammuan, for example. Generally in this book we have used the French 'x'

instead of the English 's' as this is more widely accepted in the country. So we use Xekong instead of Sekong. But where an 'English' spelling has gained acceptance – for example in the case of Paksé rather than Pakxé – we have kept the 's'. In either instance we provide alternative spellings where appropriate.

noticeably and significantly different from Thai, the major influence on the Lao language today remains that of Thai.

Dance, drama and music

Lao music, songs and dances have much in common with those of the Thai. Instruments include bamboo flutes, drums, gongs, cymbals and pinched or bowed string instruments shaped like banjos. The national instrument is the *kaen*, a hand-held pipe organ. It is made from bamboo and is similar in appearance to the South American pan pipes. Percussion is an important part of a Lao orchestra and two of the most commonly used instruments are the *nang nat*, a xylophone and the *knong vony*, a series of bronze cymbals suspended from a wooden frame. The *seb noi* orchestra – a consortium of all these instruments – is used to introduce or conclude vocal recitals. The *seb gnai* orchestra includes two big drums and a Lao-style clarinet as well; it was used in royal processions and still accompanies certain religious ceremonies.

Despite the lack of written notation, many epic poems and legends have survived to the present day as songs, passed, with the composition itself, from generation to generation. Early minstrels took their inspiration from folklore, enriched by Indian myths. Traditional Lao music can now only be heard during performances of the *Phra Lak Phra Lam*, the Lao version of the Indian epic the Ramayana. Many of the monasteries have experts on percussion who play every Buddhist sabbath. There is also a strong tradition of Lao folk music, which differs between tribal groups.

Secular songs, drawing largely on Lao literature for inspiration, are known as *mau lam* and can be heard at festival time not just in Laos but also in Northeast Thailand (where they are known as *mor lam*), which is also, culturally, 'Lao'. Indeed, there has been something of a Lao cultural revival in Northeast Thailand and some of the best performers are based there. It is also the best place to pick up cassette tapes of famous *mor lam/mau lam* singers.

In Vientiane and the provincial capitals, younger Lao tend to opt for western-style pop. To the raucous strains of the likes of Joan Jett and the Blackhearts – with the lyrics roughly translated into Lao – local bands entertain Levi-clad dancers well into the early hours in Vientiane's discos and nightclubs. The Communist leadership have become increasingly concerned at this invasion of western and Thai culture and there has been an attempt to limit the quantity of non-Lao music that is played in clubs and karaoke bars. The authorities have dictated that only a certain proportion of songs can be non-Lao and there are cultural police who occasionally check that these rules are being observed.

Classical Lao theatre and dance have Indian origins and were probably imported from the Cambodian royal courts in the 14th century. Thai influence has also crept in over the years.

Religion

Theravada Buddhism

Theravada Buddhism, from the Pali word *thera* ('elders'), means the 'way of the elders' and is distinct from the dominant Buddhism practised in India, Mahayana Buddhism or the 'Greater Vehicle'. The sacred language of Theravada Buddhism is Pali rather than Sanskrit, Bodhisattvas (future Buddhas) are not given much attention and emphasis is placed upon a precise and 'fundamental' interpretation of the Buddha's teachings, as they were originally recorded. By the 15th century, Theravada Buddhism was the dominant religion in Laos – as it was in neighbouring Siam (Thailand), Burma (Myanmar) and Cambodia. Buddhism shares the belief, in common with Hinduism, in rebirth. A person goes through countless lives and the experience of one life is conditioned by the acts in a previous one. This is the Law of Karma (act or deed, from Pali *kamma*), the law of cause and effect. But, it is not, as commonly thought in the West, equivalent to fate.

For most people, nirvana is a distant goal and they merely aim to accumulate merit by living good lives and performing good deeds such as giving alms to monks. In this way the layman embarks on the Path to Heaven. It is also common for a layman to become ordained, at some point in his life (usually as a young man), for a three month period during the Buddhist Rains Retreat.

Monks should endeavour to lead stringently ascetic lives. They must refrain from murder, theft, sexual intercourse, untruths, eating after noon, alcohol, entertainment, ornament, comfortable beds and wealth. They are allowed to own only a begging bowl, three pieces of clothing, a razor, needle, belt and water filter. They can only eat food that they have received through begging. Anyone who is male, over 20 and not a criminal can become a monk.

The 'Way of the Elders', is believed to be closest to Buddhist as it originally developed in India. It is often referred to by the term 'Hinayana' (Lesser Vehicle), a disparaging name foisted onto Theravadans by Mahayanists. This form of Buddhism is the dominant contemporary religion in the mainland Southeast Asian countries of Laos, Thailand, Cambodia and Myanmar (Burma).

In Theravadan Buddhism, the historic Buddha, Sakyamuni, is revered above all else and most images of the Buddha are of Sakyamuni. Importantly and unlike Mahayana Buddhism, the Buddha image is only meant to serve as a meditation aid. In theory, it does not embody supernatural powers and it is not supposed to be worshipped. But, the popular need for objects of veneration has meant that most images *are* worshipped. Pilgrims bring flowers and incense and prostrate themselves in front of the image. This is a Mahayanist influence which has been embraced by Theravadans.

Buddhism in Laos

The Lao often maintain that the Vientiane area converted to Buddhism at the time of the Moghul emperor Asoka. This seems suspiciously early and is probably untrue. The original stupa at That Luang, so it is claimed, was built to encase a piece of the Buddha's breastbone provided by Asoka. Buddhism was undoubtedly practised before Fa Ngoum united Lane Xang and created a Buddhist Kingdom in the mid-14th century. He was known as the Great Protector of the Faith and brought the Phra Bang, the famous golden statue – the symbol of Buddhism in Laos – from Angkor in Cambodia to Laos.

Buddhism was gradually accepted among the lowland Lao but many of the highland tribes remain animist. Even where Buddhism has been practised for centuries, it

In Siddhartha's footsteps: a short history of Buddhism

Buddhism was founded by Siddhartha Gautama, a prince of the Sakya tribe of Nepal, who probably lived between 563 and 483 BC. He achieved enlightenment and the word buddha means 'fully enlightened one', or 'one who has woken up'. Siddhartha Gautama is known by a number of titles. In the west, he is usually referred to as The Buddha, that is the historic Buddha (but not just Buddha); more common in Southeast Asia is the title Sakyamuni, or Sage of the Sakyas (referring to his tribal origins).

Over the centuries, the life of the Buddha has become part legend, and the Jataka tales which recount his various lives are colourful and convoluted. But, central to any Buddhist's belief is that he was born under a sal tree, that he achieved enlightenment under a bodhi tree in the Bodh Gaya Gardens, that he preached the First Sermon at Sarnath and that he died at Kusinagara (all in India or Nepal).

The Buddda was born at Lumbini (in present-day Nepal), as Queen Maya was on her way to her parents' home. She had had a very auspicious dream before the child's birth of being impregnated by an elephant, whereupon a sage prophesied that Siddhartha would become either a great king or a great spiritual leader. His father, being keen that the first option of the prophesy be fulfilled, brought him up in all the princely skills – at which Siddhartha excelled – and ensured that he only saw beautiful things, not the harsher elements of life.

Despite his father's efforts Siddhartha saw four things while travelling between palaces – a helpless old man, a very sick man, a corpse being carried by lamenting relatives and an ascetic, calm and serene as he begged for food. The young prince renounced his princely origins and left home to study under a series of spiritual teachers. He finally discovered the path to enlightenment at the Bodh Gaya Gardens in India. He then proclaimed his thoughts to a small group of disciples at Sarnath, near Benares, and continued to preach and attract followers until he died at the age of 81 at Kusinagara.

In the First Sermon at the deer park in Sarnath, the Buddha preached the Four Truths, which are still considered the root of Buddhist belief and practical experience: suffering exists; there is a cause of suffering; suffering can be ended; and to end suffering it is necessary to follow the 'Noble Eightfold Path' – namely, right speech, livelihood, action, effort, mindfulness, concentration, opinion and intention.

Soon after the Buddha began preaching, a monastic order – the Sangha – was established. As the monkhood evolved in India, it also began to fragment into different sects. An important change was the belief that the Buddha was transcendent: he had never been born, nor had he died; he had always existed and his life on earth had been mere illusion. The emergence of these new concepts helped to turn what up until then was an ethical code of conduct, into a religion. It eventually led to the appearance of a new Buddhist movement, Mahayana Buddhism which split from the more traditional Theravada 'sect'.

Despite the division of Buddhism into two sects, the central tenets of the religion are common to both. Specifically, the principles pertaining to the Four Noble Truths, the Noble Eightfold Path, the Dependent Origination, the Law of Karma and nirvana. In addition, the principles of non-violence and tolerance are also embraced by both sects. In essence, the differences between the two are of emphasis and interpretation. Theravada Buddhism is strictly based on the original Pali Canon, while the Mahayana tradition stems from later Sanskrit texts. Mahayana Buddhism also allows a broader and more varied interpretation of the doctrine. Other important differences are that while the Thervada tradition is more 'intellectual' and self-obsessed, with an emphasis upon the attaining of wisdom and insight for oneself, Mahayana Buddhism stresses devotion and compassion towards others.

is usually interwoven with the superstitions and rituals of animist beliefs. Appeasing the spirits and gaining merit are both integral features of life. Most highlanders are animists and the worship of *phi* or spirits has remained central to village life throughout the revolutionary years, despite the fact that it was officially banned by the government. Similarly, the *baci* ceremony – when strings representing guardian spirits are tied around the wrists of guests – is still practised throughout Laos.

In the late 1500s, King Setthathirat promoted Buddhism and built many monasteries or *wats*. Buddhism was first taught in schools in the 17th century and prospered until the Thai and Ho invasions of the 18th and 19th centuries when many of the wats were destroyed. With the introduction of socialism in 1975 Buddhism was banned from primary schools and people prohibited from giving alms to monks. With the increasing religious tolerance of the regime it is now undergoing a revival and many of the wats are being rebuilt and redecorated. Males are expected to become monks for three months or so before marriage, usually during Buddhist Lent. All members of the priesthood are placed under the authority of a superior – the *Phra Sangharaja*– whose seat was traditionally in the capital of the kingdom.

In line with Buddhist tradition, materialism and the accumulation of personal wealth is generally frowned on in Laos. Poverty is admired as a form of spirituality. This belief proved rather convenient for the Communist regime, when it was taken to extremes. Today, in the new capitalist climate, the traditional attributes of spirituality sit uncomfortably with Laos' increasingly bourgeois aspirations.

Buddhism, as it is practised in Laos, is not the 'other-worldly' religion of western conception. Ultimate salvation – enlightenment, or *nirvana* – is a distant goal for most people. Lao Buddhists pursue the Law of Karma, the reduction of suffering. Meritorious acts are undertaken and demeritorious ones avoided so that life and more particularly future life, might be improved. 'Karma' is often thought of in the West as 'fate'. It is not. It is true that previous karma determines a person's position in society, but there is still room for individual action – and a person is ultimately responsible for that action. It is the law of cause and effect.

It is important to draw a distinction between 'academic' Buddhism, as it tends to be understood in the West and 'popular' Buddhism, as it is practised in Laos. In Laos, Buddhism is a 'syncretic' religion: it incorporates elements of Brahmanism, animism and ancestor worship. Amulets are worn to protect against harm and are often sold in temple compounds. In the countryside, farmers have what they consider to be a healthy regard for the spirits *(phi)* and demons that inhabit the rivers, trees and forests. Astrologers are widely consulted by urban and rural dwellers alike. It is these aspects of Lao Buddhism which help to provide worldly assurance and they are perceived to be complementary, not in contradiction, with Buddhist teachings.

Most Lao villages will contain a 'temple', 'monastery' or *wat* (the word does not translate accurately). The wat represents the mental heart of each community and most young men at some point in their lives will become ordained as monks, usually during the Buddhist Rains Retreat, which stretches from July to October. Previously this period represented the only opportunity for a young man to gain an education and to learn how to read. An equally important reason for a man to become ordained is so that he can accumulate merit for his family, particularly for his mother, who as a woman cannot become ordained.

As in Thailand, Laos has adopted the Indian epic the *Ramayana* (see page 297), which has been the inspiration for much Lao art and sculpture. Complete manuscripts of the Lao *Ramayana* – known as the *Phra Lak Phra Lam*, used to be kept at Wat Phra Kaeo and Wat Sisaket.

Buddhism under Communism

Buddhism's relationship with Communism has been complex and usually ambivalent. As the Pathet Lao began their revolutionary mission they saw in the country's monks a useful means by which to spread their message. Many monks, though they may themselves have renounced material possessions and all desires, were conscious of the inequalities in society and the impoverished conditions in which many people lived their lives. Indeed most of them came from poor, rural backgrounds. In addition many monks saw themselves as the guardians of Lao culture and as the US became more closely involved in the country so they increasingly felt that it was their job to protect the people against the spread of an alien culture and mores. Therefore, right from the start, monks had a natural sympathy with the ideals of the Pathet Lao. Indeed, significant numbers renounced their vows and joined the revolution. Others stayed on in their monasteries, but used their positions and the teachings of the Buddha to further the revolutionary cause. The Pathet Lao, for their part, saw the monks as a legitimizing force which would assist in their revolutionary efforts. Monks were often the most respected individuals in society and if the Pathet Lao could somehow piggy-back on this respect then they too, it was reasoned, would gain in credibility and respect. The Rightist government also tried to do the same, but with notably less success.

With the victory of the Pathet Lao in 1975, their view of the *sangha* (monkhood) changed. No longer were monks a useful vehicle in building revolution; overnight they became a potential threat. Monks were forced to attend re-education seminars where they were instructed that they could no longer teach about merit or *karma*, two central pillars of Buddhism. Their sermons were taped by Pathet Lao cadres to be scrutinized for subversive propaganda and a stream of disillusioned monks began to flee to Thailand. So the *sangha* was emasculated as an independent force. Monks were forced to follow the directives of the Lao People's Revolutionary Party and the *sangha* came under strict Party control. Monasteries were expected to become mini-cooperatives so that they did not have to depend on the laity for alms and they were paid a small salary by the State for undertaking teaching and health work. In short, the LPDR seemed intent on undermining the *sangha* as an independent force in Lao society, making it dependent on the State for its survival and largely irrelevant to wider society. The success of the Pathet Lao's policy of marginalization can be seen in the number of monks in the country. In 1975 there were around 20,000 monks. By 1979 this had shrunk to just 1,700.

However before the *sangha* could sink into obscurity and irrelevance, the government eased its policy in 1979 and began to allow monks and the *sangha* greater latitude. In addition and perhaps more importantly, the leadership embraced certain aspects of Lao culture, one of which was Theravada Buddhism. The memorial to the revolutionary struggle in Vientiane, for example, was designed as a Buddhist *that* (stupa) and government ministers enthusiastically join in the celebration of Buddhist festivals.

Christianity in post-1975 Laos

Growing religious tolerance has also rekindled Christianity. While many churches in provincial towns were turned into community centres and meeting halls after the revolution, Vientiane's Evangelical Church has held a Sunday service ever since 1979. But Christians have only felt free to worship openly in recent years and recent events have shown that even this 'freedom' comes with qualifications. In 1989 the first consultation between the country's Christian leaders (Protestant and Roman Catholic) was authorized by the government – it was the first such meeting since 'liberation'.

Government representatives and two leaders of the Buddhist Federation were also invited to attend – ironically both were Hmong.

Foreign missionaries were ejected from Laos in 1975. But with indigenous priests and missionaries now operating in the countryside (many under the guise of non-governmental aid organizations), church leaders predict the rapid growth of Christianity – they say there are around 17,000 Christians in the country. Not many Buddhists have converted to Christianity but it seems to be growing among the animist hilltribes. The US Bible Society has recently published a modern translation of the Bible into Lao, but tribal language editions do not yet exist. The shortage of bibles and other literature has prompted Christian leaders to 'offer unsolicited gifts' to the department of religious affairs to ease restrictions on the import of hymn books and bibles from Thailand.

While there is more freedom to worship today than during the pre-reform period, there is still a sense in the leadership that Christians are a political threat. In 1998 the authorities arrested 44 Christians, among them three Americans, for conducting unauthorized church services in people's private homes. The Americans were expelled but the Laotians were thrown in prison. This sort of knee-jerk over-reaction usually ends up being counter-productive. The US Congress responded to what they saw to be religious persecution by blocking an economic agreement that was likely to significantly boost textile exports to the US. (China gets away with these sorts of things because it is a powerful and important country; Laos is weak and unimportant.) The fact that the leadership in Laos is hyper-sensitive to such issues was reinforced in November 1999 when six Christian leaders were reportedly arrested and imprisoned for planning a pro-democracy rally along with around 100 other activists.

Land and environment

Geography

Laos stretches about 1,000 km from north to south, while distances from east to west range from 140 to 500 km. The country covers an area of 236,800 sq km – less than half the size of France and just a third of the size of Texas. Only 24% of the population live in towns and the country has the lowest population density in Asia with 22 people per sq km. The population is 5.2 million (2000) and is growing at 2.6% a year (average, 1995-2000).

Rugged mountains cover more than three-quarters of the country and with few all-weather roads (there are just 4,000 km of sealed roads in the entire country), rivers remain important communication routes. Historically, the Mekong River has been the country's economic artery. On its banks nestle Laos' most important cities: in the north the small, colourful former royal capital of Luang Prabang, further south the administrative and political capital of Vientiane and farther south still the regional centres of Thakhek, Savannakhet and Pakse.

Laos is dominated by the Mekong River and the Annamite chain of mountains which both run southeast towards the South China Sea. Flowing along the borders of Laos are 1,865 km of the 4,000 km-long Mekong River, the country's main thoroughfare. The lowlands of the Mekong valley form the principal agricultural areas, especially around Vientiane and Savannakhet and these are home to the lowland Lao – sometimes argued to be the 'true' Lao. The Mekong has three main tributaries: the Nam Ou and Nam Tha from the north and the Nam Ngum, which flows into Vientiane province.

Much of the northern half of Laos is 1,500 m or more above sea level and its karst limestone outcrops are deeply dissected by steep-sided river valleys. Further south, the Annamite chain has an average height of 1,200 m. Heavily forested, rugged mountains form a natural barrier between Laos and Vietnam. Most of the country is a mixture of mountains and high plateau. There are four main plateaux: the Xieng Khouang plateau, better known as the Plain of Jars, in the north, the Nakai and the limestone Khammuan plateau in the centre and the 10,000 sq km Bolovens Plateau to the south. The highest peak is the 2,800 m Bia Mountain, which rises above the Xieng Khouang plateau to the northeast.

Mekong River: mother river of Southeast Asia

The Mekong River is one of the 12 great rivers of the world. It stretches 4,500 km from its source on the Tibet Plateau in China to its mouth (or mouths) in the Mekong Delta of Vietnam. On 11 April 1995 a Franco-British expedition announced that they had discovered the source of the Mekong – 5,000 m high, at the head of the Rup-Sa Pass, and miles from anywhere. Each year, the river empties 475 billion cubic m of water into the South China Sea. Along its course it flows through Myanmar (Burma), Laos, Thailand, Cambodia and Vietnam – all of the countries that constitute mainland Southeast Asia – as well as China. In both a symbolic and a physical sense then, it links the region. Bringing fertile silt to the land along its banks, but particularly to the Mekong Delta, the river contributes to Southeast Asia's agricultural wealth. In former times, a tributary of the Mekong which drains the Tonle Sap (the Great Lake of Angkor and Cambodia), provided the rice surplus on which that fabulous empire was founded. The Tonle Sap acts like a great regulator, storing water in time of flood and then releasing it when levels recede.

The first European to explore the Mekong River was the French naval officer Francis Garnier. His Mekong Expedition (1866-68), followed the great river upstream from its delta in Cochin China and in the process 'discovered' the lost ruins of Angkor, tropical jungles, tribal groups, and much else besides. Of the 9,960 km that the expedition covered, 5,060 km were 'discovered' for the first time. The motivation for the trip was to find a southern route into the Heavenly Kingdom – China. But they failed. The river is navigable only as far as the Lao-Cambodian border where the Khone rapids make it impassable. Nonetheless, the report of the expedition is one of the finest of its genre.

Today the Mekong itself is perceived as a source of potential economic wealth – not just as a path to riches. The Mekong Secretariat was established in 1957 to harness the waters of the river for hydropower and irrigation. The Secretariat devised a grandiose plan incorporating a succession of seven huge dams which would store 142 billion cubic m of water, irrigate 4.3 million ha of riceland, and generate 24,200MW of power. But the Vietnam War intervened to disrupt construction. Only Laos' Nam Ngum Dam on a tributary of the Mekong was ever built. Now that the countries of mainland Southeast Asia are on friendly terms once more, the Secretariat (now known as the Mekong River Commission) and its scheme have been given a new lease of life. But in the intervening years, fears about the environmental consequences of big dams have raised new questions. The Mekong Secretariat has moderated its plans and is now looking at less ambitious, and less contentious, ways to harness the Mekong River. Nonetheless, several new dams have been constructed on tributaries of the Mekong and many more are at various stages of planning.

Climate

For the best time to visit, see page 19 The rainy season is from May through to September-October; the tropical lowlands receive an annual average rainfall of 1,250 mm a year. Temperatures during these months are in the 30s°C. In mountainous Xieng Khoung Province, it is cooler and temperatures can drop to freezing point in December and January. The first half of the dry season, from November to April, is cool, with temperatures between 10° and

Background

The universal stimulant – the betel nut

Throughout the countryside in Southeast Asia, and in more remote towns, it is common to meet men and women whose teeth are stained black, and gums red, by continuous chewing of the 'betel nut'. This, though, is a misnomer. The betel 'nut' is not chewed at all: the three crucial ingredients that make up a betel 'wad' are the nut of the areca palm (Areca catechu), the leaf or catkin of the betel vine (Piper betel), and lime. When these three ingredients are combined with saliva they act as a mild stimulant. Other ingredients (people have their own recipes) are tobacco, gambier, various spices and the gum of Acacia catechu. The habit, though also common in South Asia and parts of China, seems to

have evolved in Southeast Asia and it is mentioned in the very earliest chronicles. The lacquer betel boxes of Myanmar and Thailand, and the brass and silver ones of Indonesia, illustrate the importance of chewing betel in social intercourse. Galvao in his journal of 1544 noted: "They use it so continuously that they never take it from their mouths; therefore these people can be said to go around always ruminating." Among westernized Southeast Asians the habit is frowned upon: the disfigurement and ageing that it causes, and the stained walls and floors that result from the constant spitting, are regarded as distasteful products of an earlier age. But beyond the élite it is still widely practised.

20°C. This gives way to a hot, dry season from March to June when temperatures soar and are often in excess of 35°C. Average rainfall in Vientiane is 1,700 mm, although in North Laos and the highlands it is much wetter, with more than 3,000 mm each year.

Vegetation

Much of Laos is forested. The vegetation is rich and diverse: a mix of tropical and subtropical species. Grassy savanna predominates on plateau areas such as the Plain of Jars. In the forests, some hardwoods tower to over 30 m, while tropical palms and mango are found in the lowlands and large stands of pine in the remote northern hills.

About half the country is still covered in primary forest but this is being seriously threatened by logging which provides Laos with more than two-thirds of its export earnings. Officially, around 450,000 cubic m are felled each year for commercial purposes, although in reality this is probably an underestimate owing to the voracious activities of illegal loggers – many of whom are Thai. A ban on the export of logs in 1988 caused official timber export earnings to slump 30% – but environmentalists claim that the ban has had little impact on the number of logs being exported. Another ban was imposed in late 1991. In addition, shifting cultivators clear an estimated 100,000 ha of forest a year. The government sees shifting cultivators (most of whom are from one of Laos' ethnic minorities) as the primary cause of forest loss and the current five year development plan has reiterated the government's commitment to 'totally eradicating' shifting cultivation. But if the situation is similar to neighbouring countries like Thailand and Vietnam then this will do little to preserve the forest because the primary culprits are commercial logging concerns.

Government reforestation programmes far from compensate for the destruction. In October 1989 the Council of Ministers issued a decree on the preservation of forests of which the people appear to be blissfully unaware. There was a half-hearted propaganda campaign to 'teach every Lao citizen to love nature and develop a sense of responsibility for the preservation of forests'.

Background

Wildlife

Mammals include everything from wildcats, leopards and tigers to bears, wild cattle and small barking deer. Laos is also home to the large Asian elk, rhinoceros, elephants, monkeys, gibbons and ubiquitous rabbits and squirrels. Ornithological life encompasses pheasants, partridges, many songbirds, ducks and some hawks and eagles – although in rural areas many birds (and other animals) have been killed for food. There is an abundant reptilian population, including cobras, kraits, crocodiles and lizards. The lower reaches of the Mekong River, marking the border between Cambodia and Laos, is the last place in Indochina where the rare Irrawaddy dolphin is to be found. However dynamite fishing is decimating the population and today there are probably just 100-200 left. Another rare denizen of the Mekong, but one that stands a greater chance of survival, is the *pa buk* catfish (*Pangasianodon gigas*) which weighs up to 340 kg. This riverbed-dwelling fish was first described by western science only in 1930, although Lao fishermen and their Thai counterparts had been catching it for many years – as James McCarthy notes in the account of his travels through Siam and Laos published in 1900. The fish is a delicacy and clearly has been for many years – its roe was paid as tribute to China in the late 19th century. Because of over-fishing, by the 1980s the numbers of *pa buk* had become severly depleted. However a breeding programme is having some success and young *pa buk* fingerlings are now being released into the Mekong.

There is an enormous problem of smuggling rare animals out of Laos, mainly to South Korea and China. In 1978, the gall bladder of a black bear from Laos was auctioned in Seoul for US$55,000. Teeth and bones of wild cats from Laos are in demand for Chinese medicine. The English-language daily, *Khao San Pathet Lao*, published a report estimating that in 1992 more than 10 tonnes of protected wild animals had been slaughtered for export in the northeastern province of Houa Phanh.

The degree to which Laos' flora and fauna are under-researched was illustrated in August 1999 when it was announced that a previously unknown species of striped rabbit had been discovered quietly nibbling the grass in the mountains dividing Laos from Vietnam. This area of Indochina has proved a veritable cornucopia of unknown animals. During the 1990s scientists have discovered one antelope, several species of deer, an ox and even a remnant herd of Javan rhinoceros, a species which was previously thought to be confined to a small corner of West Java.

Books

Books on Southeast Asia

www.thailine.com/lot us is the homepage of White Lotus, a Bangkok-based publishing house specializing in English language books (many reprints of old books) on the region including early travel accounts of Laos

Dingwall, Alastair *Traveller's Literary Companion to South-east Asia* (1994) In Print: Brighton. Experts on Southeast Asian language and literature select extracts from novels and other books by Western and regional writers. The extracts are annoyingly brief, but it gives a good overview of what is available.

Dumarçay, Jacques *The Palaces of South-East Asia: Architecture and Customs* (1991) OUP: Singapore. A broad summary of palace art and architecture in both mainland and island Southeast Asia.

Fraser-Lu, Sylvia *Handwoven Textiles of South-East Asia* (1988) OUP: Singapore. Well-illustrated, large format book with informative text.

Higham, Charles *The Archaeology of Mainland Southeast Asia from 10,000 BC to the Fall of Angkor* (1989) Cambridge University Press: Cambridge. Best summary of changing views of the archaeology of the mainland.

Keyes, Charles F *The Golden Peninsula: Culture and Adaptation in Mainland Southeast Asia* (1977) Macmillan: New York. Academic, yet readable summary of the threads of continuity and change in Southeast Asia's culture. The volume has been recently republished by Hawaii University Press, but not updated or revised.

King, Ben F and Dickinson, EC *A Field Guide to the Birds of South-East Asia* (1975) Collins: London. Best regional guide to the birds of the region.

Miettinen, Jukko O *Classical Dance and Theatre in South-East Asia* (1992) OUP, Singapore. Expensive, but accessible survey of dance and theatre, mostly focusing on Thailand, Myanmar and Indonesia.

Osborne, Milton *Southeast Asia: an Introductory History* (1979) Allen & Unwin: Sydney. Good introductory history, clearly written, published in a portable paperback edition. A new revised edition is not on the shelves.

Rawson, Philip *The Art of Southeast Asia* (1967) Thames & Hudson: London. Portable general art history of Myanmar, Cambodia, Vietnam, Thailand, Laos, Java and Bali; by necessity, rather superficial, but a good place to start.

Reid, Anthony *Southeast Asia in the Age of Commerce 1450-1680: the Lands below the Winds* (1988) Yale University Press: New Haven. Perhaps the best history of everyday life in Southeast Asia, looking at such themes as physical well-being, material culture and social organization.

Reid, Anthony *Southeast Asia in the Age of Commerce 1450-1680: Expansion and Crisis* (1993) Yale University Press: New Haven. Volume 2 in this excellent history of the region.

Rigg, Jonathan *Southeast Asia: the Human Landscape of Modernization and Development* (2002, 2nd edn) London: Routledge. A book which covers both the market and former command economies (ie Myanmar, Vietnam, Laos and Cambodia) of the region. It focuses on how people in the region have responded to the challenges and tensions of modernization.

SarDesai, DR *Southeast Asia: Past and Present* (1989) Macmillan: London. Skilful but at times frustratingly thin history of the region from the 1st century to the withdrawal of US forces from Vietnam.

Steinberg, DJ *et al In Search of Southeast Asia: a Modern History* (1987) University of Hawaii Press: Honolulu. The best standard history of the region; it skilfully examines and assesses general processes of change and their impacts from the arrival of the Europeans in the region. A new edition is being prepared.

Tarling, Nicholars (edit) *Cambridge History of Southeast Asia* (1992) Cambridge: Cambridge University Press. Two-volume edited study, long and expensive with contributions from most of the leading historians of the region. A thematic and regional approach is taken, not a country one, although the history is fairly conventional.

Waterson, Roxana *The Living house: an Anthropology of Architecture in South-East Asia* (1990) OUP: Singapore. An academic but extensively illustrated book on Southeast Asian architecture and how it links with lives and livelihoods. Fascinating material for those interested in such things.

Books on Laos

Connors, Mary *Lao Textiles and traditions* Oxford University Press.

Art

Evans, Grant *Laos: Culture and Society* (1999) Chiang Mai, Thailand: Silkworm Books. Edited volume written by assorted scholars of Laos. Highly informed; good for those who really want to know about the country.

Culture & society

Raintree Books, Pang Kham Road, Vientiane, stocks a reasonable selection of dictionaries and 'teach yourself' books.

Marcus, Russell (1983) Charles E Tuttle Co, USA. Perhaps the best Lao-English/English-Lao dictionary, but costs around US$20. Order it from www.worldlanguage.com

Dictionaries & teach yourself Lao books

Background

Werner, Klaus *Learning and Speaking Lao*. Useful and cheaper than Marcus (about US$12).

Phone Bouaravong *Learning Lao for Everyone* locally produced and comes with tapes.

Economics, politics & development

Dommen, Arthur J *Laos: Keystone of Indochina* (1985) Boulder: Westview Press. Out of date now in terms of the economic picture that is painted, but a reasonable overview.

Grant Evans *Lao Peasants under Socialism* (1990) New Haven: Yale University Press. The definitive account of farmers in modern Laos. A new edition has been published by Silkworm Books in Chiang Mai (Thailand), updated to take into account economic changes brought about by the New Economic Mechanism.

Evans, Grant (edit) *Laos: Culture and Society* (1997) Chiang Mai, Thailand: Silkworm Books. A book due to be published in 1997; should provide the most comprehensive account of Laos' culture(s) and society. The editor, Grant Evans, is one of the world's foremost scholars of Laos.

Håkangård, Agneta *Road 13: A Socio-economic Study of Villagers, Transport and Use of Road 13 S, Lao P.D.R.* (1992) Development Studies Unit, Department of Social Anthropology, Stockholm University. A shortish monography examining how road 13, the main north-south highway, is affecting people's lives along the route. Only for the really interested.

Ivarsson, Soren, Svensson, Thommy and Tonnesson, Stein *The Quest for Balance in a Changing Laos: A Political Analysis* (1995) Nordic Institute of Asian Studies (NIAS) report no. 25, NIAS, Copenhagen. A study which examines the question of Laos' role and place within the wider region and its quest for 'equi-distance' between the powers of the area.

Stuart-Fox, Martin (edit) *Contemporary Laos* (1982) St Lucia: Queensland University Press. A useful overview of Laos up to 1980. By dint of its publication date, though, it cannot cover important events since the LPDR effectively gave up its attempt to build a revolutionary state.

Stuart-Fox, Martin *Laos – Politics, Economics and Society* (1986) London: Francis Pinter. Out of date now in terms of the economic picture that is painted, but a good single volume summary of the country providing broad-brush historical and cultural background too.

Stuart-Fox, Martin *Buddhist Kingdom, Marxist State: the Making of Modern Laos* (1996) Bangkok: White Lotus. Really a collection of Stuart-Fox's various papers published over the years and brought up-to-date. Possibly the single best volume to take. It is particularly good on recent history – from the emergence to the victory of the Pathet Lao in 1975 and developments since then. Widely available in Bangkok.

Tapp, Nicholas *Sovereignty and Rebellion: the White Hmong of Northern Thailand* (1989) Oxford University Press: Singapore. Scholarly study of the tensions under which the Hmong are forced to live their lives. Fieldwork is Thai-based, but much of the ethnography is relevant to Laos too.

Trankell, I-B *On the Road in Laos: an Anthropological Study of Road Construction and Rural Communities* (1993) Uppsala Research Reports in Cultural Anthropology, No 12, Uppsala University, Uppsala. A research monograph; like Håkangård's volume; really only for the very interested.

Zasloff, J J and Unger, L (edits) *Laos: Beyond the Revolution* (1991) Macmillan, Basingstoke. Edited volume with a mixed collection of papers; some of the economics/politics chapters are already rather dated.

Food

Phia Sing *Traditional recipes of Laos* (1995) Totnes, Devon, UK: Prospect Books. The best Lao cookbook available. The recipes were collected by the chief chef at the Royal Palace in Luang Prabang, Phia Sing, who recorded them in the 1960s. They have been translated into English and made West-friendly by replacing some of the more esoteric ingredients.

Vientiane Guide, published by the Women's International Group. Available from bookshops in Vientiane. Invaluable if proposing to live in the country, with handy tips on how to rent a house, employ domestic servants, schools and so on.

Guides

Manich Jumsai, ML *A New History of Laos, Bangkok* (1971) Chalermnit Books. This history is very standard in approach and uncritical in terms of the material that is recounted. There are some good stories here, but it should not be taken at face value. It is widely available in Bangkok and relatively cheap.
Stuart-Fox, Martin and Kooyman, Mary *Historical Dictionary of Laos* (1992) New York: the Scarecrow Press. Takes, as the name suggests, a dictionary approach to Laos' history which is fine if you are looking up a fact or two, but doesn't really lend itself to telling a narrative.
Stuart-Fox, Martin *A History of Laos* (1997) Cambridge: Cambridge University Press. Most up-to-date history of the country by one of the handful of non-Laotian historians of Laos. Concentrates on the modern period,
Toye, Hugh *Laos – Buffer State or Battleground* (1968) London: Oxford University Press.

History

Castle, Timothy *A War in the Shadow of Vietnam: US Military Aid to the Royal Lao Government 1955-1975* (1993) New York: Columbia University Press.
Grant Evans & Kelvin Rowley *Red Brotherhood at War, Vietnam Cambodia & Laos since 1975* (1990) Verso.
Grant Evans *Yellow Rainmakers: Are Chemical Weapons Being Used in Southeast Asia* (1983) Verso.
McCoy, Alfred W *The Politics of Heroin: CIA Complicity in the Global Drugs Trade* (1991) Lawrence Hill/Chicago Review Press. Originally published at the beginning of the 1970s, it is the classic study of the politics of drugs in mainland Southeast Asia.
Parker, James *Codename Mule: Fighting the Secret War in Laos for the CIA* (1995) Annapolis, Maryland: Naval Institute Press. Another book to add to the growing list that recount the personal stories of the Americans fighting in Laos. Much of it deals with the fighting on the Plain of Jars.
Robbins, Christopher *Air America: the Story of the CIS's Secret Airlines* (1979) New York: Putnam Books. The earlier of Robbins' two books on the secret war. Made into a film of the same name with Mel Gibson in the starring role.
Robbins, Christopher *The Ravens: Pilots of the Secret War of Laos* (1989) New York: Bantam Press. The best known and the most thrilling read of all the books on America's secret war in Laos. The story it tells seems almost incredible.
Warner, Roger *Back Fire: the CIA's Secret War in Laos and its Link to the War in Vietnam* (1995) New York: Simon and Schuster. The best of the more recent books recounting the experiences of US servicemen in Laos.

Indochina War

Background

De Carne, Louis *Travels in Indochina and the Chinese Empire* (1872) London: Chapman Hall. Recounts De Carne's experiences in Laos in 1872, some years before the country was colonized by the French.
Garstin, Crosbie *The Voyage from London to Indochina* (1928) Heinemann. Hilarious, rather irreverent account of a journey through Indochina.
Hoskin, John *The Mekong* (1991) Bangkok: Post Publishing. A large format coffee table book with good photographs and a modest text. Widely available in Bangkok.
Lewis, Norman *A Dragon Apparent: Travels in Cambodia, Laos and Vietnam* (1951) One of the finest of all travel books; now reprinted by Eland Books but also available second-hand from many bookshops.

Travel & geography

Maugham, Somerset *The Gentlemen in the Parlour: a Record of a Journey from Rangoon to Haiphong* (1930) Heinemann: London. An account of Maugham's journey through Southeast Asia, in classic limpid prose.

McCarthy, James *Surveying and Exploring in Siam with Descriptions of Laos Dependencies and of Battles against the Chinese Haws* (1994) White Lotus: Bangkok. Reprint of an account first published in 1900 telling of the travels of Englishman James McCarthy who was employed by the government of Siam as a surveyor and adviser; an interesting book to read when travelling, particularly, in the north and northeast.

Mouhot, Henri *Travels in Indochina* (1986) Bangkok: White Lotus. An account of Laos by France's most famous explorer of Southeast Asia. He tried to discover a 'back door' into China by travelling up the Mekong, but died of Malaria in Luang Prabang in 1860. The book has been republished by White Lotus and is easily available in Bangkok; there is also a more expensive reprint available from OUP (Kuala Lumpur).

Stewart, Lucretia *Tiger Balm: Travels in Laos, Cambodia and Vietnam* (1998) London: Chatto and Windus.

Magazines *The Far Eastern Economic Review* (weekly). Authoritative Hong Kong-based regional magazine; their correspondents based in each country provide knowledgeable, in-depth analysis particularly on economics and politics.

Newsletters *Indochina Newsletter* (monthly) from Asia Resource Centre, c/o 2161 Massachusetts Avenue, Cambridge, MA02140, USA.

Background

Footnotes

Useful words and phrases

Greetings

yes/no	men/baw	**A little, a bit**	noi, hoi
thank you/	kop jai/	**Where?**	you-sigh?
no thank you	baw, kop jai	**How much is…?**	Tow-dai?
hello/goodbye	suh-bye-dee/lah-gohn	**It doesn't matter**	baw penh yang
What is your name?	Chow seu yang?	**never mind**	
My name is…	koi seu….	**Pardon?**	kow toat?
Excuse me, sorry	ko toat	**I don't understand**	Kow baw cow-chi
Can/do you speak	Koy pahk pah-sah	**How are you?**	Chao suh-bye-dee-baw?
English?	anhg-geet?	**not very well**	baw suh-bye

The hotel

What is the charge	Kit laka van nuang	**Does the room have**	Hong me nam
each night?	taw dai?	**hot water?**	hawn baw?
Is the room	Hong me ai yen baw?	**Does the room have**	Me hang ap nam baw?
air conditioned?		**a bathroom?**	
Can I see the room	Koi ko beung hong dea?	**Can I have the bill**	Koi ton han bai hap?
first please?		**please**	

Travel

Where is the	Sa ta ni lot phai yu sai?	**Is it far?**	Kai baw?
train station?		**Turn left/turn right**	leo sai/leo qua
Where is the	Sa ta ni lot mee yu sai?	**Go straight on**	pai leuy
bus station?		**River**	Xe Se, Houei/Houai
How much to go to…?	Khit la ka taw dai…?	**Town**	Muang/Mouang
That's expensive	pheng-lie	**Mountain**	phou
Will you go for…kip?	Chow ja pai…kip?		
What time does the	Lot mea oak jay mong…?		
bus/train leave for…?			

Restaurants

Can I see a menu?	Kho beung lay kan arhan?	**Where is a restaurant?**	Lahn ah hai you-sigh?
Can I have…?	Khoy tong kan…?	**Breakfast**	arhan sao
I am hungry	Koy heo kao	**Lunch**	arhan athieng
I am thirsty	Koy heo nahm	**It costs….kip**	Lah-kah ahn-nee…kip
I want to eat	Koh yahk kin kao		

Time

in the morning	muh-sao	**today**	muh-nee
in the afternoon	thon-by	**tomorrow**	muh-ouhn
in the evening	muh-leng	**yesterday**	muh van-nee

Days

Monday	Van Chanh	**Friday**	Van Sook
Tuesday	Van Ang Khan	**Saturday**	Van Sao
Wednesday	Van Pud	**Sunday**	Van Arthid
Thursday	Van Pa Had		

Numbers

1	nung	9	cow	100	hoy
2	song	10	sip	101	hoy-nung
3	sahm	11	sip-et	150	hoy-nah-sip
4	see	12	sip-song	200	song-hoy
5	hah	20	sao	1,000	phan
6	hoke	21	sao-et	10,000	sip-phan
7	chet	22	sao-song	100,000	muun
8	pet	30	sahn-sip	1,000,000	laan

Basic vocabulary

airport	deune yonh	**hotel**	hong
bank	had xay	**island**	koh (or) hath
bathroom	hong nam	**market**	ta lath
beach	heva	**medicine**	ya pua payad
beautiful	ngam	**open**	peud
bicycle	loht teep	**petrol**	nahm-mahn-eh-sahng
big	nyai	**police**	lam louad
boat	quoi loth bath	**police station**	poam lam louad
bus	loht-buht	**post office**	hong kana pai sa nee
bus station	hon kay ya	**restaurant**	han arhane
buy	sue	**road**	tha nonh
chemist	han kay ya	**room**	hong
clean	sa ard	**shop**	hanh
closed	arte	**sick (ill)**	bo sabay
cold	jenh	**silk**	mai
day	vanh (or) mua	**small**	noy
delicious	sehb	**stop**	yoot
dirty	soka pox	**taxi**	loht doy-sanh
doctor	than mah	**that**	nahn
eat	kinh	**this**	nee, ahn-nee
embassy	Satan Tood	**ticket (air)**	pee yonh
excellent	dee leuth	**ticket (bus)**	pee lot mea
expensive	pheng	**toilet**	hong nam
food	ah-han	**town**	nai mouang
fruit	mak-mai	**very**	lai-lai
hospital	hong moh	**water**	nam (or) nah
hot (temp)	hawn	**what**	men-nyung

Useful phrases

dinner	kao leng
breakfast	kao sao
lunch	kao tiang
too much	lai pawd
tasty	saierb

Glossary

Amitabha   the Buddha of the Past
Amulet   protective medallion
Arhat   one who has perfected himself
Avadana   Buddhist narrative, telling of the deeds of saintly souls
Avalokitsvara   also known as Amitabha and Lokeshvara, the name literally means 'World Lord'; he is the compassionate male Bodhisattva, the saviour of Mahayana Buddhism and represents the central force of creation in the universe
Bai sema   boundary stones marking consecrated ground around a bot
Ban   village; shortened from muban
Batik   a form of resist dyeing
Bhikku   Buddhist monk
Bodhi   the tree under which the Buddha achieved enlightenment (*Ficus religiosa*)
Bodhisattva   a future Buddha. In Mahayana Buddhism, someone who has attained enlightenment, but who postpones nirvana to help others reach it.
Boun   Lao festival
Brahma   the Creator, one of the gods of the Hindu trinity, usually represented with four faces, and often mounted on a hamsa
Brahmin   a Hindu priest
Bun   to make merit
Caryatid   elephants, often used as buttressing decorations
Champa   rival empire of the Khmers, of Hindu culture, based in present day Vietnam
Chao   title for Lao kings
Charn   animist priest who conducts the basi ceremony in Laos
Chat   honorific umbrella or royal parasol
Chedi   religious monument (often bell-shaped) containing relics of the Buddha or other holy remains
Chenla   Chinese name for Cambodia before the Khmer era
Deva   a Hindu-derived male god
Devata   a Hindu-derived goddess
Dharma   the Buddhist law
Dok sofa   frond-like construction surmounting temple roofs in Laos. Over 10 flowers means the wat was built by a king
Dtin sin   decorative border on a skirt
Dvarapala   guardian figure, usually placed at the entrance to a temple
Funan   the oldest Indianised state of Indochina and precursor to Chenla

Ganesh   elephant-headed son of Siva
Garuda   mythical divine bird, with predatory beak and claws, and human body; the king of birds, enemy of naga and mount of Vishnu
Gautama   the historic Buddha
Geomancy   the art of divination by lines and figures
Gopura   crowned or covered gate, entrance to a religious area
Hamsa   sacred goose, Brahma's mount; in Buddhism it represents the flight of the doctrine
Hinayana   'Lesser Vehicle', major Buddhist sect in Southeast Asia, usually termed Theravada Buddhism
Hor kong   a pavilion built on stilts where the temple drum is kept
Hor latsalot   chapel of the funeral cart in a Lao temple
Hor song phra   secondary chapel
Hor takang   bell tower
Hor tray/trai   library where manuscripts are stored in a Lao or Thai temple
Hor vay   offering temple
Ikat   tie-dye method of patterning cloth
Indra   the Vedic god of the heavens, weather and war
Jataka(s)   the birth stories of the Buddha; they normally number 547; the last 10 are the most important
Kala (makara)   a demon ordered to consume itself; often sculpted with grinning face and bulging eyes over entranceways to act as a door guardian; also known as kirtamukha
Kathin/krathin   a one-month period during the eighth lunar month when lay people present robes and gifts to monks
Ketumula   flame-like motif above the Buddha head
Kinaree   half-human, half-bird, usually depicted as a heavenly musician
Kirtamukha   see kala
Koutdi   see kuti
Krishna   incarnation of Vishnu
Kuti   living quarters of Buddhist monks in a temple complex
Laterite   bright red tropical soil/stone commonly used in Khmer monuments
Linga   phallic symbol and one of the forms of Siva. Embedded in a pedestal

shaped to allow drainage of lustral water poured over it, the linga typically has a succession of cross sections: from square at the base through octagonal to round. These symbolise, in order, the trinity of Brahma, Vishnu and Siva

Lokeshvara see Avalokitsvara

Mahabharata a Hindu epic text

Mahayana 'Greater Vehicle', major Buddhist sect

Maitreya the future Buddha

Makara mythological aquatic reptile often found with the kala framing doorways

Mandala a focus for meditation; a representation of the cosmos

Mara personification of evil and tempter of the Buddha

Matmii Lao cotton ikat

Mat mi see matmii

Meru sacred or cosmic mountain at the centre of the world in Hindu-Buddhist cosmology; home of the gods

Mondop from the sanskrit, *mandapa*. A cube-shaped building, often topped with a cone-like structure, used to contain an object of worship like a footprint of the Buddha

Muang administrative unit

Muban village, usually shortened to ban

Mudra symbolic gesture of the hands of the Buddha

Nak Lao river dragon, a mythical guardian creature (see naga)

Naga benevolent mythical water serpent, enemy of Garuda

Naga makara fusion of naga and makara

Nalagiri the elephant let loose to attack the Buddha, who calmed him

Nandi/nandin bull, mount of Siva

Nirvana release from the cycle of suffering in Buddhist belief; 'enlightenment'

Nyak mythical water serpent (see naga)

Pa kama Lao men's all-purpose cloth

paddy/padi unhulled rice

Pali the sacred language of Theravada Buddhism

Parvati consort of Siva

Pathet Lao Communist party based in the northeastern provinces of Laos until they came to power in 1975

Pha biang shawl worn by women in Laos

Pha sin piece of cloth, similar to sarong

Phi spirit

Phra sinh see pha sin

Pra Lam Lao version of the Ramayana

Pradaksina pilgrims' clockwise circumambulation of holy structure

Prah sacred

Prang form of stupa built in Khmer style, shaped like a corncob

Prasada stepped pyramid (see prasat)

Prasat residence of a king or of the gods (sanctuary tower), from the Indian prasada

Quan Am Chinese goddess of mercy

Rama incarnation of Vishnu, hero of the Indian epic, the *Ramayana*

Ramakien Lao version of the *Ramayana*

Ramayana Hindu romantic epic

Sakyamuni the historic Buddha

Sal the Indian sal tree (*Shorea robusta*), under which the historic Buddha was born

Sangha the Buddhist order of monks

Sim/sima main sanctuary and ordination hall in a Lao temple complex

Singha mythical guardian lion

Siva the Destroyer, one of the three gods of the Hindu trinity; the sacred linga was worshipped as a symbol of Siva

Sofa see dok sofa

Sravasti the miracle at Sravasti when the Buddha subdues the heretics

Stele inscribed stone panel

Stucco plaster, often heavily moulded

Stupa chedi

Tam bun see bun

Tavatimsa heaven of the 33 gods at the summit of Mount Meru

Thanon street

That shrine housing Buddhist relics, a spire or dome-like edifice commemorating the Buddha's life or the funerary temple for royalty

Theravada 'Way of the Elders'; major Buddhist sect also known as Hinayana Buddhism ('Lesser Vehicle')

Traiphum the three worlds of Buddhist cosmology – heaven, hell and earth

Trimurti the Hindu trinity of gods: Brahma, the Creator, Vishnu the Preserver and Siva the Destroyer

Tripitaka Theravada Buddhism's Pali canon

Ubosoth see bot

Urna the dot or curl on the Buddha's forehead, one of the distinctive physical marks of the Enlightened One

Usnisa the Buddha's top knot or 'wisdom bump'

Vahana 'vehicle', a mythical beast, upon which a deva or god rides

Viharn assembly hall in a Buddhist monastery

Vishnu the Protector, one of the gods of the Hindu trinity

Index

Shorts

Maps

Map symbols

Administration

—·—· State border
□ Capital city
○ Other city/town

Roads and travel

▬▬ Freeway
━━ Main highway
── Sealed road
- - - - Unsealed roads of variable quality
······ Footpath
↦▬ Railway with station

Water features

≈ River
◯ Lake
▨ Beach, dry river bed
≋ Ocean
〰 Waterfall
〜 Reef
⚑ Ferry

Cities and towns

▫ Sight
█ Sleeping
● Eating
▨ Building
▬ Main through route
── Main street
── Minor street
▭▭ Pedestrianized street
→ One way street

⋈ Bridge
▨ Park, garden, stadium
✦ Airport
⑤ Bank
🚏 Bus station
✚ Hospital
🏪 Market
🏛 Museum
⊚ Police
✉ Post office
ℹ Tourist office
♱ ♁ Cathedral, church
⛽ Petrol
◉ Internet
⛳ Golf
🅿 Parking
Ⓐ Detail map
◀Ⓐ Related map

Topographical features

◯ Contours (approx), rock outcrop
�山 Mountain
⊥⊥⊥ Escarpment
⊼⊼⊼ Gorge

Other symbols

∴ Archaeological Site
♦ National park/wildlife reserve
✿ Viewing point
🍷 Winery
▲ Campsite
🌳 Mangrove

Credits

Footprint credits
Text editor: Tim Jollands
Map editor: Sarah Sorensen

Publishers: James Dawson and
Patrick Dawson
Editorial Director: Rachel Fielding
Editorial: Stephanie Lambe,
Sarah Thorowgood, Claire Boobbyer,
Felicity Laughton, Caroline Lascom
Production: Jo Morgan, Mark Thomas,
Emma Bryers, Davina Rungasamy
Cartography: Claire Benison,
Kevin Feeney, Robert Lunn
Design: Mytton Williams
Marketing and publicity:
Rosemary Dawson, La-Ree Miners
Sales: Ed Aves
Advertising: Debbie Wylde,
Lorraine Horler
Finance and administration:
Sharon Hughes, Elizabeth Taylor,
Leona Bailey
Distribution: Pam Cobb, Mike Noel

Photography credits
Front cover: Impact Photo Library
Back cover: Impact PhotoLibrary
Inside colour section: Impact Photo
Library, Eye Ubiquitous, Lindy Hickman,
La Belle Aurore, Robert Harding Picture
Library, Art Directors and TRIP

Print
Manufactured in Italy by LegoPrint

Publishing information
Laos Handbook
3rd edition
© Footprint Handbooks Ltd
December 2002

ISBN 1 903471 39 7
CIP DATA: A catalogue record for this
book is available from the British Library

® Footprint Handbooks and the Footprint
mark are a registered trademark of
Footprint Handbooks Ltd

Published by
Footprint Handbooks
6 Riverside Court
Lower Bristol Road
Bath BA2 3DZ, UK
T +44 (0)1225 469141
F +44 (0)1225 469461
E discover@footprintbooks.com
W www.footprintbooks.com

Distributed in the USA by
Publishers Group West

All rights reserved. No part of this
publication may be reproduced, stored in
a retrieval system, or transmitted, in any
form or by any means, electronic,
mechanical, photocopying recording, or
otherwise without the prior permission of
Footprint Handbooks Ltd.

Neither the black and white nor coloured
maps are intended to have any political
significance.

Every effort has been made to ensure that
the facts in the Handbook are accurate.
However, travellers should still obtain
advice from consulates, airlines etc about
travel and visa requirements before
travelling. The authors and publishers
cannot accept responsibility for
any loss, injury or inconvenience
however caused.

Acknowledgements

With special thanks to John and Valerie Middleton.
Patrick Gilbert, Thailand
Prof Stefano Magistretti, UK
Steve Scott, UK
Yves Mauboussin, France
Andreas Kucher, Germany
Vic Cowling, Laos
Dieter Neuschafer, Switzerland
Priscilla Nuttall, UK
Berit Johns, Norway
Natasha Nicholas
Peter Standing, UK
Pany Saignavongs, Laos
Lisa Ferguson
Mark Owen, USA
Catherine and Ian Sheldrake, UK

Keep in touch

Footprint feedback

We try as hard as we can to make each Footprint Handbook as up-to-date and accurate as possible but, of course, things always change. Many people write to us - with corrections, new information, or simply comments.

If you want to let us know about an experience or adventure - hair-raising or mundane, good or bad, exciting or boring or simply something rather special - we would be delighted to hear from you. Please give us as precise information as possible, quoting the edition number (you'll find it on the front cover) and page number of the Handbook you are using.

Your help will be greatly appreciated, especially by other travellers. In return we will send you details about our special guidebook offer. Email Footprint at:
laos3_online@footprintbooks.com

or write to:
Elizabeth Taylor
Footprint Handbooks
6 Riverside Court, Lower Bristol Road
Bath BA2 3DZ UK

www.footprintbooks.com

Dip in and keep on the pulse with what Footprint are up to online.

- Latest Footprint releases
- Entertaining travel articles and news updates
- Extensive destination information for inspiration and trip planning
- Monthly competitions
- Easy ways to buy Footprint guides

Complete title listing

Footprint publish travel guides to over 120 countries worldwide. Each guide is packed with practical, concise and colourful information for everybody from first-time travellers to travel aficionados. The list is growing fast and current titles are noted below.

Available from all good bookshops

www.footprintbooks.com

(P) denotes pocket Handbook

Latin America & Caribbean

Argentina Handbook
Barbados (P)
Bolivia Handbook
Brazil Handbook
Caribbean Islands Handbook
Central America & Mexico
  Handbook
Chile Handbook
Colombia Handbook
Costa Rica Handbook
Cuba Handbook
Cusco & the Inca Trail Handbook
Dominican Republic Handbook
Ecuador & Galápagos Handbook
Guatemala Handbook
Havana (P)
Mexico Handbook
Nicaragua Handbook
Peru Handbook
Rio de Janeiro Handbook
South American Handbook
Venezuela Handbook

North America

Vancouver (P)
Western Canada Handbook

Africa

Cape Town (P)
East Africa Handbook
Libya Handbook
Marrakech & the High Atlas
  Handbook
Morocco Handbook
Namibia Handbook
South Africa Handbook
Tunisia Handbook
Uganda Handbook

Middle East

Egypt Handbook
Israel Handbook
Jordan Handbook
Syria & Lebanon Handbook

Australasia

Australia Handbook
New Zealand Handbook
Sydney (P)
West Coast Australia Handbook

Asia

Bali Handbook
Bangkok & the Beaches
  Handbook
Cambodia Handbook
Goa Handbook
India Handbook
Indian Himalaya Handbook
Indonesia Handbook
Laos Handbook
Malaysia Handbook
Myanmar (Burma) Handbook
Nepal Handbook
Pakistan Handbook
Rajasthan & Gujarat Handbook
Singapore Handbook
South India Handbook
Sri Lanka Handbook
Sumatra Handbook
Thailand Handbook
Tibet Handbook
Vietnam Handbook

Europe

Andalucía Handbook
Barcelona Handbook
Berlin (P)
Bilbao (P)
Bologna (P)
Copenhagen (P)
Croatia Handbook
Dublin Handbook
Dublin (P)
Edinburgh Handbook
Edinburgh (P)
England Handbook
Glasgow Handbook
Ireland Handbook
London Handbook
Madrid (P)
Naples (P)
Northern Spain Handbook
Paris (P)
Reykjavik (P)
Scotland Handbook
Scotland Highlands & Islands
  Handbook
Spain Handbook
Turkey Handbook

Also available

Traveller's Handbook (WEXAS)
Traveller's Healthbook (WEXAS)
Traveller's Internet Guide (WEXAS)

Footnotes

Tailor made specialists to
Laos

Regent Holidays
(UK) Limited
15 John Street
Bristol BS1 2HR
Telephone:
+44 (0)117 921 1711
Fax:
+44 (0)117 925 4866

email: regent@regent-holidays.co.uk   www.regent-holidays.co.uk

Advertiser's index

Join Bangkok Airways on an innovative heritage tour of **4** historic kingdoms. From the City of Angels, Bangkok, fly to the first capital of Thailand, Sukhothai. Then explore Luang Prabang, the ancient capital of Laos. Next stop Hué, the former capital of Vietnam, and from there on to Siem Reap in Cambodia, home of the legendary Angkor Wat, before returning to Bangkok. Five great experiences in one great tour* of the Mekong region. Exclusively with Bangkok Airways.

Footnotes

'UNESCO World Heritage Sites :
Sukhothai (Thailand), Luang Prabang (Laos),
Hue' (Vietnam) and Angkor (Cambodia)

*Tour starting in July 2002

For more information of the tour, please contact

DIETHELM TRAVEL	Tel : + 66 2 255 9150-70	E-mail : dto@dto.co.th
INDOCHINA SERVICES	Tel : + 66 2 255 4001-7	E-mail : info@is-intl.com
MEKONGLAND	Tel : + 66 2 256 7176-9	E-mail : mekongld@mekongland.com
PINK ROSE HOILDAYS	Tel : + 66 2 255 8966	E-mail : info@pinkroseholidays.com

FRANKFURT OFFICE   Tel : (49 69) 133 77 565/566 Fax : (49 69) 133 77 567   E-mail : bkkair.fra@t-online.de
BANGKOK HEAD OFFICE Tel : +66 2 229 3434/3456 Fax : +66 2 229 3450/3454 E-mail : pg@bangkokair.co.th

www.bangkokair.com

Trails of Asia

Journey through lost kingdoms and Hidden history of Southeast Asia and let Asian Trails be your guide!

Blazing new paths in travel

Choose Asian Trails, the specialists in Southeast Asia.
We will organise your holiday, hotels, flights and tours to the region's
most facinating and undiscovered tourist desinations.
Contact us for our brochure or log into
www.asiantrails.net or www.asiantrails.com

CAMBODIA: No. 33, Street 240, P.O. Box 621, Phnom Penh
Tel: (855 23) 216 555, Fax: (855 23) 216 591, E-mail: asiantrails@bigpond.com.kh

INDONESIA: JI. By Pass Ngurah Rai No. 260, Sanur, Denpasar 80228, Bali
Tel: (62 361) 285 771, Fax: (62 361) 281 515, E-mail: willem@asiantrailsbali.com

LAO P.D.R.: Unit No. 5, Baan Sokpaluang, Muang Sisatanak, P.O. Box 8430, Vientiane
Tel: (856 21) 351 789, Fax: (856 21) 351 789, E-mail: atrailsv@laotel.com

MALASIA: Wisma UOA II, Suite No. 9-11, 9/F, JI. Pinang, 50450 Kuala Lumpur
Tel: (60 3) 2710 1215, Fax: (60 3) 2710 1216, E-mail: res@asiantrails.com.my

MYANMAR: 73 Pyay Road, Dagon Township, Yangon
Tel: (95 1) 211212, 727422, 705982, Fax: (95 1) 211670, E-mail: res@asiantrails.com.mm

THAILAND: 15th Floor, Mercury Tower, 540 Ploenchit Road, Bangkok 10330
Tel: (662) 658 6080-9, Fax: (66 2) 658 6099, E-mail: res@asiantrails.org

VIETNAM: Unit 721 7/F Saigon Trade Center, 37 Ton Duc Thang St., D. 1, Ho Chi Minh City
Tel: (84 8) 9 10 28 71-3, Fax: (84 8) 9 10 28 74, E-mail: asiantrails@hcm.vnn.vn

Footnotes

Laos

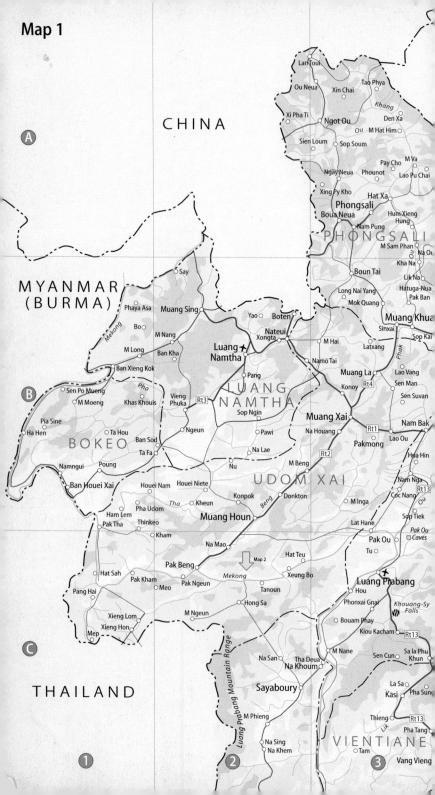

Map 1

Gulf of Tonkin

○ Axen

Pahai ○

dap

○ Chakeuy Tay   Ka Reen ○

○ Kaleum

Xe Kong

SEKONG

Ban Phon   Dak Chung ○
○ Sekong   ○ Cha Van   Dak Klao ○
○ Nam Hang

un
an   ○ Thakkanat   Kamane

Thac Kie ○

○ Keng Say   ○ Sala Tin Toc   Van Tat ○
lovens
lateau   ○ Sakke

Attapeu   ○ Xaisetha
○ Pa-am
Sau
○ Phya Ha   Rt18   Tasseing ○
ATTAPEU
○ Chom

Kong My ○
Phia Ka Nleng ○

VIETNAM

CAMBODIA

N

0 km   20
0 km   20

A

B

C

4   5   6

For a different view of Europe, take a Footprint

New pocket Handbook series:
Bilbao, Bologna, Copenhagen, Madrid, Naples, Berlin,
Reykjavik, Dublin, Edinburgh. Also available: Cape Town,
Havana, Barbados, Sydney, Vancouver

Discover so much more...
Listings driven, forward looking and up-to-date. Focuses on
what's going on right now. Contemporary, stylish, and innotive
approach providing quality travel information.